GENE AUTRY WESTERNS

by
Boyd Magers

Ruth -

Gene Back In The Saddle!

— Boyd Magers

Published by
Empire Publishing, Inc.
3130 US Highway 220
Madison, NC 27025
Phone: 336-427-5850 • Fax: 336-427-7372
www.empirepublishinginc.com

Library of Congress Control Number: 2007929678
ISBN Number: 978-0-944019-49-8

Published and printed in the United States of America
1 2 3 4 5 6 7 8 9 10

Dedication

Dedicated to the memory of Alex Gordon.

Contents

Acknowledgments

Les Adams, Karla Bulhman, Joe Collura, Ned Comstock at University of Southern California, Bobby Copeland, Brian Dalrymple, Michael Fitzgerald, Jimmy Glover, Alex Gordon, Doug Green, Gordon Gregersen, G. D. Hamann, Maxine Hansen, Jimmy Hawkins, Whitey Hughes, Irynne Isip, Alun Jones, Dick Jones, Rhonda Lemons, Jack Lewis, Leonard Maltin and his MOVIE CRAZY publication, Kim Mansfield, Jack Mathis, Austin Muttie Mewse, Ray Nielsen, Evy and Michael Patrick, Barry Rellaford, Jerry Schneider, O. J. Sikes, Jon Guyot Smith, Richard Smith III, Lillian Spencer, Jack Williams, Nick Williams, Tinsley Yarbrough. And a special thanks to my wife, Donna Magers, without whose patience and understanding this book could not have been accomplished.

Foreword by Dick Jones

It was 1948 and I was trying to re-establish myself in Hollywood after being "out of sight—out of mind" from doing a radio show in New York City for three years…then serving in the Army for two years, when Gene Autry put out the word that he was looking for me to meet with him at his office in Hollywood.

An appointment was made and I arrived 15 minutes early as I was anxious to find out what this meeting was all about. I had never met or talked to him before and was a little awed and skeptical until Mr. Autry told me of his upcoming color film "The Strawberry Roan" featuring his horse Champion, and that he had decided I was the only "kid" he would let ride his horse in the film as was called for in the story. Naturally, I let him know I was available and would like to work in his movie. Contracts were signed. I was given a script, wardrobe worked out and off to Sedona, Arizona, where a third of the show was filmed. The interior scenes were filmed in Hollywood at Columbia Studios and the exterior of the ranch was photographed on location out in Placerita Canyon, just northwest of the San Fernando Valley where another one third of the film was shot. That was the best job I had in 1948 and I later realized how truly

Gene Autry and Dick Jones say "goodbye to the Old West" in a relaxing moment between scenes from Gene's last motion picture, "Last of the Pony Riders."

blessed I was at that first meeting with Mr. Gene Autry.

Later, in 1950, after returning from Gallup, New Mexico, at the finish of filming the Errol Flynn movie "Rocky Mountain" for Warner Bros., Mr. Autry called me into his office, in the all new Flying A studio in Hollywood and related his plans for a television series called "Range Rider", to star the long and lean, very athletic Jock Mahoney. He needed a teenage type sidekick to help the storyline. Well, as I was the oldest teenager in Hollywood with the ability to handle the action in the series that was contemplated, I, of course, indicated I was available and eager to work in his new show. That was the beginning of a long and wonderful adventure of working for and with Gene Autry on many of his feature films and dozens of his TV shows. Plus co-starring with Gene and Jocko at the Houston, Texas, "Fat Stock" Rodeo, then on to Madison Square Gardens, two times and up to Boston Gardens for their big rodeos. This led to a great friendship and working relationship that is beyond description. I like to tell those that ask, "What was it like to work with Gene Autry"—I let them know without hesitation that Mr. Autry was easy to work with, calm, never seemed to get overly excited, never blew his top or raved and ranted. He surrounded himself with the best in the business from Mandy Schaefer with years of experience in motion picture production, Mitchell Hamilburg, an astute business manager and talent agent; these made up the main body of Flying A Pictures Inc. His film crew was considered the best, with Lou Gray Assistant producer calling the shots from the field and William Bradford, cinematographer, with a canny eye for keeping everything in frame and in focus down to the maintenance and cleanup crew. They were all family of which I was considered a part, and great to work with. To reiterate, Gene Autry was the best boss a guy could ever want *and* his checks never bounced.

After filming 76 "Range Riders", Jocko moved on to other venues and I remained under contract to Flying A. Gene wasn't through with me yet as he had another western series in mind, so he put me in the short-lived TV oater "Buffalo Bill Jr." with a little girl, Nancy Gilbert, as the "sidekick" mainstay. It was pure action, shoot 'em up and tear 'em up storyline with some humor from "Pappy" Cheshire, the adult stabilizing influence in the show.

Between shooting the "B B Jr." series, I played various parts in several of Gene's shows. That was very prudent business action by Mr. Autry, as I was receiving a weekly salary, so, instead of letting me just sit around on off days becoming stale, I was put to work in his other shows until my contract expired and I was free to seek other jobs.

So, now you have some idea how I entered into this position of Boyd asking me to write a foreword to his book on Gene's film and television works. So take a deep seat, a long rein and we'll get on with looking at an historic career.

This is not a storybook or adventure novel about the accomplishments of the man, the star, the singing cowboy, it is a documentary of the movies and television shows

Gene was in from the very first through the very last feature film, aptly titled "The Last of the Pony Riders".

This is *the* ultimate Gene Autry book. It is factual, diligently researched and a chronological listing of all Gene's feature films and filmed television shows. This book has everything you ever wanted to know about Gene's work on the big silver screen and television films. It contains cast, crew and behind the scenes personnel that go into producing the finished product. Much of this information comes from Boyd's personal files of some 30 years collecting data and the complete files kept by Gene's staff at his office in North Hollywood which was provided to Boyd for his perusal. Boyd's fetish for facts and detail over "hearsay" information is challenged and applied in the preparation of this book.

Now, enjoy the fact that you have the facts on Gene Autry's career in and on films.

In conclusion, I would like to thank you Boyd Magers for asking me to write a foreword to your work. I am honored and deeply appreciative for the opportunity to express my gratitude to Mr. Autry, to you Boyd and to all the wonderful people of Flying A for a truly blessed career working with and for Gene Autry.

September, 2006

"Look Ma, no hands!" Dick Jones rears up on Storm while making the "Range Rider" TV series. The horse's name in the series was Lucky. Note: no cantleboard on the saddle.

Rockin' To and Fro—
A Few Words Before Saddling Up…

GENE AUTRY WESTERNS presents a detailed account of Gene's movie and TV appearances, the songs included, cast and production credits, synopses, costs, locations, and more. Often included are remembrances of making the films from Gene, other cast members and directors as well as comments on how the film was received by theater owners.

This book is not intended to delve into Gene's personal appearances, his radio show, business interests, recording career or personal life. We'll leave those aspects of Gene's multi-faceted career to other researchers and authors.

Although accurate records of full casts, including stuntmen, financial records indicating production costs, and general production notes were researched at the Autry Entertainment office, the Margaret Herrick Motion Picture Academy Library, the University of Southern California, and Republic files owned by Jack Mathis, they are sporadic. Therefore, you will notice some films have a more complete cast listing or more detailed information than others. Due to fires at Gene's Melody Ranch, production notes available for evaluation are hit and miss. Some production records were spared and are totally complete, others are lost to the ages.

You'll find that character names shown in the cast listings may not always be mentioned on screen. Often character names were assigned to minor players although that name is never actually spoken on screen. If, through our research of production material, we were able to assign a name to a character, even if it is not spoken on screen, we listed that name as assigned.

A film's budget as noted is the studio's planned amount allotted for production of a picture. The negative cost is the actual amount of money spent to produce the film. When noted, a domestic film rental is the film rental money paid to distributors in the United States and Canada.

For the various "What the Exhibitor Had to Say" notes, these were excerpted from various issues of MOTION PICTURE HERALD tradepapers. Often, you'll note many months—sometimes years—difference in time from when one of Gene's westerns was released and when it actually played a specific theater. Distribution of movies in the '30s and '40s was quite different than it is today when thousands of prints of a movie are released simultaneously all over the country. During Gene's time, only a few hundred prints of a picture were struck and then "bicycled" around the country from theater to theater. Some of the very late Exhibitor comments even came from a re-release of one of Gene's westerns.

All else should be self-explanatory.

I believe by looking back at Gene's westerns in chronological order you will see the development of a star—a man who over three decades kept both youngsters and adults entertained. Gene was a man who changed the face of screen westerns, fired the imagination of the world and truly became America's Favorite Cowboy.

Gene Autry Beginnings

Gene Autry, as singer, actor, songwriter, musician, businessman and just plain humanitarian, has consistently embodied, stood for and symbolized decency and fair play. His devotion to the American free enterprise system allowed him to live out a classic rags-to-riches success story. Patriotism for Gene Autry meant more than words in a song; he gave three years at the height of his career to serve his country during World War II. The honors and awards Gene Autry has received over the course of his long and successful life are legion, and all well-deserved.

Critics have often derided Gene's films because they felt the music diluted the action. Critics never truly grasped Gene's grassroots appeal in a Depression era world that cried out for an escapist blending of music, action and comedy. Gene developed an unbeatable combination. His gentle,

natural voice painted pictures of a western landscape while his boyish, sincere, almost vulnerable on-screen charm won over scores of females; yet he could be forceful and demanding enough when it came to the action sequences to lure in the young and older male audiences.

The self-made career rise of Gene Autry was nothing short of spectacular, but cannot be fully appreciated or understood unless some of his early life is known, for he was not born with a silver spoon in his mouth.

Born Orvon Grover Autry on September 29, 1907, about six miles outside of Tioga, Texas, at Indian Creek in Cooke County, his grandfather was a pastor at Indian Creek Baptist Church for several years. Gene's father, Delbert, was variously a farmer, livestock dealer and horse trader. Earnings were meager, causing the family to frequently

Gene Autry and his Oklahoma Cowboys.

move. Over the next several years they spent time, and Gene attended school during various years, in Achille, Oklahoma; Tioga, Texas; Ravia, Oklahoma and Pilot Point (near Tioga). According to high school yearbooks, Gene dropped out of school early in the 10th grade at Tioga, at which time he landed a full time job with the railroad.

Over the years, the family increased to four as Gene was followed by two sisters, Veda and Wilma, and younger brother Dudley, born October 9, 1919, in Achille.

Gene was exposed to the traditions of the west by his father, to music by his mother, Nora, and to singing by his grandfather who put Gene in the church choir at a young age.

As a young man he was determined to escape from the poverty he experienced as a child and driven to succeed. Always good with numbers, he took correspondence courses in accounting and learned the Morse Code to heighten his chances of landing a job with the railroad. Gene worked as a helper for the railway company in Tioga, Texas, from June 1924 to March 1925. At that time he was hired by J. M. Puckett personally and paid by him to work around the station as the company did not pay helpers. But the money he was getting could not support him and he was trying for something better within the railroad. On June 14, 1925, Orvon Grover Autry filled out his application for the railroad in Sapulpa, Oklahoma, and began working as an assistant telegraph operator at Weleetka, Oklahoma on June 18, 1925. Over time, working various stations up and down the Frisco line in Oklahoma, the dreary, lonely work and long evenings led him to use his idle time to become a more accomplished guitar player. His music turned from hobby to passion as he began to see it as a way out of the dusty Oklahoma prairie.

Acting on a mother's tip to look up her sons Johnny and Frankie Marvin if he went to New York seeking a singing career, Gene found both brothers to be welcoming and helpful to the fledgling singer in late 1928.

After a test recording in New York, Gene took the advice of Frankie Marvin and others to return home to Oklahoma and get some experience.

Returning to the Sooner State he obtained a job singing on KVOO radio in Tulsa, billed as Oklahoma's Yodeling Cowboy, while wisely keeping his telegrapher job with the railroad.

In the fall of 1929 Gene returned to New York once again in search of a record contract, which this time he successfully obtained with Victor. His first record, "My Dreaming of You", was cut in October 1929 and released in early 1930.

Gene continued to record for a variety of labels, with much of his repertoire in the mold of the then popular country blues singer Jimmie Rodgers. But, by the end of 1931, Autry was becoming aware he must forge his own musical identity.

In October 1931 Gene recorded the song that became his springboard to success. "That Silver Haired Daddy of Mine" became a runaway hit and led to his joining the cast of the "WLS Barn Dance" in Chicago. Now with a million selling record and being billed as Oklahoma's Yodeling Cowboy on WLS, in April 1932 Gene finally walked away from the Frisco Railroad telegrapher job and never looked back—only ahead. He began to tour the Midwest extensively.

It was at this time, April 1, 1932, that he married Ina Mae Spivey, the niece of his songwriter friend and collaborator, Jimmy Long.

Autry spent three years, 1931-1934, on WLS and the network National Barn Dance.

Then Hollywood came calling…

Songbook published in 1932 while Gene was with The National Barn Dance on WLS, Chicago.

In Old Santa Fe
<u>Mascot, November 1934</u>

Producer .... Nat Levine
Supervising Producer .... Victor Zobel
Director .... David Howard; Joe Kane
                 (uncredited)
Original Story .... Wallace MacDonald, John
                 Rathmell
Screenplay .... Colbert Clark, James Gruen
Photography .... Ernest Miller, William
                 Nobles
Film Editor .... Thomas Scott
Sound Engineer .... Terry Kellum

SONGS: "As Long As I've Got My Dog" (music and lyrics unknown)—sung by Ken Maynard on screen (voice doubled by Bob Nolan). Reprised by George Hayes; "Someday in Wyoming" (aka "Wyoming Waltz") (music and lyrics by Gene Autry)—sung by Gene Autry; "Mama Don't Like Music" (music and lyrics by Gene Autry, Smiley Burnette)—sung by Smiley Burnette; "Down In Old Santa Fe" (music and lyrics by C. Harold Lewis)—sung by Gene Autry, Smiley Burnette and party guests.

RUNNING TIME: 63½ minutes

FILMING DATES: September 17 to late September 1934

LOCATIONS: Noah Beery Sr.'s "Paradise" ranch; Palmdale desert area

CAST:

Actor	Character
Ken Maynard	Ken "Kentucky" Maynard
Tarzan	Tarzan (Ken's horse)
Evalyn Knapp	Lila Miller
H. B. Warner	Charlie Miller
Kenneth Thomson	Matt Korber (aka Chandler)
Wheeler Oakman	Tracy
George Hayes	Cactus Barnes
George Chesebro	Nick
George Burton	Red
Gene Autry	Gene (square dance caller/ singer)
Smiley Burnette	Accordionist/singer
Edward Hearn	Outlaw
Stanley Blystone	Outlaw Hank
Silver Tip Baker, Dick Botiller, Frank O'Connor	Party guests
Horace B. Carpenter	Guest
Jim Corey	Deputy
Art Dillard, Wes Warner	Ranch hands
Frank Ellis	Deputy playing cards
Jack Jones	Musician
Jack Kirk, Tracy Layne, Cliff Lyons	Cowhands
Frankie Marvin	Band musician
William McCall	Doctor
Jack Rockwell	Sheriff
Wally West	Cowhand at party

STUNTS: Jack Jones, Cliff Lyons, Wally West.

THE FILM: A seminal B-western, important for what it foreshadowed. It marks the beginning of the end for star Ken Maynard and the beginning for Gene Autry.

It was the starring silent westerns Maynard made in the '20s for First National (soon absorbed by Warner Bros.) that made him a cowboy star of the first rank. When he moved over to Universal in 1929 he was in peak condition, his horsemanship was spectacular. After a brief slide at Tiffany and World Wide in the early '30s, Ken was back on top at Universal once again by 1933, making $10,000 a week—a truly tidy sum in the wake of the depression. But there were problems, all of which stemmed from Ken's stubborn, demanding nature—abetted by his fondness for booze. Ken could be a mean drunk. And he drank a lot. He was temperamental, belligerent; he wanted things done his way and flew into temper tantrums when they were not. Ken parted company with Universal in 1934 because they wouldn't give him his way. Nat Levine, owner of tiny Mascot, picked him up immediately, still at $10,000 per week. Levine had big things planned for Ken but after "In Old Santa Fe" and the "Mystery Mountain" serial, Levine too let Ken go because Ken's low boiling point had become far too difficult to deal with, abusive when drunk and argumentative on the set when things weren't to his personal satisfaction.

Levine had planned to star Ken in "The Phantom Empire" but gave it to Gene Autry whose seven minute musical segment midway in "In Old Santa Fe" (for which he was paid $75) had generated positive feedback. Gene sings "Someday in Wyoming" also known as "Wyoming Waltz", Smiley Burnette clowns "Mama Don't Like Music" and Gene returns for "Down In Old Santa Fe", a song Levine bought and named the picture after even though nothing in the story takes place in Santa Fe. Interesting to note, touches of the Jimmie Rodgers influence in Gene's voice still linger on. Within a year or so, Autry's popularity eclipsed not only Maynard's, but all the other cowboy stars.

Maynard was now 40 and, because of his drinking, was becoming increasingly pudgy. Larry Darmour signed him for an independent series of eight released through Columbia. From there it was all downhill—fast—at Grand National, Colony and finally Monogram as part of the Trail Blazers. Even there his demanding ways caused his exit from that low-budget work. It makes one wonder—what if Ken had been more agreeable with Levine and not been dropped in 1934 before Mascot was absorbed into Republic…would Ken have been "the Singing Cowboy" Autry became? Would Bob Nolan have continued to dub Ken's singing voice as he does in "In Old Santa Fe"?

The film gives us not only the birth of Gene Autry (and Smiley Burnette) but marks a career turning point for George Hayes as well. His crotchety old characters in John Wayne Lone Star westerns had convinced Hayes this was his best shot at stardom. His loveable old grump persona comes to fruition in "In Old Santa Fe" as Cactus. Producer Harry Sherman was impressed enough with Hayes' role that he hired him for his Hopalong Cassidy films in 1935.

With an obviously better than average B-western budget, "In Old Santa Fe" is set in the modern day west on a dude ranch owned by Charlie Miller (H. B. Warner) and his daughter Lila (former Wampus Baby Star Evalyn Knapp) whom Ken takes a shine to. Also arriving at the ranch is slick eastern gangster Chandler (Kenneth Thomson) whose father was once an associate of Miller's, so Chandler blackmails Miller into turning over half the ranch to him.

Realizing Maynard is a threat to him, he and his henchman Tracy (Wheeler Oakman) at first rig a horse race so that Ken loses his prize palomino, Tarzan, and later frame Ken for the murder and robbery of a stage driver.

Granted, the final denouement reveals a few off-screen actions we weren't privy to, but overall—with an

exceptionally exciting horse race, a good script, some quite funny lines, Gene and Smiley's unbilled musical interlude midway, and a quick pace, it's an especially entertaining picture.

Indeed, with its fantasy blend of old and new—cars and horses, gangsters and cowboys, music and western action—the film truly foreshadowed the Autry films with all of these ideas carried over into his pictures.

For "In Old Santa Fe", director David Howard was hired on loan from Fox but his contract expired before the film was completed, so Joe Kane finished up the picture uncredited.

As a footnote to Maynard, he may not have been the first cowboy to sing on screen, but he was in the forefront of popularizing the breed. However, after "In Old Santa Fe" and the advent of Autry, he never sang on screen again. Maynard's final years were spent in virtual poverty with his boozing becoming increasingly worse. Interestingly, one of his greatest benefactors was Gene Autry who had idolized Ken long before this film. Gene never allowed Maynard to be aware of his monetary support in Ken's final years. Ken died a physical wreck at the Motion Picture Hospital in 1973. He was the biggest enigma in westerns—handsome, romantic and charming on one hand yet troublesome and demanding on the other. So much so that it eventually cost him his career.

NOTES AND COMMENTS: Although credited to Norman S. Hall, the teleplay of Gene's TV episode "Six Shooter Sweepstakes" (10/1/50) is a direct swipe from the plot of "In Old Santa Fe".

FILM COMMENTS: *Nat Levine:* "I received a half dozen letters from Autry during 1933 asking for an opportunity to work for me in anything I would suggest in pictures. Autry's name value at the time was limited to an independent radio station in Chicago, practically an unknown with questionable ability. On one of my trips East, I stopped off in Chicago, not to meet Autry, but for business I had with my distributor. But I did get to meet Autry and he virtually begged me for an opportunity to come to Hollywood and work in pictures. While he was nice looking, it seemed to me he lacked the commodity necessary to become a western star: virility! I was not impressed and tried to give him a nice brush-off, telling him I would think about it. For a period of six months he wrote to me continually, conveying that he would do anything for the opportunity. Autry was completely raw material, knew nothing about acting, lacked poise, and was awkward. A couple of days after his arrival I had him at my home and invited my production staff to meet him. The next day all my associates questioned my judgment in putting him under contract. They thought I was slipping. But I persisted, and for the first four months he went through a learning period. We had at that time in our employ a professional dramatic and voice teacher, and Autry became one of her pupils. He wasn't much of a horseman either, so I had Tracy Layne and Yakima Canutt teach him how to ride." [1]

"We made the deal and he came to Hollywood with his musician-friends. I got Autry at $100 a week, Smiley Burnette at $75, Frankie Marvin at $60."[2]

"We constantly strove to be pathfinders, 'The Phantom Empire' was one of the innumerable productions which proved it. Here was science fiction that would be readily acceptable today, and not considered old-fashioned." [1]

Ken Maynard: "Gene got his start in my pictures. Ol' Gene became a big star; today he's a multimillionaire. I'm happy for him. He was one fine young fellow."[3]

Gene Autry: "Ken (Maynard) wasn't the easiest guy in the world to work with. He had a bad reputation of getting along with the other actors. But my first picture was with him, and he treated me just as nice as you could possibly treat anybody, and when I started making my own pictures, he did everything he could to help me…show me little tricks and things like that."[4]

CAST BIO: The man that started Gene Autry—and Smiley Burnette—on their road to success was born Nathaniel Levine in New York City on July 26, 1899. Even as a boy he was called Nat, and it is by that name we have come to know the man who became known as "King of the Serial Makers" at Mascot.

At age 13, a job as an office boy with the Marcus Lowe theatre chain in New York instilled in Nat an interest in the film industry.

In his early 20's he became sales manager with a firm that distributed Felix the Cat animated cartoons out of Kansas City.

Nat Levine

After two years with the Winkler organization, Levine obtained the rights to an unreleased silent feature, "Every Woman's Problem", and released the picture independently. Only four months after its release Levine had grossed four times his original investment, proving to himself feature distribution was where his future lay.

By 1927 he formed Mascot Pictures and established office space at 6001 Santa Monica Blvd. in Hollywood. Determined to make his tiger-and-globe trademark into one of the most famous logos in Hollywood, Levine set up a nationwide distribution network—an area he was well versed in by the time he formed his own company.

Levine displayed an amazing talent for turning out decent serials and, later, features for $15,000-$30,000. He also had a winning skill in obtaining talent…talent that was either on the descent or ascent in the business. Levine's first release was in January 1927, the silent 10 chapter serial "The Golden Stallion" starring Lefty Flynn. After five more silent serials, Levine courageously released the first silent/sound chapterplay. In other words, "King of the Kongo" ('29) was released in both a traditional silent version and a sound version for theaters then so equipped.

Mascot serials were always successful box office and dozens more followed in the '30s, along with some 16 features. Oddly, though many of Levine's serials were western-themed, the only Mascot feature western was Ken Maynard's "In Old Santa Fe", which introduced Gene Autry to the movie-going public.

The response was favorable and Levine quickly gave Gene and Smiley brief roles in Ken Maynard's "Mystery Mountain" serial, then took a chance and starred Gene in Mascot's biggest budgeted (to that time) serial, "The Phantom Empire".

In 1933 Levine leased the shuttered former Mack Sennett studio at 4024 Radford in North Hollywood. Hindsight tells us he should have bought the property, but he did not.

By then Consolidated Film Laboratories had been processing virtually every foot of film Mascot turned out. That fact gave Consolidated's president, Herbert J. Yates, an accurate measuring stick by which to calculate Levine's success.

In 1935 Yates approached Levine with an offer, merge Mascot, Monogram, Consolidated Labs and several small independents into a new company to be called Republic Pictures, with Levine to be an important executive in the studio operation. Thus was Republic formed. John Wayne's "Westward Ho" was their first release in August 1935, followed shortly by Gene's "Tumbling Tumbleweeds" in September with Levine as producer.

Within the first year Yates and Levine banded together to buy out the Monogram share, giving Levine 50% ownership in Republic.

An inveterate gambler at heart, Levine now found himself able to wager on most any game—or horse—he chose. Restlessness within Levine to conquer new cinematic worlds led him to resign from Republic on February 2, 1937, allowing Yates to buy him out for a reported $1 million. Levine stayed on with Republic for several months to tie up loose ends but Armand Schaefer immediately took over as producer on Gene's pictures. Yates immediately took sole control, installing Moe Siegel in April as President and brother Sol as executive superintendent.

With plenty of money and time on his hands, Levine soon squandered his fortune at the racetrack.

Smiley Burnette and Gene Autry are featured in Ken Maynard's "In Old Santa Fe."

review them. However, I'll have to break over and say a good word for this western. It drew better than average business and pleased. Created a lot of com-ment. Play it on Saturday."

—H. M. Johnson, Avon Theater, Avon Park, Georgia (June 1935)

"Here is an exceptionally good western with fine singing and music. My patrons enjoyed it very much. If you want a fine outdoor picture date this one. It is good."

—S. H. Rich, Rich Theater, Montpelier, Ohio (July 1935)

"One of the best westerns played in this theater. Many favorable comments from patrons. Pleased our Friday and Saturday patrons 100 percent, and did good business."

—Robert Wygent, Heights Theater, Houston, Texas (October 1935)

In the ensuing years, Levine joined MGM for a brief time as a producer. His tenure as studio manager at ZIV-TV was a bit longer but by 1962 he was a theater manager for California Sterling Theatres, retiring after ten years. The man who jump-started Gene Autry's career never regained the lofty status he once held at Mascot and Republic.

When his health started to deteriorate he was admitted to the Motion Picture Country Home in Woodland Hills where he died on August 6, 1989.

WHAT THE EXHIBITOR HAD TO SAY: "At last they have learned how to make westerns. Pulled and pleased 100 percent. More like."   —G. Carey, Strand Theater, Paris, Arkansas (February 1935)

"I have recently made it a point not to review the westerns, as they are pretty much the same sort and it is useless to

"This one was old, but there is still good action. One of Gene Autry's first pictures, also Smiley Burnette. George "Gabby" Hayes is in it too. They are all good. Good for midweek business. Sound fair, as the recording was done a good while ago."

—Frank D. Fowler and Jack LaGrande, Princess Theater, Mocksville, North Carolina (February 1948)

SOURCES:

1. Tuska, Jon. *The Vanishing Legion.* McFarland, 1982. p. 156, 160.

2. Fernett, Gene. *Next Time Drive off the Cliff.* Cinememories Pub., 1968. p. 80.

3. *Western Clippings #27.* January/February 1999. p. 35.

4. "Melody Ranch Theater" showing of "Prairie Moon" on Nashville Network, 1987.

Mystery Mountain
Mascot serial, December 1934

CHAPTER TITLES: 1) The Rattler 2) The Man Nobody Knows 3) The Eye That Never Sleeps 4) The Human Target 5) Phantom Outlaws 6) The Perfect Crime 7) Tarzan the Cunning 8) The Enemy's Stronghold 9) The Fatal Warning 10) The Secret of the Mountain 11) Behind the Mask 12) The Judgment of Tarzan

Producer ....Nat Levine
Supervising Producers ....Armand Schaefer, Victor Zobel
Directors.....................................Otto Brower, B. Reeves Eason
Original Story and ....Sherman Lowe, Barney Sarecky, B. Reeves Eason, Bennett Cohen
   Screenplay
Photography ....Ernest Miller, William Nobles
Music Theme...............................Lee Zahler
Supervising Editor ....Wyndham Gittens
Film Editor ....Earl Turner
Sound Engineer ....Terry Kellum
Art Director................................Ezra Paul
Special Effects and ....J. Laurence Wickland
   Miniatures
   LOCATIONS: Bronson Canyon; Iverson's
   BUDGET: $65,000
   NEGATIVE COST: $80,000

CAST:

Actor	*Character*
Ken Maynard	Ken Williams
Tarzan	Tarzan (Ken's horse)
Verna Hillie	Jane Corwin
Sid (Syd) Saylor	Breezy Baker
Edward Earle	Frank Blayden
Hooper Atchley	Dr. Edwards
Edward Hearn	Lake
Al Bridge	Tom Henderson
Bob Kortman	Rattler Henchman Hank
Lew Meehan	Rattler Henchman Red
George Chesebro	Rattler Henchman Anderson
Tom London	Rattler Henchman Morgan
Frank Ellis	Rattler Henchman Hughes
Jim Mason	Rattler Henchman Davis
Lynton Brent	Mathews, Telegrapher
Gene Autry	Thomas, Lake teamster (Chs. 6-8, 12)
Smiley Burnette	Lake teamster (Chs. 6-7, 12)

Don Brodie, Steve Clark,
 Francis Sayles ....Construction Workers
Tommy Coats ....Guard
Edmund Cobb ....The Rattler when masked
Jim Corey ....Corwin teamster Jim
Dick Dickinson, Curley
 Dresden, Al Haskell,
 Pascale Perry, Robert Walker,
 Wes Warner, Slim Whitaker .....Rattler Henchmen
Jack Evans, William Gould,
 Lee Shumway, Wally Wales .....Corwin teamsters
Carmencita Johnson ....Little Jane Corwin
Sam Lufkin..................................Lake Ranchhand Guard
Philo McCullough.......................Fake deputy
Lafe McKee ....Jim Corwin
Art Mix..Art, Lake teamster
Jack Rockwell ....Jack Jones, Corwin
 teamster
John "Pegleg" Wallace .... Pegleg Steve
Roger Williams ....Workman

STUNTS: Cliff Lyons (double for Ken Maynard);
Yakima Canutt.

THE FILM: When the B&L Railroad builds a tunnel that will put the Corwin Transportation Company out of business, the father of Jane Corwin (Verna Hillie) is the first person in a long line of people who are mysteriously murdered. Behind these murders is the sinister Rattler. Ken Williams (Ken Maynard), special investigator for the railroad, is determined to discover the identity of The Rattler. Ken learns The Rattler has a grand scheme to control transportation in the area. Of course, the Rattler's real identity is not unveiled until Chapter 12.

Fast paced and stuffed with exciting action and stunts, "Mystery Mountain" is one of Mascot's best serials. Although it went $15,000 over its $65,000 budget due to Maynard's insistence on making the picture as though he were still at Universal, it proved to be Mascot's most profitable serial to date, grossing close to $1 million.

Gene Autry and Smiley Burnette appear briefly in Chapters 6, 7, 8 and again quickly in Chapter 12. Oddly, perhaps prophetically, it is Gene who fires a rifle at Ken at the end of Chapter 6, thereby ending the chapter.

The Phantom Empire
Mascot serial, February 1935

CHAPTER TITLES: 1) The Singing Cowboy 2) The Thunder Riders 3) The Lightning Chamber 4) Phantom Broadcast 5) Beneath the Earth 6) Disaster From the Skies 7) From Death to Life 8) Jaws of Jeopardy 9) Prisoners of the Ray 10) The Rebellion 11) A Queen In Chains 12) The End of Murania

Producer ....Nat Levine
Production Supervisor..................Armand Schaefer
Directors......................................Otto Brower, B. Reeves "Breezy" Eason
Assistant Director.........................William Witney
Original Story...............................Wallace MacDonald, Gerald Geraghty, Hy Freedman (Freidman), (Maurice Geraghty -uncredited)
Screenplay Continuity..................John Rathmell, Armand Schaefer
Photography ....Ernest Miller, William Nobles
Added Photography ....William Bradford; Ellis "Bud" Thackery
Music..Lee Zahler, Henry Hadley, Hugo Risenfeld, Charles Dunworth and Ferdinand Herold's "Zampa Overture"
Musical Director ....Arthur Kay
Film Editor...................................Earl Turner
Associate Editor ....Walter Thompson
Sound Dept...................................Terry Kellum
Costumes.....................................Iris Burns
Set Decorations ....Mack D'Agostino, Ralph M. DeLacy, Jack Coyle
Special Effects.............................Howard Lydecker Jr., Gordon Schaefer, Billy Gilbert

SONGS: "Uncle Noah's Ark" (music and lyrics by Gene Autry, Smiley Burnette)—sung by Gene Autry, Smiley Burnette and Radio Rangers in Ch. 1, Gene and Radio Rangers in Ch. 12; "That Silver Haired Daddy of Mine" (music and lyrics by Gene Autry, Jimmy Long)—sung by Gene Autry in Ch. 1; "I'm Oscar, I'm Pete" (music and lyrics by Gene Autry, Smiley Burnette)—sung by Gene Autry, Smiley Burnette, William Moore in Ch. 2; "No Need to Worry" (music and lyrics by Gene Autry, Smiley Burnette)—sung by Radio Rangers in Ch. 4; "Uncle Henry" (music and lyrics by Gene Autry, Smiley Burnette)—sung by Gene Autry in Ch. 4; "I'm Getting a Moon's Eye View of the World" (music and lyrics Gene Autry, Smiley Burnette)—sung by Gene Autry in Ch. 8; "My Cross Eyed Gal" (music and lyrics by Gene Autry, Jimmy Long)—sung by Radio Rangers in Ch. 8; "Just Come on Back" (music and lyrics by Gene Autry, Smiley Burnette)—sung by Radio Rangers in Ch. 12.

RUNNING TIME: Ch. 1 is 30 minutes, all others run 18-20 minutes

FILMING DATES: Late 1934

LOCATIONS: Bronson Canyon; Iverson Ranch; Agoura Ranch; Griffith Observatory; Mack Sennett lot in San Fernando Valley

BUDGET: $70,000–$75,000

CAST:

Actor	*Character*
Gene Autry	Gene Autry
Frankie Darro	Frankie Baxter
Betsy King Ross	Betsy Baxter
Dorothy Christy	Queen Tika
Wheeler Oakman	Argo (Muranian High Chancellor)
Charles K. French	Mal
Warner Richmond	Rab
J. Frank Glendon	Prof. Beetson
Lester "Smiley" Burnette	Oscar
William Moore (aka Peter Potter)	Pete
Edward Piel Sr.	Dr. Cooper
Jack Carlyle	Saunders
Chuck Baldra	Deputy

Stanley Blystone ....Gaspar (Muranian
                                        television operator)
Don Brodie...................................Radio technician
Bob Burns, Jim Corey, Tracy
    Layne, Don Wayson ....Muranians
Fred Burns...................................Muranian priest
Bob Card ....Deputy
Lane Chandler, Bruce Mitchell....Muranian guards
Ray Corrigan, Slim Whitaker.......Thunder Riders
Frank Ellis..................................Thunder guard leader
Henry Hall...................................Muranian High Priest
Frankie Marvin.............................Frankie, Musician
Jack Jones, Ken Card, Loyal
    Underwood, Jad Dees, Aleth
    Hansen (aka Lem Giles),
    Charley Quirk, Ezra Paulette,
    Henry Braeholder (aka Hank
    Skillet) ....Musicians
George Magrill.............................Lt. Paul
Bobby Nelson..............................Junior Thunder Rider
Dick Rush....................................Sheriff
Richard Talmadge ....Thunder Rider captain
Wally Wales ....Thunder guard
Wally West ....Muranian soldier
Jay Wilsey ....Thunder guard
George Burton.............................Lt. Adar
Hal Boyer ....Capt. Ord
??..Tom Baxter
Cora Shannon..............................Guest with hearing aid
Pico ....Gene's Horse

STUNTS: Ken Cooper, Richard Talmadge, Jack Jones, George Magrill, Wally West.

THE FILM: Nat Levine was the motion picture entrepreneur at the head of Mascot Pictures who specialized in serials and B-features in the $30,000-$50,000 range. Mascot made the first sound serial in 1929, "King of the Kongo", and a total of 31 serials between 1927 and 1935. Levine used stars on their way down (Harry Carey, Ken Maynard, Bob Custer, Tom Mix), non-actor names from the sporting or circus world (Clyde Beatty, Red Grange) and stars to be (John Wayne, George Brent, Boris Karloff, Johnny Mack Brown—and Gene Autry).

Levine met Gene in Chicago in 1933 and put he, Smiley Burnette and Frankie Marvin under contract to Mascot for $100, $75 and $60 a week respectively. Then Mascot released its only feature western "In Old Santa Fe" starring Ken Maynard and featuring a ranch-party sequence with Gene, Smiley and Frankie. Under Levine's guidance Gene spent four months studying with an acting coach and training with two great stuntmen/horsemen, Yakima Canutt and Yancey Lane.

By this time, Levine was ready to star Ken Maynard in a serial, "Mystery Mountain". Unbilled and barely recognizable in minor roles are Autry and Burnette. Maynard, accustomed to higher standards at Universal

where he'd had his own production company, was not happy with Levine's fast-filming, lower budget way of working. The serial went over its four week schedule and budget. When it was over, Maynard and Levine agreed to part company.

However, Levine had already planned a second Maynard serial, "The Phantom Empire". He'd been grooming Gene Autry and the response to Gene from audiences who'd seen "In Old Santa Fe" was positive, so he elected to go with his instincts to star Gene as a singing radio cowboy in an expensive (by Mascot standards) 12 chapter combination western/science-fiction cliffhanger. Levine was actually hedging his bet. By combining two disparate genres, if "Phantom Empire" failed or alienated audiences with its Sci-Fi elements, the serial could certainly be counted on to succeed as a western. Oddly, line producer Armand Schaefer was against the whole idea and threatened to quit. Fortunately, he did not, for he and Gene became fast friends and worked together in business right up until the end of Gene's film career.

The original story was concocted by former silent star Wallace MacDonald. When talkies came in he played secondary roles and began writing scripts at Columbia, soon becoming story editor at Mascot. He later supervised writers at Republic and still later became a producer at Columbia.

A wilder, more preposterous screenplay had never been produced and a less likely, unknown star could hardly be imagined. Levine backed up Gene with juvenile stars Frankie Darro and Betsy King Ross, both daredevil riders. Darro was a seasoned actor who had already starred in five serials for Levine's Mascot ("Vanishing Legion", '31; "Lightning Warrior", '31; "The Devil Horse", '32; "The Wolf Dog", '33; "Burn 'Em Up Barnes", '34). Cute, freckled, 12 year old "World's Champion Trick Rider" Betsy King Ross came to Hollywood in '33 to appear in "Smoke Lightning" with George O'Brien, then co-starred at Mascot in Johnny Mack Brown's "Fighting with Kit Carson" serial ('33).

Fortunately for Levine and Mascot, for Gene and Smiley, and for all of us, the wild, preposterous combination was a rousing success, catapulting Gene to stardom nearly overnight and laying the foundation for a tremendous lifelong multi-million dollar career for Autry. Shrewdly, Levine heralded "The Phantom Empire" as "Mascot's greatest chapter-play achievement." And that it was—combining Murania, a futuristic subterranean city five miles beneath the surface peopled by a super-scientific race ruled by a beautiful queen, with the Thunder Riders, a hard-riding horde of juvenile horsemen with a "To the Rescue" motto, and singing western radio star, Gene Autry. Thrown into the mix were robots, television, death-rays, flame guns, airplanes, rich radium deposits sought by a devious band of scientists, the murder of Gene's partner, broad comedy and country music. How could it fail to entertain a Depression era audience anxious for escapism?

The complex, yet somehow basic, plot has discredited scientist Professor Beetson (J. Frank Glendon) seeking the entrance to the lost kingdom of Murania, rich in radium deposits. On the pretense of a vacation, Beetson and his cohorts come to Radio Ranch, a resort owned by Gene Autry and his partner, Tom Baxter. Radio Ranch is kept solvent by its daily radio broadcasts featuring Gene and his Radio Rangers. Unless Gene appears on the air each day at 2pm for the radio show, the radio contract will be cancelled and the ranch will be lost. (This ridiculous subplot later finds Gene broadcasting remotely from a shack and even an airplane!)

Smiley Burnette, William Moore, Betsy King Ross, Gene Autry, Frankie Darro, and musicians at Radio Ranch.

Baxter's teenaged youngsters, Frankie (Darro) and Betsy (King Ross), organize a group of Junior Thunder Riders after nearly being captured by the masked and caped Muranian horsemen who sound like thunder when they ride to the surface world.

With tourists and Radio Ranch in full swing, Beetson is prevented from going about his nefarious business of searching for the vast radium deposits they have detected. His plan is to get rid of Gene and see Radio Ranch deserted. Beetson murders Tom Baxter during a radio broadcast and frames Gene.

Meanwhile, far beneath the earth's surface, in Murania, Queen Tika (Dorothy Christy) observes everything that is taking place by means of radium-controlled television. She determines the only way to protect her kingdom is to do away with Gene, leaving nothing at Radio Ranch to attract tourist–surface dwellers.

Eventually, Gene, Frankie and Betsy fall into the hands of the Muranians with Tika ordering Gene's execution. Saved by treacherous Muranian Prime Minister Argo (Wheeler Oakman), Gene and his friends escape several perils and fight their way back to the surface.

Argo has planned a revolt to overthrow Queen Tika, but it rages out of control, destroying Murania and all its people.

Returning to Radio Ranch in time for his daily broadcast, Gene tricks a confession from Beetson and saves the day for all concerned.

For sheer lunacy, innocence and zany charm, there are few serials that can top "The Phantom Empire". It also was a groundbreaking serial, establishing a vogue for science-fiction chapterplays like "Flash Gordon" a year later and popularizing the new genre of singing cowboy westerns headed up by Gene himself.

Autry's rapid-fire success is startling. Taking a hard look at his qualities, we find a young cowboy singer not exactly blessed with striking good looks or assertive virility. Compared to men like Maynard, Jones, O'Brien, even the fledgling Wayne, Gene hardly seemed the type for hard action sequences. He possessed a quiet, pleasing personality, but, at this time, minimal acting ability. As a horseman, he compared unfavorably with Maynard, Jones, Gibson and others. He did write good cowboy ballads and sang in a pleasant style. Gene's rapid surge to three decades of stardom is proof "star quality" in the eyes of the public cannot be defined.

Gene's horsemanship by the time of "The Phantom Empire" was acceptable, his acting is basic with an emphasis of precise enunciation at the expense of expression, but comes across fine in the raw musical sequences. Most importantly, and a lasting key to Gene's success, he comes across as a pleasant, likeable average guy.

Oscar (Smiley Burnette) and Pete (William Moore) (later disc jockey Peter Potter) provide low grade, feeble attempts at comedy relief as two klutzy cowboy musicians. If "Phantom Empire" has a drawback, their irritating antics are it.

One of four entrances to a mine tunnel in Bronson Canyon in Griffith Park became the secret entrance to Murania with an attached makeshift papier-mâché and plaster door painted to match the rocky cliffside.

To simulate Murania, cast and crew converged on the newly built Griffith Observatory and Planetarium in Griffith Park. "The Phantom Empire" was filmed there the year construction was completed, with the observatory playing the underground city. The futuristic design of the structure was ideal to portray the architecture of a futuristic city. Gene did battle with Muranians on various exterior walkways and steps against the backdrop of the facility's copper roof, bronze doors and art deco walls.

As was customary in serials, two directors were employed to spell each other on alternate days. Both Otto Brower and "Breezy" Eason were veteran action specialists. Eason's early work includes the chariot race in 1926's "Ben Hur". Brower later directed action sequences in "Charge of the Light Brigade" ('36). Serving as assistant director was Levine's 19 year old office boy, William Witney, soon to become a top action director in his own right.

Some props, such as death rays and lab equipment (some of it generated by Kenneth Strickfadden who also designed lab equipment and sets for "Frankenstein", '31, "Mask of Fu Manchu", '32, "Flash Gordon", '36 and many others) were quite impressive. Less so were the robots, more comical than menacing. Understandable when one realizes the seven robot suits were located at Western Costume having made their initial appearance in MGM's 1933 musical comedy, "Dancing Lady" with Joan Crawford. They seemed even more out-of-place in 1952 when Columbia resurrected them for their "Captain Video" serial. The vast Muranian cityscape was the talented miniature work of Howard Lydecker Jr., then 23, soon to become a legend in the special effects field.

To achieve the impressive effect in Chapter 12 of Murania being destroyed, frames from the film were enlarged onto glass stereopticon plates coated with a thick emulsion. When heated, the emulsion oozed downward while cameras filmed the deteriorating image in slow motion.

NOTES AND COMMENTS: Two feature versions of "The Phantom Empire" were released in April 1940. "Radio Ranch", adapted by Gerald and Maurice Geraghty, from Mascot, and the less common "Men With Steel Faces" released simultaneously in New York by Times Films. Both ran 70 minutes. Oddly, in England, "The Phantom Empire" was issued as "It Couldn't Possibly Happen".

In 1979 NBC premiered a midseason replacement series called "Cliffhangers", a weekly show comprised of three separate segments seeking to recapture the fun and escapism of yesteryear. One segment, "The Secret Empire", owes everything to "The Phantom Empire". A frontier marshal and his young companion discover a futuristic city hidden underground. Sound familiar? NBC representatives fervently denied any knowledge of "The Phantom Empire" or any inspiration derived from the '35 serial. No matter. By then "The Phantom Empire" had passed into public domain. Anyone who cared

Gene's in trouble far beneath the Earth's surface in Murania.

to use material connected with the film was perfectly legal to do so.

FILM COMMENTS: Gene Autry: "The first time I saw Smiley Burnette I was playing a little town (in Illinois), Champaign-Urbana. I had an accordion player and he became sick, so I went to the manager of the theater and said, 'Do you happen to know of an accordion player around here?' And he said, 'Down here about 15 miles in Tuscola, Illinois, there's a guy that plays accordion, he sings and he's pretty good. His name is Smiley Burnette.' So I gave Smiley a call. I asked how much he was making. He said, 'About $15 a week and my gasoline.' I offered him about $40 a week and his expenses when I was on tour. Smiley said, 'You've just hired yourself a man.' We drove down there and I met Smiley at a drugstore and believe it or not he was driving a little Austen car. We went out to his home and he played the piano, the handsaw and he sang and did everything—and bugged his eyes out. And I said, 'I think you'll be all right so I hired Smiley and he worked with me on WLS (radio) in Chicago for about two years and then I had a chance to go to Hollywood and I brought Smiley out with me."[1]

WHAT THE EXHIBITOR HAD TO SAY: "Here is something different in serials. Based on the fantastic ideas made popular by the comic strips such as 'Buck Rogers' and 'Flash Gordon'. Started this on a hot Sunday but it is building and holding those who started it. It is well done with more plot than most serials. Just showed the third episode. The producers deserve credit for this new idea in serials and the clever manner in which this has been produced."

—J. E. Stocker, Myrtle Theater,
Detroit, Michigan (June 1935)

"The picture ("Radio Ranch" feature version) was old and in bad condition, but the patrons ate it up."

—Mel Jolley, Columbia Theater,
St. Thomas, Ontario, Canada (November 1941)

SOURCES:
1. "Melody Ranch Theater" showing of "Phantom Empire" feature ("Radio Ranch") on Nashville Network, 1988.

NAT LEVINE *presents*
GENE AUTRY in "RADIO RANCH"

A MASCOT REISSUE

A Feature Version of the Serial Motion Picture "Phantom Empire"

Smiley Burnette, Gene Autry, William Moore, and Gene's musicians must appear on the air daily or their contract will be cancelled. The lobby card is from the featurized version of "The Phantom Empire" serial.

Tumbling Tumbleweeds
Republic, September 1935

Producer ....Nat Levine
Supervisor ....Armand Schaefer
Director ....Joseph Kane
Assistant Director.........................Mack V. Wright
Original Story..............................Alan Ludwig
(pseudonym for
Armand Schaefer)
Screenplay....................................Ford Beebe
Photography ....Ernest Miller
Supervising Editor ....Joseph H. Lewis

Film Editor ....Lester Orlebeck
Sound Engineer ....Terry Kellum
Sound Effects ....Roy Granville
Musical Director ....Abe Meyer

SONGS: "I'll Yodel My Troubles Away" (music and lyrics by Gene Autry and Smiley Burnette)—sung by Gene Autry; "Cowboy Medicine Show" (music and lyrics by Smiley Burnette)—sung by Gene Autry and troupe; "Corn-Fed and Rusty" (music and lyrics by Smiley Burnette)—sung by Smiley Burnette; "Ridin' Down the Canyon" (music and lyrics by Smiley Burnette and Gene Autry)—sung by Gene Autry (duet with himself on record); "That Silver Haired Daddy of Mine" (music and lyrics by Gene Autry and Jimmy Long)—sung by Gene Autry; "Tumbling Tumbleweeds" (music and lyrics by Bob Nolan)—sung by Gene Autry.

RUNNING TIME: 61 minutes
FILMING DATES: July 6 to 12, 1935
LOCATIONS: Victorville, California, desert area; Monogram Ranch townsite
BUDGET: $15,344
NEGATIVE COST: $18,801

CAST:

Actor	*Character*
Gene Autry ....Gene Autry
Smiley Burnette ....Smiley
Lucille Browne............................Jerry Brooks
George Hayes...............................Dr. Parker
Norma Taylor ....Janet Brooks
Edward Hearn ....Barney Craven
Eugene Jackson...........................Eightball
Jack Rockwell ....McWade
George Chesebro..........................Henchman Connors
Frankie Marvin............................Shorty
Slim Whitaker ....Foreman Higgins
Joseph Girard ....Autry Sr.
Charles King ....Blaze Williams
Cornelius Keefe ....Harry Brooks
Tom London................................Sykes
George Burton..............................Sheriff Manton

Bartlett A. Carre, Bob Card..........Deputies
Tommy Coats, Ken Cooper,
   Tracy Layne, Cliff Lyons,
   Bud McClure, Bud Pope ....Henchmen
Henry Hall....................................Nester Leader
Chuck Baldra ....Nester Rider
Frank Brownlee............................Cattleman
Ralph Bucko, Roy Bucko,
   Wally West...............................Posse Riders
Horace B. Carpenter....................Town Drunk
Steve Clark, Archie Ricks............Cowhands
Oscar Gahan................................Musician
Otto Hoffman, Fred Parker,
   Herman Hack............................Nesters
Iris Meredith................................Girl
Lou Morphy, George Morrell,
   Tom Smith, Jack Hendricks......Townsmen
Arthur Thalasso............................Blacksmith
Champion.....................................Gene's horse

STUNTS: Ken Cooper (for Gene Autry), Cliff Lyons, Tommy Coats.

THE FILM: Republic publicity announced, "The singing idol of the air now becomes the troubadour of the trails" and "Radio's singing cowboy takes to the saddle in a musical action drama."

It was a classic gamble by the newly formed Republic with a practically unknown to the screen singing cowboy in an all new genre that introduced songs and background music to the standard B-western format. Certainly cowboys like Bob Steele and others had sung on-screen before, but Gene Autry's first feature film in a lead role was shrewdly constructed as a traditional western with songs introduced

naturally through a medicine show element. Surrounded by an array of behind the scenes talent that would go on to distinguished careers of their own, Gene acquits himself well, although he is very stiff and obviously not quite yet comfortable delivering some of the called-for forceful lines of dialogue. Gene clearly doesn't yet know what to do with his hands. However, he appears much more at ease in the musical and more relaxed scenes as his natural instincts take over. Gene isn't helped by a ridiculous amount of makeup, making him look like a refugee from the silent era. Gladly, this was remedied in the next couple of features. By contrast, Gene's sidekick, Smiley Burnette, seems a screen natural, complementing screen veteran George Hayes nicely without getting in the way.

The prologue to "Tumbling Tumbleweeds" reads, "In the Old West there was no law. Men came, saw good land and took what they wanted—the stronger divided empires. Later arrivals asked only for water and a plot of ground where they might live in peace. These were the nesters. And the great land lords hated them. From the hatred came bitter range warfare."

Gene Autry returns home after a five year absence as a singer with Dr. Parker's Medicine Show troupe, which includes Parker (George Hayes), Smiley Burnette, Eightball (black actor/dancer Eugene Jackson) and Shorty (Frankie Marvin), only to find his best friend, Harry Brooks (Cornelius Keefe) accused of the murder of Gene's rancher father, with whom Gene had a quarrel before he left town years ago. Eventually, through Brooks' wife (Norma Taylor), Gene discovers Brooks sold water rights to Gene's father, water rights town big-shot Barney Craven (Edward Hearn) desired for himself, so he killed Gene's father and framed Brooks.

Gene plants a trap for Craven and his henchmen, giving an opportunity for a slam-bang free-for-all fight with a dozen or more men involved while the runaway medicine show wagon careens along at breakneck speed.

Besides this exciting finale, there's a terrific action sequence at the start with plenty of music and excitement throughout the picture. The romance angle is slight for this first entry with Gene reuniting, after five years away, with blonde Lucille Browne. Highlight of the film gives Gene a chance to sing his record hit "That Silver Haired Daddy of Mine" just as he learns of his father's death.

"Tumbling Tumbleweeds" laid the template for many similar features to follow and exhibitors raved to trade papers about the mixture of action, music and comedy and asked for more, leading Republic to release two more Autry westerns in 1935, nine in 1936

Gene Autry confronts Edward Hearn while George Hayes, Lucille Browne and Smiley Burnette gather around.

The crowd watches as Gene Autry grapples with George Chesebro and Jack Rockwell holds off Tom London.

and seven to eight per year from there on.

"Tumbling Tumbleweeds" led to a host of singing cowboy imitators, but only Roy Rogers and Tex Ritter came within shouting distance.

"Tumbling Tumbleweeds" became a picture of worldwide historic significance.

NOTES AND COMMENTS: According to Republic files, Gene's original three year pact with six month options started at $100 per week with "Tumbling Tumbleweeds" and rose to $350 by mid 1938. From then on he was signed to yearly contracts, the first covering the 1938-1939 period calling for $6,000 each for the first two pictures and $10,000 each for the remainder. (See "The Old Barn Dance".)

No small reason for the success of "Tumbling Tumbleweeds" is the myriad of young talent behind the camera. Director Joseph (Joe) Kane, born in 1894 in San Diego, came to directing by way of film editing. His work was speedy, but always clean and fast-moving. He took time with action sequences, then moved things along by completing several pages of dialogue rather quickly. Producer Nat Levine saw his potential and moved him up from the cutting room to director on the first three

Joe Kane.

Autry pictures. Kane went on to direct dozens of Autry, John Wayne, Roy Rogers and Bill Elliott westerns for Republic until the studio folded in 1959. From there he moved easily into TV. He died in 1975.

Screenwriter Ford Beebe, born in Grand Rapids, Michigan, in 1887, was first a newspaper reporter in San Diego. By 1914, he was writing scenarios for the young Universal studio who quickly moved him up to scripting western shorts and features as well as serials. Beebe also wrote four of Ken Maynard's First National starrers before arriving at Nat Levine's Mascot to work on several serial scripts as well as move into directing. When Mascot was folded into Republic he stayed long enough to script "Tumbling Tumbleweeds" then moved to Columbia, Universal and others, turning out excellent work on dozens of features. Beebe reunited briefly with Gene during the TV era to helm several episodes of Flying A's "Adventures of Champion". Shortly before his 90th birthday he died in 1978.

Best known as an executive producer, Armand "Mandy" Schaefer, born August 5, 1898, in Tavistock, Ontario, Canada, entered the film industry in 1924 as a property man for Mack Sennett after serving in the U.S. Army tank corps during WWI. By the early '30s he was directing low budget westerns and serials for various studios, including Mascot. With the merger of Mascot into Republic, Nat Levine appointed Mandy supervising producer on the Autry series. Under the pseudonym of Alan Ludwig, Schaefer developed the original story for "Tumbling Tumbleweeds". It was the beginning of a long and close relationship between Mandy and Gene, who appointed him president of his Flying A production company in 1947 when Gene moved over to Columbia. With the advent of TV, Mandy served as producer on all of Gene's TV productions. Schaefer died September 26, 1967.

Cinematographer Ernest "Ernie" Miller was one of the most respected cameramen in the business having cut his teeth on low budget westerns and action pictures beginning in 1921. Like the others, he was working with Nat Levine when Mascot merged into Republic. He stayed with Republic, working on many Autry features, up through 1945 when he moved over to PRC and Lippert, finally finishing out an illustrious 33 year career in 1954 with several Bill Elliott Allied Artists westerns.

Supervising film editor Joseph H. Lewis was born of Russian parentage in New York City in 1907. At 17 he joined his older brother who was working at MGM as an editor. Leaving there in '35, he became chief cutter at the dynamic

Mascot. He was another of the Mascot veterans to join Republic when Mascot folded into the new studio. Following a salary dispute, he eventually joined Universal doing outstanding work as a director on Bob Baker and, later, Johnny Mack Brown B's. He later helmed several critically acclaimed film noir pictures before moving heavily into TV with some of the best directed episodes of "The Rifleman" and other TVers. Joe died at 93 August 30, 2000.

Working under Lewis was film editor Lester Orlebeck (1907-1970) from Sheboygan, Wisconsin, who found a home with the fledgling Republic and never strayed. Mostly he was an editor on over 100 Republic westerns, but did try his hand at directing eight Three Mesquiteers westerns in '40-'41. Finding he preferred editing, he remained with Republic til 1948, moving over to TV in the '50s to work on "Gunsmoke", "Wanted Dead or Alive", "Gilligan's Island" and others.

"Hold it!" Frankie Marvin, Slim Whitaker, Gene Autry, Jack Rockwell and Smiley Burnette put a stop to badmen trying to rough up Eugene Jackson.

Worthy of note is the curious fact that, though the film is supposedly set in the old west (the prologue states this), when Gene returns home "five years later" he is a recording star. However, the story continues to unfold as if in the old west again. It's an interesting point as very soon Republic would begin to ponder over which time period to set their singing cowboy sensation in—old or modern west. The other studios whose singing cowboys sprung up like weeds—Dick Foran, Fred Scott, Bob Baker, George Houston, Tex Ritter, James Newill, Eddie Dean—had no doubts about this, keeping their cowboy boots firmly planted in the old west. As we will see, Republic had other ideas.

A 1935 tie-in promotion to the film included a song writing contest sponsored by Sam Fox Publishing Company, publisher of Bob Nolan's "Tumbling Tumbleweeds", and Republic with the winner to have his or her song published by Sam Fox.

A novelization of "Tumbling Tumbleweeds" was to appear in a new Street and Smith pulp publication, MOVIE ACTION.

At the time "Tumbling Tumbleweeds" was released, Gene had a hit recording of the Bob Nolan tune on the Melotone label (a subsidiary of the American Record Corporation), backed up by "Old Missouri Moon".

Many reference books list the Sons of the Pioneers (with Bob Nolan and Roy Rogers) as being in the cast of "Tumbling Tumbleweeds", but they do not appear in the film. The confusion no doubt arises from the title song which was written by Nolan.

Promotion-wise, Republic offered to theatre owners a 10x2' likeness of Gene Autry for lobby display, a song

sheet, gum-backed postage stamp giveaways with a portrait of Gene for sticking on letters and a crayon coloring set in a 3x6" envelope with three crayons.

Working titles for the picture before Republic settled on "Tumbling Tumbleweeds" were "Melody Trail", "Singin' Cowboy", "Red River Valley", "Galloping Ministrel", "Song of the Six-Gun", "Tex Comes A'Singin'" and "Sagebrush Troubadour". Several of these found their way onto the screen as later Autry film titles.

Reissued while Gene was in the service during WWII, more "modern" images of Gene were used on much of the re-release advertising for "Tumbling Tumbleweeds" to make the film appear to be more current to the movie-going public. According to the re-issue pressbook, Gene turned down a $5,000 offer to endorse a cigarette because of the possible effect it might have on his young fans.

Smiley Burnette and Gene Autry wrote the beautiful "Ridin' Down the Canyon" on the back of a magazine while he and Gene were driving out to California. Since neither could read or write music, in the next town they came to they had someone put it to music. The song is currently in the U. S. Congressional Hall of Fame as being one of the top 10 most beautiful ballads.

FILM COMMENTS: *Gene Autry:* "I returned to Hollywood in early 1935, to stay, and to strike paydirt in 'Tumbling Tumbleweeds'. It was the first of a genre, the first western plotted and sold around the main character's ability to sing. The Autry image was established in that film almost 100%. It was tinkered with in minor ways; on occasion I wore a Tim McCoy style neckerchief, three feet of white silk. But, for the most part, the Autry of 'Tumbling Tumbleweeds' was the Autry of 1947's 'Robin Hood of

Texas'.[1]

"It was the first picture Republic made. They only had two stars in those days, me and a young guy by the name of John Wayne. Sometimes it was rather hard to blend songs and action, but we managed to do it.[2]

"It has been pointed out frequently that the cowboy sings about almost everything but his mother. The only explanation I can give about this is that they are so essentially masculine they lean a great deal more toward the paternal side of the family. They respect virility and action. Perhaps this is the reason for 'Silver Haired Daddy of Mine' being more popular than other numbers. When 'Silver Haired Daddy of Mine' passed the one million mark, Columbia records gave me the first gold record that was ever made. The publicity department thought it was time to celebrate so they all got together and said I think we ought to give Gene a gold record. It kinda set the stage.[3]

"Remember Mary Ford? (Later) she was a member of my radio troupe. Mary and her husband, Les Paul, hit it big with their multiple-track recordings in the '50s. I used it, for the first time, I am told, with an early version of the title song from 'Tumbling Tumbleweeds'. The multiple track allowed me to sing both the lead and the tenor; in other words, my own harmony."[4]

Lucile Browne (misspelled Lucille in the film's credits): "Gene had a rabid enthusiasm for baseball. Girls' softball was the rage then. There were small parks all over town. Jim (husband/actor James Flavin) and I invited Gene to go with us to a game. He was to meet us at the park and we would save him a seat. He arrived after the game started. We were sitting high up in the bleachers so he had to climb through the crowd to reach us. He was all decked out in one of his fancy cowboy outfits. At that time, it was rare to see one off the set. You can imagine the comments and razzing he took. Jim and I wanted to sink through the seats. Little did we realize, then, that he was starting a new era by being the first really popular singing cowboy."[5]

CAST BIOS: Gene Autry and Smiley Burnette's friendship was based on common struggles, mutual respect, similar interests and the genuine nature of both men. Fate, persistence and Lady Luck all had a share in their first meeting.

Lester Alvin Burnette was born March 18, 1911, in Summum, Illinois. His parents were both ordained ministers of the Christian Church who moved to Monticello, near Urbana, when Smiley was young.

Living next to a couple who were musicians with access to various instruments, Lester was allowed to borrow an instrument, go off and learn how to play it, a task he took to naturally. By nine, Lester could play ten instruments and by 22 he had mastered as many as 50. He learned music by ear and eventually could play up to 105 instruments.

Lester dropped out of school due to family financial needs and never finished the 9th grade. To help support the family he worked at a variety of jobs, eventually finding his true calling with WDZ radio in Tuscola, Illinois. One of his tasks was to read the daily newspaper comic strips using multiple character voices. Seeking a name for himself on a children's program, he came up with Smiley. It stuck.

In December 1932, Gene, working at Chicago radio's WLS (World's Largest Store), was under contract to Sears and Roebuck. Finding himself in need of an accordion player, he was told about Smiley in downstate Illinois. Gene phoned Smiley, increased his salary and a lifelong friendship and bond was formed.

Smiley joined Gene's organization in early 1933, made public appearances with Gene and worked on several recording sessions. Initially, Smiley worked with Gene as part of his group on WLS, then in December 1933 he officially became a member of the WLS National Barn Dance. The following year, the pair headed west to provide a musical interlude for Ken Maynard's "In Old Santa Fe". They also had bit parts in Mascot's Ken Maynard serial "Mystery Mountain". Upon completion of these films, they headed back to WLS.

While on tour in Wisconsin, two contract offers arrived for Gene and Smiley from Mascot's Nat Levine to star in the 12 chapter serial "The Phantom Empire". Feature pictures followed.

Smiley and newspaper columnist Dallas MacDonnell met and were married in October 1936. Over the years the couple adopted four children, all from Tennessee.

When Gene entered the service during WWII, Republic cast Smiley in several Roy Rogers pictures, along with those of Eddie Dew, Bob Livingston and Sunset Carson. When Columbia offered Smiley more money he exited Republic in 1944, moving over to Columbia's Durango Kid series with Charles Starrett in 1946. When that series ended in 1952, Gene was now producing his own pictures at Columbia, so the pair was reunited for Gene's final feature westerns.

In 1953 Gene Autry said, "Smiley is not only one of my oldest friends, but he's one of the busiest and most talented

Gene Autry and Smiley Burnette made a perfect B-Western team beginning with their first film, "Tumbling Tumbleweeds."

Smiley Burnette as he looked in later days with Gene and in the Charles Starrett/Durango Kid Westerns.

western actors in the business. He's had more than 300 songs published. A mutual friend recommended Smiley when I needed a good accordionist and I hired him. That was the best hunch I ever played. When I came to Hollywood six months later to make my first picture, Smiley came along and was immediately signed for a supporting role. To appear anywhere now without Smiley by my side would be like trying to get by without my right arm."[6]

By the same token, Smiley Burnette once said, "I enjoyed working in pictures with Gene. He feels if an actor steals the picture, it makes for a good picture. All he wants is the picture to be a Gene Autry picture. I never had a cross word from him in all the years I worked with him, and I know of times I tried his patience. He'll never know how grateful I am to him for all he's done for me, and if I told him, he would think I was gushy, so I don't tell him."[7]

As an insight into Smiley's personality, Gene offered, "Smiley had a big party over at his house one time, sent everybody invitations and he said be sure and bring a shovel. So everybody came over with a shovel. When they got there, we found out he was digging a swimming pool (laughs) and he had everybody out there diggin' that swimming pool for him. That tied about anything I ever heard. (Laughs)"[8]

Smiley continued to do personal appearances all over the country when the films ended and once again came before the camera for TV's "Petticoat Junction" series in September 1963, becoming known to a new generation as Charlie Pratt, the Cannonball engineer. Finishing his scenes for the last show of the '66-'67 season, he was hospitalized in Encino, California, and died of leukemia February 16, 1967.

Smiley's original hat and shirt were placed in the Cowboy Hall of Fame in Oklahoma City in 1962. He was inducted into the Western Music Association Hall of Fame in 1998 and was honored with a star on Hollywood's Walk of Fame in 1986.

Pretty, blue-eyed Lucile Browne has the distinction of being Gene's first leading lady in a feature film. Born March 18, 1907, in Memphis, Tennessee, following education at the National Park Seminary in Washington DC, she became an artist's model in New York and Chicago. After securing stage work with a Chicago stock company Browne worked in films from 1929 til the mid '40s and again briefly in 1950. She later became president of the Screen Extras Guild. The co-star of six serials and eight westerns was married to actor James Flavin in 1932. Their deaths in 1976 were only weeks apart.

The inimitable George Francis Hayes, born May 7, 1885, in Wellsville, New York, was the only member of his family to get the acting bug. His father was a hotel man, his brother Clark was an oilman, while his other brother William was involved in the stock business in Idaho. As a young man, Hayes worked in a circus and played semi-pro baseball. He appeared in vaudeville and on the legit stage, primarily in stock companies. Although he'd made several films in the '20s, he lost most of his money in the 1929 stock market crash and returned to movies that year at which time he made "Rainbow Man" for Paramount. By the time of "Tumbling Tumbleweeds" Hayes had already made a name for himself as both comic sidekick and heavy in westerns seeing duty opposite Harry Carey, Bob Steele, Rex Bell, John Wayne and others. Hayes joined the Hopalong Cassidy series in 1936 as Windy Halliday before returning to Republic, honing his personification of Gabby Hayes to a T in a string of Roy Rogers and Bill Elliott B-westerns. He worked in two other westerns with Gene, "In Old Monterey" ('39) and "Melody Ranch" ('40).

In real life, he was the exact opposite of the character he played on film. He was well read, well groomed, serious and highly philosophical. Hayes died February 9, 1969.

The importance of producer Armand "Mandy" Schaefer to Gene Autry's career is immeasurable. Mandy started with Gene as a co-writer and supervising producer on "The Phantom Empire" under the auspices of Mascot head Nat Levine. When next Levine tried to sell Schaefer on the idea of starring Gene in a new series of B-westerns, ones with as much music as gunplay and action, Schaefer threatened to quit, believing the idea ridiculous. However, Mandy hung in there as producer of "Tumbling Tumbleweeds" and with its staggering box office success was quickly convinced of Gene's popularity and that of the singing-cowboy western. Mandy produced Gene's first 15 Republic titles from 1935 to 1937, as well as "In Old Monterey" in 1939.

When Gene returned from WWII, Schaefer produced the first three of Gene's Republic films.

Gene recognized Mandy's producing talent, knew he liked and could depend on him, thereby signing Schaefer to an exclusive contract as producer of all his Columbia westerns.

Armand Schaefer.

When Gene moved into television with his Flying A Productions, Schaefer was at the helm as producer of not only "The Gene Autry Show", but as producer on every show Gene developed—"The Range Rider", "Death Valley Days", "Annie Oakley", "Buffalo Bill Jr." and "The Adventures of Champion".

As stated, Armand L. Schaefer was born August 5, 1898, in Tavistock, Ontario, Canada. Immigrating to the U.S. with his family in 1905, by 1920 he was living in Spokane, Washington, with his father, Fred, who was employed as a laborer in the fuel industry.

Schaefer entered pictures in 1924 with the Mack Sennett Studio as assistant prop man to director Roy Del Ruth. He soon moved to the Christie's organization as prop man, electrician, grip, set dresser, whatever was needed. He was learning a trade in the burgeoning motion picture industry.

With Action Pictures for Pathé he was assistant director on over 50 silent westerns starring Buffalo Bill Jr., Wally Wales and Buddy Roosevelt.

As sound came in, Schaefer freelanced as assistant director and/or director on low budget westerns and serials, soon joining Nat Levine's Mascot as a director and supervising producer…which is where he first encountered Gene.

After producing the first 15 Autry features, Republic moved Mandy over to a variety of other films from 1938-1946, which is when Gene returned from service. Over the years, he was Republic's most prolific producer, amassing 68 producing credits.

As stated, when Gene set up his production facilities with Flying A, Mandy was hired exclusively as producer.

Gene Autry and Republic president Herbert J. Yates while on tour in England in 1939.

When Flying A wrapped up production, Mandy retired to Newport Beach, California, where he died at 69 on September 26, 1967.

Born August 24, 1880, in Brooklyn, NY, and educated at Columbia University, Herbert J. (John) Yates, the cigar-chomping force behind Republic Pictures, spent his early adulthood as a salesman for the American Tobacco Company and for Liggett and Myers as an account executive. At the beginning of WWI Yates took his first stab at motion picture production with a handful of silent films in 1915. That led him to create Consolidated Film Industries in 1922, a far more lucrative venture.

In 1933, slapstick producer Mack Sennett fell on hard times, filing for bankruptcy. Mascot owner Nat Levine leased the studio at 4024 Radford in North Hollywood.

In 1935 Yates approached Levine with an offer. Since Mascot as well as Monogram and several small independents were customers of his film lab, to which they owed considerable money, Yates convinced Mascot, Monogram, Liberty, Chesterfield and Invincible to merge under the wings of the Republic eagle in mid 1935.

This merger, however, was not one of equals, so Trem Carr and W. Ray Johnson departed Republic in 1937 to reform their Monogram Pictures. Yates also bought out Levine's interest in 1937.

Yates' reign at Republic lasted until 1959 when he was ultimately ousted by stockholders who'd grown increasingly dissatisfied with him. Much of the resentment centered around Yates' seemingly blatant favoritism of his Czechoslovakian ice-skating wife, Vera Hruba Ralston, whom he repeatedly cast in big, expensive films that often lost money due to her lack of acting skills. Also, Yates stubbornly refused to license Republic's film library to television, a mistake that initially cost the company thousands of dollars. Fortunately, Yates eventually realized television's potential and licensed the Republic library to TV and even produced several TV series ("Stories of the Century", "Frontier Doctor", "Adventures of Dr. Fu Manchu") in the mid '50s. However, with no strong production head and faced with the onslaught of television in an era of declining theater revenue, Republic's sprawling studio became more valuable as real estate. By May of 1959 Yates called it quits, leasing the studio to Lippert Pictures. CBS-TV became the studio's principal lessee in 1963, purchasing the property in April 1967.

As an understanding of how Yates operated, Gene stated, "Herb Yates had two personalities. When you were with Herb Yates socially, he was one of the finest hosts you could ever be with. He took me to England in 1939; he was a perfect gentleman, perfect host, spent money… I've been with him to nightclubs, been with him playing golf. When you play golf with him he wouldn't let you ever tip a caddie. I've seen him tip a caddie $100 like it was nothin'. But when you walked into his office and sat on the other side of that desk, he was tough. He'd argue with you over $1."[9]

An extremely wealthy man, Yates died on February 3, 1966.

WHAT THE EXHIBITOR HAD TO SAY: "A picture no exhibitor need have reluctance in booking. A worthy successor to "In Old Arizona"; with more emphasis on hard riding and gunplay. Gene Autry sings several songs he has popularized with his recordings and displays a pleasing personality. This well produced film was strong at the box office and received excellent audience response."

—J. W. Noah, New Liberty and Ideal Theaters,
Ft. Worth, Texas (November 1935)

"'Tumbling Tumbleweeds' has all the earmarks of a major studio western. We popularized Gene Autry with the serial 'The Phantom Empire', and had a ready-made audience. We had an extra large children's attendance, larger than the usual Thanksgiving matinee. This was double billed with 'Front Page Woman' and the show pleased old and young."

—J. E. Stocker, Myrtle Theater,
Detroit, Michigan (December 1935)

"I had more profit left on 'Tumbling Tumbleweeds' than I did 'Top Hat'. And that is saying a-plenty. People came to see this picture that I had never seen in the theatre before. And all left satisfied."

—M. S. Porter, Orpheum Theater,
Nelsonville, Ohio (January 1936)

SOURCES:

1. Autry, Gene with Herskowitz, Mickey. *Back In the Saddle Again.* Doubleday, 1978. p. 40.

2. "Melody Ranch Theater" showing of "Tumbling Tumbleweeds" on Nashville Network, 1987.

3. *Tumbling Tumbleweeds* pressbook. 1935.

4. Autry, Gene with Herskowitz, Mickey. *Back In the Saddle Again.* Doubleday, 1978. p. 52.

5. Audio interview with Robert Malcolmson. 1970.

6. *Who's Who in Western Stars #3.* Dell Pub., 1953. p. 31.

7. *Western Clippings #27.* January/February 1999. p.35.

8. "Melody Ranch Theater" on Nashville Network, 1987.

9. "Melody Ranch Theater" showing of "Robin Hood of Texas" on Nashville Network, 1987.

Melody Trail
Republic, October 1935

Producer ....Nat Levine
Supervisor ....Armand Schaefer
Director ....Joseph Kane
Original Story..............................Sherman Lowe and
                                  Betty Burbridge
Screenplay...................................Sherman Lowe
Photography ....Ernest Miller
Supervising Editor ....Joseph H. Lewis
Film Editor..................................Lester Orlebeck
Sound Engineer...........................Terry Kellum
Sound Effects ....Roy Granville
Original Music ....Lee Zahler

SONGS: "Hold On Little Dogies, Hold On" (music and lyrics by Gene Autry and Smiley Burnette)—sung by Gene Autry; "On the Melody Trail" (music and lyrics by Smiley Burnette)—sung by Gene Autry; "Way Down On the Bottom" (music and lyrics by Smiley Burnette)—sung by Smiley Burnette; "A Lone Cowboy On a Lone Prairie" (music and lyrics by Gene Autry and Smiley Burnette)—sung by Gene and the girls; "Western Lullaby" (music and lyrics by Gene Autry and Smiley Burnette)—sung by Gene, Smiley and the girls; "My Neighbor Hates Music" (music and lyrics by Smiley Burnette)—sung by Smiley Burnette; "Where Will the Wedding Supper Be" (music and lyrics by Gene Autry and Smiley Burnette)—sung by Gene and the cast.

    RUNNING TIME: 61 minutes
    FILMING DATES: August 21-27, 1935
    LOCATIONS: Rodeo scenes shot at Pendleton, Oregon, rodeo; Jack Garner Ranch
    BUDGET: $15,075
    NEGATIVE COST: $18,386

CAST:

Actor	*Character*
Gene Autry	Gene Autry
Ann Rutherford	Millicent "Millie" C. Thomas
Smiley Burnette	Frog Millhouse
Wade Boteler...............................	Timothy T. Thomas
Willy Castello	Frantz
Al Bridge.....................................	Matt Kirby
Fern Emmett................................	Nell
Marie Quillan	Perdita
Gertrude Messinger......................	Cuddles
Abe Lefton	Rodeo Announcer
Tracy Layne	Henchman Slim
Baby Shah	Baby Ricca
Jane Barnes	Helen
Tex Cooper, Tom Smith	Townsmen
George DeNormand	Henchman Pete
Marion 'Mary Ann' Dowling.......	Sally
Oscar Gahan, Frankie Marvin, Wes Warner, Al Taylor..............	Rustlers
Herman Hack	Henchman
Chick Hannon, Joe Yrigoyen	Riders
Fred Parker..................................	Storekeeper
Ione Reed	Mamie
Montie Montana..........................	Rodeo Rider on Paint Horse
Chuck Baldra	Rodeo Employee
Champion.....................................	Champion
Buck (dog)	Souvenir

    STUNTS: Joe Yrigoyen, Ken Cooper (Gene's double), George DeNormand, Cliff Lyons.

THE FILM: A much lighter touch is applied to Gene Autry's second feature, "Melody Trail", setting the tone for the series by blending music, comedy and western action into a more modern day west with cars and dude ranches involved.

This film is noteworthy in the fact that two firsts occur. Smiley Burnette, Gene's sidekick, is given the screen name of Frog Millhouse, which he continued to use throughout the series, and Gene's horse Champion receives on-screen billing and is called by name several times in the film.

Gene's acting continued to improve, as he seemed more at ease, more natural, in dialogue exchanges.

After winning a $1,000 purse in the bronco-riding event at a rodeo, Gene Autry and his pal Frog Millhouse are asleep when a gypsy (Willy Castello) steals the money. Now broke, Gene, having been smitten by Millicent Thomas whom he spotted at the rodeo, and Frog accept jobs as cooks, even though they know absolutely nothing about the culinary arts, at the Triple T Ranch, owned by Millicent's strong-willed rancher father (Wade Boteler). Suspected of rustling, which they are, the cowboys of the ranch, headed up by sneering ex-foreman Matt Kirby (Al Bridge) are let go and replaced by a group of girls. Meanwhile, Millicent's loveable but kleptomaniac Saint Bernard, Souvenir, "steals" the baby belonging to the gypsy (who made off with Gene's rodeo winnings) and his wife Perdita (Marie Quillan). As Millicent is caring for the child, the gypsy, Frantz, arrives at the ranch looking for his baby. Not noticing Millicent has returned the baby to Frantz, Gene and Smiley observe Frantz leaving, and, assuming he is a kidnapper, give chase, eventually discovering he is the thief who stole Gene's money. This turn of events resolved, Gene helps the cowgirls by capturing Kirby and his rustlers.

NOTES AND COMMENTS: The original Champion, the horse Gene rode in all his future pre-war Republic westerns, made his debut in "Melody Trail". (For more see the special section on all the various Champions.) Abe Lefton, billed as the World's Most Famous Rodeo Announcer, has a prominent spot in the early-on rodeo scenes which were filmed during a performance at Pendleton Oregon. Lefton often appeared live at rodeos with Gene and in film performances where rodeo footage was needed.

The 200 pound dog Buck, a cross between a Newfoundland and a Saint Bernard, was first seen on-screen in "Call of the Wild" in 1935 with Clark Gable and Loretta Young. Buck also appeared in Republic's 14 chapter 1936 serial, "Robinson Crusoe of Clipper Island", Republic's Three Mesquiteers western "The Trigger Trio" ('37) and Laurel and Hardy's "Swiss Miss" ('38), among others.

Although Gene marries leading lady Ann Rutherford in a mass ceremony at the end of the film, they do not kiss. That screen *first* for Gene was reserved for another film.

As with "Tumbling Tumbleweeds", when "Melody Trail" was re-issued, updated images of Gene were used in advertising to make the film seem more current.

FILM COMMENTS: *Ann Rutherford:* "I made more money than Gene Autry! I was earning $150 a week; Gene only got $100 a week while Smiley Burnette received $50. And that's the only time I ever made more money than Gene Autry! (Laughs) He had what my mother used to say was a 'come out of the kitchen' singing voice. You stopped what you were doing to listen. Gene was a lovely man, but he was one cowboy who couldn't ride a horse! He virtually invented the 'singing cowboy.' Actually, he wasn't a cowboy at all—he worked as a telegraph clerk at a train station in Oklahoma. He had a radio show, and when Will Rogers came by, Gene asked him to 'tune in and hear me.' Gene had a good quality to his voice. He wrote Nat Levine, head of Mascot, who didn't answer his letters. But Gene was persistent—eventually Nat Levine himself stopped off—at the radio station—and heard Gene and Smiley and the gang. They had a young flavor and charisma about them that Levine liked. He bought them all for peanuts! (Laughs) He started Gene off in a science fiction serial at Mascot, 'Phantom Empire' (1935), just before it turned into Republic. I have held Gene up to young players all these years as the prime example of making the most of everything you have. On this picture with Gene, his wife Ina was very busy between takes having Gene sign pictures for his fans. She had a little filing system. Gene took the best care of his fans. Gene

Gene confronts Al Bridge in a tense moment from "Melody Trail." (That's Gene's old friend Frankie Marvin on horseback behind the extra in the black hat.)

had a theory, even then. He said if these kids like you, you get 'em when they're 9-10 years old, and you're nice to them and send back your picture, they're gonna like you when they're grown up, and their kids are gonna like you. And it's proven true."

"I was only 16 years old. I didn't drive. They didn't have limos, they'd delegate an electrician or whoever was going by our apartment to pick me and my mother up and take us to the set. We'd hit that studio at 5 o'clock in the morning, be on the set at 7 or 8, as early as possible. Frequently, we weren't shooting on a set, so they'd put us in a car and drag us 30-40 miles out in the boondocks someplace. And you'd work there in the dust and heat all day. When the sun went down they'd bring you back—but you didn't go home. That's when you did the interior shots."

"Smiley Burnette was probably the most talented young man, musically, I ever met, with the possible exception of Mickey Rooney. Smiley could look you in the eye and write a song about what he wanted to tell you. He'd sing it to you. I can see him now with his accordion—what he called his 'Stomach Steinway'—and his guitar or git-fiddle. He never had formal lessons, but there was not an instrument he could not get music out of."[1]

Gene Autry: "Until 'Melody Trail', the females in westerns usually numbered one, only, and wore slacks. My second feature film, and most of those that followed, had pretty gals hanging all over the corral and often clad in either majorette costumes, or the forerunner of the mini. Whose idea this was I don't recall, but I'm willing to take credit for it."[2]

Regarding the six-gun bit so prominent on Champion, Gene explained, "I knew a fella back in Ardmore, Oklahoma, that always was working on bits and things like that. He came up with an idea to get a bridle bit made out of guns. I thought at first I'd take a regular .45 and have it split, but that was too heavy, we couldn't do that. Then I tried to make one out of metal, stainless steel, but it was still too heavy. Finally, I went over to an aluminum place and I asked 'em if they could cast an aluminum bit for me and they said they could. So I had them cast an aluminum bit just like a six shooter. For a while I had a hackamore made out of it. I just kept on experimenting with it until we wound up with the bit Champion always used."[3]

CAST BIOS: Vivacious Ann Rutherford is best remembered as Carreen, one of Scarlett O'Hara's sisters in "Gone With the Wind" in '39. However, it's the Golden Boot Award winner's four westerns opposite Gene Autry for which she's fondly recalled by western devotees. Born November 2, 1920, in Toronto, Ontario, Canada, she is the daughter of a former Metropolitan Opera singer. Movies were not her initial entertainment medium; she first appeared on Los Angeles radio. That led to a role in Mascot's "Waterfront Lady" ('34). (Incidentally, music cues from that film are reused in "Melody Trail".) In 1935, Mascot co-starred Ann with Grant Withers in the 15 chapter serial, "The Fighting Marines" and cast her in "Melody

Gene Autry, Ann Rutherford and Buck the dog strike a "Melody Trail" pose.

Trail", her first with Gene. Moving over to MGM, Ann was Andy Hardy's girlfriend Polly Benedict in the popular Hardy Family series from 1938-1942, as well as appearing in "Gone With the Wind". She later worked at 20th Century–Fox and again at Republic. Ann was "Blondie" on radio for the 1949-1950 season in the role originated by Penny Singleton. She was also heard regularly on "The Eddie Bracken Show" as Eddie's girlfriend between 1945-1947. Several TV shows closed out her screen career. Today, Ann is often a popular guest at various western film festivals.

Gene's regular stuntman double in his earliest films, through mid 1939, was Kenny Cooper.

Virgil Kenneth Cooper was born April 2, 1896, to dirt farmer parents in Olaton, Kentucky (southeast of Owensboro—Hwy 878—on the Rough Caney River). Earlier Kenny's Dad, Edwin, had been a livery stable driver.

By 1917, at 21, Kenny had migrated west to South Dakota where he was cowboying and breaking horses. He met and married Helen Belle Potter of South Dakota in 1919.

Somehow, the brown-eyed, black-haired Cooper arrived in Hollywood by the late '20s and was stunting in silent westerns. His first sound work appears to be in "Beau Bandit" ('30 RKO) with Rod LaRocque and George Duryea (aka Tom Keene).

Cooper continued to find work at various studios until

1935 when he became part of Republic's talented stunt team, doubling not only for Gene but for Robert Livingston in many of the Three Mesquiteers westerns.

Two well known stuntmen, Yakima Canutt and Whitey Hughes, have both described Cooper as a bit of a "joker" and "prankster". Stuntman Jack Williams, whom Cooper got into the "business" on a Johnny Mack Brown Mascot serial, "Fighting With Kit Carson" ('33), recalls, "Cooper was a bronc rider and a helluva stuntman. He was also very mischievous, a great gagster." Williams also said Cooper was not very cautious about the care of his clothing when dressed in Autry's fancy duds. "He'd lay around in a bale of hay or some such until he was called to double Gene, then have to do the scene in rumpled clothing."[4]

One of Cooper's younger brothers, Gordon (1907-1993) was employed for years as a laborer in the film business.

Kenny worked until the mid '50s when everyone seems to have lost track of the talented stuntman.

Cooper died March 6, 1989, in San Diego, California.

WHAT THE EXHIBITOR HAD TO SAY: "Would like to buy 100 westerns as good as Republic's 'Melody Trail'. Has everything a small town and country patronage house could ask for in a western."
—Harlan C. Dodd, Charlestown Theater, Charlestown, Indiana (November, 1935)

"Something a little different. Western fans seemed to go for it."
—M. F. Bodwell, Paramount Theater, Wyoming, Illinois (January 1936)

"A swell New Year's show. Couldn't have had a better crowd or better picture. My crowd are Autry fans."
—Mrs. Gene Michael, Van Theater, Van, West Virginia (January 1936)

"This is a splendid western. Good riding, good comedy, great singing. This man Autry has personality, voice and everything to please the people and they begin to ask for his pictures. That is going some these days."
—Bert Silver, New Silver Theater, Greenville, Michigan (February 1936)

"Very fine western. The 'cowgirls' were a very pleasing novelty."
—Sammie Jackson, Jackson Theater, Flomaton, Alabama (March 1936)

"This boy Autry is there. Can ride like nobody's business. Sing, can he sing, and this little boy with him keeps right up with Gene or a little ahead of him."
—W. H. Brenner, Cozy Theater, Winchester, Indiana (May 1936)

SOURCES:

1. "Melody Ranch Theater" showing of "Melody Trail" on Nashville Network, 1988; and *Western Clippings #27.* January/February 1999. p. 4.

2. Autry and Herskowitz. *Back in the Saddle Again.* p. 52.

3. "Melody Ranch Theater" showing of "Sons of New Mexico" on the Nashville Network, 1987.

4. Interview with author. 2005.

Sagebrush Troubadour
<u>Republic, December 1935</u>

Producer ....Nat Levine
Supervisor ....Armand Schaefer
Director ....Joseph Kane
Assistant Director.......................Leonard Kunody
Second Assistant Director...........William Witney
Original Story............................Oliver Drake
Screenplay..................................Oliver Drake and Joseph
      Poland
Photography ....Ernest Miller and Jack
      Marta
Supervising Editor ....Joseph H. Lewis
Film Editor ....Lester Orlebeck
Sound Engineer...........................Terry Kellum
Sound Effects ....Roy Granville

SONGS: "Way Out West in Texas" (music and lyrics by Gene Autry)—sung by Gene Autry; "On the Prairie" (music and lyrics by Smiley Burnette)—sung by Gene Autry; "End of the Trail" (music and lyrics by Gene Autry and Smiley Burnette)—sung by Gene and Smiley; "Hurdy Gurdy Man" (music and lyrics by Smiley Burnette)—sung by Tommy Gene Fairey; "My Prayer For Tonight" (music and lyrics by Smiley Burnette)—sung by Gene, Smiley and cast; "Looking for the Lost Chord" (music and lyrics by Smiley Burnette)—sung by Smiley Burnette; "I'd Love a Home In the Mountains" (music and lyrics by Smiley Burnette and Gene Autry)—sung by Gene Autry.

RUNNING TIME: 58 minutes
FILMING DATES: October 26 to November 2, 1935
LOCATIONS: Kernville, California; Monogram Ranch; Pasco Ranch; Republic cave set
BUDGET: $17,274
NEGATIVE COST: $18,621

CAST:

Actor	*Character*
Gene Autry	Gene Autry
Barbara Pepper	Joan Martin
Smiley Burnette	Frog Millhouse
Fred Kelsey	Hank Polk
J. Frank Glendon	John Martin
Hooper Atchley	Henry Nolan
Julian Rivero	Pablo
Denny Meadows (aka Dennis Moore)	Lon Dillon
Tom London	Sheriff
Frankie Marvin	Deputy
Art Davis	Musician
Tommy Gene Fairey	Tommy—singer on organ grinder
Tex Phelps	Cowhand at Party
Bud Pope, Wes Warner, Al Taylor	Deputies
Jack Rockwell	Ranger Captain
Edward Mariott	Stage Driver
Joe Yrigoyen	Rider
Oscar Gahan, Morgan Brown	Men
Leonard Kunody, N. Mathias, Slim Metcalf, Russell Frank, Charlie Sargent, G. W. Burnette, Wally Howe, Henry De Silva, George Morrell, Jack Harvey, Mrs. Earl Waggener, Geraldine Bunke, Blanche Hance, Lillian Castle, Dorothy Woods, Harry Hay, Art Taylor, Al Slvan, Rene LaPre, Robert Hall, Bill Stahl, Harry Fraser, Salvador Murgi, Jack Fendrich, Grant Davis, Wally Rose, Harry Denny, Bruce Randall, Jack Noyes, Harold Johnson, Dave Daggett, Virginia Myers, Helen Gibson, Suzanni Derri, Lew Dutch, Otto Kupp, Dorothy Trail, Maxine Greenwood, Beulah Blust, Dianne Gardner, Betty Kimbrough, Margo Burns, Betty Eagan, Lois Hassett, Linda Landi, Lillian Francis, Virginia Neville, Christine Hull, Sada Brown, Sally Cleaves, Jannette West	Extras
Champion	Champion

STUNTS: Ken Cooper (Gene's double); Art Dillard, Jack Long, Wes Warner (Barbara Pepper double).

THE FILM: Gene seems more comfortable with dialogue, a bit more natural and self assured and there are flashes of the wide-grinned boyish charm that served him so well in later pictures. There is no doubt on-screen good chemistry between Gene and leading lady Barbara Pepper. At one point early in the picture, after she has crowded Gene off the road, he turns her over his knee and spanks her thoroughly. At the close of the film Gene receives his first screen kiss, although Barbara Pepper initiates the buss.

Rumors still persist to this day that Gene never kissed the girl. These misconceptions no doubt arise from the fact many viewers have probably never watched Gene's earliest features. Fan magazine and newspaper columnists in the very late '30s and early '40s when Gene was at his peak often concluded Gene never kissed his leading lady. As late as 1964, a movie mag reported Gene canceled a proposed cameo on the TV series "Burke's Law" because the script called for him to "break his life-long rule" and kiss Dorothy Lamour. True Gene Autry devotees know better; "Sagebrush Troubadour" and others to follow prove it. At the end of this film, leading lady Barbara Pepper impetuously grabs Gene and kisses him in the final fadeout. Although she initiates the buss, it is the first sequence of its kind in an Autry western. In Gene's next film, "The Singing Vagabond" ('36), he kisses young Ann Rutherford, making that the first screen kiss initiated by the singing cowboy. Another kiss occurs at the conclusion of "Oh, Susanna!" ('36) as Gene kisses Frances Grant. Yet again, in "The Big Show" ('36) Gene kisses Kay Hughes. Also in the guise of Tom Ford, Gene has a kissing scene in the film within the film with actress Mary Russell. In "The Old Corral" ('36) Gene and Hope (later Irene) Manning kiss at the fadeout. Still more, at the conclusion of "Round-Up Time in Texas" ('37) Gene kisses Maxine Doyle. Whether producers elected to cease the screen kisses themselves or whether Gene's young fans wrote in enough to cause the producers to change their policy we do not know, but there are no more passionate smooching scenes in Gene's films after "Round-Up Time in Texas". An only-implied off-screen kiss does exist at the conclusion of "Rootin' Tootin' Rhythm" ('37) with leading lady Armida. Then there is the famous "almost-kiss" scene in "South of the Border" ('39) after Gene has saved senorita Lupita Tovar's runaway. Young Mary Lee urges Gene to kiss her as the prince did to wake up sleeping beauty, but as Gene approaches Lupita, he decides better of it, shaking his head, "Nah." Also of note, in "Shooting High" ('40), in the film within a film, Gene reluctantly receives a screen kiss from starlet Kay Aldridge but does not return the buss. Negative advance publicity prompted Republic to delete a kiss between Gene and Ann Miller in "Melody Ranch" ('40) but, again, it *is* implied off-screen. The only other kisses in Gene's films come years later. Jo Dennison gives Gene a friendly-gesture thank-you kiss on the cheek during a lakeside

Smiley Burnette seems oblivious while Barbara Pepper is about to impetuously kiss Gene Autry near the end of "Sagebrush Troubadour."

picnic in "Beyond the Purple Hills" ('50). But here again, this doesn't really qualify as a true screen smooch. Then Gail Davis kisses Gene on the cheek in "Texans Never Cry" ('51) and at the end of "Pack Train" ('53). Kathleen Case extends an affectionate show of gratitude in Gene's final feature, "Last of the Pony Riders" ('53), but these are certainly not kisses in which Gene actively participates. By the time Gene was producing his own features at Columbia, his highly publicized non-kissing "policy" was so widely reported that a publicity campaign was developed around a proposed kissing scene with Elena Verdugo for "The Big Sombrero" ('49). But that never made it to the screen.

Not only did Gene kiss six of his leading ladies in the mid '30s, he also "married", on screen, Ann Rutherford in "Melody Trail" ('35) and "Comin' 'Round the Mountain" ('36). The impression at the end of "Red River Valley" ('36) is that he's married to Frances Grant. The same for Lois Wilde in "The Singing Cowboy" ('36). Gene marries Kay Hughes in the final scene of "Ride Ranger Ride" ('36). But after '37, Gene's screen romances remained ambiguous, leaving all to the imagination of the viewer.

The story is a developing murder mystery, worthy of oriental detective Charlie Chan, with a wild action-packed finish. Gene and Frog are undercover Rangers assigned the task of tracking down the murderer of Joan Martin's (Barbara Pepper) old, half-blind grandfather, throttled to death with a guitar-string. Reaching town, Gene begins to receive ridiculously high offers for a swayback horse in his possession, which he eventually discovers is a key to the murder. Seems the swayback automatically knows the way to a hidden gold mine discovered by Martin's blind grandfather, leading all five murder suspects to scheme to own the horse. During a barn dance, the old horse is positioned so it will attract the killer.

NOTES AND COMMENTS: "Sagebrush Troubadour" affords Smiley Burnette a grand opportunity to display his ability with a variety of musical instruments—trombone, clarinet, ocarina, trumpet, etc.

"Sagebrush Troubadour" includes an unusual sequence of Gene being thrown off Champion as the horse steps in a gopher hole. Don't believe any other feature allowed Gene to be unhorsed.

The swayback horse, George, was owned by Lionel Comport who was paid $150 for the unique animal's use. Gene Autry remembered, "That old swayback horse appeared in the film 'Mrs. Wiggs of the Cabbage Patch' ('34 Paramount). We used that same horse."[1]

Kenny Cooper once again doubled Gene and was paid $200.

Gene's longtime friend Frankie Marvin, featured one way or another in nearly all of Gene's films, was paid $45 for playing a deputy and for caring for Gene's horse, Champion. Frankie also picked up $12.50 for retakes.

Exteriors were shot in the Kernville, California, area where 15 extras, 17 horsemen, 3 children and 8 women were hired locally by J. L. Wofford, owner of the oft-used Wofford Ranch in the Kernville area.

Smiley Burnette's father, George W. Burnette, worked as an extra in nearly every film Smiley made at Republic.

Three year old Tommy Gene Fairey was paid $10 to "sing" the Smiley Burnette tune "Hurdy Gurdy Man".

FILM COMMENTS: *Pat Buttram:* "Smiley Burnette had a circus going on inside of him all the time."[2]

Oliver Drake: "(Producer) Nat (Levine) had signed up the sensational singing star Gene Autry, and Mandy

There's a little horse trading going on between Denny Meadows (aka Dennis Moore), livery barn owner Fred Kelsey and Gene Autry.

(Schaefer) said they had made two pictures with Autry that were smash hits, 'Tumbling Tumbleweeds' and 'Melody Trail'. Mandy gave me a small office on the lot and loaned me a secretary from the secretarial pool whenever I needed one. It felt like home because Autry's main director was Joseph Kane, whom I'd known from the old Pathé days. Another director, Mack Wright, had been my assistant at one time; and half the crew on the lot had worked for me at various times, or I had known them. I felt right at home, and started to work on the first Autry story, which was called 'Sagebrush Troubadour'. During the end of 1935, I finished 'Sagebrush Troubadour', and worked on another picture called, 'The Singing Vagabond'. I also wrote some of the songs for the pictures."[3]

CAST BIOS: Leading lady Barbara Pepper, who goes down in history as giving Gene Autry his first on-screen kiss, was born in 1916 in New York City where her father managed the famous Astor Hotel. In 1933 she appeared on stage in Florenz Ziegfeld's last "Follies" as well as on screen in the Eddie Cantor extravaganza "Roman Scandals" for Samuel Goldwyn. She was in George White's "Scandals" on stage as well. A role in King Vidor's highly acclaimed "Our Daily Bread" with Tom Keene followed in 1934.

Following "Sagebrush Troubadour" she began to gain weight, and drifted into wise-cracking supporting roles, as she is in Gene's next film, "The Singing Vagabond" where she's Smiley Burnette's love interest rather than Gene's. Last seen in "My Fair Lady" ('64), she died in 1969 at only 53.

A side of Gene Autry not always recognized is his loyalty to old friends. Frankie Marvin and Gene Autry's close association began when Gene was just starting his career on the radio as Oklahoma's Yodeling Cowboy. Oklahoma born brothers Frankie and Johnny Marvin were popular vaudeville entertainers when young Gene showed up at their New York apartment in the late '20s. They befriended the young Oklahoman, tutored him and sent him back to Oklahoma for more seasoning. Gene never forgot this friendly gesture, and when he made it good a few years later, he sent for Frankie and Johnny Marvin and made them an integral part of his growing organization. "In 1953," Gene stated, "Frankie Marvin and I have been working together ever since our old radio and vaudeville days back in Chicago. When I first met him he was appearing in a vaudeville act with his brother, Johnny, in New York. (Later) I needed a guitarist, and since he was about the best in the business, I made him an offer to join my radio show. When I came west to go into the picture business Frankie came with me."[4]

Johnny Marvin became associated with Gene in a business capacity while Frankie became a trusted musician and actor somewhere in sight in nearly every one of Gene's films.

John Senator Marvin was born in Butler, Oklahoma, in 1897 and Frankie joined him January 27, 1904. Frankie, the youngest of seven, was raised on a farm; attending high school in Kingman, Kansas, then became a barber for eight years. By the time Frankie was barbering, Johnny was headlining in New York and recording for Victor. He returned to get his kid brother into the business with him. In 1927 they went back to New York working together on the stage. Johnny became well known as a song writer and Frankie as a steel guitar and ukulele

Frankie Marvin.

player and comedian. When Gene came to New York he looked up the boys who proceeded to help him learn some of the ins and outs of the business. When Gene later started working in Chicago and needed a good steel guitar man, he sent for Frankie. Frank returned to New York after working with Gene for awhile and picked up with Johnny again. As Gene's career progressed and he entered the movie business he again sent for Frankie. Frankie played steel guitar on Gene's "Melody Ranch" radio show, on his recordings and the soundtrack for most of his movies and appeared in small roles in nearly all of Gene's movies.

During the war, while Johnny was entertaining troops in the South Pacific, he contracted a tropical malady that resulted in his death in December 1944.

Frankie's steel guitar playing became one of the consistently recognizable components of the Autry sound on tour and on Gene's "Melody Ranch" radio show. Marvin died in January 1985.

WHAT THE EXHIBITOR HAD TO SAY: "These Autry westerns are the outstanding pictures of the season. They are tops in all ways. I am also referring to 'Melody Trail' and 'Sagebrush Troubadour'. Give these pictures your preferred playing time and watch the crowds roll in. As business getters these pictures are ahead of Cantor, Astaire and (Ginger) Rogers and a lot of the big stars. Republic sells these pictures at a just rental so as to leave you a profit."
—M. S. Porter, Orpheum Theater, Nelsonville, Ohio (January 1936)

"If your customers like Autry this is your show. As usual he gets them up in the air, then brings them down again with his songs." —Mrs. Gene Michael, Van Theater, Van, West Virginia (January 1937)

SOURCES:

1. "Melody Ranch Theater" showing of "Sagebrush Troubadour" on Nashville Network, 1988.

2. "Melody Ranch Theater" showing of "Tumbling Tumbleweeds" on Nashville Network, 1988.

3. Drake, Oliver. *Written Produced and Directed by Oliver Drake.* Hale-Ken Enterprises, 1990. p. 37.

4. *Who's Who in Western Stars #3.* Dell Pub., 1953. p. 32.

The Singing Vagabond
Republic, December 1935

Producer ....Nat Levine
Supervisor ....Armand Schaefer
Director ....Carl Pierson
Assistant Director.......................B. Reeves Eason
Original Story.............................Oliver Drake
Screenplay..................................Betty Burbridge and
                                   Oliver Drake
Photography ....William Nobles
Supervising Editor ....Joseph H. Lewis
Film Editor.................................Lester Orlebeck
Sound Engineer...........................Terry Kellum
Sound Effects..............................Roy Granville
Musical Supervisor ....Arthur Kay

SONGS: "Lou'sianna Belle" (music and lyrics by Stephen Foster)—sung by a minstrel chorus; "De Camptown Races" (music and lyrics by Stephen Foster)—sung by Robinson Neeman and extras; "Singing Vagabonds" (music and lyrics by Oliver Drake, Herb Myers)—sung by Gene Autry and his Singing Plainsmen; "Honeymoon Trail" (music and lyrics by Oliver Drake, Herb Myers)—sung by Gene Autry, Ann Rutherford and troupe; "Farewell Friends of the Prairie, Farewell" (music and lyrics by Smiley Burnette)—sung by Gene Autry, Ann Rutherford and cast; "Wagon Train" (music and lyrics by Gene Autry and Smiley Burnette)—sung by soldiers and girls.

    RUNNING TIME: 56 minutes
    FILMING DATES: November 16-29, 1935
    LOCATIONS: Calabasas, California, area ranch; Republic backlot
    BUDGET: $35,270
    NEGATIVE COST: $35,388

CAST:

Actor	*Character*
Gene Autry	Captain Tex Autry
Ann Rutherford	Leticia "Lettie" Morgan
Smiley Burnette	Frog Millhouse
Barbara Pepper	Honey
Niles Welch	Judge Forsyth Lane
Grace Goodall	Aunt Hortense
Henry Roquemore	Otto Spaeth
Allan Sears	Utah Joe
Warner Richmond	Buck LaCrosse
Frank LaRue	Colonel Seward
Ray Bernard (aka Ray Corrigan)	Orderly–Pvt. Hobbs
Bob Burns	Buffalo
Chief John Big Tree	White Eagle
Tom Brower	Old Scout
Edmund Cobb	Officer
Chief Thunder Cloud	Young Deer
Charles King	Henchman Red
Jack Ingram, Frankie Marvin	Singing Plainsmen
George Letz (aka George Montgomery)	Soldier
Robinson Neeman	Jerry Barton
Celia McCanon	Dolly
Marion O'Connell, Marie Quillan, Elaine Shepherd, Janice Thompson, June Thompson	Showgirls
Sherry Tansey	Wagon Driver
Iron Eyes Cody	Indian
Jim Corey	Raider
Bill Yrigoyen	Settler
Wes Warner	Army Enlistee
Tracy Layne	Army Officer
Frank Ellis	Hearing Observer
Champion	Champion

STUNTS: Cliff Lyons, Ken Cooper (Gene's double), George Montgomery.

THE FILM: Gene Autry altered his character name only one time at Republic; he is Ranger Captain Tex Autry in this film. The only other name change for Gene was on loan-out to 20th Century–Fox for "Shooting High" ('40).

    With a budget more than double what Gene's first three films had cost, producer Nat Levine was still experimenting with the format for Gene's pictures, placing him firmly in the old west of 1860 for "The Singing Vagabond". This and "Comin' 'Round the Mountain" two films later no doubt convinced Levine and others that Gene was not best suited to costume westerns. Gradually, Republic was coming to the realization that Gene's unique singing cowboy appeal needed a milieu and environment all its own, a sort of never-never land of mixed ingredients. Meantime, there were several "straight" westerns like this as Gene felt increasingly at home in front of the camera. But even that "at homeness" involved a bit of an awkward country manner that, in itself, endeared Gene Autry to audiences.

"The Singing Vagabond" finds Gene (and his sidekick Frog Millhouse, who has less to do than usual) in buckskins as Captain Tex Autry, head of the Army Civilian Scouts known as the Singing Plainsmen. Rescuing a wagon train from an Indian attack, Gene meets dainty Lettie Morgan (Ann Rutherford), heir to a rich St. Louis family fortune, who is running away from a former fiancée by joining the company of a show troupe. Troublemakers Utah Joe (Allan Sears) and Buck LaCrosse (Warner Richmond) are stirring up the Indians to attack incoming settlers so Joe and LaCrosse can grab off the territory for themselves. When horses are stolen from the Army post, Tex is framed as a traitor and condemned to death. Aided by Frog and his Singing Plainsmen, Tex escapes and eventually captures the renegades and clears his name.

NOTES AND COMMENTS: Barbara Pepper, Gene's leading lady in the previous feature, is here relegated to a lesser part, being romanced by Smiley Burnette.

Western fans will recognize Ray Bernard—soon to be known as Ray "Crash" Corrigan in Republic's Three Mesquiteers series—as Pvt. Hobbs, the Colonel's orderly.

This was the first Autry picture to introduce background music to the action sequences, including Von Gluck's oft-used "Dance of the Furies" for action sequences.

The scene in "The Singing Vagabond" of the Indians crossing a river with bluffs in the background is stock footage from Tim McCoy's MGM silent "War Paint", made in 1926. The footage later turned up in McCoy's "End of the Trail" at Columbia in '32 and reappeared countless times as stock footage for westerns and serials clear into the 1950s. The scene was originally filmed on the Little Wind River at the Wind River Indian Reservation, a few miles north of Lander, Wyoming.

FILM COMMENTS: *Ann Rutherford:* "George Montgomery was in 'The Singing Vagabond' but he didn't mention it to me when we did 'Orchestra Wives' ('42) together seven years later. He didn't want me to know he was George Letz at that time. (Laughs) George was a good looking kid; a good actor; fun; wonderful, dear and sweet with two wonderful kids by Dinah Shore. His talents are unlimited—as a sculptor, furniture-maker—whatever it was, George was excellent at doing it!"[1]

Screenwriter Betty Burbridge: "I wrote many of Gene's pictures and never could understand it. Gene was a smart businessman in a flashy western suit. Here was a dear man who had no acting ability and knew it. But through a combination of circumstances, he became a star almost overnight and shrewd businessman that he turned out to be, he put it to work to his own advantage, formulating his own 'Ten Commandments' to guide his screen character. I can only explain his great success as the result of a rugged schedule of personal appearances; he was the first screen cowboy star to embrace the personal appearance tour so completely.

"Gene was a success in the record business before he came to the screen and that must have helped. It was hard to write for him, as Autry scripts had to be written for about four main character parts, to help carry him along. Gene was a very nice person and realized that his talent as a screen cowboy was slight.

"Gene always used his own name on-screen, but celluloid Autry was no rough-and-tumble cowpoke. His screen character had both manners and social graces, moving smoothly in the company of ruffians or society leaders, and accepted by both. Easing himself through sticky situations with a song or two, Gene never fought anyone older or smaller than himself, didn't drink or smoke, and never cussed—he was the best darned Boy Scout you'll ever find. To him, romance meant simply another song, preferably around a campfire, under the western moon or riding along beside the heroine while strumming his guitar.

Ranger Captain Gene Autry contronts troublemaker Allan Sears. Behind Gene are Chief Thunder Cloud and Ray Bernard (later Corrigan.)

"His clothes were as far removed from the reality of western garb as Hollywood could make them, and regardless of what he was involved in doing, seldom lost their neat press and *never* got dirty. His aim with a six-shooter was uncanny and unerring; if the scriptwriter so desired, he could disarm the villain with a single shot while riding at breakneck speed, but chases were always more exciting if you let the opposing sides bang away at each other for awhile, and the chief villain always had to come to his bitter end at Autry's hand."[2, 3]

CAST BIOS: One of the most respected and proficient screenwriters of B-westerns from the '20s to the '40s was Betty Burbridge.

Born December 7, 1895, in San Diego, California, she was stagestruck from a young age and broke into movies as a leading lady in 1913 while still in her teens. As Elizabeth Burbridge she appeared in some 40 films for Essanay, Bison, Triangle and other early companies.

By 1923 Betty had given up most of her acting aspirations and was writing a syndicated newspaper column under the byline of Prudence Penny Jr., commenting on such diverse subjects as interior decorating, numerology and ad-

A SATURDAY EVENING POST (9/6/41) ad for Smith Corona says "Betty Burbridge first learned to type. . . began writing stories, movie scripts and plays. Then came success as a scriptwriter for Gene Autry, one of the best liked movie stars. 'I sincerely urge folks to learn typing and recommend a Corona or L. C. Smith typewriter,' says Miss Burbridge."

vice to the lovelorn.

About this time, producer Lester F. Scott Jr. was forming Action Pictures. As Betty had written a few scripts in 1917-1918 and had a way with words, Scott hired her to become his scriptwriter for the low budget silents of Buddy Roosevelt, Buffalo Bill Jr. and Wally Wales. The 30 plus scripts she wrote for Scott set in motion a screenwriting career that ran through 1950, winding down with Gene Autry's Flying A TV productions.

From 1924 through the close of Action Pictures' existence, Betty wrote the majority of Scott's films. She then went under contract to Pathé in 1929. As sound came in she freelanced, writing potboilers for Rex Lease, Bob Custer, Jack Perrin, Tom Tyler and others.

Burbridge found a home at Republic in 1935, contributing the story to Gene's "Melody Trail" and the screenplay to "The Singing Vagabond". In all, Betty worked on 13 of Gene's westerns up through 1940. She rejoined Gene in 1950, contributing scripts for three of his TV episodes.

Meantime, the prolific writer worked on nearly 100 movies between 1935 and 1949, turning out stories and scripts for The Three Mesquiteers, Charles Starrett, Jimmy Wakely, The Cisco Kid, Sunset Carson, Monte Hale and Russell Hayden among others.

The talented Burbridge died at 91 on September 19, 1987, in Tarzana, California.

Throughout the '30s the snide, snarling presence of Warner Richmond elicited instantaneous boos from front row kids as he menaced Tex Ritter, Jack Randall, John Wayne and others, including Gene Autry in "The Singing Vagabond". Richmond had previously worked with Gene in "The Phantom Empire" and would again in "Prairie Moon".

Werner Paul Raetzmann was born in Racine (or

possibly Reedsburg), Wisconsin, in 1886. After working in stock companies, he came to New York's old Vitagraph Studios, first appearing on the screen in 1912.

In the developing years of silent films, Richmond had romantic leads and second leads in dozens of films, critics taking special note of his work in "Tol'able David" in 1921.

With the advent of sound, he turned to vicious villains in six serials and numerous westerns.

His career was severely curtailed in 1940 when he suffered a serious head injury when he fell from his horse during a chase scene on a Tex Ritter picture in Prescott, AZ. The left side of his face was paralyzed for some time until constant massaging eventually restored his reflexes after three years.

Richmond made a few more westerns in the late '40s but eventually retired to the Motion Picture Home where he died at 62 in June 1948.

WHAT THE EXHIBITOR HAD TO SAY: "Our patrons enjoyed this musical western and we received no complaints. It is as well produced as the previous Autry films."
— J. W. Noah, New Liberty and Ideal Theaters, Fort Worth, Texas (February 1936)

"I can't add anything to this picture in way of praise any more than I have the others of this series. They are so far ahead of other pictures this year that I lack words to describe them. If other companies would drop a lot of their society dramas and add a number of this type of picture, us small town exhibitors would have something to live for."
— M. S. Porter, Orpheum Theater, Nelsonville, Ohio (March 1936)

SOURCES:

1. Magers, Boyd and Fitzgerald, Michael. *Ladies of the Western.* McFarland, 2002. p. 246.

2. *Under Western Skies.* December 1983. p. 47, 51.

3. *Film Collector's Registry.* Vol. 2, #1. (January/ February 1970) interviews with Betty Burbridge by Kalton C. Lahue.

Red River Valley
Republic, March 1936

Producer ....Nat Levine
Supervisor ....Armand Schaefer
Director ....B. Reeves Eason
Assistant Directors ....Leonard Kunody and
                           Bill Stroback
Second Assistant Director ....Bill Witney
Screenplay and Original Story .....Stuart and Dorrell
                           McGowan
Photography ....William Nobles
Supervising Editor ....Joseph H. Lewis
Film Editor ....Carl Pierson
Sound Engineer...........................Terry Kellum
Musical Supervisor ....Harry Grey
Production Manager....................Al Wilson

SONGS: "Yodeling Cowboy" (music and lyrics by
Gene Autry)—sung by Gene Autry; "Red River Valley"
(public domain)—sung by Gene Autry; "Fetch Me Down
My Trusty Forty-Five" (music and lyrics by Smiley
Burnette)—sung by Smiley Burnette; "Construction Song"
(music and lyrics by Sam H. Stept)—sung by construction
workers; "Red River Valley" (public domain)—sung by
George Chesebro, men in saloon and Gene Autry.

RUNNING TIME: 56 minutes

FILMING DATES: January 21-28, 1936. Pickup shots
on Republic backlot January 31 and February 6, 1936.

LOCATIONS: Yuma, Arizona, Territorial Prison;
Trem Carr Ranch; Joe Yrigoyen Ranch in Burbank; Laguna
Dam on Colorado River; Imperial Sand Dunes near Yuma,
Arizona; Republic backlot

BUDGET: $19,173

NEGATIVE COST: $23, 692

CAST:

Actor	*Character*
Gene Autry	Gene Autry
Smiley Burnette	Frog Millhouse
Frances Grant	Mary Baxter
Boothe Howard	Steve Conway
Jack Kennedy	Mike
Sam Flint	George Baxter
George Chesebro	Bull Dural
Charles King	Sam
Eugene Jackson	Iodine
Edward Hearn	Sheriff Ed
Frank LaRue	Hartley Moore
Ken Cooper	Henchman Long
Frankie Marvin	Henchman Becker
Tracy Layne	Hank–Rancher
C. E. Anderson, Monty Cass, Milburn Morante	Townsmen
Chuck Baldra, Jack Montgomery, Pascale Perry	Barflys
Hank Bell, Earl Dwire, William McCall, George Morrell, Chris Allen, Charles Schaeffer	Ranchers
Horace B. Carpenter, Oscar Gahan, Herman Hack, Cactus Mack, Al	

Taylor, Jay Wilsey, C. Bishop,
Jack Hendricks, Harry Fraser,
Toby West.................................Construction workers
Missouri Royer.............................Deputy
Joe Cochin, George "Rusty"
Fellowes, John "Snake" Wilson,
Cheyenne Martin......................Workers
Lloyd Ingraham............................Old Rancher
Rose Plummer..............................Old Rancher's Wife
Helen Gibson, Ann Purcher,
Nora Bush, Phoebe Rand,
Cora Shannon...........................Women
J. P. Lockney, Irwin Collins, Ray
Bernard (aka Ray Corrigan),
G. W. Burnette, Art Reenan,
Tex Dale, Cap Fields, John
Lucky, C. Fisher.......................Men
Jean Dabney, Ray Hobart,
Roland Smith............................Musicians in Saloon
Roy Bucko..................................Cowboy
Frank Jocelyn..............................Piano Player
Duke Lee.....................................Dealer
Ronald Burke, Mickey Nelson.....Children
C. L. Sherwood............................Bartender
Red Larkin, Harry Alton, Ed
Zimmer, Ed Ray, Wally Howe..Westerners
Fletcher Clark..............................Teacher
Jack Donovan..............................Office Director
Lottie Hildebrand.........................Mother
Champion....................................Champion

STUNTS: Ken Cooper (double for Gene Autry); Jean Criswell (double for Frances Grant); Wally West, Stub Musselman, Joe Yrigoyen, Bill Yrigoyen, Bud Pope, Ed Jauregui, Andy Jauregui, Jay Wilsey.

THE FILM: Directed by "Breezy" Eason with the lightning pace of a serial, "Red River Valley" is perhaps the most exciting, vigorous, tightly knit entry in the series. In the action finale Reeves throws everything in. There are scenes of construction workers battling with everything and anything available to them. Even the heavies are polished off rather brutally in a train wreck.

The prologue reads, "Drought—the grim enemy that almost devastated once prosperous farm and ranch lands. Men have learned the bitter lessons of unpreparedness. Throughout stricken areas today, they are rallying forces to fight back with their only weapon—water."

Republic liked scripts about drought and irrigation schemes, it was a recurring plot device in several Autry, Roy Rogers and Three Mesquiteers westerns. It created empathy in the rural areas where such problems were truly taking place.

"Red River Valley" concerns such a scheme in which shrewd, suave Steve Conway (Boothe Howard) is secretly scheming to destroy the local ranchers' hopes of bringing water to the parched valley. Howard is a colorless heavy, with acting honors going to George Chesebro as his uncouth, loud mouthed, unshaven henchman Bull. Bull is busted at every turn by Gene who even forces him at the point of a gun to sing "Red River Valley" in a saloon when Bull is urging threatening workers to halt progress on the irrigation project. "There," says Gene at the conclusion of the song, "Don't you feel better? Nothing like a song!"

After delivering a herd of cattle to the irrigation company, Gene and Frog (Smiley Burnette) become interested in the plight of the ranchers, agreeing to take on the dangerous task of ditch rider for the irrigation company. Gene must deal with sabotage, attempted attacks on his life, payroll robberies and much more before he brings the shady men to justice.

NOTES AND COMMENTS: When "Red River Valley" was reissued it was retitled "Man of the Frontier" so as not to cause confusion with the 1941 Roy Rogers film of the same name.

Once again, Ken Cooper doubled and did stunts for Gene. He was paid $200 a week in comparison to actors

Gene Autry and George Chesebro are about to come to blows as Chesebro and Charles King (left of Gene) try to stir up trouble over the irrigation project. Gene's friend Jack Kennedy stands by.

48

Smiley Burnette provides a little musical accompaniment while Gene Autry romances leading lady Frances Grant.

George Chesebro who received $75; Charles King—$60; Sam Flint—$160; Eugene Jackson—$50; Frances Grant—$125; Jack Kennedy—$125; Frank LaRue—$30; Boothe Howard—$100 and Edward Hearn—$35. The musicians in the saloon earned $12.50 plus overtime. Frankie Marvin earned an extra $10 by doing a bulldog stunt.

While making a scene in the Yuma area in which a wagon was to cross a railroad track, a small train engine was supposed to hit the wagon but the timing was off. The wagon was on the track when the train collided with it sending a wagon wheel hurtling 20 feet into the air landing atop an expensive $100,000 camera, crushing it. Two cameramen fortunately escaped injury. Only one camera remained for filming. The saving grace that kept the company on schedule came about as 20th Century Fox was doing some desert shooting on "Under Two Flags" ('36) in the sand hills near Yuma. The Fox unit had almost 15 cameras. Arrangements were made to borrow a couple of cameras for Republic's use.

FILM COMMENTS: *Gene Autry:* "'Red River Valley' had a good mix, I thought, of action, music, comic foolery, and plot. In many ways it was the most typical of the early Autrys, pitting me against a banker conniving to grab the town water rights, a kind of TVA Goes West."[1]

In 1988, on his TNN TV show, "Melody Ranch Theater", Gene Autry humorously recalled one lengthy scene that involved a dangerous, rigorous sprint across Laguna Dam.

Gene said, "I had a rope around George Chesebro. He had to walk across that dam, and I was following. The dam was two or three feet wide; there was about a foot of water running over that dam, and it was slippery, (like) trying to walk on a sidewalk with ice on it." Autry went on to relate Chesebro "had been drunk all night, and the water was making him dizzy." George frantically pleaded with Autry, "Gene, hold on to me. I'm going over." Since there was no sound on that part of the picture, Gene retorted to Chesebro, "Go ahead! I don't care if you go over." Evidently feeling himself in peril, Autry added "it was all I could do to stand up with my boots on in that water anyway." Meanwhile, still panicky, Chesebro kept reminding Gene, "Don't turn loose of that rope." Although Chesebro is shown drowning on screen, he finally made it across Laguna Dam out of lens range.[2]

CAST BIOS: "Our Gang" producer Hal Roach took one look at his childish, fuzzy afro and nicknamed him Pineapple. Child actor Eugene Jackson was born on Christmas Day, 1916, in Buffalo, New York. After a 1923 film debut, he gained fame as Farina's older brother, Pineapple, in six of Roach's "Our Gang" comedies. In 1926 Jackson went to work as the only black child in Mack Sennett's Buster Brown comedies. He danced on the street in the Academy Award winning "Cimarron" in '31 and was featured dancing in three Gene Autry westerns, perhaps the best of which is "Red River Valley" where he dances on the bar and a roulette wheel.

During the TV era, Jackson worked on TV's "Julia" and Redd Foxx's "Sanford and Son". In later years he taught dance at studios he started in Compton and Pasadena. Jackson died of a heart attack October 26, 2001.

WHAT THE EXHIBITOR HAD TO SAY: "Up to the usual average of this star which have been coming through very good."
—J. E. Stocker, Myrtle Theater, Detroit, Michigan (May 1936)

"All I can say is that this is what they wanted. At any rate, it grossed more money than any of the Big Specials that we have shown in the past 18 months. What more could anyone ask of it?"
—G. A. Van Fradenburg, Valley Theater, Manassa, Colorado (July 1936)

SOURCES:
1. Autry with Herskowitz. p. 52.
2. "Melody Ranch Theater" showing of "Red River Valley" on Nashville Network, 1988.

Comin' 'Round the Mountain
Republic, April 1936

Producer ....Nat Levine
Supervisor ....Armand Schaefer
Director ....Mack V. Wright
Assistant Director........................Arthur Lueker
Original Story.............................Oliver Drake
Screenplay..................................Oliver Drake, Dorrell
  and Stuart Mc-Gowan
Photography ....William Nobles
Supervising Editor ....Joseph H. Lewis
Film Editor................................Lester Orlebeck
Sound Engineer...........................Terry Kellum
Musical Supervisor ....Harry Grey

SONGS: "She'll Be Comin' 'Round the Mountain" (Public Domain)—sung by Gene Autry and men; "Don Juan of Sevillio" (music and lyrics by Sam H. Stept)—sung by Smiley Burnette; "Chiquita" (music and lyrics by Sam H. Stept)—sung by Gene Autry; "When the Campfire is Low on the Prairie" (music and lyrics by Sam H. Stept)—sung by Gene Autry and men at campfire.

RUNNING TIME: 56 minutes

FILMING DATES: February 26 to March 4, 1936

LOCATIONS: Lone Pine, California; Olanchi (10 miles south of Lone Pine); Pio Pico ranch house; Republic adobe set

BUDGET: $19,572

NEGATIVE COST: $21,537

CAST:

Actor	*Character*
Gene Autry ....Gene Autry
Ann Rutherford ....Dolores Moreno
Smiley Burnette ....Frog Millhouse
(Le) Roy Mason ....Matt Ford
Raymond Brown ....Caldwell
Ken Cooper ....Henchman Slim
Tracy Layne ....Henchman Butch
Robert McKenzie ....Marshal John Hawkins
Laura Puente ....Dancer
Hank Bell ....Man in matador skit
Dick Botiller................................Man who retrieves bull

Steve Clark, Jack Montgomery,
  Artie Ortego..............................Men at remount station
Jim Corey, Wes Warner ....Henchmen
Frank Ellis...................................Joe at relay station
John Ince ....Race starter
Frank Lackteen............................Eagle Feather
Frankie Marvin, Chuck Baldra ....Ranch hands
Montie Montana..........................Roper
Stanley Blystone ....Betting man
Pop Kenton..................................Dan
Al Hart ....Henry
Joe Yrigoyen ....Stage Driver
Jack Kirk, Blackjack Ward,
  Pascale Perry ....Extras
Roy Bucko ....Race Judge
Bob Card ....Sharpshooter
Champion....................................El Diablo

STUNTS: Ken Cooper (double for Gene Autry), Wes Warner, Joe Yrigoyen.

THE FILM: Republic, still experimenting with the perfect format for Gene Autry, returned him to buckskins and the old west as a Pony Express rider for "Comin' 'Round the Mountain".

This is the first film in which Champion has a major role as El Diablo, a beautiful wild horse integral to the plot.

Pony Express rider Gene Autry fights against scheming ranch owner Matt Ford (LeRoy Mason) who is after the contract to sell horses to the Pony Express company. Gene also befriends lovely Dolores Moreno (Ann Rutherford) whose ranch is about to be sold for non-payment of taxes. After Gene finds and tames the wild horse, El Diablo, he suggests mustangs have more endurance than Ford's thoroughbreds and proposes a cross-country race to prove his point. Ford tries every way he can to sabotage the race, but, naturally, El Diablo (Champion) wins the fabulously exciting race finale.

NOTES AND COMMENTS: The sprawling, historic ranch house of Pio Pico, California's first Spanish Governor,

was then a 142 year old adobe. Today it is preserved on the eastern outskirts of Los Angeles as a state historic park museum, a memorial to California's historic Spanish regime.

Eagle-eyed western fans will recognize the sequence where Gene tames the wild horse, El Diablo (played by Champion), by hanging around his neck as being a "stock shot" actually performed earlier by stuntman legend Yakima Canutt doubling for western star Harry Carey in the Mascot serial, "The Devil Horse" ('32).

Smiley's song of the matador "Don Juan of Sevillio" was later used by Burnette in a Durango Kid B-western.

Irving Greig and Charles Hadlett, Hollywood trick and tap dance artists on roller skates, are inside the comical bull used in the matador sequence.

FILM COMMENTS: *Gene Autry:* "'Comin' 'Round the Mountain' was one of just (three) films I made for Republic actually set in the old west. My retreat from the buckskin western was no accident, but based on my belief that the public found me more convincing as Singin' Gene than as a Pony Express rider. This one was also notable for the fact that it produced my first screen kiss, with Ann Rutherford. The year was 1936 and it worked so well that we came right back and tried it again, four years later,

with Ann Miller. And they cut the scene. But that's another story.[1]

"Champion came from Oklahoma. I had him trained to do tricks like to take a bow, and to pray, and things like that. We started building Champion to where he was as popular with the kids—or maybe more popular, than I was. He turned out to be a great horse and photographed like a million dollars. To start with, when I made a picture, I used to travel with the picture and get on the stage. Champion was on the stage with me. I used to sing 'Old Faithful' to him. About the middle of the song he'd come out from the wings and I'd feed him carrots. When I'd finish the song he'd turn around and walk off the stage."[2]

CAST BIOS: The screenwriting brothers Dorrell and Stuart McGowan began to script Gene Autry westerns at Republic in 1936 with "Red River Valley". They went on to write a total of 16.

Dorrell was born November 30, 1899, in Chicago, Illinois. His brother Stuart was born August 17, 1904, in the Windy City. The brothers began in the movie business as pie throwers for comic producer Mack Sennett.

Over the years the brothers also scripted many rural comedies for the Weaver Brothers and Elviry, Roy Acuff, several Roy Rogers titles and bigger budget westerns for

Dorrell McGowan.

Stuart McGowan.

Gene Autry doesn's seem at all intimidated by LeRoy Mason, as Marshal Robert McKenzie restrains Mason's gun hand.

Bill Elliott and Vaughn Monroe. Turning to TV, they worked on "Death Valley Days" and "Sky King". At times, they also tried their hand at directing and producing.

On their team work, Dorrell explained, "My brother was the typewriter guy. I had a hard time writing with a pencil. We did a lot of 'em together. He always waited for me to say 'whatta we gonna do today?' and I'd have to come up with an idea. We tried to keep it more modern, going on the present time, rather than invent something that didn't happen. Read the newspapers every day…anything that was interesting and a little bit different that we could make a story around, with some action, where you could fit Gene into it correctly."[3]

Dorrell died in September, 1997, and Stuart in September, 1999.

"Comin' 'Round the Mountain" was the first of nine films in which handsome and usually well dressed suave heavy LeRoy Mason was pitted against Gene Autry.

Born July 2, 1903, in Larimore, North Dakota, Mason entered films at 21 in 1924 working in several Tom Tyler silents.

During WWII Mason was in the Signal Corps in 1942 but was discharged due to poor health.

Mason suffered a heart attack while filming Monte Hale's "California Firebrand" and was taken to a Van Nuys, California, hospital on September 12, 1947. He died there of heart disease October 13, 1947.

Tracy Layne was one of the primary trainers of Champion. Born February 12, 1890, in a sod shanty on the plains near Newport, Nebraska, his parents soon moved to Oregon. At 15 Tracy ran away from home to work in a Washington logging camp where he drove a team of mules. Over the next several years Layne worked at many jobs, including herding cattle and horses at a Pendleton, Oregon, ranch. He briefly studied law, wrote beautiful poems of the high country range and, possessed of an Irish tenor voice,

sang at rodeos in Oregon.

Twenty-seven when WWI broke out, he and several buddies enlisted and fought in famous battles such as Belleau Woods and Verdun.

Returning home in 1919 he herded cattle and worked on the railroad. Married by age 30, he was in Los Angeles in 1924 where he met cowboys he'd known in Pendleton who'd come to Hollywood to work in movies.

Becoming an actor in silent westerns, he met Ken Maynard who hired Tracy to train his nine matched Palomino horses, one of them being Ken's famous Tarzan.

Meeting Gene in 1935, the singing cowboy asked Tracy to find him a lead horse like Maynard's. When the horse was located, they named him Champion and Tracy taught him many tricks.

A year or so later, at 45, Layne went to work for himself, purchasing a superb sorrel stallion he named Zane. Training him, Tracy found the horse work with Elizabeth Taylor, John Wayne, Clark Gable, Dick Powell, Gary Cooper and others. It is Zane who kicks out a gate in "Comin' 'Round the Mountain" for which Layne was paid $200.

When Zane became too old to work, Universal Studios hired Layne to train a mule who became Francis the Talking Mule.

At 60 Layne retired from training and films in 1950 and headed home to Oregon, buying a small place on the Columbia River in Umatilla. At 89 he sold the home and lived with his daughter and her husband in Gladstone. Layne died of cancer in a Portland hospital

Tracy Layne.

Smiley Burnette, Ann Rutherford, and Gene Autry on location in Lone Pine, California.

at 92 on November 1, 1981, marking the end of a long adventurous life.

WHAT THE EXHIBITOR HAD TO SAY: "This excellent picture, as all the other Autry films, did excellent business at the box office. This picture received more laughs from the audience than Autry's previous productions for Republic. If your patrons enjoy Gene Autry, then you can do good business with this picture. We posted displays in the lobby two weeks in advance which had all the people taking notice. If we were selling reserved seats on this picture, we would have had every seat in the house sold within three or four hours. We did excellent business on a three day run. This Autry production is well balanced. Music and action runs about equal throughout the production. Excellent recording."

—John Westland, New Liberty and Ideal Theaters,
Fort Worth, Texas (May 1936)

"These are the subjects that fill up the empty seats in a small town that has now entered its seventh year of drought and poor prices for wheat. Very good drawing card, but why so short if they are not on a double bill, which very few small towns can afford to have, especially in Western Canada."

—A. L. Dove, Bengough Theater,
Bengough, Saskatchewan, Canada (September 1936)

"Autry is a comer with us and this was one okay show. Also it seems that the photography is 100 percent over a year ago. This picture is good enough to put by a poor co-feature."

—S. A. Kimball, Sokokis Theater,
Limerick, Maine (February 1937)

"Like the usual run of Autrys. Good for an Autry crowd and they always come back for more of him."

—Mrs. Gene Michael, Van Theater,
Van, West Virginia (March 1937)

"Very fine western entertainment with plenty of action and a good supporting cast. Autry sings very well in this one. These kind of westerns are the ones that help build up the weekend."

—W. M. Redmond, Uptown Theater,
Glendive, Montana (April 1937)

SOURCES:

1. Autry with Herskowitz. p. 52.

2. "Melody Ranch Theater" showing of "Tumbling Tumbleweeds" on Nashville Network, 1987.

3. "Melody of the West", American Movie Classics. October 1994.

The Singing Cowboy
Republic, May 1936

Producer.......................................Nat Levine
Supervisor ....Armand Schaefer
Director......................................Mack V. Wright
Original Story ....Tom Gibbons
Screenplay.................................Dorrell and Stuart
                                                  McGowan
Photography ....William Nobles, Edgar
                                                  Lyons
Supervising Editor ....Joseph H. Lewis
Film Editor.................................Lester Orlebeck
Sound Engineer..........................Terry Kellum
Musical Supervisor ....Harry Grey

SONGS: "There's an Empty Cot in the Bunkhouse" (music and lyrics by Gene Autry)—sung by Gene Autry; "Ya-Hoo" (music and lyrics by Oliver Drake)—sung by Gene Autry, Smiley Burnette and boys; "We're On the Air" (music and lyrics by Harry Grey)—sung by Gene and the boys; "True Blue Bill" (music and lyrics by Gene Autry)—sung by Gene Autry; "Rainbow Trail" (music and lyrics by Smiley Burnette, Oliver Drake)—sung by Gene Autry and Lois Wilde; "Down in Slumberland" (music and lyrics by Smiley Burnette)—sung by Smiley Burnette; "The New Jassackaphone" ("Listen to the Mockingbird") (Public Domain, new lyrics by Smiley Burnette)—sung by Smiley Burnette; "Washboard and Room" (music and lyrics by Frankie Marvin)—sung by Frankie Marvin; "My Old Saddle Pal" (music and lyrics by Gene Autry)—sung by Gene Autry; "I'll Be Thinking of You, Little Gal" (music and lyrics by Gene Autry)—sung by Gene Autry.

RUNNING TIME: 56 minutes
FILMING DATES: April 1-10, 1936
LOCATIONS: Brandeis Ranch; Iverson Ranch
BUDGET: $19,894
NEGATIVE COST: $22,312

CAST:

Actor	*Character*
Gene Autry	Gene Autry
Smiley Burnette	Frog Millhouse
Lois Wilde	Helen Blake
Lon Chaney Jr.	Martin

Ann Gillis ....Lou Ann Stevens
Earle Hodgins ....Prof. Pandow
Harvey Clark ....Henry Blake
John Van Pelt...............................Steve Stevens
Earl Eby ....Herbert Trenton
Ken Cooper ....Henchman Bill
Harrison Greene ....Mayor Hawkins
Jack Rockwell ....Sheriff
Tracy Layne ....Henchman Kirk
Patricia Caron.............................Miss Kane
Art Davis....................................Pete
Oscar Gahan...............................Tom—Autry Cowhand/
   Musician
Alfred P. James...........................Justice of the Peace
Jack Kirk ....Jack—Autry Cowhand/
   Musician
Wes Warner ....Autry Cowhand/
   Musician
Frankie Marvin...........................Shorty
Charles McAvoy ....Detective Johnson
George C. Pearce.........................Dr. C. M. Hill
Fred "Snowflake" Toones ....Horn player
Champion ....Champion

STUNTS: Ken Cooper (double for Gene Autry), Joe Yrigoyen.

THE FILM: Featuring an unsurpassed bevy of new songs, the aptly titled "The Singing Cowboy" fits well with Gene Autry's worldwide popularity at this point, coming one year before his title of #1 Cowboy star at the box office as voted by the exhibitors of America in their annual money makers poll.

Furthermore, the fresh, new medium of television (along with radio, cars and city slickers) is prominently featured in the storyline long before sets were commonly owned in the mid '50s. All this serves to return Gene to his unique singing cowboy fantasyland. With its perfect blend of modern and old west and an emphasis on music (11 songs) and comedy more than the land-grab plot, this becomes the first film to "define" the Autry mystique.

Five year old Lou Ann Stevens (Ann Gillis) is seriously injured in a barn fire purposely set by crooked Martin (Lon Chaney Jr.) who kills his partner, Stevens (John Van Pelt), during the melee. Martin desires to own the ranch for himself as he's discovered gold on the property. After Gene Autry saves Lou Ann's life he discovers she needs a delicate operation. To pay for this, Gene and Frog (Smiley Burnette) set out to raise the money by organizing a western music band, The Covered Wagon Boys, and convince a coffee company to sponsor them on the radio and TV.

To further his plans to take over the ranch, Martin steals Gene's Television Troubadours show wagon, hoping to break Gene's contract with the coffee company. Covered Wagons plunging through the canyons create a breathtaking, spectacular finale.

NOTES AND COMMENTS: According to Republic production notes, Gene Autry was paid $810 for this picture while Smiley Burnette earned $250. Leading lady Lois Wilde received $75 and Lon Chaney Jr. $140. Kenny Cooper, again stunting for Gene, earned $200. Glib Earle Hodgins was paid $125 while young Ann Gillis got $60 for her role.

Leading lady Lois Wilde, a famous Ziegfeld girl in his Follies shows, remained in touch with Gene over the years and shortly before her death in 1995 phoned Flying A Pictures Vice President Alex Gordon at the Autry office suggesting a reunion with Gene in a show she was planning in Las Vegas. Unfortunately, Gene's busy schedule with the Anaheim Angels and Miss Wilde's encroaching age and approaching death made this wonderful idea impossible.

Wilde was also seen in Republic's "Undersea Kingdom" serial in '36 and other westerns opposite Rex Bell, Jack Randall and Hopalong Cassidy.

During a broadcast, Smiley Burnette plays a weird instrument strapped to a mule he calls a Jassackaphone while, as a separate number, Frankie Marvin

"The Singing Cowboy"—Gene Autry serenades leading lady Lois Wilde.

plays a washboard with weird things attached.

Gene fractured his right arm when Lon Chaney Jr. flung him against canyon rocks during a furious fist fight which, incidentally, is not seen in the film.

FILM COMMENTS: *Gene Autry:* "In case anyone still didn't know I was a cowboy star, and I sang, the studio decided to take the direct approach. I was asked once what "The Singing Cowboy" was about, and I replied, 'Oh, about sixty-five minutes.' But the action was clearly secondary to the songs, ten of them, including 'Listen to the Mockingbird'.[1]

"1936 was way before commercial television came along. I think they had a few experimental stations, so some of our writers showed up with the idea of doing television. It was way ahead of its time. Lon Chaney Jr. worked with me in that picture. He was a fine actor, but of course he had a tough job because everyone remembered his father. His father was one of the greatest character actors in the world. So Lon Chaney Jr. had a tough job to follow his father and everybody expected him to be just as fine an actor as his father."[2]

Ann Gillis: "I was in that burning barn! My mother nearly had a fit and thought for sure I was a goner. Of course, the technical crew was, as usual, superb and I was never in one moment's danger." [3]

WHAT THE EXHIBITOR HAD TO SAY: "This picture recaptures the mood of the earlier Autry westerns in emphasizing music and novelty situations. It received a perfect audience response and withstood the onslaught of a heat wave. We recently had the pleasure of becoming personally acquainted with Autry, whose quiet and unassuming manner makes him just as impression off screen as on."

—J. W. Noah, New Liberty and Ideal Theaters, Fort Worth, Texas (July 1936)

"This was not produced on a large scale, but how the western fans ate it up. Comedy, music, a few thrills and spills and they come out telling you how good it was. After playing some of the million dollar babies, we small town exhibitors have to shoot in a western to make up the loss."

—John J. Metzger, Oriental Theater, Beaver City, Nebraska (August 1936)

"From my observation after showing 'Singing Cowboy' and 'Oh, Susanna', Autry is the best bet an exhibitor can make, for in my estimation Autry will be greater than Tom Mix was in his palmist days in silent pictures. Autry's combination of singing and riding makes a happy medium for clicking at the box office. This is my first comment on any product in 26 years in business here, but I feel credit is due, even though Republic is a newcomer in the business."

—Johnnie Griffin, Orpheum Theater, Chinook, Montana (February 1937)

"Autry musical westerns outdraw all other pictures so typed. Of course they please; otherwise they wouldn't do so."

—C. E. Morrow, Morrow's Theater, Decatur, Illinois (February 1937)

SOURCES:

1. Autry with Herskowitz. p. 53.

2. "Melody Ranch Theater" showing of "The Singing Cowboy" on Nashville Network, 1987.

3. *Western Clippings* #70. March/April 2006. p. 18.

Guns and Guitars
Republic, June 1936

ACTION . . . luring the killers into the trap!

THRILLS . . . unarmed—trapped by a bandit band!

SURPRISES . . . singing a song while bullets deal death!

Ride the adventure trail with your singing saddle star!

GENE AUTRY

"GUNS and GUITARS" with Smiley Burnette and CHAMPION

Directed by Joseph Kane
Supervised by Robert Beche
Original Story and Screen Play by Dorrell & Stuart McGowan

Produced by NAT LEVINE

A REPUBLIC PICTURE

Producer	Nat Levine
Supervisor	Robert Beche (and Armand Schaefer uncredited)
Director	Joseph Kane
Assistant Director	Ray Culley
Second Assistant Director	Red Jones
Original Story	Dorrell and Stuart McGowan
Screenplay	Dorrell and Stuart McGowan
Photography	Ernest Miller
Supervising Editor	Murray Seldeen
Film Editor	Lester Orlebeck
Sound Engineer	Terry Kellum
Script Clerk	William Witney
Musical Supervisor	Harry Grey

SONGS: "Ridin' All Day" (music and lyrics by Smiley Burnette)—sung by Gene Autry; "Cowboy Medicine Show" (music and lyrics by Harry Grey)—sung by Gene Autry and troupe; "I've Got Fine Relations" (music and lyrics by Smiley Burnette)—sung by Smiley Burnette; "Guns and Guitars" (music and lyrics by Oliver Drake)—sung by Gene Autry; "Dreamy Valley" (music and lyrics by Oliver Drake and Harry Grey)—sung by Gene Autry.

RUNNING TIME: 57 minutes
FILMING DATES: May 3-9, 1936
LOCATIONS: Republic Western Street; Jack Garner Ranch
BUDGET: $20,220
NEGATIVE COST: $20,365

CAST:

Actor	Character
Gene Autry	Gene Autry
Smiley Burnette	Frog Millhouse
Dorothy Dix	Marjorie Miller
Earle Hodgins	'Doctor' Parker
J. P. McGowan	Dave Morgan
Tom London	Conners
Charles King	Sam
Frankie Marvin	Shorty
Eugene Jackson	Eightball
Jack Rockwell	Sheriff Ed Miller
Ken Cooper	Deputy
Tracy Layne	Henchman Ed
Wes Warner	Henchman Al
Jack Kirk	Cowhand Dan
Art Davis	Fiddle player Art
Jim Corey	Henchman Buck
Pascale Perry	Frank Hall
Al Taylor	Cowhand Red
Frank Straubinger	Henchman Joe
Jack Don	Sing Lee
Victor Adamson, Art Dillard, George Morrell, Blackjack Ward	Townsmen
Roy Bucko, Bob Card	Henchmen
Bob Burns	Jenkins
Jack Evans	Man at show
Harrison Greene	Dr. Schaefer
Eva McKenzie, Rose Plummer	Townswomen
Lou Morphy	Deputy

George Plues, Francis Walker ......Cowhands
James Sheridan.............................Man at show
Herman Hack, Francis Walker,
   Emma Tansey, Ralph Bucko.....Extras
Horace Carpenter ....Drunk
Champion ....Champion

STUNTS: Ken Cooper (Gene's double), Francis Walker, Joe Yrigoyen.

THE FILM: Expert action director Joe Kane is back and the 57 minutes pass like a breeze as Gene and Smiley are back as part of a medicine show as they were in "Tumbling Tumbleweeds". The ultimate "medicine show man" Earle Hodgins lands a terrific role stealing most of the laughs from Smiley Burnette. Eugene Jackson is along to do a dancing act again while soon-to-be PRC cowboy star Art Davis fiddles in the background.

Traveling with Doc Parker's medicine show, Gene and Frog are drawn into a conflict over the quarantine of cattle infected with Texas Cattle Fever and the unscrupulous ranchers led by leading citizen Morgan (J. P. McGowan) masterminding the dirty work of Conners and Sam (Tom London and Charles King).

When the sheriff is supposedly murdered and Morgan attempts to have his own man (Pascale Perry) elected, Gene upsets their apple cart by running for the position himself—and is elected, eventually exposing Morgan's plans.

One of the most delightful scenes in Gene's early films comes as he runs afoul of bullies Conners and Sam. Conners warns Gene if he's not out of town by 5 o'clock he'll fill him full of holes. The hour arrives with Gene still there entertaining on the medicine show stage. Conners and Sam, who have been drinking in the bar, in a display of their "toughness" throw beer steins through the bar window and step through the broken glass. Still holding beers they weave their way to where Gene is singing and stand sneering and loudly applauding as he finishes. Fun to see is Charlie King trying to keep a straight face through all of this. Gene then quietly tells the ruffians a little story about Dr. Parker's medicine, about a gunfight on the Panhandle, then draws his own gun and shoots a bottle of Doc Parker's elixir from Conners' hand. Completely backed down by what they believed was a timid "singing cowboy", the pair sneak away, tails between their legs.

Take note of the exciting finale in which Gene (actually stuntman Kenny Cooper) takes a wild spill on Champion, but both get right back up to continue the chase.

Leading lady Dorothy Dix is fairly colorless with little to do.

NOTES AND COMMENTS: Surviving Republic production notes indicate Gene Autry was paid $1,050 for "Guns and Guitars" while saddlepal Smiley Burnette earned $300. Leading lady Dorothy Dix and "Professor" Earle Hodgins gathered $125 apiece. Unscrupulous J. P. McGowan earned $145 while his right-hand man, Tom London, was paid $85. Oddly, lesser billed Charlie King got $100. Gene's usual double, Kenny Cooper, earned $225 plus an extra $65 for some "bulldog" stunts. Director Joseph Kane received $450 and production supervisor Armand Schaefer was paid $500 (although screen credit—for whatever reason—went to Robert Beche). For the screenplay, Dorrell and Stuart McGowan divided $850.

The song "Cowboy Medicine Show", briefly reprised here, originated in Gene's first film "Tumbling Tumbleweeds".

FILM COMMENTS: *Gene Autry:* "If one had to pick an example of the slice-of-life plots that tended to pop up in my films, 'Guns and Guitars' would probably serve. I did not engage, for the most part, in such mundane activities as saving the old homestead or chasing bank bandits. While my solutions were a little less complex than those offered by FDR, and my methods a bit more direct, I played a kind of New Deal cowboy who never hesitated to tackle many of the same problems: the dust bowl, unemployment, or the harnessing of power. This may have contributed to my popularity with the 1930s audiences."[1]

CAST BIOS: The two "dog-heavies" of "Guns and Guitars" are two of the most respected, most popular with

Gene puts the cuffs on unscrupulous J. P. McGowan and Tom London.

viewers, and most prolific badmen in B-western history.

During a career that spanned 48 years beginning in 1915, Tom London made some 550 movies and close to 100 TV episodes, many with Gene Autry, including Gene's first feature "Tumbling Tumbleweeds" right on through Gene's TV episodes in 1954.

London was born Leonard Clapham August 24, 1889, in Louisville, Kentucky. Working as a salesman he made his way to Chicago where he went to work as a prop man for the William Selig film company. When Selig moved his company to the warmer climate of California, Leonard Clapham went along with him. A friendship with Universal star J. Warren Kerrigan got him onto the Universal lot where he worked from 1916 til about 1924. Changing his name to Tom London in 1925, he rustled cattle, shot sheriffs in the back and functioned as a screen badman opposite Tom Mix, Ken Maynard and other silent screen cowboy heroes.

When sound came in, Tom's hearty, slightly nasal, but deep baritone voice easily made the transition to sound. Developing a reputation as a true professional, he was cast constantly in westerns and serial after serial.

As he grew older, he turned more and more to character roles. As TV came along, now 61 in 1950, Tom left the owlhoot roles to younger guys and concentrated on portraying grizzled old-timers, sheriffs, scouts and the like.

Jock Mahoney, later TV's "Range Rider" for Gene's Flying-A TV productions called Tom "The most underrated actor in town. The most patient, most professional actor I've ever known, as well as a kind, giving man."

London wound his career in 1961, then passed away at his home in North Hollywood on December 5, 1963.

Charles King is, without a doubt, the preeminent badman of '30s and '40s B-westerns.

Affectionately known by his fans as "Blackie", Charles Lafayette King was born February 21, 1895 in Hillsboro, Texas. By age 20, Charlie was in Hollywood with his earliest supposed work as an extra in "Birth of a Nation" in 1915. His first documented film work is in 1921.

Before Charlie became established in westerns, he had a run at being a comedian in Universal's popular Mike and Ike two-reel comedy shorts of the late '20s. These comedic talents were often brought to the fore in playing badmen roles.

With the advent of sound, Charlie found himself ensconced and well received in hordes of B-westerns opposite Ken Maynard, Bob Steele, Tex Ritter, Gene Autry and others.

Buster Crabbe remembered Charlie as "A big man… agile as a cat and strong as an ox. He moved like a gazelle. He fought a lot of the movie cowboys and always lost, but I doubt any of them could have whipped him in a real fight. If he had been more serious about his career, and laid off the booze, he might have been a big star. He certainly had the talent."

During his final years, Charlie appeared as an extra on early episodes of "Gunsmoke", supplementing his income working as a security guard at Menasco Steel Company in the San Fernando Valley.

With over 400 films to his credit, the heavy we loved to hate died May 7, 1957, at 62 of a hepatic coma brought on my cirrhosis and chronic alcoholism.

To B-western movie goers of the '30s and '40s, brash, glib Earle Hodgins represented the perfect portrait of the fast talking old west medicine show pitchman. In close to 50 films dressed in a frock coat, string tie and stovepipe hat, Hodgins was a medicine show pitchman, circus barker, sideshow spieler or con man of some sort. He stole scene after scene from stars and sidekicks alike in countless films.

Outlaw Charlie King has Smiley Burnete "wrapped up" while vicious J. P. McGowan has the drop on Gene. Standing behind McGowan are Earle Hodgins and Dorothy Dix. .

George Earle Hodgins was born in Payson, Utah, October 6, 1893, and was educated at first in Salt Lake City. His mother, Minta, was remarried to a William Old by 1910 and the family moved to Oakland, California, where Old was a prompter in the mining business.

How Hodgins came to show business and perfected his medicine show pitchman spiel is unknown, but census records indicate by 1928 he was employed in San Francisco as a "theatrical actor".

His first film was "The Sport Parade" in 1932, but he gained much notoriety with his stock-doubletalk as Doc Carter in John Wayne's "Paradise Canyon" ('35 Lone Star).

"The Singing Cowboy" ('36) was Hodgins' first of nine (counting one TV episode) screen appearances with Autry.

With over 300 movie credits and some 75 TV appearances, Hodgins' last role was on "Gunsmoke" in 1963.

The ultimate snake oil pitchman died of a heart attack April 14, 1964, in Los Angeles, California.

WHAT THE EXHIBITOR HAD TO SAY: "Agreeable western entertainment that should satisfy on a Friday-Saturday date. Autry's loyal following came in full force and gave this picture a satisfactory response."
—J. W. Noah, New Liberty and Ideal Theaters, Fort Worth, Texas (September 1936)

"Good entertainment for the younger set. Not very much music, which puts Autry over. Need more songs."
—A. L. Dove, Bengough Theater, Bengough, Saskatchewan, Canada (January 1937)

"Gene Autry never disappoints me. This is old but it has the usual Autry draw. You can't go wrong when you play Autry. Business good. —Nick Raspa, State Theater, Rivesville, West Virginia (March 1946)

SOURCES:
1. Autry with Herskowitz. p.53.

Oh, Susanna!
Republic, August 1936

Producer ....Nat Levine
Supervisor ....Armand Schaefer,
                                      Robert Beche
                                        (uncredited)
Director ....Joseph Kane
Original Story............................Oliver Drake
Screenplay.................................Oliver Drake
Photography ....William Nobles
Supervising Editor ....Murray Seldeen
Film Editor................................Lester Orlebeck
Sound Engineer.........................Terry Kellum
Musical Supervisor ....Harry Grey

SONGS: "Dear Old Western Skies" (music and lyrics by Gene Autry)—sung by Gene Autry; "Honeymoon Trail" (music and lyrics by Oliver Drake, Herb Myers)—sung by Gene Autry; "Oh, Susanna" (music and lyrics by Steven Foster)—sung by Gene Autry, Smiley Burnette and The Light Crust Doughboys; "Tiger Rag" (music and lyrics by La Rocca)—sung by The Light Crust Doughboys; "They Never Come Through With the Ring" (music and lyrics by Herb Myers, Oliver Drake)—sung by Smiley Burnette, Earle Hodgins; "Ride On Vaquero" (music and lyrics by Oliver Drake, Fleming Allen, Harry Grey)—sung by The Light Crust Doughboys; "Where a Water Wheel Keeps Turning On" (music and lyrics by Sam Stept, Oliver Drake)—sung by Gene Autry, Frances Grant; "As Our Pals Ride By" (music and lyrics by Fleming Allen)—sung by The Light Crust Doughboys.

    RUNNING TIME: 59 minutes
    FILMING DATES: June 1; July 12-18, 1936
    LOCATIONS: Lone Pine, California; Kernville, California; Saugus train station; Iverson Ranch; Newhall Land and Farming Company in Piru, California; Café exteriors on Ventura Blvd; Republic backlot
    BUDGET: $25,329.01
    NEGATIVE COST: $28,243

CAST:

Actor	*Character*
Gene Autry	Gene Autry aka Tex Smith
Smiley Burnette	Frog Millhouse
Frances Grant	Mary Ann Lee
Earle Hodgins	Prof. Ezekial Daniels
Donald Kirke	Flash Baldwin
Boothe Howard	Wolf Benson
The Light Crust Doughboys	(including Bert Dodson, Dick Reinhart, Marvin "Smokey" Montgomery)
Edward Peil Sr.	Sheriff Cole
Clara Kimball Young	Aunt Peggy Lee
Frankie Marvin	Henchman Hank
Carl Stockdale	Jefferson Lee
Roscoe Gerall	Irate Farmer
Roger Gray	Sage City Judge
Fred Burns	Cottonwood Sheriff Jones
Walter James	Sage City Sheriff Briggs
Lew Meehan	Pete, Baldwin's henchman/driver
Fred "Snowflake" Toones	Train Porter
Silver Tip Baker, Edward Coxen, Rube Dalroy, Mur-dock MacQuarrie	Sage City Townsmen
Roy Bucko, Tommy Coats, Tom Smith	Mineral Springs Deputies
Horace B. Carpenter	Sage City Blacksmith
Jack Clifford	Sage City Office Deputy
Curley Dresden, Bud Pope, Tracy Layne, Jay Wilsey	Sage City Deputies
Earl Dwire	Excited Sage City Townsman
Oscar Gahan	Sage City Barber
Ray Henderson	Sage City Townsman on bench
Alfred P. James	Justice of the Peace
Jack Kirk	Sage City Deputy/Lee Ranch Hand
William McCall	Sage City whittling Townsman

Merrill McCormick, Wes Warner.Cottonwood Deputies
Bruce Mitchell ....Train Conductor
George Morrell...........................Sage City Telegrapher
Pascale Perry...............................Knife Act Assistant
Bob Reeves ....Ranch Guest
Billie Bellpart..............................Lady
Ann Lee Roberts, Dave Daggett,
   Mary McCreary, J. C. McGovern .Extras at Ranch house
Tom Martin, Leon Lord, J.
   Lockhart, J. Jackson, P.
   Cunning, R. Wells, Gordon
   Dodds, B. McGarry, B. Sullivan,
   Jack Moyes, R. Smith, A. R.
   Cody, B. E. Johnstone ....Men
Walter Wilson, C. Brinelley,
   Duke Lee ....Deputies
N. Thalan, Maryan Curtis,
   M. Ladd ....Train Passengers
Spencer Chan ....Chinaman
Tip O'Neil ....Old Timer
George French............................Butcher
Wally Howe.................................Bearded man
Joy Winthrop...............................Spinster
Pinky Barnes, C. Howell..............Bit Men
Arbella Jones..............................Colored Mammy
Bill McCall, Lawrence
   Underwood, Paul Boggs...........Villagers
Sam Simone, Babe Green, Bill
   Dill, Walter Clinton ....Men in Street Clothes
M. McChrystal, D. Jensen L.
   Landi, J. Castle, A. Stombs, L.
   Monroe, R. Messinger, E.
   Reynolds, E. Beck ....Girls in Riding Habits
A. Garon, P. Easterday ....Waitresses
George Kidwell...........................Policeman
George Reed...............................Fireman
Sam Costa, Steve Callahan, Ed
   Peil Jr., S. Hedlond ....Cowboys
Estelle Bennett, Irene Dehn ....Women
O. Callaway, M. Clark, D. Woods,
   V. Eubanks, E. Sturgeon...........Women in Street
Clothes
G. Dodds, R. Hall, Buel Jameson,
   J. Garwood, E. Pine, R.
   Laughton, J. P. Middleworth ....Doughboys
Champion....................................Champion

STUNTS: Yakima Canutt, Tommy Coats, Jay Wilsey, Joe Yrigoyen, Wally West, Pierre Valim (double for Boothe Howard), Kenny Cooper (double for Gene Autry); Jack Kirk (double for Smiley Burnette); Eileen Goodwin (double for Frances Grant).

THE FILM: Again set in the mythical west, "Oh, Susanna!" continued Gene Autry's string of 1936 hit westerns. The lighthearted film pokes mild fun at itself and its cowboy hero. Every opportunity is taken to emphasize

Oh, woe is me! Smiley, Earle Hodgins and Gene are in jail again. And with no guitar!

Gene is a radio star. Once again, "Professor" Earle Hodgins steals many of the picture's laughs from Smiley Burnette.

Killer Wolf Benson (Boothe Howard) escapes from a sheriff's posse, boards a passenger train, knocks out and robs radio singer Gene Autry of his clothes and identification. He then hurls Gene's unconscious body off the train and assumes Gene's identity. Found beside the railroad tracks, Gene is befriended by Frog (Smiley Burnette) and Professor Daniels (Earle Hodgins), a traveling two-man show. When Gene, now in the garb of the notorious killer tries to explain his plight to the sheriff, he is believed to be Benson, jailed and ordered hanged. Meanwhile, Benson, pretending to be Autry, goes to a dude ranch run by an old friend of Gene's who has not seen him in years. When Jefferson Lee (Carl Stockdale) sees through Benson's ruse, Lee is killed and robbed. The family, including Lee's daughter Mary Ann (Frances Grant) believe the killer to be Gene Autry. Arriving at the ranch as an entertainer, under an assumed name, Gene finally brings Benson and his cohorts to justice.

It's all good fun, with Smiley and Earle Hodgins forming a sort of comedy duo. As a pair they are quite funny, and it's a pity Republic didn't continue the casting for awhile.

The songs are great, the action terrific, what more could a viewer want?

NOTES AND COMMENTS: An unfortunate accident occurred July 14 in the Kernville vicinity when several cast members were shaken up aboard their bus after overturning on a soft shoulder. Assistant to the associate producer Bob Beche sustained severe injuries—a broken arm, cuts and bruises that resulted in admittance to a Bakersfield hospital. Five other passengers required medical assistance.

"Honeymoon Trail", heard on the radio here, was previously used in "The Singing Vagabond".

Bert Dodson, of The Light Crust Doughboys (organized in 1930) was later one of the three Cass County Boys who were with Gene for years on radio, three TV tours and in the movies.

Listen closely early in the picture for a reference-joke

made about crooner Bing Crosby.

Richard Smith III detailed in WESTERN CLIPPINGS #35 (May/June 2000) Gene Autry's initial legal dispute at Republic which lasted 60 days during mid-1936 before he made "Oh, Susanna!" Part of Gene's *modus operandi* in his big contract battle was to hastily exit Studio City for an extended personal appearance tour and line up other possible paying projects that eventually forced Republic to initiate extensive court action against him. Once Republic and Autry were reunited, acceptable terms for a new contract would be just about always in the cowboy's favor. "Gene Autry signatured his initial feature contract with Mascot May 17, 1935. Then President Nat Levine merged his small movie company June 11 into the new Republic Pictures Corporation which had officially organized March 28, 1935. Autry's three-year pact was immediately transferred to Republic whereby he was paid $100 each week for eight annual B-westerns with six-month options involving $50 raises. Gene's association at the freshman studio went smoothly during the premier '35-'36 season through his 8th oatuner, 'Guns and Guitars'. Immediately, Autry began noting the small salary he earned from Republic was not in line with his studio value. The singing cowboy also reacted negatively at making a 9th western ("Oh, Susanna!") before his picture season officially ended June 30, 1936. Meanwhile, Republic ordered Gene to report to the film set May 20. Autry, instead, left Sunday evening May 17 for a three-month personal appearance tour to include Texas, Oklahoma and other southern states. He prepared these schedules on the premise Republic was unwilling to discuss contractual revisions. Autry's speedy departure caught the studio off guard. Thinking well ahead, Gene also thought of participation in radio as well as personal appearances that could gross him approximately $1,000 a week in both entertainment mediums. The singer was set to reach New York City and negotiate a stage tour for Fall 1936. Additionally, allegedly, he became receptive to film offers from other movie outfits of around $3,500 per picture. Meantime, Republic stopped Gene Autry's tour at Pittsburg, Kansas, May 26 with a federal court restraining order. A May 29th temporary injunction followed. These court rulings kept Gene from being able to engage in other show business ventures apart from his Republic contract. The studio wanted $9,444.37 from Autry, the amount, it claimed, already spent for preparation of his "Oh, Susanna!" a show-cause hearing to make the original federal order permanent was postponed to June 9 as Autry had not been found for presentation of his summons. Meanwhile, the temporary restraint remained in effect. Responding in federal court June 5 to Republic producer Nat Levine that his services were not special or unique, Autry, acting through attorneys, stated the new movie period wasn't set until July 1. He informed Republic of his impending tour which Republic supposedly approved. Gene also asserted a separate oral contract maintained the cowboy was not obligated for more than the allotted number of movies. On June 16, a federal judge ordered the temporary injunction remain against Gene, provided Republic post a $20,000 bond within five days. Now, Autry wanted $900 back wages from studio coffers, plus $1,000 per week for the period of personal appearances interrupted unwarrantably. An ironclad restraining order was lodged against Autry on June 19. However, by late June, the judge amended his previous ruling in the studio's injunction giving Gene an opportunity to make phonograph recordings and appear on the radio. July 2 was set for deciding the possible permanent injunction as Gene was to be Chicago-bound to discuss a radio hookup with Sears Roebuck. Republic entered general denial July 1 to every Autry counterclaim. Despite extensive finger pointing and wagging of tongues from the opposing sides over a two month period, both came together July 7 and settled their differences, resulting in court-action dismissal. Autry and Republic smoked the peace pipe July 8. The cowboy signed a fresh seven-year contract to mainline eight pictures every 365 days that allowed Republic the right for two more movies from Autry as added compensation, and a weekly salary rise with yearly increases. Gene couldn't make outside features under this new arrangement, but had the right to all proceeds from personal appearances, radio, records and music publishing. Four days later (7/12/36), Republic cameras rolled on 'Oh, Susanna!'."

Killer Boothe Howard (center) has led them on a merry chase pretending to be Gene, but at last Sheriff Edward Peil, Sr., Gene, Smiley, Frances Grant and Earle Hodgins have caught up with the culprit.

FILM COMMENTS: *Gene Autry:* "With 'Oh, Susanna!' we began what was to become a policy for most of the movies I did at Republic: employing various country music groups, usually regional, with at least some radio fame. The Light Crust Doughboys were first, out of Fort Worth, only a few years away from seeing their leader, Pappy Lee O'Daniel, elected governor of Texas. The music in my previous films had been supplied by Smiley, myself, and a few, uncredited, backup musicians."[1]

Kay Hughes was originally scheduled to be Gene's leading lady, but was replaced by Frances Grant. On the first day of shooting in Lone Pine, Kay was injured. "They asked me if I could ride and I said sure. I'd been on a horse, but only in a riding stable. It was the first scene I did… they put me on this horse with a bunch of cowboys and we had to run into camera range and stop abruptly in a ditch. Everybody stopped but me! I went over the horse's head and hurt my arm and back. I still have a scar on my elbow. I had to go home, so I didn't do my first Gene Autry. Also, at the same time, the bus went off the road and overturned. Several members of the troupe were injured (two grips, a propman and Robert Beche). We all went back together to the studio. I remember Al Teeter was on the bus going back. He was one of the crew and wrote songs. I still have some of the songs he wrote. He never did publish them. I think he went to Disney later on."[2]

CAST BIOS: Leading lady Frances Grant, who was also in "Red River Valley", gets to harmonize with Gene in "Oh, Susanna!" and shares a kiss with him at the fade-out.

Born Stella Fortier in Roxbury, Massachusetts, on February 15, 1909, the 5' 4" Frances Grant became a Ziegfeld Follies dancing partner to dancer/entertainer Hal LeRoy and entered films as a hoofer in 1934.

After making several westerns, she became a dance instructor in the '40s and '50s working on such films as "Mrs. Mike" ('49) and "Fancy Pants" ('50).

She died in Lexington, Massachusetts, on February 20, 1982.

WHAT THE EXHIBITOR HAD TO SAY: "A tip-top western. When Gene Autry pictures appear on our screen, the money hand in the ticket office begins to circle the dial. The more Gene sings the better our patrons like it. Autry pictures will do no injustice to any exhibitor."
—E. I. Hawkins, Hawkins Theater, Newellton, Louisiana (March 1937)

"A good show, but hope we will see a better show in his next picture." —Rudolf Duba, Royal Theater, Kimball, South Dakota (July 1937)

"These semi-westerns do well for us. People will accept them who do not care for ordinary westerns, and they seem to satisfy the western fans also."
—G. A. Van Fradenburg, Valley Theater, Manassa, Colorado (July 1937)

"Our second Autry picture and nearly doubled receipts over his first one. Looks like he'd be a sure bet for Saturday."
—A. N. Miles, Eminence Theater, Eminence, Tennessee (November 1937)

SOURCES:
1. Autry with Herskowitz. p. 53.
2. Magers and Fitzgerald. *Westerns Women.* McFarland, 1998. p. 111.

Ride Ranger Ride
<u>Republic, September 1936</u>

Producer ....Nat Levine
Supervisor ....Armand Schaefer
Director ....Joseph Kane
Assistant Director.......................Louis Germonprez
Original Story..............................Bernard McConville and
         Karen DeWolf
Screenplay.................................Dorrell and Stuart
McGowan
Photography ....William Nobles
Supervising Editor ....Murray Seldeen
Film Editor.................................Lester Orlebeck
Sound Engineer..........................Terry Kellum
Script Clerk...............................R. G. Springsteen
Musical Supervisor ....Harry Grey

SONGS: "Ride Ranger Ride" (music and lyrics by Tim Spencer)—sung by Gene Autry and Rangers; "Goin' Down the Road" (music and lyrics by The Tennessee Ramblers)—sung by The Tennessee Ramblers; "The Bugle Song" (music and lyrics by Smiley Burnette)—sung by Smiley Burnette; "Yellow Rose of Texas" (Traditional)—sung by Gene Autry and the Rangers; "On the Sunset Trail" (music and lyrics by Sam H. Stept, Sidney Mitchell)—sung by Gene Autry; "Marche Militaire" (Public Domain by Franz Schubert)—sung by Smiley Burnette and Max Terhune; "Song of the Pioneers" (music and lyrics by Tim Spencer)—sung by wagon train troupe.

RUNNING TIME: 63 minutes

FILMING DATES: August 12-18, 1936

LOCATIONS: Agoura Ranch and surrounding mesa; Republic backlot

BUDGET: $25,865

NEGATIVE COST: $26,801

CAST:

Actor	*Character*
Gene Autry	Gene Autry
Smiley Burnette	Frog Millhouse
Kay Hughes	Dixie Summeral
Monte Blue	Duval, aka Chief Tavibo
George J. Lewis	Lt. Bob Cameron
Max Terhune	Scout Rufe Jones
Robert E. Homans	Colonel Summeral
Lloyd Whitlock	Major Crosby
Chief Thunder Cloud	Little Wolf
William J. Blair, Dick Hartman, Fred "Happy" Morris, Garnett "Elmer" Warren, Kenneth L. "Pappy" Wolfe, Cecil "Curley" Campbell	The Tennessee Ramblers
Joe de la Cruz	Bob Tail Horse
Jack Cheatham	Jailer Wilson
Marie Astaire	Goldie
I. Stanford Jolley	Settler
Frankie Marvin	Ranger
Nelson McDowell	Proctor
Frederick Blanchard	Governor Mathews
Phillip Armenta	Great Bear
Art Davis	Orderly
Iron Eyes Cody, Red Star, High Eagle, Sonny Chorre, Shooting Star, Greg Whitespear, Sky Eagle, Joe Marcellina, Humming Bird, Silver Moon, Little Pine, Pete Tapia, Bahe Denet, Alex Shoulders, Augie Gomez	Comanche Warriors
Frank Todd, Ben Fields, Al Brinker, Dan Fitzpartick, Tex Sale, Phil Harrison, Frank Stanley, Cleve Monroe, John Caldwell, C. P. Fisher, Frank Santley, Pinky Barnes	Cowboys
Roscoe Gerall	Guard
Iris Boles, Helen Gibson	Wagon Train Women
Sam Lufkin	Guard
George Godfrey	Man
Eddie Contreras	Peon
Mrs. Armenta, J. Maillard, Rose Plummer	Women
Carlos Ruffino, Ramon Ross, Gilberto Galvan, Alfred Palacio, Bill Melendez	Vaqueros
M. Ruiz, Alvira Canto	Spanish Women
Al Boles, Arthur Singley, Robert Thomas, Pat Henry, Jack Trent	Cavalrymen

REPUBLIC PICTURES
presents

GENE AUTRY

IN

'RIDE, RANGER, RIDE'

with

SMILEY BURNETTE
THE TENNESSEE RAMBLERS

PRODUCED *by* NAT LEVINE

DIRECTED *by* JOSEPH KANE
ORIGINAL STORY *by* BERNARD McCONVILLE
and KAREN DeWOLF
SCREEN PLAY *by* DORRELL *and* STUART McGOWAN

A REPUBLIC PICTURE

Gene battles Monte Blue while Lieut. George J. Lewis battles off more Indians in this title card scene.

Bud Pope......................................Settler
Al Brinker, Red Carlin, Phil
   Harris, Charley Ekdrich, Silver
   Tip Baker, Tex Phelps...............Scouts
Robert Burns, Bob Mitchell, Art
   Taylor, Jack Carlisle, Harry
   Fraser, Jimmy Ellard, J.C.
   McGovern, Cliff Moore, Harry
   Harris, G. W. Burnette, Jack
   Ingram, Warren Smith ....Civilians
Joan Barckay, Helen Leslie,
   Elaine Waters, Bobbie LaSalle,
   Billie Hirsch ....Girls
Morgan Brown ....Waiter
A. W. Newington........................Bartender
J. N. Pacheco, Mario Prado, C.
   Guerrero, Frank Montejano......Musicians
Bill Yrigoyen, Joe Yrigoyen, Steve
   Callahan, Ed Jauregui, Sam Costa,
   Bill Maul, Jim Shepard, Tom Carter,
   Al Duncan, George Cole, Tom
   Gillibrand, Harry Wellingham, Bill
   Gafney, Bob La Berge, Bob Brown,

Jack Trent, Pat Henry, Art Dillard,
   George Fiske, Robert Hall, Walter
   Wilson, Bud Pope, Al Boles,
   Bill Drake ....Riders
Champion....................................Champion

STUNTS: Al Boles (double for Max Terhune and Monte Blue), Ken Cooper (double for Gene Autry), Joe Yrigoyen, Jack Leonard, Jack Ingram, Charles Sullivan, Roy Moore

THE FILM: Another pure western, "Ride Ranger Ride" puts Gene back in the old west as a Texas Ranger who joins the Cavalry when the rangers are disbanded. Troopers Rufe Jones (Max Terhune) and Frog Millhouse (Smiley Burnette) join Gene in the Army. A rivalry for the affections of the Colonel's daughter, Dixie (Kay Hughes), develops between Gene and Lt. Bob Cameron (George J. Lewis). Ordered to make peace with the Indians, Lt. Cameron has Gene sent along with the detachment. In a skirmish, Gene shoots his way out and is later sighted by the Colonel for breach of discipline and for fighting with the Colonel's interpreter, Duval (Monte Blue), who is actually an Indian spy. Mustered out of the Army, Gene and his pals must round up the troublemakers and reveal Duval's double-life to Colonel Summeral (Robert E. Homans).

Max Terhune's first screen assignment serves him well, completely overshadowing Smiley's somewhat limited role in this feature. The Indians are treated pretty roughly, but then so is Smiley in a running gag with Little Wolf (Chief Thunder Cloud) who is trying to scalp him. Terhune also generates genuine laughs in a recurring bit involving sneeze-causing snuff.

NOTES AND COMMENTS: Script clerk R. G. Springsteen (1904-1989) from Tacoma, Washington, became a noted director of Republic westerns in the mid-'40s.

George J. Lewis took quite a tumble from his horse according to production notes, landing on his shoulder. Fortunately, he was not seriously injured.

A week before filming commenced, Gene received unspecified injuries in an overturned car accident near Roswell, New Mexico.

FILM COMMENTS: Gene Autry: "Over the years, I am told, 'Ride, Ranger, Ride' has become a collector's item, in the unexplained way that those things often happen. This one is valued as the other of the two Autry scripts at Republic, placed in the period of the American frontier. I leave the U.S. Cavalry, rejoin the Texas Rangers, and expose the traitor who instigated an Indian uprising. I know. Why does a synopsis, even your own, always sound like a blurb for a movie ad?"[1]

Kay Hughes: "We were coming back from location in the limo and Gene was singing to me. I thought, 'Oh, dear, do I have to listen to this?' At the time, I didn't think he had a very good voice. Now, I realize he's a wonderful singer, I really do. But at the time, you know, he was just singing. He wasn't trying to make a pass, he was just singing."

Kay was Gene's 4th leading lady to give him an on-screen kiss. Although it was her first screen kiss, she says she wasn't nervous. "It was just another scene. There's so

Gene and Kay Hughes.

many people around, you just do it and don't think anything of it. But there was something funny about that scene. It was at the end of the picture. I was sitting on a rock. Gene was supposed to pull me up and we were supposed to kiss. He didn't pull me up, so I pushed myself up with my hands. I had to push myself up to kiss him! But they didn't do another, just one take and that was it."[2]

CAST BIOS: For the musical group in "Ride Ranger Ride" Republic hired one of the most popular old-time string bands in the country, The Tennessee Ramblers. Dick Hartman (1898-1962) apparently organized the band at KDKA radio, Pittsburgh, Pennsylvania, about 1928. The band began to hit their stride around 1933 when the Ramblers went to WHEC radio, Rochester, New York. In 1934, the company sent them to WBT, Charlotte, North Carolina, which became their primary base of operations. They began recording for Bluebird in 1935 and made two films with Gene Autry, "Ride Ranger Ride" and "Yodelin' Kid From Pine Ridge". Hartman departed the group in 1938 and other personnel changed by the time the group made later films with Tex Ritter, Dale Evans, Roy Acuff and Charles Starrett. At the time of this film the personnel were Dick Hartman of Burlington, West Virginia, who began in radio in 1922; William J. Blair of New Martinsville, West Virginia; fiddler Kenneth L. "Pappy" Wolfe of near Leesburg, Virginia, who started playing fiddle and calling square dances at the age of seven; bassman Fred "Happy" Morris of Carroll County, Georgia; fiddler Garnett "Elmer" Warren out of Mount Airy, North Carolina; and tenor banjo/steel guitarist Cecil Campbell.

Max Terhune made his film debut in "Ride Ranger Ride". Robert Max Terhune was born February 12, 1891, on a farm near Franklin and Amity, Indiana, and was educated in Chicago schools. Originally known as "The Hoosier Mimic" Max began as a solo act in 1920, among his vaudeville tricks were magic, juggling, ventriloquism and imitations of every known animal or fowl. Max joined the WLS National Barn Dance in 1931 which is where he met Gene and Smiley. Established in Hollywood, Gene remembered Max's talent and sent for him to be in "Ride Ranger Ride". Max is also featured in Gene's "The Big Show" and "Manhattan Merry-Go-Round".

On the Orpheum vaudeville circuit his ventriloquist's dummy was named Skully Null but he became Elmer Sneezeweed when Max joined the Three Mesquiteers series in 1936 at Republic as Lullaby Joslin, a role he played in 21 films, leaving in 1939 to become the comic sidekick in The Range Busters series at Monogram. As Alibi he made 24 in that series. In the late '40s he co-starred in several with Johnny Mack Brown. As an expert card manipulator, it is Max's hands you see for a close-up card scene doubling Clark Gable in "The King and Four Queens" ('56). His last screen appearance was as a doctor in "Giant" ('56).

Max died of a stroke (preceded a week earlier by a

heart attack) on June 5, 1973, in Cottonwood, Arizona.

This was George J. Lewis' first feature with Gene, but he later worked in "Twilight On the Rio Grande", "The Big Sombrero", "Wagon Team" and nearly a dozen of Gene's TV episodes.

The dashing, black-haired Lewis was born December 10, 1903, in Guadalajara, Mexico, to American parents who left the country for Brazil to evade the Mexican revolution when George was six. Two years later, the family moved to Wisconsin. His father, who guarded shipyards during WWI, was out of the service living in Coronado, California, where George finished high school and became interested in dramatics.

By 1923 he was in Hollywood appearing in silent films. Shortly after "Ride Ranger Ride" George headed east where he appeared in numerous plays and on radio. By 1939 he was back in Hollywood and became one of the best known of the western and serial badmen, his vivid black mustache always lending a cunning note to his evil undertakings.

George ended a 44 year career in 1966 and devoted full time to his thriving real estate business from which he retired in 1980.

George died at his home in Rancho Santa Fe, California,

on December 8, 1995, two days shy of his 92nd birthday.

Kay Hughes, born in Los Angeles, California, in 1914, desired to be a dancer but an illness requiring several operations when she was a teenager prevented that from becoming a reality. Kay entered films in 1935 and was Gene's leading lady twice in 1936, in "Ride Ranger Ride" and "The Big Show". She'd been scheduled to do "Oh, Susanna!" but was injured. (See "Oh, Susanna!" Film Comments.)

By the late '30s Kay had moved from Republic to Universal, eventually leaving films by the mid '40s. In later years, she lived with her husbands, there were three, in Tulsa, Oklahoma, St. Louis, Missouri, and Reno, Nevada.

Kay died in Desert Hot Springs, California, at 84 on April 4, 1998.

WHAT THE EXHIBITOR HAD TO SAY: "When better westerns are made Gene Autry will make them. All Gene Autry pictures do a fine business for us."

—Gavin Bros., American Theater, Stevensville, Montana (December 1936)

"Not nearly as good as most Autry pictures but better than the average musical western. Why don't they give this guy a better break while he is still popular?"

—Roy Pringle, Eureka and General Theaters, Fabens, Texas, (February 1937)

"A very good musical western. As good as the rest of the Gene Autry pictures we played, and they were all plenty good for the theatre. Packed house whenever we play a Gene Autry picture. Better than most specials."

—Fischer & Bichler, Mattray Theater, Strasburg, North Dakota (September 1937)

"This did better than the average Autry reissue. Max Terhune was very good in this. He used to be about as popular as Smiley Burnette is here. Wonder why some company hasn't made some westerns with him lately?"

—S. T. Jackson, Jackson Theater, Flomaton, Alabama (March 1946)

SOURCES:
1. Autry with Herskowitz. p. 53.
2. Magers and Fitzgerald. Westerns Women. McFarland, 1999. p. 111-112.

Scout Max Terhune points the way for Gene and George J. Lewis.

The Big Show
<u>Republic, November 1936</u>

The Beverly Hill Billies, Smiley Burnette; "Happy Go Lucky Vagabonds" (music and lyrics by The Light Crust Doughboys)—sung by The Light Crust Doughboys; "I'm Mad About You" (music and lyrics by Sam Stept and Ted Koehler)—sung by Gene Autry and Smiley Burnette; "Ride Ranger Ride" (music and lyrics by Tim Spencer)—sung by a chorus of Texas Rangers; "Lady Known as Lulu" (music and lyrics by Sam Stept and Ned Washington)—sung by The Jones Boys; "Wild and Wooley West" (music and lyrics by Sam Stept and Ted Koehler)—sung by Gene Autry, Smiley Burnette, Max Terhune and Elmer, Sally Payne, Sons of the Pioneers; "Nobody's Darlin' But Mine" (music and lyrics by Jimmie Davis)—sung by Gene Autry; "Roll Wagons Roll" (music and lyrics by Tim Spencer and Carl Winge)—sung by The Sons of the Pioneers; "Old Faithful" (music and lyrics by Michael Carr and James Kennedy)—sung by Gene Autry.

RUNNING TIME: 70 minutes

FILMING DATES: September 14 to October 9, 1936

LOCATIONS: Texas Centennial in Dallas, Texas; Iverson Ranch; Joe Yrigoyen Ranch; Republic backlot

BUDGET: $35,955

NEGATIVE COST: $34,632

Producer ....Nat Levine
Supervisor ....Armand Schaefer
Director ....Mack V. Wright
Assistant Director........................Louis Germomprez
Original Story..............................Dorrell and Stuart
                               McGowan
Screenplay...................................Dorrell and Stuart
                               McGowan
Photography ....William Nobles and
Edgar Lyons
Supervising Editor ....Murray Seldeen
Film Editor ....Robert Jahns
Sound Engineer...........................Harry Jones
Musical Supervisor ....Harry Grey

SONGS: "The Martins and the Coys" (music and lyrics by Weems and Cameron)—sung by Gene Autry,

CAST:

Actor	Character
Gene Autry ....Gene Autry
Gene Autry ....Tom Ford
Smiley Burnette ....Frog Millhouse
Kay Hughes..................................Marion Hill
Sally Payne..................................Toodles Brown
William Newell ....Lee Wilson
Max Terhune ....Ventriloquist
Charles Judels ....Schwartz

Sons of the Pioneers: Tim
   Spencer, Bob Nolan, Len Slye,
   Hugh Farr, Karl Farr.................Sons of the Pioneers

The Jones Boys ....Singers

The Beverly Hill Billies: Elton
   Britt, Charlie Slater, Jad Dees,
   Ezra Paulette, Lem Giles,

Aleth Hansen, Rudy Sooter ......Singers
The Light Crust Doughboys:
   including Bert Dodson, Dick
   Reinhart, Marvin "Smokey"
   Montgomery ....Singers
Rex King ....Fred Collins
Harry Worth ....Tony Rico
Mary Russell ....Mary (Ford's leading lady)
Christine Maple............................Miss VanEvery
Jerry Larkin.................................Henchman Blackie
Jack O'Shea ....Henchman Joe
Wedgewood Nowell....................Movie director
Antrim Short ....Assistant Director
June Johnson ....Studio secretary
Grace Durkin................................Pretty Girl
Captain Leonard Pack ....Himself
Richard Beach.............................Studio Assistant
Horace B. Carpenter....................Studio gateman
Cornelius Keefe, Martin
   Stevenson ....Studio actors
Jeanne Lafayette...........................Studio actress
Tracy Layne ....Henchman
Frankie Marvin, Art Davis ....Movie lot Cowboy
Art Mix.......................................Studio Stunt Double
Frances Morris ....Studio Script Girl
Helen Servis................................Studio actress Helen
The SMU 50...............................Southern Methodist
                         University Marching
                         Band
Sam Costa ....Mary's Truck Driver
Ervin Collins ....Indian/and/Grip
Jimmy Shepard............................Indian/and/Settler
Joe Yrigoyen ....Settler/and/Cowboy/
                         and/Indian
Bill Yrigoyen, Ed Jauregui, Bob
   LaBerge, Bill Gafney, Don
   Sterling, Bud Hecker, Billy
   Lewis ....Cowboys
Edwin Lanford ....Rickshaw Puller
Jack Ingram.................................Cameraman
Tex Wilson, Shorty Hendricks .....Carpenters
Cypryan Paulette..........................Boom Man
Martin Provenson........................Radio Announcer
Richard Godfrey..........................Trapper
Fred Hartman, Vic LaCardo, Ben
   Heideman, Lewis Wood, James
   Springer, Charles Hopkins,
   William Bartley, Herman
   Woods, Dick Scott....................Men
Christine Maple............................Elizabeth
Morgan Brown ....Make-up Man
Flora Roberts...............................Lady
Helen Huntington.........................Girl
30 Texas Rangers ....
Champion....................................Champion

STUNTS: Ken Cooper (double for Gene Autry);

Jack Kirk (double for Smiley); Cliff Lyons, Bill Yrigoyen, Joe Yrigoyen, Sam Costa, Wally West, Helen May (double for Kay Hughes), Art Davis (double for Harry Worth).

THE FILM: "The Big Show" is one of Gene Autry's most unusual westerns. And it was just this type of unusual material that made Gene the biggest cowboy star in the country. A high-gear mixture of action, comedy, music and fun, including a huge cast that featured, not one, but four musical groups, all filmed before the backdrop of the 1936 Texas Centennial Exposition in Dallas. It's also the first Autry film to run 70 minutes; it would be three years before Republic elevated Gene again to lengthier titles with "In Old Monterey" ('39).

"The Big Show" is truly witty and funny at times, including humorous bits by not only Smiley Burnette, but former vaudevillian William Newell as a Mammoth Pictures press agent; Ziegfeld Follies comedienne Sally Payne in several slapstick pratfalls for her first screen role (she later co-starred in several films with Roy Rogers); noted stage and screen comedian Charles Judels as a look-a-like for Republic prexy Herbert J. Yates; and least, but not last, Mary Russell as conceited film actor Tom Ford's leading lady who delivers some hilarious comebacks to the ego-driven Ford.

The whole picture is reminiscent of the wonderful screwball comedies of the '30s, yet composed of a wonderful layering of genre elements. Here we have a film within a film—Republic Pictures poking satirical fun at themselves…Gene being made an honorary Texas Ranger on film while they believe he is Tom Ford when Gene actually was awarded that distinction…a dual role for Gene…urban gangsters who try to escape dressed as cowboys by riding a stagecoach alongside a man-made lagoon at the actual 1936 Texas Centennial and a diverse mix of music from pure western to Jimmie Davis country to

A movie within a movie. Cameras roll while Gene (as actor Tom Ford) plays a scene with Mary Russell.

the Jones Boys, a hip harmonizing black vocal quintet and the 50-strong Southern Methodist University chorus. To complete the absurdity there's Smiley Burnette following a chase by pulling a rickshaw. Only Gene Autry could pull all these divergent elements together and make it work as a joyful movie-going experience unlike no other B-western ever made.

The plot, for the record, has Gene playing a dual role as Mammoth Pictures' arrogant, egotistical cowboy star Tom Ford and his dead-ringer stunt double, Gene Autry. When Ford goes fishing, publicity man Lee Wilson (William Newell) talks Gene into impersonating Ford at 'The Big Show', the Texas Centennial. Trouble erupts on all fronts when Gene sings on the radio when everyone believes Ford can't sing a note. Mammoth Studios, thinking Ford can sing after all, announces in VARIETY they're now going to make musical westerns. A gangster, Tony Rico (Harry Worth) to whom Ford owes a gambling debt, comes looking for Gene (believing him Ford), as does Ford's fiancée *and* the real Ford when he discovers the deception. Worse, when Gene's girl Marion Hill (Kay Hughes) believing him to be Ford, learns of the deception, she leaves him, causing Gene, in order to win her back, to reveal the deception to all the world on the radio.

Meanwhile, Rico and his boys had hoodwinked Wilson out of $25,000 and are making their getaway. This leads to a wild, fun-for-all, merry chase across the Centennial to capture the crooks and recover the money.

"The Big Show" totally charms us with its playful mix of on-location setting, music, sly inside industry humor and low budget inventiveness. No wonder it became one of Gene's biggest hits and led to him being voted by exhibitors by the end of 1936 as the No. 1 Cowboy Star at the nation's box office.

NOTES AND COMMENTS: "The Big Show" is an historic archive with Republic taking a full film crew to the Texas Centennial Exposition in Dallas from September 15-September 19, 1936. The actual Exposition ran from June 6 to November 29, 1936. The idea for the big event to celebrate the birth of the Lone Star Republic first came about in a speech by Governor James Stephen Hogg in 1900. Hogg's idea took root, but not without considerable political wrangling. Houston,

San Antonio and Dallas were pitted in competition to be host city but it was Big D that came up with the money, an existing infrastructure in Fair Park and strong civic leadership. Dallas contributed $7,791,000. The legislature kicked in $3 million and the U.S. Congress matched that amount. The post office put out a special 3¢ stamp and the U.S. mint coined commemorative half dollars. The exposition opened on June 6, 1936, with twin themes of history and progress. When the expo shut down on November 29 it had seen close to six and a half million visitors.

The opening credits have some interesting views of the Exposition in Fair Park. George Dahl was the Centennial architect who designed and built the Exposition in 10 months, including a face-lift of the 1908 Coliseum which became the Administration Building, now the Women's Museum.

When Gene and his friends arrive at the Exposition, scenes are shown of the Sinclair Dinosaur Exhibit, the Midway and the Federal Building (currently the Tower Building). As they arrive at the Main Gate the GM Exhibits Building in the present Music Hall at Fair Park can be viewed in the background. Note the streetcars which, in 1936, all led to the Centennial.

During the parade you can see the Hall of State and Humble's Hall of Texas Heroes Exhibit Building as well as the Ford Motor Company exhibit building in the background. Grand Place now occupies that location.

During the parade and as "Tom Ford" is presented with an honorary commission in the Texas Rangers (which in real life Gene Autry was presented) you can glimpse the Federal (Tower) Building, Varied Industries Building (presently the Automobile Building), the Hall of State and Esplanade of State. The "mob of teenagers" scene is in front of the Hall of State.

The Jones Boys perform in the Gulf Oil Company Radio Studios Building which was located between the present Automobile Building and the Old Mill Restaurant. In addition to having live broadcasts on the radio networks, the programs were broadcast on an elaborate public address system referred to as "Singing Towers" which were structured all over the park.

There are also some scenes that take place in the Livestock Building.

Most spectacular are

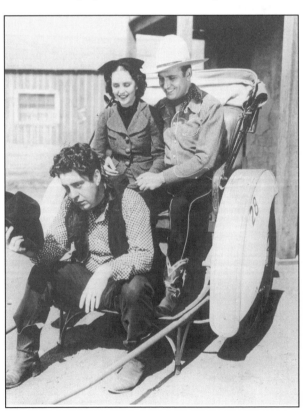

Kay Hughes, Gene and Smiley do a little clowning around between scenes of "The Big Show."

the actual scenes from a pageant about Texas history, "The Cavalcade of Texas", which was performed on the world's largest outdoor stage at the time, a 300 x 170 foot stage with mountains and bluffs reaching 60 feet in the air. It was at about the present location of the State Fair Coliseum. The Cavalcade was managed by A. L. Vollman who produced another show for the '37 Expo and went to San Francisco in '39 and '40. The water spray you'll see in "The Big Show" was used as a sort of "curtain" between acts.

As Tony Rico and his hoods stash their loot, you'll note the Gulf Spray or Sidney Smith Fountain which is now in front of the Music Hall. Smith was one of the early founders of the State Fair of Texas.

As Rico and his boys go on stage with other real performers there are actual scenes from the finale of The Cavalcade of Texas. The public address system announces "Texas Under Six Flags" with a display of men on horseback carrying flags onto the stage—Spain, France, Mexico, Lone Star of Texas, Stars and Bars of the Confederacy and "The Stars and Stripes Forever." Gene rides to the top of "the mountain" on the site with the American Flag.

The chase scene that follows features passing views of the Cotton Bowl, the midway, Ford Exhibits Building, Texaco Exhibits Building, Christian Science Monitor Exhibit Building, "Forbidden City" attraction, even a brief glimpse of the funnels of the steamship Normandie from the daring "Streets of Paris" French revue. The rickshaw ends up in the lagoon in front of the Museum of Fine Arts, presently Science Place. (These historic notes and research were provided by Robert T. Paige of Irving, Texas.)

There's a hilarious inside joke in "The Big Show". A Herbert J. Yates (president of Republic) look-a-like, Mr. Schwartz, president of Mammoth Pictures, hears Gene sing and believes it's his "star" Tom Ford. He proclaims on the phone to publicity man Lee Wilson, "From now on we're making nothing but musical westerns. What? They won't go over? Why, a year from now every studio in the business will be making 'em." Later a one-sheet of Gene Autry in "The Singing Cowboy" is seen to complete this inside joke.

Mary Russell, who plays Tom Ford's wisecracking leading lady, injured her back during the filming of her covered wagon scene.

The Governor of Texas, James V. Allred, almost made his film debut in "The Big Show". The film suffered several rain delays and one of those caused the Governor to cancel his flight from the capital in Austin to Dallas. A gentleman who represents the Governor awards Tom Ford, actually Gene, an honorary commission in the Texas Rangers. However, Governor Scholz of Florida does appear as an "extra" in the picture as he was a guest of the Exposition.

Leonard Pack, one of the most colorful characters of Texas, is introduced with his famous horse, Texas, to Gene in "The Big Show". Pack, a Captain of the Texas Rangers for

40 years, was in charge of policing The Texas Centennial grounds in Dallas. Pack took his horse Texas to nearly every state in the union advertising the Exposition.

This is one of the scant few B-westerns whose plotline is actually about making B-westerns. Others in the sub-genre include: "Quick Trigger Lee" ('31) with Bob Custer, "Scarlet River" ('33) with Tom Keene, "Thrill Hunter" ('33) with Buck Jones, "Mystery Ranch" ('34) with Tom Tyler, "Cowboy Star" ('36) with Charles Starrett, "Hollywood Roundup" ('37) with Buck Jones, "Hollywood Cowboy" ('37) with George O'Brien, "Shooting High" ('40) with Gene Autry, "Chatterbox" ('43) with Joe E. Brown, "Twilight On the Prairie" ('44) with Johnny Downs, "Bells of Rosarita" ('45) with Roy Rogers, "Ding Dong Williams" ('46) with James Warren, "Out California Way" ('46) with Monte Hale, "Under California Stars" ('48) with Roy Rogers, "Sons of Adventure" ('48) with Russell Hayden, "Grand Canyon" ('50) with Richard Arlen, "Kid From Gower Gulch" ('50) with Spade Cooley and "Hoedown" ('50) with Jock Mahoney.

Playing a small part as a studio secretary was June Johnson who was the young daughter of Chic Johnson of the popular comedy team of Olsen and Johnson.

FILM COMMENTS: *Gene Autry:* "No B-westerns had been produced with bigger budgets, or released with more fanfare and publicity, than mine. The Rogers films of the war years and the Hopalong Cassidys from Paramount were about the only others that had anything resembling a promotion campaign. Certain of my pictures were treated as special entries, rather than as the-next-in-an-endless series. The first to rate this handling was 'The Big Show,' filmed on location at the Texas Centennial. That means we did the background shots and some of the specialty acts in Dallas.

"'The Big Show' marked my only dual role. I appeared as a kind of snooty film star named Tom Ford, whose

Gangster Harry Worth (in black) and henchman Jerry Larkin have the drop on Gene and pal William Newell.

double and stunt man happened to be Gene Autry. With the exception of my part as a henchie in 'Mystery Mountain', and a later film at Fox, this was the only other time I played a character whose name was not my own.

"This time we featured not one but five musical groups: Sons of the Pioneers, the Light Crust Doughboys (whose star, Bob Wills, had just quit to go out on his own), the Beverly Hill Billies, the Jones Boys, and the SMU band. By loading up the credits, and designating the movie as an 'Autry Special', Republic found that it could charge the exhibitors more than the usual flat rate. This discovery inspired a number of 'Autry Specials'."[1]

CAST BIOS: The credit for turning Republic's latest Gene Autry picture into truly a 'Big Show' goes to director Mack V. Wright, born in Princeton, Indiana, March 9, 1894.

By 1914 he was acting in small roles in Hollywood silent pictures. After serving in WWI, he returned to the film capital and worked steadily for Universal for the next few years, acting and, eventually, directing.

Forming a friendship with producer/director J. P. McGowan, Wright worked as an actor in a slew of low budget features for McGowan.

With the dawn of sound, Wright spread his wings as screenwriter and assistant director. In 1932 his first sound directorial job came with John Wayne's "Haunted Gold" and two other Wayne westerns for Warner Bros.

His talent noticed, Wright was hired by the newly formed Republic and helmed Gene Autry's "Comin' 'Round the Mountain" in '36. "The Singing Cowboy", "The Big Show" and "Rootin' Tootin' Rhythm" followed before he was assigned to the Three Mesquiteers series.

Leaving Republic in '37, Wright moseyed on to helm westerns with Kermit Maynard and the Rough Riders and several with Bill Elliott and Buster Crabbe, as well as lower-echelon comedies and musicals at Universal.

He wound up his career in the '50s by working as a production manager on TV's "Sea Hunt".

Moving to Boulder City, Nevada, he was retired when he died at 71 on August 14, 1965.

WHAT THE EXHIBITOR HAD TO SAY: "Absolutely tops in westerns. Mr. and Mrs. Exhibitor, if you aren't running these Autrys, you are depriving your patrons of something they deserve."   —L. B. Jarrell, Ritz Theater, Columbia, Louisiana (December 1936)

"This picture broke my Saturday house record. When Gene Autry comes to my theatre, I know I will do above average business. That should be enough for any exhibitors who play action pictures."   —Elgin Ramsey, Dixie Theater, Tracy City, Tennessee (January 1937)

"'The Big Show' depends almost entirely upon the Texas Centennial backgrounds for its entertainment strength,

which wavers precariously when Autry sings such a hot-cha un-western number as 'I'm Mad About You'. We would say that the popularity of this player has been due to his singing ability, pleasing personality and the intriguing titles given his films, not his story material, which has with but two exceptions been exceedingly trite. The novelty of a western star singing has carried Autry this far and won him a public that is beginning to compare his efforts with those of the Hopalong Cassidy series, noteworthy because of their fine production values and story strength. Are you listening, Republic?"

—J. W. Noah, New Liberty and Ideal Theaters, Fort Worth, Texas (February 1937)

"Now here is an Autry that is the greatest western I have ever seen. The background is laid at the Texas Centennial and is outstanding. Autry surpasses everything he has made with this one. The patrons were very well pleased, and so were we with the box office report."

—W. M. Redmond, Uptown Theater, Glendive, Montana (March 1937)

"This is an Autry special. It's good. Will do business. But it lacks the action and rough and tumble of other westerns. But still let's have more Autrys."

—Cecil Ward, Bassett Theater, Bassett, Virginia (February 1937)

"Good show. The first Gene Autry picture played in our house and it must have satisfied. First western we played on Sunday, the town being deserted, and yet we have done average business. Thanks, Gene."

—Rudolf Duba, Royal Theater, Kimball, South Dakota (July 1937)

"Nothing remarkable about this picture, as far as I can see. But the way they come to see these Autry pictures is remarkable. This one comes very near to a high for the past year."   —G. A. Van Fradenburg, Valley Theater, Manassa, Colorado (August 1937)

"While I did not consider this as good as some other Autry pictures, it did more than average business against a street carnival. Seemed to please almost 100%. This Autry boy is just about tops among the big money getters."

—L. R. Creason, Palace Theater, Eufaula, Oklahoma (October 1937)

"Just bring Gene Autry to town and here come the people. He still rates the best box office western star in my theater."

—Cleo Manry, Buena Vista Theater, Buena Vista, Georgia (October 1944)

SOURCES:

1. Autry with Herskowitz. p. 54-55.

The Old Corral
Republic, December 1936

Producer ....Nat Levine
Supervisor ....Armand Schaefer
Director ....Joseph Kane
Original Story.............................Bernard McConville
Screenplay..................................Sherman Lowe and
    Joseph Poland
Photography ....Edgar Lyons
Supervising Editor ....Murray Seldeen
Film Editor................................Lester Orlebeck
Sound Engineer...........................Harry Jones
Musical Supervisor ....Harry Grey

SONGS: "The Old Corral" (music and lyrics by Walter Hirsch)—sung by Gene Autry; "Five Man Band" (music and lyrics by Smiley Burnette)—sung by Smiley Burnette; "Down Along the Sleepy Rio Grande" (music and lyrics by Len Slye)—sung by the Sons of the Pioneers; "He's Gone, He's Gone Up the Trail" (music and lyrics by Tim Spencer)—sung by the Sons of the Pioneers; "With All My Heart" (music and lyrics by J. Strauss)—sung by Hope Manning; "In the Heart of the West" (music and lyrics by Gene Autry and Fleming Allen)—sung by Hope Manning and Gene Autry; "Money Ain't No Use Anyway" (music and lyrics by Gene Autry)—sung by Gene Autry; "Silent Trails" (music and lyrics by Tim Spencer)—sung by the Sons of the Pioneers; "So Long Old Pinto" (music and lyrics by Oliver Drake)—sung by Gene Autry and the Sons of the Pioneers.

RUNNING TIME: 57 minutes
FILMING DATES: October 19-26, 1936
LOCATIONS: Kernville; Iverson Ranch; Republic backlot
BUDGET: $26,379
NEGATIVE COST: $27,378

CAST:

Actor	*Character*
Gene Autry	Sheriff Gene Autry
Smiley Burnette	Deputy Frog Millhouse
Hope Manning	Eleanor Spencer aka Jane Edwards
Sons of the Pioneers: Tim Spencer, Len Slye (aka Roy Rogers), Bob Nolan, Hugh Farr and Karl Farr	O'Keefe Brothers
Cornelius Keefe	Martin Simms
Lon Chaney Jr.	Garland
John Bradford	Mike Scarlotti
Milburn Morante	Clem Snodgrass
Merrill McCormick	Frank—Scarlotti Henchman
Charles Sullivan	Scarlotti Henchman
Buddy Roosevelt	Tony—Scarlotti Driver
Lynton Brent	Dunn—dealer
Frankie Marvin	Wife-beating prisoner
Ed Platt	Oscar—gas station attendant
Lou Fulton	Elmer—Stuttering gas station attendant
Jerry Jerome	Tony Pearl
Bob Card	Townsman
Ken Cooper	Pete
Jim Corey	Prisoner
Jack Evans	Townsman applauding O'Keefe Brothers
Harrison Greene	Emcee at the celebration
Herman Hack	Barfly
Jack Ingram	Irate Gambler with gun
Rose Plummer	Townswoman
Marc Cramer	Bus Driver
Lew Kelly	Red
Frank Mills	Gang Member
Max Hoffman Jr.	Man
Carmen LaRoux	Rita Gonzales—Dancer
Tito Renaldo	Pedro Tanya—Dancer
Murdock MacQuarrie, Bud McClure	Townsmen
Al Taylor, Joe Yrigoyen	Posse Riders
Abe Lefton	Announcer
Wally West, Jack Hendricks	Extras
Champion	Champion

74

STUNTS: Ken Cooper (double for Gene Autry); Joe Yrigoyen.

THE FILM: Noteworthy on several counts, "The Old Corral" is remembered for the fight, a brief scuffle actually, between Gene Autry and Roy Rogers—then still Leonard Slye of the Sons of the Pioneers who made their second film appearance after backing up Charles Starrett in Columbia's "Gallant Defender" ('35). After rolling down a hill, Gene asks Slye if he can still sing. When Slye nods affirmatively, Gene tells him to go ahead and Slye offers a brief yodel. That sequence has been repeated endlessly on various documentaries about both Gene and Roy.

The story has nightclub singer Eleanor Spencer (Hope Manning) fleeing Chicago after witnessing a murder committed by her boss, gangster Mike Scarlotti (John Bradford). Arriving out west in Turquoise City, supposedly incognito, but with her picture in all the papers, she is recognized by crooked nightspot owner Martin Simms (Cornelius Keefe) who hires Eleanor to sing in his joint while he notifies Scarlotti of her whereabouts hoping to collect a reward from the gangster. Singing sheriff Gene Autry, already troubled locally by the O'Keefe Brothers (the Sons of the Pioneers), and his deputy Frog Millhouse (Smiley Burnette) come to Eleanor's aid and round-up the gangsters amidst a wild cattle stampede.

The simple plot is nothing more than a device to hang the songs and some action on, but the fun, music and complete escape from reality make up for that. The worst blight on the picture is a very unfunny stuttering "comedy sequence" with two gas station attendants, Oscar and Elmer

who also polluted the Three Mesquiteers' "Gunsmoke Ranch" ('37) and "The Painted Stallion" serial ('37) before Republic wisely got rid of the team.

NOTES AND COMMENTS: In England, where a Tex Ritter film with "The Old Corral" title had been shown, Republic changed the title of this film to "Texas Serenade".

Although rodeo announcer Abe Lefton is usually credited as being in this picture, he is no where to be seen in prints viewed. According to production notes he was paid $40 for his work, which apparently ended up on the cutting room floor. Meanwhile, Buddy Roosevelt, low budget B-western star of the '20s and '30s, worked for $45 for four days as Scarlotti's driver. Cornelius Keefe, first seen with Gene in "Tumbling Tumbleweeds", earned $200; John Bradford was paid $125; Milburn Morante $60; Lon Chaney Jr. $125; and stuntman Ken Cooper, doubling for Gene, received $200.

"The Old Corral" was Hope Manning's first film. Born Inez Harvout July 17, 1912, in Cincinnati, she changed her name to Irene Manning when she signed with Warner Bros. in the early '40s. She died May 28, 2004, of heart disease.

Smiley Burnette married newspaper columnist Dallas MacDonnell on October 26, 1936.

FILM COMMENTS: Born Inez Harvout, *Hope Manning* said, "The first thing they did at Republic was to change my name—to Hope Manning. The head of publicity, Het Manheim, was a nice little Jewish man who came up with the moniker—giving us both the initials of HM. We soon fell in love and married but the marriage didn't last. He was based in New York, and I was traveling all over the place. Since I was a singer, you'd have thought I would be put in a musical, right? (Laughs) Well, the first thing I heard was (in a mocking, nasal voice) 'Bak 'n thuh saddle, agin' and I was cast opposite Gene Autry in his latest picture. I was astonished, but as years passed, I felt so blessed to have appeared in the film—it has so many admirers and is well remembered, even today! It is very heartwarming. (Gene and I) We did kiss but it wasn't his first. (Laughs) We did do the kiss all right, and the cameras were acranking. *But*, when we did it, the crew laughed so loud and so hard, I thought the kiss might be removed! Gene could kiss his horse, but not his leading lady! (Laughs) I thought I would sing in the picture, of course, and I even wrote a song for me to do

An historic moment — Gene Autry gets the drop on Len Slye (right) —later to become Roy Rogers at Republic. At the time Roy was a member of the Sons of the Pioneers. That's Pioneer Karl Farr in the center.

Gene and leading lady Irene Manning.

in the film. But, Cy Feuer, head of the musical department at Republic, told me Gene would never go for it. No way. It wasn't simple enough for a western…it was too uppity, I guess. (Laughs) One bit of advice Cy did give me was something I used for the rest of my career. Cy said to 'Keep it simple.' Gene was very nice; this was still pretty early in his career, but he'd made it big and *fast*, so what he wanted was the way it went. No song by me, for instance. There was *no* chemistry between us and I was never asked to do another film with him. (Laughs)" As for Smiley Burnette, "I called him 'Smelly' Burnette—he was always perspiring and he, well frankly, he stunk! (Laughs)."[1]

Gene Autry: "A lot of the program westerns back in those days, in the days of Mix, Buck Jones, a lot of the silent stars, the girl didn't have too much to do. When I came in and became the singing cowboy, we tried to get a better part for the girl, that way you could always get better names. We'd get girls that could sing some, and the plots had the girl inheriting a ranch, or had to settle her father's estate, things of that sort. If you had a part for a girl with more for them to do, you'd get better names. That's one of the reasons we did that."[2]

CAST BIOS: The best western music group ever, the Sons of the Pioneers, were consistently climbing their own popularity polls in the late '30s with records, public appearances and on film. No other group had as profound an effect on western music as did the Son of the Pioneers. Their lyrical musical portraits literally define the romanticized west.

After various stables at success, individually and sometimes partially collectively, Leonard Slye (Roy Rogers), Vern (Tim) Spencer and Bob Nolan formed the Pioneer Trio in 1933. also known simultaneously as the Gold Star Rangers on KFWB radio in Los Angeles. Texas fiddler Hugh Farr was soon added in late '33 or early '34. His brother Karl added a distinctive guitar sound to the group by March 1935.

Their melodic harmony was quickly recognized and first utilized in an El Brendel comedy short "Radio Scout" ('35 Vitaphone). Several other short subjects and their first feature, "The Old Homestead" ('35 Liberty), followed.

Columbia then signed the group in late 1935 to backup Charles Starrett in his new series of B-westerns. Also during this period the Pioneers appeared in a couple of musical westerns with Dick Foran, the next "singing cowboy" on the screen after Gene Autry.

Bob Nolan sold his famous "Tumbling Tumbleweeds" song to Republic for a paltry $100 under a non-exclusive license to exploit the song both as the title for Gene Autry's first musical western and as a song to be used within the film.

In 1936, Republic used the Sons of the Pioneers in Gene's all-star "The Big Show" but gave them a larger spotlight and speaking parts in "The Old Corral".

The group continued to co-star with Charles Starrett at Columbia but it was their last involvement with Republic until 1941 when the group left Columbia to re-join their old friend who had emerged from the group to become Roy Rogers, Republic's second singing cowboy, with "Under Western Stars" in 1938.

As we'll see, during that tenure at Republic (12/41 to 9/48) they managed one more film with Gene, "Call of the Canyon" ('42).

Down through the years the personnel that made up the Sons of the Pioneers changed many times but the Sons of the Pioneers' brilliant musical legacy has endured to this day.

WHAT THE EXHIBITOR HAD TO SAY: "Our box office jumps every time we play Gene Autry westerns. This is the best western star we are using. Autry pictures gross with the biggest pictures we play."

—Gavin Brothers, American Theater, Stevensville, Montana (January 1937)

"This was doubled with 'The General Died at Dawn' and is on par with the usual Gene Autry pictures. This program did above average business for us."

—J. E. Stocker, Myrtle Theater, Detroit, Michigan (February 1937)

"We couldn't see anything in this Autry opus. At any rate, his personality failed to click with our folks and the production value was way below standard."

—L. A. Irwin, Palace Theater, Penacook, New Hampshire (May 1937)

76

"Here are the comments received while playing this one: 'Gene Autry is not so hot.' 'As a cowboy he don't fit the saddle.' 'Singing he is A-1, but he acts as if he's cocksure of himself.' All I have to say is he does the trick nevertheless at the box office."   —Jno. S. Erickson, Rex Theater,
Iron Mountain, Michigan (August 1937)

SOURCES:

1. *Western Clippings* #62. November/December 2004. p. 16.

2 "Melody Ranch Theater" showing of "Ride, Ten-derfoot, Ride" on Nashville Network, 1987.

Round-Up Time in Texas
<u>Republic, February 1937</u>

Producer	Nat Levine
Supervisor	Armand Schaefer
Director	Joseph Kane
Assistant Director	Ray Culley
Original Screenplay	Oliver Drake
Photography	William Nobles
Supervising Editor	Murray Seldeen
Film Editor	Lester Orlebeck
Sound Engineer	Harry Jones
Musical Supervisor	Harry Grey

SONGS: "When the Bloom Is On the Sage" (music and lyrics by Vincent and Howard)—sung by Gene Autry and cowboys; reprised by Gene Autry, The Cabin Kids, Smiley Burnette; "Old Chisholm Trail" (Traditional)—sung by Gene Autry; "Drink Old England Dry" (Traditional)—sung by Maxine Doyle and men in saloon; "Uncle Noah's Ark" (music and lyrics by Gene Autry and Smiley Burnette)—sung by Gene Autry and Smiley Burnette; "Prairie Rose" (music and lyrics by Sidney Mitchell)—sung by Gene Autry; "Jacob Drink" (Polish Traditional)—sung by John Holland; "African Chant" (Traditional)—sung by extras; "Moon of Desire" (music and lyrics by Republic staff)—sung by Gene Autry; "Voice Improvisation" (music and lyrics by Republic staff)—sung by Smiley Burnette and Cabin Kids; "She'll Be Comin' 'Round the Mountain" (Traditional)—sung by Chorus; "On Revival Day" (music and lyrics Andy Razof)—sung by The Cabin Kids; "Cave Man" (music and lyrics by Smiley Burnette)—sung by Gene Autry; "Dinah" (music and lyrics by Harry Akst, Sam Lewis, Joe Young)—sung by The Cabin Kids and Smiley Burnette.

RUNNING TIME: 58 minutes
FILMING DATES: November 7-14, 1936
LOCATIONS: Iverson Ranch; L.A. River; Republic backlot
BUDGET: $26,658
NEGATIVE COST: $29,441

CAST:

Actor:	*Character:*
Gene Autry	Gene Autry
Smiley Burnette	Frog Millhouse
Maxine Doyle	Gwen Barclay
Cabin Kids	Chief Bosuto's children
LeRoy Mason	John Cardigan
Earle Hodgins	Barkey McKlusky
Dick Wessel	Cragg Johnson
Buddy Williams	Chief Bosuto
Elmer Fain	Macle, Chief's son
Cornie Anderson	Namba
Frankie Marvin	Shorty
Ken Cooper	Tex Autry
John Holland	Singer in Saloon
Jim Corey	Bill
Al Ferguson	Captain Banning
Slim Whitaker	Corporal
Carleton Young	Man who gives diamond news
Billy Franey	Man with cigar
Jack Kirk	Cook
Al Knight	Native
George Morrell	Dealer
Charles Murphy	Reports gate open
Jack C. Smith	Henchman
Al Taylor, George Plues	Ranch hands
Art Davis	Cowhand
Ray Corrigan	Gorilla
Rudy Sooter	Musician
Herman Hack	Barfly
Champion	Champion

STUNTS: Ken Cooper (Gene's double).

THE FILM: "Round-Up Time in Texas" is one of the weirdest westerns ever made, and many would agree a low point in Gene's film career. Other screen cowboys traveled afield, Smith Ballew to Hawaii, Hopalong Cassidy to South America, but nobody went to the lengths of Gene Autry who wound up in South Africa with a herd of horses. Jive-singing black children. Smiley Burnette in blackface and a sarong. Ray "Crash" Corrigan in his ape suit. A native chieftain in a top hat. Natives in fright wigs. Completely ludicrous. Patrons must have exited the theater scratching

78

their heads, "What *was* that?" "Round-Up Time in Texas" has to be seen to be believed. It's to Gene's credit that he still had an audience for his next picture after they'd seen this losing conbobulation.

When Gene's brother Tex (Ken Cooper) wires him from South Africa that he and his partner have discovered a diamond mine there, Gene and Frog (Smiley Burnette) hurry across the ocean to help him, only to discover the partner murdered and Tex missing and blamed for the killing. Gene's suspicions that local saloon owner Cardigan (LeRoy Mason) is actually the guilty party continue to mount, especially after Cardigan has Gene and Frog framed for illicit diamond buying. Meanwhile, Gwen (Maxine Doyle), a singer at Cardigan's saloon, is the daughter of Gene's murdered partner and is secretly trying to find her father's killer. As she and Cardigan head for the diamond mine, Gene and Frog elude the police and reach Cardigan's party where the entire group is captured by savage Zulu natives. From there, director Joe Kane and writer Oliver Drake play the rest mainly for laughs with a wild mix of lions, a gorilla, be-bop African singers, cockney auctioneers and leftover stock footage from Republic's "Darkest Africa" serial ('36). A real misfire here.

NOTES AND COMMENTS: When Gene and Smiley sing in the South African bar, the song they choose is "Uncle Noah's Ark"—very nostalgic as it was the primary song used in their first starring vehicle, "The Phantom Empire" serial.

Leading lady Maxine Doyle (1915-1973), an acrobatic dancer at MGM, was married to Republic director William Witney. She earned $125 a week for her role in "Round-Up Time in Texas". Other salaries included $200 weekly to LeRoy Mason, $150 to Earle Hodgins and $225 to Ken Cooper as Gene's stunt double.

For the gorilla scenes with Smiley Burnette, producer Armand Schaefer used some stock footage from Republic's "Darkest Africa" serial ('36) then hired Ray Corrigan and his $3,600 ape outfit which was made from millions of strands of human hair. The costume reportedly took eight people four months to make, as each hair was put in individually. Mechanical contrivances in the head allowed Corrigan to "ape" the gorilla's actions.

Gene Autry was ranked third Money Making Western Star of 1936 according to boxoffice reports by American Theatre exhibitors as listed in the tradepaper MOTION PICTURE HERALD survey released in January 1937.

Gene, leading lady Maxine Doyle and the talented Cabin Kids. In real life, Doyle was married to Republic director William Witney.

Buck Jones was #1 and George O'Brien was #2, followed by Gene at #3, William Boyd at #4 and Ken Maynard at #5. A mention by exhibitors for first place was credited with 10 points, second place with 9 points, and so on down to one point for a ballot for tenth place. Jones received 942 points, O'Brien 910 points, Gene 672 points, Hoppy 618 points, Maynard 578 points. A total of 34 western stars made the poll with at least one point.

FILM COMMENTS: *Gene Autry:* "In those days, Republic had a rule about titles. If it was catchy, use it. Never mind if it didn't fit the story. So you will understand when I tell you 'Round-Up Time in Texas' takes place in Africa. Wild horses, a diamond mine, and a savage tribe of Zulus are the key elements. A group called the Cabin Kids provided the background music, and if you wish to know how long ago this was, all you need to be told is that a Republic press release described them as 'a really swell group of pickaninnies'."[1]

CAST BIOS: Gene Autry spotlighted the Cabin Kids in two films, "Round-Up Time in Texas" and his next, "Git Along Little Dogies". Outstanding as religious Negro singers in the South, hailing from Asheville, North Carolina, the brother/sister quintet soon graduated to radio, appearing with Paul Whiteman and Rudy Vallee, then screen work in "Hooray For Love" ('35 RKO) with Ann Sothern and "Mississippi" ('35 Paramount) with Bing Crosby.

Four of the five youngsters are brothers and sisters: Frederic Hall, approximately 6; James Hall, 11; Winifred Hall, 8 and Helen Hall, 10. Ruth Gamble, 12, rounds out the group.

WHAT THE EXHIBITOR HAD TO SAY: "Another good Autry, though not in comparison with 'The Big Show'."

—L. B. Jarrell, Ritz Theater
Columbia, Louisiana (February 1937)

"We have just received the glossy paper pamphlet which Republic flatteringly calls a press sheet on 'Round-Up Time in Texas'. Exhibitors in buying the product of this company are well aware that the complete sales are usually made on the strength of the Autry pictures, yet this star is apparently in the studio doghouse judging by the press sheets and advertising material prepared for his productions. While sermonizing, we might also mention the shoddy story material the producers are inflicting upon the star in trading upon his popularity that is beginning to show slight signs of decline."

—J. W. Noah, New Liberty and Ideal Theaters,
Fort Worth, Texas (February 1937)

"Excellent singing by Autry and Smiley Burnette. Each Autry picture does more business than the preceding one and is a real box-office tonic. This particular picture is perhaps his poorest. Autry and Burnette turn in their usual fine performances but the South African scenes are so patently false that it spoils the picture."

—Ted Stump, Elted Theater,
Absarokee, Montana (April 1937)

"Gene Autry is by far the best western star we have for consistent drawing power. Autry pictures draw almost as many patrons as the so-called "A" pictures from the other producers. This picture is full of action, you'll like it."

—W. Gavin Bros., American Theater,
Stevensville, Montana (March 1937)

SOURCES:
1. Autry with Herskowitz. p. 55.

Git Along Little Dogies
Republic, March 1937

Producer ....Armand Schaefer
Director ....Joseph Kane
Assistant Director.........................Louis Germonprez
Original Screenplay ....Dorrell and Stuart
                                         McGowan
Photography ....Gus Peterson
Supervising Editor ....Murray Seldeen
Film Editor.................................Tony Martinelli
Sound Engineer...........................Terry Kellum
Musical Supervisor ....Harry Grey

SONGS: "Git Along Little Dogies" (Traditional)—sung by Gene Autry, Maple City Four Smiley Burnette; "Honey, Bringing Honey to You" (music and lyrics by Smiley Burnette)—sung by Smiley Burnette; "Chinatown" (music and lyrics by Jean Schwartz)–sung by Gene Autry and Maple City Four; "If You Want to be a Cowboy" (music and lyrics by Fleming Allen)—sung by Gene Autry and Maple City Four; "Calamity Jane" (music and lyrics by Will and Gladys Ahern)—sung by Will and Gladys Ahern; "Stock Selling Song" (music and lyrics by Harry

Grey, Raoul Kraushaar)—sung by the Maple City Four; Medley: "Wait For the Wagons" (music and lyrics by R. H. Buckley), "Red River Valley" (Traditional), "She'll Be Comin' 'Round the Mountain" (Traditional), "Long, Long Ago" (music and lyrics by Thomas Haynes Bayly), "Oh, Susanna" (music and lyrics by Stephen Foster), "Goodnight Ladies" (Traditional), "He's a Jolly Good Fellow" (Traditional)—all sung by Gene Autry, Maple City Four and townsfolk; "After You've Gone" (music and lyrics by Henry Creamer and Turner Layton)—sung by The Cabin Kids; "In the Valley Where the Sun Goes Down" (music and lyrics by Sam H. Stept and Sidney Mitchell)—sung by Gene Autry; "Happy Days Are Here Again" (music and lyrics by Milton Ager)—sung by entire cast.

RUNNING TIME: 66 minutes
FILMING DATES: February 3-17, 1937
LOCATIONS: Kernville; Iverson Ranch; Placerita Canyon; Republic backlot
BUDGET: $35,983
NEGATIVE COST: $36,171

CAST:

Actor	Character
Gene Autry ....Gene Autry
Smiley Burnette ....Frog Millhouse
Maple City Four: L. G. Patterson, Al Rice, Art Janes, Fritz Meissner..........................Singing Ranch hands
Judith Allen ....Doris Maxwell
Weldon Heyburn ....George Wilkens
William Farnum ....Maxwell
Willie Fung ....Sing Low
Carleton Young ....Nick, holdup man
Will Ahern, Gladys Ahern............Radio show per-formers
The Cabin Kids ....Sam Brown's children
Frankie Marvin...........................Henchman at oil rig
Sam McDaniel ....Sam Brown
Frank Ellis, Bob Burns, Jack C. Smith, Charles O'Connor, Tracy Layne, Bert Mitchell, Col. E. B. Nix, Fred Fuller ....Ranchers

Frank Austin.................................Man who gets ten shares
Silver Tip Baker ....Townsman (with white handlebar mustache)
Chuck Baldra, Ken Card..............   Musicians
Lynton Brent ....Holdup man
Fred Burns....................................Bank Customer
Horace Carpenter ....Clem
Jane Keckley ....Clem's wife
Art Davis ....Fiddle player in contest radio program
Earl Dwire, Charles Murphy, ...Townsmen
Helen Gibson ....Dwire's wife
Oscar Gahan.................................Guitar player
Oscar "Dutch" Hendrian..............Abductor
Jack Kirk ....Ed, Rancher
Lydia Knott, Eva McKenzie ....Townswomen
Monte Montague ....Barfly making challenge
Buck Morgan................................Barfly
George Morrell.............................Storekeeper
G. Raymond Nye ....Sheriff
Eddie Parker................................Tool shed henchman
Pascale Perry...............................Henchman driving car
Rose Plummer..............................Rancher's wife
Charles Sullivan ....Henchman
Al Taylor ....Vehicle man
Robert Homans ....Garrett
Frank Darien ....Pete
Kenneth Thomson.........................Elwood
Morgan Brown ....Man with car
Williard Willingham, Emmett Crero, Ralph Willingham, Gardner Sheehan, Glen Johnson, Frank Yrigoyen, Wally Howe, Marvin Shannon, Roy Fisk, Art Felix, Jay Owen, Herman Hack, Jack Hendricks, Wade Walker, Frank Walsh, Harry Alton, Jack Davis, Al Steele, Harry Fly, Frank Beckman, Tex Dale, Jim Scoby...Men
Bruce Mitchell ....Riley
Pete Logan, Ray Johnson, Harry Willingham, Pete Johnson........Sheriff's Posse
Sam Lufkin, Robert Anderson .....Drillers
Opal Callaway, Agnes Burke, Adabelle Driver, Irene Kalish, Viola Dinsmore........................Women
Viola Porter ....Housewife
F. D. Brookledge ....Banjo player at Radio Contest
Marcell Borquin ....Bass player at Radio contest
Jeff Gladhill.................................Piano player at Radio contest
Pete De Grosso............................Singer
Champion.....................................Champion

STUNTS: Ken Cooper (Gene's double); Jean Criswell (Judith Allen's double); Eddie Parker, Joe Yrigoyen, Jack Kirk.

THE FILM: One of Gene's best-loved films, "Git Along Little Dogies" is a fast-moving and amusing story about the efforts of honest people to protect themselves from would-be swindlers trying to sell stock in an apparently worthless oil well. The plotline resonated well in rural post-depression America.

"Git Along Little Dogies" is significant in that it was the first of Gene's films that presented his leading ladies as spunky girls who did things their way and often gave Gene a hard time with a "taming of the shrew" plotline rather than the hapless heroines of other B-westerns. This theme, in a changing America of the late '30s, also resonated well, especially with the women in the audience, and became a recurring and popular theme in future Autry pictures.

Gene Autry strongly opposes the drilling of an oil well fearing it will pollute the drinking water of the local rancher's cattle. Meanwhile, local radio station owner Doris Maxwell (Judith Allen) is promoting the sale of stock in the well for her father (William Farnum) who has embezzled $25,000 to support the project. Rivals at first, Gene and Doris eventually join forces to defeat George Wilkens (Weldon Heyburn), the smooth swindler in charge of drilling who is stalling on bringing in the well. He expects to take over the well when the option held by Doris' father expires.

NOTES AND COMMENTS: The popularity of the community sing on radio stations across the country in the late '30s was incorporated into Dorrell and Stuart McGowan's "Git Along Little Dogies" script in a very enthusiastic scene as Gene attempts to forestall the attempt of Weldon Heyburn to secure a personal lease on a valuable oil well. Gene engages the entire audience in a rousing seven

Gene and Smiley do a gun-to-gun clowning around between takes.

tune songfest, then selling stock shares with a song from the Maple City Four. With song lyrics emblazoned across the screen, and urgings to sing along by Gene, the melodious infection invariably spread throughout the theater resulting in complete audience participation.

This was the first of Gene's films without the involvement of producer Nat Levine, who had originally brought both Gene and Smiley to Hollywood. From its inception, Herbert J. Yates ruled Republic with an iron hand. Nat Levine's Mascot had been part of the merger that formed Republic in 1935, but on February 2, 1937, he announced he would be exiting Republic at the completion of the season, which he did on October 3, moving to MGM for a brief while, then into relative obscurity. With Levine's departure, Yates installed Moe Siegel as president of Republic Productions with his brother Sol Siegel soon named producer of serials and Gene Autry westerns.

Note how the oil and mud splashes on Gene's clothing vary from scene to scene. Obviously filmed in more than one take.

In England exhibitors found the title "Git Along Little Dogies" to have little relevance to English audiences, so the film was retitled "Serenade of the West".

Fred "Snowflake" Toones, often credited in this title as playing Sam Brown, is *not* in "Git Along Little Dogies". The Sam Brown role is essayed by talented actor Sam McDaniel.

Comedians Candy Candido and Otto "Coco" Heimel were originally contracted to appear in "Git Along…" but by mutual consent their agreement was cancelled less than a week after signing the contract. Obviously, they were replaced by the dance team of Will and Gladys Ahern.

Talented Judith Allen was paid $425, the most any leading lady had made thus far in an Autry film, while Weldon Heyburn earned $400 a week. The rope/dance Ahern team gathered $200 per day for their specialty act and stuntman Ken Cooper once again earned $250. William Farnum made $150 and Willie Fung $100.

FILM COMMENTS: *Gene Autry:* "How delicately the *love angle* was treated in most of my movies was vividly reflected in 'Git Along Little Dogies.' The rules were clear: almost no clinches, no embraces, were allowed. I could put my arm around the heroine's waist only if necessary to save her from falling over a cliff. Believe me, when your audience consisted mainly of women who craved romance, and small boys who hated it, a compromise was required to please both.

"In 'Git Along Little Dogies', Judith Allen, who had once played opposite W. C. Fields (in 'The Old Fashioned Way' in '34), had the part of the insolent young thing. In one scene she drove her car through a pool of oil, laughing as she splattered me from head to foot. And now I quote from a review of the film: 'Gene jumps on Champion, chases the auto, and brings it to a stop by shooting a tire. The heroine states that he is no gentleman. Gene puts a bullet through another tire. She attacks him. Gene picks her up and drops

Gene's accused of a bank robbery he didn't commit and handcuffed by Sheriff G. Raymond Nye while Judith Allen, Weldon Heyburn (the real villain) and rancher Jack Kirk look on.

her into a brook…After dropping her in the water; he is allowed to be slightly contrite. He lets the girl talk him into putting on the spare tires. While he is at work, she jumps on Champion and rides away.

"Now my grade school public relished all this, while the grown-ups could see that the foundation was being laid for a beautiful romance. But it was essential the love interest be disguised. One boo, or hiss, or raspberry, could cause five hundred hearts to freeze.

"A final word about 'Little Dogies'. In it, we hit the ecology trail. We opposed the drilling of an oil well out of fear it would spoil the cattle's drinking water."[1]

Judith Allen: "While the (film) is very exciting, I personally don't encounter many rigorous moments. I'm pushed in a pond once by Autry, but that's only for a short sequence, and anyway I enjoyed the plunge."[2]

CAST BIOS: Born Marie Elliott February 8, 1911, in New York City, Judith Allen's zealous ambition as a child was to be a snake charmer or a gypsy. However, when she grew up, various beauty contests led to modeling and stage work before she was heralded as Cecil B. DeMille's new discovery for "This Day and Age" ('33). She'd made some 20 films before coming to Republic as one of Gene's more talented leading ladies in "Git Along Little Dogies" and "Boots and Saddles". Allen "retired" in 1940, but briefly returned to the screen in 1950. She died of heart failure October 5, 1996, in Yucca Valley, California.

The Maple City Four, a popular radio quartet, brought close harmony to their Midwest listeners for over a quarter of a century. The group was formed in LaPorte, Indiana, in 1924 and their talent led to a spot on WLS' fledging "National Barn Dance" in late 1926. Called the "Marx Brothers of Radio", the Maple City Four mixed comedy songs, skits, weird instrumentals, barbershop harmony and light patter. Gene brought the foursome to Hollywood for a select spot in "Git Along Little Dogies" and used them again in "The Old Barn Dance". Pat Buttram chuckled, "They could sing good but they were crazy. They played practical pranks on everybody."[3] The group was also in Roy Rogers' first starrer, "Under Western Stars" in '38. The group remained a favorite on stage, at corporate events, and on WLS well into the '50s.

WHAT THE EXHIBITOR HAD TO SAY: "Good Autry picture. Print was worn and poor."

—G. S. Caporal, Yale Theater, Oklahoma City, Oklahoma (May 1942)

SOURCES:

1. Autry with Herskowitz. p. 55-56.

2. "Git Along Little Dogies" pressbook.

3. "Melody Ranch Theater" showing of "Git Along Little Dogies", 1987.

Rootin' Tootin' Rhythm
Republic, May 1937

Title card for "Rootin' Tootin' Rhythm" pictures not only Gene and Smiley but cast members Monte Blue, Hal Taliaferro and Frankie Marvin (lower left).

Producer ....Armand Schaefer
Director ....Mack V. Wright
Assistant Director.......................Louis Germonprez
Original Story............................Johnston McCulley
Screenplay...................................Jack Natteford
Photography ....William Nobles
Supervising Editor ....Murray Seldeen

Film Editor ....Tony Martinelli
Sound Engineer...........................Terry Kellum
Musical Supervisor ....Raoul Kraushaar

SONGS: "The Old Home Place" (music and lyrics by Fleming Allen, Jack Natteford)—sung by Gene Autry, Smiley Burnette, Charlie Meyers, Al Clauser and His Oklahoma

Outlaws and others; "Little Black Bronc" (music and lyrics by Al Clauser, Tex Hoepner)—sung by Smiley Burnette, Al Clauser and His Oklahoma Outlaws; "I Hate to Say Goodbye to the Prairie" (music and lyrics by Gene Autry)—sung by Gene Autry; "Mexicali Rose" (music and lyrics by Helen Stone, Jack B. Tenney)—sung by Gene Autry; "Trail of the Mountain Rose" (music and lyrics by Al Clauser, Tex Hoepner)—sung by Al Clauser and His Oklahoma Outlaws; "Dying Cowgirl" (music and lyrics by Gene Autry)—sung by Smiley Burnette; "Mexicali Rose" (music and lyrics by Helen Stone, Jack B. Tenney)—sung by Gene Autry, Armida.

RUNNING TIME: 61 minutes
FILMING DATES: March 10-20, 1937
LOCATIONS: Lone Pine; Palmdale/Lancaster area; Republic backlot
BUDGET: $23,500
NEGATIVE COST: $33,034

Diminuitive Armida cowers as rustler leader Monte Blue holds a gun on Gene.

CAST:

Actor	Character
Gene Autry	Gene Autry
Smiley Burnette	Frog Millhouse
Armida	Rosa Montero
Monte Blue	Joe Stafford
Al Clauser and His Oklahoma Outlaws: Al Clauser, Slim Phillips, Tex Hoepner, Don Austin, Larry Brandt	Singing cowhands
Hal Taliaferro	Buffalo Brady
Ann Pendleton	Mary Ellen
Max Hoffman Jr.	Jed, the Apache Kid
Charles King	Jim Black
Frankie Marvin	Hank, Gene's foreman
Nina Campana	Ynez
Charles Meyers	Charlie, boy dancer
Dick Botiller	Cowhand at wanted poster
Art Davis	Fiddler
Curley Dresden	Slim, wounded cowhand
Karl Hackett	Sheriff Miles Palmer
Henry Hall	Lige Palmer
Milburn Morante	Barfly
George Morrell, Cliff Parkinson	Ranchers
Pascale Perry	Pedro
Frank Straubinzier, Buck Spencer, Augie Gomez	Cowboys
Buck Connors, Roy Bucko	Cattlemen
Champion	Champion

STUNTS: Yakima Canutt, Ken Cooper (double for Gene), Buck Spencer (double for Smiley), Augie Gomez (double for Armida).

THE FILM: Directed by Mack V. Wright with what seems to be an overabundance of musical numbers and comedy, it finally slips into much action before concluding, most unusually, not with a shot of Gene or Smiley, but of heroine Armida, misty-eyed, watching Gene ride away.

The coincidence driven plot has Gene and his partner Buffalo (Hal Taliaferro) owning a ranch where their cattle are being rustled. Gene and Frog (Smiley Burnette) take off after the rustlers, as do Buffalo and the ranch hands in a separate party. In a total comedy of errors Gene and Frog come across the clothes of two notorious outlaws (Max Hoffman Jr., Charles King) who, themselves, have swapped clothes with two deputy sheriffs they have killed. Dressed in outlaw clothes, Gene and Frog are mistaken for the real outlaws and the outlaws are taken to be sheriffs. Nonsensical misadventure follows complicated misadventure as Gene and Frog run across the ranch of rustler leader Stafford (Monte Blue) and his niece and stepdaughter (Armida, Ann Pendleton). An unusual mixture of music, comedy and action, owing much again to the screwball comedies popular in the '30s.

NOTES AND COMMENTS: Outstripping Judith Allen's salary for "Git Along Little Dogies", petite (4' 11"), fiery Mexican born (1913) actress Armida (Vendrell) was paid a whopping $750 to emote opposite Gene in "Rootin' Tootin' Rhythm". Armida's "star" quickly faded and she returned to live in Mexico around 1950. Meanwhile, stuntman Ken Cooper earned his usual $250 per week, Monte Blue was paid $250, Max Hoffman Jr. $175, Hal Taliaferro $150, Ann Pendleton $100, Charles King $90 and Al Clauser and his Oklahoma Outlaws received $1,250 (divided five ways) for two weeks work.

British Lion Film Distributors, who handled Republic product in England and Ireland, thought "Rootin' Tootin' Rhythm" was too difficult for British audiences to comprehend, so they changed the release title to "Rhythm On the Ranch".

Gene stated that Armida (and later Adele Mara) helped him to sing Spanish lyrics to film songs.

Working title for this film was "Rough Ridin' Rhythm", a title later used for a Kermit Maynard western in 1937.

Gene introduces the song "Mexicali Rose" in this film, a song he'd later use as a title tune in 1939.

Visiting Al Clauser and His Oklahoma Outlaws, who were from WHO, Des Moines, Iowa, WHO's sportscaster Ronald Reagan spent his very first day on a movie set during the filming of this picture.

Director Mack V. Wright and cameraman William Nobles took full advantage of a real storm at Lone Pine turning it into a stunning chase sequence.

FILM COMMENTS: *Gene Autry:* "'Rootin' Tootin' Rhythm' was based on a story by Johnston McCulley, the creator of Zorro. But the only Spanish influence was provided by my leading lady, Armida, a Lupe Velez type. The plot was another of those mistaken-identity-through-a-clothes-swap things I got involved in, more than once."[1]

CAST BIOS: Al Clauser was born in 1911 in Manito, Illinois, and by 1934 he and his Oklahoma Outlaws were radio stars on WHO, Des Moines, Iowa. They met Gene during his pre-movie days at WLS in Chicago. Once Gene had become established and was using regional talent in his films, Clauser telegraphed Autry. Gene remembered him and brought he and the boys to Hollywood to appear in "Rootin' Tootin' Rhythm". Unfortunately, further film work did not develop and they returned to WHO, then moved to WCKY in Cincinnati, then WHBF in Rock Island, Illinois, and finally settled at KTUL in Tulsa, Oklahoma, in 1942 where they became a western swing band at night while working days at Spartan Aircraft. After WWII, Clauser added young female vocalist Clara Ann Fowler to his group. She later became recording star Patti Page. In later years, Clauser became the very popular Uncle Zeke on a KTUL-TV children's program. Retiring in 1976 after 34 years at KTUL, he died March 3, 1989.

WHAT THE EXHIBITOR HAD TO SAY: "Another Autry that did exceptional business. Largest Saturday matinee in 20 years. The only trouble with these Autry pictures is that you can't get the kids out as long as you run the show. Some stayed from 10:30am to 5pm. Many of my patrons know Autry personally, as he was raised near here. However, his pictures are not as good as some other westerns we play.

—L. R. Creason, Palace Theatre,
Eufaula, Oklahoma (November 1937)

SOURCES:
1. Autry with Herskowitz. p. 56.

Yodelin' Kid From Pine Ridge
Republic, June 1937

Producer ....Armand Schaefer
Director ....Joe Kane
Assistant Director........................William O'Connor
Original Story...............................Jack Natteford
Screenplay...................................Jack Natteford, Stuart McGowan, Dorrell McGowan
Photography ....William Nobles
Supervising Editor ....Murray Seldeen
Film Editor..................................Lester Orlebeck
Sound Engineer...........................Terry Kellum
Musical Supervisor ....Raoul Kraushaar

SONGS: "Sing Me a Song of the Saddle" (music and lyrics by Gene Autry and Frank Harford)—sung by Gene Autry; "Hittin' the Trail" (music and lyrics by William Lava, Jack Stanley)—sung by Gene Autry; "Georgia Rodeo" (music and lyrics by Fleming Allen)—sung by Gene Autry, Tennessee Ramblers, Smiley Burnette; Medley of: "Molly Put the Kettle On" (Traditional), "Red River Valley" (Traditional), "When a Circus Comes to Town" (music and lyrics by Fleming Allen), "She'll Be Comin' 'Round the Mountain" (Traditional)—all sung by the Tennessee Ramblers; "Down In Santa Fe" (music and lyrics by Gene Autry)—sung by Gene Autry; "Swing Low, Sweet Chariot" (Traditional)—sung by Negro men/women.

RUNNING TIME: 59 minutes
FILMING DATES: April 22-30, 1937
LOCATIONS: Keen Camp; Lake Sherwood; Republic backlot
BUDGET: $31,230
NEGATIVE COST: $31,269.03

CAST:

Actor	Character
Gene Autry	Gene Autry
Smiley Burnette	Colonel Millhouse
Betty Bronson	Milly Baynum
LeRoy Mason	Len Parker
Charles Middleton	Autry Sr.
Russell Simpson	Bayliss Baynum
The Tennessee Ramblers: Dick Hartman, W. J. Blair, Charles (Cecil) Campbell, Fred "Happy" Morris, Garnett "Elmer" Warren, Kenneth "Pappy" Wolfe	Themselves
Lillian Leatherman, Lucille Leatherman	Tennessee Rambler Girls
Jack Dougherty	Jeff Galloway
Guy Wilkerson	Zeke
Frankie Marvin	Luke
Henry Hall	Sheriff Martin
Fred "Snowflake" Toones	Sam
Al Taylor	Turpentiner Hank
Jack Evans, Oscar Gahan, Herman Hack, Lou Morphy	Turpentiners
Charles Brinley, Bob Burns, Jack Kirk, Hal Price	Cattlemen
Ralph Bucko, Roy Bucko	Cowhands
Jack Ingram	Blake
Jim Corey, Lew Meehan	Henchmen
Art Dillard, Bert Dillard, Buck Morgan, Wally West	Rodeo spectators
Art Mix	Autry impersonator
Jack Montgomery	Joe
Bill Nestell	Rustler's camp cook
Bud Osborne	Deputy Carter
Rose Plummer	Townswoman
Archie Ricks	Card-playing Hench-man
Tom Smith	Rodeo stage driver
Loren Riebe	Clown
Bill Yrigoyen, Gunnard Johnson, Pete Logan, Frank Yrigoyen, Raymond Preddy, Ed Jauregui, Frankie Gordon, Roy Screwdriver, Marvin Shannon, Al Martin, Leonard Trainer, Elmar Napier, Glenn Johnson, Ray Johnson, Holloway Grace, Jack Kirk, E. W. Napier, Duke Lee, Charles Brinley, George Morrell	Turpentiners and Cattlemen

Forrest Dillon, Bud McClure ....Rustlers
Champion ....Champion

STUNTS: Ken Cooper (double for Gene Autry); Bobbie Kashade and Gertie Messenger (doubles for Betty Bronson); Loren Riebe, Bill Yrigoyen, Yakima Canutt, Cliff Lyons, Wally West.

THE FILM: Continuing to experiment and place Gene Autry in unusual and different environments, "Yodelin' Kid From Pine Ridge" is nicely photographed with some of the best riding and fancy mounting sequences yet seen by Gene. Set in the turpentine forests of Georgia where, the prologue explains, "contrary to general belief many large cattle ranches are to be found." This unusual "western" is a partial reworking of Gene's first, "Tumbling Tumbleweeds", having Gene banished by his father only to return sometime later with a Wild West show to find his father murdered.

Sporting a mustache, Smiley Burnette plays more of a character than in previous films as Colonel Millhouse, owner of the Wild West show.

We are also afforded, for the first time, a chance to see Gene put Champion through some of his tricks.

Involved in a feud between cattlemen, who want land for grazing, and the mountain folk, known as The Turpentiners, Gene quarrels with his cattleman father (Charles Middleton), who believes the Turpentiners responsible for recent cattle rustling, over treatment of the mountain folk, and is banished by his Dad. A few years later, now a rodeo star, Gene returns to Pine Ridge with Col. Millhouse's Wild West show to find his sweetheart, Milly Baynum (Betty Bronson), still waiting for him and his father near bankruptcy from the continued raids of the rustlers led by Len Parker (LeRoy Mason). With the help of his Wild West Show buddies, Gene goes after the rustlers when his father and Milly's father (Russell Simpson) are murdered.

As a heroine, diminutive Betty Bronson at first seems incongruous to Autry, looking to be about 16 years old, but one then realizes child-brides were not uncommon in the rural hills of Georgia. And in actuality, Bronson was 30 in 1937, the same age as Autry.

Republic was still experimenting with the Autry persona, swinging back and forth from Old West to modern times, not quite sure how to properly handle the valuable property they had on their hands. "Yodelin' Kid From Pine Ridge" is a fascinating attempt for something a bit different. Within the year, Republic settled on their standard Autry-fantasy and films like this were not to be seen again.

NOTES AND COMMENTS: Dorrell and Stuart McGowan's original script title was "The Singing Kid From Pine Ridge" but was changed when Republic's legal

Gene's in jail again as leading lady Betty Bronson and a mustachioed Smiley Burnette try to reason with Sheriff Henry Hall.

department found that Warner Bros. objected, citing their 1936 Al Jolson film "The Singing Kid".

In England 'Yodelin' Kid…" was changed to "Hero of Pine Ridge".

Villain LeRoy Mason was paid $250 for six days work as was leading lady Betty Bronson. Stuntman Ken Cooper received $250 doubling Gene for eight days. Russell Simpson earned $125 per day and Charles Middleton $100 a day while Fred Toones only made $12.50 per day. (Production notes do not indicate how many days these actors were employed, probably only one or two.) Dick Hartman's Tennessee Ramblers received $1,200 for the picture (six men, two girls). Former silent cowboy star Jack Daugherty (credited onscreen as Jack Dougherty—his true legal name) was paid $125 for three days work. In addition, Republic paid $50 per day for the use of 225 head of cattle.

Young director Bill Witney came off Republic's "The Painted Stallion" serial ('37) to direct two scenes for "Yodelin' Kid", the ones where Gene chases LeRoy Mason over a cliff into the river.

With more gunfire than in any prior Autry film, according to the Motion Picture Association of America Collection at the Academy of Motion Picture Arts and Sciences, Production Code Administration Director Joseph Breen cautioned Republic about the amount of violence in the script. After the film was completed, the PCA rejected it because of the length of the battle between the cattlemen and turpentiners. It was approved in late May 1937 after it had been re-edited and the offensive sequences toned down.

Gene used "Sing Me a Song of the Saddle" in several films, plus, it was also his "Melody Ranch" radio show theme before he switched to "Back In the Saddle Again."

The Tennessee Ramblers, since making their first film not quite a year previously with Gene, "Ride Ranger Ride", had added a singing girl duo to their act, Lillian and Lucille

Leatherman. Perhaps this was ill-advised as the ladies seem to sing off-key.

FILM COMMENTS: *Gene Autry:* "The screen's original Peter Pan, Betty Bronson, a major star of the silent era, attempted a comeback in 'Yodelin' Kid From Pine Ridge'. (The script may have convinced her it wasn't worth it. She retired soon after that.) But a supporting cast of real quality included two veterans, Charles Middleton of 'Ming the Merciless' fame and Russell Simpson, a few years away from Pa Joad in 'Grapes of Wrath'." [1]

CAST BIOS: Playing Gene's father here is Charles Middleton, forever remembered by screen audiences as Ming the Merciless in a trilogy of Flash Gordon serials at Universal. Born October 7, 1879, in Elizabethtown, Kentucky, his first taste of show business was in carnivals and circuses and then vaudeville. Middleton's deeply lined, cruel visage was perfect for heavies in all types of films.

In describing Middleton's personality, veteran heavy himself, Tris Coffin explained, "Square is not exactly the word for him but it's pretty near—and I don't mean to be depreciating because that was his personality. He was very quiet and, as I recall, he didn't mix too much with the rest of us. If there was anything going on that was fun, he was most likely not in it. There was nothing unfriendly about him but he was sort of a loner—on the set at least; I don't know anything about his private life." [2]

After a nearly 30 year career of over 200 movies, including Gene's "Shooting High" in 1940, Middleton died of heart disease April 22, 1949, at a Los Angeles hospital.

WHAT THE EXHIBITOR HAD TO SAY: "This is the best Gene Autry picture in some time. It gives the customers plenty of people, action, plus a Wild West show, the singing they expect from Gene Autry, also specialties by the Tennessee Ramblers. Smiley Burnette also helps along nicely. Business on this was above average. This was doubled with "50 Roads to Town".

—J. E. Stocker, Myrtle Theater, Detroit, Michigan (October 1937)

"Last of the Gene Autry pictures on the 1936-'37 program. This one did good business here. Republic has the best westerns. Played this one with "Elephant Boy", a fine double bill."

—C. J. Schultz, Orpheum Theater, Tremonton, Utah (August 1937)

At last — Gene's got the goods on rustlers Jack Dougherty and LeRoy Mason.

SOURCES:

1. Autry with Herskowitz. p. 56.

2. Magers, Boyd; Nareau, Bob; Copeland, Bobby. *Best of the Badmen.* Empire, 2005. p. 222.

Public Cowboy No. 1
Republic, August 1937

Producer ....Sol C. Siegel
Director ....Joe Kane
Assistant Director........................Harry Knight
Original Story..............................Bernard McConville
Screenplay...................................Oliver Drake
Photography ....Jack Marta
Supervising Editor ....Murray Seldeen
Film Editors ....Lester Orlebeck, George Reid
Sound Engineer...........................Terry Kellum
Musical Director ....Raoul Kraushaar

SONGS: "Wanderers" (music and lyrics by Paul Francis Webster, Felix Bernard)—sung by Gene Autry; "The West Ain't What It Used to Be" (music and lyrics by Fleming Allen)—sung by Gene Autry; "Heebie Jeebie Blues" (music and lyrics by Oliver Drake, Harry Grey)—sung by Smiley Burnette; "I Picked Up the Trail to Your Heart" (music and lyrics by Fleming Allen)—sung by Gene Autry; "Defective Detective From Brooklyn" (music and lyrics by Oliver Drake, Fleming Allen)—sung by Smiley Burnette; "Old Buckaroo" (music and lyrics by Fleming Allen)—sung by Gene Autry.

RUNNING TIME: 60 minutes
FILMING DATES: June 18-28, 1937
LOCATIONS: Kernville; Republic backlot; Paulson Packing Co. in San Fernando, California
BUDGET: $40,829
NEGATIVE COST: $39,812

CAST:

Actor	*Character*
Gene Autry	Gene Autry
Smiley Burnette	Frog Millhouse
Ann Rutherford	Helen Morgan
William Farnum	Sheriff Matt Doniphon
Arthur Loft	Jack Shannon
Frankie Marvin	Deputy Stubby
House Peters Jr.	Jim Shannon
James C. Morton	Eustace P. Quackenbush
Maston Williams	Thad Slaughter
Frank LaRue	Judge
Milburn Morante	Ezra
Ray Bennett	Collins, Airplane spotter
Jack Ingram	Larry (murdered rancher)
Douglas Evans	Radio Announcer
Charles Brinley, Frank Ellis	Townsmen
Bob Burns	Rancher
Jim Mason, George Plues, Henry Isabell, Art Dillard	Rustlers
King Mojave	Steve (thug)
Hal Price	Rancher Bidwell
Walter Murray	Doc
Ed Cecil	Lawyer
Bob Lawson	Airplane pilot
William Walker	Joe
Irving Wofford, John Wofford, Richard Herren, Cad Murrel, Pierce Murrel, John Garret, Charles Murphy, Arthur Wilson, Woodie Woodford, Ernie Daniels	Riders at Kernville
Tom Smith, Fred Schaefer, Lew Matzo, Ernie Daniels, Carey Loftin	Motorcycle Riders
Curley Dresden, Vinegar Roan, George Plues, Bob Reeves, Art Mix	Riders
Champion	Champion

STUNTS: Ken Cooper (double for Gene Autry); Lucille Wofford (double for Ann Rutherford); Art Dillard, Bill Yrigoyen, Ray Johnson, Pete Logan.

THE FILM: There's a dash of just about every sort of entertainment ingredient in "Public Cowboy No. 1", with the "Autry format" now fully established. The screenplay gives Gene's vocal talents full opportunity to shine, as well as his unique flare for romancing the girl. Along with abundant comedy from Smiley Burnette (including a bit where he and Frankie Marvin don a cow-outfit and get mixed up with the real cattle) and a full-out action finale, this is a very entertaining Autry western.

As the deputy of aging Sheriff Doniphon (William Farnum), Gene Autry believes in the old fashioned methods of catching modern cattle rustlers on wheels who employ an airplane spotter and carry off their raids using refrigerator trucks. It's at this point there is one quite brutal scene of beeves being slaughtered. With the raids causing a crisis among ranchers and townsfolk, the citizens demand Sheriff Doniphon's retirement while they bring in a "progressive" New York detective. But eventually Gene, in love with pretty newspaper editor Helen Morgan (Ann Rutherford), proves the cowboy on horseback is still better for catching range rustlers than the mechanized modernization of the New Yawk defective.

NOTES AND COMMENTS: Ann Rutherford, who had appeared with Gene in three previous films, was now under contract to MGM. Republic paid MGM to loan her out for "Public Cowboy No. 1". Meanwhile, William Farnum received $300 for a week's work and Arthur Loft $250. Stuntman Ken Cooper, continuing to double Gene in the rough scenes, earned his usual $250.

Gene Autry had just been voted the #1 western star at the boxoffice by the exhibitors of America, therefore the title of this movie is an obvious reflection of that honor more than anything in the plot of the film. Regarding that honor Gene told columnist Erskine Johnson, "I like being a screen cowboy. I'm best suited for that. I like to please kids and cowboy actors usually enjoy longer careers than drawing room idols."[1] Gene was offered roles by every studio in town but turned them all down to stay at Republic.

With every film, Smiley's "costume" comes ever closer to what we all seem to remember; in "Public Cowboy No. 1" he turns his hat brim upward.

With slight changes, the song "Defective Detective from Brooklyn" was re-cycled by Oliver Drake for Rod Cameron's "Riders of the Santa Fe" at Universal in 1944.

FILM COMMENTS: *Gene Autry:* "We were grinding out a picture on an average of every six weeks, one after another like link sausage. Strung together and laid bare, some of the ideas seem silly today and some were, even then. But many were fresh and inventive. In 'Public Cowboy No. 1', we used a short wave radio set to foil a cattle rustling ring that was directed from an airplane. This was 1937, remember. The movie was later re-created as a Big Little Book. That was a compliment, I guess.

"By then we had practically formed our own stock company, whose cast included such semi-regulars as William Farnum, another silent screen idol, who re-established himself in the 'good sheriff' roles."[2]

House Peters Jr.: "Overall, I'd rate my experience working on 'Public Cowboy No. 1' very pleasant. However, in the story there is a meatpacking plant conspicuously labeled Chicago and Western Packers. This was not a façade

Smiley Burnette, Sheriff William Farnum, deputy Frankie Marvin, newspaperwoman Ann Rutherford and Gene Autry in a happy moment during "Public Cowboy No. 1."

on a studio backlot. It was a real slaughterhouse located at the north end of Sepulveda Boulevard in the San Fernando Valley. Our scenes at this place were shot during a summer heatwave of about 100 degrees in the shade. The stench was overpowering.

"On a more positive note, I can't say enough good things about Gene Autry. In all the years I was to act with him, he was always prepared and ready to work when he came on the set. Gene didn't waste other people's time and treated everyone with respect, unlike some others I've worked with over the years.

"This was my first picture of what would be many with Gene, both features and television. He was most considerate and pleasant on his pictures in the early days. Later, when the Flying A Company was formed, he was most kind to all those who worked for his company, from producer Mandy Schaefer and associate producer Lou Gray, to the directors, cameramen, actors and actresses. In return, he was well-liked by most actors and crew who worked with him."[3]

Ann Rutherford, when asked if she received a bonus from MGM for being loaned back to Republic, "Are you

out of your gourd? (Laughs.)"[4]

CAST BIOS: Stage trained William Farnum appeared in over 150 movies from 1912 to 1952; "Git Along Little Dogies" was the first of six he made with Gene Autry. Born on the Fourth of July, 1876, in Boston, Massachusetts, his father trained his three sons, William, Dustin and Marshall, in the profession. William made his stage debut at the age of ten (1886) in Richmond, Virginia, in a production of "Julius Caesar" starring Edwin Booth. His first New York appearance was in 1896 with his first major success in the title role of "Ben Hur" in which he toured for five years. Coming to films in 1912, he won the coveted role of Roy Glenister in Selig's soon to be classic adaptation of Rex Beach's novel THE SPOILERS. (The tale has been filmed a total of five times.) It is the final reel fight between Farnum and Tom Santschi in the original that gave the film its enduring fame. Farnum rose to become one of the highest paid stars in Hollywood when he joined Fox, starring in a series of Zane Grey adaptations. Suffering an injury in 1924's "The Man Who Fights Alone" at Paramount, an

Gene rescues Ann Rutherford from crooked Arthur Loft who's attempting to use the girl as a hostage.

operation was necessary. In a coma for four months, he was not expected to live. His medical bills amounted to $2.5 million. The stock market crash of 1929 took what was left. After a four year hiatus, during which time brother Dustin died, William Farnum returned to the screen in 1930. Although now 54, his fine speaking voice enabled him to find plenty of character player work, mostly in westerns. Working right up until the end, the fabulous Farnum died of cancer June 5, 1953.

Round-faced, heavy-set, balding Arthur Loft played crooked politicos, bankers and other fast talking scam artist business-types while masquerading as a respectable citizen. In "Public Cowboy No. 1" Loft portrays the local wholesale meat dealer who is actually head of the rustlers. Of Loft's 225 or so movies from 1932-1948, only three dozen were westerns, but his appearance in one always signaled underhanded deeds for Gene Autry, Roy Rogers, Don Barry and others. Hans Peter Loft was born May 25, 1897, in Ouray, Colorado, of Danish heritage. He first came to Hollywood in 1932. Loft's other westerns with Autry are "Rhythm of the Saddle", "Back In the Saddle" and "Down Mexico Way". The dependable actor was only 49 when he died of a heart attack January 1, 1947, at his home in Los Angeles.

WHAT THE EXHIBITOR HAD TO SAY:
"I want to report on 'Yodelin' Kid From Pine Ridge' and 'Public Cowboy No. 1'. These are the poorest Autry pictures I have played. They are cheaply produced with practically no story, poor direction, and no appeal in any way. This isn't my opinion alone but it is taken from remarks from patrons. Republic certainly has slipped on these Autry pictures since Nat Levine quit producing them. And they (Republic) have the nerve to call 'Public Cowboy No. 1' a special when it isn't even a good Saturday western. I am not writing this in any criticism of Autry as I realize he has done the best he could with that they gave him to work with. But if Republic doesn't improve these pictures they are going to ruin Autry. My business was off practically one-half for three pictures, and for no other reason then they were poorly and cheaply made pictures."
—M. S. Porter, Orpheum Theater, Nelsonville, Ohio (October 1937)

"Played to a nice Saturday and Sunday business. This first Autry picture of the '37-'38 product is just as good or even a little better than last year's. Good enough for any day of the week." —Fischer and Bichler, Mattray Theater, Strasburg, ND (November 1937)

"This is a very poor picture but there was no complaint from the Autry fans. Did a fair Saturday business."
—Roy W. Adams, Mason Theater, Mason, Michigan (August 1938)

"Another great western with the un-beatable Gene Autry."
—George Khattar, Casino Theater, Whitney Pier, Sydney, Nova Scotia, Canada (March 1939)

SOURCES:
1. *Los Angeles Examiner.* June 10, 1937.
2. Autry with Herskowitz, p. 56.
3. Peters Jr., House. *Another Side of Hollywood.* Empire, 2000. p. 76.
4. Magers, Boyd and Fitzgerald, Michael. *Ladies of the Western.* McFarland, 2002. p. 244.

Boots and Saddles
Republic, October 1937

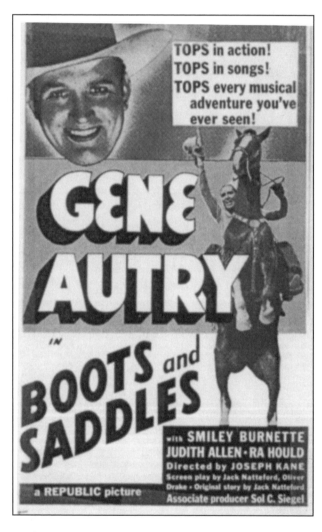

SONGS: "Salud Vaquero" (music and lyrics by Aaron Gonzalez Jr.)—sung by large group at Spanish fiesta; "Take Me Back to My Boots and Saddle" (music and lyrics by Walter G. Samuels, Leonard Whitcup, Teddy Powell)—sung by Gene Autry and Spanish fiesta crowd; "Ridin' the Range" (words and music by Gene Autry, Fleming Allen, Nelson Shawn)—sung by Gene Autry and studio chorus; "Dusty Roads" (music and lyrics by Smiley Burnette)—sung by Smiley Burnette; "Cielito Lindo" (Traditional)—sung by Cecilia Callejo; "The One Rose That's Left in My Heart" (words and music by Lane McIntire, Del Lyons)—sung by Gene Autry; "Why Did I Get Married" (music and lyrics by Carson Robison)—sung by Gene Autry.

RUNNING TIME: 59 minutes
FILMING DATES: July 30 to August 9, 1937
LOCATIONS: Lone Pine; Republic backlot
BUDGET: $42,179
NEGATIVE COST: $43,483

CAST:

Actor	Character
Gene Autry	Gene Autry
Smiley Burnette	Frog Millhouse
Judith Allen	Bernice Allen
Ra Hould	Spud aka Edward, Earl of Grandby
Guy Usher	Colonel Allen
Gordon (Bill) Elliott	Jim Neale
John Ward	Henry "Windy" Wyndham
Frankie Marvin	Shorty
Chris-Pin Martin	Greeter at Fiesta
Stanley Blystone	Sergeant
Bud Osborne	Joe Larkins
Lynton Brent	Officer
Cecilia Callejo	Spanish Café singer
Jerry Frank	Army Sentry
Merrill McCormick	Bushwhacker
Nelson McDowell	Constable
Bob Reeves	Neale Henchman
Al Taylor	Bushwhacker

Producer	Sol C. Siegel
Director	Joe Kane
Assistant Director	William A. O'Connor
Original Story	Jack Natteford
Screenplay	Jack Natteford, Oliver Drake
Photography	William Nobles
Film Editor	Lester Orlebeck
Musical Director	Raoul Kraushaar

Fenton "Duke" Taylor ....Henchman
Billy Arnold ....Captain
Mike Martin ....Juan
Joe de la Cruz.............................Jose
Ken Cooper ....Carriage Driver
Eduardo "Lalo" Guerrero and Los
    Carlistas ....Spanish singers
Champion ....Champion

STUNTS: Ken Cooper (Gene Autry double), Yakima Canutt, Fenton "Duke" Taylor, Bill Yrigoyen.

THE FILM: Sporting the hit songs "Take Me Back to My Boots and Saddle" and "The One Rose That's Left in My Heart" plus some other good tunes, and superb direction once again from Joe Kane, "Boots and Saddles" emerges as a real turning point in Gene's film career. Gene is in fine voice, with his confident presence and easy, smiling amusement with certain situations on screen more evident than ever before. He also now seems to know what to do with his hands, often snugging up his gloves. We also begin to witness the beginnings of Smiley Burnette's "official"

wardrobe.

The story, about the orphaned British Earl of Grandby (Ra Hould) who has to depend on his ranch foreman, Gene Autry, to save his ranch from nasty mortgage holder Jim Neale (Bill Elliott, sporting a mustache), is more fun and foolishness than serious power struggle. Gene decides to win a contract to break and sell horses to the Army in order to save the ranch. With identical bids submitted by both Gene and Neale, a cross-country race is planned to decide the winner. All the while, Gene manages another "taming of the shrew" romance with the daughter, Bernice Allen (Judith Allen), of the Army post's Colonel (Guy Usher).

NOTES AND COMMENTS: A year from now Gordon "Bill" Elliott became a major B-western star himself, first at Columbia, then at Republic.

"The One Rose That's Left in My Heart" is the favorite song of Gene's second wife, Jackie Autry.

Twelve year old Ra Hould (Richard Arthur Hould), a youngster from New Zealand, made his U.S. film debut in 1936 and soon signed an MGM contract under the name Ronald Sinclair as a possible threat to Freddie Bartholomew.

All's well that ends well with Gene and Champion, young Ra Hould, Judith Allen and her screen father Col. Guy Usher.

However, after a few films, Sinclair became a top film editor, was heavily involved with American International Pictures during its formative years, and was also president of the California branch of the Humane Society of the U.S. He died of respiratory failure at the Motion Picture Home in 1992.

FILM COMMENTS: *Gene Autry:* "The heavy in 'Boots and Saddles' was Gordon Elliott, and there is a point to be made here about movie luck and people who persevere. Elliott had knocked around since 1929, playing mostly dress extras. After this film, Columbia made a serial called 'The Great Adventures of Wild Bill Hickok', and gave Elliott the starring role. The studio renamed him Wild Bill Elliott, he later became the screen's second Red Ryder, and he was still around in the early fifties when the B-western began its final spasm. By then the cowboy hero drank when he felt like it, beat up the villain while holding a gun on him, and wore his six-shooter reversed in the holster, with the butt forward. (Elliott may have been the first to wear them in that fashion.)" [1]

Columnist *Jimmy Starr:* "Theatre managers tell me Gene Autry is the biggest outdoor hit they have played since Bill Hart and Tom Mix heydays." [2]

WHAT THE EXHIBITOR HAD TO SAY: "Another great western from Autry. Played this on Christmas Day and was not a least bit worried or disappointed. Thanks, Gene."

—George Khatter, Casino Theater, Whitney Pier, Sydney, Nova Scotia, Canada (December 1938)

"At the risk of getting murdered by fellow exhibs., I am forced to report that in my town these babies are getting weaker and weaker per each issue. 'Springtime in the Rockies' being the only good one in the last four or five. If it wasn't for Smiley Burnette these pics would flop so hard there wouldn't even be a thud. Or maybe I'm all wet. They say 'Old Barn Dance', 'Gold Mine In the Sky' are much better. They may be. We'll see."

—R. D. Fisher, Cozy Theater, Cabool, Missouri (February 1939)

"A Good Autry western. You're OK too, Smiley. Autry sings the popular 'The One Rose' in this."

—C. H. Collier, Globe Theater, Drew, Mississippi (February 1939)

"Gene Autry is tops for westerns here. However, we are not doing any good with Autry reissues."

—Mrs. O. E. Brumley, Pal Theater, Chatham, Louisiana (June 1943)

"Autry is still good and people will pay to see him."

—Raymond Krutsinger, Rialto Theater, Lyndon, Kansas (July 1943)

"Autry is business. Even though some are corny, they still do from average to better-than-average business."

—J. N. Allison, Dana Theater, Dana, Indiana (November 1943)

"These Autry reissues have so far held up midweek playing dates. We did way above average business."

—Leroy Strandberg, Roxy Theater, Hinchley, Minnesota (April 1944)

SOURCES:
1. Autry with Herskowitz, p. 57.
2. Starr, Jimmy. Column in *Los Angeles Evening Herald Express*. August 4, 1937.

Manhattan Merry-Go-Round
Republic, November 1937

Producer ....Harry Sauber
Director ....Charles F. Reisner
Assistant Director.......................George Sherman
Director of New York Sequence ..John Auer

Screenplay ....Harry Sauber from
                    Frank Hummerts'
                    musical revue
Original Musical Review ....Frank Hummert
Photography ....Jack Marta
Supervising Editor.....................Murray Seldeen
Film Editor ....Ernest Nims
Costumes ....Eloise
Furs...Willard H. George
Jewelry ....Mauboussin, Trabert &
                    Hoeffer Inc./Miss
                    Geva's wardrobe by
                    Muriel King
Art Director ....John Victor Mackay
Musical Directors ....Alberto Columbo and
                    Harry Grey

SONGS: "Manhattan Merry-Go-Round" (music and lyrics by Sammy Cahn, Saul Chaplin)—sung by studio singers; "Have You Ever Been To Heaven" (music and lyrics by Peter Tinturin, Jack Lawrence)—performed by Phil Regan and Ted Lewis and his Orchestra; "I Owe You" (music and lyrics by Peter Tinturin and Jack Lawrence)—performed by Phil Regan and Louis Prima and his Orchestra; "When My Baby Smiles At Me" (music and lyrics by Ted Lewis, Bill Monro, Andrew Sterling, Harry Von Tilzer)—performed by Ted Lewis and his Orchestra; "I'm a Musical Magical Man" (music and lyrics by unknown)—performed by Ted Lewis and his Orchestra; "All Over Nothing At All" (music and lyrics by Peter Tinturin and Jack Lawrence)—performed by Kay Thompson and her Ensemble; "Minnie the Moocher" (music and lyrics by Cab Calloway)—performed by Cab Calloway and his Cotton Club Orchestra; "Mama, I Wanna Make Rhythm" (music and lyrics by Walter Kent, Jerome Jerome, Richard Byron); "It's Round-Up Time In Reno" (music and lyrics by Gene Autry, Jack Owens, Jack Lawrence)—sung by Gene Autry, Smiley Burnette, Frankie Marvin.

RUNNING TIME: 82 minutes

FILMING DATES: August 4-18, 1937; September 22-23, 1937

98

CAST:

Actor	*Character*
Phil Regan	Jerry Hart
Leo Carrillo	Tony Gordoni
Ann Dvorak	Ann Rogers
Tamara Geva	Madame "Charlie" Charlizzini
James Gleason	Danny The Duck
Ted Lewis and His Orchestra	Themselves
Cab Calloway and His Cotton Club Band	Themselves
Kay Thompson and Her Radio Choir	Themselves
Joe DiMaggio	Himself
Henry Armetta	Spadoni
Luis Alberni	Martinetti, the Impressario
Max Terhune	Himself—the Ventriloquist
Smiley Burnette	Frog, the Accordion Player
Louis Prima and His Band	Themselves
Gene Autry	Himself
Jack Adair	Eddie
Dorothy Arnold	Dancer
Stanley Blystone, Hal Craig	Detectives
Gennaro Curci	Michael Angelo
Virginia Dabney	Woman
Anna Demetrio	Charlizzini's Maid
Neal Dodd	Minister
Ralph Edwards	Radio Man
Sam Finn	Speed
Al Herman	Blackie
Jack Jenny and His Orchestra	Themselves
Selmer Jackson	J. Henry Thorne
Eddie Kane	McMurray, Manager of Manhattan Merry-Go-Round Nightclub
Joe King	Chief of Detectives
The Lathrops	Themselves, Group Performers
Whitey's Lindy Hoppers	Themselves, Dancers to Cab Calloway's music
Frankie Marvin	Gene Autry Band Musician
Nellie V. Nichols	Mamma Gordoni
Moroni Olsen	Jonathan "Joe"
Bob Perry	Baldy
Rosalean and Seville	Themselves, Group

Leo Carrillo, Tamara Geve, Gene Autry, Phil Regan, Ann Dvorak, James Gleason.

	Performers
Gertrude Short	Danny's Nightclub Date
Thelma Wunder	Dorothy
Art Davis	Gene Autry's Fiddler

THE FILM: In Gene Autry's own words, "Republic broke new ground in 'Manhattan Merry-Go-Round' when I became the first cowboy to rate a guest star billing." [1]

This filmusical is a radical departure for Gene, now the #1 western star at the boxoffice. It was a time in Hollywood when movies with musical guest stars were hot at the boxoffice. Lavishly produced and studded with name talent, the slight storyline has gangster Tony Gordoni (Leo Carrillo) inheriting a record company and forcing singer Jerry Hart (Phil Regan) to use his charm and persuade opera star Madame Charlizzini (Tamara Geva) to join the company. Jerry succeeds, but almost loses his fiancée Ann (Ann Dvorak) in the process. Jerry winds up singing at Gene Autry's ranch before everyone is reunited.

Gene Autry and Smiley Burnette are guest stars in cameo roles, appearing basically in only the last 10 minutes of the movie. Gene sings one song and has some dialogue with Leo Carrillo, James Gleason and Phil Regan.

SOURCES:
1. Autry with Herskowitz. p. 57.

Springtime In the Rockies
Republic, November 1937

Producer ....Sol C. Siegel
Director ....Joe Kane
Assistant Director.......................Bill O'Connor
Original Screenplay ....Gilbert Wright,
                                    Betty Burbridge
Photography ....Ernest Miller
Film Editor ....Lester Orlebeck
Musical Director ....Alberto Columbo

SONGS: "Give Me a Pony" (music and lyrics by Gene Autry, Frank Harford)—sung by Gene Autry; "When It's Springtime in the Rockies" (music and lyrics by Woolsey, Saver, Taggart)—sung by George Chesebro, Gene Autry, cowboys; "Vitamine D" (music and lyrics by Smiley Burnette)—sung by Polly Rowles, Ula Love, Ruth Bacon, Jane Hunt; "The Moon is Riding" (music and lyrics by Winston Tharp, Leon Leonardi)—sung by Gene Autry and girls; "Sing Your Song Cowboy" (music and lyrics by Jimmy Lefevre, Vincent Caruso)—sung by Jimmy Lafevre's Saddle Pals; "Way Down Low" (music and lyrics by Smiley Burnette)—sung by Smiley Burnette; "There'll Be a Hayride Weddin' In June" (music and lyrics by Gene Autry, Johnny Marvin)—sung by Gene Autry, cowboys and girls; "Down In the Land of Zulu" (music and lyrics by Gene Autry, Johnny Marvin)—sung by Smiley Burnette, Ula Love, Ruth Bacon, Jane Hunt; "Buffalo Gals" (Traditional)—sung by Jimmy Lafevre's Saddle Pals; "You're the Only Star in My Blue Heaven" (music and lyrics by Gene Autry)—sung by Gene Autry.

RUNNING TIME: 60 minutes
FILMING DATES: September 11-22, 1937
LOCATIONS: Republic back lot; Keen Camp; Jack Garner Ranch; Lake Hemet
BUDGET: $46,309
NEGATIVE COST: $49,516.31

CAST:

Actor	*Character*
Gene Autry ....Gene Autry
Smiley Burnette ....Frog Millhouse
Polly Rowles ....Sandra Knight
Ula Love....................................Sylvia "Silly" Parker

Ruth Bacon.................................Peggy Snow
Jane Hunt ....Jane Hilton
George Chesebro.........................Thad Morgan
Al Bridge....................................Briggs
Tom London................................Tracy
Edward Hearn ....Jed Thorpe
Frankie Marvin...........................Autry Musician/
                                  Cowhand
William Hole...............................Bub
Edmund Cobb ....Sheriff
Fred Burns..................................Rancher Harris
Jimmy Lafevre's Saddle Pals ....Musical ranch hands
Jim Corey, Victor Cox, Jack Kirk .. Cowboys
Art Davis ....Slim, Autry Musician/
                                  Cowhand
Art Dillard, Lou Morphy.............Cowhands
Robert Dudley.............................Barn dance MC
Frank Ellis, Howard Hickey,
    Buck Spencer...........................Ranchers
Oscar Gahan, Johnny Luther........Autry Musicians/
                                  Cowhands
Stuart Hamblen ....First Truck Driver
Bud McClure, Bob Burns ....Ranchers
Lew Meehan.................................Deputy
George Montgomery....................Cowboy at dance
Bill Nestell ....Truck Driver
Bud Pope.....................................Townsman
Jack Rockwell ....Sheriff of Sage City
Rudy Sooter ....Autry Musician/
                                  Cowhand
Nellie Walker ....Townhall girl
Buster Steele...............................Autry Ranch hand
Curley Hoagg ....Autry Musician/Ranch
                                  hand
Adele Wilde ....Cowgirl
Jack Daly.....................................Jim
Ken Cooper, Bill Yrigoyen ....Furniture deliverers
Champion....................................Champion

STUNTS: Ken Cooper (double for Gene); Buck Spencer (double for Smiley); Nellie Walker (double for Polly Rowles); Hazel Burns, Joe Yrigoyen, Bill Yrigoyen.

THE FILM: "Springtime in the Rockies" was Gene's last 1937 release and it signaled a watershed in his career, for he was on a collision course with Republic president Herbert J. Yates. It would all come to a head in 1938 after one more film. In the meantime, "Springtime…" confirmed, if confirmation was needed, that Autry was in top form.

The plot is more screwball comedy with another taming of the shrew romance as ranch foreman Gene encounters lots of sheep double dealing and ranch mixups when he tries to show Eastern ranch owner and animal husbandry agricultural college graduate Sandra Knight (Polly Rowles) and her singing gal-pals that sheep and cattle won't mix. No amount of persuasion can stop Knight from bringing sheep to her ranch until crooked cattle dealer Thorpe (Edward Hearn) starts to take advantage of the situation. Along the trail to straightening out the mix-ups, we even get to hear perennial badman George Chesebro sing a few bars of the title song—at Gene's pistol point, after which Gene remarks, "It's hard to sing and be mean at the same time."

Gene finished 1937 as the undisputed number one cowboy in Hollywood, outstripping all the oldtimers and all of the new singing cowboy contenders. To some it was still a mystery. Buck Jones reckoned it would never last. But to millions of Gene Autry fans it was no mystery, they loved Gene. There is no doubt that, single-handed, he was the cause of Republic being a healthy profit-making organization.

NOTES AND COMMENTS: The plot of "Springtime In the Rockies" was recycled by Republic for Roy Rogers' "Utah" in 1945.

Capable, attractive Polly Rowles, in her only western, was paid $350 while Al Bridge earned $150 per week and Ula Love, George Chesebro and Tom London all took home $100 each. Jane Hunt made $75.

Several filming delays took place. A new camera had to be sent up from the studio when the one being used at Keen Camp was punching holes in the film. There were also four hour delays on two different days due to dark cloud cover. Buster Steele was injured in a riding scene and one sheep broke a leg.

"You're the Only Star in My Blue Heaven" was the favorite song of Gene's first wife, Ina. The song was reprised several times in Gene's features and TV series.

Gene and Smiley are about to force badman George Chesebro to sing a few bars of "When It's Springtime in the Rockies."

FILM COMMENTS: *Gene Autry:* "I kept two horses always saddled up in case we had to do a lot of chases. I didn't like to ride Champion in too many chases, because he would get hot and sweaty and lathered then he wouldn't stand very good for close-ups."[1]

CAST BIOS: For 39 years in over 400 features and some 33 serials, the lean, nasty, sneering, snarling presence of George Chesebro menaced cowboy stars from silent days on through the demise of the B-westerns in 1954. Chesebro's hatchet-faced badmen knew no boundaries, they were at every studio—Columbia, Republic, Universal, Monogram, PRC down to the lowliest independents. His best role opposite Gene Autry is, undoubtedly, "Springtime in the Rockies" although he made a total of seven westerns with the singing cowboy.

Born July 29, 1888, in Minneapolis, Minnesota, George Newell Chesebro started his acting career in a local stock company in 1907. Vaudeville was next, touring the Orient and singing with a musical comedy group from 1911-1913. He continued to perform in vaudeville and stock upon his return to the U. S. in 1913 until coming to Hollywood in 1915.

For the next few years he played male leads opposite popular female performers until he entered the U.S. Army for service in WWI. Upon his discharge, he continued as a leading man in serials and westerns.

Shifting to villainous character roles, Chesebro imperiled various silent stars thereby setting the pattern for the rest of his career, rustling cattle, bushwhacking sheriffs, manhandling ladies and plotting all manner of land grabs.

The end of his screen skullduggery came on May 28, 1959, at 70, when the beloved George Chesebro died at his home in Hermosa Beach, California, from heart failure brought on by hypertension and arteriosclerosis.

Chesebro's fellow screen owlhoot, Pierce Lyden, observed, "George Chesebro, with that voice that commanded attention, was always good to work with—and happy to be around—like the time an assistant director said to a group of us one morning, 'What a rotten, no good, tough looking bunch of outlaws.' And George says, 'You ain't seen no outlaws, buddy, until you've seen my in-laws.'"[2]

WHAT THE EXHIBITOR HAD TO SAY: "Did not do the business I expected. Western pictures not so hot in this community. These features are too short for a good story as we don't run double bill entertainment."
—Arthur L. Dove, Bengough Theater,
Bengough, Saskatchewan, Canada (April 1939)

"Will be glad when these ancient Autry films are finished. They used to be tops for our Saturday program, but our patrons are tired of seeing the same thing all over again."
—A. Zach Culler, New Theater,
North, South Carolina (May 1946)

"I waited all week for this one and wasn't disappointed. The patrons came in to see a good picture and didn't go away disappointed. Everybody was happy, including me."
—Harry T. Wachter, Gentry Theater,
Gentry, Arkansas (August 1946)

SOURCES:

1. "Melody Ranch Theater" showing of "Back In the Saddle" on Nashville Network, 1987.

2. Lyden, Pierce. *The Movie Badmen I Rode With.* Self published, 1988.

The Old Barn Dance
Republic, January 1938

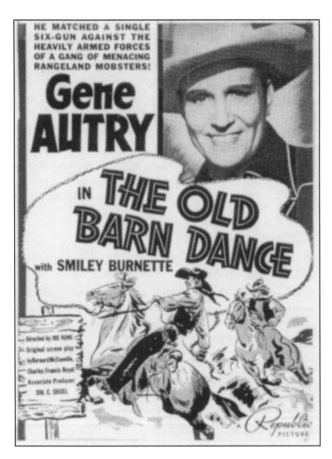

Producer ....Sol C. Siegel
Director ....Joe Kane
Assistant Director.........................Harry Knight
Original Screenplay ....Bernard McConville,
         Charles F. Royal
Photography ....Ernest Miller
Film Editor ....Lester Orlebeck
Production Manager.....................Al Wilson
Unit Manager ....Arthur Siteman
Musical Director ....Alberto Columbo

SONGS: "Ten Little Miles" (music and lyrics by Peter Tinturin and Jack Lawrence)—sung by Gene Autry, Smiley Burnette, Frankie Marvin; "Old Nell" (music and lyrics by Frankie Marvin)—sung by Smiley Burnette; "Rocky Mountain Rose" (music and lyrics by Joan Jasmyn, William Tracey, M. K. Jerome)—sung by Gene Autry; "Square Dance Call" (Traditional)—sung by Roy Rogers; "Eating Wax" (music and lyrics by Abner Wilder)—sung by Walt Shrum's Colorado Hillbillies; "She'll Be Comin' 'Round the Mountain" (Public Domain)—sung by Stafford Sisters; "At the Old Barn Dance" (music and lyrics by Peter Tinturin and Jack Lawrence)—sung by Gene Autry and cast; "Then and Now" (music and lyrics by Smiley Burnette)—sung by Gene Autry; "Roamin' Around the Range" (music and lyrics by Smiley Burnette)—sung by Gene Autry; "The New Jassackaphone" to the tune of "Listen to the Mockingbird" (Public Domain with new lyrics by Smiley Burnette)—sung by Smiley Burnette; "You're the Only Star in My Blue Heaven" (music and lyrics by Gene Autry)—sung by Gene Autry; "The Green Grass Grew All Around" (aka "The Tree In the Wood") (Public Domain)—sung by The Maple City Four; "The Lady Wants to Dance" (music and lyrics by Walter Hirsch, Lou Handman)—sung by Gloria Rich; "Old Chisholm Trail" (Public Domain)—sung by Gene Autry and Walt Shrum's Colorado Hillbillies.

RUNNING TIME: 60 minutes

FILMING DATES: November 27 to December 9, 1937

LOCATIONS: Lone Pine; Republic backlot; Kernville

BUDGET: $49,191

NEGATIVE COST: $50,179

CAST:

Actor	*Character*
Gene Autry ....Gene Autry
Smiley Burnette ....Frog Millhouse
Helen Valkis (aka Joan Valerie) ...Sally Dawson
Sammy McKim...........................Johnny Dawson
Walt Shrum and his Colorado Hillbillies: Walt Shrum, Cal Shrum, Rudy Sooter, Robert "Pappy" Hoag, Tony Fiore, Rusty Cline, Abner Wilder, Vic Luiggili Spatafore, Toby Stewart..Musicians

The Stafford Sisters: Christine
  Stafford, Pauline Stafford, June
  Schaefer..................................Singers
Maple City Four...........................Comic Singers
Dick Weston (aka Roy Rogers)....Square Dance Caller
Ivan Miller ....Thornton
Earl Dwire..................................Clem Hanley
Hooper Atchley ....Maxwell, Finance Co.
                          Manager
Ray Bennett................................Buck, Thornton's
                          Gunman
Carleton Young ....Peabody, Thornton's
                          Henchman
Frankie Marvin, William Cowdry,
  Howard Hickey, George
  Guessford ....Autry Cowhands
Earle Hodgins..............................Terwilliger
Gloria Rich, Bob Nolan ....Singers
Bill Nestell, Fred Burns ....Farmers
Victor Adamson, George
  Montgomery ....Men
Frank Darien ....Dawson
Neal Hart....................................Sheriff Wilson
Jack Rockwell ....Reagan
Francis Sayles ....Carson, Tractor Owner
Jimmy Hollywood........................Rancher
Jack Kenny...................................Tractor Salesman
Forrest Dillon ....Cowboy
Helen Holmes, Helen Gibson ......Women
Bill Yrigoyen...............................Tractor Driver
Bob Card, Chuck Baldra, Bob
  Burns, Rudy Sooter, Fred
  Burns, Merrill McCormick,
  Bud McClure ....Extras
Champion....................................Champion

STUNTS: Art Dillard, Buck Spencer, Nellie Walker, Fred Kennedy, Ken Cooper (Gene's double).

THE FILM: 1938 proved to be the year that confirmed Gene Autry's position as Hollywood Cowboy King as he saw his popularity spreading to take in audiences who would not normally come to see B-western films. These audiences didn't go to see Gene's films just for western action, they went to hear him sing and display his easy-going, bashful charm. It was Gene's 24th movie appearance in five years, but it would be six months before he made another picture. The problem stemmed from Republic president Herbert J. Yates' "block booking" of Gene's films. (See details in the Notes and Comments section.)

Filled with terrific (and plentiful) music, the plot of "The Old Barn Dance" seeks to link up the early encroachment of the machine age, tractors, upon the western horse era of the rural farmer. As horse traders, the business of Gene Autry and Frog Millhouse (Smiley Burnette) is virtually ruined when the tractor company owned by unscrupulous Thornton (Ivan Miller) begins

cutting into their horse sales. In order to secure a lucrative advertising contract with Thornton, who appreciates Gene's music, radio station owner Sally Dawson (Helen Valkis) enlists Gene to make broadcasts for her radio station but tricks him into the contract with lies and secretly recorded broadcasts. Gene finds himself unwittingly promoting the merits of tractors, which the farmers then buy en masse. Then as harvest time approaches, Thornton begins to foreclose on the farmers who can't meet the payments. The farmers turn on Gene, whom they believe to have bilked them. Learning what has happened, Gene and the boys raid the radio station, destroying all the recordings of Gene's songs that have been used. However, a recording secretly made by Sally's kid brother, Johnny (Sammy McKim), that incriminates Thornton, is inadvertently also destroyed. Luckily (and actually impossible) Sally and Johnny piece the totally smashed record back together and, with Gene, expose the company for the swindlers they truly are.

In one telling scene, Gene sings "Rocky Mountain Rose" astride Champion in the middle of the street while adoring townsfolk listen—just as they were in the theaters. It's a perfect Autry moment. There's plenty of other music from the Maple City Four, Stafford Sisters and Walt Shrum and his Colorado Hillbillies (including brother Cal Shrum). The acceptance by rural audiences of this hillbilly and barn dance music obviously helped pave the way for Republic's series of Weaver Brothers and Elviry rural-music comedy/dramas. Roy Rogers, still using the name Dick Weston, is a square dance caller at the barn dance.

NOTES AND COMMENTS: Gene was at loggerheads with Republic president Herbert J. Yates. The studio had been paying him around $5,000 a picture and he felt his importance warranted $25,000, the amount Paramount offered him for one picture. "They pay Buck Jones $15,000 a picture, Bill Boyd gets $12,500 and George O'Brien about $15,000," Gene told THE HOLLYWOOD CITIZEN NEWS. "But all the boxoffice polls show I'm in first place among the cowboys, so I think I'd oughta get as much, or pretty near those other fellows."[1] "The Old Barn Dance" was sold by Republic as a "special", meaning a higher film rental rate to exhibitors than regular Autry releases. Also, unknown to Gene at the time, Republic "block-booked" his films so exhibitors wanting to play them (and everyone did) had to pay for the studio's entire annual output of approximately 45 films of varying subject matter. Block-booking was legal at the time and many studios utilized the policy. Anti-trust laws broke up the practice in the late '40s. Learning of this policy soured Gene on Republic and it led to a contract dispute. Historian Richard Smith III described the chain of events in WESTERN CLIPPINGS #27. "Not only was the movie cowboy desirous of more folding money, due to big box-office profits his westerns were reaping, but Gene wanted to amend his contract to guarantee Republic wouldn't attempt to collect half the money he made from endorsements, radio or public appearances. Also, after hearing one movie distributor

A rare behind-the-scenes shot as the Republic camera crew gets ready to film the next scene with Gene and Smiley at Lone Pine, California.

complain that a whole Republic film season package was required for purchase in order to obtain eight Gene Autry features, Autry immediately demanded Republic president Herbert J. Yates quit such policy and listen to his other complaints. Yates refused. Gene did not show up for the first day's shooting (12/27/37) on a new oater, 'Washington Cowboy', which caused his immediate suspension from Republic. He later made an appearance two days hence for camera chores, but said no screenplay was prepared, which resulted in a contract breach. Reportedly, Gene gave the studio until January 5 to start a new film.

"Now officially on strike, Gene headed out on a personal tour of the southwest and midwest, always one step ahead of the process server with a subpoena. DAILY VARIETY and VARIETY (1/18/38) printed Autry's gripes as Republic and the cowboy had attorneys arguing in their respective behalves. Paramount and 20th Century-Fox were ready to best Republic's top offer to Gene for new musical westerns if he were free to make such a deal.

"As January progressed, Autry was willing to exchange peace overtures with the studio if it met his monetary demand to offset the financial loss he incurred in an earlier two picture Paramount deal before this walkout.

"Autry squeezed in a N.Y.C. trip to negotiate a 32 week Downey Brothers circus deal at $4,000 every seven days. By Jan. 26, Gene's feud with Republic widened even further as the cowboy wired a statement from Nashville refuting studio claims his pictures weren't moneymakers and 'Republic, if it wants to make adjustments with exhibitors, can get more money for my releases and still sell its other product at reasonable prices.'

"A Nashville court judge stymied Gene further Jan. 27, issuing an injunction requested by Republic's attorneys to restrain him from appearing in films, vaudeville, radio, or stage shows until his present studio contract was concluded. Gene circumvented this for awhile by having the other members of his troupe and his horse Champion on stage while he paid his admission like any other patron and held receptions for the customers in the foyer. The system was not overly successful, as theatre managers felt uneasy in the realization they were outwitting a Federal court.

"DAILY VARIETY (1/31/38) stated Yates was willing to allow Autry to buy out his remaining Republic pact if he apologized for the Nashville statement. But should Gene fail to comply, Yates said he would follow through on legal proceedings, and reminded Gene the studio had already invested $500,000 in him.

"Burned up with the injunction, Autry lost another round February 2 in a Nashville federal court when it refused to dissolve the legal restraint. Autry waited in limbo, but eventually, by mid-March, was negotiating with Republic's Yates, producer Sol Siegel and distribution chief James Grainger. At this point, Gene made some money outside the bounds of the Republic dispute upon sale of his 3½ acre Olive Street ranch in Burbank to Cinecolor Inc. for construction of a new film laboratory.

"Unless Republic met his salary demands by April 9, Gene was prepared to trek to South America on a 20-week tour not covered by the U. S. injunction. Such a trip never materialized. On April 21, the cowboy was back in Nashville to await statements from Yates and Republic executive Moe Siegel in a new effort to dissolve the injunction. Although its results were not mentioned in the trades, this hitch must have been settled satisfactorily, as by May 2 the studio commenced its four day annual sales convention at the Hollywood Roosevelt Hotel, promoting its '38-'39 product, including eight Autry westerns. Republic film distributors howled about the six-month famine in Autry movies and wanted assurance from Yates himself the cowboy was on the studio's payroll for the next year.

"The night of May 2, Gene had a serious discussion with Yates and Secretary-treasurer George C. Schaefer. Two days later, some 300 Republic convention delegates cheered the cowboy's official return to Republic ranks where he publicly buried the hatchet in a rousing ceremony by walking on stage arm-in-arm with Yates.

"Gene's new and better terms with Republic resulted in

big salary raises. Starting with the '38-'39 season, he was to be paid $6,000 each for the first two pictures and $10,000 per film on the remainder, although Gene had to give way on his demands that Republic cease block booking. Several years later the U.S. government passed an anti-trust law outlawing block booking. Anxious to realize big bucks once again on Gene's movies, Republic wasted no time placing him back in the saddle with his initial post-strike feature, 'Gold Mine In the Sky'."[2]

"Washington Cowboy", the next film Gene was to make, was retitled "Under Western Stars", and elevated Leonard Slye (aka Dick Weston) to stardom as Roy Rogers. Released in 1938, Gene's perennial sidekick Smiley Burnette remained in the film as did Gene and Johnny Marvin's composition "Dust". According to the HOLLYWOOD REPORTER (April 13, 1938) Gene subsequently sued Republic for $25,000 for unauthorized use and dramatization of the lyrics to "Dust" which is sung in the film by Rogers during the screening of a film about the effects of a drought. The suit over the song was settled out of court prior to Gene's return to work at Republic. Incidentally, Johnny Marvin's "Dust" was nominated for an Academy Award in 1938 but lost out to "Thanks for the Memory".

In his autobiography, BACK IN THE SADDLE AGAIN, Gene explained the situation this way. "I have powerful memories of 'The Old Barn Dance', for reasons only indirectly related to the movie. It was the last I would make for six months. After a final, tiresome hassle with Herb Yates over my contract, (I) took a walk.

"I am by nature slow to anger. But once convinced I have been wronged, and my feet planted, you cannot budge me with a tractor. A man broke enough, long enough, often develops a keen sense of his worth and does not mind fighting to get it. But my quarrel with the studio was not entirely over dollars. I had signed my first contract, with Nat Levine with this understanding: If I proved myself, and made money for Republic, I would be rewarded.

"By 1937 I had moved up to first place in the box office polls for western stars. My pictures didn't play the luxury, four-thousand-seat theaters. They played the rural flea pits and the little independent houses, with 800 seats or less. But people were standing in line and I went out to meet them. I made personal appearances all over the country, drumming

That secret recording, held by young Sammy McKim, spells the end for crooked Ivan Miller — and Gene lets him know it. Leading lady Helen Valkis is on the right.

up business for the eight films a year we were rolling out.

"Herb Yates had taken over the company. Republic profits soared. My salary had jumped to $5,000 a film, but there were strings. My contract contained a clause that entitled the studio to half of any money I received from endorsements, radio or public appearances. No attempt had been made to collect and I was assured that none would. But at the end of the year I wanted the contract amended. I didn't want some lawyer rediscovering those rights later and deciding they should be enforced.

"I might have made none of this an issue, if not for a policy Republic had put quietly into effect. It was called block buying. I found out about it between pictures, on the road, when I stopped by the office of a local film distributor. 'If we want a Gene Autry film, we have to buy the entire studio line. That's a lot of loot. They're using your films to push whatever else they got going.'

"I confronted Herb Yates. I wanted that practice stopped, those clauses removed, and, while I was about it, a fairer share of the profits my pictures were producing. That was the wrong approach to take with Yates. But if there was a better one I didn't know it.

"He was not unkind or ungenerous. But like a lot of studio bosses of that era, his vanity was such that he would resist doing what was right rather then yield to what he saw as pressure.

"Socially, he was the best of company. He could pick up everybody's tab in a night club, lay down a thousand dollars, and think nothing of it. The next day, across his desk, if you were asking for a raise, he would throw dollars around like they were manhole covers.

"I had a new picture scheduled to start in two weeks, to be called 'Washington Cowboy'. When I walked out of his office, we both knew I wouldn't be there when the cameras rolled. The trade papers made it sound like a range war.

"So I had gone on strike. It was the only weapon you had if you got into a scrap about your contract. But my idea of a strike was to keep busy and keep moving. A moving target is harder to hit. Any cowboy knew that.

"Now began a chase scene that topped anything we had done on the screen. I told George Goodale to book a tour going east, as many dates and towns as he could line up.

"Of course, when I failed to show up for the first day's shooting on 'Washington Cowboy', the studio suspended me. Yates said he would make the film without me and create a new cowboy star. That was when they gave a screen test to Leonard Slye, who had appeared in a couple of my pictures as Dick Weston, and whose name was soon to be Roy Rogers. They changed the title of the movie to 'Under Western Stars'.

"Yates had threatened to break me—'if you won't work here, you won't work anywhere.' The studio took out an injunction to prevent me from appearing on stage until my contract had been fulfilled. We hit the road, through Arizona, New Mexico and Texas, always one step ahead of the process server.

"Republic followed us all over the country, but they didn't catch up until the tour reached Nashville. The injunction was a temporary one and Republic took me into court, in Nashville, to make it permanent.

"Months had flown by. Now the rest of the tour had to be canceled. My prospects were not bright. But as Smiley often kidded me: 'Whenever the wolf came to the door, Autry ended up with a fur coat.'

"Back in Los Angeles, I was getting help from a powerful lobby. Republic's distributors were holding their annual convention and they climbed all over Herb Yates. It was going on six months since an Autry movie had been released. They made it sound not like a business problem, but a national famine. Many of them had gone along with the block buying, to the extent they would buy a package of 20, my eight plus twelve others, and ship back the ones they didn't want without using them. Now they demanded some assurance I would be working for Republic next year. Otherwise, they warned Yates, their theaters would be in trouble.

"At that point, Yates called. Our attorneys got together and worked out a compromise. In a curious way, there were no hard feelings. All he had done was call me disloyal and threaten to ruin me. In return, I had called him a cheap skate and a tyrant. In those years, in Hollywood, no one took anyone else seriously. So we played golf.

"My salary was raised to $10,000 a film (escalating to 15 and 20 over the next seven years), and the clauses I found objectionable were removed. The package deals continued; they were by then too entrenched to undo. And I gave my permission, which they needed, for the song I had written, 'Dust', to be sung by Roy Rogers, in a movie that had been scheduled for me."[3]

"The Old Barn Dance" was one of Gene's films re-issued while he was serving in the Air Force during WWII. Re-released in 1943, Republic hoped it would help keep Gene's name before the public during his absence from making films.

Tractors and farm implements used in this production were furnished exclusively by International Harvester Company.

Harvester company heavy Ivan Miller earned $300 for his work in the picture, $50 more than leading lady Helen Valkis. Earle Hodgins, who had much larger roles in earlier Autry films, also made $250 even though his role here amounts to one scene. Raphael (Ray) Bennett got $125 a week while Jack Rockwell and Carleton Young collected $100 each. Walt Shrum's Colorado Hillbillies were paid $1,000 as a group (9 members). The Stafford Sisters made $150 a day and recorded their song tracks two days before filming.

There are several in-jokes or unique product placements to watch for in "The Old Barn Dance". A Mobilgas sign is blatantly displayed in one scene, a forerunner of today's rampant product placement in movies. Also, in the scene when Gene saves young Sammy McKim, look for the Republic B-western movie posters on the side of a building.

One is from "A Lawman Is Born" ('37) with Johnny Mack Brown and another is from a Three Mesquiteers western. Is it an in-joke when Smiley announces the big barn dance will be held at Corrigan's barn? Joshing Republic star Ray Corrigan?

Although he's a bad guy in the picture, Ivan Miller as harvester company owner Thornton makes a valid observation as he watches Gene sing. He whistles lowly and remarks, "Say, that boy's got something those farmers understand." Nothing could be truer.

On November 30, during the filming, a realistically staged mob scene involving the principals and many extras went awry leaving Gene with a wrenched shoulder, Smiley with a sprained left wrist and Colorado Hillbillies' fiddler Robert Hoag with a fractured right leg. As well, stuntman Fred Kennedy had his foot stomped on by a horse, Fred Burns wounded his arm in a buckboard wreck and bit player Bill Cowdry sustained a mashed foot as two horses jammed together. Forty of the bunched horses in some scenes were caught up in the riotous frenzy, stampeding into a residential area of Republic's backlot. When North Hollywood police failed to catch the horses, Republic's cowhands pitched in to corral them.

Champion's trailer, 50 feet long and 25 feet high, was wired with electricity to ward off strangers from opening a door or window when they shouldn't. The wiring resulted from an attempted theft of Gene's prized horse while on location filming "The Old Barn Dance".

Leading lady Helen Valkis, born July 15, 1911, changed her name briefly to Helen Hughes, then settled on Joan Valerie from late 1938 on. She'd made two westerns earlier in '37 opposite Dick Foran, but "The Old Barn Dance" was her last western. She became better known as a blonde sophisticate type in the early '40s. She left films in 1952 and died as the result of a broken back suffered in an auto accident in early 1983.

FILM COMMENTS: *Sammy McKim:* "My first meeting with Gene was on the Republic lot, shooting pictures of signing my contract (using Gene's back for publicity releases). He was a pleasant guy and wished me success in films. This was summer of 1937. Later that year, I had the juvenile lead with Gene and Smiley Burnette in 'The Old Barn Dance' and had a number of scenes with Gene, including one in which he rescued me from being trampled by a herd of cattle stampeding through town, catching me up on Champion just in time. Gene was an excellent rider. 'The Old Barn Dance' finished shooting just before Christmas. Republic made arrangements for Gene to lead the Hollywood Christmas Parade on Champion along with Smiley and me on horseback. Helen Valkis rode up on Santa's sleigh. I was on a frisky little gray and white pinto, who was a little hard to rein in. Somewhere along the parade route on the famous Hollywood Blvd., I heard Gene's voice, with a laugh 'Hey, Sammy—are you supposed to lead this parade?' I hadn't realized it, but I looked around to see Gene and Smiley some distance behind me! I was embarrassed—and got back into line!"[4]

Cal Shrum: "Gene Autry emphasized the use of popular radio bands in his films. (My brother) Walt and I took the band and headed for Hollywood with hopes of being in a Gene Autry movie.

"We thought all we had to do was walk into Republic Studios and they would put us in movies. Well, it didn't work out that way. They wouldn't even let us in the gate.

"After a few days in Hollywood, we were forced to return home due to a shortage of funds. Determined to be in movies, several months later we returned to Hollywood and once again returned home in defeat.

"Our whole group came to one decision, to give up the idea of being in movies. However, that decision changed in just a few weeks. We had just finished a performance at the Tower Theater in Kansas City. As we were backstage packing up, this gentleman walked in and said, 'I'm Sol Siegel, the producer of the Gene Autry movies, and I would like to have you boys in my next film.' I explained we had already been out there two times and couldn't get past the gate. He then wrote me a note and handed it to me saying, 'You won't have any problem now.'

"At the time we had about twenty dates booked; most

Gene and Smiley with Walt Shrum and his Colorado Hillbillies. Cal Shrum is directly behind Gene.

of them would be good paying jobs. Back then we worked on a percentage basis, and $100 a night for the whole band was considered good money. We made a gamble, but one I've never regretted. I had all our dates cancelled, and we left for Hollywood again, but this time for a screen test.

"This time we found the gateman at Republic more receptive. "We arrived at studio two where Gene Autry, Smiley Burnette and Mr. Siegel were summoned. Gene immediately sensed our nervousness and came over and started talking to us. Then he said, 'Boys, do me a song.' We did our best number, and before we finished Gene nodded his head to Mr. Siegel. A few minutes later Gene said, 'You boys will be in my next movie.'

"We signed a contract with Republic to appear in their next Gene Autry release, 'The Old Barn Dance'. The first few days were spent in the studio doing musical arrangements. We, as a group, got $75 for every original song contributed to a film. This was in addition to the $75 a week we each received as contract players.

"After all the music was completed, we were directed to the wardrobe department where we were outfitted, guns and all. Then the whole troop traveled 200 miles to Lone Pine to begin shooting the picture.

"Having been brought up on a ranch and practically 'raised in the saddle' proved beneficial to Walt and me. We were originally hired as musicians, but our riding ability put us in the spotlight with Gene and Smiley all through the film.

"Our script called for several big fights. The studio offered doubles but we said we'd do our own fighting. That was sure a mistake, one of our band suffered a broken ankle and another twisted his back.

"Republic (cast us again in another) Autry feature, 'Blue Montana Skies'. At this time (my brother) Walt and I went our separate ways. He kept the band and I went on forming a group called Cal Shrum and His Rhythm Rangers."[5]

CAST BIOS: Child star Sammy McKim was featured in two of Gene's films, "The Old Barn Dance" and "Rovin' Tumbleweeds". Born in North Vancouver, British Columbia, Canada, on December 24, 1924, Sammy was the second of five children. The family moved to first Seattle, then California in 1934. While Sammy and his grandfather were visiting a cousin who worked at MGM, a casting agent became impressed with Sam's All-American-boy look and he was soon in the movies with an unbilled role in "This Is the Life" ('35). Many westerns and serials at Republic and Columbia followed. Sammy's passion as a boy was art and, after service in WWII, he enrolled in art school. Called to duty in Korea, he continued his education

afterward and obtained a job in the art department at 20th Century–Fox. He soon joined the Walt Disney organization where he remained for 32 years as an illustrator/designer. Sam died of a heart attack July 9, 2004, near his home in Sunland, California.

WHAT THE EXHIBITOR HAD TO SAY: "The best Autry picture to date. Business plenty good when we play an Autry. Will click anywhere on a Friday-Saturday date."
—G. W. Barber, McCrory Theater, McCrory, AR (August 1938)

"There is a Santa Claus and I don't mean maybe. Played this with Laurel and Hardy comedy and they came in droves. Gene, I want to thank you from the bottom of my heart for the merriest Christmas I ever had, and look forward to playing every one of your pictures in 1939."
—A. G. Miller, Lyric Theater, Atkinson, NE (December 1938)

"Better than the average run of westerns. The best Autry that I have played to date, although parts of some were spoiled by a bad print. We small town exhibitors are always on the end of the stick and most prints are badly worn. However, can recommend this only on a double bill. I happen to be one of those fortunate not to run double bills and these features are really too short."
—A. L. Dove, Bengough Theater, Bengough, Sakatchewan, Canada (June 1939)

"I played this on a weekend double bill and it served perfectly. Business above average and it pleased all my customers."
—Charles A. Brooks, Ritz Theater, Marshfield, Missouri (February 1943)

"Have played all the Autry reissues to good business. This was no exception."
—A. E. Eliasen, Koronis Theater, Payneville, Minnesota (December 1943)

"A satisfactory western, but failed to draw as well as some of the other Autry reissues."
—A. B. Pierce, Crumpler Theater, Crumpler, West Virginia (March 1946)

SOURCES:
1. *Hollywood Citizen News.* March 19, 1938.
2. *Western Clippings #27.* January/February 1999. p. 31-32.
3. Autry with Herskowitz. p. 59-63.
4. *Western Clippings #27.* January/February 1999. p. 8.
5. Shrum, Cal. *Presenting Cal Shrum.* Self pub-lished, 1986. p. 4-6.

Gold Mine In the Sky
Republic, July 1938

Producer ....Charles E. Ford
Director ....Joe Kane
Assistant Director.......................Harry Knight
Original Story.............................Betty Burbridge
Screenplay ....Betty Burbridge, Jack
                    Natteford
Photography ....William Nobles
Film Editor ....Lester Orlebeck
Production Manager....................Al Wilson
Unit Manager ....Arthur Siteman
Musical Score.............................Alberto Columbo

SONGS: "Hummin' When We're Comin' 'Round the Bend" (music and lyrics by Al Columbo, Eddie Cherkose)—sung by Gene Autry, Smiley Burnette, Jack Kirk, Fred Toones, cowboys; "There's a Gold Mine In the Sky" (music and lyrics by Nick and Charles Kenny)—sung by Gene Autry and a cowboy chorus; "That's How Donkeys Were Born" (music and lyrics by Smiley Burnette, Eddie Cherkose)—sung by Smiley Burnette and Golden West Cowboys; "Spring Song" (music by Felix Mendelssohn, Public Domain)—performed by the Stafford Sisters; "Dude Ranch Cowhands" (music and lyrics by Gene Autry, Fred Rose, Johnny Marvin)—sung by Gene Autry, Smiley Burnette, Stafford Sisters, Golden West Cowboys; "I'd Love to Call You My Sweetheart" (music and lyrics by P. Ash, J. Goodwin, Larry Shay)—sung by Gene Autry; "Hike Yaa" (music and lyrics by Smiley Burnette)—sung by Smiley Burnette, Gene Autry and cowboys; "Tumbleweed Tenor" (music and lyrics by Smiley Burnette, Eddie Cherkose)—sung by Smiley Burnette and Golden West Cowboys; "As Long as I Have My Horse" (music and lyrics by Gene Autry, Fred Rose, Johnny Marvin)—sung by Gene Autry.

    RUNNING TIME: 60 minutes
    FILMING DATES: May 21 to June 9, 1938
    LOCATIONS: Jack Garner Ranch; Keen Camp; Republic backlot; Lake Hemet; Acton Railroad Depot
    BUDGET: $55,950
    NEGATIVE COST: $59,515

CAST:

Actor	Character
Gene Autry	Gene Autry
Smiley Burnette	Frog Millhouse
Carol Hughes	Cody Langham
J. L. Frank's Golden West Cowboys (Frank A. "Pee Wee" King, Daisy Rhodes, Everett "Abner" Sims, Oral Rhodes, C. E. "Jack" Skaggs, Milton Estes)	Cowhands/Musicians
Craig Reynolds.............................	Larry Cummings
Cupid (Helen) Ainsworth.............	Jane Crocker
LeRoy Mason...............................	Red Kuzak
Frankie Marvin.............................	Cowhand Joe
Robert Homans	"Lucky" Langham
Eddie Cherkose	Sykes
Ben Corbett	Spud Grogan, Jailbird
Milburn Morante	Mugsy Malone, Jailbird
Jim Corey	Henchman Chet
George Guhl.................................	Constable Cy Wheeler
Stafford Sisters............................	Themselves (Singers)
Al Taylor	Henchman Red
Charles King	Painter
John Beach...................................	Ranch Hand Al
Tommy Coats................................	Ranch Hand Buck
Art Dillard, Matty Roubert, Bob Woodward.........................	Cowhands
Earl Dwire....................................	Station Agent
Herman Hack, Joe Whitehead, Maston Williams.......................	Henchmen
Lew Kelly.....................................	Judge
Jack Kirk, Fred "Snowflake" Toones	Cooks
George Montgomery	Ranch Hand Tom
George Plues	Henchman Oscar
Maudie Prickett, Anita Sharp-Bolster..........................	Ranch Guests
Worth Crouch	Ranch Hand Hank
Bob Card......................................	Ranch Hand Slim
Joe Yrigoyen	Ranch Hand Pete

Roy Bucko ....Henchman Black Mike
Bud McClure..............................Henchman Rattlesnake
                                                          Pete
Harold A. Martin ....Carter
Brandon Beach............................Guest
Champion....................................Champion

STUNTS: Joe Yrigoyen, Nellie Walker, Jack Kirk (double for Smiley Burnette), Ken Cooper (double for Gene Autry).

THE FILM: With his initial post strike feature the full Gene Autry mythical west has arrived, packed with entertainment. All the blended elements of modern and old west, music, comedy and action are intermingled. Even his Martin guitar now says Gene Autry on it. With his hat brim pinned back, Smiley Burnette is totally in character with his checkered shirt, black string tie and woeful looking white horse, Nellie.

Directed by Joe Kane, "Gold Mine in the Sky" is an Autry favorite with its classic title song and another taming of the shrew plotline.

Young eastern girl Cody Langham (Carol Hughes) has been left a western ranch by her late father (Robert Homans) who, knowing his headstrong daughter, appoints ranch foreman Gene Autry as administrator of his will. Cody wants to marry unscrupulous Chicago playboy Larry Cummings (Craig Reynolds) and sell the ranch, but needs Gene's approval to do so. Gene sees through the phony Larry who, discovering the value of the ranch property, plots to get rid of Gene by sending to Chicago for racketeers led by Red Kuzak (LeRoy Mason). With Frog's help, Gene exposes Larry and brings Cody to her senses.

With "Gold Mine In the Sky", Gene's fans were ably compensated for their six month wait for Gene to return to the screen.

NOTES AND COMMENTS: This is the first Autry film in which we notice Smiley Burnette has painted a ring around his horse Nellie's left eye. It's just there; no mention is made of it. Gene recalled, "(That) horse would run every time he'd hear a bell or a whistle. He was an old fire horse. They had to have a horse that would definitely distinguish himself so they painted a ring around his eye. We just left it on every picture we made after that and he became really established with Smiley."[1] In later years at Columbia with Charles Starrett, Smiley called the horse Ringeye but at Republic the horse was referred to simply as Nellie or Black Eyed Nellie.

Heavyset comedienne Cupid (Helen) Ainsworth gave up acting by 1942 and became a famous actor's agent representing, among others, Guy Madison of TV's "Wild Bill Hickok" fame.

Columnist Walter Winchell is mentioned in the dialogue of "Gold Mine in the Sky" placing the time-frame of the film firmly in the late '30s.

An age old slapstick gag of a man painting a building and being continually splashed with mud by cars continually racing by is used very effectively here due to the comedy talents of actor Charlie King (who usually played heavies on screen).

The final fight scene with Craig Reynolds took over three hours to film. During either this, or another fight scene, on May 31 Gene suffered several deep cuts to both knees. When the wounds became aggravated and infected Gene was laid up for five days while the company shot around him.

The Golden West Cowboys were paid $250 a week. Also earning that amount were Robert Homans and LeRoy Mason. The Stafford Sisters received $350 as did Cupid (Helen) Ainsworth.

FILM COMMENTS: *Pee Wee King:* "I believe I was the first Opry performer to make a movie, and I made four of them. The first one was Gene Autry's 'Gold Mine In the Sky'. Before Gene left Louisville in 1934 for Hollywood, he said to me, 'By God, if I make it out there, you're going to be with me. We'll make a movie together. By (1938) we were hotter than a pistol at the Grand Ole Opry and were attracting big audiences wherever we played.

"On Friday, May 13, 1938, the Golden West Cowboys and I were getting ready to start our road show at the high school auditorium in New Hope, Alabama. As usual, we were a little anxious, but on this particular evening we were more

Telegrams often bring good news — but not this one for Gene and Smiley. Peeking over the saddle is future star George Montgomery, just getting his feet wet in the movie business in several of Gene's films.

nervous than ever. We had been waiting all day for a call from Hollywood telling us whether we had been invited to appear in Gene's movie, 'Gold Mine In the Sky'. Just before we went on stage, the telephone switchboard operator burst into the auditorium out of breath, saying, 'Mr. King, Gene Autry is waiting to talk with you on the telephone.' I asked the band to cover for me until I got back. Fifteen minutes later I returned and announced to the boys and the audience, 'Gene Autry wants us to come to Hollywood and make a movie with him, and he wants us there by Wednesday.' The band was so excited and hyped up, I think we gave the best concert of our career that night. After the show, we hurried back to Nashville to prepare for our trip.

"We all went in two cars, packed like sardines. We drove straight through in our four-door Chevys, stopping only to eat and gas up and switch drivers.

"We arrived exhausted but safe and excited. We didn't have much time to rest because we had to report to the studio right away. The musical director sketched out the songs we were going to play in the movie. Smiley Burnette came in and said, 'I'll answer any questions you have when you come over to my house.' I said, 'Oh, are we coming over to your house?' He said, 'Yes, we'll rehearse the songs for the movie, and we're having a steak and salad cookout tonight to welcome you. I make the best Caesar salad in Hollywood.' And I believe he did. What a place he had! I'd never seen a house like that—fifteen closets full of clothes. He and his wife Dallas were wonderful to us. After dinner we rehearsed the songs that he and Gene had written for the movie.

"We were in California for about four weeks, and what a thrill it was. (We) went out to film the exterior shots for the movie in studio buses and got settled in cabins which were our quarters while we were on location. We spent some time rehearsing and some time in front of the cameras, but mostly we spent time waiting. We were able to spend a little time horseback riding in the mountains. We were in a lot of the scenes, but didn't have much to say because we were usually playing music.

"Most of the Golden West Cowboys were very inexperienced with horses, and we needed to improve our riding skills. One time all of us were mounted when the (assistant) director came over and said, 'Hold it. I want Pee Wee's band to dismount and stand over there. You are being paid to act and make music, not to ride horses. If you get hurt on the horses, it will cost us money.' We said, 'We want to ride the horses.' He said, 'You want to risk getting hurt and delaying production, costing us money?' We said again, 'We want to ride the horses.' So we learned to ride horses, some of us better than others.

"Only two horses got hurt, and that was the fault of the cowboy riders. In one place the horses reared back and threw the riders when they balked at a rattlesnake nest. The horses ran on through the bushes and got skinned up a bit, but nobody in the cast or crew got snake bit.

"Gene wanted to do his own stunts, but he knew what he was doing. He was an excellent horseman. He did his own riding and took his own falls and did his own fighting. He loved the fight scenes and got a big kick out of all the action. Gene did have one accident while we were shooting the movie, part of a fight scene. He was supposed to jump off his horse onto another guy and they would tumble down a hill. (The assistant director) wanted the stuntman to take the fall, but Gene insisted he wanted to do it himself. When he was jumping out of his stirrups, he got his legs crossed and fell to the ground on his knees. He had to be taken to the hospital in Hollywood and didn't get back for two days. While he was gone, we shot around his scenes, which was hard to do, since he was in most of the movie.

"All the guys that worked for Gene just loved him. They worshipped him. Smiley told me that once he was working with Gene on a movie right before Christmas, and the producer decided to stop production for a couple of weeks. It bothered Gene that the actors and crew wouldn't have paychecks just before Christmas, so he turned a piece of his bad luck into their good fortune. Gene got his knees injured in a fight scene and had to spend a week recovering, but he made sure everyone got paid for the time he was laid up. That's the kind of guy he was.

"I've always tried to learn from people who know more than I do about things. For example, Smiley had been in a number of movies already and he knew the ropes. He taught me how to make sure I got included in the scenes and wound up on the screen. 'Stay close to Gene,' he advised me. I wanted to make sure my face was on the screen, not on the cutting room floor. Every time I saw a camera come on, I

While filming "Gold Mine in the Sky," Gene and J. L. Frank's Golden West Cowboys appeared on Eddie Cantor's radio show. Daisy Rhodes and Pee Wee King are directly behind Gene.

put on my best stage smile and edged toward Gene. While we were shooting the first scene inside the dance hall, Gene walked on the set and saw me standing there with my white cowboy suit on. He said, 'Kid, who told you to wear a white suit?' I said, 'Nobody. This is all I brought. We came here directly from the Opry.' He said, 'I know you wear it on the stage at the Opry, but I'm the only one who wears a white suit in my movies. Now you get on up to the costume wagon and get another suit.' I said, 'But Gene, that's way up the hill, and I'll never make it back in time to shoot this scene. Anyway, I'll bet they don't have a suit in my size.' Gene said, 'Okay, we'll figure out something. You go over there to the piano and make believe you're playing.' So I went over that way, but I watched where Gene and the leading lady would be coming to, and I shifted toward that spot. It took some fancy footwork and twisting around, but I did it. Later, when I led the band, I got Gene to come over to where we were. I said, 'Gene, with all this noise I can't hear you from over there. Come over here so I can hear your cues.' That's what he did, and that's why I'm in so many of the scenes.

"The accordion I took to Hollywood was a new thousand dollar instrument with rhinestones all over it that spelled out my name. In one scene where I'm supposed to be riding on the stagecoach, Smiley said, 'Kid, you want to be seen, so we'll put you up there on top next to the driver.' The driver was Joe Yrigoyen, who was also one of Gene's doubles. As I was climbing up, the director saw me and said, 'No, we can't let you get up there. It's too dangerous. You might fall off.' I pleaded with him and finally Smiley said, 'Oh, once we get him up there, he won't fall off. We can boost him up, then haul up his accordion and put it in his lap, then strap him to the seat. He'll bounce around, but he won't fall off.' So with the help of a young extra named George Montgomery, they hoisted me up and strapped me in with my accordion.

"The scene went off without a hitch, and there I am on top of the stagecoach as it's coming around a hill, playing 'She'll Be Comin' 'Round the Mountain' on my accordion. Actually, I'm pretending to play the song because, of course, we recorded the actual music for the sound track later in the studio.

"The girls weren't allowed to wear wristwatches, rings, or any kind of jewelry, and there I am on top of the stagecoach with my rhinestone accordion glittering in the sun. It was a lot of fun, but I'm sure no real westerner ever had an accordion like that.

"We had to be up and ready for makeup by five o'clock every morning. Then we'd sit around and wait for our scenes to come up. Sometimes they'd ring the dinner bell and we hadn't done one thing. We'd get off under a tree or tent and talk or play cards.

"Frankie Marvin, who was Gene's steel guitar player and right-hand man, was also a prankster. One day our cook, a big, heavyset black fellow, called out, 'Come and get it.' At the same time Frankie came running down to the chow wagon holding up something long and snakelike,

hollering, 'There's a snake over there by the chuckwagon.' The cook lit out running, then saw that Frankie was holding a rubber hose, and said, 'Don't you ever do that trick again. If I had stumbled into that hot tub of water over there, I'd be boiled by now.' On location, we generally had sandwiches for lunch, but for dinner we'd have steaks or pork chops or chicken and delicious hot homemade bread.

"When 'Gold Mine In the Sky' opened in Nashville, at a first-run theater, we played a concert in connection with it. Gene was a smart businessman and knew how to squeeze the most money from a movie. He chose popular bands like ours from large cities to be in his movies, and he named movies after popular songs—such as 'Gold Mine In the Sky' and 'South of the Border'. But his best formula for success was this, as he said: 'Surround yourself with good, talented, hard-working people, and you're bound to be successful.' Gene loved to make money, but he loved the work he did to make it."[2]

Gene Autry (regarding the presence of strong-willed women in his films): "That may have been due, in no small part, to the presence of such screenwriters as Betty Burbridge, Luci Ward, and Connie Lee. We didn't exactly use them because they were experts on the west. Whatever their formula, those films were about the only ones in the B-western category, up to then, that had a mass appeal to women.

"The touch of Betty Burbridge was evident again on 'Gold Mine In the Sky', my first movie after my strike against Republic had ended. For the third time in less than a year, the plot had me riding herd on a spoiled heiress. That was a favorite of Betty's, who had already milked it pretty good back in the silent film days.[3]

"There was fun on that picture. There was about four or five girls that worked at the ranch (The Stafford Sisters). They had a cabin where all these girls stayed. One night LeRoy Mason, Kenny Cooper and Frankie Marvin went up there and they took some kind of cheese that smelled awful. They put it all in the bed, bed sheets and pillowcases. The girls went back there and said something's wrong. They all came back down to the main dining room and called me over. They said, 'Gene, we can't stay in that place…Smells like a skunk is in there or something. We can't stand that smell.' Everybody started laughing. When I found out what it was, they had to transfer those girls to another cabin. (Laughs) So, sometimes it was hard work but we had a lot of fun too." [4]

CAST BIOS: Frank "Pee Wee" King co-wrote with Redd Stewart "The Tennessee Waltz" in 1947. He also helped introduce several instruments to the Grand Ole Opry.

Born February 18, 1914, of Polish-German heritage, he grew up in the polka and waltz culture of Wisconsin, changing his name from Kuczynski to King. He first played accordion at 15 and later formed Frankie King and the King's Jesters. Gene first used Pee Wee as a fill-in musician on a midwestern fair in late 1932. Pee Wee stayed with Gene on "The National Barn Dance" and "Conqueror Record Time" for about two months before returning home to re-form his own band. King rejoined Gene's organization for about eight months in 1934 when Gene was working out of Louisville, Kentucky. When Gene left for California, King started his own band once again, re-naming it Pee Wee King and His Golden West Cowboys. By 1936 he was performing on WNOX (Knoxville, Tennessee) radio then moved to Nashville for a ten year run on the Grand Ole Opry.

Of the over 400 songs he wrote, his biggest hits were "Slow Poke", "You Belong to Me", "Bonaparte's Retreat", "Changing Partners" and "Tennessee Waltz".

In 1970 Pee Wee was inducted into the Songwriters' Hall of Fame and in 1974 he became the 23rd member of the Country Music Hall of Fame.

Pee Wee suffered several strokes and died March 7, 2000, in Louisville, Kentucky.

"Gold Mine In the Sky" was the first of three features Carol Hughes made with Gene Autry. It would have been four had Gene not gone on strike allowing Roy Rogers to star in "Under Western Stars" ('38) in which Carol was the leading lady.

Carol was in Gene's next film, "Man From Music Mountain" as well as "Under Fiesta Stars" in 1941.

Best known for replacing actress Jean Rogers as Dale Arden in the third and last of Universal's "Flash Gordon" serials in 1940, she had begun in "George White's 1935 Scandals".

Married to actor Frank Faylen in 1936 until his death in 1985, she continued to work into the mid '50s.

The mother of actress Carol Faylen, Carol was the former mother-in-law of talkshow host Regis Philbin.

At 85, she died August 8, 1995.

Lyricist, comedy writer and part-time actor Eddie Cherkose was born May 25, 1912, in Detroit, Michigan.

Coming to Hollywood writing comedy for radio, by 1937 he was steadily employed writing music and lyrics at Republic.

For "Gold Mine In the Sky" he had an acting role and helped write three of the songs. He went on to write songs for several other Autry pictures.

During his career he contributed songs to some 50 pictures and wrote gags for Abbott and Costello, Olsen and Johnson, Spike Jones, the Ritz Brothers and Charlie McCarthy.

He died at 87 April 21, 1999, of natural causes in Studio City, California.

WHAT THE EXHIBITOR HAD TO SAY:
"Another good picture from Republic, the Reliable. To us Burnette is the whole show. An excellent Autry that drew only average."
—A. J. Inks, Crystal Theater, Ligonier, Indiana (February 1939)

"Better than average western and Burnette is at least half the show."
—Sam Kimball, Cornish Theater, Cornish, Maine (May 1939)

SOURCES:
1. "Melody Ranch Theater" showing of "The Singing Hill" on the Nashville Network, 1987.
2. Hall, Wade. *Hell Bent for Music.* University Press of Kentucky. 1996. p. 190-197.
3. Autry with Herskowitz. p. 66.
4. "Melody Ranch Theater" showing of "Gold Mine In the Sky" on Nashville Network, 1987.

Eastern girl Carol Hughes is none too happy that the foreman of her ranch, Gene Autry, has been made executor of her late father's estate — especially when, in their first meeting, Gene has to bail her out of jail for hitting a pig with her car. The fellow jailbirds are familiar character players Ben Corbett and Milburn Morante while the jailer/ judge is Lew Kelly.

Man From Music Mountain
Republic, August 1938

Producer	Charles E. Ford
Director	Joe Kane
Original Story	Bernard McConville
Screenplay	Betty Burbridge, Luci Ward
Photography	Jack Marta
Film Editor	Lester Orlebeck
Production Manager	Al Wilson
Unit Manager	Arthur Siteman

SONGS: "Little Deserted Town" (music and lyrics by Gene Autry, Johnny Marvin, Fred Rose)—sung by Gene Autry; "Man From Music Mountain" (music and lyrics by Eddie Cherkose, Peter Tinturn, Jack Lawrence)—sung by Gene Autry, Smiley Burnette and cowboys; "Love, Burning Love" (music and lyrics by Gene Autry, Johnny Marvin, Fred Rose)—sung by Smiley Burnette, Frankie Marvin, Rudy Sooter, Gene Autry; "All Nice People" (music and lyrics by Smiley Burnette)—sung by Smiley Burnette with Polly Jenkins and her Plowboys; "I'm Beginning to Care" (music and lyrics by Gene Autry, Johnny Marvin, Fred Rose)—sung by Gene Autry; "She Works Third Tub at the Laundry" (music and lyrics by Smiley Burnette)—sung by Smiley Burnette and Sally Payne; "Goodbye Pinto" (music and lyrics by Gene Autry, Johnny Marvin, Fred Rose)—sung by Gene Autry with Polly Jenkins and her Plowboys.

RUNNING TIME: 58 minutes
FILMING DATES: June 28 to July 8, 1938
LOCATIONS: Iverson's; Jauregui Ranch; Republic backlot
BUDGET: $48,008
NEGATIVE COST: $54,814

CAST:

Actor	Character
Gene Autry	Gene Autry
Smiley Burnette	Frog Millhouse
Carol Hughes	Helen Foster
Sally Payne	Patsy
Ivan Miller	John Scanlon
Ed Cassidy	William Brady
Lew Kelly	Bowdie Bill
Howard Chase	Abbott
Albert Terry	Buddy Harmon
Frankie Marvin	Larry
Earl Dwire	Lew Martin
Lloyd Ingraham	George Harmon
Lillian Drew	Mirandy Higgins
Al Taylor	Henchman Hank
Joe Yrigoyen	Henchman Pete
Polly Jenkins and Her Plowboys	Themselves
Chris Allen	Chris Blake
Chuck Baldra	Autry cowhand-musician
Horace B. Carpenter	Land buyer
Eddie Cherkose	Musician
Dick Elliott	Harkness
Oscar Gahan	Saloon fiddle player
Ruth Gillette	Fatima
Gordon Hart	Madame Fatima's confederate Tom
Earle Hodgins	Madame Fatima's pitchman
Cactus Mack	Autry cowhand-musician
Bud McClure	Deputy
Merrill McCormick	Tex
Fred Parker, Tex Phelps	Townsmen
Hal Price	Quartzville Bartender
Lee Shumway	Sheriff
Rudy Sooter	Ranch hand Steve
Henry Isabel	Joe
Edward Hart	Bus Driver
James Lucas	Stooge
Walter Murray	Judge Bronson
Willa Pearl Curtis	Lady
Jack Kirk, Jack Lafever	Ranch hands
Champion	Champion

STUNTS: Ken Cooper (double for Gene), Jack Kirk (double for Smiley), Joe Yrigoyen.

THE FILM: "Man From Music Mountain" is the last Autry film to be directed by the talented Joe Kane before

Republic moved him over to helm the Roy Rogers series.

The modern aspects of the story almost overpower the western elements at times, although Kane manages to get things back on track with some wild windup action.

An abundance of music somewhat reduces the amount of action, and many feel some of Gene's later '30s films were "overcrowded" with novelty numbers, often from Smiley Burnette—but also Gene. Mind you, in this one, with a group like Polly and her Plowboys, you can expect some oddities. Gene was ill-served by many of the musical groups Republic gave him at this period, different every film and mostly forgettable. However, Gene and Smiley managed to push them to the background in most cases, but it might have been better if Gene had been given a good, solid, steady singing group to back him, as did the Cass County Boys during Gene's Columbia days.

Excellent plot, diverging far from the beaten formula path, has the Western Development Company, run underhandedly by John Scanlon (Ivan Miller) and William Brady (Ed Cassidy), inducing ranchers to convert their assets into cash to buy sites in Gold River, long deserted by the miners, promising them electricity is coming when Boulder Dam opens. Shares in the played-out Betsy Lee Mine are offered as extra bait. The swindlers plan a clean-up and quick exit but Gene Autry out schemes the schemers.

"Man From Music Mountain" takes its place as one of Gene's most entertaining westerns to this point.

NOTES AND COMMENTS: Lynne Roberts was originally scheduled to be Gene's leading lady in "Man From Music Mountain" but was replaced by Carol Hughes in the role of Helen because Roberts had not completed her work in Republic's "Dick Tracy Returns" serial ('38).

Ten year old Albert Terry plays Buddy. His pinto pony, Half Pint, valued at $100, was included in Terry's $75 a week salary. Polly Jenkins and her Plowboys earned $250 a week with a three week guarantee. Carol Hughes was signed at $500 a week on a two week guarantee. Sally Payne drew $150 a week; Ivan Miller earned $257.10 a week; Ed Cassidy $100 a week; Lloyd Ingraham $175 a week; Earl Dwire $125 a week; and Gene's stuntman Kenny Cooper was now up to $300 a week.

In 1943 Joe Kane directed another Republic western also entitled "The Man From Music Mountain" with Roy Rogers. Its plot is entirely different. To avoid confusion when both films were released to television, the Rogers film was retitled "Texas Legionnaires".

Polly Jenkins and Her Plowboys were stars on WKTV-TV, Utica, New York. The musically accomplished Jenkins played piano, organ, vibraphone, accordion and xylophone.

FILM COMMENTS: *Screenwriter Betty Burbridge:* "I'd say Gene's chief charm was that little-boy quality— and the way his eyes never leave the face of the person to whom he's speaking. Then, too, I think his love of color in his riding clothes is another indication of this boyishness. He loves gay colors, so he wears 'em."[1]

Albert Terry is a young orphan left in Gene's care while pretty Carol Hughes is the town's hairdresser Gene is trying to help.

116

CAST BIOS: Originally known as the "Sunshine Girl" of artist's models, perky, tomboyish Sally Payne came to Hollywood and made her debut in a 1934 MGM short subject. Starting at Republic in 1936, she made two with Gene, "The Big Show" and "Man From Music Mountain" before becoming a staple in Roy Rogers' westerns as of 1940. Gale Storm, who was in two with Sally and Roy, found her "a lovely person and very professional."[2]

After a divorce from radio gag writer William Telaak in 1941 and marriage to Western Airlines Chairman Arthur F. Kelly in 1942, Sally left the screen, returning only briefly to appear in three early '50s "Kit Carson" TV episodes.

Kelly merged Western with Delta and became a top executive with that airline until his retirement.

Turning to art, Sally painted oils and illustrated a series of SMALL STAR STORY children's books. For years, Sally owned the Bookworm bookstore in Brentwood, California.

She died May 8, 1999, of a massive stroke at her Bel-Air, California, home.

WHAT THE EXHIBITOR HAD TO SAY: "A great Saturday picture that stood them in the aisles. Business about double average Saturday. Smiley Burnette turns in his most comical performance. In the future I'm going to play all Autry's on Tuesday-Wednesday dates. Just let your patrons know Autry is going to play and they'll do the rest. Don't forget, fellows, this is the kind of picture that makes the cashier think she's playing a piano instead of punching a ticket machine." —Sam Schlwetz, Rialto Theater, Three Rivers, Texas (January 1939)

"A good drawing picture that has nothing to recommend it but the pulling power of Autry." —A. J. Inks, Crystal Theater, Ligonier, Indiana (January 1939)

"Definitely not as good a picture as 'The Old Barn Dance'. We had several walkouts on it. Gene Autry alone won't be enough for our patrons. He needs story and casting support. They nearly forgot to include the talented troupe, Polly Jenkins and Her Plowboys, after giving them billing. They are good and could have helped entertain if they'd been given any footage at all. The way this story worked out, so far as we can see, all concerned would have been just as

Gene and Champion, Sally Payne and Carol Hughes.

well off if Autry had kept out of their town. True, the crooks sold them a supposedly worked-out mine but after all was said and done 'thar still was gold in them thar hills.'" —L. A. Irwin, Palace Theater, Penacook, New Hampshire (February 1939)

"Plenty kicks. Kids all ask when's amateur night again. My patrons boo these shows. One woman came out and asked why Smiley Burnette didn't change shirts once in a while in the picture. His shirt was wet from sweat. Used on double feature. No business." —Ray S. Hanson, Fox Theater, Fertile, Minnesota (March 1939)

"Good entertainment but only for double bills. What a good producer could do with this star if he was in feature length productions. My patrons enjoy the singing of this star, also the orchestra; the little lady playing the bells was a big hit but not enough of her playing to suit my crowd." —A. L. Dove, Bengough Theater, Bengough, Saskatchewan, Canada (September 1939)

"I can always depend on Autry to keep my patrons smiling and to keep my business going. This is as great as the newest one he made in 1942. Lots of good songs by Autry and Frog." —Nick Raspa, State Theater, Lowington, North Carolina (December 1945)

SOURCES:
1. *Autry's Aces.* December 1952-Feb. 1953. p. 14.
2. Interview with author. 1999.

Prairie Moon
Republic, October 1938

Producer ....Harry Grey
Director ....Ralph Staub
Assistant Director.........................Tommy Flood
Screenplay....................................Betty Burbridge,
         Stanley Roberts
Photography ....William Nobles
Film Editor..................................Lester Orlebeck
Musical Director ....Raoul Kraushaar
Production Manager.....................Al Wilson

SONGS: "Rhythm of the Hoofbeats" (music and lyrics by Gene Autry, Johnny Marvin, Fred Rose)—sung by Gene Autry, Smiley Burnette, cowboys; "The Girl In the Middle of My Heart" (music and lyrics by Eddie Cherkose, Walter Kent)—sung by Gene Autry; "In the Jailhouse Now" (music and lyrics by Jimmie Rodgers)—sung by Gene Autry, Smiley Burnette; "Welcome Song" (music and lyrics by Eddie Cherkose, Walter Kent)—sung by the schoolchildren; "The West, a Nest and You" (music and lyrics by Leroy

Yoell, Billy Hill)—sung by Gene Autry and barn dance audience; "Story of Trigger Joe" (music and lyrics by Eddie Cherkose, Walter Kent)—sung by Smiley Burnette.

RUNNING TIME: 58 minutes

FILMING DATES: August 25 to September 6, 1938

LOCATIONS: Brandeis Ranch; Iverson Ranch; Republic backlot

BUDGET: $49,992

NEGATIVE COST: $60,185

CAST:

Actor	Character
Gene Autry	Gene Autry
Smiley Burnette	Frog Millhouse
Shirley Deane	Peggy Shaw
Tommy Ryan	Willie "Brains" Barton
Walter Tetley	Hector "Nails" Barton
David Gorcey	Clarence "Slick" Barton
Stanley Andrews	Frank Welch
William Pawley	Jim "Legs" Barton
Warner Richmond	Mullins
Ray Bennett	Hartley
Tom London	Henchman Steve
Bud Osborne	Henchman Pete
Jack Rockwell	Sheriff
Peter Potter	Bandleader
Art Baker	Judge Dean
Buster (Brad) Slaven	Mortimer Larkin
Fred Burns	Townsman
Bob Card	Bass player
Tommy Coats, Curley Dresden, Al Taylor, Chuck Baldra, George Plues	Rustlers
Jim Corey	Posse rider
Jack Kirk	Man outside Sheriff's Office
Frankie Marvin	Autry cowhand; Stooge in whip act
Merrill McCormick	Henchman Saunders
Mira McKinney	Mrs. Higgins
Lew Meehan	Henchman Jake
James C. Morton	Man on stoop in Chicago
Hal Price	Police captain
Dan Thompson	Himself (whip act)
Dan White	Henchman Joe
N. E. Hendrix, Forrest Burns, Roy Bucko, Jack Montgomery, Harry Willingham, Fenton "Duke" Taylor, Cecil Kellogg	Riders
Guy Willis	Captain Gilroy
William Cody	Dan Thompson
Max Marx	Henchman Regan
Alice Thurston	Mrs. Welch
Rudy Sooter	Guitar player
Champion	Champion

Gene and Smiley agree, they have their hands full with these tough Chicago kids — David Gorcey, Tommy Ryan and Walter Tetley.

STUNTS: Ken Cooper (Gene's double); Jack Kirk (Smiley's double); Fritz Johanet (Tommy Ryan's double); William E. Gaffney (Walter Tetley's double); Robert J. Folkerson (David Gorcey's double); Tommy Coats, Duke Taylor, Joe Yrigoyen.

THE FILM: New Autry producer Harry Grey and new director Ralph Staub turned out what might be termed "The Dead End Kids Out West". Obviously inspired by Warner Bros.' success with "Dead End" ('37), Gene straightens out three tough Chicago kids—one of them even played by original Dead End Kid Leo Gorcey's brother, David Gorcey.

Deputy Sheriff Autry agrees to take care of the ornery three sons of an old friend, Jim Barton (William Pawley), who turns out to be the head of a gang of rustlers, when he is shot and killed avoiding capture. The boys are not the least bit impressed with ranch life and make things miserable for Gene's sweetheart and school teacher Peggy Shaw (Shirley Deane).

Cattle rustler Frank Welch (Stanley Andrews) covertly wins the young hoodlums regard, promising to let them into his gang while secretly planning to adopt the boys, thereby gaining control of the Barton ranch to carry on his rustling activities.

Despite the fact the boys resent Gene as a "flatfoot", they finally wake up to the brutal Welch and appreciate Gene as a guardian.

NOTES AND COMMENTS: Republic's "Lone Ranger" serial, also released in 1938, is referred to by the kids.

The role of Judge Dean is played by Art Baker who became famous with his "You Asked for It" TV show in the '50s.

Director Ralph Staub was paid $1,250 to direct the picture. Leading lady Shirley Deane earned $400 a week;

Stanley Andrews made $450; Warner Richmond $175; William Pawley $350 and both Walter Tetley and David Gorcey received $200 a week. It's assumed Tommy Ryan, a slightly bigger name at the time, made a bit more but production files were incomplete on his salary.

Pre-production title was "Pony Boy".

Gene's parade mount, Texas, died of undisclosed causes September 8, 1938. Gene had been grooming him to replace Champion when the time came to retire Champ.

CAST BIOS: Esteemed French born composer and splendid musical director Raoul Kraushaar worked on over 30 Gene Autry westerns. Born in France in 1908, the son of an orchestra musician, Kraushaar lived with his aunt after his mother died, and as a teenager stowed away on a ship bound for New York. In 1926 he studied musical arranging at Columbia University and in the '30s moved to Los Angeles

Raoul Kraushaar.

to launch his career at Republic as an assistant to music department head Cy Feuer. "Instated as Feuer's right hand man," writes Jack Mathis in REPUBLIC CONFIDENTIAL, "Kraushaar mainly acted as administrative assistant while doing some composing, conducting, orchestrating and hiring of musicians for recording sessions."[1] Both Feuer and Kraushaar joined the armed forces for WWII in mid 1942. Afterward, Raoul only worked on two Sunset Carson Bs at Republic before moving on to other films, including a long stint at Monogram/Allied Artists. He later wrote wonderful theme music for "Hopalong Cassidy", "Lassie", "The Fugitive" and "The Untouchables" TV shows and was musical director on "Bonanza". He provided music for cartoons such as "Yogi Bear" and "Huckleberry Hound" and even did music for Nintendo games at Moby Games as late as 1988.

At 93, Kraushaar died October 13, 2001, in Pompano Beach, Florida.

WHAT THE EXHIBITOR HAD TO SAY: "The usual offering for this team and that means tops. We liked it and so did all the fans. It has action, music, romance and comedy. We doubled this with 'The Night Hawk' and it brought us the largest gross in years. We not only stood

them up but had to turn many away. Thanks to you, Gene, and a salute to you, Smiley."

—R. V. Rule, Gym Theater, Beverton, Michigan (January 1939)

"Just lately we have noticed the last Autry pictures not doing so good as six months ago. This may be due to weather conditions for they still have plenty of boxoffice left."

—Harland Rankin, Plaza Theater, Tilbury, Ontario, Canada (February 1939)

"Another not up to the standards of this series. Autry's pictures used to be our best boxoffice bets but lately they have fallen off considerably. Patrons complain they are all the same basic formula. Without Smiley Burnette, I'm afraid they would not be the pictures they are."

—M. R. Harrington, Avalon Theater, Clatskanie, Oregon (February 1939)

"An Autry that was no better or worse than his previous attempts. His pictures are all the same but still he draws them, so why comment. We feel that Smiley is 90% of the shows and Autry gets the credit. An excellent combination."

—A. J. Inks, Crystal Theater, Ligonier, Indiana (February 1939)

"After hearing about the drawing knockouts (of Gene Autry), my patrons have never given him a very big tumble. Plenty of good singing and some action but so far as we are concerned he is just another western star with a price on his pictures." —Mayme P. Musselman, Princess Theater, Lincoln, Kansas (April 1939)

"Gene very good as usual and pleased. Cannot see where this star will outdraw Dick Foran or Buck Jones."

—George Khattar, Casino Theater, Whitney Pier, Sydney, Nova Scotia, Canada (August 1939)

"Dear Gene, this is a good western, but you're getting too modern." —C. H. Collier, Globe Theater, Drew, Mississippi (September 1939)

SOURCES:

1. Mathis, Jack. *Republic Confidential.* Mathis Advertising. 1999. p. 239.

120

Rhythm of the Saddle
Republic, November 1938

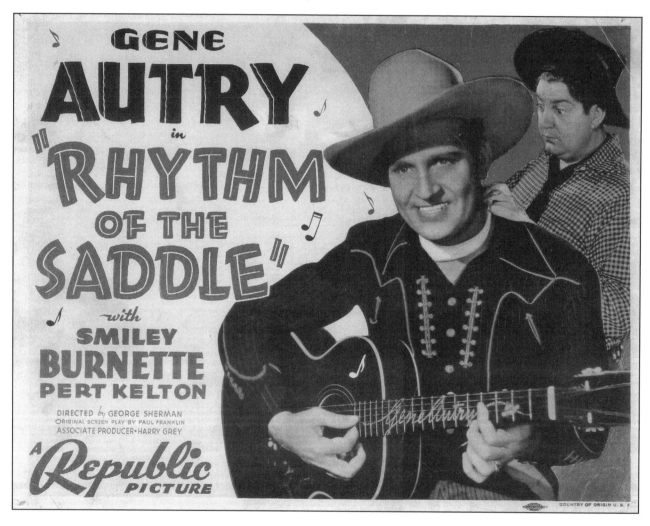

Producer ....Harry Grey
Director ....George Sherman
Assistant Director.........................William O'Connor
Screenplay....................................Paul Franklin
Photography ....Jack Marta
Film Editor ....Lester Orlebeck
Musical Director ....Raoul Kraushaar
Production Manager...................Al Wilson

SONGS: "Merry-Go-Roundup" (music and lyrics by

Gene Autry, Fred Rose, Johnny Marvin)—sung by Gene Autry; "Oh, Ladies" (music and lyrics by Gene Autry, Fred Rose, Johnny Marvin)—sung by Gene Autry, Smiley Burnette; "When Mother Nature Sings Her Lullaby" (music and lyrics by Larry Yoell, Glen J. Brown)—sung by Gene Autry with Virginia Dabney and anonymous girl singers; "The Old Trail" (music and lyrics by Gene Autry, Fred Rose, Johnny Marvin)—sung by Gene Autry, Smiley Burnette and cowboys; "Let Me Call You Sweetheart" (music and lyrics by Beth Slater Whitson, Leo Friedman)—sung by Gene

Autry, Smiley Burnette.

RUNNING TIME: 58 minutes

FILMING DATES: September 23 to October 4, 1938

LOCATIONS: Iverson Ranch; Republic backlot

BUDGET: $50,513

NEGATIVE COST: $53,920

CAST:

Actor	Character
Gene Autry	Gene Autry
Smiley Burnette	Frog Millhouse
Pert Kelton	Aunt Hattie
Peggy Moran	Maureen McClure
LeRoy Mason	Jack Pomeroy
Arthur Loft	Clyde Chase
Ethan Laidlaw	Tex Robinson
Walter DePalma	Henchman Leach
Archie Hall	Henchman Rusty
Eddie Hart	Alec
Eddie Acuff	Dixie Erwin
William Bailey	Rancher at race
Al Taylor	Henchman Shorty
Chuck Baldra, Jack Kenny	Henchmen
Roy Bucko	Stage race Judge
John Beach	Ranch Hand
Fred Burns	Rancher
Bob Card	Man at meeting
Horace B. Carpenter	2nd Rodeo Judge
Curley Dresden	Stage race Judge
Lester Sharpe	Doctor
Jack Kirk	Sheriff Williams
Tom London	Red Malone
Jim Mason	Henchman
Art Mix, Francis Walker	Rodeo Hands
Montie Montana	Rodeo Trick Rider (stock footage)
Fred Parker	1st Rodeo Judge
Carl Stockdale	Rodeo Spectator
Emmett Vogan	Rodeo Announcer
Art Wenzel, Rudy Sooter	Musicians
Roger Williams	Race Official
Douglas Wright	Announcer
Joe Yrigoyen	3rd Stagecoach Driver
Fenton "Duke" Taylor, Art Dillard, Oscar Gahan, Frankie Marvin, Carl Cotner	Gene's Riders
Beatrice Brenner	Connie, cigarette girl
Virginia Dabney	Mistress of Ceremonies
Douglas Wright and Company	Horse act
Bud Pope, Bob Wilke, Leonard Penn	Extras
Champion	Champion

STUNTS: Ken Cooper (Gene's double); Jack Kirk

Gene's in a confrontation with gambling house owner LeRoy Mason who's been operating a crooked roulette wheel, cheating Peggy Moran (standing) and her aunt, Pert Kelton.

(Smiley's double); Bill Yrigoyen, Joe Yrigoyen.

THE FILM: "Rhythm of the Saddle" is a rather tepid affair, a mixture of rodeos and nightclubs with no standout songs. However, a thrill-packed stagecoach race pitting Gene against the bad guys climaxes the picture. This type of race was a big favorite with Republic producers and was often featured—many times intercut with stock shots from such sequences in other Republic westerns.

Gene Autry is foreman of a ranch owned by Maureen McClure (Peggy Moran) on which is being held the annual Frontier Week rodeo celebration. Gambler Jack Pomeroy (LeRoy Mason) and his crowd, owning a rival ranch, are anxious to get the contract for next year's rodeo. Pomeroy stages a series of "accidents" to make the current event a failure. While the big stagecoach race to determine who is awarded the next year's contract is being run, Frog Millhouse (Smiley Burnette) operates a device to get a secret recording of a conversation between the crooks which eventually trips them up.

NOTES AND COMMENTS: Setting this film clearly in 1938, Gene makes an offhand remark about television—still very early in its development.

Working title for this film was "Rodeo Buster".

Look quickly—when Sheriff Williams (Jack Kirk) is on the phone in his office, you can glimpse a wanted poster on which is a picture of John Wayne.

FILM COMMENTS: *George Sherman:* "When I was first assigned to direct one of Gene's pictures I wanted to meet Gene and find out what he was like, how he reacts. I met Gene, and I started to shoot the picture and I discovered he had a very unusual quality. He was able to project his own particular personality on the screen. It's very hard to do for a lot of people. It was a naturalness and he seemed so normal that the reaction of the other people put them very much at ease. It was an interesting sidelight to the man. The other side of the coin was Smiley Burnette. With Smiley I had what were commonly called creative differences (laughs) because Smiley had a tendency to overact and mug in front of the camera and I was trying to keep him down. One day, I said, 'Smiley, you got that hat with the brim up, you got a shirt that's checkered that's bagging over your belly, your pants are down below your hips, you got a gun down here, you got a horse with a circle around his eye—what the hell more do you need? You don't have to mug in front of the camera. The stuff that's written for you is funny, just play it as it's written, don't try to force the comedy, let it play naturally.' But they were wonderful pictures. (Gene and Smiley) complemented each other."[1]

Peggy Moran: "Gene was the star of the first movie I ever had a lead in. He was very polite, very nice, but distant. I went to an interview for 'Rhythm of the Saddle'. My agent told me, 'Whatever they ask you, tell them yes—you can do it.' Naturally they asked if I could ride and I told them 'yes' although I really couldn't. So, I practiced for about a week. When we started the picture I could hardly sit down. My whole fanny was sore and blistered! Gene knew I couldn't ride, so he kept by me, in case I should have any trouble. I never knew him very well, but a few years ago, I saw him and brought a picture of us both. He signed it 'To Peggy, a swell leading lady.' It was the scene where I am sitting on a rock and he is serenading me with 'Let Me Call You Sweetheart,' which is something I couldn't be in real life, as he was, of course, married."[2]

George Sherman.

CAST BIOS: The directing career of George Sherman spawned 40 years from 1937-1977.

Born in New York on July 14, 1908, Sherman came to Hollywood in his 20's working his way up through the ranks from errand boy to assistant director for Sol Lesser produced westerns starring Smith Ballew and George O'Brien in the early '30s. Signing up with Republic in 1937 he began guiding the action packed Three Mesquiteers westerns, eventually directing 19 in the series.

New Autry producer Harry Grey, searching for new directorial talent now that Republic had moved Joe Kane over to the Roy Rogers films, tried Sherman out on "Rhythm of the Saddle".

Gene Autry in his BACK IN THE SADDLE AGAIN biography described George as "…about the size of a popcorn kernel, but he was an artist. Like Howard Hawks,

he had a taste for give-and-take dialogue and the tongue-in-cheek approach to making films."[3]

Sherman's superior work at the reins always stood out and he went on to helm some of Gene's best and biggest late '30s hits—"Mexicali Rose", "Colorado Sunset", "Rovin' Tumbleweeds" and "South of the Border"—before Republic assigned him to their Don Barry series and more with the Three Mesquiteers.

Sherman later moved to Columbia and Universal on dozens of A-pictures. One of his last films was "Big Jake" in 1971 with John Wayne.

Sherman died of heart and kidney failure March 15, 1991, in Los Angeles, California.

WHAT THE EXHIBITOR HAD TO SAY: "These Autry pictures have always been crowd pullers for us, but a few more like this one and we'll have to look for another western star to satisfy the lovers of horse operas. For the first time patrons walked out and their comments clearly indicated their feelings, the gist of which seemed to be that Autry was getting too swellheaded for his actual talents. Even the dialogue had everyone in the cast heaping praises on his head. It was just too much to swallow."

—M. R. Harrington, Avalon Theatre,
Clatskanie, Oregon (February 1939)

"Perfect entertainment. Personally enjoyed it very much. I don't believe Gene is doing quite as well as he used to do. But we have no complaints."

—Harland Rankin, Plaza Theater,
Tilbury, Ontario, Canada (February 1939)

"Not up to Autry's standard but still a good draw. Smiley Burnette pleases our patrons. You never miss on Autrys."

—R. A. Moore, State Theater,
Clarence, Iowa (February 1939)

"An excellent western that drew less than average business. Smiley Burnette again is the whole show."

—A. J. Inks, Crystal Theater,
Ligonier, Indiana (April 1939)

"Very good western. Good business, but a worn print."

—Eddie Ornstein, Rialto Theater,
Marengo, Indiana (February 1942)

"It was a good show but too short of running time. We played two of Columbia's two-reel comedies, but it was still too short. Smiley was really funny in this."

—Jerry Abbott, Masonic Theater,
New Castle, Virginia (October 1949)

"The usual Autry reissue. Gene looks so young in the film that many people commented on it. My gross was slightly below average with perfect weather."

—Fred G. Weppler, Colonial Theater,
Colfax, Illinois (May 1950)

SOURCES:

1. "Melody Ranch Theater" showing of "Carolina Moon", 1988.

2. *Western Clippings #27.* January/February 1999. p. 5; and *Western Clippings #9* January/February 1996, p. 21.

3. Autry with Herskowitz. p. 105.

Gene's just discovered his pal Smiley making a recording of a proposal to Pert Kelton, with whom Smiley is secretly smitten. That recording device is what eventually traps the bad guys.

Western Jamboree
Republic, December 1938

Producer ....Harry Grey
Director ....Ralph Staub
Assistant Director........................Kenneth Holmes
Original Story.............................Pat Harper
Screenplay...................................Gerald Geraghty
Photography ....William Nobles
Film Editor.................................Lester Orlebeck
Musical Supervisor ....Raoul Kraushaar
Production Manager....................Al Wilson

SONGS: "The Cowboy's Dream" (Public Domain)—sung by Gene Autry and cowboys; "Cielito Lindo" (Public Domain)—sung by Gene Autry, Smiley Burnette; "Balloon Song" (music and lyrics by Johnny Marvin, Eddie Cherkose)—sung by Smiley Burnette; "Old November Moon" (music and lyrics by Gene Autry, Johnny Marvin)—sung by Gene Autry; "I Love the Morning" (music and lyrics by Johnny Marvin, Eddie Cherkose)—sung by Gene Autry, Smiley Burnette, Frankie Marvin, cowboys; "When the Bloom Is On the Sage" (music and lyrics by Nat Vincent, Fred Howard Wright)—sung by Gene Autry, others.

RUNNING TIME: 56 minutes
FILMING DATES: October 18-27, 1938
LOCATIONS: Iverson Ranch; Republic backlot
BUDGET: $55,462
NEGATIVE COST: $63,462

CAST:

Actor	*Character*
Gene Autry ....Gene Autry
Smiley Burnette ....Frog Millhouse
Jean Rouverol..............................Betty Haskell
Esther Muir ....Duchess
Joe Frisco ....Frisco
Frank Darien ....Dad Haskell
Margaret Armstrong....................Mrs. Gregory
Harry Holman ....Doc Trimble
Edward Raquello........................Don Carlos
Bentley Hewlett ....Randolph Kimball
Kermit Maynard...........................Slim
George Wolcott ....Walter Gregory
Ray Teal ....McCall

Jack Perrin....................................Tobin
Jack Ingram.................................Farrell
Davison Clark ....VanFleet
Eddie Dean.................................Thompson
Frank Ellis...................................Ranch hand
Lew Kelly....................................Mark, taxi driver
Wilbur Mack ....J. W. Gillingham,
                                         Lawyer
Frankie Marvin.............................Shorty, Ranch hand
Jack Montgomery.........................Sheriff
Herman Hack ....Henchman
Jack Hendricks, Ray Jones, Art
Mix, George Morrell, Fred Parker,
Francis Walker, Curley Dresden,
Art Davis, George Plues...............Extras
Champion....................................Champion

STUNTS: Ken Cooper (Gene's double).

THE FILM: An interesting cast populates this otherwise minor Gene Autry western. It marks the film debut of Eddie Dean who later became a singing cowboy star himself at PRC from 1945-1948. This film and "Prairie Moon" were directed by Ralph Staub who produced and directed the popular one reel "Screen Snapshots" series for Columbia in the '30s. Leading lady Jean Rouverol became a successful author after the Communist scare blacklisted her from screen activity. Kermit Maynard, brother of the more famous B-western star Ken Maynard—with whom Gene made his first film, "In Old Santa Fe"—had his own B-western series for Ambassador from 1934-1937. Kermit had now turned to supporting roles and worked clear into the '60s TV era. He also became a representative for the Screen Extras Guild. Jack Perrin had been a leading man in silent westerns and starred in several independent talkies from 1930-1936 but now, like Maynard, had turned to supporting roles. Joe Frisco made his name on the vaudeville stage as a dancer (a sample of his terpsichorean talent is seen here). He soon added his stuttering voice to the act and became a popular comedian. He's also seen in "Ride, Tenderfoot, Ride".

Gene Autry, as foreman of a ranch, agrees to a ruse to help an elderly friend who has lied in letters to his daughter Betty (Jean Rouverol) back East, telling her he is a wealthy rancher. When they arrive out west, Gene helps her Dad (Frank Darien) deceive his daughter, her prospective bridegroom and his haughty mother into believing the ranch is the old man's. Gene and his friends pretend to turn the place into a dude ranch. However, the ruse is interrupted by both the arrival of the true owner and some unscrupulous crooks who have discovered helium gas on the range and plot to steal it for a foreign power.

NOTES AND COMMENTS: Working title of the picture was "Bloom on the Sage".

Gene sings the popular Spanish tune "Cielito Lindo", the first of many instances where he sang in Spanish for his Latino audiences as well as American lovers of Spanish language music.

Weekly salaries for talent ran a bit higher on "Western Jamboree" with Esther Muir earning $400 a week. Jean Rouverol was at $350 a week with Harry Holman, Edward Roquello and Margaret Armstrong receiving $300. Kermit Maynard got $175 and Jack Perrin $75 as opposed to newcomer Eddie Dean at $125. George Wolcott earned $175 a week. Stuntman Ken Cooper was again at $300 a week.

"When the Bloom is on the Sage" was first heard in "Roundup Time in Texas" in 1937.

FILM COMMENTS: *Jean Rouverol:* "I remember only that Gene Autry was as white as a flounder. I have never seen a western actor who looked less like one. He was white and soft and I thought, 'What in God's name ever enabled this man to become a star?' The music helps. What I did learn on that picture was that…I was shooting a scene with Smiley Burnette, who was the comedian; I couldn't understand how I always managed to end up with my back to the camera. The cameraman called me over and said, 'Don't let Smiley do this to you. He's upstaging you.' I didn't know enough about camera…and I probably wasn't narcissistic enough to care, but I was puzzled…never happened on the stage. The cameraman said, 'Don't let him. Complain.' So I did, aloud to everybody! I learned, subsequently, Smiley

Gene with leading lady Jean Rouverol.

did that to everybody he worked with. *Everybody!* That's the only time in my experience it ever happened. I never saw it again with anybody else."[1]

Gene Autry: "Our last film that year was 'Western Jamboree', and it brought me together with one of the funniest humans Hollywood ever knew. The name Joe Frisco might draw a blank look today, but no one in his trade was ever more widely quoted. People collected Joe Frisco stories and held them like old coins, waiting for the value to go up. Joe palled around with Smiley and Pat Buttram, the two sidekicks of my movie years. He had a heart as big as a blimp and whatever Joe had—clothes, booze, or debts—he shared. And Joe stuttered. That wasn't what made him funny, but it didn't detract any. He was a racetrack junkie. Went there almost every day. One afternoon he left the set early and headed for Santa Anita. There he ran into Bing Crosby, who made the mistake of asking how he was doing. 'N-n-n-not so g-g-g-good,' he said, reaching out a hand. 'L-l-lend me a sawbuck.' Bing slipped him a twenty-dollar bill. After the next race they met near the paddock and Bing said, 'How'd you do, Joe?' 'N-n-n-not so g-g-g-good,' he said. 'G-g-g-gimme another sawbuck.'

"Finally, Frisco bet a long shot and the horse came home at something like 35 to 1. Later, Bing walked into the bar and there Frisco was, a pile of money on the counter, holding court and buying drinks for his friends. When Crosby walked in Joe motioned him over, peeled off two twenties, and said, 'S-s-s-say, kid, s-s-s-sing me a song.'"[2]

WHAT THE EXHIBITOR HAD TO SAY: "Another good Autry. Plenty of action, humor and good western songs is what my patrons expect in a good western and the Autrys give them what they want."

—A. E. Eliasen, Rialto Theater,
Paynesvile, Minnesota (January 1939)

"Average western drama which pleased good business."
—E. M. Freiburger, Paramount Theater,
Dewey, Oklahoma (January 1939)

"Republic should spend a little more money on Autry productions. Smiley Burnette draws the laughs. Low gross due to bad weather." —R. A. Moore, State Theater,
Clarence, Iowa (March 1939)

"A good western and with Smiley Burnette these seem to satisfy but I sure would like to know where all that business is the salesman and exhibitor reports said were being done by Autry. My Friday and Saturday programs just don't do it any more."

—Mayme P. Musselman, Princess Theater,
Lincoln, Kansas (June 1939)

SOURCES:

1. Magers, Boyd and Fitzgerald, Michael. *Ladies of the Western.* McFarland, 2002. p. 235.

2. Autry with Herskowitz, p. 66.

Home On the Prairie
Republic, February 1939

Producer ....Harry Grey
Director ....Jack Townley
Assistant Director.........................William O'Connor
Original Story...............................Paul Franklin
Screenplay....................................Charles Arthur Powell,
                                                        Paul Franklin
Photography ....Reg Lanning
Film Editor...................................Lester Orlebeck
Musical Supervisor ....Raoul Kraushaar
Production Manager....................Al Wilson

SONGS: "There's Nothing Like Work" (music and lyrics by Smiley Burnette, Eddie Cherkose)—sung by Smiley Burnette; "I'm Gonna Round Up My Blues" (music and lyrics by Gene Autry, Johnny Marvin)—sung by Gene Autry, dance guests and Rodeoliers; "She'll Be Comin' 'Round the Mountain" (Public Domain)—sung by the Rodeoliers; "Moonlight on the Ranch House" (music and lyrics by Walter G. Samuels)—sung by Gene Autry; "Big Bull Frog" (music and lyrics by Walter G. Samuels)—sung by Gene Autry.

RUNNING TIME: 59 minutes

FILMING DATES: December 10-30, 1938

LOCATIONS: Keen Camp and Garner Valley; Republic backlot; Jauregui Ranch; Placerita Canyon Road; Stretch of railroad between Fillmore and Saugus

BUDGET: $55,344

NEGATIVE COST: $60,265

CAST:

Actor	*Character*
Gene Autry	Gene Autry
Smiley Burnette	Frog Millhouse
June Storey	Martha Wheeler
George Cleveland	Jim Wheeler
Jack Mulhall	Dr. Sommers
Walter Miller	Belknap
Gordon Hart	H. R. Shelby
Hal Price	Sheriff
Earle Hodgins	Professor Wentworth
Ethan Laidlaw	Carter (henchman)
John Beach	Tom Ross (henchman)
Jack Ingram	Wilson (henchman)
Bob Woodward	Madden
Sherven Brothers Rodeoliers	Themselves
Chuck Baldra	Deputy Joe
Fred Burns	Tall party guest
Burr Caruth	Doctor Phillips
Art Dillard, Al Taylor, Chuck Baldra, Frankie Marvin, Curley Dresden	Deputies
Olin Francis	Loading dock official
Dorothy Vernon	Party guest
Helen Servis	Ruthie
Carl Seilers	Off-screen Punch and Judy man
George Plues	Thug
Champion	Champion

STUNTS: Ken Cooper (double for Gene); Jack Kirk (double for Smiley); Bob Woodward.

THE FILM: Gene Autry's westerns often worked

Gene's Westerns often included some unusual elements not found in other Westerns — such as an elephant that helps rescue Gene and Smiley from jail.

topical themes of the '30s and '40s into the plots, keeping them fresh by skipping the time worn elements that brought westerns to a low point at the nation's box offices in the early '30s. In a plot reminiscent of "Guns and Guitars", Gene and Frog (Smiley Burnette) are livestock inspectors who report evidence of the dreaded hoof and mouth disease and thus prevent shipment of infected cattle. They are accused of favoritism when they try to help an old rancher (George Cleveland) and his attractive daughter (June Storey) whose cattle appear to be diseased and are doomed to be destroyed. Through investigation, Gene finds another rancher (Walter Miller) has planted a diseased steer on his friend's ranch, thus making it appear the epidemic started there.

NOTES AND COMMENTS: Working title of the picture was "Ridin' the Range".

For the first time in an Autry picture, Republic moved the production credits to the end of the film rather than up front with the cast listings.

Stuntman for Gene Autry, Ken Cooper, once again earned $300. Other weekly salaries were $250 to Walter Miller; $200 each to June Storey and George Cleveland; $150 to Jack Mulhall; $100 to Ethan Laidlaw; $75 to Jack Ingram. Paul Eagle's elephant Nee Pa—and a horse named Mike—were paid $300 a week.

The female Boston Bulldog, Squeezy, was owned by Curley Twifford.

FILM COMMENTS: *June Storey:* "Gene was marvelous. While I was filming with Gene, my parents were going through a divorce and I was just devastated. Gene served as my friend, brother and protector. He was my pillar of strength during that period. He was a very relaxed individual, easy to work with, and easy to get along with. He could be very businesslike. He did become an empire builder. Gene claimed he was not particularly bright but surrounded himself with people who knew more then he did. Friends and people were more important to Gene than things. During the time I worked with Gene, his beautiful home burned, destroying many of his awards and valuable items. Gene's wife, Ina, had been cleaning the rug with gasoline when the fire started. Gene was on the set taking a snooze when everyone expressed their sorrow to Gene, and he told us it was only things that were destroyed and he still had his most important possessions, his friends. I had spent quite a bit of time around Will Rogers, and I thought Gene had some of Will's philosophy."[1]

Gene Autry: "'Home on the Prairie' marked the first appearance of June Storey, a pretty little blonde from Canada, as my favorite rein-holder. June was Smiley Burnette's favorite audience. He had a conviction, it was almost a religious belief, that your feet were the key to your physical and mental health. Whenever people looked tired, Smiley would bathe and massage their feet. He carried a pail around with him on the set. June thought it was a very generous thing for Smiley to do and took frequent advantage of the service.

"Still in her teens, June was one of those people who wanted to nominate you for a prize anytime you did a good deed. I found a tiny kitten once, I'm not sure where, just abandoned on the street, I guess. I brought it to the shooting that day in a sock—it was no bigger than a man's hand—and held it in my lap between scenes. June loved to tell people about that. 'Have you heard,' she'd ask, 'about Gene and the little kitten he carried around in a sock?'

"And whoever it was would wait, just wait for the rest of the story or the punch line or whatever, and that would be it. There wasn't any more."[2]

Gene manhandles henchman Ethan Laidlaw while Smiley holds a gun on the other two — Bob Woodward and George Plues.

CAST BIOS: Co-starring with Gene Autry in ten of his westerns at the height of his career ('39-'40) has assured June Storey a lasting and prominent niche in western leading lady history.

The pretty blonde with the sparkling personality was born April 20, 1918, in Toronto, Canada. Her father was a forest ranger whose health necessitated a move for his family to near Tyler Lake, Connecticut, when June was only five.

In 1930 the family was visiting relatives near Laguna Beach, fell in love with the area and moved there. "In high school I knew the son of director Chuck Reisner. When I met him, he got me into a picture with Jimmy Durante over on Balboa, playing a college student in the background of 'Student Tour' ('34). Then my uncle,

who was well known back east, arranged for a test at Fox for me. They thought the test was horrible but that I showed imagination, so they put me under contract and I studied for four years under Florence Enright."[3]

In June 1935, June signed a seven year contract with 20th Century–Fox where several other films followed with a major break in "In Old Chicago" ('38). "When the picture was previewed, Sol Siegel from Republic attended and told me they were looking for a leading lady for cowboy star Gene Autry. He asked me if I would be interested in trying out for the part. I was athletic and could ride a horse, so I thought I would enjoy the role. I requested and was granted my release from 20th Century–Fox." June's first was "Home on the Prairie".

Following her days at Republic, June freelanced. "I appeared in several other films. Among them were 'Strange Woman' ('46) with Hedy Lamarr, 'Killer McCoy' ('47) with Mickey Rooney and 'Snake Pit' ('48) with Olivia de Havilland. In about 1947, I purchased a 450 acre ranch on the Rogue River in Oregon. It was located about four miles from a ranch owned by Ginger Rogers. While there, I had a

radio show that was sponsored by a local dairy.

"In 1950, on a foggy night, after attending a Kiwanis meeting, I was involved in a terrible accident. A truck, illegally overloaded with redwood logs and with its lights off, hit my car. I was severely injured. My head was cut, and my leg was broken and slammed into the glove compartment. I was within inches of being decapitated. I was not expected to live—when I did live, I was not expected to walk again. The doctor told me to keep thinking that I could move my leg. I worked hard at following his advice and eventually I did move my leg. Through the care and inspiration I received from the doctors and nurses, I fully recovered. I grew quite a bit spiritually during this ordeal and developed a deep sense of commitment to help others. I decided to become a nurse.

"I did things backwards: I went to work for a doctor at Laguna Beach. I worked for free for my training. Then I worked at a nursing home, then I went to college to get a nursing degree."

Somewhere during this time, June was either divorced or widowed from her husband and left with a son and daughter. For 10 years she was nurse to the wife of the man who became her second husband. When the man's wife died in '79, June married her employer, Lincoln Clark, an engineer.

June attended several film festivals in the late '80s before her death from cancer December 18, 1991. She always said, "It is a real tribute to the fans who maintain an interest in this part of Americana. I'm happy I was part of it."[3]

WHAT THE EXHIBITOR HAD TO SAY: "Autry doesn't rate here like he has in past. Still a good bet but set your sights on Roy Rogers." —R. A. Moore, State Theater, Clarence, Iowa (April 1939)

"My first Autry but it surely won't be my last. Best weekend business in months. More power to you, Gene, keep up the good work. I can't wait till I play your next one." —Don Bloxham, Palace Theater, Exira, Iowa (September 1939)

"We don't seem able to sell this Autry in a big way but our regulars like him and when we satisfy our weekend patrons, that means they will be back more often when they get some cash. Our Friday and Saturday business is definitely off because our farmers are broke and don't come to the show." —Mayme P. Musselman, Princess Theater, Lincoln, Kansas (September 1939)

SOURCES:
1. Interview with author.
2. Autry with Herskowitz. p. 67.
3. Interview with author.

Mexicali Rose
Republic, March 1939

Producer ....Harry Grey
Director ....George Sherman
Assistant Director........................Phil Ford
Original Story.............................Luci Ward and Connie Lee
Screenplay...................................Gerald Geraghty
Photography ....William Nobles
Film Editor.................................Tony Martinelli
Musical Supervisor ....Raoul Kraushaar
Production Manager....................Al Wilson

SONGS: "Mexicali Rose" (music and lyrics by Helen Stone, Jack B. Tenney)—sung by Gene Autry; "Robin Hood" (music and lyrics by Walter G. Samuels)—sung by Gene Autry; "You're the Only Star in My Blue Heaven" (music and lyrics by Gene Autry)—sung by Gene Autry; "My Orchestra's Driving Me Crazy" (music and lyrics by Smiley Burnette)—sung by Smiley Burnette; "El Rancho Grande" (music and lyrics by Del Moral, Emilio Uranga)—sung by Gene Autry, Smiley Burnette, Noah Beery, riders.

RUNNING TIME: 59 minutes
FILMING DATES: January 25 to February 11, 1939
LOCATIONS: Palmdale area yucca tree groves; Corriganville; Monogram Ranch; Oil well scenes possibly at Mentryville, near Newhall; Republic backlot
BUDGET: $56,375
NEGATIVE COST: $68,620

CAST:

Actor	*Character*
Gene Autry	Gene Autry
Smiley Burnette	Frog Millhouse
Noah Beery Sr.	Pedro Valdez
Luana Walters..............................	Anita Loredo
William Farnum	Padre Dominic
William Royle	Robert Carruthers
LeRoy Mason..............................	Harley Blythe
Wally Albright.............................	Tommy Romero
Kathryn Frye	Chalita Romero
Roy Barcroft...............................	McElroy
Dick Botiller...............................	Manuel, Valdez rider
Vic Demourelie	Hollister
John Beach	Henchman Brown
Henry Otho.................................	Mexican officer
Josef Swickard	Gonzales
Joe Dominguez, Al Haskell, Merrill McCormick, Tom Steele	Valdez Riders
Sherry Hall	Guest at the Fiesta
Jack Ingram, Frank O'Connor	Investors
Tom London...............................	Mexican Police officer
Frankie Marvin...........................	Henchman Smith
Eddie Parker...............................	Henchman
Al Taylor	Henchman Jones
Fred "Snowflake" Toones	Cook
Cesar Miro	Broadcast Announcer

Suzanne Kaaren ....Oil Company Secretary
George DeNormand ....Joe (truck driver)
Barry Hays ....Henchman Richards
George Magrill ....Thug
Chuck Baldra, Art Felix, Joe
   Garcia, Roy Brent, Tex Terry,
   Earl Askam, Marty Faust, Al
   Haskell, Cliff Parkinson, Henry
   Wills, Bob Card, Bob Wilke,
   Bert LeBaron, George Magrill .Men
Champion ....Champion

STUNTS: Ken Cooper (Gene's double); Henry Wills, Jack Kirk (Smiley's double).

THE FILM: After several mediocre releases, Gene needed a big smash—and "Mexicali Rose" was it. On-screen Gene quite obviously seems to be having fun in this picture, and the enjoyment is infectious. "Mexicali Rose" captured everything that made Gene the most popular cowboy star. All the ingredients are here, a popular title song and another big hit by Gene, Smiley's slapstick comedy, the kind of crooked business execs post-Depression audiences loved to hate, a sufficient amount of action for the pure western buffs, a charming leading lady, and a sentimental storyline.

It's a simple tale, set in Mexico, of a poor Mexican padre (William Farnum) trying to help his orphan children while defending the land against shady oil company executives who want the land for oil. Hired as a radio singer, Gene soon discovers his show's sponsor is crooked. With the aid of a colorful music-loving bandido (Noah Beery in a charming performance), Gene and Frog (Smiley Burnette) save the orphanage.

NOTES AND COMMENTS: Salaries ranged from $750 per week for Noah Beery to $75 for Tom London. William Farnum drew $300 a week while William Royle and LeRoy Mason were both at $200. Roy Barcroft earned $125, Dick Botiller $100 and Suzanne Kaaren's brief role was worth $200 a week. Leading lady Luana Walters was loaned from Paramount for $150 a week.

A fictionalization of "Mexicali Rose" appeared in MOVIE STORY magazine in May of 1939.

Gene originally introduced his big hit song "Mexicali Rose" in "Rootin' Tootin' Rhythm" in 1937. He also reprised "You're the Only Star in My Blue Heaven" from "Springtime In the Rockies", also 1937.

FILM COMMENTS: *Gene Autry:* "Whenever one of my films had the same title as a current best-selling song, such as "Mexicali Rose", the exhibitors always knew that Republic was going to hit them with a slightly higher tab. The reason being that these were usually shot on a bigger budget, and Yates liked to get back the money they spent for the rights to the song.

"But I believe this one was worth the price of the ticket. The cast included Noah Beery Sr., who could chew up as much scenery as his brother, Wallace. And we laid three big ones on them in the music department. In addition to the title song; we brought back 'You're the Only Star in My Blue Heaven' and introduced 'El Rancho Grande'. That last one had more ay-yi-yi-yi's than even Desi Arnaz in his prime."[1]

CAST BIOS: One of the great character villains of the silent and sound screen, Noah Beery Sr., was in reality a kind, gentle, charitable man, but he could personify evil with his broad-faced grin and chortling laugh emanating from his rotund 6' 1½" 230 pound frame. "The real make-up for a character must come from within," he once explained. "It is the result of studying the man until you can feel as he must feel—then your body, your whole features will become responsive to your own mental picture."[2]

Born Noah Nicholas Beery February 17, 1882, in Smithville, Missouri, his father was reportedly of Swiss descent and worked as a police officer. Noah was the elder brother of the more famous of the acting Beery brothers, Wallace Beery. Noah grew up on a farm in western Missouri and reportedly went to grade school in Kansas City with outlaw Jesse James' son.

Still a boy, he sold lemon drops to actors at the Gillis Theater in Kansas City. Amused by his already booming, deep voice, various actors urged him to cultivate it and go on the stage, which he did at the youthful age of 16.

Possessed of a rich singing voice, after some lessons, Beery performed for a year in the Kansas City area and for a week at the

In Mexico, Gene and Smiley befriend Padre William Farnum and his niece Luana Walters who are being put upon by crooked oil promoters.

fashionable Hammerstein's Resort in New York State as well as at Kansas City's Electric Park.

Finding he preferred melodrama, he scored a moderate success in a three year tour of a "Trail of the Lonesome Pine" production with brother Wallace. By 23, he was touring for a year with "As Ye Sow", eventually playing for a month on Broadway.

In 1910 Beery married Marguerite Walker Lindsey, a stage actress. They had a son who died. The second child, Noah Lindsey Beery (later called simply Noah Beery Jr.) was born August 10, 1913, in New York. Seriously ill for months, doctors advised a milder climate so the Beerys moved to Florida where Noah Sr. made some early films and worked at any job he could find until the family finally reached California in 1917 where he found film work immediately, eventually appearing in over 110 silents.

As talkies came in, Beery was in his late 40s, and even with his powerful voice and fabulous persona, his star began to slip—although he worked in nearly 90 films on through 1945.

His wife died in 1935 but 1940 saw his son Noah Jr. join with another respected Hollywood family when he married Maxine Jones, daughter of Buck Jones.

Beery was residing in a New York City hotel in 1946 while playing the role of Tammany Hall's Boss Tweed in a stage production of "Up In Central Park". Taking a two-week vacation from the play to visit California where he, his brother Wallace, and Wallace's daughter, Carol Ann, were to appear together on a Lux Radio Theatre presentation, Noah suffered a fatal heart attack and on April 1 died in his brother's arms. He was 64.

WHAT THE EXHIBITOR HAD TO SAY: "What a relief

Dick Botiller, John Beach, William Royle, Noah Beery, Sr. and Gene in a tense moment from "Mexicali Rose."

it is to run a western of this kind. He is one cowboy that certainly elevated westerns to a higher plane. I do not know how it is with other houses, but with my house, when you show Gene Autry, I show it to the same crowd of people that I do to some special outstanding attraction. Business always good in anything that Gene makes."

—Bud Davis, Ritz Theater,
Roanoke, Alabama (August 1939)

"One of the better Autry reissues. They seem to satisfy and I seldom previously have played them all."

—Charles A. Brooks, Ritz Theater,
Marshfield, Missouri (August 1943)

SOURCES:
1. Autry with Herskowitz. p. 68.
2. Magers, Boyd; Nareau, Bob; Copeland, Bobby. *Best of the Badmen.* Empire Pub., 2005. p. 44.

Blue Montana Skies
Republic, May 1939

Producer	Harry Grey
Director	B. Reeves Eason
Assistant Director	Phil Ford
Original Story	Norman S. Hall, Paul Franklin
Screenplay	Gerald Geraghty
Photography	Jack Marta
Film Editor	Lester Orlebeck
Musical Supervisor	Raoul Kraushaar
Production Manager	Al Wilson

SONGS: "Rockin' In the Saddle" (music and lyrics by Gene Autry, Fred Rose, Johnny Marvin)—sung by Gene Autry, Smiley Burnette and cowboys; "'Neath the Blue Montana Sky" (music and lyrics by Gene Autry, Fred Rose, Johnny Marvin)—sung by Gene Autry, cowboy chorus; "Old Geezer" (music and lyrics by Gene Autry, Fred Rose, Johnny Marvin)—sung by Smiley Burnette, Gene Autry; "Famous Men of the West" (music and lyrics by Fred Rose, Johnny Marvin, Eddie Cherkose)—sung by Gene Autry, Walt Shrum and His Colorado Hillbillies; "I Just Want You" (music and lyrics by Gene Autry, Fred Rose, Johnny Marvin)—sung by Gene Autry.

RUNNING TIME: 56 minutes
FILMING DATES: March 8-30, 1939
LOCATIONS: Big Bear; Lake Sherwood, Agoura Ranch; Morrison Ranch; Republic backlot
BUDGET: $58,857
NEGATIVE COST: $65,613.91

CAST:

Actor	Character
Gene Autry	Gene Autry
Smiley Burnette	Frog Millhouse
June Storey	Dorothy Hamilton
Harry Woods	Hendricks
Tully Marshall	Steve
Al Bridge	Marshal
Glenn Strange	Bob Causer
Dorothy Granger	Millie Potter
Edmund Cobb	Joe Brennan
Robert Winkler	Wilbur Potter
Jack Ingram	Henchman Frazier
Augie Gomez	Blackfeather
John Beach	Mountie Corporal
Walt Shrum and his Colorado Hillbillies: Walt Shrum, Cal Shrum, Tony Fiore, Frank Wilder, Virgil Dehne, Robert Hoag, Rusty Cline	Musicians
Allan Cavan	Jim, Customs officer
Curley Dresden	Henchman Davis
Elmo Lincoln	Mack, Trading Post man
Frankie Marvin	Cookie
Jack Montgomery	Henchman Dennis
Moe Malulo	Maloo
Al Haskell	Henchman
Bud Wolfe, Don Roberts, Ted Mapes	Mounties
Eddie Cherkose	Hotel clerk
Pat Frahm, Johnny Treece, Arthur Roberti, Ethan Laidlaw, Knute Erickson, Leon Brace, Rudy Sooter, Wally West, Jack Kenny, Art Dillard, Ray Jones, Jack Hendricks	Extras
Champion	Champion

STUNTS: Ken Cooper (Gene's double); Jack Kirk (Smiley's double); Nellie Walker (June's double); C. H. Adams (standby double); J. Scott (dog team driving double for Gene); Bill Yrigoyen.

THE FILM: A nice change of atmosphere in a more traditional western for Gene, even though the story is set in Canada with Gerald Geraghty's tight script bringing some straight outdoor action back to Gene's films.

Up in the North Country to sell cattle, fur thieves murder Gene's partner (Tully Marshall). The only clue to the murderer is the initials "HH" which the dead man has carved on a stone. This leads Gene and pal Frog (Smiley Burnette) to a nearby dude ranch where he finds Dorothy Hamilton (June Storey) a half owner along with the man who is the head of the smugglers (Harry Woods).

Gene holds a gun on fur thieves Al Haskell, Glenn Strange and Moe Malulo while trading post owner Elmo Lincoln disarms Augie Gomez. Lincoln was the first screen Tarzan in 1918.

The climax has Gene creating an avalanche on a snow-covered mountain to trap the smugglers below.

NOTES AND COMMENTS: Original working title for the film was "Yankee Doodle Cowboy".

Plagued by bad weather and no sunlight, "Blue Montana Skies" finished nine days behind schedule, giving it a lengthy 23 day shoot.

Director B. Reeves "Breezy" Eason was paid $1,599 for "Blue Montana Skies". Curiously, his middle name was misspelled "Reaves" on screen. Gene's saddle pal Smiley Burnette maintained his $1,000 per picture salary. Character player Tully Marshall earned $201 per day on a two day schedule. Al Bridge and Dorothy Granger were both hired at $150 a week with Glenn Strange at $100 and leading lady June Storey upped to $250 a week. Walt Shrum and his Colorado Hillbillies were paid $800 for the length of the picture, to be divided between the seven of them.

351 fur pieces were rented for $350. Their total value was $3,000 and consisted of 10 gray wolf, 2 white fox, 5 silver fox, 10 coyote, 10 imitation fox and over 300 Canadian hares in bundles.

On location Smiley Burnette bedeviled director "Breezy" Eason, as well as the cast and crew, by saying "smur fugglers" instead of "fur smugglers". Some retakes were needed.

FILM COMMENTS: *June Storey:* "I never knew Smiley off the set but he was a wonderful person to work with. He and his wife 'adopted' 3 or 4 children and arranged for something like 39 orphan children to be placed in homes. Smiley was a humble person who cared deeply for children. He had a little habit of taking a bowl of hot water…he said, 'This is gonna make you feel a lot better'…and he'd massage and put your feet in hot water. He and Gene were great together. Even off screen he could make Gene laugh and keep everybody relaxed. We all got along very well. I think, during the war years, it relaxed people to see these light movies with Gene and Smiley, myself—all getting along, having fun with what they were doing. There was no professional jealousy; we just did it on a daily basis. Gene was very relaxed. He had a good philosophy and that becomes very contagious. I was the youngest on the lot and they loved to tease me. I'd just blush at hardly anything at all. They kind of treated me special."[1]

Gene Autry: "We had a bit of trouble with the horses because a lot of them had never seen snow, so it was quite a problem. Champion, you had to walk him around a little while and he'd pick up his feet like he was walking on something that was hot. At first he didn't want to run, but we soon got him used to that."[2]

Property man H. B. Phillips in a memo to production manager Al Wilson: "Mr. Eason asked Smiley Burnette to take off his ring inasmuch as he was in his Indian costume, so he gave me the ring to hold for him. But when we got through Saturday afternoon, he left in such a hurry that he did not pick up his ring, and when I got home Saturday night, I still had the ring in my pocket. So I took it along with me to Big Bear Monday, March 13. I put the ring on my finger so that I might have it with me to give back to him. However, we were up in the snow, and Bill Stratton and I were busy with the bundles of furs, tying and untying them. It was very cold at Big Bear in the snow, and I had to take off my gloves about six or seven times to tie and untie the furs. One of those times that I took off my gloves was when I must have lost the ring."[3]

CAST BIOS: Jack Ingram was one of the top heavies in B-westerns for 20 years from the mid '30s to the mid '50s, appearing in over a dozen of Gene's features and several of his TV episodes.

When the cameras were rolling he rustled, robbed, cheated and killed with wild abandon, yet in real life he felt everything had a right to live and would not even harm an ant or bee. He felt it was his duty to set a good example off screen and conducted himself accordingly. He constantly laughed and joked.

John Samuel Ingram was born November 15, 1902, in Chicago, Illinois, to Irish parents. Orphaned as an infant, he spent his boyhood on his uncle's farm in Wisconsin where he acquired his love of animals and his riding abilities. Then the family moved to Dallas, Texas.

At the young age of 15 and anxious to join the Army, with consent he lied about his age and enlisted, serving with the 8th Field Artillery overseas where he was wounded and gassed. He spent two years recuperating at a French hospital. After WWI, Jack enrolled at the University of Texas to study law, but eventually became more interested in performing. He became a regular member of a successful traveling minstrel show and later joined and toured the country with Mae West's stage shows.

Spotted on Broadway in West's "Diamond Lil" ('28), he was signed by Paramount in '29 because of his knowledge of horses and his ability to perform difficult stunts.

While performing a leap from a high rock onto a horse in "Charge of the Light Brigade" ('36), the horse shied, throwing Jack's timing off. When he fell he broke his arm. He'd begun doing bit roles in Republic westerns in '35 but by '36 moved seriously into acting fulltime.

1944 was a banner year for Jack. Not only did he make 22 movies and three serials, he found time to marry Eloise (Lou) Fullerton, a Hollywood columnist and publicist. They purchased 200 acres of what had been part of the old

Prolific screen heavy Jack Ingram and Gene — wearing a gorgeous Hudson Bay coat.

Charlie Chaplin estate. The property had previously been purchased by Dave O'Brien and James Newill (The Texas Rangers at PRC). They sold the property to Ingram, whom they knew well from his many badman roles in their series.

With the help of several pals, Ingram built a western street set which included a well-landscaped house that became Ingram's home. Dozens of westerns and TV episodes were lensed at Ingram's ranch, including several of Gene's TV episodes.

Selling the property in 1956, Jack moved to Encino, bought a 55 ft. yacht, berthed at Long Beach Harbor, and enjoyed himself during retirement. He also rented the yacht to film companies, including ZIV's "Sea Hunt".

While fishing at their lodge in Oregon, Jack suffered a heart attack and was hospitalized for a month. Returning to California, his recovery was slow and one of the nicest and one of the busiest men in westerns and serials (with or without his mustache) suffered a second heart attack and died at West Hills Doctor's Hospital in Canoga Park, California, February 20, 1969.

WHAT THE EXHIBITOR HAD TO SAY: "Gene Autry is just the same actor as when he started but still does business. Smiley Burnette says 'whoopee' and all the audience yells." —C. L. Niles, Niles Theater, Anamosa, Iowa (July 1939)

"Still doing business on these Gene Autry reissues." —E. M. Freiburger, Paramount Theater, Dewey, Oklahoma (February 1946)

"Good western. Good print, too. In the last few weeks I have played a Tex Ritter, an Autry reissue and a Rogers. The Tex Ritter western did the best business." —S. T. Jackson, Jackson Theater, Flomaton, Alabama (December 1946)

SOURCES:
1. Interview with author.
2. "Melody Ranch Theater" showing of "Blue Mon-tana Skies" on Nashville Network, 1987.
3. Republic inter-office memo from prop man H. B. Phillips to production manager Al Wilson, dated March 17, 1939.

Mountain Rhythm
Republic, June 1939

Producer ....Harry Grey
Director ....B. Reeves Eason
Assistant Director........................Phil Ford
Original Story.............................Connie Lee
Screenplay..................................Gerald Geraghty
Photography ....Ernest Miller
Film Editor................................Lester Orlebeck
Musical Supervisor ....Raoul Kraushaar
Production Manager....................Al Wilson

SONGS: "Highways Are Happy Ways" (music and lyrics by Larry Shay)—sung by Gene Autry, Smiley Burnette, Jack Pennick, Ferris Taylor; "It Makes No Difference Now" (music and lyrics by Floyd Tillman, Jimmie Davis)—sung by Gene Autry; "It Was Only a Hobo's Dream" (music and lyrics by Gene Autry, Fred Rose, Johnny Marvin)—sung by Gene Autry, Smiley Burnette; Medley: "Old MacDonald"/"Old Gray Mare"/ "Long, Long Ago"/"Oh, Dem Golden Slippers"/"Put On Your Old Gray Bonnet" (Public Domain with "Bonnet" music and lyrics by Murphy, Wenrich)—sung by Gene Autry, Smiley Burnette, hotel guests; "Gold Mine In Your Heart" (music and lyrics by Gene Autry, Fred Rose, Johnny Marvin)—sung by Gene Autry; "Knights of the Open Road" (music and lyrics by Gene Autry, Fred Rose, Johnny Marvin)—sung by hobos; "Put On Your Old Gray Bonnet" (music and lyrics by Murphy, Wenrich)—sung by Gene Autry, June Storey, Smiley Burnette, Maude Eburne, Jack Pennick, Ferris Taylor, hobos.

RUNNING TIME: 59 minutes
FILMING DATES: April 21 to May 6, 1939
LOCATIONS: Iverson Ranch; Walker Ranch; Jauregui Ranch; Republic backlot; Barney Oldfield's Resort
BUDGET: $60,199
NEGATIVE COST: $65,326.64

CAST:

Actor	*Character*
Gene Autry	Gene Autry
Smiley Burnette	Frog Millhouse
June Storey	Alice
Maude Eburne	Ma Hutchins
Ferris Taylor	Judge Homer Worthington
Walter Fenner	Cavanaugh
Jack Pennick	Rocky
Hooper Atchley	Daniels
Bernard Suss	MacCauley
Ed Cassidy	Sheriff Dalrymple
Jack Ingram	Carney
Tom London	Deputy Tom
Roger Williams	Kimball
Frankie Marvin	Burt
Al Taylor	Foreman Andy
Slim Whitaker	Deputy Lem
Silver Tip Baker	Rancher
John Beach	Henchman Reynolds
Bob Burns	Bob Plummer (Rancher)
Curley Dresden	Henchman Pete
Herman Hack, Murdock MacQuarrie, Lou Morphy	Townsmen
J. Harrison	Chauffeur
George Allen	Bus Driver
Tex Driscoll	Old Timer
Bill Nestell	Truck Driver
Art Mix	Henchman
Jack Baxley	Parkinson, Govern-ment auctioneer
Brandon Beach	Banker
George Taylor	Bud, hobo
C. L. Sherwood, Francis Sayles	Hobos
Bill Yrigoyen	Hay Wagon driver
Ralph Douglas	Frankie, bellhop
Elmo Lincoln	C. L. Boggs, cattle broker
Jim Corey, Victor Cox, Dirk Thane, Duke Lee, Howard Hickey, Floyd Pruitt, Arthur Roberts, Gwen Seager, Horace Carpenter, Roy Bucko, George Sowards, Augie Gomez, George Morrell, Wally West, Jack Hendricks, Bud McClure	Extras

Gene saves the ranch for Smiley's aunt, Maude Eburne (left), as he and deputy Tom London force a confession from henchman Jack Ingram.

Spade Cooley, Oscar Gahan.........Musicians
Champion....................................Champion

STUNTS: Ken Cooper (Gene's double); Jack Kirk (Smiley's double); Nellie Walker (June Storey and Maude Eburne's double); Joe Yrigoyen; Bill Yrigoyen.

THE FILM: "Mountain Rhythm" proves anything goes in an Autry picture. Here we have a dude ranch mixed with singing hobos rounding up cattle on bicycles!

In this only average Autry western, Gene and Frog Millhouse (Smiley Burnette) come to the aid of Frog's Aunt (Maude Eburne) when she and other ranchers are in danger of losing their ranches to Cavanaugh (Walter Fenner), an eastern promoter who wants to develop a dude ranch on the land. Cavanaugh is trying to drive the stockmen from the valley by arranging for a government sponsored public auction. Gene helps the ranchers pool their cash to bid on the property, but it is stolen by Cavanaugh's henchmen. However, with the help of hobos Gene and Frog have befriended, they stage a round-up, obtaining enough cattle to buy the land and save the valley.

NOTES AND COMMENTS: Gene Autry was now drawing $10,000 per picture with Smiley Burnette earning $1,000 per film. June Storey, now a regular in the Autry pictures, was upped to $500 a week. Maude Eburne also drew

$500 a week while Walter Fenner and Ferris Taylor got $250. Jack Pennick was at $200, Bernard Suss $175, Jack Ingram $75, Roger Williams $66, Tom London $75, Ed Cassidy $100 and director Eason was hired at $1,500.

CAST BIOS: B. Reeves Eason was a top action director who began directing westerns in 1915.

Born in New York October 2, 1886, Eason ran a produce business before entering stock and vaudeville as a performer. When he first came to motion pictures in 1913 it was as an actor, but he soon gravitated to directing.

In 1927 he supervised the chariot races in MGM's original "Ben Hur".

Known in the business as "Breezy" because he breezed through his action sequences with truly incredible speed, he often averaged 50-60 set-ups a day.

Eason preferred to be the sole director of pictures he worked on; therefore he primarily relegated himself to B-films, becoming one of the best fight and chase specialists in the industry.

When sound came in, Eason directed ten serials for Mascot, including Gene's "Phantom Empire" in 1935. He returned to helm Gene's "Red River Valley" in '36 and two with Gene in 1939, "Blue Montana Skies" and "Mountain Rhythm".

In later years Eason became a noted second-unit action director on such big films as "Charge of the Light Brigade" ('36), "Adventures of Robin Hood" ('38), "Man of Conquest" ('39), "Gone With the Wind" ('39), "They Died With Their Boots On" ('47), "Northwest Stampede" ('48), "Dallas" ('50), and others.

Retiring in 1952, Eason died of a heart attack June 9, 1956, in Sherman Oaks, California.

WHAT THE EXHIBITOR HAD TO SAY: "Good picture, good business. I played two MGM's, a Paramount and a Warner picture this week and this is the first one which did me any business. Too much Fourth of July, I guess."

—E. M. Freiburger, Paramount Theater, Dewey, Oklahoma (July 1939)

Colorado Sunset
<u>Republic, July 1939</u>

Smiley is smitten with Barbara Pepper in this scene on the title card for "Colorado Sunset." Frankie Marvin (in black hat) is behind Burnette, while singer Patsy Montana smiles behind Pepper.

Producer ....William Berke
Director ....George Sherman
Original Story............................Luci Ward, Jack
                       Natteford
Screenplay..................................Betty Burbridge, Stanley
                       Roberts

Photography ....William Nobles
Film Editor..................................Lester Orlebeck
Musical Supervisor ....Raoul Kraushaar
Production Manager....................Al Wilson

SONGS: "Colorado Sunset" (music and lyrics by L.

Wolfe Gilbert, Con Conrad)—sung over credits by a studio chorus; "On My Merry Old Way Back Home" (music and lyrics by Walter G. Samuels)—sung by Gene Autry, Smiley Burnette, CBS-KMPC Texas Rangers; "Cowboys Don't Milk Cows" (music and lyrics by Smiley Burnette)—sung by Smiley Burnette; "I Want to Be a Cowboy's Sweetheart" (music and lyrics by Patsy Montana)—sung by Patsy Montana; "Poor Little Dogie" (music and lyrics by Gene Autry, Fred Rose, Johnny Marvin)—sung by Gene Autry; "Beautiful Isle of Somewhere" (music and lyrics by J. Fearis)—sung by Gene Autry and others; "Autry's Your Man (Campaign Song)" (music and lyrics by Walter G. Samuels)—sung by Smiley Burnette, the CBS-KMPC Texas Rangers and others; "Seven Years With the Wrong Woman" (music and lyrics by Bob Miller)—sung by Gene Autry; "Colorado Sunset" (music and lyrics by L. Wolfe Gilbert, Con Conrad)—sung by Gene Autry, June Storey, others.

RUNNING TIME: 65 minutes

FILMING DATES: June 1-14, 1939

LOCATIONS: Keen Camp; Corriganville; Morrison Ranch; Garner Ranch and nearby Horner Ranch; Republic backlot

BUDGET: $77,483

NEGATIVE COST: $78,657.50

CAST:

Actor	Character
Gene Autry	Gene Autry
Smiley Burnette	Frog Millhouse
June Storey	Carol Haines
Barbara Pepper	Ginger Bixby
Larry "Buster" Crabbe	Dave Haines
Robert Barrat	Doc Rodney Blair
Patsy Montana	Patsy
The CBS-KMPC Texas Rangers:	
Clarence Hartman, Paul Sells, Francis Mahoney Jr., Roderic May, Gomer Cool, Edward Cronenbold, Herbert Kratoska, Robert Crawford	The Texas Troubadours
Purnell Pratt	Mr. Hall
William Farnum	Sheriff George Glenn
Kermit Maynard	Rufus Drake
Jack Ingram	Clanton
Elmo Lincoln	Dairyman Burns
Frankie Marvin	Ranch hand
Al Taylor	Henchman Stagg
Chuck Baldra	Cowboy
Reginald Barlow	Dairyman Casey
Fred Burns	Radio listener
Budd Buster	Ira
Ed Cassidy	Dairyman
Francis Ford	Street drunk
Jack Kirk, Ralph Peters, Jack Kenny	Husbands
Ethan Laidlaw	Brent, Man who puts up poster
Murdock MacQuarrie	Dairyman Jones
George Morrell, Roy Bucko	Radio listeners
Betty Mack	Mrs. Evans
Jane Keckley	Mrs. Brown
Dorothy Curtis	Mrs. Debs
Rose Plummer	Woman listener
Slim Whitaker	Cigar recipient
Bill Yrigoyen	Dairyman Dillon
Frank Ellis	Dairyman Horner
Gale Gillin	Woman
Margurite Cole, Polly Barley	Wives
Elise Dolph	Hall's Secretary
Johnny Tresch, Forrest Dillon, Augie Gomez, George Plues, Henry Morris, John Beach, Curley Dresden, Shannon Davidson	Heavies
Victor Cox, Jack Montgomery, John Wade	Extras
Champion	Champion

STUNTS: Joe Yrigoyen (Gene's double); Jack Kirk (Smiley's double); Jimmy Van Horn, Clem Fuller, Vernon Harrington, Jack Shannon, Ted Wells, Willard Willingham, Buell Bryant, Nick Nichols, Bill Yrigoyen.

THE FILM: Gene Autry was coming into a period of his strongest popularity with "Colorado Sunset", a top-notch western with all the elements that made him number one at the western boxoffice poll in 1939. 1940 would find him ranked 4th in the list of *all* Hollywood stars.

Directed with flair by George Sherman, "Colorado Sunset" "clicks" from the instant Gene, Frog (Smiley Burnette) and The Texas Troubadours (CBS-KMPC Texas Rangers) ride into camera view singing the happy, upbeat "On My Merry Old Way Back Home".

Disappointment sets in when they discover Frog (in absolute top form here) has mistakenly purchased a dairy farm. Winding up in the milk business puts them squarely in the midst of a dairy war with local veterinary Doc Blair (Robert Barrat) and his henchmen, local deputy Dave Haines (Buster Crabbe) destroying dairymen's milk before it gets to market unless they join the crooks' protection racket. A local radio station, run by Carol Haines, Dave's sister, inadvertently broadcasts "veterinary bulletins" from Blair which are actually coded messages to Blair's men instructing them where to strike the dairymen's milk runs. After the Sheriff (William Farnum) discovers Blair's scheme and is murdered, Gene is persuaded to run for the office against the crooked Dave Haines.

The finale spotlights a spectacular running battle with the bad guys and becomes one of the biggest action windups of any Autry picture.

All told—simply one of Autry's best.

NOTES AND COMMENTS: Buster Crabbe was loaned out by Paramount at $750 a week for this film as

Both running for sheriff, Gene is at odds with Buster Crabbe. June Storey on the left, Barbara Pepper on the right.

a heavy, which he seems to relish. Meanwhile, main heavy Robert Barrat was paid more than any player had previously been allotted on an Autry film, $1,500 a week. Other weekly salaries fell in line—Barbara Pepper at $400, June Storey at $500, Jack Ingram $75, Kermit Maynard $150, Betty Mack $100 and William Farnum signed on at $100 a day. The CBS-KMPC Texas Rangers were hired as a group for $400 a week.

This is the first picture Republic figured in a 20% overhead as the script was constantly being revised as it went along, including an extra day's filming. The original cost of $69,000 was based on the first draft of the script.

While filming on June 3 at Jack Garner's Ranch, a small brush fire occurred as a result of some bailed hay used in fire scenes that smoldered into flames twelve hours after the fire was thought to have been extinguished. A forest ranger was present at all times with the company, but since the fire broke out at 5am, no one was present. Republic production department employee Harry Knight answered a summons to appear before the Justice of the Peace in nearby Hemet on June 14. He waived trial and was fined $100.

This is the first film in which we see Gene in a business suit.

FILM COMMENTS:

Gene Autry: "The decision had been made to tour the British Isles starting in late July 1939. We turned them out so fast in the first half of the year it was like watching a nickelodeon. One of them was 'Colorado Sunset', which had as supporting actors Elmo Lincoln, the screen's first Tarzan, and Buster Crabbe, one of his successors. This may have been the only western ever made with two ex-Tarzans in the cast. That may not be the stuff of legends, but it should win a trivia contest. In the movie, Buster hid behind a mustache. He was then starring as Flash Gordon. Somehow, the studio thought his fans would be less upset at his losing to Autry in a one-on-one, if he looked less like Flash.[1]

"Patsy Montana was a delightful, warm-hearted person and a wonderfully talented performer. I was very pleased that she agreed to sing her hit song 'I Wanna Be a Cowboy's Sweetheart' and play a role in 'Colorado Sunset'. Of course, she earned a gold record for that terrific song. No one could sing it like she could. Patsy and I only made that one film together; however, she remained a close and special friend throughout the years."[2]

WHAT THE EXHIBITOR HAD TO SAY: "A very good western with plenty of good music by the KMPC Rangers and Patsy Montana. It seems like this added music sure is a big help and the Autry westerns are getting better. We don't break any house records with Autry but our patrons are pleased."   —Mayme P. Musselman, Princess Theater, Lincoln, Kansas (December 1939)

SOURCES:
1. Autry with Herskowitz. p. 68.
2. Letter from Gene Autry to *People* Magazine, October 30, 1996.

In Old Monterey
Republic, August 1939

Producer ....Armand Schaefer
Director ....Joe Kane
Assistant Director...........................Phil Ford
Original Story.................................Gerald Geraghty,
                        George Sherman
Screenplay......................................Gerald Geraghty,
                        Dorrell and Stuart
                        McGowan
Photography ....Ernest Miller

Film Editor...................................Edward Mann
Musical Supervisor ....Raoul Kraushaar
Production Manager....................Al Wilson

SONGS: "It Happened in Monterey" (music and lyrics by Billy Rose, Mabel Wayne)—sung by Gene Autry; "Born In the Saddle" (music and lyrics by Gene Autry, Johnny Marvin)—sung by Gene Autry; "My Buddy" (music and lyrics by Gus Kahn, Walter Donaldson)—sung by Gene

Autry, Hoosier Hot Shots; "It Looks Like Rain"/"Skeleton Rag" (music and lyrics by W. Hall)—sung by Hoosier Hot Shots, Smiley Burnette; "Tumbling Tumbleweeds" (music and lyrics by Bob Nolan)—sung by Gene Autry and The Ranch Boys; "Little Pardner" (music and lyrics by Gene Autry, Fred Rose, Johnny Marvin)—sung by Gene Autry; "Virginia Blues" (music and lyrics by E. Erdman, Fred Meinke)—sung by Hoosier Hot Shots; "Columbia, the Gem of the Ocean" (Public Domain)—sung by Gene Autry, Gabby Hayes, June Storey, townspeople; "Vacant Chair" (music and lyrics by George Root)—sung by June Storey, Gene Autry.

RUNNING TIME: 73 minutes

FILMING DATES: June 18 to July 3, 1939

LOCATIONS: Lone Pine; Kernville; Railroad tracks at Castaic Junction and Piru; Republic backlot; Big T Plant of Consumers Rock and Gravel Co. (Borax plant) at San Fernando Blvd. and Dexter; Lasky Mesa in Calabasas

BUDGET: $89,994

NEGATIVE COST: $98,723

CAST:

Actor	*Character*
Gene Autry	Sgt. Gene Autry
Smiley Burnette	Frog Millhouse
June Storey	Jill Whittaker
George "Gabby" Hayes	Gabby Whittaker
The Hoosier Hot Shots: Charles "Gabe" Ward, Ken Trietsch, Paul "Hezzie" Trietsch, Frank Kettering	Musicians/Soldiers
Sarie and Sallie: Margaret Waters (Sallie), Edna Earle Wolson (Sarie)	Themselves
The Ranch Boys: Ken Carson, Joe "Curley" Bradley, Jack Ross	Singers/Cowhands
Stuart Hamblen	Bugler
Billy Lee	Jimmy Whittaker
Jonathan Hale	Huntley Stevenson
Robert Warwick	Major Clifford B. Forbes
William Hall	Gilman
Eddy Conrad	Club Marine owner
William H. Reed	Lt. Walsh
Edward Earle	Captain Vaughn
Lee Prather	Colonel Haskell
Jack Kenney	Sgt. Newsom
Fred Burns	Rancher Fred Blake
Victor Cox	Rancher
Neal Dodd	Clergyman
Curley Dresden	Rancher Marshall
Frank Ellis	Rancher Saunders
Rex Lease	Orderly
Jack O'Shea	Miner
Hal Price	Wagon driver
Ted Mapes	Army Sentry
Barry Hays	Field operator
Lynton Brent	Workman
Dan White	Townsman
Garland Lincoln	Train Engineer
Robert Blair	Train Fireman
Rudy Sooter	Musician
Gilman Shelton, Geraldine Peck, Nick Nicholl, Joe Phillips, Rex DeWitt, Bill Smith, Harry Leroy, Bill Brown, Jim Corey, Jim Mason, George Montgomery, Roy Bucko, Ralph Bucko, Harry McClintock, Curley Dresden, Chuck Baldra, Cactus Mack, Jack Hendricks, Pascale Perry, Bob Wilke	Extras
Johnny Tresh, Frankie Marvin, Leonard "Shorty" Woods, Bill Yrigoyen, Herman Hack, Jack Shannon	Cavalrymen
Champion	Champion

STUNTS: Joe Yrigoyen (Gene's double); Jack Kirk (Smiley's double); Nellie Walker (June's double); Henry Morris (Gabby's double); Jack Long, Tom Steele, Bill Yrigoyen, Wally West, Art Dillard, Jay Wilsey, Carey Loftin, Charles Thomas, Duke York, George Allen, Eddie Parker, Bert LeBaron.

THE FILM: With the longest running time (73 minutes) and largest cost ($98,723) yet afforded a Gene Autry western, Republic was clearly moving their number one star into a higher category of picture. Republic was steering Gene's films away from the traditional B-western programmer; with bigger budgets and better casts they were aiming at A-theater playdates.

To handle the picture, Republic executive producer Armand "Mandy" Schaefer stepped back in as actual line producer of "In Old Monterey". Mandy hadn't served in that position since 1937's "Yodelin' Kid From Pine Ridge". Schaefer also brought back director Joe Kane who hadn't worked with Gene for a year since he'd been moved over to the Roy Rogers series. Dorrell and Stuart McGowan were also reunited with Gene, helping Gerald Geraghty polish his script which dramatically dealt with the real-life war clouds gathering in Europe at a time when America was still deeply isolationist. Newspaper headlines at the start of the picture proclaim "Entire World in an Arms Race" and "War Threat Stirs Europe". Released shortly after the 4th of July, patriotism was clearly on Republic's mind with "In Old Monterey".

With war looming, the Army Air Corps needs to purchase ranch land for a bombing range but ranchers led by Gabby Whittaker (George "Gabby" Hayes) are unwilling to sell the land they have worked hard to develop. Sgt. Gene Autry is sent undercover by the Army to persuade the ranchers to sell and move without a fight.

Unscrupulous Huntley Stevenson (Jonathan Hale),

Crooked foreman William Hall hands out more bad news to Gene and ranchers George "Gabby" Hayes, Fred Burns and Frank Ellis.

Even though the patriotic approach is laid on a bit heavy handed, it no doubt served its purpose in 1939. The only other drawback to one of Gene's best pictures is a preponderance of comedy material from WSM, Nashville, Radio's Sarie and Sallie, the Hoosier Hot Shots and Smiley Burnette. However, a fast action finish and Gene's warbling of the classic "Tumbling Tumbleweeds", the touching "My Buddy", and the title tune serve to offset these overages.

NOTES AND COMMENTS: Republic had originally scheduled Ward Bond for the role of mine foreman Gilman. For whatever reason, he was replaced by William Hall at $350 a week. Gabby Hayes worked for $515.62 a week, the same figure he was getting on the Roy Rogers pictures according to Republic production notes. The Hoosier Hot Shots each received $562.50 a week on a two week guarantee—$4,500 for two weeks. Jonathan Hale made $750, Billy Lee $250, Robert Warwick $500, stuntman Joe Yrigoyen $300 and Sarie and Sallie $100 each per week.

The Hoosier Hot Shots were a very popular comic novelty group on WLS' "National Barn Dance", having joined the Chicago radio program in 1933. Before signing with Republic, several heated Western Union telegrams were sent back and forth between Chicago and Hollywood. Fellow members of "The National Barn Dance", Lulu Belle and Scotty, had appeared in Roy Rogers' Republic film "Shine On Harvest Moon" in 1938. Apparently, Lulu Belle and Scotty were not pleased with their treatment as a May 29, 1939, telegram from Earl Kurtz of Artists Bureau Inc. in Chicago, representing the Hot Shots read, "They (Hot Shots) want some assurance that the picture will not be like Lulu Belle and Scotty's and that they will not be handled in the same careless way." E. H. Goldstein, Republic General Manager, replied, "The fact we are intending to spend more money on this Autry picture than we have spent on any Autry ever produced should be sufficient assurance for the Hot Shots that we would do nothing that would hurt (them). Have talked with Mandy Schaefer who is producing the picture and he tells me the Hot Shots have the best parts ever written into any of our pictures for a guest act." The Hot Shots then signed the contracts but apparently included a clause totally unacceptable to Republic as noted in Goldstein's later telegram to Kurtz also on May 29, 1939. "We are sorry but we cannot under any circumstances agree to the changes as no studio in California would place themselves in the position which in substance is that if an artist does not like something in the script they can walk out or if they are asked to do something in a picture they don't like they will refuse. Such a paragraph is completely out.

president of the Atlas Borax Company, is informed the government won't pay his price for his mine, that the price is too high and the government appraisal is fair. In defiance, Stevenson has his foreman (William Hall) keep the ranchers stirred up so public sentiment will force the government to pay a higher price.

Gene and Frog (Smiley Burnette) show the ranchers and townspeople war newsreels depicting tragic scenes in China and Spain. In a out-of-the-norm all-out patriotic pitch for a western, Gene argues the United States could be victimized by high altitude bombing if the Army doesn't develop better weapons, which is why the Army needs the bombing range.

Stirred by patriotism, Gabby confesses he was thinking only of himself and not the 140 million other people in the country. Proclaiming he owes his country an apology, Gabby leads the throng in singing "Columbia, the Gem of the Ocean".

But Gene's victory is short-lived when Stevenson's men dynamite the Whittaker ranch, killing young Jimmy Whittaker (Billy Lee), and blame the tragedy on the Army's bombing runs.

Leading lady June Storey has had little to do up until the death of her little brother in the bombing sequence. At this point, she becomes bitterly antagonistic to Gene, making him look and feel guilty in a way seldom seen in his westerns. That sense of responsibility is underlined by the remorseful singing of "The Vacant Chair" sung by both Gene and June Storey. Gene completes the film as June looks on with complete disdain. This is more than the usual romantic misunderstanding seen in Gene's films.

Gene must now prove Stevenson's sabotage and win back the support of the ranchers.

This refers to paragraph three which they inserted. Please take this up with the boys immediately and have them wire us if they are satisfied with original contract," which the Hot Shots did. And they were as well represented in "In Old Monterey" as any group had been in an Autry picture.

Gene Autry's triumphant six week good will tour of the British Isles began August 3, 1939, after sailing from New York on July 26.

Oddly, Gene had a bit of trouble securing a passport for this tour to England and Ireland as he couldn't prove he was born. His native Tioga, Texas, did not issue birth certificates at the time Gene was born so the cowboy had to round-up his family physician. Locating the doctor after an intensive search, affidavits from five residents of Tioga who were living when Gene was born were eventually secured.

Upon arrival in London, Gene sent a telegram to syndicated columnist Bosley Crowther which read, "Arrived in London. Tremendous reception. A-ridin' high. Yippee."[1]

The tour was the brainstorm of publicist Bill Saal whom Gene termed "A wild man, but one of the finest PR men I ever saw." Accompanying Gene and Saal was Republic president Herbert J. Yates and, of course, Champion. In his autobiography, BACK IN THE SADDLE AGAIN, Gene recalled, "Through the entire tour, of course, Champion was treated with a courtesy and respect given few other American entertainers. They asked me to bring him to a luncheon in my honor at the Savoy Hotel in London and I did. I led him through the lobby of that elegant hostelry, where the princes of Europe have met, and later he walked among the tables at my reception, while the startled guests protected their plates."[2]

To say Gene's reception in England was overwhelming would be an understatement. He was mobbed by a throng of thousands who jammed the streets of London to see Gene

and Champion for the British premiere at the Tottenham Court Road Paramount Theater of "Colorado Sunset". Upon leaving the theater the crowds were so thick Gene and Bill Saal had to jump to the roof of a smallish British car to make their exit onto the street. Unable to move from there, they found themselves slowly sinking down as the roof slid down into the center of the car. Later, unable to locate the owner, they felt guilty but could do nothing about it at that point.

Meanwhile, war clouds were gathering over Europe. Gene was in Liverpool the day the Nazis marched into Poland. As he wrote in his autobiography, "But all of that, the war talk, the guns going off in our imagination, had something to do with the size of the crowds and the emotion they showered on us. It was a kind of last hurrah, I guess. People had a sense of their lives changing, of time running out on make-believe things. In Dublin, when we paraded through town with Champion, 300,000 lined the streets to watch, what was then thought to be a world record for anyone less than a Pope."[3]

The crowd in Dublin was within about 50,000 of the entire population of the city at that time. Gene's appearance at the Theatre Royal in Dublin broke all records with $22,000 in one day, topping Gracie Fields, England's number one comedienne by $4,000.

Gene and his group returned home by plane on September 14.

So impressed were they by Gene, the British government ordered Gene's entire schedule of 1939 features for showing to their soldiers.

FILM COMMENTS: *Gene Autry:* "'In Old Monterey' was considered another big picture that year, mainly because you didn't find Smiley Burnette, Gabby Hayes, and myself working together very often. Gabby was wonderful, always with a yarn to spin.

"According to some critics, the only drawback to the film was that you also got the Hoosier Hot Shots, a western forerunner of Spike Jones and his City Slickers. This was another group out of WLS radio. They made strange noises with rub-boards, slide whistles, pig bladders, and whoopee cushions. Hezzie, the comedian of the group, could also wiggle his ears. 'Are you ready, Hezzie?' was their trademark. Their biggest hit was, 'I've Got Tears in My Ears From Lying on My Back in Bed While I Cry Over You'.[4] The only act that could follow the Hoosier Hot Shots was Champion (Chuckles)."[5]

June Storey: "Republic producer Mandy (Armand) Schaefer's daughter's name was Jill, so he had me named that for 'In Old Monterey'."[6]

WHAT THE EXHIBITOR HAD TO SAY: "Here is the series that never fails us. We have found the best spot for them is on bank nights."

—E. C. Arehart, Strand Theater, Milford, Iowa
(October 1939)

Gene and Smiley seem to have more important things on their minds than June Storey's dress caught in the door.

Thousands of people turned out to greet Gene Autry upon his arrival in London, England.

"Not as good as his usual picture, but pleased our audience."　　　　—George S. Caporal, Yale Theater, Oklahoma City, Oklahoma (January 1940)

"This was brought back to better business than the first time."　　　　—Miss Cleo Manry, Buena Vista Theater, Buena Vista, Georgia (January 1943)

SOURCES:
1. Bosley Crowther column, August 3, 1939.
2. Autry with Herskowitz. p. 71.
3. ibid. p. 72.
4. ibid. p. 68.
5. "Melody Ranch Theater" showing of "In Old Monterey" on Nashville Network, 1987.
6. Interview with author.

Rovin' Tumbleweeds
Republic, November 1939

Producer ....William Berke
Director ....George Sherman
Assistant Director.......................Harry Knight
Screenplay.................................Betty Burbridge, Dorrell
                           and Stuart McGowan
Photography ....William Nobles
Film Editor................................Tony Martinelli
Musical Supervisor ....Raoul Kraushaar
Production Manager...................Al Wilson

SONGS: "Ole Peaceful River" (music and lyrics by Johnny Marvin)—sung by Gene Autry and flood victims; "Away Out Yonder" (music and lyrics by Johnny Marvin)—sung by Gene Autry, others; "On the Sunny Side of the Cell" (music and lyrics by Johnny Marvin, Fred Rose)—sung by Smiley Burnette and Pals of the Golden West; "Paradise In the Moonlight" (music and lyrics by Gene Autry, Fred Rose)—sung by Gene Autry and Pals of the Golden West; "Back In the Saddle Again" (music and lyrics by Gene Autry, Ray Whitley)—sung by Gene Autry and Pals of the Golden West; "Rocky Mountain Express" (music and lyrics by C. H. Tobias, H. Tobias, A. Von Tilzer)—sung by Pals of the Golden West, Smiley Burnette; "Hurray" (music and lyrics by Eddie Cherkose, Smiley Burnette)—sung by Smiley Burnette; "A Girl Like You" (music and lyrics by Johnny Marvin)—sung by Gene Autry.

RUNNING TIME: 64 minutes

FILMING DATES: September 19 to October 2, 1939

LOCATIONS: Burro Flats; Corriganville; Chatsworth Railroad Station; Republic backlot

BUDGET: $72,387
NEGATIVE COST: $ 74,013

CAST:

Actor	*Character*
Gene Autry	Gene Autry
Smiley Burnette	Frog Millhouse
Mary Carlisle	Mary Ford
Douglass Dumbrille	Stephen Holloway
Pals of the Golden West: Nora Lou Martin, Ray "Bud" Jackson, Howard Russell, Larry Shaw, Harold Pulliam..............	Singers
William Farnum	Senator Timothy Nolan
Lee "Lasses" White.....................	Storekeeper
Ralph Peters	Satchel
Gordon Hart	Congressman Fuller
Vic Potel....................................	Man in store
Jack Ingram................................	Blockade boss Blake
Sammy McKim............................	Eddie
Reginald Barlow	Higgins
Eddie Kane.................................	Congressman
Guy Usher	Charles H. Craig
Fred Burns.................................	Rancher Taylor
Horace B. Carpenter....................	Radio listener
Ed Cassidy	Sheriff
Tom Chatterton	Speaker of the House
Maurice Costello.........................	Ways and Means Committee member
Frank Ellis..................................	Angry Rancher Morgan
Charles K. French	Committee member
Jane Keckley	Mrs. Casey
Crauford Kent	Congressman Hutton
Jack Kirk	Man with Gene
Bud McClure..............................	Migrant
Joe McGuinn..............................	Henchman
Art Mix......................................	Brawler
Chuck Morrison	Man at packing company
Horace Murphy	Jailer
Bud Osborne	Man from Development Corporation
Rose Plummer.............................	Rancher's wife

Harry Semels.................................Peanut Vendor
David Sharpe................................Reporter
Lee Shumway...............................Congressman Ran-dolph
Forrest Taylor..............................Casey
Tex Terry......................................Angry Rancher Berg
Fred "Snowflake" Toones ....Porter
Slim Whitaker.............................Migrant
Dan White....................................Townsman
Billy Byrne..................................Jimmy (schoolboy)
Imboden Parrish..........................Reporter
Brandon Beach............................Politician
Joe Sully.....................................Hamburger Stand man
Nina Gilbert................................Mrs. Nolan
Jean DeBriac...............................Ambassador Roget
John P. Wade...............................Chairman of Committee
Frankie Marvin, Kermit Maynard,
   William Nestell, Robert Barry,
   Jack Gallagher, Betty Mack,
   Frank Meredith, Herberta Wil-
   liams, Marguerite Cole, Bob
   Burns, Hank Worden, Francis
   Sayles, Augie Gomez, Bob
   Wilke ....Extras
Champion....................................Champion

STUNTS: Joe Yrigoyen (Gene's double), Jack Kirk (Smiley's double), Dave Sharpe.

THE FILM: Republic seemed bent on a patriotic/topical spree with Gene Autry. After their war preparedness theme of "In Old Monterey", they next borrowed a theme from the Jimmy Stewart/Frank Capra classic "Mr. Smith Goes to Washington" ('39 Columbia) and sent Gene off to Congress where he encountered constant difficulties in getting his flood control bill introduced.

The film is a perfect example of the real life situations and problems farmers, migrants and ranchers faced, most of whom were Gene's biggest movie-going audience in rural areas.

The crusading congressman plot deviates from the "usual" Autry formula and was received badly at first, many thinking Gene was out of place in Washington, but history has been kind to it and most viewers now regard it as an Autry classic. As a social commentary on the times it has much to say, even if the pure western elements are muted. Actually, many western fundamentals were moderated in Gene's later Republic pictures, but that's exactly one of the several differences which set Gene apart from the plethora of other B-western heroes and consequently

put him in the #1 position at the boxoffice…along with his winning smile, genuine warmth, charismatic personality and fabulous singing.

When floods lay waste to the Green River Valley, Gene Autry, Frog Millhouse (Smiley Burnette) and the other ranchers are forced to abandon their homes. Moving to neighboring Rand County, the migrants are met with hostility by the citizens who feel threatened by the influx of the disposed who are forced to work for low wages.

With the backing of radio station KYX, Mary Ford (charming Mary Carlisle) gets Gene a job singing on the radio in order to finance relief efforts.

Unknown to all, Holloway (Douglas Dumbrille), owner of the Randville Development Corporation, is conspiring with Congressman Fuller (Gordon Hart) to block a flood control bill in Washington until he can drive the ranchers out and buy up their land for taxes.

When the people become disenchanted with Fuller, Holloway sneakily throws his support behind the popular radio star and convinces Gene to run for Congress on a flood control platform. Holloway believes he can control Gene once the fledging congressman reaches Washington.

Elected, and in Washington, along with Frog and Mary as his secretary, Gene is stymied by bureaucratic red tape at every turn.

Defeated in his efforts to pass a flood control bill, Gene returns home in the midst of another torrential downpour. As Gene manages to bring the townspeople and the migrants together to fight the raging water and avoid disaster, even Holloway finally realizes the importance of flood control and agrees to make restitution and support Gene's bill.

NOTES AND COMMENTS: Republic liked the title

Congressman Gene Autry and Mary Carlisle rally the people to band together and fight the raging floodwaters in the climax to "Rovin' Tumbleweeds."

Obviously Gene's fed up with the underhanded dealings of Douglas Dumbrille (right) and Congressman Gordon Hart.

"Washington Cowboy". They assigned it to, what turned out to be Roy Rogers' first film after Gene went on strike, "Under Western Stars" ('38). They also assigned it to what was eventually released as "Rovin' Tumbleweeds". Another working title for this picture was "Raiders of the Wasteland".

As many times in previous Autry films, contemporary subjects or names are mentioned. "Rovin' Tumbleweeds" contains a reference to the great race horse Seabiscuit and a RADIO GUIDE magazine (with Gene on the cover) is shown.

The first performance on film by Gene of his most famous song, "Back in the Saddle Again", is in "Rovin' Tumbleweeds". The song, as written by Ray Whitley, was first featured in George O'Brien's "Border G-Man" ('38 RKO).

Floods actually inundated California's Imperial Valley in early 1939, which may have given Betty Burbridge and the McGowans the idea for their story. At any rate, authentic newsreel footage of the flood and refugee evacuation procedures were incorporated into "Rovin' Tumbleweeds".

Douglas Dumbrille pulled in $1,000 for the picture with William Farnum getting $100 a day. Other weekly payments were: Gordon Hart $200; Jack Ingram $100; Sammy McKim $125; Fred Toones $125; the Pals of the Golden West $66 each, and stuntman Joe Yrigoyen $300.

FILM COMMENTS: *Sammy McKim:* "I don't remember too much about this picture, except one scene where leading lady (Mary Carlisle) was thrown from her horse, ripped her pants and didn't want to come out of the bushes when Gene came along—too modest! I told Gene I had my swimsuit under my Levi's and volunteered *my* pants for her. She accepted (leaving me in my shirttails!) All according to the script! Gene was 'all business' on

the various sets—knew his lines and didn't give the director any trouble (like a few stars had reputations for). Gene was respected and well-liked. Walt Disney Imagineering (where I worked for 32 years as an illustrator-designer) designed much of the display areas for the Autry Western Heritage Museum. Gene came over once for an initial meeting. Van Romans, who was coordinating things, didn't know I'd been an actor and knew Gene. He said he'd call me into his office next time Gene came over—but Gene never made a second trip. However, I did meet Gene's wife, Jackie, at one later meeting, at which I gave her a large 'get well card' I'd made for Gene, was a number of Disney people's signatures. Gene had fallen, broken his hip and was recuperating at home. Van Romans arranged for Gene's coming to Disney's for my retirement party (Jan. '87), but Gene had fallen again and aggravated the same hip. He couldn't come, but signed my official retirement card with many of my fellow workers—and sent along a color 8x10 photo of himself with '6-shooters' drawn, signed to me with warm personal regards."[1]

Mary Carlisle: "'Rovin' Tumbleweeds" is considered one of Gene's best films, and I do agree. He was a nice man to me. A charming man. Romance? Heavens, no! I wasn't married at the time but I never became much interested in other people that way—except for my husband, James Blakely, who did work as an actor in the '30s."[2]

CAST BIOS: Ray Whitley is country music's almost forgotten jack-of-all-trades. He starred in movies, designed instruments, wrote songs and organized bands. Music he wrote over 30 years ago has made it into today's top 10 tunes.

Born in Atlanta, Georgia, on December 5, 1901, Ray grew up in Alabama. In his early life Ray spent time as a Texas ranch hand, iron worker, electrician, taxi driver, structural steel worker and with the Navy.

As construction work declined in the depression of the '30s, Ray put his singing voice and guitar playing to work, organizing the Range Ramblers band. Later Whitley bands were the Six-Bar Cowboys, the Oklahoma Wranglers and the Rhythm Wranglers.

In 1935 Ray signed with Decca and his recordings took on a western flavor and led to a movie career.

It was during his movie making days that Whitley wrote the classic "Back In the Saddle Again". "We were scheduled to record the music for a motion picture at 7am that morning, but the telephone rang at 5am, and it was my producer at the studio calling to tell me to come up with another song before the 7am recording session because they were one song short. As I hung up the phone, I told my wife,

Gene and songwriter / singer Ray Whitley who composed what became Gene's themesong, "Back in the Saddle Again."

Fred Rose.

of hit songs for Gene's films and records. Gene termed him "the best song doctor I ever knew."[4]

Knowles Fred Rose was born in Evansville, Indiana, August 24, 1898. His parents separated soon after he was born and Fred grew up with relatives in St. Louis where he supplemented the family income by playing piano for tips in local saloons.

By 1917 he was in Chicago where he found similar work in the rough bars on the Windy City's south side.

During the '20s Rose made his name as a successful song writer, authoring or co-authoring pop and jazz hits like "Red Hot Mama". During these same years he also made piano rolls; broadcast on Chicago radio stations and recorded for the Brunswick label.

Moving to Nashville, between 1933 and 1938 he shopped his songs to music publishers. In 1936 he scored his first western/pop hit with "We'll Rest at the End of the Trail" recorded by Tex Ritter, the Sons of the Pioneers and Bing Crosby.

Out of this came his association with Gene Autry from 1938-1942 in Hollywood. Gene referred to Fred as "gifted" and said they "worked well together, often sitting down and designing a song for a particular movie scene."[5]

In 1942 Rose joined country music giant Roy Acuff in founding Acuff-Rose Publications, Nashville's first major country-music publishing company.

Rose continued to pen songs such as "Blue Eyes Crying In the Rain" and served as MGM's Nashville-based A&R man.

He was responsible for bringing the genius of Hank Williams to MGM, and many other artists to Capitol and RCA Victor.

Rose died December 1, 1954. He was posthumously elected to the Country Music Hall of Fame in 1961, the first year the honor was bestowed by the Country Music Association.

WHAT THE EXHIBITOR HAD TO SAY: "A fair picture. By all means not one of Autry's best, but it will do."
—P. S. Caporal, Mayflower Theater, Oklahoma City, Oklahoma (February 1940)

'Well, they need another song, so I'm back in the saddle again.' She quickly replied, 'Well there's your title—'Back in the Saddle Again'.' So I sat down and started working on it and in less than an hour, I had the melody and a verse finished." Ray performed the song in "Border G-Man" ('38 RKO) starring George O'Brien. "But the song would have been just another song without the help of my friend and co-writer, Gene Autry," Ray explained. "Gene recorded the song on Columbia Records and 'Back in the Saddle Again' became his theme song."[3] Gene sang it in "Rovin' Tumbleweeds" and it was later the title song of Gene's 1941 Republic film "Back In the Saddle" and has been his theme song since.

Fred Rose and Whitley wrote songs together, including "I Hang My Head and Cry" and "Ages and Ages Ago". Many of their collaborations were used in the Tim Holt films and the Whitley shorts. Inspired by Whitley and country-western music, Rose later moved to Nashville and launched the famous Acuff-Rose music publishing company.

Whitley's last film was a role in "Giant" ('56). He died February 21, 1979.

Fred Rose was a principal figure in the rise of the Nashville music industry between 1942 and 1954 in the roles of music publisher, song writer, producer and talent scout. But before all that, he and Gene Autry wrote a host

SOURCES:

1. *Western Clippings* #27. January/February 1999. p. 8.

2. Interview with author. 1998.

3. Interview with Gerald F. Vaughn. 1973.

4. "Melody Ranch Theater" showing of "Under Fiesta Stars" on Nashville Network, 1987.

5. Autry with Herskowitz, p. 26.

South of the Border
Republic, December 1939

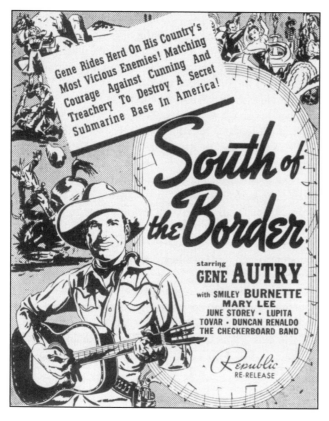

lyrics by Jimmy Kennedy, Michael Carr)—sung by Gene Autry; "Moon of Manana" (music and lyrics by Johnny Marvin)—sung by Gene Autry; "Girl of My Dreams" (music and lyrics by Sunny Clapp)—sung by Gene Autry; "Goodbye Little Darlin'" (music and lyrics by Gene Autry, Johnny Marvin)—sung by Gene Autry, Mary Lee; "Merry-Go-Roundup" (music and lyrics by Gene Autry, Fred Rose, Johnny Marvin)—sung by Mary Lee; "When the Cactus Blooms Again" (music and lyrics by Gene Autry, Johnny Marvin)—sung by Gene Autry and the Checkerboard Band; "The Horse Opry" (music and lyrics by Fred Rose, E. G. Nelson)—sung by June Storey, Gene Autry; "Fat Caballero" (music and lyrics by Smiley Burnette)—sung by Smiley Burnette.

RUNNING TIME: 71 minutes

FILMING DATES: October 30 to November 11, 1939

LOCATIONS: Palmdale area; Republic backlot; Corriganville; oil field located in Baldwin Hills near LAX

BUDGET: $75,947

NEGATIVE COST: $80,342

Producer ....William Berke
Director ....George Sherman
Assistant Director.........................Harry Knight; George Webster
Original Story..............................Dorrell and Stuart McGowan
Screenplay....................................Betty Burbridge, Gerald Geraghty
Photography ....William Nobles
Film Editor...................................Lester Orlebeck
Musical Supervisor ....Raoul Kraushaar
Production Manager....................Al Wilson

SONGS: "Come to the Fiesta" (music and lyrics by Art Wenzel)—sung by Gene Autry, Smiley Burnette and The Checkerboard Band; "South of the Border" (music and

CAST:

Actor	Character
Gene Autry	Gene Autry
Smiley Burnette	Frog Millhouse
June Storey	Lois Martin
Lupita Tovar	Dolores Mendoza
Mary Lee	Patsy
Duncan Renaldo	Andreo Mendoza
Frank Reicher	Don Diego Mendoza
Alan Edwards	Saunders
Claire DuBrey	Duenna
Dick Botiller	Pablo
William Farnum	Padre
Selmer Jackson	American Consul
The Checkerboard Band: Clyde "Buddy" Gilmore, Wesley Patterson, Sid Sherman, George Thall, Art Wenzel	Musicians
Sheila Darcy	Rosita
Curley Dresden	Bandit Chico

Reed Howes	Henchman Weber
Charles King	Bandit Mike
Rex Lease	Radio Operator Flint
Bud Pope	Mexican Rurale
Hal Price	Ship Captain
Julian Rivero	Juan
Slim Whitaker	Carlos
Bill Yrigoyen	Henchman
Augie Gomez	Coachman
Joe De La Cruz	Driver
Trini Varella	Fortune Teller
Almeda Fowler	Matron
Danton Ferraro	Customs Inspector
Tony Martelli	Ship Steward
Chuck Baldra, Jim Corey, Bess Flowers, Frankie Marvin, Merrill McCormick, George Montgomery, Buck Moulton, Jack O'Shea, Jack Perrin, Ernest Sarracino, Francisco Maran, Bud McClure, Herman Hack	Extras
Champion	Champion

STUNTS: Joe Yrigoyen (Gene's double), Jack Kirk (Smiley's double), Nellie Walker (June's double); Bill Yrigoyen; Duke York.

THE FILM: Initially, the fanciful plot of "South of the Border" promises great romance with its fortune teller's dream-like beginning and the hugely popular song, then turns quite different with its tale of foreign agents fomenting revolution down Palermo way, submarine bases

The famous "near kiss" between Lupita Tovar and Gene.

and all, threatening the Pan American neutrality act.

Government agents Gene Autry and Frog Millhouse (Smiley Burnette) are dispatched south of the border to foil the plans of foreign spies trying to start a revolution in (fictional) Palermo to obtain control of American oil concessions and establish a submarine refueling base.

To his dismay, Gene learns the brother (Duncan Renaldo) of the beautiful senorita (Lupita Tovar), whom Gene has fallen in love with, is a renegade patriot involved with the saboteurs.

On the way to Palermo, Gene is followed by a teenage waif, Patsy (Mary Lee), who insists on calling him "Daddy".

Gene also becomes involved with Lois Martin (June Storey), an unwitting cantina dancer accomplice of the spies.

Successfully winning out over the plotters, Gene is less successful when he returns home to find Tovar has turned her affections toward the nunnery to atone for the indiscretions of her renegade brother.

Director George Sherman fills the picture with smart showmanship, capturing both the plaintive romance as well as the melodrama with equal assurance, turning "South of the Border" into Gene's biggest hit film to date, and as history would prove, of all time.

NOTES AND COMMENTS: Young Mary Lee, in her first of nine pictures with Gene Autry, was paid $250 a week on a two week guarantee on loan-out from orchestra leader Ted Weems. Lupita Tovar also earned $250 a week while Claire DuBrey and Alan Edwards earned (some would argue) inflated for their worth compared to Lee, Tovar and Storey, respective weekly payments of $400 and $375. Frank Reicher, in his brief role, was paid even more—$600 for a week's work. Dick Botiller, Rex Lease and Slim Whitaker each drew $100 a week. William Farnum's pivotal role of the Padre earned him $500.

Gene first heard the title tune, "South of the Border", during his personal appearance tour of the British Isles in August 1939. Two songwriters, Jimmy Kennedy and Michael Carr, who had never been to America or Mexico, and who had never seen a cowboy, came backstage in Dublin, Ireland, where Gene was appearing with a song they wanted him to record. The song writing duo had already written such hits as "Red Sails in the Sunset", "Harbor Lights" and "Isle of Capri". Gene recognized a hit tune and persuaded Republic Pictures boss Herbert J. Yates to buy it for a movie. It became one of Gene's biggest hits.

Likewise, Gene's duet with his cute new co-star, "Goodbye, Little Darlin'", is a stand-out.

Although it cast no aspersions on Mexico or its people, "South of the Border" was banned by Mexico in the summer of 1940 for showing anywhere within its borders. Mexico's government was supersensitive to American releases which, it thought, would detrimentally affect their country and citizens.

After completion of "South of the Border", Gene made

South of the border, Gene's got the drop on troublemaker Duncan Renaldo while Smiley and Mary Lee lend support.

a tour of the World's Fair amusement zone on November 22, 1939, where he was crowned 'King of the Cowboys' by Ruth Mix, daughter of Tom Mix, at a Wild West Show and Rodeo.

Gene began his long-running CBS radio show "Melody Ranch" for the Wrigley gum company on January 7, 1940. Gene explained, "Indirectly, I brought home something else from that tour (of the British Isles). P. K. Wrigley happened to be in Dublin the day Champion and I paraded through town. At the time, he had been thinking about a radio show for Doublemint gum to sponsor. He went back to his advertising agency in Chicago and told them of an unbelievable sight he had witnessed, a singing cowboy who drew 300,000 people in the streets of Dublin.

"I was on the set of "Shooting High" when I answered a telephone page. The call was from Danny Danker, of the J. Walter Thompson agency, the man who made Lux toilet soap famous. When I put down the phone I turned to Carl Cotner and Frankie Marvin, who had bit parts in the film, and said, 'Hey, stick your fiddles in the car tomorrow. We're going to do an audition for CBS for a radio show for the Wrigley people.' The three of us walked into the CBS studios on Sunset Boulevard the next day. Out of that came 'Melody Ranch'. We went on the air with it in 1940. It lasted sixteen good years."[1]

According to Gene on his "Melody Ranch Theater" Nashville Network TV series, his initial salary for the radio show was $1,500 a week which eventually rose to $5,000 per week after 16 years.

FILM COMMENTS: *June Storey:* "Didn't Mary Lee have a great voice? Very natural actress. She didn't have a reputation of *knowing* her chalk marks, it just came out of her like a fountain. 'South of the Border' was popular because everyone loved the song. There was great support in the cast of Gene's films. How could you not enjoy Mary

Lee or Gene's singing? Or the humor of Smiley?" Of course it was Herbert J. Yates who ran Republic. Papa Yates, as we used to call him either lovingly or unlovingly, (laughs) had his own way, shall we say. He looked like a little eagle to me. (Laughs) I wasn't afraid of him. I think I was too stupid to be afraid. He used to go ice skating with a little tam (a French looking hat) on the side of his head. (Laughs) One of the things I proposed to Papa Yates was that Nellie Walker, the stunt girl, who was having kind of a rough time, I suggested, with all the work she was doing at Republic, he should put her under contract. She would work more and (it would) give her a steady income. So I just walked into this office and said, 'Why don't you give Nellie a contract?' And he did. I have the impression it was the first time a stunt person in Hollywood had been given a contract, they were usually paid by the stunt, or by the picture.

"When I was in high school, there were 48 youngsters in the glee club. And guess who was asked to leave because they were throwing the entire class off key? (Laughs) Watch 'South of the Border'...well, I always had a very small voice, a small singing voice, it didn't carry very far, and not always on key. So they decided to always dub over it with someone else's voice but I *should* sing on camera because it makes you appear more natural, as you're singing the words. So, where we're singing at the table in the cantina, I look up and all the fellas up on the lights, the grips, everybody, are kidding, holding their noses, 'Oh, how awful'...sticking their fingers in their ears! 'Ooh, get her off!' (Chuckles) My little tiny voice...Gene started to laugh in the scene. I couldn't keep a straight face 'cause every time I'd look a little bit away from Gene, they're all making these terrible gestures at me. So Gene's smiling in that scene on film was not only because he was enjoying what he was doing but he was laughing 'cause the whole crew was making fun of me. You'll never see such a happy group of singers! No—I don't sing well at all!"[2]

Gene Autry: "Mary Lee was about nine years old when her father took her to one of my shows and I met her backstage. At that time neither of us suspected our trails would cross again. A few years passed and Mary blossomed into a beautiful teenager with a wonderful singing voice. I heard her perform with the Ted Weems Orchestra and I knew this little girl was hitched to a big star. I was right. Mary appeared in 'South of the Border' and fans took her to their hearts right away. From that first movie, through numerous others. Mary charmed and sang her way into our lives. It wasn't only the movie fans that loved her; the cast and crew did too. It was hard not to! She was a ray of sunshine, a talented firebrand of energy, and she could sing like an angel."[3]

Mary Lee: "Gene Autry and Smiley Burnette were on the WLS Barn Dance program out of Chicago on Saturday nights, but during the week they toured the regional towns on one-night stands. When they came to Ottawa (Illinois), Daddy took me backstage and Mr. Autry shook hands with me and gave me one of his songbooks. I didn't dream, then, that one day I would be fortunate enough to appear in Mr.

Gene and 15 year old Mary Lee made a perfect team and were extremely popular with audiences.

Autry's pictures. Mother and I flew out to Hollywood. Our plane was about four hours late, arriving at four in the morning. Mr. and Mrs. Autry were at the airport to meet us, and took us to their home to spend the night. Two days later, I reported to the studio for my first picture, 'South of the Border'."[4]

Lupita Tovar: "Gene became a Top Ten box office star. That picture made a lot of money! Gene was a lovely cowboy. A lovely person, such a gentleman. Smiley, his sidekick, was always nice. I particularly remember the little girl, Mary Lee—such a talent, and the other leading lady, June Storey, who was very pretty." As for the famous near-miss-kiss scene with Gene in the carriage, "It *was* in the script. Gene Autry *never* kissed a girl; he was very pure for the kids. Today we would have been doing more than kissing. (Laughs)"[5] (Obviously Lupita was unaware of Gene's earlier films with kissing scenes.)

CAST BIOS: The super talented brown-haired, brown eyed Mary Lee was only 15 when she began co-starring with Gene Autry.

Mary Lee Wooters was born in Centralia, Illinois, October 24, 1924. Her father was a barber and moved the family to Ottawa, Illinois, where he also sang on radio with Mary's older sister, Vera. Soon Mary began to join in as the trio performed at local gatherings.

In May 1938, a ballroom manager arranged an audition for Mary with popular bandleader Ted Weems, best known for his recording of "Heartaches". Weems approved and hired the then 13 year old.

While appearing with Weems at the Avalon Ballroom on Catalina Island, Warner Bros. talent scouts heard Mary

and signed her for a role in "Nancy Drew, Reporter" ('39) with Bonita Granville and Frankie Thomas.

Gene heard the 4' 11", 100 pound Mary singing one of his songs with Weems and arranged for her to co-star with him in "South of the Border". Her wonderful singing voice and delightful screen presence became Republic's answer to Judy Garland at MGM and Deanna Durbin at Universal as she appeared in nine of Gene's films and later two with Roy Rogers.

Mary's sister Vera worked for Autry as one of his secretaries. Her older sister, Norma Jean Wooters, was also blessed with singing and acting ability and was seen in two Charles Starrett B-westerns at Columbia, "Bad Men of the Hills" ('42) and "Fighting Buckaroo" ('43). Their father worked for years as a caretaker at Gene's home, and later offices, at 1098 Bluffside Dr. in N. Hollywood.

Mary Lee's melodious voice was silenced professionally when she married an Army sergeant in late 1943 and left showbiz behind to rear two children, Phillip and Laura.

For many years she worked with the Southern California Good Sam Club.

At 71, Mary died on June 6, 1996, in the Agoura Hills, California, area.

WHAT THE EXHIBITOR HAD TO SAY: "One of the best Autry pictures we have ever played and in my opinion Mary Lee stole the show. She is a marvelous singer. Here's hoping we see more of her." —Fred Basha, Palace Theater, Corner Brook, Newfoundland, Canada (March, 1941)

"Good old Gene Autry, they still like him."
—Harland Rankin, Plaza Theater, Tilbury, Ontario, Canada (April, 1944)

"I doublebilled 'King of the Cowboys' with Roy Rogers with 'South of the Border' and advertised a Rogers versus Autry program to standing room only. Roy and Gene tied for honors but I got the do-re-mi."
—Ella Lindenau, Arthur Theater, Lemont, Illinois (April 1944)

SOURCES:

1. Autry with Herskowitz. p. 74-75.

2. Interview with author.

3. Gene Autry comments written 2/9/98 for Varese Sarabande CD, "Gene Autry With His Little Darlin', Mary Lee".

4. *Western Clippings #27.* January/February 1999. p. 36.

5. *Western Clippings #43.* September/October 2001. p. 20.

Rancho Grande
Republic, March 1940

Gene and leading lady June Storey (to Gene's right) with the Pals of the Golden West.

Producer ....William Berke
Director ....Frank McDonald
Assistant Director........................Harry Knight
Original Story..............................Peter Milne, Connie Lee
Screenplay...................................Bradford Ropes, Betty Burbridge, Peter Milne
Photography ....William Nobles
Film Editor.................................Tony Martinelli
Musical Supervisor ....Raoul Kraushaar

Production Manager.....................Al Wilson

SONGS: "Rancho Grande" (music and lyrics by Del Moral, Emilio Uranga)—sung by studio singers over the credits, then by Gene Autry and the Brewer Kids. Reprised several times throughout the film, once to include Smiley Burnette; "Whistle" (music and lyrics by Gene Autry, Johnny Marvin)—sung by Mary Lee, Gene Autry, Pals of the Golden West; "Dude Ranch Cowhands" (music and lyrics by Gene Autry, Fred Rose, Johnny Marvin)—sung by Gene Autry, Smiley Burnette, ranch hands; "Swing of the Range" (music and lyrics by Johnny Marvin, Harry Tobias)—sung by Mary Lee; "There'll Never Be Another Pal Like You" (music and lyrics by Gene Autry, Johnny Marvin)—sung by Gene Autry; "Ave Maria" (public domain)—sung by The Boys' Choir of St. Joseph's School; "I Don't Belong In Your World" (music and lyrics by Gene Autry, Johnny Marvin, Fred Rose)—sung by Gene Autry; "You Can Take the Boy Out of the Country" (music and lyrics by Smiley Burnette)—sung by Smiley Burnette.

RUNNING TIME: 67 minutes

FILMING DATES: February 7-21, 1940

LOCATIONS: Bronson Canyon; train tunnel beneath Topanga Canyon Road just south of Santa Susanna Pass Road; Republic backlot; Janss Ranch in Thousand Oaks; cattle pens (most likely) at Piru, west of Saugus, California; Chatsworth depot

BUDGET: $76,573

NEGATIVE COST: $75,754

CAST:

Actor	Character
Gene Autry	Gene Autry
Smiley Burnette	Frog Millhouse
June Storey	Kay Dodge
Mary Lee	Patricia "Patsy" Fairfield Dodge
Dick Hogan	Tom Dodge
Ellen Lowe	Effie Tinker
Ferris Taylor	Emory Benson
Rex Lease	Joe Travis
Joseph DeStefani	Jose
Ann Baldwin	Susan Putnam
Pals of the Golden West: Nora Lou Martin, Ray "Bud" Jackson, Howard "Slim" Russell, Larry Shaw, Harold "Lucky" Pulliam	Pals of the Golden West
Boys' Choir of St. Joseph's School	Choir
Roy Barcroft	Madden
The Brewer Kids	Themselves
Horace B. Carpenter	Justice of the Peace
Jack Ingram	Adams
Edna Lawrence	Rita
Bud Osborne	Joe, Croupier
Slim Whitaker	Cowboy who announces wreck
Chuck Baldra	Cowhand Bill
Roscoe Ates	Cowhand Tex
Hank Worden, Augie Gomez, John Treesh, Frankie Marvin, Hank Bell, Cactus Mack	Cowhands
Mildred Shay	Miss Dolan
Marguerite Cole	College Girl #3
Ross Latimer	Dudley
Bill Carey	Alex
Richard Webb	Steve
Eva Puig	Mother Hernandez
Nick Thompson	Father Hernandez
George Volk	Padre
George DeNormand, Bill Yrigoyen, Eddie Parker	Nightclub Bouncers
Ann Bradley	Girl at club
Jim Corey, Ray Jones, William Nestell, Pascale Perry	Extras
Champion	Champion

Mary Lee and Gene.

STUNTS: Joe Yrigoyen (Gene's double); Jack Kirk (Smiley's double); Nellie Walker (June's double); Eddie Parker, Bill Yrigoyen.

THE FILM: By now Gene Autry was at the height of his power as a movie star. Scorn his westerns some might, but he was way out ahead in fan popularity and at the boxoffice. He was singing his best, the rounded, drawling tones he had developed when coming to Hollywood had completely superseded the nasal, Jimmie Rodgers-style of his former years. His was now a sophisticated sound, styled to suit the cowboy/crossover image. Gene could sing western, country and pop, all in his own fashion. His acting style came from his own easy personal charm. By now he and Smiley Burnette were a team in the same league as Laurel and Hardy, Abbott and Costello, Rogers and Astaire and others. Republic was giving Gene top budgets, hit songs and running times of around 70 minutes. His films played not just to rural areas and B-theaters, but in larger venues, and not just here at home but all over the world. Republic and Gene had created a screen image, they knew what pulled the audience in, even if many critics and even co-workers often could not understand it.

Eschewing action and emphasizing music, Gene's friendly nature, Smiley's comedy and the sweet charms of June Storey and Mary Lee, "Rancho Grande" is a very enjoyable film that could be widely appreciated by audiences not usually attracted to westerns. Republic continued to follow this magic formula with Gene's films and even employed it with Roy Rogers when Gene was in the service for WWII. They knew it worked.

As foreman of the vast Rancho Grande, Gene Autry is saddled with the late owner's three Eastern bred grandchildren, Kay and Tom (June Storey, Dick Hogan), both spoiled, madcap college types, and their younger, more level-headed kid sister Patsy (Mary Lee). Gene tries to impress them with the importance of what they possess, the work ethic and what an unfinished irrigation project will mean to settlers in the valley. However, Kay and Tom are more interested in having a good time. All the while, Gene is trying to save Rancho Grande from foreclosure by sneaky lawyer Benson (Ferris Taylor).

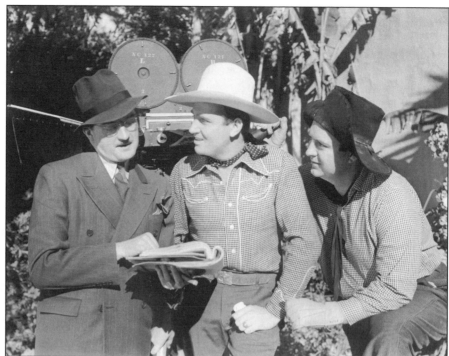

Director Frank McDonald goes over the script with Gene and Smiley.

NOTES AND COMMENTS: Dick Hogan, who specialized in youthful roles, was loaned out to Republic by RKO at $250 a week on a two week guarantee.

Cowboy actor and singer Chuck Baldra, 50, was killed when a train smashed into his car on May 14, 1949. Baldra tried to stop at the tracks but his brakes apparently failed. Accident took place at Sherman Way and Laurel Canyon Blvd. in North Hollywood. The eastbound train carried Baldra's sedan 145 feet, demolishing it. Beginning about 1930, Baldra was in westerns with numerous stars. He often was heard singing around a campfire with Jack Kirk and Glenn Strange.

The joyful "Rancho Grande" had been heard previously in "Mexicali Rose". Gene and Republic liked it well enough, with its south of the border appeal, to feature it here as the title tune.

Gene's "Melody Ranch" radio show on May 19, 1940, guest starred June Storey in a radio recreation of "Rancho Grande".

CAST BIOS: Director Frank McDonald was born November 9, 1899, in Baltimore, Maryland.

A former traffic manager for the Armour and Southern Pacific railroad, McDonald came to Hollywood as a dialogue director at Warner Bros. in 1934 after a 17 year career on the stage as an actor/stage manager/director/and playwright. Working in stock companies in more than 25 cities, he began to direct at Warners in 1935. He landed at Universal in 1938, then Republic in 1940. His first

with Gene was "Rancho Grande" followed by "Gaucho Serenade", "Carolina Moon", "Ride, Tenderfoot, Ride" and "Under Fiesta Stars".

When McDonald was engaged to direct Gene's westerns, Republic president Moe Siegel instructed him not to "direct" Autry's performances lest it cramp the proven personality appeal of Gene's naturalness. With this in mind, McDonald simply and tactfully informed cast members in each scene what Autry would be doing and how they were to respond.

McDonald also helmed several of the Weaver Brothers and Elviry pictures and a string of eight Roy Rogers pictures at Republic before returning to the Autrys after the war with "Sioux City Sue" and "Twilight On the Rio Grande".

He continued to work, primarily at Monogram in the '50s before turning heavily to TV with some 16 episodes of Gene's TV series as well as "Death Valley Days", "Annie Oakley", "Wyatt Earp", "Champion", "Get Smart", "Flipper" and other TVers.

Not only did he "hate the mornings"[1] according to Gene, stuntlady Alice Van told writer Francis Nevins, "McDonald hated westerns, he hated the sun, he hated the wind and the dust and the dirt. He just wasn't a western type. He hated them but they always put him on westerns. He loved to go out at night and have dinner and go to nightclubs and shows, and he hated to get up early in the morning. Everything he hated, he did…we used to all laugh." Van told Nevins McDonald was highly allergic to the sun and, when working outdoors, he'd wear a huge hat to cover his face, a bandana to protect his neck, and half-gloves for his hands, with only the fingers sticking out and getting exposed.[2]

Although Dick Jones didn't become a regular member

of the "Autry stock company" until Gene's Columbia films, he certainly worked with McDonald on many of his "Range Rider" and "Buffalo Bill Jr." TV series for Flying A Productions. "McDonald was one of the top directors Autry ever had around. Very humorous individual. I was sitting in a blacked out set as he came strolling in with his swagger stick, big puffy scarf he always wore under his jacket, and his fedora hat, brim turned up. He walked in there and looked around at the set. It had one of those deer heads over the door. He stands there a moment, contemplating this and says, so seriously, 'That sucker must have been going awfully fast to get stuck that far.' (Laughs) He would save Autry an awful lot of film. He'd start on the master shot, then cut into it for individuals, very few camera moves… he'd get it all done very professionally. He always wore a store hat with the brim curled up, a large silk scarf—very dressy, he'd puff it out of his sport coat. Truthfully, he was a boudoir director. On action, he'd leave it up to the people who knew what they were doing. He'd say, I want to get this angle, that angle, he blocked it out, and we—and the stunt guys—choreographed it."[3]

Actress Evelyn Keyes once said, "I've never seen anyone as terrified of directing as Frank McDonald."[4] Nevertheless, his body of film and TV work is immense.

He died March 8, 1980, in Oxnard, California.

FILM COMMENTS: *Mildred Shay:* "Gene Autry was a darling man. He spoke very fondly of (his former leading lady, Judith Allen) to me. He was angry that Cecil B. DeMille had blacklisted Judy all because she wouldn't sleep with him. I wouldn't sleep with DeMille either but I guess the fact (wealthy New York lawyer) Joseph A. Shay was my daddy I escaped unharmed. Gene and I got on so well partly because I knew how to ride a horse, he detested those blonde bits of fluff who failed to know the difference between the back and the front of a pit pony."[5] (Shay was married three times, the last to a British Cavalry and Guard officer, Geoffrey Steele, a descendant of Mary Queen of Scots. They had one daughter who married Gordon Waller, half of the '60s pop music duo Peter and Gordon. Shay, 94, died October 15, 2005.)

WHAT THE EXHIBITOR HAD TO SAY: "This reissue did not please nor draw as well as the other Autry pictures. There was entirely too much singing and not much action."
—James C. Balkcom Jr., Gray Theater, Gray, GA (August, 1946)

SOURCES:

1. "Melody Ranch Theater" showing of "Sioux City Sue" on Nashville Network, 1987.

2. Interview with Francis Nevins. Circa '80s.

3. Interview with author. February 2006.

4. Interview with Michael Fitzgerald. November 2005.

5. Interview with Austin Mutti-Mews. June 2004.

Shooting High
20ᵗʰ Century–Fox, April 1940

Executive Producer	Sol M. Wurtzel	Photography	Ernest Palmer
Associate Producer	John Stone	Film Editor	Nick DeMaggio
Director	Alfred E. Green	Sound Engineers	Eugene Grossman, William H. Anderson
Assistant Director	Charles Hall		
2ⁿᵈ Unit Director	Otto Brower	Set Decorations	Thomas Little
Original Screenplay	Lou Breslow, Owen Francis	Art Direction	Richard Day, Lewis Creber
Contributing Writers	Harry Akst, Joseph Hoffman, Frances Hyland, Lester Ziffren	Costumes	Helen A. Myron
		Musical Supervisor	Samuel Kaylin
		Production Manager	William Koenig

Choreographer...........................Nick Castle, Geneva Sawyer

SONGS: "Wanderers" (music and lyrics by Felix Bernard and Paul Francis Webster)—sung by Gene Autry, Jane Withers; "In Our Little Shanty Town of Dreams" (music and lyrics by Gene Autry, Johnny Marvin)—sung by Gene Autry, Jane Withers; "There's Only One Love In a Lifetime" (music and lyrics by Gene Autry, Johnny Marvin, Harry Tobias)—sung by Gene Autry; "Little Old Band of Gold" (music and lyrics by Gene Autry, Charles Newman, Fred Glickman)—sung by Gene Autry.

RUNNING TIME: 66 minutes

FILMING DATES: November 18 to December 16, 1939

LOCATIONS: 20th Century–Fox backlot; Santa Susanna Pass; Corriganville

CAST:

Actor	Character
Jane Withers	Jane Pritchard
Gene Autry	Will Carson
Marjorie Weaver	Marjorie Pritchard
Frank M. Thomas	Calvin Pritchard
Robert Lowery	Bob Merritt
Kay Aldridge	Evelyn Trent
Hobart Cavanaugh	Clem Perkle
Jack Carson	Gabby Cross
Hamilton MacFadden	J. Wallace Rutledge
Charles Middleton	Hod Carson
Edward Brady	Mort Carson
Tom London	Eph Carson
Eddie Acuff	Andy Carson
Pat O'Malley	Sam "Lem" Pritchard
George Chandler	Charles Pritchard
Bob Card	Storekeeper Dave Pritchard
LeRoy Mason	Russ, First Crook
Lee Moore	Bert, Second Crook
Harold Goodwin	Third Crook
George Chesebro	Man Getting a shave
Frank Ellis	Rufe Pritchard
Dick French	Movie Crewman with fake money
Frank McCarroll	Hiram Pritchard, known as "Deef and Dumb"
Ivan Miller	Attorney Sanders
Kathryn Sheldon	Hotel woman
Georgia Simmons	Aggie
Emmett Vogan	Surveyor McCormick
Budd Buster, Foxy Callahan, Jess Cavan, Johnny Luther, Herman Nowlin, Pascale Perry, Snub Pollard, Herman Willingham, Henry Wills, Merrill McCormick, Ray Jones, Hank Worden, Frankie Marvin, Carl Cotner	Townspeople

Champion...................................Champion

STUNTS: Henry Wills.

THE FILM: "Shooting High" was Gene's first feature away from his home lot of Republic. Gene and the Republic heads considered it a good move as the film would be seen in theaters not normally playing Gene Autry pictures. Juvenile box office star Jane Withers had enough clout to persuade all parties to make the co-starrer. The sensational teaming certainly made the venture a success although Autry fans preferred Gene in familiar surroundings and missed the presence of Smiley Burnette.

In those unfamiliar surroundings Gene was not at his best. Cast as Will Carson (the only picture where he did not play "himself"), grandson of the local town hero frontiersman, Gene appeared uneasy and when called upon to show emotion in a few dramatic scenes, managed only a baffled, bewildered expression.

An old feud that originated with the grandparents of the Prichards and the Carsons who live in Carson's Corners flares up again when town banker Calvin Pritchard (Frank M. Thomas) tries to put a highway through where the local monument to frontiersman Will Carson stands.

When a movie company comes to town to film the life story of old Will Carson, Gene at first doubles for, then takes the place of the egotistical cowboy star (Robert Lowery), captures gangsters who rob the local bank, and settles the family feud all while winning the hand of Marjorie Pritchard (Marjorie Weaver), the older sister of match-making Jane Pritchard (Jane Withers).

Gene as Will Carson.

160

Director Alfred Green, who had never made a western, may have wondered what he got himself into with Jane Withers and Gene Autry.

Jack Carson is his usual blustery self as the movie producer and the cast includes a host of wonderful character players.

It should be noted, Gene reluctantly receives a screen kiss from starlet Kay Aldridge (later to gain fame at Republic in the "Perils of Nyoka" serial ['42]).

NOTES AND COMMENTS: The songs in this 20th Century–Fox departure were all new with the exception of "Wanderers" which was reprised from "Public Cowboy No. 1" ('37).

According to Jane Withers Gene received $25,000 for "Shooting High", twice the salary Republic was paying him, but this figure is unsubstantiated.

By this time Autry merchandising was everywhere—cowboy outfits, Big Little Books, a "Bandit Trail" game, toothbrush, stationary portfolios, the Gene Autry Sunday newspaper strip from Waltham Features Syndicate in New York, scarves, novelty balloons and Gene's "Melody Ranch" radio show on 66 CBS stations.

The working title of the picture while in development at Fox was "Jubilo" based on a Will Rogers silent film. Originally planned to star Tony Martin and Joan Davis, the script was retooled to fit Jane Withers and Gene.

FILM COMMENTS: *Jane Withers:* "Joseph Schenck was then head of 20th Century–Fox. I wanted to do a film with Gene Autry, so I called Mr. Schenck. He told me Gene was Republic's biggest star and they'd never loan him to Fox. So, I asked if he would loan me to Republic but he told me I was the number 6 box office draw in the country, and Fox would never loan me to another studio. He did agree it was a great idea, it would be box office dynamite!

"I just had to do a picture with Gene Autry, so I put it in my prayers. Then I called Republic. When the studio operator answered, I told her I would like to talk to the head of the studio—(I didn't even know his name at the time). She said, 'Little girl, a lot of people would like to talk to Mr. Yates, but he's a busy man.' I told her, 'Well, I'm a busy girl. My name is Jane Withers, and could you please connect me?' The operator screamed '*The* Jane Withers, the actress? I am sure Mr. Yates would be thrilled to speak with you.' Mr. Yates was in an important conference, but she said she'd take a note into him; he'd definitely want to talk to me. I waited for awhile and finally he came on the phone. 'Hello, is this little Jane Withers? I'm Herbert Yates and I am a big fan of yours!' I told him I had a terrific idea—I wanted to make a picture with Gene Autry—and he said he'd love to borrow me. I had to explain that Mr. Schenck wouldn't loan me and thought he wouldn't loan Gene, but that I had a great idea and that, Honest Injun, I would not take up more than 15 minutes of his time. He had a board meeting, but I was getting out of school at noon and could meet him around 2:30. He said he'd explain to the others and leave the meeting when I arrived. True to his word, Mr. Yates left the meeting. I explained that perhaps Fox could loan Republic two or three of their stars in exchange for Gene, since neither studio would loan us to the other outright. He thought that was a good idea, so we called Fox.

Mr. Schenck's secretary said he was in an important meeting. I told her if she went in and slipped him a note, saying Jane Withers was at Republic in Mr. Yates' office, he might come out and talk to us. And he did! I wouldn't take no for an answer. Not when I knew this would be good for everyone concerned. I was afraid Mr. Schenck would be mad at me, but he wasn't! He thought it a wonderful idea! Mr. Yates told him he had a very determined young lady with a very credible idea!

"It was like having a baby—it took nine months to put the deal through, but three of Fox's stars were loaned to Republic in exchange for Gene. And, as I thought, the picture was enormously successful! It was one of the biggest box office pictures of the '39-'40 season. I was happy as a lark to finally get

In between scenes, to Gene's amusement, Jane Withers offers Champion a carrot to munch on.

to work with Gene Autry. We remained friends ever since. When he would be on the road, he would carve things and send them to me. I have a little slide ornament he made from the horn of a cow—it is white with two turquoise eyes. I have it beside a little gold watch with engraving he gave me, which I haven't worn since I was a little girl. I kept the little box he sent it in. The inscription reads 'For Janie—love and kisses from two-gun Autry.' I have three scarves he wore in 'Shooting High'. He got all his costumes after his pictures. I have Gene's shirt—embroidered, and a pastel plaid and a brown earth-colored one."[1]

Kay Aldridge: "Gene was a kind and considerate man. He made everyone feel at ease. I was very comfortable working with him. I think Jane Withers had a crush on him—everyone liked him."[2]

Gene Autry: "For 'Shooting High', the studio had loaned me to 20th Century–Fox, whose hot property then was a child actress named Jane Withers. Years later, she would appear on television commercials as Josephine the plumber. For one of the rare times in my career, I took second billing and played a character other than myself. In the movie, I doubled for a stuffed-shirt cowboy star played by Robert Lowery. The cast also included Jack Carson, as a high-powered press agent. A couple of scenes in the film dealt with making a film, and this gave what happened on the set a slightly madcap quality.

"The film within the film has Lowery (as the cowboy star) going through the motions, until it came time for the rough stuff. The director would yell 'Cut!' and then I would replace Lowery. That is what you saw on the screen. What happened next, of course, was that the real stuntman replaced *me*. I never objected to doing my own stunts. But this was just good business. If a boxoffice name got his tail bone busted during a movie and couldn't continue, someone would be out big money."[3]

CAST BIOS: Dixie's Dainty Dewdrop, Jane Withers, was born in Atlanta, Georgia, April 12, 1926. She had her own radio show at 4 in Atlanta and, before long, was in Hollywood by age 6.

Her big break came when 20th Century–Fox needed an opposite "type" for Shirley Temple's "Bright Eyes" ('34). The rest is history.

With her first starring film, "Ginger" ('35), Jane quickly rose to be a Top 10 boxoffice champ during the late '30s.

Jane enjoyed less popularity in teenage ingénue roles and retired in 1947, but returned for a terrific character role in "Giant" in 1956.

She made a small fortune from her late-in-life portrayal of Josephine the Plumber in a long running series of TVmercials.

SOURCES:
1. *Western Clippings #27.* January/February 1999. p. 33.
2. *Cliffhanger #10.* 1989. p. 53.
3. Autry with Herskowitz. p. 75.

Gaucho Serenade
Republic, May 1940

Producer ....William Berke
Director ....Frank McDonald
Assistant Director.........................Harry Knight
Screenplay...................................Betty Burbridge,
Bradford Ropes
Photography ....Reggie Lanning
Film Editor ....Tony Martinelli
Musical Supervisor ....Raoul Kraushaar
Production Manager....................Al Wilson
Choreographer.............................Fred Velasco

SONGS: "Headin' For the Wide Open Spaces" (music and lyrics by Gene Autry, Johnny Marvin, Harry Tobias)—sung by Gene Autry, Smiley Burnette; "Give Out With a Song" (music and lyrics by Connie Lee)—sung by Mary Lee; "A Song at Sunset" (music and lyrics by Gene Autry, Johnny Marvin)—sung by Gene Autry, Mary Lee; "Gaucho Serenade" (music and lyrics by James Cavanaugh, John Redmond, Nat Simon)—sung by Gene Autry and people in the cantina; "Wooing of Kitty McFuty" (music and lyrics by Smiley Burnette)—sung by Smiley Burnette; "The Singing

Hills" (music and lyrics by Mack David, Dick Sanford, Sammy Mysels)—sung by Gene Autry; "Keep Rollin', Lazy Longhorns" (music and lyrics by Gene Autry, Johnny Marvin)—sung by Gene Autry, Mary Lee, Smiley Burnette, chorus.

RUNNING TIME: 67 minutes

FILMING DATES: March 21 to April 8, 1940

LOCATIONS: Lake Hemet and highway area; San Fernando Valley area; Republic backlot

BUDGET: $77,885

NEGATIVE COST: $83,633

CAST:

Actor	Character
Gene Autry	Gene Autry
Smiley Burnette	Frog Millhouse
June Storey	Joyce Halloway
Duncan Renaldo	Don Jose
Mary Lee	Patsy Halloway
Clifford Severn Jr.	Ronnie Willoughby
Lester Matthews	Frederick Willoughby
Smith Ballew	Buck Benson
Joseph Crehan	Edward Martin
William Ruhl	Carter
Wade Boteler	Rancher
Ted Adams	E. J. Jenkins
Wendell Niles	Radio Announcer
The Velascos (Fred and Mary)	Mexican dancers
Jose Eslava's Orchestra	Themselves
Chuck Baldra	Ranch Hand
Fred Burns	Cowhand
Ed Cassidy	Customs officer
Kernan Cripps	Police Broadcaster
Joel Friedkin	Station Master
Olaf Hytten	School headmaster
Jack Kirk	Gas Station attendant
George Lloyd	Steve (Willoughby's cellmate)
Tom London	Sheriff Tom Olson
Frankie Marvin	Gas station owner
Walter Miller	George Blake
Gene Morgan	Head Stevedore
Julian Rivero	Mexican rancher
Ralph Sanford	Motorcycle cop
Harry Strang	State Policeman #1
Frank Meredith	State Policeman #2
Al Taylor	Deputy
Fred "Snowflake" Toones	NYC Pier worker
Hank Worden	Jalopy-driving farmer
Fred Schaefer	Motor cop
Schuyler Standish, Douglas Wheatcroft	English boys
Walter Merrill	Deck Steward
Tex Terry	Rancher
Steve Benton	Policeman
Ralph Bucko, Jim Corey, Joe Dominguez, Sam Appel, Victor Cox, Bob Card, Cliff Parkinson, Roy Bucko; Rosa Turich	Extras
Champion	Champion

STUNTS: Joe Yrigoyen (Gene's double); Jack Kirk (Smiley's double); Nellie Walker (June's double).

THE FILM: Gene Autry at the peak of his career, giving the public exactly what they expected in an Autry film with his relaxed, reassuring personality in one of his absolute best films. As written by Betty Burbridge and Bradford Ropes, "Gaucho Serenade", basically a "road picture", contains some of the wittiest dialogue (and obvious ad libs) and scenes of all Gene's films.

Burbridge was a well-respected western film scripter while Ropes wrote others for Gene (and Roy Rogers) and went on to script other comedy films, including two for Abbott and Costello ("Time of Their Lives" ['46] and "Buck Privates Come Home" ['47]).

This utterly charming picture has down-and-out rodeo stars, Gene and Frog (Smiley Burnette), leaving New York for California by car and horse trailer only to discover that young English-boy Ronnie Willoughby (Clifford Severn Jr.) has stowed away with them believing they are there to pick him up and take him to his father's ranch. Willoughby has just arrived by steamship to reunite with his father, Frederick Willoughby (Lester Matthews) whom he believes to own Rancho San Quentin, not realizing his father has been railroaded on an embezzlement charge by crooked members of Western Packing Co. Edward Martin and George Blake (Joseph Crehan, Walter Miller) and is in *prison* San Quentin. In order to prevent Willoughby from testifying against the crooks, they send their flunkies, Jenkins and Carter (Ted Adams, William Ruhl), out to kidnap the boy. Joyce Halloway (June Storey) and her kid sister Patsy (Mary Lee) appear "on the road" with Gene and Smiley as a runaway bride and her young sister. Gene collects them in his caravan, eliciting one fun mishap after another, including an amateur talent show sequence at Gaucho Cantina, headed up by a very animated, energetic Duncan Renaldo.

Watch for the incident where Smiley wades in the lake to retrieve June Storey from her car she's just driven into the water. Smiley, unscripted, actually steps into a pothole and you can see Gene, on shore, burst into laughter, although Smiley recovers with a quick ad-lib.

Former 20th Century-Fox B-western star Smith Ballew appears as a suitor for Storey, but finally announces he's been called by Hollywood to become a western movie star.

It's quite obvious everyone concerned was having a great deal of fun while making "Gaucho Serenade"—and it's contagious.

NOTES AND COMMENTS: Working title of this film was "The Old Mill Stream". A later edited television release was "Keep Rollin'".

Smith Ballew, Gene's friend and romantic rival in

"Gaucho Serenade", was a big band singer out of Palestine, Texas, whom producer Sol Lesser tapped to make B-westerns at 20th Century–Fox in 1937. His series did not "click" and was dropped in 1938 after only five features.

One of the two English schoolmates of Clifford Severn Jr. is played by Douglas Wheatcroft, born August 12, 1926, in Seattle, Washington. This is very likely his first film. He shortened his name to Douglas Croft and caught plum roles as a young James Cagney in "Yankee Doodle Dandy" ('42) and a young Gary Cooper in "Pride of the Yankees" ('42). He then co-starred as Robin, the Boy Wonder, in Columbia's "Batman" serial in '43. His career spiraled downward and by 1947 he'd left Hollywood.

During the exciting, well-staged action climax, watch Gene chase a train com-mandeered by the heavies and transfer from a galloping Champion to the train without the aid of a stuntman-double. Unusual that Republic would allow the star of the film to perform this dangerous stunt himself.

Weekly salaries for the supporting cast ranged from $750 a week for Lester Mathews to $75 a week for motor cop Frank Meredith. Clifford Severn Jr. was paid $250; Mary Lee $400; Walter Miller $225 and Smith Ballew $300.

According to HOLLYWOOD REPORTER news items in late '39 and early '40, Republic originally purchased the title "Grand Ole Opry" from WSM Radio in Nashville, Tennessee, as a starring vehicle for Gene Autry. For unknown reasons it became a vehicle for the rural musical-comedy team of The Weaver Brothers and Elviry, released in June 1940.

FILM COMMENTS: *June Storey:* "During 'Gaucho Serenade' we were up at Lake Hemet. Once I had to excuse myself because we were away from the facilities. Consequently, (smiles) I came down with the most unbelievable case of poison ivy you've ever seen. I had welts all over and a 104° temperature. We were staying in tiny little cottages with little wood stoves. The assistant director would come in around about 4 in the morning, sneak in carefully and build up a fire in the stove. I usually shared my hut with my stand-in and the lady who did some of my riding for me, Nellie Walker. So the fire had been built, then about 6 in the morning I saw a hand come in the door holding a real large pair of long wool underwear, complete with sleeves. Tossed them on the floor and I heard

Gene and Smiley discuss what to do with thugs Ted Adams and William Ruhl while Clifford Severn Jr., Mary Lee and June Storey cower by the horse trailer.

Smiley, Gene, and June Storey convince fugitive Lester Matthews it's best for he and his son Clifford Severn Jr., to turn himself in.

Gene's voice say, 'Here. Wear this.' The idea was to wear the underwear to protect my clothes from the poison ivy. However, the underwear was wool and made the itching worse. I had some horseback riding scenes and I was just in misery! Well, there was a little English fellow in 'Gaucho Serenade', Clifford Severn Jr., his father was a doctor in South Africa, and he had me go on a diet. He said an alkaline diet is the way you have to go. He put me on black olives and cottage cheese, and I cannot eat black olives to this day! (Laughs) Cottage cheese once in a while."

Yet another incident on "Gaucho Serenade". June has just driven her car into the water... "In the scene, Smiley was carrying me out from the car and he stepped into a pothole. (Laughs) Everyone was budget minded, if my wedding gown had gone into the mud it would have shut down production. It cracked Gene up and he started to laugh til tears rolled down his cheeks. (Laughs) Smiley tried to cover up, which he did quite well."[1]

CAST BIOS: Announcer/writer/producer Wendell Niles was born December 29, 1904, in Twin Valley, Minnesota. He attended the University of Montana and New York University before entering radio as an orchestra leader in 1923.

On radio, at various times, he was the announcer on "The Chase and Sanborn Hour", "Al Pearce and His Gang", "The Don Ameche Show" and Gene Autry's "Melody Ranch".

Starting in films in 1932, he often was heard (not always seen) as a radio newscaster or police broadcaster. Niles also narrated many film shorts, such as "Screen Snapshots", and coming attraction movie trailers. For television he was the announcer, for a time, on "Let's Make a Deal", "Truth or Consequences" and others.

His brother, Ken Niles, was also a radio and voice-over talent.

Niles died March 28, 1994, in Toluca Lake, California.

Duncan Renaldo, who became famous as TV's "Cisco Kid", had excellent roles in three of Gene's westerns—"South of the Border", "Gaucho Serenade" and "Down Mexico Way".

His birth year, likely 1904, and heritage are cloudy. He never knew his parents or what his ethnic roots were, possibly Rumanian, Russian, Portuguese or Spanish.

Early in the '20s he entered the U.S. on a temporary 90-day seaman's permit. When the 90 days were up he'd gotten his foot in the door of the movie business and stayed. By 1931, MGM's "Trader Horn" had made him a star.

A few years later he was arrested as an illegal immigrant and spent most of 1934-'35 in prison. A key figure in his release was Republic president Herbert J. Yates who signed Duncan to a seven year contract in 1937, first casting him in serials and by 1939 as Renaldo, a member of the Three Mesquiteers.

His Republic contract up in 1944, Renaldo moved on to portray the Cisco Kid in a series of Monogram and United Artists features and then on TV from 1950-1956. He died in 1980.

Walter Miller had been one of the top paid leading men in silent serials before changing lanes to become a dastardly villain in talkies during the '30s. He and heroine Allene Ray were the most famous team in ten silent serials for Pathe between 1925-1929.

Born Walter Corwin Miller March 9, 1892, in Dayton, Ohio, he apparently spent a portion of his youth in Atlanta, Georgia, before being educated at Manual Training High School in Brooklyn, New York, where he began a stage career at 17 playing juvenile leads with stock companies and in Vaudeville.

In 1910, after closing a short season with a stock company in Troy, New York, he was offered a leading man role in films by small independent Reliance. He remained with them only a year before returning to stage work with the Hall Stock Company.

By 1912 he was back in Hollywood, briefly with D. W. Griffith before moving to some class features at Fox and Metro as well as work at a handful of independents.

Never really becoming a major star, it was Miller's ten serials with Allene Ray that endeared him to a legion of fans in the '20s. He was earning $1,000 a week, top pay for a serial star at the time.

Walter Miller.

When sound came in he was quickly signed in '29 by Nat Levine at Mascot for the lead in "King of the Kongo" which was released in both sound and silent versions. In all, Miller made six serials for Mascot, ten for Universal, two for Columbia and two at Republic.

While filming Gene Autry's "Gaucho Serenade" on a Thursday, he and a fellow actor agreed to pull no punches in a fight scene. Over the next two days he continued to complain of a pain in his back during the filming when, while doing some closeups on Saturday March 30, 1940, Walter Miller suffered a massive heart attack and collapsed on the Republic backlot. He died a short time later at the Hollywood Receiving Hospital.

Virtually all Miller's scenes had been shot, so he remains prominent in the film even though Republic oddly removed him from the credits.

WHAT THE EXHIBITOR HAD TO SAY: "The average Autry musical western that always goes over big with our patrons." —Fred Basha, Palace Theatre, Corner Brook, Newfoundland, Canada (October 1941)

"The public in our situation criticize these pictures but I noticed that most of them stayed after seeing our feature attraction. The criticism on this was mild. Many patrons here doubtless follow the musical classics, but I could not help being amused at people keeping time with their number elevens during the singing of a western ballad. Business fair." —Simon Galitiziki, Coed Theater, Topeka, Kansas (December 1941)

"These reissues are going all right but do not do any extra business. They are far ahead of the average western, however, and I have no complaints." —Charles A. Brooks, Ritz Theater, Marshfield, Missouri (July 1943)

SOURCES:
1. Interview with author.

Carolina Moon
Republic, July 1940

Producer ....William Berke
Director ....Frank McDonald
Assistant Director........................Harry Knight
Original Story.............................Connie Lee
Screenplay..................................Winston Miller
Photography ....William Nobles
Film Editor ....Tony Martinelli
Musical Supervisor ....Raoul Kraushaar
Production Manager.....................Al Wilson

SONGS: "Carolina Moon" (music and lyrics by Benny Davis, Joe Burke)—sung by studio singers over the credits, reprised by Gene Autry, Smiley Burnette, Mary Lee; "At the Rodeo" (music and lyrics by Gene Autry, Johnny Marvin, Harry Tobias)—sung by Gene Autry, Jimmie Lewis and his Texas Cowboys; "Me and My Echo" (music and lyrics by Connie Lee)—sung by Mary Lee; "Swanee River" (music and lyrics by Stephen Foster)—sung by Scott Crinoline Choir; "Dreaming Dreams That Won't Come True" (music and lyrics by Gene Autry, Johnny Marvin, Harry Tobias)—sung by Gene Autry, June Storey; "Say Si Si" (music and lyrics by Ernesto Lecuona, Stillman, Francia Luban)—sung by Gene Autry, June Storey, Mary Lee; "Climbin' Up D'Mountain" (Public Domain)—sung by Scott Crinoline Choir.

RUNNING TIME: 65 minutes

FILMING DATES: May 20 to June 4, 1940

LOCATIONS: Corriganville; Keen Camp; Riviera Country Club; Elysian Park stood in for race track and rodeo grounds; an Encino home stood in for the Wheeler home; Republic backlot

BUDGET: $77,711

NEGATIVE COST: $77,991.55

CAST:

Actor	*Character*
Gene Autry	Gene Autry
Smiley Burnette	Frog Millhouse
June Storey	Caroline Stanhope
Mary Lee	Patsy Stanhope
Eddy Waller	Colonel Stanhope
Hardie Albright	Henry Wheeler
Frank Dae	Colonel Jefferson
Terry Nibert	Evangeline Jefferson
Robert Fiske	Barrett
Etta McDaniel	Mammy
Paul White	Billy
Fred Ritter	Davis (landowner)
Ralph Sanford	Nelson (logging foreman)
Jimmie Lewis and His Texas Cowboys	The Lone Star Cowboys
Eddie Kane	Bank President
Mary Kenyon	Ranch Girl
Jack Kirk	Thompson (landowner)
Scott Crinoline Choir	Choir Singers
Horace Murphy	Barber
John P. Wade	Weston (landowner)
Burr Caruth	Elderly Man
Chuck Baldra	Slim
Cactus Mack	Hank
Frankie Marvin	Jim
Shannon Davidson	Pete
Ben Carter	Butler
Joey Ray	1st Bookie
Joe Devlin	2nd Bookie
Milton Kibbee	Rodeo Announcer
Thelma Long	Negro Woman
Charles Moore	Negro Man
Mildred Shay	Woman
Walter Soderling	Notary
Fred "Snowflake" Toones	Sam
Fred Burns	Rodeo Official
Nellie Walker	Nellie
Eddie Foster, Billy Wayne, Carl Cotner	Extras
John Beach, Bob Card, Art Dillard, Augie Gomez, Henry Morris, Jim Massey, Pascale Perry, Jim Corey, Curley Dresden	Rodeo Cowboys
George Becker, Phil Bloom, Jack Buchanan, Russell Custer, Joe Chambers, Harry Dean, P. Deasy, Jay Guedalia, Al Haskell,	

Bill McGowan, Johnny Powers,
Bill Wilkus, M. Welch ....Loggers
Champion ....Champion

STUNTS: Joe Yrigoyen (Gene's double), Jack Kirk (Smiley's double), Nellie Walker (June's double).

THE FILM: Producer William Berke deviated even more from the stereotype western formula in "Carolina Moon", taking Gene Autry and Smiley Burnette to the deep South, ringing in some Negro spirituals, a fox hunt and pleasure riding by the Southern gentry.

The yarn has rodeo cowboys Gene Autry and Frog Millhouse (Smiley Burnette) caught in the mesh of a situation down South involving possible losses by old time plantation owners of their property to a neighborhood schemer pretending to be their friend (Hardie Albright). He's actually only after the lumber on the land.

June Storey is very acceptable as a high-strung, proud Southern gal bent on saving the family fortune and the plantation of her father (Eddy Waller). Mary Lee is Storey's vivacious younger sister. Comedy elements come from Terry Nibert as a southern belle on the lookout for a husband—Frog. Frank Dae is a blustery southern gentleman ever on the lookout for an old fashioned duel—and again Frog is the target.

NOTES AND COMMENTS: Billed as Jimmie Lewis and his Texas Cowboys, the group was later, and better, known as Texas Jim Lewis and his Texas Cowboys, a popular novelty band who played a contraption he called a "hootnanny", a large collection of Claxon horns, bulb hooters, washboards, dishpans, mouth organs and musical spoons all hitched to a frame that closely resembled a sawhorse.

Dolly Waldorf was the voice double for June Storey. (See "South of the Border" for June's opinion of her singing voice.) Dolly appeared in James Cagney's "Something to Sing About" ('37 Grand National) as a member of the singing group Three Shades of Blue.

The 16 member Scott Crinoline Choir recorded both the spiritual numbers heard in "Carolina Moon" May 14, 1940, at the Ross Snyder Playground and were paid $11 each for their work. Carlyle Leon Scott, the leader, received $25.

Top weekly salary went to villain Hardie Albright at $400. Eddy Waller earned $350, Frank Dae $300, Etta McDaniel $200.

Elysian Park where the race track and rodeo grounds scenes were filmed was set aside for public use when Los Angeles was founded in 1781. At 600 acres, it's the second largest park in L.A. after Griffith Park.

On Gene's "Melody Ranch" radio show for September 15, 1940, leading lady June Storey helped Gene recreate "Carolina Moon".

Smiley Burnette's regular horse, Black Eyed Nellie, does not appear with him in any scenes for this movie.

WHAT THE EXHIBITOR HAD TO SAY: "Not one of Autry's best by any means but they turned out for it anyway."
—H. D. Furnice, Casey Theater,
Casey, Iowa (August 1941)

"Played repeat showing to average business. Not the best Autry, but still good. I'd like to know what type piano June Storey was playing while Autry was singing the "Si Si" number. Did anyone notice its sound?"
—Sammie Jackson, Jackson Theater,
Flomaton, Alabama (September 1941)

"A small town life-saver that we always do well on and made more popular with the singing of Mary Lee who is well liked here."
—Fred Basha, Palace Theater,
Corner Brook, Newfoundland (December 1941)

"A fairly good Autry. Better than his other ones."
—George S. Caporal, Yale Theater,
Oklahoma City, Oklahoma (April 1942)

"This was as good as any Autry picture. A fair and carnival were in town, but it was so cold that they came to the show to keep warm."
—Jerry L. Abbott, Masonic Theater,
New Castle, Virginia (September 1949)

Gene's doing all he can to help plantation owner Eddy Waller (left) in his business dealings with banker Eddie Kane.

Ride, Tenderfoot, Ride
Republic, September 1940

Producer ....William Berke
Director ....Frank McDonald
Assistant Directors ....Harry Knight, Bill O'Connor
Original Story.............................Betty Burbridge, Connie Lee
Screenplay...................................Winston Miller
Photography ....Jack Marta
Supervising Editor ....Murray Seldeen
Film Editor..................................Lester Orlebeck
Musical Supervisor ....Raoul Kraushaar

Production Manager.....................Al Wilson

SONGS: "When the Work's All Done This Fall" (Public Domain)—sung by Gene Autry; "Eleven More Months and Ten More Days" (music and lyrics by Arthur Fields and Fred Hall)—sung by Gene Autry, Smiley Burnette; "Woodpecker Song" (music and lyrics by Harold Adamson, D. Lazzaro)—sung by Gene Autry, Mary Lee; "That Was Me By the Sea" (music and lyrics by Smiley Burnette)—sung by Smiley Burnette; "Ride, Tenderfoot, Ride" (music and lyrics by Johnny Mercer and Richard A. Whiting)—sung

by Gene Autry, Mary Lee and June Storey; "Leanin' On the Ole Top Rail" (music and lyrics by Charles and Nick Kenny)—sung by Gene Autry; "Oh! Oh! Oh!" (music and lyrics by Gene Autry, Johnny Marvin)—sung by Cindy Walker, Mary Lee and the Pacemakers; "On the Range" (music and lyrics by Gene Autry, Johnny Marvin)—sung by Gene Autry and others.

RUNNING TIME: 65 minutes

FILMING DATES: June 28 to July 12, 1940

LOCATIONS: Lake Hemet area; Palmdale area; Chatsworth Railroad Station; Agoura Ranch area; Corriganville Ranch; Republic backlot

BUDGET: $74,965

NEGATIVE COST: $74,443

CAST:

Actor	Character
Gene Autry	Gene Autry
Smiley Burnette	Frog Millhouse
June Storey	Ann Randolph
Mary Lee	Patsy Randolph
Warren Hull	Donald Gregory
Forbes Murray	Henry Walker
Joe McGuinn	Henchman Martin
Joe Frisco	Stuttering haberdasher
Isabel Randolph	Emily Spencer
Herbert Clifton	Butler Andrews
Mildred Shay	Stewardess
Si Jenks	Sheriff
Cindy Walker	Singer
The Pacemakers: Reginald Barlow, Stephen Carr, George Sherwood, Lee Shumway	Jones, Anderson, Taylor and Evans (respectively)
Walter Soderling	Darien
Gertrude Messinger	Miss Robinson
Chuck Morrison	Jones (trucker)
Frank O'Connor	Perry
Fred Burns	Rancher Allen
Ray Cooke	Airline Ticket Clerk
Curley Dresden	Spectator
Dick Elliott	Airport agent
Franklyn Farnum	Cattleman #1
Jack Kirk	Ranch foreman
Cactus Mack	Henchman
Wilbur Mack	Husband on phone
Frankie Marvin, Augie Gomez	Cowhands
Hal Price	Rancher
Fred "Snowflake" Toones	Train porter
Slim Whitaker	Cattleman #2
Hank Worden	Henry Haggerty
Ray Jones	Cattleman #3
Bob Burns, Bud McTaggert, Harold Daniels, Harold Gerard, Ed Peil Sr., Fred Ritter, Tex Terry, Jimmie Fox, Cliff Parkinson	Extras
Dorothy Curtis	Wife #2
Lucile Browne	Marcia, swimsuit guest
Jack Perrin	Workman
Betty Farrington	Woman #2
Phyllis Gordon	Woman #1
Lucille Hoose	Girl #3, Betty Lee
Benadetta Landers	Girl #2, Joan
Duke Lee	Rancher
Tony Marsh	Radford Boy #2
William Nestell	Cattleman
Netta Packer	Wife #1
Patti Sacks	Girl #4, Eleanor
Robert Wayne	Radford Boy #1
Cecil Weston	Wife #3
Champion	Champion

STUNTS: Joe Yrigoyen (double for Gene Autry); Jack Kirk (double for Smiley Burnette); Nellie Walker (double for June Storey).

THE FILM: There's not much rough and tough action in "Ride, Tenderfoot, Ride", but it still has more of a western flavor than "Carolina Moon", although music and amusement are uppermost in the screenplay which involves yet another twist on the "taming of the shrew" plotline.

Gene Autry inherits a large meat packing company but finds its business life threatened by the scheming of a rival concern headed up by Ann Randolph (June Storey) and her conniving general manager Donald Gregory (Warren Hull). When Gene refuses to sell out so the Randolph company can take over his rich distribution contracts, Ann uses her womanly wiles to convince Gene to sell. Ann's kid sister Patsy (Mary Lee) learns Gene is being duped and warns him.

Running his company in open competition to the Randolph organization, Gene uses old-time methods like parades and music to build back his customers.

Crooked manager Gregory tries dirty work, only to end up in jail with the two companies merging through romance.

Snappy and fast-paced. All in all, one of Gene's most popular and entertaining outings.

NOTES AND COMMENTS: The late Alex Gordon, once vice president of Flying A Pictures, assessed Gene's popularity quite accurately. "In the days of early western movies, youthful audiences consisted mainly of young boys at the children's matinees. Most girls were bored by the familiar and repetitious action, chases and gunfights, with the leading lady reduced to helpless distress waiting for the hero to rescue her and the ranch. Gene Autry changed all that.

"With the advent of musical westerns pioneered by Gene, his ever increasing fan mail (99% from teenage girls and older women) proved that the feminine sex filled theater seats when his pictures played, and they stampeded for seats at his personal appearances, tours, rodeos, and bought his records and songbooks by the millions.

"Ride, Tenderfoot, Ride" is what June Storey, Gene and Mary Lee are singing as they ride along the trail.

"That did not mean that the westerns' male audiences turned their backs on Gene's movies. On the contrary, the enticing combination of action, musical interludes and slight romantic suggestions proved to be an unbeatable draw. Gene's natural performances, always playing himself, made the difference. No other singing cowboy could copy that. Gene was the same on and off screen as his audience discovered. After just 22 starring movies, Gene was voted the No. 1 western star at the box office by the exhibitors of America in their annual polls. Three years later, in 1940, Gene was voted the fourth biggest box office attraction in the entire United States, right behind Mickey Rooney, Spencer Tracy and Clark Gable.

"In a bow to Gene's vast female audience that constantly craved for more romance in his movies, Betty Burbridge and Connie Lee, successful script writers in the western genre, were signed to script the movie that was to provide his female fans with their favorite of them all, 'Ride, Tenderfoot, Ride'. Based on the hit song by Johnny Mercer and Richard Whiting, this 1940 release has Mary Lee posing as Gene's young bride in order to cut the plane fare back from boarding school to half rate. Gene is dubious about the plan but she persuades him, to the raised eyebrow reaction of the other passengers. Patsy, in a brand new upswing hairdo, gets on well with Gene for what he thinks is a short duration, but upon her arrival home she tells her big sister that she and Gene are 'that way' about each other and June hasn't a chance! The sister feud is one of the funniest sequences in the picture in which June Storey and Gene do some tall wrangling as the rival owners of a large meat packing concern."[1]

The purported photo of a baby Gene Autry on the front page of the DAILY ENTERPRISE mockup newspaper seen early in the picture is actually a photo of Carolyn Hays, daughter of Earl Hays of Earl Hays Press. Since 1915 the company supplied, and still does to this day, printed props, newspaper mockups, wanted posters, etc. to motion picture studios.

Strangely, Cindy Walker, one of the top western music composers for Gene and others, including "Blue Canadian Rockies", is featured here as a singer only and has none of her own compositions in this movie.

Screenwriter Winston Miller had earlier worked on Gene's "Carolina Moon" and was previously an uncredited contributor to "Gone With the Wind" ('39). He went on to write several for Charles Starrett at Columbia and Roy Rogers at Republic before graduating to A-films such as "My Darling Clementine" ('46), "Relentless" ('48), "Station West" ('48), "Rocky Mountain" ('50), "Boy From Oklahoma" ('54) and "April Love" ('57), among others.

For the airplane interior, Republic received from American Airlines a Douglas Flagship mockup.

Warren Hull was best known at this time for his portrayals of the Spider, Mandrake the Magician and the Green Hornet in four Columbia serials. He became even better known in the late '40s-early '50s as the host of radio and TV's popular game show "Strike It Rich".

Taking an active interest in the affairs of his community, Smiley Burnette was unanimously chosen honorary mayor of Studio City about this time.

FILM COMMENTS: *Mary Lee on Gene Autry's appeal:* "Mr. Autry's so *natural*. The folks that like Mr. Autry most, the middle class ranchers and people in the country, see a slice of their own lives in his pictures, and that's why they enjoy them. He's so nice—he's always nice to everyone." [2]

Songwriter Cindy Walker: "I never did know him real, real well, but he was always a wonderful artist and I always appreciated that he did quite a few of my songs. He was always glad to listen to any of my songs I brought him and he did about ten. He did 'Here's to the Ladies', a beautiful recording of 'Blue Canadian Rockies', 'Cowboy Blues', 'It's A Shame We Didn't Talk It Over', 'Over and Over Again', 'Silver Spurs On the Golden Stairs' and 'I Was Just Walkin' Out the Door'. The first time we ever met was when Larry Crosby, Bing's brother, took me over to meet Gene. They wanted some pictures made. I'll never forget, Gene was sitting in his den with his feet propped up and had on his white socks. Larry introduced me to Gene, but he never did get up or move his feet off of the desk. (Laughs) Larry told him Bing had just recorded a song of mine—'Lone Star Trail'. Asked Gene if he'd mind having his picture made with me. He said, 'No, I wouldn't mind.' Then he said somethin' better. Said, 'They're bringing up Champion. How 'bout that?' I said, 'Yeah, that's the one I want my picture made with.' (Laughs) Not thinking how it sounded! Larry Crosby looked at me just like my Papa would, 'What a thing to say.' I didn't mean anything wrong, I just loved horses. So I have two lovely pictures of me with Champion.

"I sang a little song in 'Ride, Tenderfoot, Ride'. It was just a bit…I didn't do nothing. So what. I don't claim to have been in the movies."[3]

WHAT THE EXHIBITOR HAD TO SAY: "Got extended playing time and wasn't sorry. Did good business. Gene seems to be the only natural left."
—Harlan Rankin, Plaza, Tilbury, and AlexanderTheaters, Wallaceburg, Ontario, Canada (January 1941)

"A good western picture with music which is a relief from the usual 'shoot 'em down, drag 'em out' westerns. Today's audiences are too educated and too sophisticated to fall for the old escapade with lots of shooting and picking unnecessary fights. That's why most western pictures released today have no public appeal, unless pictures like 'Ride, Tenderfoot, Ride', a western without a single shot or a single fight and still a very good western picture. Business above average."
—Harry Tishkoff, Empress Theater, Rochester, New York (March 1941)

"This one did not draw as well as we expected."
—Ray Peacock, Onalaska Theater, Onalaska, Washington (September 1941)

"One of the best Autry's played yet. Bucked a basketball game, Christmas shopping and the war. Yet one of the best week-ends to date."
—E. L. Ornstein, Rialto Theater, Marengo, Indiana (December 1941)

SOURCES:

1. Movie Facts and Trivia compiled for Gene Autry Entertainment by Alex Gordon.

2. "Ride, Tenderfoot, Ride" pressbook.

3. Interview with author.

June Storey's business manager, Warren Hull (left) is planning a little trickery for Gene while Gene is busy with Storey's kid sister Mary Lee and two of the pretty poolside girls.

Melody Ranch
Republic, November 1940

Producer	Sol C. Siegel
Director	Joseph Santley
Assistant Director	George Blair
Original Screenplay	Jack Moffitt, F. Hugh Herbert, Bradford Ropes, Betty Burbridge
Special Comedy Sequences for Jimmy Durante	Sid Kuller, Ray Golden
Photography	Joseph August
Supervising Editor	Murray Seldeen
Film Editor	Lester Orlebeck

Art Director	John Victor Mackay
Wardrobe	Adele Palmer
Musical Director	Raoul Kraushaar
Special Music and Lyrics	Jule Styne, Eddie Cherkose
Production Manager	Al Wilson

SONGS: "Melody Ranch" (music and lyrics by Eddie Cherkose, Jule Styne)—sung by Gene Autry; "Rodeo Rose" (music and lyrics by Jule Styne, Eddie Cherkose)—sung by Gene Autry; "Welcome to You" (music and lyrics by Eddie

Cherkose, Jule Styne)—sung by Mary Lee and children; "Torpedo Joe" (music and lyrics by Eddie Cherkose, Jule Styne)—sung by Mary Lee; "We Never Dream the Same Dream Twice" (music and lyrics by Gene Autry, Fred Rose)—sung by Gene Autry and Ann Miller; "My Gal Sal" (music and lyrics by Paul Dresser)—sung by Ann Miller; "Back to the City Again" (parody of "Back In the Saddle Again") (music and lyrics by Gene Autry, Ray Whitley, Eddie Cherkose)—sung by Joe Sawyer, Horace MacMahon; "Call of the Canyon" (music and lyrics by Billy Hill)—sung by Gene Autry; "What Are Cowboys Made Of" (music and lyrics by Eddie Cherkose, Jule Styne)—sung by Joe Sawyer, Horace MacMahon; "Vote For Autry" (music and lyrics by Eddie Cherkose, Jule Styne)—sung by Jimmy Durante, Mary Lee.

RUNNING TIME: 84 minutes

FILMING DATES: September 16 to October 5, 1940

LOCATIONS: Lone Pine; Republic backlot; Mammoth Lakes area

BUDGET: $181,275

NEGATIVE COST: $177,520

CAST:

Actor	Character
Gene Autry	Gene Autry
Jimmy Durante	Cornelius Jupiter Courtney
Ann Miller	Julie Shelton
Barton MacLane	Mark Wildhack
Barbara Jo Allen	Veronica Whipple
George "Gabby" Hayes	Pop Laramie
Jerome Cowan	Tommy Summerville
Mary Lee	Penny Curtis
Joe Sawyer	Jasper Wildhack
Horace MacMahon	Bud Wildhack
Clarence Wilson	Judge "Skinny" Henderson
William "Billy" Benedict	Slim
Kidoodlers	Barbershop Quartet
Maxine Ardell	Majorette
Billy Bletcher	Scarlet Shadow radio voice
Priscilla Bonner	Saloon hostess
Veda Ann Borg	Radio Station Receptionist
Ralph Bucko	Henchman
George Chandler	Taxi Driver
Edmund Cobb	Autry voter
Tex Cooper	Betting Townsman
Curley Dresden	Autry Rider
Dick Elliott	Sheriff Barstow
Frank Hagney	Man who asks for quiet
Donald Haines	Page Boy
Lloyd Ingraham	Ed, Bartender
Jack Ingram	Radio cast member
Tiny Jones	Trolley passenger
Jane Keckley	Indignant Trolley passenger
William Nestell	Rifle Shooter
Jack Kirk	Entertainer on bus
Tom London	Henchman Joe
Frankie Marvin	Mandolin player
Merrill McCormick	Henchman Charlie
John Merton	Henchman Ten-Spot
Horace Murphy	Loco (cowboy radio actor)
Post Park	Windy, Stage Driver
Slim Whitaker	Voter
Art Dillard	Bystander
Dub Taylor	Xylophone player
Carl Cotner	Musician
Burr Caruth, Ruth Gifford, Herman Hack, Chick Hannon, Art Mix, Frank McCarroll, Jack Montgomery, Bob Card, Tom Smith, Ray Teal, Wally West, Jim Corey, Roy Bucko, Bob Folkerson, Jimmy Fox, Marie Leon, Francis Sayles, Ted Wells, Pascale Perry, Bob Woodward, Jack O'Shea, Chuck Baldra, Gerald Oliver Smith	Extras
Champion	Champion

STUNTS: Yakima Canutt, Joe Yrigoyen (double for Gene Autry); Wally West.

THE FILM: With a title based on Gene's popular new radio program, Republic planned to use "Melody Ranch"

Gene, Ann Miller, Jimmy Durante and George "Gabby" Hayes are about to convince hoodlums Horace MacMahon and Joe Sawyer to do a little vocalizing.

to boost Gene into first-run theaters. Costing $177,520 to produce, it was Republic's most expensive Autry film to date. The extravagant "Special" boasted a big cast headed by veteran comedian Jimmy Durante who, with his trademark gnarled phraseology, had started in vaudeville and remained a star through the arrival of television with his own show in the '50s. However, Durante's antics, especially an extended courtroom scene, proved unfunny and out of place in an Autry film. He was *not* a hit with Autry fans who preferred the homespun humor of Smiley Burnette as Gene's sidekick. They resented his absence from "Melody Ranch" (the only Autry feature at Republic not to include Smiley) as well as objecting to the over abundance of tap dancing, barbershop harmony, and zany comedy from Barbara Jo Allen (aka Vera Vague, the squeaky-voiced, man crazed, old maid character Allen created in the '30s and played on radio with Bob Hope, Edgar Bergen and Jack Carson). The result was, even with all the money spent, with all the added frills, a disjointed, slow-moving 84 minute film that did not appeal to the followers of Gene's usual unpretentious rangeland fun-fests.

Starting off with Gene Autry's radio program setting,

old friend Pop Laramie (George "Gabby" Hayes) and young Penny (Mary Lee) invite Gene to return to his hometown of Torpedo as guest of honor at the town's Frontier Days celebration. Gene's agent/pal Corney (Jimmy Durante) persuades Gene to accept, believing the publicity will counteract the damage done to Gene's radio ratings which has come about through the lackadaisical attitude on his program of Julie Shelton (Ann Miller), a debutante with theatrical aspirations.

Gene finds Torpedo racket-ridden and run by his childhood enemies, the three Wildhack brothers (Barton MacLane, Joe Sawyer, Horace MacMahon). After being made honorary sheriff, Gene finds he has gone soft as a radio star and is beaten in a fight with the gangster brothers.

Humiliated because life in Hollywood has softened him, Gene works out and trains so that in their next encounter he emerges victorious. It's in this mix that the most charming moments of the film arrive—and they're not from Durante, Miller, Allen or any of the high-priced stars, but from Sawyer and MacMahon. After besting Gene in an on-the-air fight, the rambunctious brothers launch into a hilarious song parody of Gene's "Back in the Saddle Again"—"Back in the City Again". Later, when Gene has toughened up and beaten the boys at their own game, he forces them to sing "What Are Cowboys Made Of".

Gene, of course, avenges himself, regains his reputation, captures the gangsters in a wild trolley-car action finale, and once again tames the shrewish leading lady.

However, Durante and Autry don't mix, and Miller's too chic and slick for an Autry heroine leaving the overall picture just too disarrayed with far too many elements foreign to Autry devotees to be enjoyable.

NOTES AND COMMENTS: To set all the rumors to rest for all time, John Wayne did *not* appear in any way, shape or form in this picture. There is nothing in the Republic files that would surely have indicated this. All the cast pay records are intact and there is nothing relating to John Wayne.

The song "Call of the Canyon" was a big hit tune for Gene at the time of this film, and was used in 1942 as a film title.

"Melody Ranch" was added to the National Film Registry in 2002 under the terms of the National Film Preservation Act for films being culturally, historically or aesthetically significant.

"Melody Ranch", Gene's 43rd movie, was produced and released by Republic as a "Special", meaning it cost theatre exhibitors more money than Gene's regular six to eight movies a year and also forced them to buy an entire year's output of about 40 Republic films if they wanted the Autrys. This film industry business practice enabled companies with big name stars and strong box-office potential to unload blocks of their other features which had weak potential box office returns onto exhibitors who would normally turn them down. The system, which spread from the U.S. to Europe, came to a virtual halt in 1948 as a result of a court decision that forced the separation of the production and exhibition functions of the industry. Gene had initially opposed the practice by Republic in 1938 during his walkout. (See "The Old Barn Dance".)

Dancing star Ann Miller had her first romantic leading lady role in "Melody Ranch". After filming a complicated love scene involving a kiss from Gene, negative advance publicity prompted Republic to cut the kiss from the final print. As Gene himself explained, "Actually we kissed there at the telephone. There was a lot of (advance) publicity over that. The public relations department at Republic put out a story I was going to be kissing Ann Miller in a picture. So they were flooded with a lot of letters from the kids saying 'Don't let Gene Autry kiss Ann Miller in the picture—that's sissy!' So finally at the last minute (Republic) said, 'You're taking a chance on it—why raise a controversy with the kids?' so they cut it all out."[1] For the rest of her life, Miller wrongly continued to insist she received Gene's first screen kiss. As we know, that priority belongs to Barbara Pepper and Ann Rutherford.

Gene Autry's horse Champion was the first horse to fly coast to coast from California to New York by plane in a specially reconstructed airliner to arrive in time for Gene's Madison Square Garden Rodeo appearance from October 20-27 after completing filming of "Melody Ranch". All but two seats of the TWA plane had to be extracted to make room for Champ to lie comfortably during the flight. John Agee, Champion's trainer, was one of the passengers on the plane.

Following the Madison Square Garden show, Gene moved on to the Boston Gardens Rodeo November 1-11.

"Gene Autry's Melody Ranch" musical variety/adventure radio program began on CBS January 7, 1940, sponsored by the William Wrigley Jr. Company, the world's largest manufacturer and distributor of chewing gum. "Melody Ranch" was initially heard for 30 minutes Sunday evenings on 67 stations coast to coast. The program enjoyed a steady run on CBS with the only break in a 16 year stint coming when Gene joined the Army Air Corps. He took his oath on the air on July 26, 1942; his show departed the following season and returned on September 23, 1945, broadcast then until May 1956. The radio program inspired the film which Wrigley firmly promoted with special trailers, displays and local dealer tie-ups. Additionally, Republic launched a reported $50,000 trade paper advertising campaign for the picture with five weeks of advertising in every trade paper. On Gene's December 1, 1940, "Melody Ranch" radio program, he and Mary Lee discussed the movie and its actors.

For his work in "Melody Ranch", Jimmy Durante was paid a whopping $4,375 a week. Ann Miller earned $1,250 a week while Barbara Allen received $1,000. Heavy Barton MacLane also got $1,250 in a binding contract that assured him absolute 3rd male billing. Director Joseph Santley earned $625 per week; George Hayes $750; Joe Sawyer and Horace MacMahon were both at $500 a week. Stunt double Joe Yrigoyen was at $425 a week.

"Melody Ranch" holds the distinction of being the lengthiest series B-western of over 2,000 such films produced from 1930-1954.

FILM COMMENTS: *Gene Autry:* "The success of our radio show led, inevitably, to a picture called 'Melody Ranch'. I don't believe any Republic film in 1940 carried a bigger budget—with the likely exception of 'Dark Command', starring John Wayne. 'Melody Ranch' was what the studio in those days modestly referred to as a blockbuster. I even had a kissing scene with Ann Miller, but when that tidbit appeared in the papers during the filming, the mail from angry and disillusioned little boys was so heavy it was cut from the movie.

"In place of romance, the kids got Jimmy Durante. As an entertainer, Durante was in a class by himself. His comedy relied not only on what he said or how he said it, but on that cement-mixer of a voice, the roll of those eyes, the thrust of that nose. He was one of the great scene stealers of all time. And when it came to reading the script, I was Sir Laurence Olivier compared to Durante. He could not read a blessed line. When you did a scene with Jimmy you just let him go, and when he finished you tried to remember enough of what he said so that your answer made sense. Sometimes it did.

"At one point in 'Melody Ranch', Horace MacMahon, who became better known for his hard-bitten cop roles, was on trial for stealing a horse. His lawyer was Cornelius J. Courtney, as played by Durante. (Yes, some of our plots did tax the imagination.) Jimmy ad-libbed the whole scene. I don't recall if we reshot the scene or not. But I thought it was funnier than the original dialogue.

"Jule Styne, with his greatest hits ahead of him, had written 'Melody Ranch' as a title song for the movie. At the time, we still didn't have a theme song for the radio show. Carl Cotner thought it was a natural and urged me to use it. But I had something else in mind. I had worked with Ray Whitley on a tune for an earlier film, and I planned to try it on the show.

"Carl thought I was making a mistake. But I shook my head and said, 'I don't think it's near the song this one is. I just have a feeling about it.' I was talking about 'Back in the Saddle Again'. That time, at least, I think my judgment held up."[2]

Director Joseph Santley: "In this one we're trying to do two things. Trying to make city audiences think maybe we're spoofing westerns—and we're also trying to make the youngsters believe it's the real thing. It's quite a chore."[3]

CAST BIOS: The exceptional song lyricist, Jule Styne, had a marvelous way with a tune. Born on the final day of 1905 in London, England, Styne started as a bandleader in Chicago, moving west during the Depression to become a vocal coach. Entering filmwork in 1938 with Ritz Brothers pictures, he soon landed at Republic composing the lyrics to Gene's "Melody Ranch" title song, in addition to several other tunes in this film as well as "Ridin' On a Rainbow" ('41), the title tune to "Down Mexico Way" ('41), "Cowboy Serenade" ('42) and music background cues for "Stardust On the Sage" ('42).

In collaboration with Sammy Cahn, Styne went on to compose dozens of standards including "Let It Snow! Let It Snow! Let It Snow!"; "The Party's Over", "Three Coins In the Fountain", "Small World", "Just In Time", "People" and "Make Someone Happy". Styne was most associated with Broadway musicals such as "Gentlemen Prefer Blondes" ('49), "Bells are Ringing" ('56) and "Gypsy" ('59). After many Tony nominations, he received two in 1968 for "Hallelujah, Baby!"

Styne was honored at the Kennedy Center in 1990. The talented, prolific songwriter died of heart failure September 20, 1994, in New York.

Leggy, black-haired Ann Miller's machine-gun tap style, once timed at 500 taps a minute, charmed stage, screen and TV audiences for almost 70 years.

Born in Chierno, near Houston, Texas, in 1919, 1923 or 1925—according to whom you believe—Jonnie Lucille Collier claimed she had to add years to her age to get jobs when she was a teenager.

Gene and Jimmy Durante give Ann Miller a little lift in between scenes.

At any rate, Ann began dancing school at the age of three to correct a bad case of rickets. When her parents divorced, she moved with her mother to California. Her father would not pay alimony and Ann's hearing-impaired mother found it difficult to work. So 14 year old Ann developed a dance routine, lied about her age, and got a dancing gig at $5 a night.

Landing a seven year contract with RKO, she made her film bow in "New Faces of 1937". Other films followed and she went to Broadway in 1939 to appear in "George White's Scandals" where she stopped the show with her Mexiconga number.

Returning to Hollywood, RKO upped her salary from $250 to $3,000 a week and made headlines by insuring her legs for $1 million.

Miller leased herself out for short stints to Republic and Columbia, which is when "Melody Ranch" was made.

After WWII Ann made waves in "Easter Parade" ('48) with Fred Astaire and landed a long term MGM contract, appearing in such hits as "On the Town" ('49) and "Kiss Me Kate" ('53). Big budget musicals faded in the '50s so Ann returned to Broadway for success in "Mame" in 1969. She toured in "Anything Goes" and returned to Broadway once more with "Sugar Babies" in 1979. Her autobiography,

MILLER'S HIGH LIFE, was published in 1972.

Miller died at 84 of lung cancer on January 22, 2004.

Director Joseph Santley made his first appearance on the New York stage at the age of two with his actress mother.

Born in Salt Lake City, Utah, in 1890, he toured with his mother in various stock companies, being billed as "The World's Greatest Boy Actor". He made his Broadway debut in 1910 with "The Matinee Idol" and played numerous other roles in New York and in roadshow productions.

He directed many short subjects for Paramount before going on to do features beginning in 1929 with "The Cocoanuts", the first Marx Brothers feature.

Santley rapidly became known as a director of light comedies and musicals, a flair he brought to his first "western" in "Melody Ranch". He later helmed "Down Mexico Way" and "Call of the Canyon" for Gene Autry.

Continuing at Republic, he also directed several of their Judy Canova comedies and other light fare.

With the advent of TV, he worked on variety shows with Ethel Merman and Jimmy Durante.

Santley died in 1971.

WHAT THE EXHIBITOR HAD TO SAY: "The best Autry to date. Played to extra good business for so close to Christmas. Autry supported by good cast but some fans missed Smiley Burnette. Ann Miller helped a lot. She is clever and easy to look at."

—N. E. Frank, Wayland Theater,
Wayland, Michigan (December 1940)

"This production did not appeal to my western fans as the out and out Autry westerns. However, opinions seemed to be divided but it is good entertainment."

—A. L. Dove, Bengough Theater,
Bengough, Saskatchewan, Canada (January 1941)

"This was certainly a disappointment for all of my patrons as well as myself. Autry never has been really popular here and his last picture ('Ride, Tenderfoot, Ride') built up his reputation a little, as it was a good picture, but after showing this I can count on losing Autry pictures from now on."

—Walter Eldred, Colfax Theater,
Colfax, California (January 1941)

"This picture gave us the biggest Sunday-Monday gross since Metro's 'Boom Town' played several months ago. Autry may be fourth in the nation, but he is just about tops in Milford."

—E. C. Arehart, Strand ,
Milford, Iowa (February 1941)

"Good old Gene. What a man at the box office. He sure gives it oomph. He is an exhibitor's dream. We tied up with Wrigley's chewing gum and 'Melody Ranch' program on radio, and did real nice business."

—Harland Rankin, Plaza Theater,
Tilbury, Ontario, Canada (February 1941)

"Every time that I complete the playing of one of Autry's pictures, I venture the hope the next one will hit the spot. The name Gene Autry still brings them in, but if they continue in the slipshod manner as they have in the past, his pictures are most certainly to suffer at the box office. Radio scripts, street cars for barricade smashers may look well enough to the makers of Autry's pictures, but the people who have rallied around his banner in recent years and the smaller theaters who have run his pictures since the beginning want him in a different type picture. At present he is the idol of the kids of America. It would be interesting to know how many pairs of kids' ears are glued to the radio for his Sunday's broadcasts. Republic has in Gene Autry some very valuable star property and I for one would like to see them put him 'Back in the Saddle Again', a picture in the glorious old west, let Gene sing some of those grand western songs with Smiley as a helper and we'll all be happier."

—E. A. Reynolds, Strand Theater, Princeton,
Minnesota (February 1941)

"This is the poorest Autry we have ever played. There is something missing when Smiley Burnette isn't along. Pretty good business against 'Boom Town'."

—Joe Schindele, Granite Theater,
Granite Falls, Minnesota (March 1941)

"I played this to average business and was very much disappointed in it. In my opinion Republic pulled another boner in this one by leaving Smiley Burnette out and trying to fill the bill for comedy relief with George Hayes. Taking Smiley away from Gene is like taking the motor out of your car. Wake up, Republic."

—Harry F. Blount, Plaza Theater,
Potosi, Missouri (March 1941)

"The people in the rural localities like Autry. He is wholesome from every angle. This film was well liked here. Business good."

—R. R. Kiefer, Kiefer's Theater,
Hardisty, Alberta, Canada (March 1946)

"One of the best yet. But about one reel too long. Hey, Hollywood, when you make westerns how about keeping 'em about 3½ reels? Give us small towners a break. Keep 'em rollin', Gene."

—Harry T. Wachter, New Gentry Theatre,
Gentry, Alabama (October 1946)

SOURCES:

1. "Melody Ranch Theater" showing of "Melody Ranch" on Nashville Network, 1987.

2. Autry with Herskowitz. p. 75-77.

3. *Hollywood Citizen News.* October 3, 1940.

Ridin' On a Rainbow
Republic, January 1941

What a lineup! Riverboat entertainers Smiley Burnette, Carol Adams, Gene, Mary Lee, Georgia Caine and Ferris Taylor.

Producer ....Harry Grey
Director ....Lew Landers
Assistant Director........................George Blair
Original Story..............................Bradford Ropes
Screenplay....................................Bradford Ropes, Doris
                                 Malloy
Photography ....William Nobles
Film Editor.................................Tony Martinelli
Musical Supervisor ....Raoul Kraushaar

Special Music and Lyrics ....Jule Styne, Sol Meyer
Production Manager.....................Al Wilson

SONGS: "Hunky Dunky Dory" (music and lyrics by Jule Styne, Sol Meyer)—sung by Gene Autry, Smiley Burnette and cowboys; "Sing a Song of Laughter" (music and lyrics by Jule Styne, Sol Meyer)—sung by Mary Lee; "What's Your Favorite Holiday" (music and lyrics by Jule Styne, Sol Meyer)—sung by Mary Lee and extras; "Be

Honest With Me" (music and lyrics by Gene Autry, Fred Rose)—sung by Gene Autry; "Steamboat Bill" (music and lyrics by Leighton Brothers, Ben Shields)—sung by Gene Autry, Smiley Burnette; "Ridin' On a Rainbow" (music and lyrics by Teddy Hall, Don George, Jean Herbert)—sung by Gene Autry; "Carry Me Back to the Lone Prairie" (music and lyrics by Carson Robison)—sung by Gene Autry, Mary Lee; "I'm the Only Lonely One" (music and lyrics by Jule Styne, Sol Meyer)—sung by Mary Lee.

RUNNING TIME: 75 minutes
FILMING DATES: November 26 to December 13, 1940.
LOCATIONS: Agoura Ranch; Morrison Ranch; likely Lake Hemet area; Republic backlot.
BUDGET: $91,854
NEGATIVE COST: $88,767

CAST:

Actor	Character
Gene Autry	Gene Autry
Smiley Burnette	Frog Millhouse
Mary Lee	Patsy Evans
Carol Adams	Sally
Ferris Taylor	Capt. Elijah Bartlett
Georgia Caine	Mariah Bartlett
Byron Foulger	Matt "Pop" Evans
Ralf Harolde	Blake
Jimmy Conlin	Joe
Guy Usher	Sheriff Jim Mason
Anthony Warde	Morrison
Forrest Taylor	Jeff Billings
Burr Caruth	Eben Carter
Ed Cassidy	Rancher Brown
Ben Hall	Attendant
Tom London	Rancher Harris
Walter Long	Bartender
Chuck Morrison	Man with bartender
Spec O'Donnell	Messenger
Hal Price	Man who has car taken
Lee Shumway, Harry Strang	Ranchers
Slim Whitaker	Café Proprietor
Harry Wilson	Cupid in Holiday Pageant (Troupe member)
Fred "Snowflake" Toones, Bob Montclair	Troupe members
Roy Hansen	Bud (Troupe member)
Arthur Furelly	Syd (Troupe member)
Connie Evans	Thelma (Troupe member)
Mary Meins	Laura (Troupe member)
Vera Burnette	Dorothy (Troupe member)
Francis Walker	Thug
Fred Ritter, Charles Murphy, Barry Hays, Lew Kelly, Loretta Lee, Vincent Lee, Glenn Turnhall, Frankie Marvin, Jack Montgomery, Edward Earle, Jim Mason, Matty Roubert, William Mong	Extras
Champion	Champion

STUNTS: Joe Yrigoyen (Gene's stunt double); Bob Woodward (double for Anthony Warde); Bill Yrigoyen (double for Ralf Harolde); Fred Schaefer.

THE FILM: "Ridin' On a Rainbow" put Gene Autry back on track with "his" patrons after the mixed acceptance of "Melody Ranch".

By now a trend was quite visible in Gene's recent offerings, and apparently appreciated by his growing audiences. The shooting is less in volume and importance while the music and light comedy elements increase in volume. The gunplay and hard riding is more a gesture and a flourish, making Gene's pictures "horse operas" in the truest sense as opposed to the casual and usual sense designated in tradepaper reviews.

The story is set in a region, not too closely defined, where open cattle range meets a big river, much like the Mississippi, with a musical showboat. But such land and cattle haven't been visible from a Mississippi riverboat in many-a-year. No matter, it's another latitude freely taken by Republic and totally accepted in the mythical world of Gene Autry.

Feeling responsible for the loss of his neighbors' money when a bank is robbed of all their recent savings, rancher Autry and pal Frog Millhouse (Smiley Burnette) set out to trace the guilty parties and recoup the losses.

They join the showboat troupe of Capt. Bartlett (Ferris Taylor) in which the brightest young entertainer, Patsy Evans (Mary Lee), is the daughter of a has-been actor (Byron Foulger) who has unfortunately gotten mixed up with the bank robbers. Her father having fled, but stubbornly loyal to him, Patsy carries the stolen funds to him and is captured by the bank robbers when she tries to persuade him to return the stolen funds.

Naturally, Gene and Frog arrive in time to save her, capture the crooks and recover the money.

In the interim, the sequences are devoted primarily to the showboat's voyage with plenty of songs, tap dancing by Sally (Carol Adams)—Gene's romantic interest—and light comedy, making for a truly delightful Autry crowd-pleaser.

NOTES AND COMMENTS: The working titles of this film were "Valley of the Moon" and "Call of the Canyon", the latter title was eventually used in 1942.

The dog Spotlight was "played" by Punky, owned by Earl Johnson who was paid $125 a week for the animal's use. Director Lew Landers earned $500 a week.

The song "Be Honest With Me", written by Gene Autry and Fred Rose, was nominated for an Academy Award as best song of 1941 but did not win, losing out to "The Last Time I Saw Paris" by Jerome Kern from MGM's "Lady Be Good". Nine songs in all were nominated.

FILM COMMENTS: *Carol Adams:* "Gene was nervous about any packages he received from fans. He had someone at the studio open them for him and only those that were safe and harmless were passed on to him. This

Smiley and Gene round-up "the gang" — unknown player, Chuck Morrison, unknown player, Francis Walker.

was in 1941, long before USA terrorists, that Gene was so cautious.

"In all of Gene Autry's films, the leading lady never had any physical contact. Romance was all flirtatious. At the end of the film you'd be singing a song together or standing on each side of Champion. An interesting aside to this was when we were called into the studio's still gallery to shoot 8x10 black and white photos, Gene wanted to have a little fun and have the photographer shoot some romantic shots for his own pleasure." [1]

Gene Autry: "During the early '40s, it must have seemed to most movie-goers that Republic couldn't make an Autry or a Rogers picture without Mary Lee cast as somebody's spoiled kid sister or resident orphan-in-trouble. 'Ridin' On a Rainbow' was one of those. It was also a western version of 'Showboat'. One of the songwriters was Carson Robison, who later made a big seller out of a small classic called 'Life Gets Teejus'. Mary Lee had started out as a young singer with the Ted Weems orchestra." [2]

CAST BIOS: The "high" period in Carol Adams' early screen career was when she received rave reviews for her tap dancing in 20th Century–Fox's "Sally, Irene and Mary" with Alice Faye and Tony Martin in 1938, even though her name wasn't even mentioned on the cast sheet.

Born March 15, 1918, in Los Angeles, her first stage hit was dancing at Lowe's State Theater at the age of seven. About this time she also appeared as a flower girl in a silent Billie Dove starrer.

Awarded a dramatic scholarship at the Martha Oatman School at a young age,

by the time she was eleven Carol was playing the Pantages Circuit with the "Hollywood Starlets".

After high school, she attended Los Angeles City College for one semester then had the opportunity to dance in "Love and Hisses" ('37 Fox). Several other film roles as a dancer followed, sometimes using the name Lurline Uller.

She went on tour as a dancer with the Leroy Prinz girls and worked for a season with bandleader Ted Lewis. Musical stage revues "Hit and Run" and "Charlot's Revue" followed. Republic signed her to a term contract from October 1940 to October 1941, utilizing her first in small roles in "Behind the News" and "Bowery Boy" (both '40).

Her first starring role was in "Ridin' On a Rainbow", giving her the opportunity to show off her tap-dancing skills. Republic featured her in four other films, including Roy Rogers' "Bad Man of Deadwood", and a serial, "Dick Tracy Vs. Crime Inc." (both '41).

Director Lew Landers was a top helmer of action movies, westerns and horror films. Born January 2, 1901, in New York City, he began working as an actor and production assistant in silent films. Under his real name, Louis Friedlander, he began directing serials at Universal in 1934, including "The Red Rider" with Buck Jones and "Rustlers Of Red Dog" with Johnny Mack Brown.

His first feature effort, "The Raven" ('35) with Boris Karloff and Bela Lugosi is probably his best work. Although the film was a success, and Friedlander might have gone on to more prestigious pictures, he somehow became stuck

Gene and Smiley try to persuade Sheriff Guy Usher to go easy on Mary Lee who is shielding her father-turned-bankrobber father.

Director Lew Landers and Gene meet with Tom Tyler who was preparing to film the classic Republic serial "The Adventures of Captain Marvel."

doing program films. When he switched to RKO in 1936, he changed his name to Lew Landers and churned out 23 B-films in three years.

Republic hired him in 1940 where he helmed three of Gene Autry's westerns, "Ridin' On a Rainbow", "Back In the Saddle" and "The Singing Hill",

Landers moved once again in 1941, landing at Columbia through 1945. Late in his career he worked for PRC, Paramount, Monogram, RKO again, American-International and others, including television work on "Kit Carson", "Tales of the Texas Rangers", "Cheyenne", "Superman" and dozens more.

Rivaling Sam Newfield, William Beaudine and others as one of the industry's most prolific B-directors, Landers work is often exceptional considering the staggering amount of his output.

Actor Robert Scott, star of the Landers directed "Black Arrow" serial in 1944, said of Landers, "Lew Landers was a nice guy. I think he was kind of disillusioned about his career, because he told me one time, 'They give me these small pictures to do and want them finished by Thursday. They don't want them good, they just want to get it out. I used to finish them on time, cut and move in...do all the things you can do to get it in the can. They come out with short-comings, not the most finished pieces of movie making in the world. But producers forget what you do for them.'"
[3]

At only 61, Landers died December 16, 1962, in Palm

Desert, California, after completing his last film, "Terrified" ('63 Crown-International).

WHAT THE EXHIBITOR HAD TO SAY: "Gene Autry is a favorite here. I still don't know why. 'Frog' (Smiley Burnette) is well liked also. In this picture he gets seasick and on a 'riverboat'. Can you beat that?"
—Ray Peacock, Onalaska Theater, Onalaska, Washington (January 1941)

"Good picture and good business. The music, dancing, and showboat background will please all."
—E. M. Freiburger, Paramount Theater, Dewey, Oklahoma (February 1941)

"Thanks to Mary Lee, this is one of the best Autrys to date. Although it will not do as good at the box office as 'South of the Border', in my opinion, it is a better picture."
—Raymond Paul, Seabreeze Theater, Beaufort, North Carolina (February 1941)

"This is a good Autry entry. Plenty of music, lots of comedy, not too much action and the two supporting stars, Smiley Burnette and Mary Lee, certainly do carry Gene Autry along. If you have a small town patronage, this will certainly please your people."
—Theodore J. Friedman, Strand Theater, Suffern, New York (April 1941)

"We don't do the land-office business on Autry that some claim, but do some extra, and they seem to like him better with each picture. The direction is improving and the pictures show results from an upped budget, and if they show a profit, that's about all we can ask out here where they wonder 'What war?'"
—Mayme P. Musselman, Princess Theater, Lincoln, Kansas (October 1941)

"All of Autry's pictures draw. I don't know why. Little Mary Lee stole this one."
—E. L. Ornstein, Rialto Theater, Marengo, Indiana (October 1941)

"Played this late and had good Saturday business."
—J. N. Wells, Wells Theater, Kingsland, Georgia (March 1942)

"This old 1941 Autry did fair business and pleased Autry fans. But there are many people who won't come out to see Autry here."
—W. R. Pyle, Dreamland Theater, Rockglen, Saskatchewan, Canada (June 1942)

SOURCES:
1. Letter to Ray Nielsen, April 2006.
2. Autry with Herskowitz. p. 77.
3. Interview with author.

Back In the Saddle
<u>Republic, March 1941</u>

THE KING OF SADDLE ADVENTURE

Back in a thrill-a-minute range hit that spells A-C-T-I-O-N

BACK in the SADDLE

starring **GENE AUTRY**

with **SMILEY BURNETTE**

MARY LEE · EDWARD NORRIS

JACQUELINE WELLS

Producer ....Harry Grey
Director ....Lew Landers
Screenplay...................................Richard Murphy, Jesse
                                     Lasky Jr.
Photography ....Ernest Miller
Film Editor................................Tony Martinelli
Musical Supervisor ....Raoul Kraushaar
Production Manager....................Al Wilson

SONGS: "Back In the Saddle Again" (music and lyrics by Gene Autry, Ray Whitley)—sung by Gene Autry; "In the Jailhouse Now" (music and lyrics by Jimmie Rodgers)—sung by Gene Autry; "Ninety-Nine Bullfrogs" (music and lyrics by Smiley Burnette)—sung by Smiley Burnette; "Swingin' Sam, the Cowboy Man" (music and lyrics by Jule Styne, Sol Meyer)—sung by Mary Lee; "When the River Meets the Range" (music and lyrics by Jule Styne, Sol Meyer)—sung by Jacqueline Wells; "When the Cactus Is In Bloom" (music and lyrics by Jimmie Rodgers)—sung by Gene Autry; "I'm An Old Cowhand" (music and lyrics by Johnny Mercer)—sung by Gene Autry, Mary Lee; "You Are My Sunshine" (music and lyrics by Jimmie Davis, Charles Mitchell)—sung by Gene Autry.

RUNNING TIME: 71 minutes
FILMING DATES: January 21 to February 4, 1941
LOCATIONS: Victorville; Iverson Ranch; Chatsworth Train Station; railroad track likely in San Fernando Valley; Republic backlot
BUDGET: $84,572
NEGATIVE COST: $87,735

CAST:

Actor	Character
Gene Autry...................................Gene Autry
Smiley Burnette ....Frog Millhouse
Mary Lee ....Patsy
Edward Norris ....Tom Bennett
Jacqueline Wells ....Taffy
Addison Richards ....Duke Winston
Arthur Loft.................................E. G. Blaine
Edmund Elton.............................Judge Bent
Joe McGuinn ....Sheriff Simpson
Edmund Cobb.............................Rancher Williams
Robert Barron.............................Ward
Robert Blair................................Tex
George Sherwood........................Wilson
Bob Lemond................................Radio Announcer
Chuck Baldra, Art Dillard, Cactus Mack, Frankie Marvin.............Cowhands
Stanley Blystone ....Station Agent Jess
Ralph Bucko, Roy Bucko, Bob Woodward.........................Ranchers
Monte Montague ....Blackjack (dealer)
Victor Cox ....Miner

Curley Dresden ....Henchman Barrett
Frank Ellis..................................Rider chasing Duke
Reed Howes ....Cowhand Slim
John Indrisano............................New York Cab driver
Frank Conklin ....Cook
Jack Montgomery........................Slade
Bill Nestell ....Drunken Miner
Jack O'Shea ....Man in bar
Pascale Perry, Harry Willingham.Townsmen
Lon Poff......................................George C. Joy, Mortician
Fred "Snowflake" Toones ....Train Porter
Phillip Trent ....Jack, Tom's New York
                                      friend
Ray Jones ....Barfly
Curley Dresden ....Thug
Carl Cotner.................................Violinist
Jack Smith..................................Piano player
Bob Burns, Bob Card, Jess Cavan,
   Ben Corbett, Jim Corey, Tom
   Ewell, Art Felix, Augie Gomez,
   Tommy Coats, Herman Hack,
   Chick Hannon, Al Haskell,
   Jack Perrin, Cliff Parkinson,
   George Sowards ....Extras

Champion...................................Champion

STUNTS: Joe Yrigoyen (double for Gene Autry); Jack Kirk (double for Smiley Burnette); Nellie Walker (double for Jacqueline Wells); Dixie Lee Hall (double for Mary Lee).

THE FILM: Reviewers hailed "Back In the Saddle" as one of Gene Autry's best—and it was—combining a great title tune and other classic Autry western songs by Jimmie Rodgers and Jimmie Davis with slam-bang action, something missing from several of Gene's more recent films.

The plot involves Gene's attempt to bring about peace between ranchers and the operator of a copper mine whose chemicals are poisoning the water supply. Ranch foreman Gene Autry and pal Frog Millhouse (Smiley Burnette) escort troublesome playboy ranch owner Tom Bennett (Edward Norris) from back East to the ranch he's inherited out West. Bennett provides nearly as much trouble for Gene as mining magnate E. G. Blaine (Arthur Loft) who pretty well runs the town of Solitude.

When Blaine refuses to accede to the Cattlemen's demands for cleaning up the drinking water, tension grows as

Radio announcer Bob Lemond, trying to interview Gene, has a hard time keeping the microphone away from Smiley who wants to "talk on that radio."

their stock continues to die of copper sulphate poisoning.

Also coming to Solitude is likeable gambler Duke Winston (Addison Richards), an old friend of Gene's, but who is after the plentiful pickings resulting from the rich copper strike. He sides with the unscrupulous Blaine.

Before Gene can get an injunction against Blaine, hotheaded Tom leads a raid against Blaine's mining operation. The raid fails and Tom is jailed on a trumped-up murder charge.

Gene strikes a bargain with Blaine to drop the injunction if Blaine will release Tom and build a pipeline diversion for the poisoned water.

Soon realizing Blaine has no intention of keeping his word, Gene resorts to gun-law but is caught in the jail with Tom which is set on fire by Blaine's henchmen.

Joined by Duke, who is fed up with Blaine's underhanded double-crossing, Gene fights back. Gene and Tom are saved when Frog stampedes a herd over Blaine and his crew but Duke is killed in the wild melee.

In his westerns, Addison Richards was never better than in Gene's "Back In the Saddle". It's really Richards' film all the way as a suave good/badman gambler. All his scenes are standouts, including the one where he smugly tells arrogant mine owner Arthur Loft, "Don't ever be alone with yourself, you wouldn't like it."

Action director Lew Landers, in his second outing with Gene, delivers an excellent picture, including an exciting sequence where Gene and the judge race a train. Gene helps the judge transfer from his horse to the train. Definitely among Gene's best.

NOTES AND COMMENTS: The film's original working title was "Song at Twilight".

Actress Margaret Tallichet was originally planned to become Gene's leading lady in this picture but her husband, director William Wyler, talked her out of it in favor of a Sun Valley vacation.

FILM COMMENTS: *Gene Autry:* "Often, of course, when one of my own songs became popular we slapped it on a movie. So 'Back in the Saddle' was released in March of 1941. Smiley was in it, as usual, and Mary Lee, and an interesting actress named Jacqueline Wells. She had talent, but was one of those who seemed doomed to work in nothing but B-westerns. She would change her screen name about every five years and start over; from Diane Duval to Jacqueline Wells to Julie Bishop. Under that name, Julie Bishop, she became a Warner's contract player

and achieved semi-stardom in the war years. She is probably best remembered as the Hawaiian hooker who fell for John Wayne in 'Sands of Iwo Jima' ('50).

"I always had one regret about 'Back in the Saddle'. If we had known what was coming in just a few months, we could have saved it for the title of my first postwar movie." [1]

Jacqueline Wells (later Julie Bishop): "I'd been under contract to Paramount in the early '30s, then Columbia for several years. I was now free-lancing and always tried to do my best. Republic must have liked me, because they hired me over and over. The pictures were well-made, and there was never any trouble. I recall no accidents or tantrums or anything like that. They were fun to do. Actually, I didn't have much to do with Gene in the film, I had more scenes with Edward Norris. Now Edward is a handsome man! He was married to Ann Sheridan. They were a fun couple. For years, Norris had a ranch in the hills of Malibu. He had show horses; not race horses. A very nice guy." Prompted to recall child actress Mary Lee, "Oh, was she a child? I thought she might have been a dwarf! (Laughs) She was odd-looking, but had a great singing voice. Funny, I don't recall her mother being on the set, so naturally I assumed she was past 18." When asked about singing on screen and how it's done, Julie said, "Usually I was dubbed but, occasionally, if it wasn't something too difficult, I was allowed to do it. They prerecord the songs, then a huge machine comes onto the stage and you lip-sync to the recording." [2]

WHAT THE EXHIBITOR HAD TO SAY: "A very good western with music. Gene was never a big bet here but we do average or better with most of his pictures. With the regular cast they draw okay but our worst flop was when they left Smiley out and put in Jimmy Durante. If you haven't played

Gene tries to convince Edward Norris it's for his own good to let Sheriff Joe McGuinn arrest him, as he'll get a fair trial. Jacqueline Wells is the girl.

it, get a date. I know the patrons will like the picture."
—Mayme P. Musselman, Princess Theater,
Lincoln, Kansas (August 1941)

"Mr. Autry, I would like to take this opportunity through this column, on behalf of the small town exhibitor, to congratulate you on being the biggest box-office attraction, for this class of exhibitor, on the screen today. Your product is a box-office tonic without comparison, as our folks from the country flock in to hear you sing. I also have heard many comments on the write-up of your life in LIBERTY,

published lately. I can recommend your product to any small town exhibitor to be the tops in box-office attraction. But one mistake, why the poor advertising accessories?"
—A. L. Dove, Bengough Theater,
Bengough, Saskatchewan, Canada (August 1941)

SOURCES:
1. Autry with Herskowitz. p. 77.
2. *Western Clippings #44.* November/December 2001. p. 19.

187

The Singing Hill

Republic, April 1941

Producer ....Harry Grey
Director ....Lew Landers
Assistant Director.......................William O'Connor
Original Story.............................Jesse Lasky Jr., Richard Murphy
Screenplay..................................Olive Cooper
Photography ....William Nobles
Film Editor.................................Les Orlebeck
Musical Supervisor ....Raoul Kraushaar
Production Manager....................Al Wilson

SONGS: "Patsy's Birthday Routine" (music and lyrics by Jule Styne, Sol Meyer)—sung by Mary Lee; "Ridin' Down That Old Texas Trail" (music and lyrics by Milt Mabre, D. Massey)—sung by Gene Autry, Mary Lee, Smiley Burnette; "Tumble Down Shack in Havana" (music and lyrics by Jule Styne, Eddie Cherkose, Sol Meyer)—sung by Virginia Dale; "Blueberry Hill" (music and lyrics by Al Lewis, Larry Stock, Vincent Rose)—sung by Gene Autry; "Let a Smile Be Your Umbrella" (music and lyrics by Irving Kahal, Francis Wheeler, Sammy Fain)—sung by Gene Autry, Smiley Burnette, Mary Lee and cowboys; "Sail the Seven Seas" (music and lyrics by Smiley Burnette)—sung by Mary Lee, Smiley Burnette; "Good Old Fashioned Hoedown" (music and lyrics by Gene Autry)—sung by Gene Autry; "The Last Round-Up" (music and lyrics by Billy Hill)—sung by Gene Autry and studio singers); "There'll Never Be Another Pal Like You" (music and lyrics by Gene Autry, Johnny Marvin)—sung by Gene Autry.

RUNNING TIME: 75 minutes
FILMING DATES: March 11-24, 1941
LOCATIONS: Jauregui Ranch; Walker Ranch; Republic backlot; Red Rock Canyon
BUDGET: $86,869
NEGATIVE COST: $87,184

CAST:

Actor	Character
Gene Autry	Gene Autry
Smiley Burnette	Frog Millhouse
Virginia Dale	Jo Adams
Mary Lee	Patsy
Spencer Charters	Judge Starrbottle
Gerald Oliver Smith	Dada
George Meeker	John R. Ramsey
Wade Boteler	Pop Sloan
Harry Stubbs	James Morgan
Cactus Mack	Cactus Mack
Jack Kirk	Flint
Chuck Morrison	Henchman Pete Dawson
Monte Montague	Rancher
Leon Belasco	Dr. Miskeroff
Fred Burns, Herman Hack, Jack O'Shea, Al Taylor, Matty Roubert, Jack Rockwell, Hal Price	Ranchers
Tommy Coats	Cowhand Hank
Art Dillard	Henchman
Frankie Marvin	Cowhand Shorty
Forrest Taylor	Rancher Walters
Vinegar Roan	Cowhand Al
Turk Greenough	Cowhand Tom
Dude Chick	Cowhand Bud
Dan White, Foxy Callahan, Roy Bucko, Jim Corey, Bob Woodward, Art Dillard, Jack Montgomery, Chuck Baldra, Bob Card	Extras
Champion	Champion

STUNTS: Joe Yrigoyen, Tommy Coats, Nellie Walker, B. Kane, Yakima Canutt.

THE FILM: Still leading western stars by a number of notches in popularity, Gene Autry receives the increased care in the handling of his productions from director Lew Landers who smoothly guides Gene Autry, Smiley Burnette and Mary Lee through their paces. Landers has spotted ten songs throughout the 75 minute running time, obviously recognizing exactly what Autry's public wants.

The cast contains several talented new faces for Gene's pictures—Virginia Dale is possibly the most eccentric heiress who ever complicated his life; George Meeker makes a smooth heavy; Spencer Charters gives authority to the kindly old judge; Gerald Oliver Smith is a humorous butler and Wade Boteler is an old rancher friend of the family. Not often is such an aggregation to be found in a budget film.

The plot deals with the plight of ranchers when the free grazing land they have used for years is about to be sold to grasping young cattle broker John Ramsey (George Meeker).

Gene, as foreman of the Circle R Ranch and head of the Cattlemen's Association, tries to make youthful Jo Adams (Virginia Dale), owner of the ranch, understand the future of all ranchers hinges on her sale of the property. But Jo is a frivolous, extravagant heiress to whom sentiment means little and stubbornly refuses to stop the sale.

In a hilarious courtroom scene, Gene has Jo declared incompetent and has himself appointed her guardian.

Ramsey has already made a $25,000 downpayment to clinch his option to buy within 60 days, and Jo has already spent the money on her debts. Therefore Gene's next problem is to raise the $25,000 to return to Ramsey in order to cancel the sale. He and the cattlemen agree to pool their herds for sale to raise the cash, but Ramsey employs gunmen to stampede the cattle and flood the valley, killing kindly old Pop Sloan (Wade Boteler) in the process.

Eventually, Jo realizes it is her own selfishness that's causing all the grief and joins with Gene to stop the sale and reveal Ramsey for the crook he is.

NOTES AND COMMENTS: Interestingly, the song, "The Singing Hills", is not in the film "The Singing Hill"—which was actually based on a similarly titled novel to which Republic bought the rights before the similarly titled song made it big. The song itself appeared in "Gaucho Serenade".

Gene introduced the classic song "Blueberry Hill", one of his top selling recordings, in this picture as well as the Broadway classic "The Last Round-Up" which originated in the musical revue "Ziegfeld Follies of 1934". Gene reprised the song as the title tune of his first Columbia production.

Former Earl Carroll showgirl, now a Paramount contractee, Virginia Dale, was loaned to Republic for "The Singing Hill". Republic originally sought to borrow Patricia Morison from Paramount but she refused the part because of what she termed the unsuitable story and because she didn't like the clothes. Paramount suspended Morison and loaned Dale to Republic instead.

The dam used in "The Singing Hill" was a Lydecker brothers' miniature first built for Ralph Byrd's "Born to Be Wild" ('38) and used in later titles such as

"Dick Tracy Returns" serial ('38) and "King of the Texas Rangers" serial ('41).

WHAT THE EXHIBITOR HAD TO SAY: "No complaints even from those who do not care for westerns. Gene usually turns out entertaining and enjoyable film fare."
—H. Goldson, Plaza Theater, Chicago, Illinois (August 1941)

"Doubled this with 'Melody and Moonlight' (Republic). Makes a grand show. Stood them in the aisles. Autry packs them in like no other star."
—J. L. Thayer, Leddy Theater, Raymond, New Hampshire (August 1941)

"Hot as it was, Autry brings them in. Don't need air-conditioning for Autry."
—Harland Rankin, Plaza Theater, Tilbury, Ontario, Canada (August 1941)

"Just up the alley for a spot like mine. These are improving all the time. Star very popular among the rural supporters."
—A. L. Dove, Bengough Theater, Bengough, Saskatchewan, Canada (December 1941)

"Liked by everyone, so that is that. An excellent picture. Music and comedy, western style. Mary Lee, the up and coming starlet, is really worth watching, and she really can sing."
—Guy G. Black, Plaza Theater, Lyons, Nebraska (February 1942)

"Was a good western and pleased my patronage very much for the weekend." —Cleo Manry, Buena Vista Theater, Buena Vista, Georgia (February 1942)

It was good while it lasted, but this was talented Mary Lee's last film with Gene.

Sunset in Wyoming
Republic, July 1941

Producer ....Harry Grey
Director ....William Morgan
Assistant Director.......................Art Siteman
Original Story.............................Joe Blair
Screenplay...................................Ivan Goff, Ann
                    Morrison Chapin
Photography ....Reggie Lanning
Film Editor.................................Tony Martinelli
Musical Supervisor ....Raoul Kraushaar
Production Manager....................Al Wilson

SONGS: "I Was Born In Old Wyoming" (music and lyrics by Carson J. Robison)—sung by Gene Autry, Smiley Burnette; "There's a Home In Wyomin'" (music and lyrics by Peter DeRose, Billy Hill)—sung by Gene Autry; "Twenty-One Years" (music and lyrics by Bob Miller)—sung by Gene Autry; "Casey Jones" (music and lyrics by T. Lawrence Seibert, Eddie Newton)—sung by Gene Autry, Smiley Burnette; "Sing Me a Song of the Saddle" (music and lyrics by Gene Autry, Frank Harford)—sung by Gene Autry.

RUNNING TIME: 66 minutes

FILMING DATES: May 27 to June 11, 1941

LOCATIONS: Placerita Canyon (Walker Ranch); Republic backlot; George Lewis mansion once located in Benedict Canyon (Beverly Hills). Logging fight scenes were probably shot either at Big Bear or Keen Camp

BUDGET: $78,803

NEGATIVE COST: $84,097

CAST:

Actor	*Character*
Gene Autry	Gene Autry
Smiley Burnette	Frog Millhouse
Maris Wrixon	Wilmetta "Billie" Wentworth
George Cleveland	Asa Wentworth
Robert Kent	Larry Drew
Sarah Edwards	Susanna Hawkins Peabody
Monte Blue	Jim Haines
Dick Elliott	Lt. Gov. Cornelius Peabody
John Dilson	Phipps
Stanley Blystone	Bull Wilson
Eddie Dew	Rancher Hal Dexter
Fred Burns	Rancher Bob Clayton
Reed Howes	Rancher
Lloyd Whitlock	Senator Blake
Nora Lane	Mrs. Blake
Earle Hodgins	Circus Advance Man
Roy Bucko, Jim Corey, Frank McCarroll, Tom Smith, Al Taylor, Bob Woodward	Ranchers
Tommy Coats	Cowhand Tommy
Eddie Dean	Cowhand Eddie
Mary MacLaren	Mrs. Haines
Frankie Marvin	Cowhand musician
James Sheridan	Townsman
Bill Nestell, Frank Ellis, Tex Terry, Ken Cooper	Loggers
Alexia Moreland	Mollie
Ralph Peters	Jailer
Lee Shumway	Fred Dexter
Alphonse Martell	1st Club Waiter
Jack Chefe	2nd Club Waiter
Gino Corrado	3rd Club Waiter
Jack Cheatham	1st Club Attendant
Bob Blair	2nd Club Attendant
Gladys Gale	Mrs. Montgomery
Arthur Stewart Hull	Mr. Montgomery
Bob Lemond	Steward
Frank O'Connor	McGovern (policeman)
Herman Hack, Augie Gomez, Buck Moulton, Matty Roubert, Bud Brown, Pascale Perry, Vinegar Roan, Chick Hannon, Chuck Baldra, Joe "Slim" Balch, V. DeCamp, Art Dillard, M. Brown	Extras
Champion	Champion

STUNTS: Joe Yrigoyen (Gene's double); Yakima Canutt, Tommy Coats, Ken Cooper, Nellie Walker, Bob Woodward, Joe Garcia.

It's all a misunderstanding, but isn't it always in Gene's pictures, as Maris Wrixon and her business manager, Robert Kent (center), have Gene and Smiley arrested much to the surprise of Wrixon's father, George Cleveland. The cop on the right is Frank O'Connor who played cops and officials in dozens of movies.

THE FILM: Songs are not too plentiful in this western which has Gene Autry handing out a lesson on overlogging and reforestation…a strong environmental theme still relevant today.

Gene is his usual engaging self and Smiley Burnette turns in some humorous sequences as a butler in the mansion of a millionaire. However, at times, the story veers off on a very silly tangent, especially with a "wild animal park" sequence that sinks to nearly Three Stooges quality.

Gene is the leader of the Valley ranchers being ruined by the stripping of the nearby mountain area of its precious timber. The ranchers face flood devastation unless reforestation is adopted by the Wentworth Lumber Company.

Gene and Frog Millhouse (Smiley Burnette) appeal directly to the owner of the company, Asa Wentworth (George Cleveland) but find him dominated by his willful, impertinent granddaughter Billie Wentworth (Maris Wrixon) who is in love with the ruthless general manager of the company Larry Drew (Robert Kent). Old Asa doesn't approve of Drew's logging tactics and secretly helps Gene and Frog concoct an elaborate plot to have nearby Mt. Warner declared a state park and wildlife refuge.

Finale features a severe storm in which Asa is washed into a mountain torrent and nearly drowned before Billie sees for herself the devastation caused by the overlogging of the mountain and is won over to Gene's side.

Once again, this wonderful, eclectic mixture of timber country, cowboys, horses, modern cars, swank country clubs, high society and music seems to have been the explicit property of Gene Autry. No other studio attempted

the same with their cowboy stars. After all, only Gene's easy-going charm and boyish charisma could carry it off without becoming ridiculous. Nobody but Gene Autry could survive in such an unconventional environment. As you view Gene's films, you realize he *was* the whole show around which the most ridiculous elements could be developed. He remained the immovable center, holding it all together, dominating the audience and slyly charming them into smiling submission.

NOTES AND COMMENTS: The working title for this film was "Under Fiesta Stars", which was used for the next Autry feature.

Logging stock footage from "Come and Get It" ('36), a Samuel Goldwyn United Artists picture starring Joel McCrea, was purchased from Samuel Goldwyn Inc.

Five songs planned for this film were not used—"Heebie Jeebie Blues", "Sweet Patootie Kitty", "Sign Up For Happy Days", "My Faith Looks Up to Thee" and "I'm a Cowpoke Pokin' Along".

Los Angeles born director William Morgan (1899-1964) began his film career as a film editor for eight years with Paramount and RKO before moving over to Republic as, first an editor on "Dark Command" ('40) with John Wayne and other films, then a director. His only westerns were seven with Gene in the early '40s. In the mid '40s he returned to editing, often working for Disney.

Maris Wrixon, on loan from Warner Bros., earned $200 a week, but top salary went to Robert Kent and George Cleveland, both at $500 a week. Sarah Edwards made $300, Dick Elliott $250, Stanley Blystone $125 and Monte Blue $200. Fred Burns, Eddie Dew, John Dilson, Frankie Marvin and Eddie Dean all were set at $75 a week.

FILM COMMENTS: *Maris Wrixon:* "I had just finished 'Too Many Husbands' ('40) and was hot. Warner Bros.—who still had me under contract—wasn't doing anything with me, so when Republic asked to use me, Warners let them.

"Gene was very professional and wonderful to work with. I remember Gene Autry kissed me on screen, which is something he didn't do very often with his leading ladies. There's a scene in 'Sunset in Wyoming' where I'm pushed into a swimming pool. I took that fall in one take—thank goodness!

"The difference between working at a major studio like WB and a medium sized studio like Republic is all the difference money can make. It's like going to a first class restaurant and McDonald's. At Republic you had to work a lot faster and it was not as elegant. Everything was economized." [1]

Gene Autry: "(Director) Bill Morgan used to be a cutter, a film editor. He cut a lot of my pictures. It's a very important part of screen production. A cutter can make a good picture or a bad picture. I think this is the first picture he directed. He became a very good director."[2]

CAST BIOS: Stalwart, durable Monte Blue, a romantic leading man in silent films, had a strong, cultivated voice that transferred well into talkies where he enjoyed a quality reputation as a noted character player for 30 years. All in all, a glorious 45 year screen career that encompassed many scoundrelous characterizations, especially in Zane Grey and Gene Autry westerns such as "Ride Ranger Ride", "Rootin' Tootin' Rhythm" and "Sunset in Wyoming".

Born Gerard Montgomery Blue January 11, 1887, in Indianapolis, Indiana, he was one-sixteenth Cherokee. The Indian translation for Monte Blue is Blue Mountain.

After Blue's father was killed in a train accident, Monte's poverty-stricken mother sent the 7 year old boy and a younger brother to an orphans home.

At 12, Monte became interested in journalism, becoming a printer's devil for the weekly orphanage newspaper. At 16 he left the home and returned to Indiana.

For the next several years Blue worked at various jobs around the country, eventually scoring a day laborer job at $1.50 a day at the D. W. Griffith studio where he began to argue to other workers that the pay was too low…that they should be paid $2.50 a day. When he noticed Griffith himself observing his tirade, he returned to his job. A few days later, Griffith approached Blue to do the same sort of haranguing for a mob scene in "The Absentee". The non-actor performed the scene in the 1915 film so well Griffith put him under contract at $10 a week, soon raised to $15, appearing in Griffith's "Birth of a Nation" ('15) and "Intolerance" ('16). With Griffith he was also a stuntman, script clerk and assistant director. As Blue could ride, he also began to double western stars for other directors.

Gaining a foothold in Hollywood, by 1923 he was under a long term contract to Warner Bros. Blue was not considered a handsome man, but his magnetic personality transferred well to the screen. The camera liked him. At last he'd found his life's work.

After making several talkies for Warner Bros. in 1929 he "retired" from the screen while he, his wife and two children took a world cruise. However, when he returned during the Great Depression, bad investments had nearly wiped out his considerable savings.

Once again, as he had so many times before, he regrouped and became one of the screen's most dependable character players.

Just prior to his death Blue was working as an advance man for the Hamid-Morton Circus which was playing in Milwaukee, Wisconsin, where he died of a heart attack, complicated by influenza, on February 18, 1963.

WHAT THE EXHIBITOR HAD TO SAY: "Doubled this with 'Mr. District Attorney'. Packed them in with these two pictures. Both of them were bang-up entertainment for our audience. Autry and Burnette are 100 per cent box office draws for this section."   —I. L. Thayer, Leddy's Theater, Raymond, New Hampshire (September 1941)

"Gene Autry is picking up here and his last two pictures have drawn better than average Friday and Saturday business. Patrons like him with Smiley Burnette, and while they are not masterpieces, there is a lot of entertainment that satisfies the small towners and farmers who make up our audience. Book it and play it; you can't go wrong."
—Mayme P. Musselman, Princess Theater, Lincoln, Kansas (November 1941)

"These Autrys are all good and have plenty of drawing power here."   —J. N. Wells, Wells Theater, Kingsland, Georgia (March 1942)

SOURCES:

1. *Western Ladies #3.* November 1997. Interview with Joe Collura.
2. "Melody Ranch Theater" showing of "Home in Wyomin'"

It takes George Cleveland's near death for daughter Maris Wrixon (center) to understand the devastation overlogging can cause. Alexia Moreland helps out while rancher Monte Blue looks on.

Under Fiesta Stars
Republic, August 1941

Producer ....Harry Grey
Director ....Frank McDonald (and
                                                George Sherman)
Assistant Director.........................Art Siteman
Original Story..............................Karl Brown
Screenplay...................................Karl Brown, Eliot
                                                Gibbons
Photography ....Harry Neumann
Film Editor.................................Tony Martinelli
Musical Supervisor ....Raoul Kraushaar

Production Manager....................Al Wilson

SONGS: "Man On the Flying Trapeze" (music and lyrics by Walter O'Keefe)—sung by Gene Autry, Smiley Burnette, Joe Strauch Jr. and rodeo cowboys; "Keep It In the Family" (music and lyrics by Smiley Burnette)—sung by Smiley Burnette and Joe Strauch Jr.; "Purple Sage In the Twilight" (music and lyrics by Gene Autry, Jule Styne, Sol Meyer)—sung by Gene Autry; "I've Got No Use For Women" (music and lyrics by Sol Meyer)—sung by Gene

Autry; "When You're Smiling" (music and lyrics by Mark Fisher, Joe Goodwin, Larry Shay)—sung by Gene Autry; "Under Fiesta Stars" (music and lyrics by Gene Autry, Fred Rose)—sung by Gene Autry.

RUNNING TIME: 65 minutes

FILMING DATES: July 8 to July 22, 1941

LOCATIONS: Upper Iverson Ranch; Bronson Canyon; Reuss Ranch on Lake Malibu; Republic backlot

BUDGET: $81,812

NEGATIVE COST: $81,916

CAST:

Actor	Character
Gene Autry	Gene Autry
Smiley Burnette	Frog
Carol Hughes	Barbara Erwin
Frank Darien	Benjamin Peabody
Joe Strauch Jr.	Tadpole
Pauline Drake	Kitty Callahan
Ivan Miller	Arnold
Sam Flint	Fry
Elias Gamboa	Jose Ortega
John Merton	Tommick
Jack Kirk	Sheriff
Inez Palange	Mrs. Romero
Burr Caruth	Dr. James Ware
Tommy Coats	Henchman Boat
Art Dillard	Henchman Mike
Frank McCarroll, Chick Hannon, Bob Woodward	Henchmen
Pascale Perry	Henchman Mason
Ernest Sarracino	Ramon Alvarez
Lee Shumway	Arthur Sloane
Hal Taliaferro	Smokey
Nina Campana	Mrs. Ortega
Charles Rivero	Carlos
Joe DeLaCruz	Pasqual
Trini Varda, Tina Menard	Mexican Women
Al Herman	Rodeo Announcer
Patsy Parsons	Little girl with Tadpole
Roy Bucko	Deputy
Frankie Marvin, Sherman Davidson, George Havens, Mike Luna, Yakima Canutt, Bill Yrigoyen, Curley Dresden, Vinegar Roan, Bud Geary	Extras
Champion	Champion

STUNTS: Joe Yrigoyen (Gene's double); Tex Terry (Smiley's double); George Havens (Joe Strauch's double); Claire Friend (Carol Hughes' double); Yakima Canutt, Bob Folkerson, Ralph Gomez, Tommy Coats, Frank McCarroll.

THE FILM: Nothing new here, "Under Fiesta Stars" is simply a retooling of "Rancho Grande" ('40) and is a rather slow moving Gene Autry picture from director Frank McDonald who had helmed some of Gene's better films in 1940 and would later direct a host of Gene's TV episodes. McDonald does the best he can with an overburdened plot that relies more on verbal plotting and counterplotting than it does on western action.

Rodeo star Gene Autry and spoiled city gal Barbara Erwin (Carol Hughes) jointly inherit late Dad Erwin's ranch and mining property. Barbara's the niece, Gene's the orphan Erwin raised. Naturally, neither can sell without the other's consent. Gene is interested in operating the mine according to Dad's wishes, thereby helping the Mexican rancheros who work there. However, Barbara wants to sell out for the ready cash. After a flirtation with Gene—and Smiley "Frog Millhouse" Burnette by Barbara's pal Kitty (Pauline Drake)—fails to dissuade him, Barbara unwittingly hooks up with unscrupulous lawyers Arnold (Ivan Miller) and Fry (Sam Flint) who plot to steal the mine from Barbara and run Gene off by force through their henchman Tommick (John Merton).

This release introduced the character of Tadpole, a junior look-a-like version of Smiley, as played by Joe Strauch Jr. in five of Gene's films (and later one with Smiley and Bob Livingston). He wasn't welcomed by Autry fans—and from the serious smacks in the head Smiley gives him here, he wasn't welcomed by the egotistical Burnette either, who probably saw Strauch as stealing screen time and laughs from him.

The mine area here is Bronson Cave, seen first in an Autry film in Gene's "Phantom Empire" serial as the entrance to the underground world of Murania.

Watch for the unique two-men-on-one-horse fight at the windup. The idea was repeated in Roy Rogers' "Man from Music Mountain" ('43).

Incidentally, an unbilled George Sherman directed an action sequence for "Under Fiesta Stars" at Bronson Canyon (the exterior of the mine) and another on the upper Iverson Ranch.

NOTES AND COMMENTS: Working title of the film was "Prairie Serenade". Because the title "Under Fiesta Stars" had already been publicized as Gene's next film, several parts with Anglo actors were recast as Mexicans and Spanish costumes were added to the mine workers. Gene also wrote the title tune to complete the South of the Border flavor.

One of the most pampered of movie stars is Gene Autry's mount, Champion, who appeared with him in all his pictures right from the beginning. The best was none too good for Champ. He was in presidential suites in hotels, in barber shops, elevators and radio stations, not to mention London's famous Savoy Hotel ballroom where he went through his paces to the delight of the swankiest West End audiences. When Champion went with Gene on personal appearance tours, he traveled in a special streamlined air conditioned and padded trailer with electric lights, hot and cold running water and a special groom.

Carol Hughes and Gene, Smiley and Pauline Drake.

CAST BIOS: Joe Strauch Jr. was chosen from a reported group of some 500 aspirants for the role of Tadpole Millhouse, Smiley's kid brother, a miniature version of Burnette himself in five Autry westerns in 1941-'42.

Unfortunately, little is known about the portly Strauch who was born May 18, 1929, in Chicago, Illinois, to Joseph and Ella Louise Strauch, both from Illinois of German/Austrian heritage. Joe Sr. was at first a farmer but by 1930 was employed in manufacturing as a gold stamper.

How and why the family came to California is unknown, but by 1936 Joe appeared in his first "Our Gang" Hal Roach kid comedy, "Two Too Young". The "Our Gang" shorts were extremely popular at the time and a likely scenario is that a talent scout spotted Joe and suggested him to Roach as "one of the kids" as the cast of the shorts was constantly evolving because the kids were usually phased out by age 10 or 11 when they became too old for the comedies. Or possibly Strauch's family submitted photos of Joe, hoping he'd be accepted by Roach.

By 1941 Joe himself was 12 and too old for the comedies. Someone at Republic (possibly scripter Karl Brown?) conceived the idea of a small fry version of "Frog" to be named "Tadpole" in "Under Fiesta Stars". The 120 lb. Strauch was selected for the role and signed to a term-picture contract at $75 a week.

The character of Tadpole did not appear in the next three Autry films, but was revived for four more titles in mid-1942 at $100 a week. Strauch's contract at that time specified he mustn't lose weight, so he reportedly drank three quarts of milk a day and was allowed to eat all the candy he wanted.

A huge aviation fan, he loved to sketch airplanes and headed up a boy's club called The Flying Yanks who built models and studied first aid. At the time he aspired to be a pilot.

After Gene entered the service in 1942 a year went by before Republic used Strauch again in one last film as Frog Millhouse's kid brother in Bob Livingston's "Beneath Western Skies" ('44).

Strauch only appeared in bit roles in two more MGM films in '47 before leaving the business. At this point it is uncertain what he did for the rest of his life but he was married and working as a salesman in a J. C. Penney store when he died of heart disease at 57 in Santa Clara, California, on May 31, 1986.

WHAT THE EXHIBITOR HAD TO SAY: "Anyone who passes up Autry misses a good bet. One of the best money makers for the smaller towns. What do we care about the cost of production? Autry with Smiley gets them in and they love it and we take the gate receipts."
—C. L. Niles, Niles Theater, Anamosa, Iowa (October 1941)

"Just a fair picture that is not up to top Autry film fare. Mr. Autry seems to be losing his popularity here. I do not know whether it is the lack of good pictures or his poor acting and

"Under Fiesta Stars" introduced Smiley's nemesis, Joe Strauch Jr. as Tadpole, a junior look-a-like of Smiley's Frog character.

appeal. Time will tell."

—Theodore J. Friedman, Strand Theater,
Suffern, NY (December 1941)

"I know Frog was getting tired of drawing the crowd along, and Tadpole is a welcome newcomer. My Autry business really picked up with this picture and I think Tadpole and Frog was the big reason. They are tops with good possibilities for my situation."

—Felix H. Tistale, Ga-Ana Theater,
Georgiana, Alabama (February 1942)

"I did swell business on this Autry picture, because I received plenty of publicity from the Rodeo in Houston. Tadpole stole the show." —Vic Stephano, Grove Theater,
Groveton, Texas (February 1942)

"Did record weekend business on this. Autry has great weekend appeal here."

—Harland Rankin, Centre Theater,
Chatham, Ontario, Canada (February, 1942)

"Autry is slipping. Better get back the old supporting cast and music they used to have."

—Guy C. Black, Plaza Theater,
Lyons, Nebraska (March 1942)

"We have just started using the Autry features. During the larger part of this picture, it looked like this was a different western, with a good supporting cast and a plausible story. But before it was over the same old hokum came to pass with some of the most impossible situations imaginable.

Maybe that's what western fans want. They seemed to like this." —Horn and Morgan, Star Theater,
Hay Springs, Nebraska (March 1942)

"Business fair. Why not use Tadpole more often? He really got the comments." —Cleo Manry, Buena Vista Theater,
Buena Vista, Georgia (March 1942)

"Dear Mr. Autry: I have consistently boosted your product as first-class entertainment for the rural community, but having just run 'Under Fiesta Stars', what a fiasco! The poorest one of your series. The patrons come to the small town theater to hear you sing, not to see you act. This release was lacking in music. You had better again introduce Mary Lee in your releases and more popular cowboy songs. To the exhibitor, I could not recommend this one. It will do you more harm than good." —A. L. Dove, Bengough Theater,
Bengough, Saskatchewan, Canada (April 1942)

"Autry brought everyone songs, thrills with Frog and his sidekick. This is the best western we have had in a long time. Play this by all means. Business good."

—Nick Raspa, State Theater,
Rivesville, West Virginia (February 1946)

"I was almost afraid to play this old timer, both from the standpoint of business and for fear I'd get a bad print. I was very much pleased by both results. Business was up 50 percent or more and I got a good print. Don't be afraid of this one, fellows. Autry fans will eat it up."

—R. L. Hall, Aztec Theater,
Van Alstyne, Texas (August 1946)

Down Mexico Way
<u>Republic, October 1941</u>

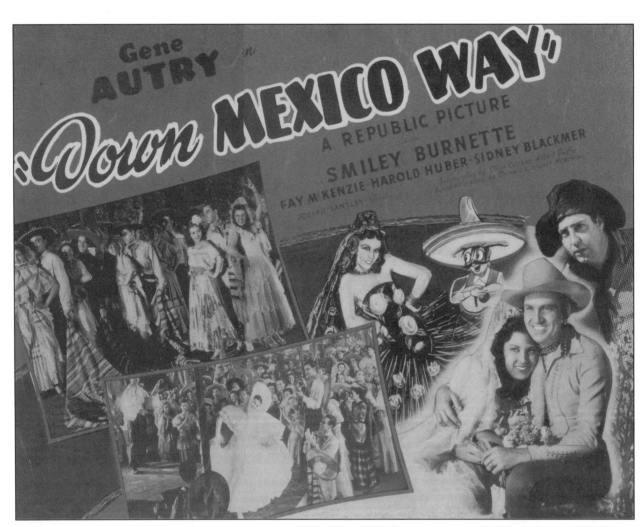

Producer ....Harry Grey
Director ....Joseph Santley
Assistant Director........................George Blair
Original Story.............................Dorrell and Stuart
                McGowan
Screenplay...................................Olive Cooper, Albert
                Duffy
Photography ....Jack Marta
Film Editor.................................Howard O'Neill
Art Director................................Ralph Oberg

Musical Supervisor ....Raoul Kraushaar
Production Manager.....................Al Wilson

SONGS: "Down Mexico Way" (music and lyrics by Eddie Cherkose, Jule Styne, Sol Meyer)—sung by studio singers, reprised by Gene Autry, Fay McKenzie, Herrera Sisters, extras; "Beer Barrel Polka" (music and lyrics by Lew Brown, Wladimir A. Timm, Jaromir Vejvoda)—sung by Gene Autry, Smiley Burnette, cast; "South of the Border" (music and lyrics by Jimmy Kennedy, Michael Carr)—sung by Gene Autry; "La Cachita" (music and lyrics by Rafael Hernandez)—sung by Fay McKenzie and the Herrera Sisters; "The Cowboy and the Lady" (music and lyrics by Arthur Quenzer, Lionel Newman)—sung by Gene Autry; "Guadalajara" (music and lyrics by Pepe Guizar)—sung by The Herrara Sisters; "A Gay Ranchero (Las Altenitas)" (music and Spanish lyrics by Juan Jose Espinosa, English lyrics by Abe Tuvim, Francia Luban)—sung by Gene Autry, Guadalajara Trio; "Maria Elena" (music and Spanish lyrics by Lorenzo Barcelata, English lyrics by S. K. Russell)—sung by Gene Autry.

RUNNING TIME: 78 minutes

FILMING DATES: August 18 to September 6, 1941

LOCATIONS: Lone Pine; Palmdale; Angeles National Forest; Republic backlot; Victorville

BUDGET: $124,947

NEGATIVE COST: $133,520.

CAST:

Actor	*Character*
Gene Autry	Gene Autry
Smiley Burnette	Frog
Fay McKenzie	Maria Elena Alvarado
Harold Huber	Pancho Grande
Sidney Blackmer	Gibson
Joe Sawyer	Allen
Andrew Tombes	Mayor Tubbs
Murray Alper	Flood
Arthur Loft	Homer Gerard
Duncan Renaldo	Juan
Paul Fix	Davis
Julian Rivero	Don Carlos Alvarado
Ruth Robinson	Mercedes
Thornton Edwards	Mexican Rurale Capt. Rodriguez
Maria Antonia Herrera, Maria Esther Herrera	The Herrera Sisters
Sam Appel	Train Conductor
Hank Bell, Fred Burns, Bob Card, Eddie Dean	Barbeque guests
Carmella Cansino, Pauqita Del Rey, Jose Manero	Dancers
Texas Jim Lewis and The Lone Star Cowboys	Singers at barbeque
Rico DeMontez, Charles Rivero, Dave Sharpe	Rurales
Esther Estrella	Flower girl
Elias Gamboa	Peon
Helen MacKellar	Miss Abby
Guadalajara Trio	Singers
Jack O'Shea	Truck passenger
Frankie Marvin, Al Haskell, Neal Hart, John Cason	Extras
Champion	Champion

STUNTS: Joe Yrigoyen (Gene's double); Tex Terry (Smiley's double); Dave Sharpe.

THE FILM: Elaborate production and exploitation plans for "Down Mexico Way", an Autry super deluxe special, weighed heavily within the thought processes of studio executives at Republic as they mapped out strategy for catapulting Gene's 44th starring feature into big box office profits. Republic obviously still remembered the banning by Mexico in 1940 of Gene's "South of the Border". Therefore the studio gave serious consideration as to how the chief villain should be pictured on-screen. The organization eliminated anyone Latin since the U.S. had a campaign of goodwill with Latin American countries. Also, the idea of showcasing a Nazi was rejected to not make it seem Mexico had started sheltering Germans. Then, there was this idea of the villain fleeing the U.S. for some crime, forcing screenwriters to reason out why Mexico would allow him to be at large. Finally, Republic settled on veteran character players Sidney Blackmer and Arthur Loft to command the dirty deeds department. Head villains established, Republic incurred another headache upon casting Mexicans themselves. So, the scenarists produced "a reformed bandit" (Harold Huber) for comedy relief. The hardnosed censorship at the Hays Office speculated Mexicans could be critical and warned Republic to exercise care on the completely lily-pure ex-badman and under no circumstances let him appear ridiculous.

Story has two swindlers, Allen (Joe Sawyer) and Flood (Murray Alper), posing as motion picture producers, selling fake stock in a movie and inducing the citizens of Sage City to invest their savings in a phony film which would star John Wayne. They promise the picture will be filmed and premiered in Sage City, thus putting the community on the map.

When Gene and Frog (Smiley Burnette) discover the producers are phonies, they trail the pair to Mexico with the aid of their genial friend and reformed Mexican ex-bandit Pancho Grande (Harold Huber).

Once in Mexico, the trio suspects Allen and Flood's cohorts, Gibson (Sidney Blackmer) and Gerard (Arthur Loft) are about to pull the same swindle on Don Alvarado (Julian Rivero), a wealthy, well-respected citizen of San Ramon who has agreed to finance the swindlers' picture in exchange for a role in the film for his lovely daughter Maria Elena (Fay McKenzie).

Maria Elena falls for Gene who warns her about the dishonest promoters. They devise a plan to expose the crooks who then make a last ditch effort to rob the bank car bringing Don Alvarado's money from Mexico City and lay the blame on Gene and his friends.

Producer Harry Grey and director Joseph Santley give "Down Mexico Way" a smart, showmanly appearance, making it one of Gene's most delicious films. Gene is ably aided and abetted by some snappy dialogue, an abundance of great tunes, a different plot, Lone Pine locations, pretty and talented Fay McKenzie in her first of five co-starrers with Gene, and a likeable reformed bandido played by Harold Huber—not to mention Smiley Burnette's always welcome contribution. Gene's second film to cost over $100,000 to produce definitely displays the higher budget on screen with

Duncan Renaldo brings news to Harold Huber, Smiley and Gene.

elaborate production and lavish musical numbers backed up by superb scoring and sharp direction.

NOTES AND COMMENTS: There is some indication Mary Lee was scheduled to return to Gene's films after a two-picture hiatus, but Republic eventually elected to feature her in non-western fare such as "Angels With Broken Wings" ('41) and "Shantytown" ('43).

Placing this film squarely in contemporary times, references are made to John Wayne as a movie star and the then popular radio show "Information Please".

Salaries ranged from $750 for the feature for Harold Huber to $600 a week for Joe Sawyer and Sidney Blackmer. Arthur Loft made $400 a week as did Murray Alper. Paul Fix was at $350 while Julian Rivero, Thornton Edwards and Duncan Renaldo were all set at $250. The twin Herrera Sisters, Maria Esther and Maria Antonia, were each paid $150 a week.

"Down Mexico Way" became the second most expensive Autry vehicle to date with a $133,520 negative cost. This higher figure occurred as the result of an endless array of background extras needed for lengthy, grand-scale musical numbers on the Republic backlot as well as inside stage shooting. Big numbers of bit players were utilized in outdoor scenes at Lone Pine's Alabama Hills and Victorville.

Gene's song "Maria Elena" led the Top 10 favorite tunes as reported by U.S. Jukebox operators 12 weeks in a row. The same tune was also in the Top 15 Best Sheet Music Sellers.

By the time "Down Mexico Way" hit the screen, Gene was the 4th biggest box office attraction in America as voted by theater exhibitors since 1939. No other star came close. No. 1 was Mickey Rooney, riding high in the Hardy Family pictures, followed by two time Academy Award winner Spencer Tracy and Clark Gable. MOTION PICTURE HERALD tradepaper (on 12/27/41) listed Gene #1 among their "Western Winners" followed by William Boyd, Roy Rogers, Charles Starrett and Smiley Burnette.

FILM COMMENTS: Dashing inside the Republic Commissary on September 2 to elude bad weather, Gene griped to visiting United Press correspondent Frederick C. Othman concerning a story on him in an unidentified national magazine which found the movie cowboy guilty of corny performances in corny movies. Gene responded bluntly, "And what I want to know is, what do they mean 'corny'? Here I try to make good, clean wholesome entertainment and the people seem to like it, but is it any more corny than that good old movie plot about the man with two wives? Or that other picture about the wife with two husbands? Corny, eh?" Gene's comments were part of a big article on "Down Mexico Way" difficulties carried in the MEMPHIS COMMERICAL-APPEAL (9/3/41) and THE WASHINGTON POST (9/4/41).

Fay McKenzie: "I loved working with Gene, he was terrific! I could sing and that was something the earlier girls couldn't do. Yates knew I had done Broadway; that helped. I could do more than smile and wave at the cowboy. Gene was a brilliant businessman. Not a fly-by-night. It was a wonderful, rich experience. He was so supportive. I had worked in pictures since I was a small child, but I was just starting to do grown-up parts at the time—and Gene was the biggest star in the world. I mean, *nobody* was a bigger star. He was topping the list throughout the world. So I was in awe—totally in awe just to be in the room where he was. I would get to the studio early, about 5, go past the publicity department, and often someone would come out and get me to sign some piece of paper. They shoved a release in my face. I never read the papers, as I was so protected by my family and never suspected anything could be wrong. One day Gene arrived at the same time I did, and saw what was happening. He ragged me all day long! 'You could have signed away your salary! That is the dumbest thing I've ever seen!' And he was right. But, my theory has always been if you expect good, you'll find it."[1]

CAST BIOS: Once described as "the girl with the blitzkrieg eyes", Gene Autry's five time leading lady in the early '40s, Fay McKenzie, was born in Hollywood, California, February 19, 1918, to show business parents, Robert and Eva McKenzie. Fay's showbiz beginning was when she was 10 weeks old and played Gloria Swanson's baby in "Station Content" ('18). Fay's father, character Robert (Bob) McKenzie, at one time had his own stock company. "The McKenzie Merry Makers", Fay laughed. "He directed as well as acted, in stock and in films. We were up at Niles, California, for about six months before we came to Hollywood. Broncho Billy Anderson, Ben Turpin, Vic Potel, it was a great group of actors. One of my earliest films was 'A Knight of the West' ('21) directed by my father. My mother wrote the story—her maiden name is correctly

Gene and leading lady Fay McKenzie.

spelled Heazlitt."

After 1924, there's a ten-year gap in Fay's credits. "That was so I could go to school and get an education." Her first picture back was "Student Tour" in '34. From there Fay went into "Sundown Trail" with Wally Wales. "Even though I was only 15 years old. (Laughs) We shot that in three days, and there was *no* script. They'd all ride one way and say this, then they'd all ride the other way and say that. (Laughs) It was very improvisational, but a great event in my life."

Then came roles in a variety of features, westerns dramas and musicals. For "Ghost Town Riders" ('38) with Bob Baker there was a sudden name change to Fay Shannon. "Later, at Republic, they wanted to change my name again—but I stalled around until the last minute and kept Fay McKenzie. But in 1938, they were searching the country for a Scarlet O'Hara. I came up with the new last name. I thought by using an Irish name, like Shannon, it might help in getting the part. (Laughs) So, for the only time, it was used in 'Ghost Town Riders'."

Fay won her first big-time recognition in 1940 with an outstanding role in the Hollywood Theater Alliance production "Meet the People" which astonished the old-timers by its duration and success, staged and acted, as it was, by a group of youngsters who had little previous stage experience. "We did it in L.A., then hit the road, and finally landed on Broadway. When they wanted to take it on tour, I preferred to return to Hollywood."

As to how she came to Republic…"My sister Lolly, who was married to Billy Gilbert, designed it. (Republic president) Herbert J. Yates was a friend. My sister said to wear just a bathing suit, draped by the pool. Yates met me, I was asked to come to the studio the next day and test and he signed me for Gene Autry's 'Down Mexico Way' which was a big, big hit for the studio. When Yates would come to California from New York, he'd call and ask me, 'Are you

happy? Is everything all right? Is anyone bothering you?' When you have the head of the studio behind you, and he was Billy Gibert's friend, you have it made!"

Briefly married to actor Steve Cochran ("The worst decision I ever made!"), they were divorced when Fay married screenwriter Tom Waldman. "The dearest, funniest, cutest guy. We have two great kids. It was the happiest time of my life, until he passed away in '85. The raising of my kids is why I quit show business, for the most part."

From then on Fay's work in films and on TV was sporadic. Today, Fay divides her time between homes in Malibu, California, and Mount Vernon, New York. "My son, Tom Waldman Jr., is a good, fine actor. He worked for MTV, doing voiceovers on things like Toys R Us. He can do every kind of accent, like me. My daughter is a writer who uses the professional name Madora McKenzie. She's married to Jonathan Kibbe, a corporate lawyer, and they live in New York. [2]

WHAT THE EXHIBITOR HAD TO SAY: "They didn't come quite as good for us on this as they usually come for an Autry picture. As far as being an Autry special, all the special that I saw about it was the extra rental charged for the specials. It was up to the Autry standard, which was good enough. It drew a good average, but it was a let-down from his other pictures." —J. E. Stocker, Myrtle Theater, Detroit, Michigan (February 1942)

"More on the elaborate scale for an Autry, with plenty of singing and action. My patrons come to hear Autry sing and this will not disappoint them. Recommend this one." —A. L. Dove, Bengough Theater, Bengough, Saskatchewan, Canada (March 1942)

"Somewhat below the Autry productions that have gone over at the box office." —A. C. Edwards, Wilston Theater, Scotia, California (March 1942)

"A weekend natural that didn't let us down. Autry did his stuff O.K." —Harland Rankin, Centre Theater, Chatham, Ontario, Canada (April 1942)

"Doesn't make much difference. If it's a Gene Autry feature, it does just about as much business and this is usually above average. This was a good Autry western with good music thrown in for those who do not care much for westerns." —Horn and Morgan, Star Theater, Hay Springs, Nebraska (August 1942)

"This Autry did the best business of any to date. 'Nuff said" —Clifton Green, Gem Theater, Lodge Grass, Montana (December 1942)

SOURCES:
1. *Western Clippings #51.* January/February 2003. p. 21.
2. Ibid. p. 20-22.

Sierra Sue
Republic, November 1941

Producer	Harry Grey
Director	William Morgan
Assistant Director	George Blair
Screenplay	Earl Felton, Julian Zimet
Photography	Jack Marta
Film Editor	Lester Orlebeck
Musical Supervisor	Raoul Kraushaar
Production Manager	Al Wilson

SONGS: "Be Honest With Me" (music and lyrics by Gene Autry, Fred Rose)—sung by Gene Autry; "Heebie Jeebie Blues" (music and lyrics by Oliver Drake, Harry Grey)—sung by Smiley Burnette; "I'll Be True While You're Gone" (music and lyrics by Gene Autry, Fred Rose)—sung by Gene Autry; "Sierra Sue" (music and lyrics by J. B. Carey)—sung by Gene Autry; "Ridin' the Range" (music and lyrics by Gene Autry, Fleming Allen, Nelson Shawn)—sung by Gene Autry and extras.

RUNNING TIME: 64 minutes

FILMING DATES: September 16 to October 1, 1941

LOCATIONS: Mammoth Lakes area; Bishop area at what is now Lake Crowley was probably used for cattle scenes; Republic backlot

BUDGET: $88,425

NEGATIVE COST: $89,897

CAST:

Actor	*Character*
Gene Autry	Gene Autry
Smiley Burnette	Frog Millhouse
Fay McKenzie	Sue Larrabee
Frank M. Thomas	Stacey Bromfield
Robert Homans	George Larrabee
Earle Hodgins	Brandywine
Dorothy Christy	Verebel Featherstone
Kermit Maynard	Jarvis
Jack Kirk	Sheriff Smith
Eddie Dean	Jerry Willis (pilot)
Hugh Prosser	Frenchy Montague
Budd Buster	Greg Travis
Rex Lease	Rex (Rancher)
Vince Barnett	Shooting gallery attendant
Roy Butler	Joe, Cannon operator
Ray Davis, Art Dillard, Frankie Marvin	Larabee men
Robert McKenzie	Dr. Ulysses Bigelow
Hal Price	Jim (Rancher)
Marin Sais	Tess (Rancher's wife)
Sammy Stein	Irate cowboy at Human Cannonball show
Ted Wells	Posseman
Horace Carpenter, Bob Wilke	Carnival Spectators
Bud Brown, Gene Eblen, Buel Bryant, Bob Remington, Sherry Allen, Eddie Cherkose, Carl Cotner, Tex Terry, Vinegar Roan	Extras
Champion	Champion

STUNTS: Joe Yrigoyen (Gene's double); Bruce Cameron (Smiley's double in acrobatic jumps into net); Tex Terry (Smiley's double); Nellie Walker (Fay McKenzie's double); Eddie Parker.

THE FILM: When poisonous devil weed infects the grazing lands of cattle country, misguided ranchers, including George Larrabee (Robert Homans), burn off every acre of the infected area—the wrong thing to do. The State Agricultural Commission sends inspector Gene Autry and pal Frog Millhouse (Smiley Burnette) to look into the problem but they encounter strong opposition and are even mistaken for bank robbers when found in possession of cash from a crashed airplane whose pilot (Eddie Dean) they were only trying to help.

Against all the opposition, Gene eventually persuades the ranchers chemical spraying is the only way to rid the grazing land of devil weed poisonous to cattle, although he has to beat up a few bully boys along the way and save the cattle from a fiery stampede at the climax.

Frog romances Larrabee's daughter, Sue (Fay McKenzie), and tries to keep Gene from dating her. This romantic rivalry results in a segment that strays too far from the main story and turns to slapstick midway as Frog becomes involved with a carnival hypnotist; eventually becoming a human cannonball.

Even though this film is set mainly outdoors, a disquieting factor was slowly coming to light during Gene's 1940-'41 films. Republic, higher budgets or not, had begun to use, if only in a small way, rear projection in some scenes. It had been done before, but only rarely.

NOTES AND COMMENTS: Actor Robert McKenzie is leading lady Fay McKenzie's real life father.

Upon completion of filming for "Sierra Sue", Gene appeared at the World's Championship Rodeo in New York City's Madison Square Garden from October 12-26. He then moved on to the Boston Garden Rodeo November 2-11.

On November 5, 1941, Carter County, Oklahoma, commissioners, at a special session, approved a change in the name of Berwyn, Oklahoma, to Gene Autry, Oklahoma. On a 90 degree day, 35,000 people gathered to view the ceremonies on November 16, 1941, as Berwyn became Gene Autry, Oklahoma, while Gene broadcast his "Melody Ranch" radio show from the newly named town.

FILM COMMENTS: *Fay McKenzie:* "Gene's pictures had such good circulation and such big audiences. It was a wonderful break for me to be in them. Smiley (Burnette) was just a love! I mean, he was the type person you just wanted to hug; he was so sweet. He was just as nice as he appears on screen. When we were on location,

he'd pick up his guitar and start singing, and pretty soon we'd all be singing together. He was just so special, and so funny—and adorable." [1]

WHAT THE EXHIBITOR HAD TO SAY: "Another good picture from Autry who always pleases on Friday and Saturday."
—C. L. Niles, Niles Theater, Anamosa, Iowa (December 1941)

"On a par with the other Autrys and did about the same amount of business. We don't stand them out but do average or better and they seem to like the singing and comedy. The picture moves right along and the kids whoop and holler, so what more could we ask for except some extra business when we pay extra rental."
—Mayme Musselman, Princess Theater, Lincoln, Kansas (February 1942)

"Double featured with 'Wild Geese Calling' from the Fox Studios to make up an excellent Friday and Saturday bill. The action fans turned out in droves and swelled the receipts to near capacity business. Everyone well pleased with results."
—A. E. Andrews, Emporium Theater, Emporium, Pennsylvania (February 1942)

"Good Autry picture, played to good business Friday and Saturday."
—Melville Danner, Kozy Theater, Granite, Oklahoma (February 1942)

"Very good Gene Autry. Played Friday, Saturday with 'Mr. District Attorney in the Carter Case', a good program drama that brought in the radio fans. Above average gross for this combination."
—Stanley Theater, Galena, Illinois (May 1942)

"The Gene Autry series still stands them up although this had plenty of action but very little singing of the popular cowboy numbers which the country folk love to hear."
—A. L. Dove, Bengough Theater, Bengough, Saskatchewan, Canada (October 1942)

Gene with Fay McKenzie.

SOURCES:
1. *Western Clippings #51.* January/February 2003. p. 21.

Cowboy Serenade
<u>Republic, January 1942</u>

Producer ....Harry Grey
Director ....William Morgan
Assistant Director........................George Blair
Screenplay....................................Olive Cooper
Photography ....Jack Marta
Film Editor ....Les Orlebeck
Musical Supervisor ....Raoul Kraushaar

SONGS: "Cowboy Serenade" (music and lyrics by

Rich Hall)—sung by Gene Autry, Smiley Burnette and cowboys (reprised by Gene, Fay McKenzie); "Nobody Knows" (music and lyrics by George R. Brown, Jule Styne)—sung by Gene Autry; "Tahiti Honey" (music and lyrics by Jule Styne, George R. Brown, Sol Meyer)—sung by Fay McKenzie; "Sweethearts or Strangers" (music and lyrics by Jimmie Davis, Lou Wayne)—sung by Gene Autry.

RUNNING TIME: 66 minutes

FILMING DATES: November 24 to December 10, 1941

LOCATIONS: Republic backlot; Bishop-Lake Crowley area; Chatsworth Railroad Station; L.A. stockyards; stretch of railway track near Chatsworth; Morrison Ranch (unconfirmed)

BUDGET: $83,486

NEGATIVE COST: $94,438

CAST:

Actor	Character
Gene Autry	Gene Autry
Smiley Burnette	Frog Millhouse
Fay McKenzie	Stephanie "Steve" Lock
Cecil Cunningham	Priscilla Smythe
Addison Richards	Asa Lock
Rand Brooks	Jim Agnew
Tristram Coffin	Dixie Trambeau
"Slim" Andrews	Pappy Vanderpyle
Melinda Leighton	Millie Jackson
Johnnie Berkes	Joe Crowley
Rick Anderson	Rusty
Ken Cooper	Bill
Bud Geary	Sam Davis (henchman)
Otto Han	Ling
Si Jenks	Sherman T. Hemmingway
Roger Kirby	Terry
Ethan Laidlaw	Fred Carson
Tom London	Checker
Frankie Marvin	Shorty
Forbes Murray	District Attorney
Hal Price	Sheriff
Loren Raker	Mr. Swallow
Forrest Taylor	Jeff Jackson
Ken Terrell	Dave
Bud Wolfe	Henchman Pete Elkins
Hank Worden	Opey
Chick Hannon	Townsman
Pascale Perry	Rancher
Fred Burns	Posseman
Tex Terry, Rod Bacon, Art Dillard, Cactus Mack, Jack Montgomery, Burt Dillard, Herman Nowlin	Extras
Champion	Champion

STUNTS: Joe Yrigoyen (Gene's double); Tex Terry (Smiley's double); Evelyn Finley (Fay's double); Clara Strong (Cecil Cunningham's double); Ken Terrell, Bud Wolfe, Bud Geary, Ken Cooper, Yakima Cunutt.

THE FILM: "Cowboy Serenade" has far less music than usual in this Olive Cooper screenplay directed again by William Morgan who was capable without being innovative. It might be noted here the striking contribution made to Gene's pictures since 1938 by musical supervisor Raoul Kraushaar who had a long association with B-westerns, culminating in his work with Bill Elliott and Wayne Morris at Monogram/Allied Artists in the early '50s. Kraushaar always provided more than effective work.

Gene Autry heads a Cattlemen's Association who appoint naïve young Jimmy Agnew (Rand Brooks) to take the collective shipment to the packing plant and handle the sale of the beef. En route by train, Agnew is fleeced by professional card sharps and is forced to pay off with the cattle shipment. Ashamed, Agnew goes into hiding.

Up to Gene to make good, and accompanied by Frog (Smiley Burnette), he gets a job on the ranch owned by Asa Lock who operates the trunk line of the railroad on which the gamblers ply their dirty deeds.

Lock's daughter, Stephanie (Fay McKenzie), ignorant of her father's involvement, assists Gene trying to prove her father honest. Lock himself pretends to play along with Gene in seeking the crooks.

Gene locates Agnew and persuades him to give himself up and make a clean breast of the entire affair so Gene will have a basis for prosecution.

Learning this, Lock gives orders for Jimmy's elimination in a car wreck but, discovering his daughter is also in the vehicle, races to prevent their fate.

With Gene's aid, the fatal crash is prevented, but Lock is himself killed. Before dying, he makes a confession absolving Agnew.

NOTES AND COMMENTS: Fay McKenzie's singing voice double in "Cowboy Serenade" and other Autry westerns was Faith Kruger. Kruger sang and essayed bit roles in Hollywood throughout the '40s in such films as "The Big Store" ('41), "DuBarry Was a Lady" ('43), "Life With Father" ('47) and "The Unsuspected" ('47), among others.

"Cowboy Serenade" was made just as the bombing of Pearl Harbor on December 7, 1941 and the outbreak of WWII took place and was Gene's first picture released after war was declared. It, therefore, was the first of six titles made by Gene before he volunteered for the U.S. Air Force in 1942.

In a rare sequence, Gene rides hell for leather being chased by a posse without wearing his hat and takes a flying leap on Champion over a wide mountainous chasm. The scene at Beale's Cut is actually from a silent Tom Mix film but edited into the Autry footage seamlessly by director/editor Morgan.

The railroad coach used in "Cowboy Serenade" was a Kimball railway coach rented from Paramount.

"Cowboy Serenade" was released in England as "Serenade of the West".

As Priscilla Smythe, character actress Cecil Cunningham made $750 a week on the film while heavy Addison Richards earned $600 a week.

According to the LOS ANGELES EVENING HERALD EXPRESS on January 14, 1942, Gene received 315,306 fan letters during 1941. Of these 210,121 came from the

Gene and Smiley confront a group of townsfolk. (L-R) Burt Dillard, Sheriff Hal Price, Slim Andrews, Forrest Taylor, Chick Hannon, Fay McKenzie, Hank Worden, Herman Nowlin, and Cactus Mack.

U.S., 80,322 from England and 20,416 from Canada. The remainder came from other parts of the world. It reportedly cost Gene over $15,000 to answer his mail, not counting the salary of three secretaries.

FILM COMMENTS: *Fay McKenzie:* Reminded there was a lot of riding in "Cowboy Serenade", "But they got a double! I *can* ride—and had learned how to ride fairly young—but I cannot do the trick stuff."

Gene and Fay were shooting "Cowboy Serenade" when Pearl Harbor was bombed. "We all heard FDR's famous speech of December 8, 1941. Then we went back to our making movies. It's kind of bizarre—but also like what happened after 9-11!" [1]

Melinda Leighton (later known as Linda Johnson): "The first western I did was with Gene Autry…'Cowboy Serenade'. I did quite a few at Republic and they wanted to put me under contract but my husband was in the service, they were sending him to San Francisco, so it was kind of a choice. Do I stay here and do that or do I go with my husband? I went with my husband, so I was out for two or three years. When I came back I kind of had to start all over again.

"Republic was not the most posh studio. I can remember doing an interior scene one time when it began to rain and the roof leaked. We had little drops of rain coming down, but we kept going. (Laughs)

"Gene Autry was very nice but he had a hard time getting off and on a horse, so they got a double for that. Of course, where *I* looked good was when a double was

doing it (for me). (Laughs) I was able to handle it pretty well, I can't remember ever doing any riding before…maybe some in Texas, but not extensively." [2]

Rand Brooks: "He certainly had a career, God love him. If you go back to when Gene was very young, Will Rogers told him to try to get into show business. Not too many people kept their name alive that long. I first met Gene in '41 doing 'Cowboy Serenade'. After the war I did three TV shows for him." [3]

WHAT THE EXHIBITOR HAD TO SAY: "Good picture and good business. Autry always pleased the Friday-Saturday crowd."
—E. M. Freiburger, Paramount Theater, Dewey, Oklahoma (January 1942)

"Good picture, but the Autrys seem to have lost that certain something that draws them in. Most always they do above average business, but not this time."
—Melville Danner, Kozy Theater, Granite, Oklahoma (March 1942)

"About on a par with the other Autrys and drew slightly better than average business on Friday and Saturday. Smiley Burnette and the old lady supplied the comedy, Gene, the music with some help from the supporting feminine lead, and we were satisfied."
—Mayme P. Musselman, Princess Theater, Lincoln, Kansas (April 1942)

"Autry's features are falling down very badly for me at the box office. This production is very short and of very little entertainment value. Another one of the Autrys that I could not recommend. No popular songs, and we miss Mary Lee in these Autry features." —A. L. Dove, Bengough Theater, Bengough, Saskatchewan, Canada (April 1942)

"One of the better Autrys. Business good."
—A. C. Edwards, Winema Theater, Scotia, California (July 1942)

SOURCES:
1. *Western Clippings #51.* January/February 2003. p. 21.
2. *Ladies of the Western.* McFarland. 2002 p. 103.
3. *Western Clippings #27.* January/February 1999. p. 7.

Heart of the Rio Grande
Republic, March 1942

Producer ....Harry Grey
Director ....William Morgan
Assistant Director.........................George Webster
Original Story...............................Newlin B. Wildes
Screenplay....................................Lillie Hayward, Winston
　　　　　　　　　　　　　　　Miller
Photography ....Harry Neumann
Film Editor..................................Les Orlebeck
Musical Supervisor ....Raoul Kraushaar

SONGS: "Let Me Ride Down in Rocky Canyon" (music and lyrics by Gene Autry, Ray Whitley, Fred Rose)—sung by Gene Autry and cowboys; "Deep In the Heart of Texas" (music and lyrics by Don Swander, June Hershey)—sung by Gene Autry, Smiley Burnette, Joe Strauch Jr., extras; "Dusk On the Painted Desert" (music and lyrics by Al Frisch, Don George, Helen Bernard)—sung by Gene Autry; "Oh Woe Is Me" (music and lyrics by Smiley Burnette)—sung by Smiley Burnette; "Rumble Seat For Two" (music and lyrics by Johnny and Frankie Marvin)—sung by Gene Autry; "Rancho Pillow" (music and lyrics by Allie Wrubel, Charles Newman)—sung by Gene Autry, Jimmy Wakely Trio; "Rainbow In the Night" (music and lyrics by Jule Styne, Sol Meyer)—sung by Edith Fellows; "Cimarron" (music and lyrics by Johnny Bond)—sung by The Jimmy Wakely Trio; "I'll Wait For You" (music and lyrics by Gene Autry, Fred Rose)—sung by Gene Autry, Fay McKenzie.

RUNNING TIME: 70 minutes

FILMING DATES: January 9-28, 1942

LOCATIONS: Bronson Cave area; Republic backlot; Iverson Ranch; Chatsworth Railroad Station; Morrison Ranch; Janss Ranch

BUDGET: $86,115

NEGATIVE COST: $92,432

CAST:

Actor	*Character*
Gene Autry	Gene Autry
Smiley Burnette	Frog Millhouse
Fay McKenzie	Alice Bennett
Edith Fellows	Connie Lane
Pierre Watkin	Randolph Lane
Joe Strauch Jr.	Tadpole Millhouse
William Haade	Hap Callahan
Sarah Padden	"Skipper" Forbes
Jean Porter	Pudge
Jimmy Wakely Trio: Jimmy Wakely, Johnny Bond, Dick Reinhart	Singing trio (Pete, Hank, Joe)
Chuck Baldra, Cactus Mack	Ranch Hands
Budd Buster	Ranch Car Driver
Edmund Cobb	Bartender
Harry Depp	Simpson
Gladys Gardner	Ellen, Schoolgirl
Gloria Gardner	Helen, Schoolgirl
Jan Lester	Betty, Schoolgirl
Patsy Fay Northup	Runt, Schoolgirl
Katherine Frye, Betty Jane Graham, Jeanne Herbers	Schoolgirls
Milton Kibbee	Connie's Taxi Driver
Nora Lane, Mady Lawrence	Secretaries
Frankie Marvin	Shorty, Wagon Driver
Frank Mills	Alice's Taxi Driver
Howard M. Mitchell	Conductor
George Reed Porter	Pilot
Allen Wood	Messenger
Ira "Buck" Woods	Porter
Kenne Duncan	Train Passenger
Champion	Champion

STUNTS: Joe Yrigoyen (Gene's double); Tex Terry (Smiley's double); George Havens (Joe Strauch Jr.'s double); Mary Ann Jackson (Edith Fellow's double); Yakima Canutt.

THE FILM: "Heart of the Rio Grande" is rated highly by Autry fans, not so by film critics. It's easy to see why. "Heart…" is one of those lazy Autry films emphasizing music, comedy and Gene's charm as he goes through another variation of his "taming of the shrew" plot, this time on a dude ranch. Villainy and action is muted but, to be perfectly frank, all that most of Gene's fans, then and now, wanted him to do on screen was to sing and look nice sitting astride Champion. Throw in a little romance, some Frog Millhouse hilarity, and that was enough. Of course, many Autry films went beyond that and added in a good plot, some riding and fighting scenes and became wonderful entertainment.

The story basically stops midway for a U.S. Savings Bond "commercial". With America now involved in WWII, a patriotic sequence shows Gene paying his ranch hands and persuading them, instead of using the money to play poker and go dancing, to buy United States Savings Bonds and Stamps. "Uncle Sam is selling a greater commodity called Liberty," Gene emphasizes. This sequence includes a great shot of a U.S. Savings Bonds poster on the back of a door.

Basically, "Heart…" is the story of schoolgirl Connie Lane (Edith Fellows) and her character rehabilitation, necessitated by the fact her millionaire industrialist father, Randolph Lane (Pierre Watkin), is just too darn busy making money to pay attention personally to the teenager's upbringing. Connie rebels at accompanying her schoolmates and her teacher, Alice Bennett (Fay McKenzie), to a dude ranch in Texas. Upon being taken there, Connie makes herself a problem for all concerned, in particular ranch foreman Gene Autry and his pal Frog Millhouse (Smiley Burnette).

Gene takes her under his paternal, understanding wing as the plot centers around his efforts to break down the resistance of the spoiled Connie, which he does with great success. Additionally, he converts Connie's money-conscious father to an appreciation of the great outdoors as opposed to the grueling existence of a business tycoon.

Subplot of Gene taking the leading lady away from a love-struck Frog closely follows the previous "Cowboy Serenade" storyline.

NOTES AND COMMENTS: Although Newlin B. Wildes is given credit for the "original story" to "Heart of the Rio Grande", the screenplay by Lillie Hayward and Winston Miller is clearly based on MGM's 1937 Freddie Bartholomew/Spencer Tracy picture "Captains Courageous" which was taken from the Rudyard Kipling novel. The spoiled brat is sent away by a wealthy father, ends up somewhere she doesn't want to be, gives everybody a hard time, finally starts to like *one* of the men (Autry/Spencer Tracy), Autry/Tracy and a semi-baddie (William Haade/John Carradine) make a bet on some competition, the brat sees a chance to get on Autry's good side by sabotaging Haade's saddle (in "Captains Courageous", Freddie Bartholomew sabotages Carradine's fishing nets), Haade/Carradine are hurt, the kid is initially proud of what she's done but then is made to understand what's happened,

Made during WWII, Republic included a patriotic plug by Gene and Smiley for U.S. Savings Bonds.

apologizes to Haade/Carradine, Haade/Carradine gets sore and tries to attack the kid, Autry/Tracy have to step in—and on it goes.

Working titles for this picture were "Dusk On the Painted Desert" and "Heart of Texas".

Character player Pierre Watkin drew $600 a week for his role while young Edith Fellows earned $400 weekly and Sarah Padden $300. Each member of the Jimmy Wakely Trio received $125 a week. Jean Porter and Joe Strauch Jr. took home $100 weekly salaries.

Once again, Faith Kruger was the singing voice double for Fay McKenzie.

The two secretaries are played by a former B-western leading lady and a B-western heroine-to-be. Nora Lane (1905-1948) began her career in 1927, making westerns with silent riders such as Fred Thomson, Tom Tyler and Ken Maynard. During the sound era she was featured in "The Cisco Kid" ('31) with Warner Baxter and other B's opposite Tim McCoy, Ken Maynard and Hopalong Cassidy. By 1942 she was essaying small character roles. On the other hand, Mady Lawrence's brief career (1941-1945) was on the upswing. In 1944 she was a leading lady in four PRC B-westerns opposite James Newill/Dave O'Brien and Buster Crabbe. She then totally disappeared from the screen.

Following completion of filming "Heart of the Rio Grande", Gene Autry appeared with his own rodeo at the Coliseum in Houston, Texas, from February 6-15.

FILM COMMENTS: *Gene Autry:* "When the planes woke up our smug, sleepy world that Sunday at Pearl Harbor,

I had one movie in progress. Originally, it had been titled 'Deep in the Heart of Texas', cashing in on the popularity of that hand-clapping number. But we ran into a problem. Universal had grabbed the rights to the title. So we had to switch at the last moment. Oddly, this was the only movie of mine in which the Jimmy Wakely Trio appeared, though they often backed me on the radio and on the road. And they wound up in Universal's picture, too, playing behind Johnny Mack Brown and Tex Ritter." [1]

Edith Fellows: "Gene Autry was a real camp, a great tease, a great practical joker. You had to be on your toes around him. In 'Heart of the Rio Grande' I'm the snotty rich girl. There's a scene where I'm supposed to be bucked off a horse. They loosened the ground and had a two-step ladder so I could roll off. Well, Gene put horse stuff on the ground! I didn't know he was doing it—the crew knew it. When the makeup person turned me around to powder me—that's when Gene did his deed. Well, he had a beautiful rawhide makeup case. So I found some of Champion's manure and put it in Gene's cold cream jar! He loved it! He was a good guy, fun, with a great sense of humor. A real OK person. I liked playing the games. I have devilment in me—we acted like two kids. He liked me striking back. However, on the second picture, he didn't kid around as much. Gene was quieter and I don't remember pranks. I guess he tested me and knew he couldn't get away with anything. A neat guy to work with. We didn't keep in touch because I moved to New York shortly after our pictures. When I came back out here, I just never did seem to run into him." [2]

Fay McKenzie: "Director William Morgan was tall, average looking, a nice man. He didn't direct you on characters; if he didn't like it, he'd just say, 'Let's try it again.'" Edith Fellows recalls Gene Autry played tricks on her when shooting "Heart of the Rio Grande". "I spoke to Edith recently and she brought that up. Gene did tell jokes, but there were no tricks on me. Maybe because she was little and I was grown, I don't know. Poor Edith—all she had was Bobby Jordan (of the Dead End Kids) to take up for her, while I always had the protection of my family. Jean Porter was also in it. She was cute as could be; a darling. Smiley Burnette, like Gene, was wonderful. I loved them both. Actually, I had known Smiley earlier. We were in a George O'Brien picture, 'Border Patrolman' ('36), shot on location in Death Valley. I was just background stuff in the picture, but it was the first time I was in a film with Smiley, years before we did all those Autry pictures together."[3]

Jean Porter: "I was in the picture all the way through but I really didn't do much. Fay McKenzie was the leading lady. A friend of mine, Edith Fellows had much more to do than I." When told Autry often played tricks on Edith, Jean was rather surprised, "Gene was good to work with. As far as I know, he didn't pull any tricks, at least not on me."[4]

Jan Lester: "When I was a teenager, I worked in motion pictures briefly. This came about when an agent saw me riding in a horse show and persuaded my mother to let me work in Gene Autry's 'Heart of the Rio Grande'. I worked under the name Jan Lester. Mother thought that more glamorous than (my real name) Mickey Black. I rode with other young girls on a ranch set for Republic. It was a fun experience. The horses were transported to a location north of the San Fernando Valley for the riding scenes. We ate delicious stew as we filmed around the campfire. While I was working, I attended a private professional school dedicated to young screen players. Our lessons were not neglected when we were on the set; time was allotted for schoolwork."[5]

CAST BIOS: Of the dozens of child actresses to grace the silver screen, many critics proclaim the most talented was Edith Fellows, who is as fine a singer as she is a thespian. Debuting in a Charlie Chase silent in 1927, Edith appeared in dozens of pictures in a wide range of genres. She had her own series, the "Five Little Peppers" while under contract to Columbia.

Born May 20, 1923, in Boston, Massachusetts, and pigeon-toed as a child, she took dancing lessons to overcome

Edith Fellows and Gene.

this and by age four had her own "one-woman" show.

Bringing Edith to Hollywood, her paternal grandmother labored tenaciously for the advancement of her granddaughter's career.

Among her important pictures are "The Rider of Death Valley" ('32) starring Tom Mix, "Jane Eyre" ('34), "Mrs. Wiggs of the Cabbage Patch" ('34) and "Keeper of the Bees" ('35). Following two films with Gene Autry in 1942, she left the screen, returning only sporadically until the '80s when she essayed the part of costume designer Edith Head in the TV movie based on the life of actress Grace Kelly and had a role in the cult horror film, "The Hills Have Eyes" ('85).

She currently lives in retirement at the Motion Picture Home in Woodland Hills, California.

In 2004 the Jimmy Wakely Trio was inducted into the Western Music Hall of Fame. Its members were Wakely, Johnny Bond and Dick Reinhart, the latter alternating with Scotty Harrell. The trio in "Heart of the Rio Grande" is composed of Wakely-Bond-Reinhart.

Jimmy Wakely was born February 16, 1914, in Mineola, Arkansas. When the family moved in 1927, Jimmy grew up in rural Oklahoma. He started his performing career as a pianist and singer in the late '30s, eventually landing on WKY radio in Oklahoma City in 1937 where he formed The Bell Boys, named after his sponsor Bell Clothing Stores.

Established as regional favorites, Gene Autry heard the group while on tour in Oklahoma and offered them help beginning a Hollywood career.

Within months of arriving in California, the group found work in "Saga of Death Valley" ('39 Republic) starring Roy Rogers and other B-westerns with The Range Busters, Don Barry, Johnny Mack Brown, Ray Whitley, Hopalong Cassidy—and then with Gene in "Heart of the Rio Grande". As Gene explained, "We made an effort to get different groups from each part of the country that were on radio. We'd bring them in for a spot in a picture. When they'd go home it'd be on the radio 'we just got back from working in a picture with Gene Autry.' So that helped our box office tremendously. Jimmy Wakely was working in Oklahoma City—WKY. He appeared with me in (this picture) and I used him on my road shows. Finally, Jimmy got an offer to star in his own pictures at Monogram."[6]

The Wakely Trio became regulars on Gene's weekly "Melody Ranch" radio program when it hit the airwaves in 1940.

By 1942, Jimmy had signed with Decca Records and later hit his stride on Capitol circa 1947.

The Trio's ability as soloists and musicians was remarkable, allowing Jimmy, Johnny and Dick to each obtain recording contracts as solo artists.

Dick Reinhart, born February 17, 1907, in Tishomingo, Oklahoma, was a gifted songwriter, instrumentalist and vocalist. Reinhart had been associated with several groups, including the Light Crust Doughboys, before joining up with Wakely.

Although Smiley wishes it wasn't so, Fay McKenzie is more interested in Gene than Smiley.

Johnny Bond, born June 1, 1915, in Enville, Oklahoma, became an important song writer ("Cimarron" among others), singer and musician. Joining with Wakely's Bell Boys, he also came to Hollywood with Wakely.

The trio stayed together until Jimmy's solo career began to take off. Whereas Jimmy's career rise became meteoric, Bond's was steadier. He remained a mainstay of Gene's "Melody Ranch" cast until the end in '56. His distinctive acoustic guitar runs became an Autry trademark on radio and recordings.

Bond later began a music publishing business with Tex Ritter and spent nearly a decade as part of TV's "Town Hall Party".

Meanwhile, Wakely launched his own series of singing cowboy films at Monogram beginning with "Song of the Range" in 1944. When the series ended in 1949, his Capitol duet with Margaret Whiting, "Slipping Around", was the #1 country song, and a huge pop hit as well.

From 1952-1958 Jimmy had his own CBS network radio show.

He formed his own record label, Shasta, in the late '50s, recording western greats such as Tex Ritter, Eddie Dean, Rex Allen—and Johnny Bond.

Wakely died September 23, 1982.

Bond died June 12, 1978.

Reinhart died December 3, 1948.

WHAT THE EXHIBITOR HAD TO SAY: "Another good Autry which pleased the Friday-Saturday fans. Autry always pulls them in here."

—E. M. Freiburger, Paramount Theater,
Dewey, Oklahoma (March 1942)

"Best Autry to date. Sings twice, 'Deep in the Heart of Texas', and the audience loved it. Women all good, and believe it or not, Gene is learning to act. He sings four good songs. Smiley Burnette and Tadpole have better parts. Play this on preferred time, get behind it and you will make yourself some money."

—C. L. Niles, Niles Theater,
Anamosa, Iowa (March 1942)

"Rather dull western."—Leon C. Boldue, Majestic Theater, Conway, New Hampshire (April 1942)

SOURCES:

1. Autry with Herskowitz. p.82.

2. *Ladies of the Western.* McFarland, 2002. p. 48-49.

3. *Western Clippings #51.* January/February 2003. p. 21.

4. *Westerns Women.* McFarland, 1999. p. 180.

5. *Good Old Days.* May 2005. Article by Jan Lester (Mickey Philips). p. 54-55.

6. "Melody Ranch Theater" showing of "Heart of the Rio Grande" on Nashville Network, 1987.

Home in Wyomin'

Republic, April 1942

Producer ....Harry Grey
Director ....William Morgan
Assistant Director........................George Blair
Original Story..............................Stuart Palmer
Screenplay...................................Robert Tasker, M.
                                      Coates Webster
Photography ....Ernest Miller
Film Editor.................................Edward Mann
Art Director................................Russell Kimball
Musical Supervisor ....Raoul Kraushaar

SONGS: "Be Honest With Me" (music and lyrics by Gene Autry, Fred Rose)—sung by Gene Autry; "Any Bonds Today" (music and lyrics by Irving Berlin)—sung by Gene Autry; "Back In the Saddle Again" (music and lyrics by Gene Autry, Ray Whitley)—sung by Gene Autry; "Tweedle-O-Twill" (music and lyrics by Gene Autry, Fred Rose)—sung by Gene Autry, Smiley Burnette; "Modern Design" (music and lyrics by Smiley Burnette)—sung by Smiley Burnette; "I'm Thinking Tonight of My Blue Eyes" (music and lyrics by A. P. Carter)—sung by Gene Autry;

"Twilight In Old Wyoming" (music and lyrics by Gene Autry, Fred Rose, Johnny Marvin)—sung by Gene Autry; "Clementine" (Public Domain)—sung by Gene Autry.

RUNNING TIME: 67 minutes
FILMING DATES: February 25 to March 14, 1942
LOCATIONS: Russell Ranch; Republic backlot; Agoura/Albertson Ranch
BUDGET: $84,006
NEGATIVE COST: $85,024

CAST:

Actor	Character
Gene Autry	Gene Autry
Smiley Burnette	Frog Millhouse
Fay McKenzie	Clementine "Clem" Benson
Olin Howlin	Sunrise
Chick Chandler	"Hack" Hackett
Joe Strauch Jr.	Tadpole Millhouse
Forrest Taylor	Pop Harrison
James Seay	Tex Harrison
George Douglas	Crowley
Charles Lane	Editor
Hal Price	Sheriff
William "Billy" Benedict	Bellboy
Ken Cooper, Bud Geary	Henchmen
Art Dillard	Bar O Rodeo Cowboy
Betty Farrington	Female fan
Tom Hanlon	Tom Hanlon (Radio Announcer)
Ray Jones	Spectator
William Kellogg, Jack Kirk, Ted Mapes, Pascale Perry, Tex Terry	Bar O Rodeo Hands
Rex Lease	Card player
Frankie Marvin, Cactus Mack, Carl Cotner, Dick Reinhart	Band Members
James McNamara	Bartlett
Lee Shumway	Bartender
Jack Montgomery	Spectator
Carl Sepulveda, Chuck Baldra, Augie Gomez, Roy Bucko, Herman Hack, Roy Butler, Cyril Ring, Bill Yrigoyen	Extras
Champion	Champion

STUNTS: Joe Yrigoyen (Gene's double); Tex Terry (Smiley's double); Evelyn Finley (Fay's double); Jack Robbins; Bill Yrigoyen.

THE FILM: "Home In Wyomin'" is a return to form for Gene Autry as murder at a Frontier Days pageant and a mysterious denouement in a deserted mine provide suspenseful entertainment in a thriller packed full of top Autry song hits—"Be Honest With Me", "Back In the Saddle Again", "Tweedle-O-Twill", "I'm Thinking Tonight of My Blue Eyes" and the patriotic "Any Bonds Today".

At one point early in the picture, newspaper reporter Clementine Benson (Fay McKenzie) refers to Gene as a phony radio star. Her editor (Charles Lane) is quick to chastise her and sum up Gene's true screen charisma "He may be a phony to a lot of so-called sophisticates, but he isn't a phony to about a million kids who copy his walk and his talk and try to pattern their life after him," Lane states. "He isn't a phony to a couple of million grown ups who see in him the living example of the modern pioneer American spirit. He isn't a phony to them."

"Home In Wyomin'" apes the popular-at-the-time murder mysteries of Charlie Chan, Sherlock Holmes and others. Radio star Gene Autry returns to his hometown to straighten out an old friend's wayward son, Tex Harrison (James Seay). Ace girl news reporter Clem Benson (McKenzie) and her hard-bitten photographer friend Hack Hackett (Chick Chandler) follow Gene to secure on-the-spot photos of the radio performer's activities even though Gene wants none of their interference after they razzed him in print.

In a high stakes poker game, Hack spots a fugitive big city racketeer, Crowley (George Douglas) who is hiding from the mob he double-crossed.

During a Frontier Days celebration, Hack is killed with the blame thrown on Tex.

In true Boston Blackie/Philo Vance fashion, Gene, after a series of difficulties with the gangsters, solves the murder mystery in a dark, claustrophobic, nightmarish old gold mine while also managing to reconcile his differences with the feisty girl reporter.

NOTES AND COMMENTS: Tom Hanlon who plays Gene's on-screen radio show announcer was actually the announcer on Gene's real Sunday night "Melody Ranch" CBS radio program.

By singing noted songwriter Irving Berlin's "Any Bonds Today" in the film, Gene was the first motion picture star to aid the U.S. Defense Bond campaign by highlighting the official song of the campaign.

At one point a humorous reference is made to another popular crooner of the day—ol' Bing Crosby.

Smiley Burnette once again employs a Jassackaphone, a weird multi-instrument strapped to a mule, something like he'd previously employed in "The Singing Cowboy" ('36).

FILM COMMENTS: *Fay McKenzie:* "Gene was a bright and marvelous man, a joy and inspiration to work with. It was wonderful for the whole family to be able to go and enjoy his films. It was such a privilege to work with Gene. It was the high point for me; a happy time. I enjoyed being with him. During the war, my sister Lolly (Ella McKenzie), her husband, my brother-in-law Billy Gilbert, and I did a tour with Gene in Arizona to entertain the troops. This was after our pictures together. I was on the American Movie Classics special which paid tribute to Gene, but unfortunately, we didn't speak to one another when it was made. I was on the East coast; Gene on the West."[1]

WHAT THE EXHIBITOR HAD TO SAY: "Another good western from Gene Autry which pleased the Friday-Saturday crowd." —E. M. Freiburger, Paramount Theater, Dewey, Oklahoma (May 1942)

"Will satisfy the Autry following."
—Leon C. Boldue, Majestic Theater, Conway, New Hampshire (August 1942)

"For two pictures previously I noted a drop off in gross and I feared Autry was slipping. He came back strong and is again "home" in any rural town he plays."
—N. J. Kennan, Park Theater, Dexter, Maine (August 1942)

"About three Autrys a year seems to be the way to make him do business. This was my second and business is very good. It's the same old stuff, but they seem to like it."
—W. R. Pyle, Dreamland Theater, Rockglen, Saskatchewan, Canada (August 1943)

"Just another Autry, if you like them. We did O.K., and no complaints. —K. John, Legion Theater, Bienfait, Saskatchewan, Canada (February 1944)

SOURCES:
1. *Western Clippings #27.* January/February 1999. p. 4.

Stardust On the Sage
Republic, May 1942

Producer ....Harry Grey
Director ....William Morgan
Assistant Director........................George Blair
Original Story.............................Dorrell and Stuart
                     McGowan
Screenplay...................................Betty Burbridge
Photography ....Bud Thackery
Film Editor ....Edward Mann
Art Director.................................Russell Kimball
Musical Supervisor ....Raoul Kraushaar

SONGS: "Perfidea" (music and lyrics by Alberto Dominguez, Milton Leeds)—sung by Edith Fellows; "Goodnight Sweetheart" (music and lyrics by Ray Noble, Jimmy Campbell, Reginald Connelly)—sung by Gene Autry; "You'll Be Sorry" (music and lyrics by Gene Autry, Fred Rose)—sung by Gene Autry; "Wouldn't You Like to Know" (music and lyrics by Smiley Burnette)—sung by Smiley Burnette; "When the Roses Bloom Again" (music and lyrics by Nat Burton, Walter Kent)—sung by Gene Autry, Edith Fellows; "I'll Never Let You Go, Little Darlin'" (music and lyrics by Jimmy Wakely)—sung by Gene Autry, Edith Fellows; Medley: "You Are My Sunshine" (music and lyrics by Jimmie Davis, Charles Mitchell), "Home On the Range" (music and lyrics by Brewster M. Higley, Daniel Kelly), "Deep In the Heart of Texas" (music and lyrics by Don Swander, June Hershey)—sung by Gene Autry, Smiley Burnette, extras.

RUNNING TIME: 65 minutes

FILMING DATES: March 24 to April 8, 1942

LOCATIONS: Republic backlot; L.A. River basin near Republic lot; Morrison Ranch (unconfirmed)

BUDGET: $86,378

NEGATIVE COST: $87,830

CAST:

Actor	*Character*
Gene Autry	Gene Autry
Smiley Burnette	Frog Millhouse
William Henry	Jeff Drew
Edith Fellows	Judy Drew
Louise Currie	Nancy Drew
Emmett Vogan	Dan Pearson
George Ernest	Curly
Vince Barnett	Abner Haskins
Betty Farrington	Mrs. Haskins
Roy Barcroft	Murphy
Tom London	McGowan
George MacQuarrie	Raymond
Griff Barnett	Larkin
Fred Burns, Frank LaRue, Frankie Marvin, Merrill McCormick, Lee Shumway, Carl Cotner	Ranchers
Ed Cassidy	Dawson
Edmund Cobb	Steve Burns
George DeNormand	Barry (Hoodlum)
Jerry Jerome	Rogers (Hoodlum)
Bert LeBaron	Wayne (Hoodlum)
Frank Ellis, Art Dillard	Men at Dance
Franklyn Farnum	Baker
Jimmie Fox	Storekeeper
Bud Jamison	Mike the Blacksmith
Rex Lease	Sheriff
Monte Montague	Cooper
Bill Nestell	Jim, Man at Wheel at Mine
Frank O'Connor	Foreman
George Sherwood	Pipeman
Tex Terry, Nellie Walker	Radio Listeners
Art Mix, Bob Woodward, Jack O'Shea, Jack Montgomery, Rose Plummer, Chick Hannon, George Sowards	Extras
Champion	Champion

STUNTS: Joe Yrigoyen (Gene's double); Tex Terry (Smiley's double); Nellie Walker (Louise Currie's double); Mary Ann Jackson (Edith Fellow's double).

THE FILM: In "Stardust On the Sage", a partial remake of 1937's "Git Along Little Dogies", there are more top tunes than tough times, running the gamut from traditional pop numbers to pure western. They're all well-chosen to appeal to the exact audience Gene and Republic

214

Asking a few questions, Smiley and Gene are about to encounter trouble at the Rawhide Mine from toughs Tom London and Roy Barcroft.

Fay McKenzie, who had been in five previous films as Gene's leading lady, was set to appear in "Stardust..." but was replaced by Louise Currie when Fay instead was cast in Republic's "Remember Pearl Harbor" set to film in May 1942.

At the end of "Stardust...", during a song medley at the radio station, Smiley Burnette conducts the orchestra, turning at one point to the movie audience and asking them to sing along as Gene performs "Deep In the Heart of Texas". The words to the song appear across the bottom of the screen. This "sing-along" gimmick was a popular short-subject feature in the '40s. Smiley used similar audience participation ideas several times at the end of the westerns he made with Sunset Carson in 1944 while Gene was in the service.

The radio station Edith Fellows and Louise Currie own is RYL. In truth, according to FCC regulations, all radio station call letters begin with W or K…none with R.

Leading lady Louise Currie took home $250 a week, while, although lesser billed, George Ernest made $375. Up and coming screen heavy Roy Barcroft, not yet signed to a term contract with Republic as he would be a year later, was paid $150 a week.

knew they were singing and playing to—even if the critics didn't understand Autry's grass-roots appeal.

Gene, the idol and town leader of the cattlemen, is deceived in business by the local agent of the packing company, Jeff Drew (Bill Henry), who uses funds derived from the sale of beef on the hoof to dabble in the development of a mining property. Gene and pal Frog (Smiley Burnette) are troubled when they learn their rancher friends are investing their hard earned funds in the hydraulic mining venture instead of cattle.

Jeff's two sisters, Nancy (Louise Currie) and Judy (Edith Fellows), lend support to him through the radio station they own and operate. They take Gene for a ride by altering what he actually said to an on-air recording promoting the sale of mining stock.

Gene aligns himself against the girls and Jeff, but eventually learns the dishonesty of mine manager Pearson (Emmett Vogan) is behind all the troubles.

In true Autry fashion, he puts the mine on a paying basis, saves the ranchers' money, protects Jeff from embezzlement charges, and wins the heart of the gal.

NOTES AND COMMENTS: Working title for this western was "Beyond the Great Divide".

Gene, Louise Currie, William (Bill) Henry.

Just how lawsuit-conscious Republic skirted the issue of naming the leading lady "Nancy Drew" without incurring legal problems from Warner Bros., who made a series of films based on the popular novels, is unknown.

One day after completing filming of "Stardust On the Sage", Gene and his Flying A Ranch Rodeo undertook a rugged schedule of personal appearances. Beginning April 9 he was at the Arena in Cleveland, Ohio, followed by the Gardens in Pittsburgh, Pennsylvania, through April 22. April 24-30 Gene appeared at the Arena in Philadelphia, Pennsylvania, followed by the Uline Ice Arena in Washington, D.C., beginning May 2. He then moved on to the Arena in New Haven, Connecticut by May 10.

FILM COMMENTS: *Louise Currie:* "Gene wasn't as much fun for me to work with as some of the others. I mean he was more stereotyped. He knew when to sing, and he had his funny man, and that kind of thing, but the girls were inconsequential. And that didn't amuse me too much. My part was so 'ick'. I didn't have enough to do. It was one of those 'hanging on the garden gate' type of roles. Gene Autry was very professional—and it was a slick production. It's just I was not too keen on my part." When told Autry and Edith Fellows played tricks on one another, Louise stated, "I intimidated Gene. I held my ground. There was no nonsense with me—no romance either. I was more sophisticated than his other leading ladies, perhaps. Gene was very proficient; there were no tricks. How do you argue with success? He had a great business head. He knew what to sell and how to sell it. He sold himself extremely well—something that most of the others, unfortunately, never could do." [1]

WHAT THE EXHIBITOR HAD TO SAY: "An excellent Autry and it means money in the bank."
—C. L. Niles, Niles Theater, Anamosa, Iowa (October 1942)

"Terrible—but business was good and they seemed satisfied."
—Ray Peacock, Onalaska Theater, Onalaska, Washington (November 1942)

"No better or worse than any of the other Autrys. They should be better."
—Arthur K. Dame, Palace Theater, Penacook, New Hampshire (December 1942)

"This Gene Autry guy has kinda gone down in my town, and it seems like Republic is putting all the responsibility on Roy Rogers, but he doesn't seem to click in my town so well. The picture was liked by all who attended."
—Sam Stephano, Grove Theater, Groveton, Texas (November 1942)

"Autry still pays all the rent for the small town boys. Hope he isn't out of circulation too long."
—Clifton Green, Green Theater, Lodge Grass, Montana (January 1943)

SOURCES:
1. *Ladies of the Western.* McFarland, 2002. p. 37.

Call of the Canyon
Republic, August 1942

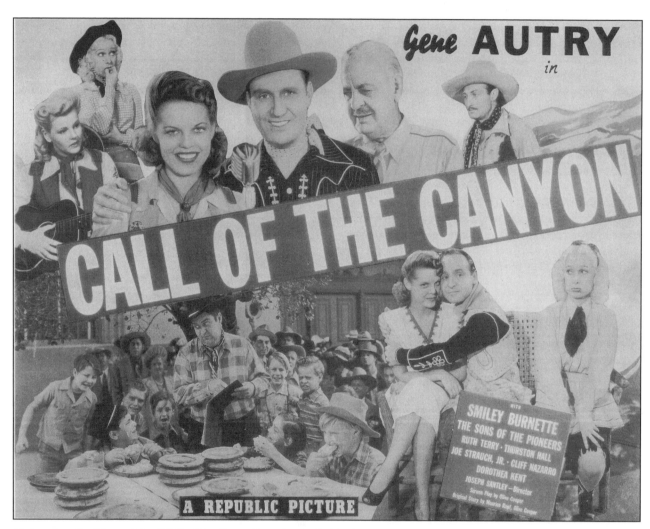

Pictured on the title card for "Call of the Canyon" are (top L-R) Muriel Barr, Dorothea Kent, Ruth Terry, Gene, Thurston Hall, John Holland. (bottom L-R) Joe Strauch Jr., Smiley and other kids, Ruth Terry, Cliff Nazarro, Dorothea Kent.

Producer ....Harry Grey
Director ....Joseph Santley
Assistant Director.......................Art Siteman
Original Story............................Maurice Rapf, Olive
                                             Cooper
Screenplay..................................Olive Cooper
Photography ....Reggie Lanning

Film Editor ....Edward Mann
Art Director.................................Russell Kimball
Set Decorations ....Otto Siegel
Musical Supervisor ....Raoul Kraushaar

SONGS: "Somebody Else Is Taking My Place" (music and lyrics by Dick Howard, Bob Ellsworth, Russ Morgan)—

sung by Gene Autry and Sons of the Pioneers; "Take Me Back to My Boots and Saddle" (music and lyrics by Walter G. Samuels, Leonard Whitcup, Teddy Powell)—sung by Gene Autry; "Coronation March" (music and lyrics by Elgar)—sung by John Holland; Medley: "Montana Plains" (music and lyrics by Patsy Montana)—sung by Gene Autry and The Sons of the Pioneers/ "When It's Chilly Down in Chili" (music and lyrics by Jule Styne, Sol Meyer)—sung by Ruth Terry/"Call of the Canyon" (music and lyrics by Billy Hill)—sung by Gene Autry; "Home Corral" (music and lyrics by Bob Nolan)—sung by The Sons of the Pioneers.

RUNNING TIME: 71 minutes
FILMING DATES: June 6-27, 1942
LOCATIONS: Bronson Canyon; Lone Pine; Republic backlot; Iverson Ranch; Burro Flats; railroad between Fillmore and Saugus; Morrison or Agoura Ranch
BUDGET: $129,808
NEGATIVE COST: $129,132

CAST:

Actor	Character
Gene Autry	Gene Autry
Smiley Burnette	Frog Millhouse
Sons of the Pioneers: Bob Nolan, Tim Spencer, Hugh Farr, Karl Farr, Pat Brady, Lloyd Perryman	Music Group
Ruth Terry	Katherine "Kit" Carson
Thurston Hall	Grantley B. Johnson
Joe Strauch Jr.	Tadpole Millhouse
Cliff Nazarro	Pete Murphy
Dorothea Kent	Jane Oakley
Edmund MacDonald	Thomas McCoy
Marc Lawrence	Horace Dunston
John Harmon	Pigeon
John Holland	Willy Hitchcock
Eddy Waller	Dave Crosby
Ray Bennett	Nash
Joy Barlow	Concertina Player
Muriel Barr	Guitarist
Bob Burns	Rancher
Budd Buster	Jim Taylor
June Earle	Violinist
Charles Flynn	Radio Technician
Carey Harrison, Fred Santley, Anthony Marsh, Broderick O'Farrell, Loren Raker, Charles Williams	Agents
Earle Hodgins	Pie Eating Referee
Frank Jaquet	Doc Hooper
Edna Johnson	Myra
Jimmie Lucas	Bus Driver
Jean Lucius	Guitarist
Frankie Marvin	Cowhand
Jeanne Strasser	Pianist
Al Taylor	Ranch Hand Al
Fred Walburn	Pie Eating Boy
Frank Ward	Skinny Thompkins
Red Knight	Red
Jack O'Shea	Pie Eating Contest observer
Audrene Brier, Gill Dennis, Johnny Duncan, Genevieve Grazis, Valmere Barman, Billie Lane, Richard Landry, Buddy Martin, Bud Mercer, Lee Morrison, Gerald Pierce, Marion Spencer, Tim Taylor, Elizabeth Ryan, Margaret Ryan, Irene Thomas, Bill Driscoll, Tim Taylor, Rosemary Wilson	Jitterbug Dancers
Bud Wolfe, Paul Power, Tex Terry	Extras
Champion	Champion

STUNTS: Joe Yrigoyen (Gene's double); Tex Terry (Smiley's double); George Havens (Joe Strauch Jr.'s double); Mary Ellen Huggins (Ruth Terry's double); Bud Wolfe.

THE FILM: Released as a "Special" by Republic, this breezy picture just before Gene's entrance into the service for WWII is full of good music, comedy and action.

Noteworthy is the fact this is only the third time the popular Sons of the Pioneers appeared in a film with Gene, for several reasons. The group had been making B-westerns with Charles Starrett at Columbia since 1935 and had just come over to Republic. They'd made "Red River Valley" in late '41 with Roy Rogers and now, possibly, Republic prexy Herbert J. Yates wanted to test the chemistry of the Pioneers with Autry. Watching Nolan and the boys in films with Roy *and* Gene, it's quite obvious Gene really didn't need the aid of the group—he could carry a picture quite well by himself—and that the camaraderie between The Pioneers and Roy was far better suited for the screen. After all, Roy had once been a member of the group. Add that to the fact Gene only made one more pre-war western, so the group really never had the opportunity to co-star further with Gene.

This is the first Autry film to boast a musical medley revue at the climax, like a Broadway musical where the performers step on stage to take a final bow. This type of reprise became a favorite of Republic president Herbert J. Yates and was frequently used in wartime Roy Rogers pictures. The practice was also picked up for the Ken Curtis/ Hoosier Hot Shots westerns at Columbia in the mid '40s.

Two story threads are woven together. One has Gene Autry leading a group of cattlemen in rebellion against the efforts of Thomas McCoy (Edmund MacDonald), the agent of a big packing company, who is trying to collect some private graft by undercutting the buying price for beef. McCoy is heavily indebted to gangster-bookies and plans to appropriate the difference between the amount the head of the packing company, Grantley B. Johnson (Thurston Hall), is willing to pay and that which McCoy will pay the cattlemen. The other plotline has Katherine "Kit" Carson (Ruth Terry), an attractive young career woman, whose future depends largely on obtaining the Johnson radio advertising account. Johnson likes the idea of a western program emanating from a real ranch, which Kit sells to him. Obliged now to prepare such a program, Kit and her company of friends frantically head west and, through a set of circumstances only believable in an Autry western, end up renting Gene's ranch from Frog Millhouse (Smiley Burnette) while Gene is out of town.

An astonished Gene, and Johnson, who has come west to check on his investment, both arrive at the same time. The beef packer magnate finds the cattlemen gunning for his scalp, so he hides his identity until he can learn the reason why. When he does, his fighting spirit drives him to beat McCoy at his own game. McCoy, desperate because of the demands of his bookie, arranges to dynamite a tunnel through which the cattle are to pass. When a rancher is killed and Tadpole (Joe Strauch Jr.) injured, Gene and Johnson join forces to secure evidence to expose and arrest McCoy.

NOTES AND COMMENTS: If you think "Montana Plains" sounds a lot like Stuart Hamblen's "Texas Plains", you're right. Although listed in Republic's music cue sheets in 1942 as "Montana Plains" written by Patsy Montana, it is an obvious rip-off of Hamblen's "Texas Plains". According to music authority O. J. Sikes, "Stuart Hamblen wrote 'Texas Plains' in 1932. He didn't record it until 1934. In the meantime, he was singing it on radio and in public performances and other artists were learning it 'by ear' and passing it around. In '32, Patsy Montana changed the title to 'Montana Plains' along with some of the lyrics to reflect her new title. She introduced 'Montana Plains' on the National Barn Dance radio show on WLS in Chicago and recorded it in '33 for RCA Victor as well, eight months before Stuart recorded 'Texas Plains' on Decca. She continued to use it as her radio theme for some time. According to Patsy, Stuart gave her permission to make the change in the title, assuming he would get royalties. However, he failed to file a separate copyright, and his name does not appear in the credits for the song in 'Call of the Canyon'. Patsy got the credit and the royalties. Oddly, Gene recorded Hamblen's 'Texas Plains', but he never recorded 'Montana Plains'. I don't know of anyone other than Patsy who recorded 'Montana Plains', but lots of people have recorded 'Texas Plains'." [1]

Top weekly salaries of $750 were paid to Thurston

Hall and Marc Lawrence. Edmund MacDonald made $500 a week while Dorothea Kent earned $350, John Harmon $300 and Eddy Waller $250 a week. The Sons of the Pioneers were each paid $200 a week.

Maurice H. Rapf (1915-2003) belonged to the Communist Party in Hollywood when he created the original story for "Call of the Canyon". "I was always on the side of the workers against the bosses," Rapf said in a WRITERS GUILD interview in 1997. You'll note that very theme in the film. Rapf later worked for Walt Disney on "Song of the South" ('46), "So Dear To My Heart" ('49) and "Cinderella" ('50), the latter of which he didn't receive credit on because by that time he'd been "blacklisted" in Hollywood during the House Un-American Activities investigations into Communism.

FILM COMMENTS: *Ruth Terry*, under contract to Howard Hughes, said, "Hughes loaned me—exclusively—to Republic. That's how I got at Republic. I did 'Call of the Canyon' with Gene Autry, my first western. Two things I remember about the picture and Gene Autry. First, I *never ever* talked to the man! He did speak to the fellows on the picture, but not with the girls. I never said *anything* to

Joe Strauch Jr., Eddy Waller, Gene, Smiley, Thurston Hall.

him, nor he to me. I don't even recall him saying 'good morning.' We just did the scenes and that was it. The other thing I remember is he kept us waiting one might. Gene was a very big star then, and he had it in his contract he wouldn't have to work after 6pm. Gene was punctual, knew his lines; always there in the morning. But on the last day of shooting, they needed another two hours. They didn't want to bring everybody back the next day for just a couple of hours shooting. They argued with Gene about breaking his rule, just this once. He firmly said 'No.' Finally, he said, 'Okay, let's eat dinner.' He never came back—he left us all there, waiting on his return—which didn't happen until the next morning! A lot of people got an extra day's pay as a result, but not me as I was under contract to Hughes. It was all business with him." [2]

Marc Lawrence: "Gene Autry created the name 'Gene Autry' as a commodity way before Marlboro Cigarettes or Coca Cola got the idea. He was clever enough to always use Gene Autry in every character he played in every film he made."[3]

Gene Autry: "Fella named Billy Hill wrote ("Call of the Canyon"). His real name was George Brown. He was from San Francisco. I met him in New York when I first started making records. I had a song called 'The Gangster's Warning'. He helped me write that. Later on I did some country songs like 'Left My Gal in the Mountains' and 'They Cut Down the Old Pine Tree' and stuff like that. Then he decided to change his name to Billy Hill, which backwards means hill-billy. (Chuckles) Just listen to the songs he wrote— 'The Last Round-Up', 'The Old Spinning Wheel', 'Wagon Wheels!', 'Empty Saddles'. A wonderful fellow."[4]

WHAT THE EXHIBITOR HAD TO SAY: "A good enjoyable Autry picture which lived up to expectations; it pleased everyone who came out and registered at the box office. We have nothing but praise for Gene's drawing power."   —Thomas Di Lorenzo, New Platz Theater,
New Platz, New York (January 1943)

"A very good Autry production, with plenty of singing and lots of action. It still takes a Gene Autry to pay off the mortgage. Play it and make some money."
—A. L. Dove, Bengough Theater,
Bengough, Saskatchewan, Canada (January 1943)

"This was a grand picture filled with laughs and music. Although I played this late it made a good weekend show. Double billed it with 'All Over Town'."
—Frank Raspa, State Theater,
Rivesville, West Virginia (June 1943)

SOURCES:
1. Email to author 7/29/05.
2. *Ladies of the Western.* McFarland, 2002. p. 269.
3. Interview with author, October, 1998.
4. "Melody Ranch Theater" showing of "Call of the Canyon" on Nashville Network, 1987.

Bells of Capistrano
Republic, September 1942

Producer ....Harry Grey
Director ....William Morgan
Assistant Director........................Art Siteman
Screenplay ....Lawrence Kimble
Photography ....Reggie Lanning
Film Editor.................................Edward Mann
Art Director................................Ralph Oberg
Interior Decorator........................Otto Siegel
Musical Supervisor ....Morton Scott
Musical Settings...........................Dave Gould

SONGS: "Forgive Me" (music and lyrics by Milton Ager, Jack Yellen)—sung by Gene Autry; "At Sundown" (music and lyrics by Walter Donaldson)—sung by Gene Autry; "Fort Worth Jail" (music and lyrics by Dick Reinhart)—sung by Gene Autry; "In Old Capistrano" (music and lyrics by Fred Stryker, Jerry Charleston)—sung by Gene Autry and extras; "Don't Bite the Hand That's Feeding You" (music and lyrics by Jimmie Morgan, Thomas Hoier)—sung by Gene Autry.

RUNNING TIME: 73 minutes

FILMING DATES: July 7-24, 1942

LOCATIONS: Republic backlot; Monogram Ranch; Agoura/Albertson Ranch; Upper Iverson Ranch; Thousand Oaks area

BUDGET: $132,288

NEGATIVE COST: $132,229

CAST:

Actor	Character
Gene Autry ....Gene Autry
Smiley Burnette ....Frog Millhouse
Virginia Grey...............................Jennifer Benton
Lucien Littlefield........................Daniel "Pop" McCracken
Morgan Conway...........................Stag Johnson
Claire Du Brey ....Melinda "Ma" McCraken
Charles Cane ....Tex North
Joe Strauch Jr. ....Tadpole Millhouse
Marla Shelton...............................Jackie Laval
Tristram Coffin...........................Jed Johnson
Jay Novello ....Jenkins
Eddie Acuff.................................Billboard Mug #1

Dick Wessel................................Billboard Mug #2
Ralph Peters ....Jailer
Al Bridge....................................Bartender, Westfall saloon
Fred Burns, Bill Nestell, Tex Terry.Barflys
Ken Christy ....Sheriff's Deputy with Attachment
William Forrest ....Durgan, Madison Square Garden Representative
Chick Hannon ....Pool Player
Howard C. Hickman ....Doctor
Ray Jones, Frankie Marvin, Jack O'Shea...........................Roustabouts
Ed Juaregui................................Brady
Joe McGuinn..............................Henchman
Tom Quinn ....Maracas Player
Julian Rivero ....Fiesta Manager
Peggy Satterlee...........................Grand Marshal
William Telaak ....Milk Truck Driver/ Henchman
Ken Terrell ....Rodeo Saboteur
Guy Usher ....Sheriff
Terrista Osta, Carlos Ramos, Fernando Ramos.....................Dancers
Augie Gomez ....Card Player
Bill Yrigoyen...............................Thug
Bob Wilke, Jack Byron, Bob Card, William Kellogg, Cactus Mack..Extras
Champion....................................Champion

STUNTS: Joe Yrigoyen (Gene's double); Tex Terry (Smiley's double); George Havens (Joe Strauch Jr.'s double); Nellie Walker (Virginia Grey's double); Bill Yrigoyen, Cliff Lyons, Post Park, Yakima Canutt.

THE FILM: "Bells of Capistrano", Gene's 56th movie, was the last he made before becoming Sergeant Gene Autry in the U.S. Air Force. It was four years before his return to the screen after flying transport planes with supplies and ammunition in the Pacific Theater of War. Gene had flown his private Cessna and Beechcraft before the War and quickly learned how to pilot larger Army planes.

Virginia Grey and Gene go over their lines between takes on "Bells of Capistrano."

During his time away, Republic re-issued many of his prior movies which kept Gene #2 at the box office behind Roy Rogers. Many of these films played in theaters—and to audiences—that had not previously played—or seen—these earlier features.

An unusually good cast, thrilling action spotted among the musical numbers—highlighted by an excitingly staged fire sequence—and a rousing Madison Square Garden patriotic rodeo production number close with Gene singing the 1915 WWI tune, "Don't Bite the Hand That's Feeding You", surrounded by an orchestral rendition of "America the Beautiful". Midway in the song Gene stops to sort of "bid goodbye" to his fans for the duration of the war by presenting a few patriotic words (penned by songwriter Sol Meyer).

The plot deals with a clash between two traveling rodeo shows, one owned by charming Jennifer Benton (Virginia Grey) and the other by ruthless Stag Johnson (Morgan Conway). By fair means or foul, Stag means to take over and absorb Jennifer's show. When the elderly couple, Ma and Pa McCracken (Claire DuBrey, Lucien Littlefield), who manage Jennifer's Worldwide Show, hire Gene Autry as a singing attraction, their Wild West Show rapidly gains new popularity, causing the rivalry between the two shows to be ratcheted up a notch. Stag stoops to violence to squash his competition with an excitingly staged fire in which Pa McCracken is seriously injured. To pay for a specialist to save McCracken's life, Gene secretly goes to work for Stag's outfit. Jennifer and her friends don't understand until Gene eventually learns of Stag's skullduggery and forces a confession from him. World Wide is saved and goes on to greater glory at Madison Square Garden.

NOTES AND COMMENTS: Notified to report for induction as a technical sergeant in the Army Air Force, Gene wound up "Bells of Capistrano" on Friday July 24 and enlisted on his "Melody Ranch" radio show July 26, 1942, taking his oath from Lt. Col. Edward Shaifer. He was due to report to Ft. Sheridan August 3.

For Gene's last film before entering the service, Republic prepared and released two unique promotional pieces. The first was a three day newspaper serialization of the film, accompanied by a photo. The second was a newspaper picture strip (four scene panels per day) in a six day format. Both were offered free to newspapers and, if found, are highly collectible today.

MOTION PICTURE HERALD's December 1942 master list of money making western stars for the past year saw Gene Autry still on top at #1, followed by Roy Rogers, William Boyd, Smiley Burnette and Charles Starrett.

FILM COMMENTS: *Gene Autry:* "The draft board called me about February and they said 'Gene, we think we're probably going to have to draft you in a few weeks for the Army. You may be in the next draft…pretty quick.' I said, 'Well, I have a lot of dates booked up because I have a brand new rodeo. I've got a lot of money tied up in it, so I'll have to do something about that. At least I'd like to fulfill all the engagements I have booked before I go into the service.' They said, 'When's your last date?' I said, 'My last date is July 4 in Chicago at Soldier's Field.' Said, 'We'll hold off

Gene takes the Army Air Corps oath from Lieut. Colonel Edward Shaifer during a "Melody Ranch" radio broadcast July 26, 1942.

drafting you til after July.' I went over and talked to Herb Yates. Said, 'Mr. Yates they tell me they're going to draft me, maybe the latest is in July. So if you wanna make any pictures you'd better get started on 'em because I am going to go in.' He said, 'I don't think you have to go because I can ask for deferment for you. We are an important industry to the Armed Services.' But there were a lot of picture people that were going into the service…Jimmy Stewart…Clark Gable… There were a lot of mothers and fathers who lived on farms taking their sons. (Friends) didn't think it would be a good idea for me to ask for a deferment. I agreed, so I went back and I told Herb Yates, 'I'm not going to ask for a deferment in any way and I don't want you to because it might be embarrassing for me later on and also for you.' He really got up in arms about that. Anyway, I decided to go into the Air Force. I told the Wrigley Company also…I was under contract with the Wrigley Company (for my radio show). I went to Hap Arnold, the commanding general of the Air Force and talked to him about going in the service. He said, 'We certainly could use you. I'd like to use you in public relations, things of that sort.' I said, 'The main thing I wanna do is be a pilot. I've got a license as a private pilot.' (Arnold) says, 'Get in the Air Force first and then we'll talk about that later.' I went ahead and did all the dates that I had, did the rodeo in Chicago, and in July I went down and enlisted in the Air Force as a private. (Gene was actually sworn in, at the Pentagon's request, on the air during the July 26, 1942, broadcast of "Melody Ranch".) Right away they assigned me to special duty, then they made me a Tech Sergeant and later went into flying. To start with I was in the Training Command but I wanted to get over into the Air Transport Command. They finally transferred me and I had to go to school and take a lot of (instruction) in flying heavier aircraft. Mr. Wrigley offered the Air Force the time if I would do a program. To tell the truth, I really didn't want to do it, but the Air Force asked me if I would do that. So I did a show for about a year. But while I was doing that I was given a chance to fly some bigger airplanes. Finally, I

got transferred over to the ferrying division, that is, I would go to the factories where they had planes, pick 'em up and deliver them all over the country. Finally, I went to Love Field and started flying the C-47s. I flew cargo and delivered other airplanes all over the world, in fact I made trips to China, India and South America. After the war in Europe was over, they didn't need pilots anymore. They started cutting off a lot of the pilots. When I talked to the Special Services Department they wanted me to take a USO troupe to the South Pacific. I'd never been (there) so I said yes. They said, 'Get a group of people together.' So I got Rufe Davis and a few others and went all over the South Pacific…almost the end of the world that way (for two months)."[1]

In fact, the 10 week "walking tour" of the Pacific Islands played approximately 85 shows to over 1,000,000 GI's arranged by the Hollywood Victory Committee. The Autry troupe visited Guam, Saipan, Tinian, Kwajelein, Angar, Peleliu, Ulitihi and Iwo Jima, covering 35,000 miles by plane in addition to the distance the troupe walked.

WHAT THE EXHIBITOR HAD TO SAY: "Just the picture for the rural communities. The patrons like it so well some stayed to see it twice." —Robert Boyd, Ohio Theater, Leipsic, Ohio (December 1942)

"Autry left our screen for the duration, we presume, in a minor blaze of glory. Business was the best for a Tuesday in many weeks and the picture is different and better than most Autrys." —Arthur K. Dame, Palace Theater, Pennacook, New Hampshire (March 1943)

"Not the Gene Autry production it is cracked up to be. It seems they have left out one of the popular favorites— Smiley Burnette—who had a very small part in this one. The Autry songs were not the favorites that he generally sings. We really looked for something outstanding on this one as it was to be his last picture before joining the Army. However, still a leading drawing card to any small town theater. Would recommend it." —A. L. Dove, Bengough Theater, Bengough, Saskatchewan, Canada (April 1943)

"Picture was very good. Played it very late. No draw on account of the late date. The people today want pictures brand new. They have the money and want the best. I have a depression house." —M. L. London, Gem Theater, East Boston, Massachusetts (May 1943)

"I can always tell if it is Autry or not by the gross receipts at night and I sure could tell this was. Did above average business and it is a good western. Autry is still tops here." —V. C. Kinchen, Avon Theater, Poteet, Texas (May 1943)

A "gag" picture taken of Gene and Rufe Davis during their 10 week USO "walking tour" of the Pacific islands after the war in Europe was ended.

SOURCES:
1. "Melody Ranch Theater" showing of "Bells of Capistrano" on Nashville Network, 1987.

"Gene's In the Army Now!"

While Gene was in the service, Republic re-released 30 of his features.[1]

"Tumbling Tumbleweeds"
"Melody Trail"
"Comin' 'Round the Mountain"
"Guns and Guitars"
"Red River Valley"
"Oh, Susanna!"
"Ride Ranger Ride"
"The Big Show"
"Git Along Little Dogies"
"Rootin' Tootin' Rhythm"
"Public Cowboy No. 1"
"Boots and Saddles"
"Springtime In the Rockies"
"The Old Barn Dance"
"Gold Mine In the Sky"

"Man From Music Mountain"
"Rhythm of the Saddle"
"Mexicali Rose"
"Blue Montana Skies"
"Colorado Sunset"
"In Old Monterey"
"South of the Border"
"Rancho Grande"
"Gaucho Serenade"
"Carolina Moon"
"Ride, Tenderfoot, Ride"
"Melody Ranch"
"Ridin' On a Rainbow"
"Back In the Saddle"
"Under Fiesta Stars"

Sources:
1. Compiled by Gordon Kay, Assistant secretary of Republic Studios.

Although he hadn't made a movie since 1942, and had been off the radio most of the time, Gene received 248,753 letters in 1945, an average of over 20,000 a month, according to the LOS ANGELES EVENING HERALD EXPRESS on January 1, 1946.

Gene made his first public appearance in California since returning from the armed forces with a 23 performance run of his Flying A Ranch Rodeo starting June 14, 1946, at the Pan-Pacific auditorium.

With nothing but Republic reissues getting into circulation during the voting period of 1945, the motion picture exhibitors' poll of "Western Box Office Champions" released December 28, 1946, by MOTION PICTURE HERALD showed Gene in third place. Roy Rogers was now #1 followed by Bill Elliott. Gabby Hayes was #4, Smiley Burnette #5 and Charles Starrett #6. An all time championship, Gene led the Western Stars Poll for six years (1937 through 1942) until he entered the service.

Gene being sworn in as a flight officer by Captain Herb Dailey at Love Field in Texas.

Sioux City Sue
Republic, November 1946

Producer ....Armand Schaefer
Director ....Frank McDonald
Assistant Director.........................Nathan Barragar
Screenplay ....Olive Cooper
Photography ....Reggie Lanning
Musical Director ....Morton Scott
Musical Score...............................Dale Butts
Film Editor ....Fred Allen
Sound ....Richard Tyler

Art Director.................................Gano Chittenden
Costume Supervision ....Adele Palmer
Set Decorations ....John McCarthy Jr.,
                                                        George Milo
Special Effects.............................Howard and Theodore
                                                        Lydecker
Makeup Supervision ....Bob Mark

SONGS: "Sioux City Sue" (music and lyrics by Dick Thomas, Ray Friedman)—sung by studio singers, reprised by Gene Autry and the Cass County Boys; "Oklahoma Hills" (music and lyrics by Leon and Woody Guthrie)—sung by Gene Autry; "Great Grand Dad" (Public Domain)—sung by the Cass County Boys; "Someday You'll Want Me to Want You" (music and lyrics by Jimmie Hodges)—sung by Gene Autry, Ken Lundy; "Red River Valley" (Public Domain)—sung by Ralph Sanford; "Old Chisholm Trail" (Public Domain)—sung by Gene Autry; "Ridin' Double" (music and lyrics by John Rox)—sung by Gene Autry; "Yours" (music and lyrics by Gonzalo Roig, Jack Sherr)—sung by Gene Autry and the Cass County Boys.

RUNNING TIME: 68 minutes

FILMING DATES: June 11-28, 1946

LOCATIONS: Republic backlot; Corriganville; Walker Ranch; Morrison Ranch; Chatsworth Lake; Lake Crowley and Lake Hemet (stock footage)

BUDGET: $175,920

NEGATIVE COST: $177,130

CAST:

Actor	Character
Gene Autry	Gene Autry
Lynne Roberts	Sue Warner
Sterling Holloway	Nelson "Nellie" Bly
Richard Lane................................	Jefferson Lang
Ralph Sanford	Big Gulliver
Ken Lundy	Jody
Helen Wallace	Miss Price
Pierre Watkin................................	G. W. Rhodes
The Cass County Boys: Jerry Scoggins, Fred Martin, Bert Dodson.............................	Musicians

George M. Carleton......................Sheriff
Harry Cheshire............................Mayor Tussie
Tristram Coffin............................Rhodes' Assistant
Kenne Duncan.............................Steve Crawley, Gulliver
                                                            Henchman
Sam Flint.....................................Doctor
Michael Hughes...........................Steve, Lang's Cartoonist
                                                            Assistant
Frank Marlowe.............................Keeno
Frankie Marvin, Forrest Burns,
    Tommy Coats..........................Cowhands
LeRoy Mason...............................Jim Dudley, Movie
                                                            Director
Edwin Mills.................................Sammy
Tex Terry.....................................Jim Bailey, Gulliver
                                                            Henchman
Minerva Urecal............................Mrs. Abercrombie, Elite
                                                            Hotel Manager
Roy Bucko, Victor Cox, Kermit
    Maynard, Pascale Perry, Bob
    Woodward ....Extras
Champion Jr. ....Champion, Wonder
                                                            Horse of the West

STUNTS: Joe Yrigoyen (Gene's double); Fred Graham (double for Ralph Sanford); Bobbie Dorree (double for Lynne Roberts).

THE FILM: Gene Autry's back in the saddle in the first of his postwar westerns following his exit from the Armed Services. Actually, Gene didn't want to make this film—in fact, he didn't want any further association with

Gene kids with leading lady Lynne Roberts just before her famous scene of a buckboard dragging her through a mud puddle with Gene in rescue pursuit.

Herbert J. Yates and Republic Pictures after he completed "Bells of Capistrano" in 1942. Gene maintained WWII service automatically voided his contract in 1942, but Yates thought otherwise and took Gene through a series of court battles into 1946, winning one decision in favor of the studio. Gene was forced back to Republic with 21 additional features to complete his old contract which had roughly three years of personal obligation left. However, Gene reached a compromise with Yates in early 1946 that required only five more B-westerns be made (at a salary of $15,000 per picture) while a higher court settled the matter. If the decision went against him, Gene agreed to fulfill his original 1938 Republic agreement. However, a final ruling in the Spring of 1947, by the time he'd finished the fifth picture, came in his favor.

These last five Republic features show evidence of minimal production values, an area over which Gene had fought continuously through the years. Gene wanted bigger budgets on all his films, not just the 'Specials', as well as a larger salary commensurate with the huge profits Republic was garnering from his features. In evidence here is stock footage over the opening credits, more use of rear screen projection, and more stock footage of a cattle drive with Gene and Champion (now actually Champion Jr.) trotting on a sound-stage treadmill.

By the time Gene returned from WWII, Smiley Burnette had exited Republic after failed attempts to saddle-partner with Robert Livingston, Eddie Dew and Sunset Carson. Smiley landed at Columbia co-starring with Charles Starrett—The Durango Kid—at a "considerable salary advance" on a new three year contract according to the HOLLYWOOD CITIZEN NEWS on January 22, 1945.

Smiley remained with Starrett till the end of his popular series in 1952, at which time, as we will see, he rejoined Gene at Columbia.

Replacing Smiley—an impossible chore—were the musical group Gene had found in Texas, the Cass County Boys, and for comedy relief, raspy voiced Sterling Holloway, for whom one must have an acquired taste. Actually, much has been written over the years about Holloway being Gene's sidekick ala Smiley in these five features. That is totally inaccurate. If one *must* assign sidekick duties to anyone in these five, it should go to the Cass County Boys who are partnered with Gene in all five. Holloway is truly only a "partner" to Gene in "Twilight On the Rio Grande". In the other four, he is simply a character actor playing various roles.

"Sioux City Sue" doesn't blaze any new trails and, some would say, was a rather muted return for Gene. Almost a comedy with its cartoon donkey and over zealous hamming from Paragon Pictures head Jefferson Lang (Richard Lane), nevertheless Gene looks good for his comeback, sings better than ever and is surrounded by some terrific songs.

Gene is a cowpoke whose singing voice brings him a Hollywood contract he really doesn't want but accepts due to the financial plight of his cattle ranch. Gene doesn't realize he's been duped by two Paragon Pictures talent scouts, Sue Warner (Lynne Roberts) and Nellie Bly (Sterling Holloway) who only want his voice for a cartoon character, Ding Dong Donkey.

Embarrassed and ridiculed when he learns of the deception, Gene heads back to his ranch, followed by Sue who is now ashamed of what she's done and wants only to make amends to the cowboy with whom she's fallen in love.

Republic Pictures president Herbert J. Yates strikes a post WWII pose with his three biggest cowboy stars — Gene Autry, Roy Rogers and Bill Elliott.

The finale finds everyone back in Hollywood following the thwarting of a plot to wipe out Gene's cattle herd by disgruntled ex-Autry cowhand Big Gulliver (Ralph Sanford).

NOTES AND COMMENTS: The "Ding Dong Donkey" cartoon work in "Sioux City Sue" was done by the Walter Lantz studio, creators of Woody Woodpecker and other cartoon characters.

Sterling Holloway was paid $1,000 a week for his role as comic relief in Gene's post-war westerns.

FILM COMMENTS: *Gene Autry:* "I had a notion about going into business for myself, setting up my own film company. My contract with the studio had expired while I was in the service, and I really didn't think Herb Yates would try to hold me to it.

"When Republic tried to claim my contract was still in force, that it had been merely in limbo during my time in the military, I did the only thing I could. I filed a lawsuit to win my release.

"The bare bones of the case were these: under California law—the Shirley Temple Law, they called it—no contract could run longer than seven years. I had signed mine in 1938, after my wildcat strike, and it had run out in 1945 while I was still in uniform. As far as I know, Olivia deHavilland had been the first to bring suit against that law, at Warner Bros. She had won the case and so I hired her lawyer.

"Our position was a simple one. No contract was valid longer than seven years, and when I went into the Air Corps I could not perform through no fault of my own, and the studio had not been required to pay me for those years so they had no services due them.

"As it turned out, a decision I had made right after my enlistment helped our case. Yates had worked out a deal with the War Department to make me available for a limited number of pictures, with the studio donating a sum equal to my salary to Armed Forces Relief. I turned it down. The money and the exposure would have been helpful and the cause was worthy, but (James) Stewart and (Clark) Gable and (Tyrone) Power, and dozens of others, weren't making movies on the side. I didn't want any sweetheart deals.

"So we filed suit against Republic to have the contract nullified. It was to be a landmark case, with large implications for the entertainment industry. It was the first case after the war of an actor returning from military duty whose contract had expired while he was in the service.

"The trial was covered by the trade papers and in the daily press. Sympathy was strong in my favor. I had been away for three and a half years, at what would have been the peak of my earning powers. The studio had gone on raking in profits, while I was knocking down a cool $135 a month. The case was heard before Judge Louis Palmer, in Los Angeles district court, I was on the stand for a solid week. And we won.

"Republic appealed the verdict and vowed to take it to the Supreme Court. (They did, and the decision was upheld.) In the meantime, I knew the legal process would take a year or more, so I went to Yates and between us we struck a bargain. Almost a bet, actually. I agreed to make five more pictures at Republic, for a percentage of the profits. If they won the case, I would finish the contract on their terms. But if I won, then I was free to go and there would be no other attempts to hold me.

"So it was done. Almost a year had passed since my Air Force discharge had come through in September of 1945.

"In the fall of 1946 I went back to work on my first Republic picture since the war: 'Sioux City Sue'. While I was away, I had lost my sidekick. Smiley Burnette had emerged as a drawing card of his own. He became the first and only supporting actor, at least in westerns, to receive top billing over the star (Sunset Carson), and a credit line that read: 'A Smiley Burnette Production.'

"But gradually Republic began to have some apparent misgivings about Smiley as a headliner. By 1945 Smiley had left Republic and signed with Columbia to co-star in the Durango Kid series with Charles Starrett. So I was in the market for a partner.

"For the Republic films I settled on Sterling Holloway, who had appeared in non-westerns in the past. He had an ambling, loose-gaited look that I liked." [1]

Sterling Holloway: "I didn't care for my role as Autry's sidekick and I really didn't care for horses. Horses and I had a mutual agreement—they hated me and I hated them. I was glad when the Autry pictures were over and I could get back to roles for which I was more suited." [2]

Fred Martin of The Cass County Boys: "We practically lived with him. We saw Gene Autry more than we saw our families for a period of about 12 years. We played in just about every city over 25,000 in the U.S. and Canada. We also went to London with him for the big spectacular at Empress Hall that lasted a month. Played Madison Square Garden and Boston Gardens every year...rodeos all over, from Spokane to Boston and all the towns in between. We were on the road anywhere from seven to eight months out of the year every year for 12 years. We played to over seven million people in seven weeks going across Canada one time. We probably appeared before more people than anybody that's ever done a show because we had such big crowds. We played four shows a day in Boston Gardens, which seated 40,000-50,000 people." [3]

CAST BIOS: The Cass County Boys co-starred with Gene in 14 features and nearly as many of his half hour TV shows. As a unit the Cass County Boys started with accordionist/keyboard player Fred Martin (born June 22, 1916, in Linden, Texas) at WFAA radio in Dallas, Texas. Soon rhythm guitarist Jerry Scoggins (born September 30, 1911, in Mt.

Pleasant, Texas), then bull fiddle player Bert Dodson, born May 27, 1915, joined him.

But, long before that, as far back as 1927, the kid from Cass County, Texas, Fred Martin was playing accordion with the well known gospel group, The Stamps Quartet. "Neil Stamps in Dallas gave me a home and education," related Fred, "and I was traveling with his quartet." Soon Fred had his own program, three 15-minute shows on WFAA, eventually becoming "a working member of the WFAA inner sanctum."

Fred recalls, "I was doing a fill-in show on WFAA when old Jerry (Scoggins) pops in one night and says, 'Let me join you.' So I just said, 'The kid from Cass County's got another kid from Cass County. Cass County Kids.' Although Jerry wasn't from Cass County. His dad was a gospel singer and that's where Jerry got his start. I knew very well who he was; he was working around Dallas with a trio called The Bumblebees. We started singing duets. Jerry was the bass singer on the Kellogg program with me in 1936. We met with old Bert Dodson. Damned good bass player, who was with the Light Crust Doughboys working out of Fort Worth." [4] Bert joined to form a trio, first called The Early Birds then The Cass County Boys, in late '36. Oddly, just prior to joining Fred and Jerry, as a member of the Light Crust Doughboys, Bert had appeared as a member of that group with Gene in "Oh, Susanna!" ('36).

Jerry, writing in the musician's union magazine, OVERTURE, recalled, "The announcer dubbed us the 'Cass County Kids'. We became very popular around Dallas and later throughout Texas. Bert had a beautiful tenor voice and could soar up to a high 'A' like a nightingale. Bert was a

Gene and the Cass County Boys (L-R) Bert Dodson (w/ bass fiddle), Fred Martin, Jerry Scoggins.

great bass player and a fine musician."

"We had a repertoire of a thousand songs," Fred explained, "special arrangements. All of us contributed to the arranging. We were all good musicians." Besides being accomplished instrumentalists, Fred Martin sang lead, Jerry Scoggins a resonant bass and Bert Dodson a lyric high tenor.

"Gene was in the service, a flyer in the Air Force (at Love Field airbase). He's actually the one who got us out of Dallas." Fred explained. "NBC wanted us to come to New York…but just on spec. Gene made a firm offer. One we couldn't turn down. So he was responsible for us coming (to Hollywood)."[4]

On "Melody Ranch Theater" in 1987 Gene said, "When I was in the Air Force I was based at Love Field for quite awhile. I got acquainted with the Cass County Boys, they were singing down there on WFAA. They were very popular in Texas. When I came back and was making pictures at Republic I called the Cass County Boys and had them to come out. They appeared on my 'Melody Ranch' radio program and in my pictures too."[5]

The boys began recording for Bluebird in the early '40s. Gene heard the trio while playing a USO hospital engagement, but just as the boys were about to sign with Gene, Bert went into the Marine Corps. Fred and Jerry were also in the service. When all were civilians again, Gene sent for the Cass County Boys who immediately joined the "Melody Ranch" radio program when it returned to the air in the fall of 1945 and began to appear in Gene's post-war Republic features and tour with Gene's road show.

In describing Gene's musical abilities, Jerry Scoggins said, "Gene had good rhythm. He wouldn't get lost when you played for him to sing. He makes you think he's singing the song right from the heart and I think he is. When he sings a love song, he's in love. It's a very sincere type of singing, which goes over with the public. Gene didn't read music, but sing it over twice, write the words down on a piece of paper and he'll do it."[6]

Unfortunately, the Cass County Boys were never well represented on record. They cut a fine group for McGregor Transcriptions, unavailable to most record buyers, and recorded for Decca and ARA but, as Fred laments, "We were never in a position to get the promotion. We made the first record, for Decca, of 'Roomful of Roses' that was recorded. Bing Crosby heard it and said he wanted to do it. Everybody got a record released (on that song) before (we did) and we were the first ones to do it. There was a running gag…every new company that started out here wanted to do an album with us. They all went broke before they released our records. (Laughs)"[4]

Besides Gene, over time, The Cass County Boys worked with singers Bing Crosby, Dick Haymes and spent a year in the mid '50s on Doye O'Dell's Los Angeles TV show. They also cut several records on Era with O'Dell. Besides working in films and on TV with Gene, the boys sang in four Charles Starrett/Durango Kid B-westerns at Columbia between 1947 and 1951 as well as appearing in "Holiday Rhythm" ('50) at Lippert and "Tucson" ('49) at 20th Century–Fox.

But primarily, as Fred Martin explained, "We spent all our time traveling. The only steady work we ever had were the years we worked in the main ballroom of the Beverly Hills Hotel for five years. Then there was a club called Rogers Ranch Club in Palm Springs, and The Last Frontier had us headlining a show in Vegas for years. It finally got to the point where we didn't want to work in Vegas, we didn't want to work in Palm Springs or the Beverly Hills Hotel— the man who worked there sold it to other interests and they closed down the room where we worked. I did music in the Biltmore downtown for a couple of years. Had a dance band down there. But it got to the point where we had lost all of our local contacts, because we were on the road all the time with Autry from '45 through '56. So we really had nothing to go back to. Having other talents, we decided just to get off the road."[4]

Fred went into business administration, Bert was in the insurance business while Jerry, though he became a stockbroker, kept a hand in music and sang the theme for the "Beverly Hillbillies" TV show, "The Ballad of Jed Clampett". The theme song was a big hit in '63. The Cass County Boys were inducted into the Western Music Hall of Fame in 1996 and received Golden Boot Awards in 1985.

Bert Dodson, 79, died October 3, 1994, in Clearwater, Florida. Jerry Scoggins, 93, died December 7, 2004, in Los Angeles.

Since 1937 Lynne Roberts (aka Mary Hart) had been making westerns with Roy Rogers, the Three Mesquiteers, George Montgomery, and the Cisco Kid before making "Sioux City Sue", her first of four with Gene.

Born in El Paso, Texas, November 22, 1919, her family came to Los Angeles when she was only nine days old. Her father was a successful sales executive who moved to California for his health. His illness drained the family finances, which is why Lynne and her two-year older brother, John, began appearing as a dance team when Lynne was only 5. The act lasted 11 years.

Meanwhile, Lynne was enrolled in Lawlor's Professional School and began to study dancing and dramatics. By the time she was seven and eight she appeared in school plays, on the stage and on radio.

She came to films at 18 in Republic's "Dangerous Holiday" in 1937. Republic then signed her to a contract on January 1, 1938, which lasted until June 1939.

Republic changed her name to Mary Hart when she made six westerns with Roy Rogers, trading on the idea of a "Rogers & Hart" team.

Moving over to 20th Century–Fox in 1940, she made a variety of films.

Republic re-signed Lynne from September 1944 to March 1948. She was Gene's leading lady in three of his five post-war Republics and was also in "The Blazing Sun" ('50) at Columbia.

Lynne retired in 1953 when she married her third

Sterling Holloway, Sheriff George M. Carleton, Gene, Lynne Roberts and Paragon Pictures exec Richard Lane in a dramatic moment from "Sioux City Sue."

husband, a brassiere manufacturer. However, that marriage also ended in divorce in 1961.

Lynne died April 1, 1978, in Sherman Oaks, California.

Sterling Holloway's physical appearance with a shock of bushy reddish-blond hair, along with his near-falsetto voice relegated him almost exclusively to comedic roles, including Gene Autry's five post-WWII westerns. However, Holloway's world wide familiarity primarily stems from his voice work on numerous Walt Disney animated films, especially Winnie the Pooh.

Born Sterling Price Holloway January 4, 1905, in the deep south of Cedartown, Georgia, he took up acting at a young age, playing comic juveniles on the stage. He was only 15 when he enrolled in the American Academy of Dramatic Arts in New York.

While a student at Georgia Military Academy he produced and acted in "The Merchant of Venice". He also played the death scene in "The Little Shepherd of the Hills" on the Chautauqua Circuit.

Graduating from the Academy, Sterling was signed in late 1923 by the Theatre Guild to play in "The Failures" on Broadway. This was followed by another play and then the popular "Garrick Gaieties" revue which ran for a year in 1925-'26. He was hailed by critics and public alike, so much so he returned for a revival of the musical revue in 1930.

Meantime, he'd made his silent movie debut in 1926. His unusual voice made him perfect for the transition to sound, playing, as usual, comedic roles, until director Lewis Milestone cast him against type in 1945 for the classic war film "A Walk in the Sun".

Following his five appearances with Gene he worked frequently on television, becoming familiar in recurring roles on "Superman", "Rin Tin Tin", "Circus Boy" and "The Life of Riley". Holloway continued to work sporadically into the early '80s.

The popular character actor died of cardiac arrest November 22, 1992.

WHAT THE EXHIBITOR HAD TO SAY: "This is the first time a good western has failed to do business. It is going very sour here in the Midwest. I think it is due to the fact that between rains the farmers are working in 24 hour shifts. It is late spring and the corn should have been in the ground a month ago, but it is still in the sacks. There is an air of pessimism that is not good. The old man climbs down about sunset and the son takes over. Wouldn't labor squawk if they had to do that. The good earth is still king pin in our economics."
—A. E. Hancock, Columbia Theater, Columbia City, Indiana (June 1947)

"Drew an above average crowd, and most of the fans seemed pleased. Makes good double bill material. One or two silly incidents spoil what was otherwise an above average musical western."
—Fred J. Hutchings, Community Theater, Leader, Saskatchewan, Canada (July 1947)

"Republic did Gene bad! This is the poorest Autry ever to show on our screen. Business good but this picture won't add to Gene's prestige in Cornell. Doubled with 'Beat the Band'."
—C. M. Hulbert, Gem Theater, Cornell, Wisconsin (August 1947)

"Love that Gene. Played Thursday-Saturday."
—George Kelloff, Ute Theater, Aguilar, Colorado (April 1949)

SOURCES:

1. Autry with Herskowitz. p. 94-97.

2. Author's audio tape of 1988 Knoxville, Tennes-see, Western Film Festival panel discussion.

3. *Western Clippings #27.* January/February 1999. p. 5.

4. Interview with author, 1995.

5. "Melody Ranch Theater" showing of "Sioux City Sue" on Nashville Network, 1987.

6. "Melody of the West". American Movie Classics. October 1994.

Trail to San Antone
Republic, January 1947

Producer ....Armand Schaefer
Director ....John English
Assistant Director........................Don Verk
Screenplay...................................Jack Natteford, Luci Ward
Photography ....William Bradford
Musical Director ....Morton Scott
Musical Score..............................Joseph Dubin
Film Editor ....Charles Craft
Sound ....Fred Stahl
Art Director................................Gano Chittenden
Costume Supervision ....Adele Palmer
Set Decorations ....John McCarthy, Earl Wooden
Special Effects.............................Howard and Theodore Lydecker
Makeup Supervision ....Bob Mark

SONGS: "(Down the) Trail to San Antone" (music and lyrics by Deuce Spriggins)—sung by Gene Autry, the Cass County Boys; "The Cowboy Blues" (music and lyrics by Gene Autry, Cindy Walker)—sung by the Cass County Boys; "Shame On You" (music and lyrics by Spade Cooley)—sung by Gene Autry, the Cass County Boys); "That's My Home" (music and lyrics by Sid Robin)—sung by Gene Autry, the Cass County Boys; "By the River of the Roses" (music and lyrics by Marty Symes, Joe Burke)—sung by Gene Autry; "The Cowboy" (Public Domain)—sung by the Cass County Boys.

RUNNING TIME: 67 minutes
FILMING DATES: August 1-20, 1946
LOCATIONS: Lone Pine; Kentucky Park Farm; Republic backlot; Totems at Monument Valley
BUDGET: $180,002
NEGATIVE COST: $204,353

CAST:

Actor	*Character*
Gene Autry ....Gene Autry
Peggy Stewart ....Kit Barlow
Sterling Holloway ....Droopy Stearns
William Henry.............................Rick Malloy
Johnny Duncan............................Ted Malloy
Tristram Coffin............................Cal Young
Dorothy Vaughan ....The Commodore
Ralph Peters ....Sam
The Cass County Boys: Jerry Scoggins (guitar), Fred Martin (accordion), Bert Dodson (bass) .Singing Ranch hands
Edward Keane ....Sheriff Jones
Frankie Marvin...........................Cowhand
Nick Stewart...............................Sandy
George Bell ....Stable visitor
Bobby Clark ....Ranch hand
Champion Jr. ....Champion, Wonder Horse of the West

STUNTS: Joe Yrigoyen (Gene's double); David Sharpe, Tom Steele, John Daheim.

THE FILM: Appearing more to be Gene Autry's first post-WWII western than "Sioux City Sue", the cowboy is welcomed home from the war by his salty housekeeper, The Commodore (Dorothy Vaughan), and three cowhand pals (The Cass County Boys) who have bought Gene a race horse as a surprise homecoming gift. Soon, everyone is made aware the horse has been stolen from neighboring rancher Kit Barlow (Peggy Stewart). Tracking down the horse thieves, Gene finds a horse trainer, Rick Malloy (William Henry), his crippled ex-jockey brother Ted (Johnny Duncan) and their eccentric pal Droopy (Sterling Holloway). Ted's career has been cut short by injuries suffered in an "accident" caused by the trickery of unscrupulous horse-trainer Cal Young (Tris Coffin).

It's up to Gene to re-establish Ted's confidence in his ability to ride in a horse race again and thwart Young's plans to sabotage the upcoming Queen's Derby which Kit needs to win in order to pay off her debts.

Spectacular horse action filmed by regular Autry cameraman William Bradford highlights the picture amidst gorgeous Lone Pine locations.

Among the thrilling stunts, Gene lassoes a runaway horse from an airplane and leaps Champion over a car with two people in it as he chases another horse.

Cass County Boys (Fred, Jerry, Bert) get introduced by Gene to pretty Peggy Stewart.

NOTES AND COMMENTS: Working title for the film was "Sergeant Gene Autry".

Stock footage of Yakima Canutt wildly holding on to a horse's head was taken from Yak's "Devil Horse" silent.

Republic added a new innovation in this Gene Autry feature by having the title's words separately flash on screen once title credits began. Only two other Republic B-westerns besides "Trail to San Antone" had the flashing word technique, Roy Rogers' "Don't Fence Me In" ('45) and "The Gay Ranchero" ('48).

Sterling Holloway was once again paid $1,000 for his role while Dorothy Vaughan earned $600 a week as did Ralph Peters. Edward Keane was at $500 a week. Stuntman David Sharpe (noticeable as Bill Henry's fight double) made $200 a week.

The airplane used was from Aeronca Aircraft Corporation of Middletown, Ohio.

After completing "Trail to San Antone", Gene appeared at the 21st annual World's Championship Rodeo in Madison Square Garden September 25-October 27.

FILM COMMENTS: *Peggy Stewart:* "Gene was fun; he had a wonderful sense of humor. It was subtle…not dry…just subtle. It popped out when you least expected it and you always did a double take. But he *was* a businessman. I have a photo of the whole camera crew sitting on the back of the camera car. (Stuntman) Joe Yrigoyen and I are sitting down on the bumper…Bill Bradford, the cameraman, is there…we're all waiting for them to water down that road up at Lone Pine so Joe (doubling Gene) can make that jump on Champion over the car. In the picture, you can see Gene very clearly, and very clearly you can see what he's reading is THE WALL STREET JOURNAL. (Laughs)

"Always…businessmen from New York found him and came way up to Lone Pine to talk. He was forever doing business, but he always had time for a sassy joke or something, especially while we were waiting for the lighting to be finished and we're just standing there and talking.

"Gene was like working with a computer. He knew his lines always, but when they'd say cut, he was talking to Harry, Joe, Tom and Clyde…telling them what stock to buy. (Laughs)

"On that car jump stunt, (Stuntman) Joe Yrigoyen) got it perfect the first time. (Chuckles) He had to or the horse would have broken his leg.

"And playing that piano in one scene (Laughs), I had two left hands faking that. The cameraman stayed back from my hands! (Laughs)" [1]

Gene Autry: "Everyone that ever worked with Peggy Stewart liked her. She was a very good lookin' girl and a nice person. She was married (at one time) to Don 'Red' Barry and he made quite a few pictures. He made the 'Red Ryder' (serial). Peggy was fun to work with, always knew her lines and looked good on a horse. Not every girl rides a horse, but she really looked good in the saddle.

"That stallion (in the picture) was called Zane, he was named after (writer) Zane Grey. Tracy Layne had a lot to do with that horse. We used all of Hudkins' (stables) horses in those days and Tracy Layne worked over there at that stable."[2]

CAST BIOS: Tris Coffin had minor roles in several earlier Autry films, but not until "Trail to San Antone" did he get a juicy part as a nasty lead heavy.

Suave and dapper, with wavy, graying hair, Tristram Coffin was one of the best dressed and handsomest heavies to work in westerns. In a Hollywood career spanning 38 years, Coffin's work ran the gamut of all film genres—he even got to be the hero in Republic's "King of the Rocket Men" serial ('49) and TV's "26 Men" ('57-'59), a series which co-starred Kelo Henderson who remembers Tris as "an accomplished veteran actor who knew his theatrical trade and portrayed his role as Ranger Captain with authority."[3]

Tristram Chalkley Coffin was born in the silver mining town of Mammoth, Utah, August 13, 1909. Tris' father was superintendent of Mammoth Mines, one of the largest silver mines in the world. Tris grew up and received his education in the Salt Lake City schools where he started acting in school plays.

After attending the University of Utah, studying medicine, he gave that up to attend, and graduate from, the University of Washington with a major in speech.

Tris had four seasons of stock in Seattle and Portland after which he entered radio. After teaching for two years at the Leland Powers School of Dramatics in Boston, Massachusetts, Tris became chief staff announcer at radio stations in Boston. In the mid-'30s in New York, Tris worked on "March of Time" and "Gangbusters" radio programs. While in radio, an RKO Hollywood scout heard him and that, coupled with his good looks, caused the scout to urge Coffin towards Hollywood.

From the beginning, Coffin worked in Monogram westerns and by the early '40s he was working at Columbia and Republic menacing Bill Elliott/Tex Ritter, Gene Autry, Roy Rogers and Russell Hayden.

Following Navy service from late '42 to early '46, Tris could be seen in 10-13 films per year from '46-'51, mostly westerns.

Describing how he became cast as a badman, Tris said, "I asked for it. I pleaded for it, and fought for it. I was doing leading man and romance roles but I loved westerns. I talked to Scotty Dunlap, who was producing westerns at Monogram, and asked him if I could do some heavies. He said, 'Tris, you're too dignified. You're strictly a leading man and romance type. You can't work in westerns as a heavy.' I said, 'Scotty, have you ever gone to a state penitentiary and looked at some of the inmates? There are lawyers, doctors, and motion picture producers; they're not all mugs.' So he said, 'Well, maybe you've got a point. I've got a script with a heavy that can be played smooth.' So he gave me the part and that was my start playing heavies and I've always loved doing them." [4]

Tris continued to work on TV and in films, mostly character parts, until 1971.

At 80, Tris died of cardiac arrest and lung cancer March 26, 1990, in Santa Monica.

Born Peggy O'Rorke in West Palm Beach, Florida, in 1923, Peggy Stewart's parents divorced when she was quite young. Her mother remarried an attorney named Stewart and Peg adopted his name.

Along with her mother and sister, Pat, the family moved to California when Peg was 12. Enamored with movies since she was a child, Peg later enrolled in the Neely Dickson Dramatic School. Living in the same apartment house was actor Henry O'Neill who took a fancy to Peg, which is easy to do, and he obtained the first film role for Peg in "Wells Fargo" ('37) as Joel McCrea's daughter.

Other film roles and a contract at Republic Pictures in 1944 followed where she co-starred with Bill Elliott, Allan Lane, Sunset Carson and others.

She married actor Don Barry in 1940 but they divorced in 1944 after having one son, Michael.

Changes at Republic saw Peggy leaving the studio in March of '47 with one of her last pictures there being Gene's "Trail to San Antone".

Freelancing, Peggy tried to get away from westerns but found herself typecast and unable to find work in other genres.

In 1953 Peggy married actor Buck Young and left the

A tense moment from "Trail to San Antone" with (L-R) Sterling Holloway (leaning against post), Johnny Duncan (mounted), Gene, Bill Henry, Peggy Stewart, Tris Coffin.

business to raise a family, two children. Keeping her hand in the business through the L.A. Theatrical community, she eventually returned to film and TV work as a character actress in the '60s.

Young died in 2000 and in 2005 Peggy retired to the Santa Clarita, California, area.

WHAT THE EXHIBITOR HAD TO SAY: "This is one of the best pictures Gene Autry ever made. Sterling Holloway keeps them laughing and the Cass County Boys furnished some good string music. Comments were good."
—L. Brazil Jr., New Theater, Bearden, Arkansas (May 1947)

"This Autry feature was a decided improvement over the reissues with this star. The production was above average and drew appreciative comments. If other productions maintain this standard they will be well worth playing."
—Fred J. Hutchings, Community Theater, Leader, Saskatchewan, Canada (May 1947)

"Doubtless due to the many Autry reissues, Gene's drawing power at the box office has been badly affected and when this happens in a theater where they prefer westerns to any other kind of product, it's time to beware. In spite of the fact we advertised it as a new Autry, it did one of the worst grosses in the past year."
—Abe H. Kaufman, Fountain Theater, Terre Haute, Indiana (November 1947)

"Used on weekend double bill. Not up to the standard set by 'Sioux City Sue'." —A. C. Edwards, Winema Theater, Scotia, California (December 1947)

"Another fair Autry. The kids go for this. We doubled this with 'Canon City' and this was a wonderful show."
—Ralph Raspa, State Theater, Rivesville, West Virginia (June 1949)

SOURCES:
1. Interview with author in mid '80s.
2. "Melody Ranch Theater: showing of "Trail to San Antone" on Nashville Network, 1987.
3. Interview with author.
4. Interview with author in 1988.

Twilight On the Rio Grande
Republic, April 1947

Producer	Armand Schaefer
Director	Frank McDonald
Assistant Director	Lee Lukather
2nd Unit Director	Yakima Canutt
Screenplay	Dorrell and Stuart McGowan
Photography	William Bradford
Musical Director	Morton Scott
Film Editor	Harry Keller
Sound	Victor B. Appel
Art Director	Frank Hotaling
Set Decorations	John McCarthy Jr. and Helen Hansard
Special Effects	Roland Chiniquy
Makeup Supervision	Bob Mark
Unit Manager	Joe Dill

SONGS: "It's My Lazy Day" (music and lyrics by Smiley Burnette)—sung by the Cass County Boys; "The Pretty Knife Grinder" (music and lyrics by Jack Elliott)—sung by Adele Mara; reprised by Gene Autry; "I Tipped My Hat and Slowly Rode Away" (music and lyrics by Larry Marks, Dick Charles)—sung by Gene Autry, the Cass County Boys, Sterling Holloway; "Twilight On the Rio Grande" (music and lyrics by Jack Elliott)—sung by Gene Autry; "The Old Lamplighter" (music and lyrics by Nat Simon, Charles Tobias)—sung by Gene Autry; "Great Grand Dad" (Public Domain)—sung by Sterling Holloway, the Cass County Boys.

RUNNING TIME: 71 minutes
FILMING DATES: January 6-25, 1947
LOCATIONS: Republic backlot; Victorville area
BUDGET: $177,351
NEGATIVE COST: $202,315

CAST:

Actor	Character
Gene Autry	Gene Autry
Sterling Holloway	Pokie
Adele Mara	Elena Del Rio
Bob Steele	Dusty Morgan
Charles Evans	Henry Blackstone
Martin Garralaga	Mucho Pesos
Howard J. Negley	Jake Short
George J. Lewis	Capt. Gonzales
Nacho Galindo	Torres
Tex Terry	Joe
The Cass County Boys: Jerry Scoggins, Fred Martin, Bert Dodson	Fred, Jerry, Bert
Keith Richards	Hart
Robert J. Wilke	Moss
Tom London	Tom, Customs Agent
Kenne Duncan	Lew Evers, Customs Agent
Frank McCarroll	Ed
Enrique Acosta	Lamplighter
Donna Martell	1st Telephone Operator
Anna Camargo	2nd Telephone Operator
Nina Campana	Mama Lopez
Elena Delarosa	Flower Girl
Carmen Gonzalez, Conchita Lemus, Linda Lombard	Girls on Balcony
George Magrill	Customs Officer
Frankie Marvin	Storekeeper at wreck
Connie Menard	Flower Girl
Alex Montoya	Police Officer
Alberto Morin	Vargo
Bud Osborne	Cody
Jack O'Shea	Mike the Bartender
Steve Soldi	Ambulance Attendant
Victor Cox, Bobby Clark	Men at Funeral
LeRoy Mason	Truck Driver Voice-over
Joaquin Elizondo	Senorita's Father
Bob Burns, Barry Norton, Gil Perkins, Jams Harrison	Extras
Champion Jr.	Champion, Wonder Horse of the West

STUNTS: Joe Yrigoyen (Gene's double); Yakima Canutt, Gil Perkins, Duke Taylor, Cliff Lyons, Fred Graham, Tex Terry.

THE FILM: Touted as "Gene saddles up for Mexico in a gay fiesta of flying fists and sparkling tunes the way only Gene can sing 'em and swing 'em," Gene Autry's third post-war Republic feature was actually a rangeland whodunit with film noirish overtones. It's Gene's best post-war Republic entry.

Gene and sidekick Pokie (Sterling Holloway in his only *true* sidekick role with Gene) attend a fiesta in a Mexican border town to locate Gene's partner Dusty (Bob Steele), ever the ladies' man.

Hotel operator Jake Short (Howard J. Negley) and his crooked attorney partner Henry Blackstone (Charles Evans) are running a smuggling operation. They intend to secretly plant refugees' jewelry on Dusty to take illegally across the border.

When Dusty fails to show up to meet Gene and the boys the next morning, Gene is faced with solving his murder and clearing his name of a smuggling charge.

Gene soon becomes involved with beautiful Cantina singer Elena (Adele Mara), whose father has also been killed, and an odd Mexican woodcutter, Mucho (Martin Garralaga), who always seems to know what is going on.

Following a mysterious path of smuggling and espionage, Gene eventually clears his partner's name and avenges his murder.

With these five post-war Republics, Gene was only biding his time until he could have his own production set-up for release through Columbia.

NOTES AND COMMENTS: Watch for the scene in which Gene turns lovely Adele Mara over his knee and spanks her after she's been throwing knives at Gene during her nightclub act.

Watch also for the scene in which Champion Jr. dances as the Cass County Boys sing.

A miscue can be noted in a "flop shot" as Gene rides Champion Jr., on a soundstage shot. Also the horse's collar suddenly appears two different times in quick close-ups after not having been noticeable in previous exterior shots. These occur following a desert chase after Adele Mara and when Mexican law officers halt Gene.

It's not the Lone Ranger, but you'll hear a touch of Rossini's "William Tell Overture" being used as background music.

Legendary stuntman Yakima Canutt was 2nd unit director for this film. Enos Edward Canutt, born November 29, 1895, on a ranch in Washington state, gained early fame when he was just a teenager on the rodeo circuit, which is where he earned the nickname "Yak" (for Yakima, Washington). Yak's 60 years before and behind the camera set the standard for achievement for stuntmen, eventually earning him a special Academy Award in 1966.

Charles Evans earned $750 a week on the film while his partner in crime Howard J. Negley was paid $500 a week. Martin Garralaga made $600 a week. Former B-western star Bob Steele took home $500. Other weekly payments varied widely: Donna Martell—$250; Ana Carmargo—$400; Nina Campana—$500; Kenne Duncan—$350; Nacho Galindo—$350; George J. Lewis—$500; Frankie Marvin—$115; Frank McCarroll—$200; Alberto Morin—$400; Bud Osborne—$250; Jack O'Shea—$250; Keith Richards—$400; Bob Wilke—$250; Tex Terry—$175.

Noted film historian Les Adams has pointed out the basic plot of "Twilight…" is yet another version of one of Republic's most-used plot devices, one which was used in "Guns In the Dark" ('37), "Rough Riders Round-Up" ('39), "The Leathernecks Have Landed" ('36) and "Remember Pearl Harbor" ('42). Revisions were made here to fit the

Gene's being accused of smuggling in this exciting moment from "Twilight on the Rio Grande." (L-R) Bert Dodson, Sterling Holloway, Jerry Scoggins, Gene (being restrained by an unknown customs agent), George J. Lewis, Charles Evans, Frank McCarroll, Tex Terry.

There's some business about knives being discussed by Gene and cantina singer Adele Mara. (Note the photo on the wall above Mara's head is of Republic star Allan Lane.

Autry mold.

Another noted film historian, Richard Smith III, pointed out the photos of Republic stars Allan Lane and Roy Barcroft on Adele Mara's dressing room wall as Gene enters the room.

On January 23, 1947, just before filming was completed on this title, the original Champion, whom Autry had ridden in all of his pictures through July 1942, died at Melody Ranch. He lived to be 17. It should be noted some sources state Champion died in early December 1946.

FILM COMMENTS: *Adele Mara:* "Gene was very sweet to me. I wasn't very fond of liquor. He would say, 'You're going to have to go places and you're going to have to drink. The thing to do is to have Scotch, tall, water. That's the best thing for you. Don't have soda. That'll last a long, long time.' He would talk to me like that all the time."

Adele at least got to demonstrate her dance expertise in a couple of Republic titles, including "Twilight On the Rio Grande", becoming her own choreographer. "Republic never paid for somebody to come in. I had to figure these things out. They'd say, 'this is the music we're going to use and this is what…' they were so cheap. I never questioned it. I just went and did it." [1]

Gene Autry: Regarding the scene in which Gene jumps Champion onto the back of a truck, Gene explained, "Champion was trained to jump up on a piano and stay there while I would sing. So when it came to this part, I was doing a chase and we did have to put a rubber matting down on the truck for him to jump on. But actually, that was a process shot. It showed a rear camera screen (that made the) truck (look like it was) driving really fast. Then I came into the scene and jumped Champ right up into the

bed of the truck, then they cut and picked us up doing the chase with the horse in the back of it." [2]

CAST BIOS: Adele Mara got her big break with bandleader Xavier Cugat and went on to great fame in Columbia and Republic films. She's adamantly "all Spanish", not half Irish as has often been written. Born Adelaida Delgado April 28, (1923?) in Highland Park, Michigan, Adele Mara (pronounced as in Theda *Bara*) "started dancing when I was eight years old. I started with tap. I loved doing it. Then I took adagio. Eventually, I got into ballet and Spanish at dancing school." [3]

Spotted at twelve or thirteen by Cugat when he was trying to get another act, the noted bandleader took her under his wing.

Upon graduation, trying her luck as a dancer in New York, she again ran into Cugat at the Paramount Theater, "He and his wife were my guardians. When he opened at the Waldorf Astoria Hotel at the Starlight Roof, I was there." [4]

Up until that time Adele had worked under her real name. Cugat shortened her first name, put three last names in a hat and out came Mara. Adele's work with Cugat led to a film contract at Columbia, then Republic from 1944 to 1951.

The advent of television brought an end to many players' term contracts and Adele's was one of them. Then married to TV scripter/producer Roy Huggins, she did some TV work but basically retired.

At 87, Huggins died of cancer in April 2002. Mara now lives in Pacific Palisades, California.

WHAT THE EXHIBITOR HAD TO SAY: "Something is the matter with the latest Autrys. His pictures haven't been as good since he came out of the Army, and business is falling off."
—Leroy Standberg, Roxy Theater,
Hinckley, Minnesota (October 1947)

"A very good action-packed western, with Gene at his best."
—James Balkcom Jr., Gray Theater,
Gray, Georgia (January 1948)

"This was very much below the Autry standard. Used on double bill with 'Moss Rose'. Business good."
—A. C. Edwards, Winoma Theater,
Scotia, California (January 1948)

SOURCES:

1. *Ladies of the Western.* McFarland, 2002. p. 153, 155.
2. "Melody Ranch Theater" showing of "Twilight On the Rio Grande" on Nashville Network, 1987.
3. *Ladies of the Western.* McFarland, 2002. p. 149.
4. *Ladies of the Western.* McFarland, 2002. p. 151.

Saddle Pals
Republic, June 1947

Producer ....Sidney Picker
Director ....Lesley Selander
Assistant Director........................Lee Lukather
Original Story..............................Dorrell and Stuart
                              McGowan
Screenplay..................................Bob Williams, Jerry
                              Sackheim
Photography ....Bud Thackery
Musical Director ....Morton Scott
Film Editor.................................Harry Keller

Sound ....Earl Crain Sr.
Art Director................................Fred Ritter
Costume Supervision ....Adele Palmer
Set Decorations ....John McCarthy Jr.,
                              Helen Hansard
Special Effects............................Howard and Theodore
                              Lydecker
Makeup Supervision ....Bob Mark
Unit Manager ....Joe Dill
Dialogue Coach...........................Andrew McLaglen

SONGS: "You Stole My Heart" (music and lyrics by Stanley Adams, Harry Susnik)—sung by Gene Autry; "Which Way'd They Go" (music and lyrics by Ray Allen, Perry Botkin)—sung by the Cass County Boys; "The Covered Wagon Rolled Right Along" (music and lyrics by Britt Wood, Hy Heath)—sung by the Cass County Boys; "Amapola" (music and lyrics by Albert Gamse, Joseph M. LaCalle)—sung by Gene Autry; "I Wish I Had Never Met Sunshine" (music and lyrics by Gene Autry, Dale Evans, Oakley Haldeman)—sung by Gene Autry.

RUNNING TIME: 72 minutes
FILMING DATES: February 28 to March 21, 1947
LOCATIONS: Lake Malibu; Republic backlot; Valsteve Ranch; Conejo Valley possibly including Russell Ranch
BUDGET: $175,032
NEGATIVE COST: $182,240

CAST:

Actor	Character
Gene Autry	Gene Autry
Lynne Roberts	Shelly Brooks
Sterling Holloway	Waldo T. Brooks Jr.
Irving Bacon	Thaddeus Bellweather
Damian O'Flynn	Brad Collins
Charles Arnt	William Schooler
Jean Van	Robin Brooks
Tom London	Dad Gardner
Charles Williams	Leslie
Francis McDonald	Sheriff
George Chandler	Dippy
Edward Gargan	Jailer
The Cass County Boys: Bert Dodson, Fred Martin, Jerry Scoggins	Bert, Fred, Jerry
Sam Ash, James Carlisle	Board Members
Bob Burns	Rancher
Paul E. Burns	Mike, Mailman
Larry Steers	1st Doctor
Edward Keane	2nd Doctor
Maurice Cass	3rd Doctor
Nolan Leary	4th Doctor
Joel Friedkin	Stimpson
Frank O'Connor	1st Buyer
Frank Henry	2nd Buyer
Ed Peil Sr.	3rd Buyer
LeRoy Mason	Cop
John S. Roberts	Messenger
Minerva Urecal	Cora Downey
Carl Sepulveda	Rancher
Frankie Marvin, Neal Hart, Kansas Moehring, Chick Hannon, Bobby Clark	Extras
Champion Jr.	Champion, Wonder Horse of the West

STUNTS: Joe Yrigoyen (Gene's double); Dave Sharpe, John Daheim, Bill Yrigoyen.

THE FILM: This virtual remake of Republic's Weaver Brothers and Elviry film "In Old Missouri" ('40) was better suited to their rural comedic style and never should have been adapted as a Gene Autry picture. As it is, it's the worst of Gene's post-war Republics with way too much silliness from nervous hypochondriac Sterling Holloway and too little western adventure.

Situation comedy plot has land corporation board members Collins (Damian O'Flynn) and Schooler (Charles Arnt) sneaking ranchers rent increases through while the goofy corporation owner, Waldo T. Brooks (Sterling Holloway) frets desperately over his health and takes off to go fishing, hastily deeding his corporation to Gene.

With power of attorney, Gene finds the corporation is in financial array leaving him to raise $50,000 as his share or everything will be lost. He realizes part of it by selling the ranch's show horses over the objections of Waldo's sister, Shelly (Lynne Roberts), then plans to raise the balance by staging a rodeo, but hi-jinks by Collins and Schooler get in his way.

Eventually, the bad guys are tricked into confessing onto a dictograph.

Youngster Jean Van had audience appeal, and if Gene had stayed with Republic she might have fit into the 'Mary Lee' mold. Lynne Roberts makes the most of a thankless role here in a script that offers more horseplay to Sterling Holloway, Irving Bacon and Charles Williams than it does horsemanship to Gene.

NOTES AND COMMENTS: Interesting to note that Gene and/or Republic employed Gene's brother, Dudley Autry, to handle men's wardrobe on this (and a few other) pictures.

Top weekly salary went to Irving Bacon at $1,000. Baddies Charles Arnt and Damian O'Flynn received $850 and $750 respectively. Minor player Paul E. Burns was also at $750 a week as was jailer Edward Gargan. Sheriff Francis McDonald got $500 a week.

FILM COMMENTS: *Jean Van:* "Unlike the feelings some actors have about working with children, I *never* got the slightest indication from Gene Autry that he felt anything but respect for me. Today I would look back and think of Gene Autry as a kind-hearted, sensitive individual. I would take him as a very, very good friend. And I would be a good friend to him, as an adult, looking back. He was helpful. He was just a very kind man."

In talking about the sequence in the film where she's in a runaway wagon which ultimately runs off a ridge into some water before Gene rescues her, Van said, "Some of it was done in the studio with the film in the background. I remember the director telling me beforehand, 'Jean, you're scared, you're very, very scared.' I do remember that water scene. I didn't know how to swim! Therefore it was very scary for me as a child. There was no double for me in that sequence, as I recall, because it was shot too close up.

"I had to learn to ride western for that movie. I recall taking lessons. There was a riding academy somewhere near Forest Lawn. That's where I went. I had only ridden

Jean Van and Gene Autry.

English before that. English riding is a different saddle. It doesn't have the horn. You use your legs a lot. The stance is you come up and you go down. You're using your legs, and it's a lot gentler. I wasn't a really good western rider, but I guess I did well enough. It was fun. It was a great horse, I remember that. A pinto."[1]

Dale Evans: "I first met Gene in the mid '30s at WHAS radio, Louisville, Kentucky. He was just as charming now as he was then. When I was on CBS radio in Chicago, a publicist with the publishing firm a friend of mine from Chicago…he and I decided we would sit down and try to write a crazy country song. 'I Wish I Had Never Met Sunshine'. We just tried to make it crazy as we could. We took it to Golden West and Gene said he would publish it with his firm if he could be one of the writers. That's a true story. He was greatly loved." [2]

WHAT THE EXHIBITOR HAD TO SAY: "This was another Autry picture that failed to click. Business off."
—A. C. Edwards, Winema Theater,
Scotia, California (January 1948)

SOURCES:
1. Interview with Ray Nielsen, August 2006.
2. *Western Clippings #27.* January/February 1999. p. 4.

Robin Hood of Texas
Republic, July 1947

Producer ....Sidney Picker
Director ....Lesley Selander
Assistant Director.......................Joe Dill
Screenplay.................................John K. Butler, Earle
                        Snell
Photography ....William Bradford
Musical Director ....Morton Scott
Orchestrations ....Nathan Scott
Film Editor.................................Harry Keller
Sound ....Fred Stahl
Art Director................................Paul Youngblood
Costume Supervision ....Adele Palmer
Set Decorations ....John McCarthy Jr.,
                        Charles Thompson
Special Effects............................Howard and Theodore
                        Lydecker
Makeup Supervision ....Bob Mark

SONGS: "Good Old Fashioned Hoedown" (music and lyrics by Gene Autry)—sung by Gene Autry and the Cass County Boys; "Goin' Back to Texas" (music and lyrics by Carson J. Robison)—sung by Gene Autry and the Cass County Boys; "Merry Go-Roundup" (music and lyrics by Gene Autry, Fred Rose, Johnny Marvin)—sung by the Cass County Boys; "You're the Moment of a Lifetime" (music and lyrics by Sergio DeKarlo, Ray Charles)—sung by Gene Autry and the Cass County Boys.

RUNNING TIME: 71 minutes

FILMING DATES: April 7-25, 1947

LOCATIONS: Iverson Ranch; Conejo Valley area possibly including Russell Ranch; Mammoth Lakes (stock footage); Republic backlot

BUDGET: $175,061

NEGATIVE COST: $174,716

CAST:

Actor	*Character*
Gene Autry	Gene Autry
Lynne Roberts	Virginia
Sterling Holloway	Droopy Haines
Adele Mara	Julie Reeves
James Cardwell	Duke Mantel

John Kellogg	Nick Castillo
Ray Walker	Detective Lieutenant Lacey
Michael Branden (aka Archie Twitchell)	Jim Prescott
Paul Bryar	Ace Foley
James Flavin	Capt. Danforth
Dorothy Vaughan	Mrs. O'Brien
Stanley Andrews	Mr. Hamby
Al Bridge	Sheriff
The Cass County Boys: Bert Dodson, Fred Martin, Jerry Scoggins	Bert, Fred, Jerry
William Norton Bailey	Chase car owner
Edmund Cobb	Deliveryman
Lester Dorr	News Photographer
Gil Perkins	Blinky Charleston, Hold-up Driver
Frankie Marvin	Guest #1
Eva Novak	Guest #2
Billy Wilkerson	Guest #3
Norma Brown	Guest #4
Opal Taylor	Guest #5
Irene Mack	Guest #6
Hank Patterson	Taxi Driver
LeRoy Mason	Voiceover
Champion Jr.	Champion, Wonder Horse of the West

STUNTS: Joe Yrigoyen (Gene's double); Ken Terrell, Duke Green, Marybelle Currie, Gil Perkins.

THE FILM: Gene Autry's last for Republic ended an association that started in 1935 and finished twelve years later, allowing for Gene's absence for WWII from 1942 to 1946.

Directed by Lesley Selander, western veteran of Hopalong Cassidy and other acclaimed westerns, "Robin Hood of Texas" moves quickly and features a strong cast including Adele Mara obviously relishing her "bad girl" role.

At one point, on the make for Gene, she even attempts

to kiss the cowboy, but he's having none of it. "Robin Hood" is a good Republic blend of modern gangsters and automobiles, a dude ranch, songs, western action and a typical Republic climax of Gene racing to cut the baddies off.

Flat broke and stranded in a small Texas town, Gene and the Cass County Boys are mistakenly arrested for complicity in a bank robbery when they were actually trying to capture the gangsters.

When a telegram arrives from the sister of Jerry Scoggins (of the Cass County Boys) that they have inherited a ranch, the police conclude the telegram is actually a coded message from the bank robbers they assume Gene and the Boys are working for. The holdup men and the loot still missing, the police release the fellows in hopes they will lead them to the rest of the gang.

Gene and the Boys meet Jerry's sister Virginia (Lynne Roberts) at the ranch and begin turning it into a dude ranch.

Meanwhile, one of the bank robbers, Duke Mantel (James Cardwell), double-crosses the rest of the gang and arrives at the dude ranch, figuring it a perfect hideout. Soon, he's followed by other members of the gang and the restful ranch becomes the scene of a hectic search for the bank loot with Gene getting unavoidably sucked deeper and deeper into the tense events.

Fred Martin, Gene, Lynne Roberts, detective Ray Walker and Jerry Scoggins gaze toward a burning barn in "Robin Hood of Texas."

All in all, Gene's last for Republic is a good mixture of sagebrush and gangsters, once again proving all westerns are not alike.

NOTES AND COMMENTS: Many stock riding shots in the spectacular climax of "Robin Hood of Texas" are taken from the climatic close in Gene's "Down Mexico Way".

James Flavin as the police captain pursuing Gene earned $1,000 a week for the film. In lesser roles, Stanley Andrews and Al Bridge were paid $750 while James Cardwell, John Kellogg, Dorothy Vaughan and Ray Walker all earned $600 apiece. Archie Twitchell (billed as Michael Branden) was at $100 less than his cohorts in crime with lesser gangster Paul Bryar at $400, as was news photographer Lester Dorr.

FILM COMMENTS: *Adele Mara:* "I loved westerns but I hated the horses. I loved to *see* horses, they're beautiful, but I was not a good rider. As a matter of fact, I was very, very bad. One of the things I had to do was ride English. They gave me lessons and I was doing fine, but when I went for the first day of shooting they gave me this enormous horse, huge in length and height. Just a *big* horse. My double said she was not going to ride that horse, it was a bad horse. They asked me to ride it. I said, 'Wait a minute, if *she* isn't going to ride it...' They said, 'Oh, she's just crazy. We're out here at the ranch and there's nothing we can do, we have to do this, don't worry about it, you've had enough lessons.' So I got on this stupid horse and he just roared out! Before I knew it, I was off the saddle and on his back, just hanging on to this thing. I was so scared! After that, I only rode into a scene and out of the scene and that was it. As little as possible.

"In this film I was a mean, nasty girl. (Laughs) I heard from a couple of the actresses that told me when they'd go up to see Yates, he would say, 'Look, you're a very good actress, but you got to get a little more sexy, like Adele.' One told me, 'If I heard your name one more time, I was going to kill you.' And I said, 'He did? He really did?' So he considered me very sexy. A lot of people did, but I didn't think of myself as sexy. All those things I used to do; I knew how bad those scripts were but it didn't bother me. I just thought, I'll try to do better than what they are. I did my very best and I loved doing it." [1]

Gene Autry: "By the time 'Robin Hood of Texas' had reached the movie houses, I had parted ways with Republic. The courts had upheld my suit and I was now free to make my own deals, and pick my own friends. We had offers from several studios." (Including Monogram who offered Gene $200,000 for four pictures per year plus a percentage of the profits after the films earned their negative costs. Two would be in color, two in black and white.) "But I wanted to form my own company, frankly, because of the tax angles. If you earned over $100,000 in those days, 85% of it was taxable. The only way to hang on to your money was to form a corporation. So I became the president and executive producer of Gene Autry Productions, and we signed a contract with Columbia to release our pictures. It was as good a deal as anyone in Hollywood had at that time. I had complete say over my films and I could take home half the profits." [2]

Gene told columnist Harrison Carroll, "It sort of makes things complete. I've been with Columbia Records since 1929; I went with Columbia Broadcasting System in 1939 and now I'm releasing through Columbia Pictures." [3]

WHAT THE EXHIBITOR HAD TO SAY: "Good old Gene. They still love him. He always satisfies his western fans."
—Harland Rankin, Beau Theater,
Belle River, Ontario, Canada (January 1949)

"As far as this point is concerned Autry is a dead duck. There has to be a strong second feature to draw the crowd. This has the same old tripe with the same rocky trail and trees passed a half dozen times in the same chase. These things are noticed, and not to advantage, either."
—Fred J. Hutchings, Community Theater,
Leader, Saskatchewan, Canada (February 1949)

"This was a little above the average Autry picture."
—Mrs. Denzil Hildebrand, Algerian Theater,
Risco, Missouri (April 1949)

SOURCES:
1. *Ladies of the Western.* McFarland, 2002. p. 155.
2. Autry with Herskowitz, p. 97.
3. *Los Angeles Evening Herald Express.* May 24, 1947.

The Last Round-Up
Columbia, November 1947
A Gene Autry Production

Producer ....Armand Schaefer
Director ....John English
Assistant Director.........................Earl Bellamy
Original Story..............................Jack Townley
Screenplay..................................Jack Townley, Earle
Snell
Photography ....William Bradford
Musical Supervisor ....Paul Mertz
Musical Director ....Mischa Bakaleinikoff
Film Editor.................................Aaron Stell
Sound Dept.................................Hugh McDowell Jr.
Art Director................................Harold MacArthur
Set Decorations ....Frank Tuttle

SONGS: "The Last Round-Up" (music and lyrics by Billy Hill)—sung by Gene Autry and studio singers; "She'll Be Comin' 'Round the Mountain" (Public Domain)—sung by Gene Autry and children; "You Can't See the Sun When You're Crying" (music and lyrics by Doris Fisher, Allan Roberts)—sung by Gene Autry and The Texas Rangers; "One Hundred and Sixty Acres" (music and lyrics by David Kapp)—sung by Gene Autry and The Texas Rangers; "An Apple For the Teacher" (music and lyrics by James V. Monoco, Johnny Burke)—sung by Gene Autry.

RUNNING TIME: 77 minutes
FILMING DATES: May 16 to June 7, 1947

LOCATIONS: Old Tucson, Arizona; Columbia Ranch; Corriganville
BUDGET: $89,559.36

CAST:

Actor	Character
Gene Autry	Gene Autry
Jean Heather	Carol Taylor
Ralph Morgan	Charlie Mason
Carol Thurston	Lydia Henry
Mark Daniels	Matt Mason
Bobby Blake	Mike
Russ Vincent	Jeff Henry
KCBS Texas Rangers: Robert "Captain Bob" Crawford, Edward "Tookie" Cronenbold, Francis "Irish" Mahaney, Roderick "Dave" May	Musicians
Roy Gordon	Homer Smith
John Halloran	Fred Taylor
Ted Adams	Harris
Jose Alvarado	Bobby Luther
Arline Archuletta	Helen Luther
Trevor Bardette	Indian Chief
Jack Baxley	Bill
Lee Bennett	Goss
George M. Carleton	Doctor
Virginia Carroll	Saleslady
John Cason	Carter
Steve Clark	Larry
Iron Eyes Cody, J. W. Cody, Art Dillard, Alex Montoya	Indians
Kernan Cripps, Frankie Marvin, Ed Peil Sr.	Ranchers
Lou Crosby	TV announcer Lou Crosby
Shug Fisher	Marvin
Jonathan Gilmore	Boy
Nolan Leary	Jake
Bud Osborne	Frank
Rodd Redwing	Louie
Frances Rey	Cora Luther

Don Kay Reynolds ....Indian Boy
Sandy Sanders ....Jim
Jay Silverheels ....Sam Luther
Blackie Whiteford ....Townsman
Billy Wilkerson ....Indian Herder
Champion ....Champion

STUNTS: Dale Van Sickel, Duke Taylor, Sandy Sanders.

THE FILM: "The Last Round-Up" is Gene Autry's first western produced by his own company, Gene Autry Productions, for release by Columbia Pictures—and it has everything a good actionful musical western should have.

Gene personally regarded it as his best—or favorite—picture, possibly because it was his own first production, or maybe because of the nature of the story with its social awareness of the Indian malnutrition plight and water rights. Certainly as a series B-western, it approaches A-feature trappings in length, production values and budget.

Gene not only brought over his favorite director of photography from Republic, William "Bill" Bradford, but top director John English gave up his producer-director spot at Republic in order to freelance and was contracted by Gene to handle directorial duties on "The Last Round-Up" as well as subsequent releases. His direction injects imaginative little bits of business into the film that add to its overall merit, such as the brief laugh-provoking baseball scene with Bobby Blake and "She'll Be Comin' 'Round the Mountain" sung by Gene and a classroom of Indian children, complete with gestures and one child who can't get them right.

Basic plot deals with the efforts of Autry to get the Indians to accept fertile new lands in exchange for the barren acreage through which a water aqueduct is to be built. Although the Indians realize their land will be useless when the aqueduct drains the river, they are reluctant to leave the land they and their forefathers have lived on for

Gene, young Bobby Blake, Jean Heather.

so long.

Local banker Mason (Ralph Morgan) and his son, Matt (Mark Daniels), are opposed to the deal for it will enable the ranchers, who will be paid a high price for their holdings, to pay off their mortgages and prevent the Masons from foreclosing on their property.

Between convincing the Indians (partly through the use of television), obtaining water rights from the ranchers and blocking the Mason's attempts to squelch the deal, Gene has his hands full.

Gene was off to an auspicious start at Columbia with a first rate, quality western that undoubtedly pleased his older fans as well as garnering new ones.

NOTES AND COMMENTS: Filming for "The Last Round-Up" was done at Old Tucson, a replica of the adobe city as it was back in 1860. Old Tucson was built in 1939 for the Columbia film "Arizona"('40). Earl Bellamy was an assistant director on that film as well as 1st assistant on "The Last Round-Up". Nearby Rattlesnake Pass, Sabino Canyon, Picture Rock and Mission San Xavier were also utilized.

Paul F. Devine, assistant to the superintendent of Los Angeles city schools, was hired to act as consultant on Indian School scenes in the picture.

1,200 head of cattle were rented for two days from nearby Tucson ranches for the stampede scenes.

One hundred Papago Indians took part in the film, coming from a reservation near Old Tucson.

Working title of "The Last Round-Up" was "Home on the Range" as stated on Gene's "Melody Ranch" radio program May 25, 1947.

Is it an inside joke? Gene, who is well known to have loved the sport of baseball, throws young Bobby Blake a ball and accidentally breaks a window.

Worldwide gross for "The Last Round-Up" up through September 1948 was $241,654.55.

FILM COMMENTS: *Gene Autry:* "My first picture (at Columbia) was 'The Last Round-Up'. That title wasn't exactly symbolic of a new beginning, but I wasn't looking for omens. I had returned from the war with a few very strong ideas of my own about making westerns. I thought the day was gone when a studio could take any fellow who wasn't tone deaf, give him a few songs in the public domain, slap a script together, and make money. I wanted to produce full-color westerns. All of them. And I told (my wife) Ina, songs would be more important than ever. But they had to be hit songs. Or original songs. But to my regret, 'The Last Round-Up' was shot in black and white. The demands on the new Technicolor Corporation had already plunged it a year behind schedule. There was another, more practical reason for using black and white. Columbia still had a lot of stock footage, desert chase scenes, and we could take advantage of that inventory by not using color. Anyway, the story line was so modern we showed TV sets in a couple of scenes. I was teamed again with (producer) Mandy Schaefer.[1]

"When I turned producer and signed with Columbia,

little did I know I was letting myself in for one continuous headache! Supervising production of a movie is more of a chore than roping an ornery broncho. So I decided I would be producer in name only. I would hitch up with a real producer to make my pictures. The producer was Armand (Mandy) Schaefer, a really smart hombre. Now, whenever anyone wants a job, offers a prop or anything, I just turn him over to Mandy who goes by the title of president of Gene Autry Productions. It's all worked out. I get to act. I get to strum the guitar. I get to ogle the lovely ladies. Mandy gets the headaches." [2]

Armand Schaefer: "I first met Gene here in Hollywood in 1933. I was the producer of Gene's first picture for Republic and produced the first 16 Autry pictures. We became very good friends, and, later, when he decided to go into business for himself, he made me a partner, and I became president of the company as well as executive in charge of all production.

"Mrs. (Ina) Autry is a very close friend of both Mrs. Schaefer and myself. We are extremely fond of her and think that she has been a great influence in Gene's success.

"Gene is exceptionally easy to get along with, has a wonderful sense of humor, and I don't think he has a nerve in his body.

"Gene is not my boss. We are partners. But, if he were, I am sure he would be a good boss. As I stated before, we are very good friends socially, play golf together, and so forth." [3]

Don Kay Reynolds: "Gene was pretty much all business. There was no foolin' around on the set, you just didn't do it. 'Course I was very young and wanted to play a bit, but that didn't work. (Chuckles) I got reprimanded by the director. (Chuckles) Gene was all business, he knew his lines and he expected everybody to know theirs. It was all like clockwork.

"Incidentally, the scene where I can't get the hand-signals right when we're all singing 'Comin' 'Round the Mountain' was in the script, it wasn't improvised. They brought me in to do that scene and from there I did 'Beyond the Purple Hills'." [4]

John English.

CAST BIOS: A Canadian who settled in Hollywood in the mid '30s, John English (1903-1969) was the co-director of some of the finest action serials ever made at Republic, titles like "Dick Tracy Returns" ('38), "The Lone Ranger" ('38), "Adventures of Red Ryder" ('40), "Drums of Fu Manchu" ('40), "Adventures of Captain Marvel" ('41), "Jungle Girl" ('41), among others. His 17 Republic serials, co-directed with William Witney, are a time capsule history of the golden age of the American movie serial.

According to Wheeler W. Dixon in THE B DIRECTORS, A BIOGRAPHICAL DIRECTORY, English "created work that was exciting, believable, and relentlessly aggressive. He did it by insisting on the reality of his world and that his actors and stuntmen play it straight, never 'down' to their mostly juvenile audience. English took his work seriously and he asked his collaborators to do the same. The results are remarkable and hold up today." [5] Gene Autry recognized these attributes and put them to good use with English helming 18 of his Columbia titles.

A slightly built man, only weighing about 120 pounds, Jack had black hair and a small neat mustache.

English had worked at MGM as a film editor on some of the Irving Thalberg pictures, most of which were blockbusters. But Jack wanted to direct. Feeling he wouldn't be afforded the opportunity at MGM where the contract directors were the best in the business, he left the powerful studio and began directing pictures for poverty row producers in 1935. He came to Republic in 1937, co-directing "Zorro Rides Again" with Witney.

Gene noticed his abilities on "Trail to San Antone" and brought Jack into

The date on the clapboard is 5/16 indicating this was the first day of filming on Gene's initial Columbia feature as the start date of "The Last Round-Up" was May 16, 1947. Preparing for the scene is director John English (probably he is the man in the suit seated on the divan) and photographer William Bradford (likely the one with the eyeshade by the camera). Tied up in the chair is Carol Thurston; beside her is Bobby Blake, Gene and Trevor Bardette (black hat). The script supervisor is most likely holding the script sitting on the divan edge. The white headed man would be the camera operator.

his Gene Autry Productions set-up at Columbia. In his biography, BACK IN THE SADDLE AGAIN, Gene lauded English by stating, "English was one of the people who put the 'move' into moving pictures. There was just nothing static about his work." [6]

Born in Boston, Massachusetts in 1899, Billy Hill grew up studying violin. At 17 he traveled west finding odd jobs in Montana, Utah and Death Valley, California.

Moving to Los Angeles in 1929, he co-wrote his first song "They Cut Down the Old Pine Tree" which Gene Autry recorded in 1930.

Written on his honeymoon for his new bride, "The West, a Nest, and You" was later set to music by Leroy Yoell and Gene Autry sang it in "Prairie Moon" ('38).

In 1933 "The Last Round-Up" became Hill's biggest hit, immediately going to #1 and staying there for nine weeks. It was recorded by a number of artists, including Gene Autry who used it first in "The Singing Hill" ('41) then as the title song of his first Columbia feature. Hill's "There's a Home in Wyomin'" was sung by Gene in "Sunset In Wyoming" ('41).

Other hits followed, including "Wagon Wheels", "Empty Saddles" and "Call of the Canyon" which was written in 1940 and used as the title tune for Gene's 1942 feature.

Hill died of heart failure in Boston, December 24, 1940.

Mischa R. Bakaleinikoff was the musical director on all but two of Gene Autry's Columbia features.

Born November 10, 1890, in Moscow, Russia, during the Tsarist era, Mischa was a music student at the time of the Russian Revolution.

Fleeing the turmoil of the Bolshevik era, Mischa came to the U.S. in 1926.

By late 1929, Mischa was in Hollywood just as the studios were finding a use for music in talking pictures. Mischa was hired as a string player in the orchestra at

Musical director Mischa Bakaleinikoff and family.

Columbia. Over time, Mischa found himself primarily playing the double bass viola on various films scores, including "Lost Horizon" ('37) where he met his wife-to-be, Helen Gilbert, the only woman cellist in the studio orchestra.

By the early '40s, Mischa was moved into the role of music director, primarily for Columbia's B-films. Although he did get to compose music for many films, his main function was as a music supervisor, conducting the recording of music that either had been written for a specific film by another composer, or more often than not, music pulled from the studio library for use in the movie at hand, and adapting the score to the needs of that film. Most of the music Mischa wrote consisted of bridge sections between existing library music to be tracked into the current movie he was working on.

For 30 years, Bakaleinikoff became one of the busiest motion picture musical directors in Hollywood, working in one capacity or another on over 325 films.

His two brothers, Constantin and Vladimir, were also musically accomplished. Constantin served as RKO's musical director for many years and Vladimir, who did work some in Hollywood for his brothers, became the assistant conductor and music advisor of the Pittsburgh Symphony Orchestra.

Bakaleinikoff was busy with film work right up to the time he died on August 10, 1960.

Paul Madeira Mertz was born September 1, 1904, in Reading, Pennsylvania where his father worked in a bakery. Unfortunately, nothing is known of his younger years, but by 1935 he was composing and arranging music, uncredited, for films at Columbia.

After service in WWII circa 1943-1944, he returned to Columbia where he worked first as musical director on the Ken Curtis/Hoosier Hot Shots westerns.

When Gene set up his Flying A Production Company at Columbia, Mertz became the musical supervisor on all 32 of Gene's Columbia westerns, working very little on other pictures.

Mertz died October 19, 1998, in Los Angeles, California.

WHAT THE EXHIBITOR HAD TO SAY: "Good old Gene. Will look for him on his tour. Still popular with us."
—Harlan Rankin, Plaza Theater, Tilbury, Ontario, Canada (January 1950)

SOURCES:

1. Autry with Herskowitz. p. 97-98.

2. "The Big Sombrero" pressbook.

3. *Autry's Aces.* January-April 1959. p. 24.

4. Don Kay Reynolds on panel discussion. Memphis Film Festival. June 2006.

5. Dixon, Wheeler W. in *The B Directors, A Biographical Directory.* Scarecrow. 1985. p. 165.

6. Autry with Herskowitz. p. 105.

The Strawberry Roan
<u>Columbia, August 1948</u>
A Gene Autry Production in Cinecolor

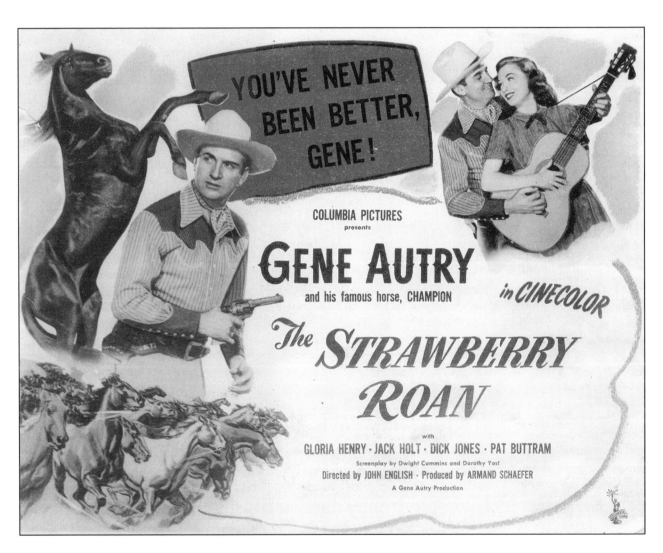

Producer ....Armand Schaefer	Sound Dept..................................Lambert E. Day
Director ....John English	Art Director ....Harold MacArthur
Assistant Director.........................Earl Bellamy	Set Decorations ....George Montgomery
Original Story..............................Julian Zimet	Hair Stylist ....Helen Hunt
Screenplay....................................Dwight Cummins,	Cinecolor Supervision.................Gar Gilbert
Dorothy Yost	
Photography ....Fred H. Jackman Jr.	**SONGS:** "The Strawberry Roan" (music and lyrics by
Musical Supervisor ....Paul Mertz	Fred Howard, Nat Vincent)—sung by Gene Autry (reprised
Musical Director ....Mischa Bakaleinikoff	by Gene Autry and Dick Jones); "Texas Sandman" (music
Film Editor ....Henry Batista	and lyrics by Doris Fisher, Allan Roberts)—sung by Gene

Autry and cowboys; "The Angel Song" (music and lyrics by Gene Autry, Curt Massey, Mary Hillard)—sung by Gene Autry; "When the White Roses Bloom" (music and lyrics by Allie Wruble, Paul Herrick)—sung by Gene Autry.

RUNNING TIME: 78 minutes
FILMING DATES: June 19 to July 18, 1947
LOCATIONS: Sedona, Arizona; Jauregui Ranch; Columbia Ranch
NEGATIVE COST: $295,547.92.

CAST:

Actor	Character
Gene Autry	Gene Autry
Gloria Henry	Connie Bailey
Jack Holt	Walt Bailey
Dick Jones	Joe Bailey
Pat Buttram	Hank
Rufe Davis	Chuck
John McGuire	Bud Williams
Eddy Waller	Steve
Redd Harper	Andy
Sam Flint	Dr. Nelson
Jack Ingram	Pete Lucas
Ted Mapes	Smitty
Eddie Parker	Jake
Champion	The Roan
Little Champ	Little Champ

STUNTS: Ted Mapes, Eddie Parker, Duke Taylor.

THE FILM: Gene Autry's personal ambition upon forming his own production company was to have his westerns produced in color and to feature hit songs. This, as Gene was to discover, meant much higher budgets at a time when the B-westerns were beginning to taper off at the box office due to the encroachment of television.

Demands on the new Technicolor Corporation put them behind schedule forcing Gene to produce "The Last Round-Up" in black and white. However, in June 1947, as filming began on "The Strawberry Roan", Columbia announced this and future Autry films would be lensed in the Cinecolor process. The color features were to be sold individually and not as a series with an ambitious schedule of three color features released per year.

However, Gene and his production company soon learned producing B-westerns in color was cost prohibitive. "The Strawberry Roan" cost nearly $300,000 and "The Big Sombrero", which began lensing about 20 days later, came in at approximately $278,000, making them the most expensive of Columbia's

over 275 produced B-westerns.

"The Strawberry Roan" ranks with the greatest of filmed horse stories, full of sentiment that tugs at the heartstrings.

The cowboys of ranch owner Walt Bailey (Jack Holt), including Gene Autry, capture the noble wild roan (Champion) stallion and attempt to gentle him. Against his father's wishes, Joe Bailey (Dick Jones), tries to ride the roan but is thrown and badly injured.

Racing away from Joe's enraged father, the horse plunges over a steep cliff and is believed dead. But Gene finds the animal and secretly nurses his wounds, hoping to bring him back to the crippled boy whose spirit is now broken.

Soon, Bailey learns what Gene has done, accuses him of rustling and posts a reward for the capture of both the roan and his former foreman. Gene, with the help of Connie (Gloria Henry), Bailey's daughter, holds out against reward hungry ranchers until Joe is able to overcome his disability and ride the roan. His father then acknowledges his mistakes.

Songs are plentiful at this early stage of Gene's Columbia career, including a long version of the famous title song. Where the film fails slightly is that Gene, smiling, charming and polite as ever, just cannot emote well enough in the dramatic scenes. With a couple of minor exceptions, it would be the last time Gene would take on a script that required of him more than his affable charm and much improved action ability. Gene's multitudinous talents simply did not include the ability to show emotion on screen.

Still, without a doubt, one of Gene's most enduring westerns and one of his most popular, primarily due to the heart warming human interest qualities.

Director John English (center with jacket) celebrated his 45th birthday June 25, 1948, while directing "The Strawberry Roan." Cast and crew gathered to sing "Happy Birthday," — led by Gene and Gloria Henry (with the cake).

NOTES AND COMMENTS: The George Montgomery noted as the set decorator on this film—and dozens of other Columbia pictures—is *not* the actor George Montgomery, nor any relation.

Important to point out, as the credit reads, "This picture was filmed under the supervision and with the cooperation of the American Humane Association." Gene always valued all animals very highly and never permitted a horse to suffer an indignity in his films.

Gene's longtime friend and radio sidekick Pat Buttram makes his film debut with Gene in "The Strawberry Roan". Pat became well known to radio audiences on the Phil Harris-Alice Faye program and his recent addition on June 13, 1948, to the weekly "Gene Autry Melody Ranch Radio Show". Pat eventually would feature in 17 of Gene's pictures and 83 of Gene's 91 TV episodes. However, Pat's role here is minor, with most of the comedy sequences falling to radio comedian (and former member of Republic's Three Mesquiteers series) Rufe Davis and his funny animal impersonations.

"The Strawberry Roan" was Gene's only released picture in 1948. He was, of course, doing his weekly radio show, but the majority of his time was dedicated to re-establishing contacts that had faded during the four years he was in the Air Force during WWII. Gene and tour manager/co-pilot Herb Green flew to cities and towns across the country to meet one on one with promoters and theater exhibitors to revive his western musical variety stage show. Gene also wanted to convince theater owners he was still a box office draw (even with the encroachment of Roy Rogers at Republic while Gene was away). And he was right. His appearance with the premiere of "The Strawberry Roan" at the Oriental Theater in Chicago broke the all-time box office record there.

Song writer Doris Fisher was known as "Queen of the Jukebox" because of all the popular songs she wrote, including "You Always Hurt the One You Love", "Tampico", and "Who Put the Blame On Mame" for the film "Gilda" ('46) starring Rita Hayworth. The daughter of noted songwriter Fred Fisher wrote "Texas Sandman" for this film and "You Can't See the Sun When You're Crying" for "The Last Round-Up". She also wrote dozens of songs for Columbia's Hoosier Hot Shots/Ken Curtis and Roy Acuff musicals. Fisher died at 87 January 15, 2003.

Following completion of "The Strawberry Roan", Gene starred at the 22nd annual World's Championship Rodeo in Madison Square Garden September 24 through October 26, 1947.

According to Erskine Johnson in his December 18, 1947, column for the L.A. DAILY NEWS, Gene allowed Champion to be ridden by Rita Hayworth in Columbia's "The Loves of Carmen", filmed at Lone Pine, California, between November 1947 and February 1948.

FILM COMMENTS: *Gene Autry:* "Our first film in color, in Cinecolor, 'The Strawberry Roan' also marked the first appearance of Pat Buttram, and the debut of Little Champ, the son of the second screen Champion. I used three different Champions in my movies (though they all had their own understudies). Little Champ's sire had been a Tennessee Walking Horse, a dark chestnut with a flaxen tail and mane, the blazed face, and four socks to his knees. He was marked exactly like the first Champion and I paid $1,500, the most I ever spent for a horse." [1]

Jack Holt: "The movie world of 20 years ago was more vivid, exciting and wacky. It reflected the tempo and spirit of those giddy days. Male stars raced up and down Hollywood Boulevard in Duisenbergs and Mercedes; feminine stars paraded in shiny black town cars a mile long, driven by haughty chauffeurs in elegant livery.

"Now, the film celebrities drive cars fresh off a Detroit assembly line. And they are too smart to risk their valuable necks speeding. I remember when Tom Mix was seen everywhere in a pure white car with his name printed on the sides. He had 'Tom Mix' spelled out in lights over the gateway to his home, and the clothes he wore made working cowboys blush.

"Today's top western star Gene Autry has four cars, but they're of standard make and color. Although he wears western suits at all times, they're made by a swank Beverly Hills tailor and are ultra-conservative in cut and color.

"In the old days, stars gave in more to their exhibitionistic tendencies. They played in public, fought in public and sometimes loved in public—and they did all three colorfully. Whether discreet or not, it certainly was glamour making. Nowadays, it seems that most stars are more conservative about their private lives than business people. They work hard, stay at home nights and save their money."[2]

Gloria Henry: "When Columbia cast me in 'The

Little Champ, Champion, Gene and Gloria Henry.

Strawberry Roan' it was a serious moment. I couldn't say no, and I didn't want to say yes. They asked, 'Can you ride?' I said, 'Sure,' because I'd learned to ride English style. (Smiles) Now there's a big difference between English and western style. They said fine. So I show up on the set and in the first scene I am to come riding in past the camera, jump down and hitch my horse on the post, yelling 'Hi Gene' as I passed. Well, when you see that in the movie, it's not me! (Laughs) Because, I got up on the horse and started off but I couldn't control the horse. He was headed straight for the camera set-up. All the camera crew dove for the side to get out of the way. Luckily I didn't knock the camera over, but when I got off, my legs were buckling and they decided I was not going to do the riding anymore.

"Later I went to Mr. Autry and told him my problem. He was cute. He told me I could ride Champion, and he would see to it personally that Champ would be very gentle and patient with me.

"Finally, Mr. Autry made me get on the horse, and off we went up the road, with Gene walking beside us. We passed three mud puddles, and I didn't land in one of them. That was when I began to relax.

"From then on, I did all right. I finally did the finishing scene at the end, but I had one more close call. Champion was very jealous of all of Gene's leading ladies. Seriously. One time we were shooting some stills out on the edge of the mountain in Sedona where the scenery is just magnificent. The still photographer had Champ in the middle, I was on one side and Gene was on the other. Gene was supposed to look sort of moon-eyed around Champ at me. Well, Champ was also looking at me. He looked at me out of the side of his eye, he moved his head over and went Whop! He tried to knock me off the mountain! (Laughs) I slipped down, but when I got up I didn't stand quite so close to him. Then, he looked over at me, took his hoof and went Stomp! Right on my foot. So we were not friends! (Laughs)

"(This picture) was the farthest I'd gone (on location) at that point and I thoroughly enjoyed it. It was just so beautiful; it was unbelievable. The thing I'll never forget is the little mining town on a hill outside of Sedona (Jerome). One night, and it might even have been the first night we were there, there was one extra car and a couple of guys on the crew and the makeup man decided to take it and go to a nightclub that was about 30 miles away, past Jerome. I don't know what that would be, but it was open and it played cowboy music. We had a great time; we drank some beer and people were dancing. It was lots of fun. I came home very tired and then had to get up early the next morning. They had no makeup room; they didn't even have a converted makeup truck like they use now. So we put my makeup on in a stretchout, one of the big cars that take people back and forth. There was practically no light and they had to put this horrible orange makeup (for the Cinecolor process used for 'Roan') on me. The first time I saw myself, I thought, 'Oh my God, I can't go out in public like this! The makeup had to be that way for the Cinecolor. I haven't seen 'Strawberry Roan' in color since it came out.

I'm not one who likes to look at myself on film.

"Dick Jones was such a darling! But I remember even more working with Jack Holt, who played his dad. He didn't want anything to interrupt a scene. Dickie was so cute; we'd tease him and we'd laugh and make jokes right up until it was time for action. And that would make Jack very upset. He'd say, 'This is serious business, now you stop this kidding around. We've got a scene to do here.' And we'd all say, 'Yes sir!'" [3, 4]

Director Earl Bellamy (assistant director on Gene's first two Columbia titles): "Gene was very dedicated, enjoyed working and tried very hard to do a good job. He had a great sense of humor. (Laughs) One funny thing he did…we were in Sedona, Arizona, for 'Strawberry Roan'…he went into the motel and threw all of leading lady Gloria Henry's furniture out into the dirt street. He was just having fun and ended up buying a whole set of furniture for the motel. He got a big kick out of that…throwing out the bed, lamps…all by himself. A lot of us stood around and watched him throw it out. (Laughs) He always got a kick out of it when he'd break into song when he was riding along. Gene always thought that was pretty funny…no matter where he was, you'd end up with a song. He was a very generous man. People who had problems, he would help them if it was worthwhile. If you had a young actress or actor, he was right there helping them. Just an all around first rate person." [5]

Dick Jones: "I was hired on 'Strawberry Roan' through a regular interview set up by my agent. They told me it was in color and a big picture. It was a big thing to me because that was my getting back into the process of filming. (Dick hadn't been before cameras since 1944.) I knew nothing about Gene Autry at the time and I doubt he knew anything about me. In the course of every day's work we got to know each other.

"I didn't do all the horse work on the picture. They had a second unit out there first with somebody dressed up like me doing those wild chases all through Sedona. We came in two or three days after that to match up the close ups. My double was probably a local. On Gene's later pictures that was all me (doing the rides and stunts).

"Jack Holt was in it. I've always admired his work. I liked being around him.

"As for Pat Buttram, anybody can get along with Pat if Pat's in a good mood. If Pat's not in a good mood, nobody can get along with him. And that's exactly the way he and Gene got along. They didn't pal around—buddy-buddy. I don't even remember Pat getting into some of the poker games.

"(Director) John English was an Englishman because of his name, but with a western sense of humor. He was very prim and proper around people upon first meeting them, then later on he got down to the nitty-gritty and was a real nice guy. He was a good action director because he took advice. He would tell the (stunt) coordinator what he wanted and the coordinator would rig it. And he gave the coordinator lots of film and lots of space to get it done."[6]

CAST BIOS: With "Strawberry Roan", Dick Jones, already a 14 year screen and radio veteran became an integral part of Gene Autry's Flying A "stock company". Dick went on to co-star with Gene in "Sons of New Mexico" ('50), "Wagon Team" ('52), "The Old West" ('52) and "Last of the Pony Riders" ('53). More importantly, Gene cast Dick as Dick West, on TV's "Range Rider". Dick co-starred with Jock Mahoney as The Range Rider on 78 30-minute episodes of the popular action-packed TV series from 1950-1953. When that series ended, Gene immediately cast Dick as the star of "Buffalo Bill Jr." for 42 half hour TV episodes which ran from 1955-1956. Meanwhile "The Boss Man", as Dick affectionately refers to Gene, kept Dick busy guest-starring on "The Gene Autry Show" and "Annie Oakley".

Dick was born February 25, 1927, in Snyder, Texas, just south of Abilene. The son of a newspaper editor, Dickie learned to ride almost before he learned to walk and, at age four, was billed in rodeos as "The World's Youngest Trick Rider and Trick Roper".

It was western star Hoot Gibson who "discovered" Dickie in 1932 at the Dallas State Fair and brought him to Hollywood for his first film, stunt work in "Wonder Bar" in 1934 with Al Jolson.

Dickie's cute good looks, vivacious energy and pleasant voice landed him more and bigger parts in not only westerns and serials but A-films such as "Babes in Toyland" ('34) with Laurel and Hardy, "Black Legion" ('37) with Humphrey Bogart and "Stella Dallas" ('37) with Barbara Stanwyck. He worked in westerns with Buck Jones (his personal favorite), William Boyd, Bob Baker, James Newill, John Wayne, George O'Brien, Kermit Maynard, Dick Foran, Jack Randall and Bill Elliott, among others.

In 1940 he had perhaps his most prominent, although unseen, role as the voice of Pinocchio in Walt Disney's animated classic. The part earned him the distinction of being named a Disney Legend in 2000.

Radio also beckoned, at 15 he took over the role of Henry Aldrich on "The Aldrich Family".

Dick served with the Army in Alaska during the final months of World War II.

It was after the war that Dick's decade long film association with Gene Autry began with "The Strawberry Roan".

Dick continued to work in films and TV into the '70s, with his last being L. Q. Jones' cult classic "A Boy and His Dog" ('75).

He's been honored with a star on the Hollywood Walk of Fame, has received the prestigious Golden Boot Award (begun by Gene's friend and co-star Pat Buttram) and was inducted into the Hollywood Stuntman's Hall of Fame.

Today, semi-retired, Dick and his wife (since 1948) Betty live in Northridge, California, and enjoy attending the many western film festivals they're invited to each year.

WHAT THE EXHIBITOR HAD TO SAY: "One of Autry's best. Wonderful color. Business far above average."
—O. Fomby, Paula Theater,
Homer, Louisiana (January 1949)

"This picture we played with Ken Maynard three times. First night I arrived late and thought the place was on fire. We are still enjoying business with Autry a fourth time."
—Harland Rankin, Plaza Theater,
Tilbury, Ontario, Canada (June 1950)

SOURCES:
1. Autry with Herskowitz. p. 98.
2. "The Strawberry Roan" pressbook.
3. *Western Clippings #27.* January/February 1999. p. 8.
4. Author's audio tape of 1988 Charlotte, North Carolina, Film Festival panel discussion.
5. Interview with author, 2002.
6. Interview with author, February 2006.

Jack Holt, Gloria Henry, Gene, Champion (as "The Strawberry Roan" of the title) and Dick Jones.

Loaded Pistols
<u>Columbia, January 1949</u>
A Gene Autry Production in Sepia Tone

Producer ....Armand Schaefer
Director ....John English
Assistant Director........................Carl Hiecke
Screenplay...................................Dwight Cummins,
                                 Dorothy Yost
Photography ....William Bradford
Musical Supervisor ....Paul Mertz
Musical Supervisor ....Mischa Bakaleinikoff
Film Editor ....Aaron Stell
Sound Dept.................................Phil Faulkner Jr.
Art Director ....Harold MacArthur
Set Decorations ....David Montrose

SONGS: "Loaded Pistols and Loaded Dice" (music and lyrics by Johnny Lange, Hy Heath)—sung by studio singers; reprised twice by Gene Autry; "Blue Tail Fly" (Public Domain)—sung by Gene Autry; "When the Bloom is On the Sage" (music and lyrics by Fred Howard, Nat Vincent)—sung by Gene Autry; "A Boy From Texas, a Girl From Tennessee" (music and lyrics by Jack Segal, Joe McCarthy Jr., John Benson Brooks)—sung by Gene Autry; "Pretty Mary" (music and lyrics by Gene Autry, Oakley Haldeman, Jim MacDonald, Bob Mitchell)—sung by Gene Autry.

RUNNING TIME: 79 minutes
FILMING DATES: May 4-22, 1948
LOCATIONS: Lone Pine; Corriganville; Columbia backlot; Iverson's Ranch
BUDGET: $69,911.19

CAST:

Actor	Character
Gene Autry	Gene Autry
Barbara Britton	Mary Evans
Chill Wills	Sheriff Cramer
Jack Holt	Dave Randall
Russell Arms	Larry Evans
Robert Shayne	Don Mason
Vince Barnett	Sam Gardner
Leon Weaver	Jake Harper
Fred Kohler Jr.	Bill Otis
Clem Bevans	Jim Hedge
Richard Alexander, "Snub" Pollard	Men at dance
The Cass County Boys: Bert Dodson, Fred Martin, Jerry Scoggins	Musicians
Hank Bell	Hank
Stanley Blystone	Ed Norton
Budd Buster, Sandy Sanders	Easy Y Ranchers
Slim Gaut	Toothless Cowhand
Frankie Marvin, John McKee	Deputies
Felice Raymond	Mrs. Kramer
Chuck Baldra, William Sundholm, Frank O'Connor, Heinie Conklin, Reed Howes, Ethan Laidlaw, Charles Murray Jr.	Extras
Champion	Champion

STUNTS: Sandy Sanders (Gene's double); Boyd Stockman; Duke Taylor.

THE FILM: The only Gene Autry film where the leading lady, Barbara Britton, is equally billed above the title in print advertising as the co-star with Gene Autry, if one chooses to overlook "Shooting High", Gene's one away from his Republic home that had Jane Withers and Gene above the title.

Song content is still high with six numbers, including the title tune which is reprised twice. But the musical spotting is so expertly done that action involvement is never slowed, a major achievement in a singing cowboy western.

The mystery content, with Gene acting much like a rangeland Charlie Chan, should appeal to the adult audience even more than the Saturday afternoon crowd. But then, Gene's films always had a high adult-audience appeal, more-so than the typical Allan "Rocky" Lane, Lash LaRue westerns of this same time period.

Young Larry Evans (Russell Arms) escapes from lynch-law after his gun has been used to kill a rancher in a poker game when the lights went out. The rancher's best friend, Gene Autry, investigates on his own and finds Larry and his pretty but fiery sister Mary (Barbara Britton) hiding in the cabin of an old miner (Clem Bevans).

Jack Holt (white jacket) and Sheriff Chill Wills (right) moderate the aftermath of a brutal fight between Gene and Fred Kohler Jr.

Believing Larry innocent, Gene keeps outwitting the posse led by Sheriff Cramer (Chill Wills) and other members of the fatal poker game including Mason (Robert Shayne) and Randall (Jack Holt) until he can discover what could be on the dead rancher's property worth committing murder for.

As in any good Charlie Chan murder mystery, Gene eventually gathers all the suspects in the poker room where the murder took place and as he's explaining why and who really killed his rancher friend, the lights go out as before and a shot is fired at Gene before he unmasks the killer in an exciting climax.

Some out of the ordinary characterizations and the murder mystery element serve to make this one of Gene's better Columbia entries.

NOTES AND COMMENTS: Working title for the picture was "Hideaway".

Gene's friend Jake Harper is played by Leon Weaver, formerly part of the rural comic family The Weaver Brothers and Elviry at Republic.

Iron-jawed Jack Holt, father of B-western star Tim Holt and B-western heroine Jennifer Holt, had been a top western star himself in silent Paramount westerns of the '20s. When his career waned in the '40s, he re-entered the Army, serving two years and attaining the rank of major before receiving a medical discharge. Still trim and fit, he returned to Hollywood in '45 and played supporting roles in westerns with his son Tim, Roy Rogers, Allan "Rocky" Lane, Bill Elliott, Rod Cameron, Don Barry, Lash LaRue, Clark Gable and two with Gene Autry—"The Strawberry Roan" and "Loaded Pistols". After a series of heart attacks, Holt died in 1951.

Fred Kohler Jr., who has a bruising scrap with Gene, is

Barbara Britton prevents brother Russell Arms from a rash decision involving Gene's life.

the son of noted western screen heavy Fred Kohler.

Roy Rogers held onto his #1 position in MOTION PICTURE HERALD'S list of "Money Making Western Stars for 1948" as polled by theatre exhibitors. Gene Autry was #2 in a reported "foto-finish". Bill Elliott was third, Gabby Hayes fourth and William Boyd fifth.

FILM COMMENTS: *Russell Arms:* "I only worked with Gene Autry in two pictures but found it a first-class experience both times. I think it reflected on Gene's personality and the fact he surrounded himself with competent, able people in his Flying A Production Company that he turned out western hit after hit. He wasn't a great actor or singer but was hugely successful in both fields as he was an exceptional business man with a warm, winning personality. He seemed to have the Midas Touch so that every venture of his came out smelling like roses!

"The first picture I did with Gene was 'Loaded Pistols' which also starred Barbara Britton. She was my sister in the film and I, as Larry, was always getting into trouble so she, naturally, turned to Gene to help me out. Which he did.

"This was fine casting because Barbara had been modeling and working in 'society' films. We all got along fine. I had a number of scenes with Gene which all seemed to go smoothly. No star treatment from Gene, only a quiet tip now and then to make things go smoother and better, tips which I was only too glad to take.

"One day out on location I was riding to get into position for the next scene when Gene, sitting in his director's chair, stopped me and struck up a conversation. Among other things he asked me if I had ever thought about making a career of being a western actor. He said I looked good sitting a horse and good in cowboy clothes and other things in that vein. I was flattered, of course, but replied that I wanted to go to Broadway and be a stage actor. I enjoyed making this film but wanted a different kind of career. Looking back I often wonder how things would have been if I had answered Gene differently." [1]

WHAT THE EXHIBITOR HAD TO SAY: "Good old Gene Autry came along on Friday and Saturday and filled the house, thus making it possible to show a profit on what would have been otherwise a bad week. Too bad the westerns on Fridays and Saturdays have to pay the freight on the alleged superdupers we play at high rental (the rest of the week)."
—E. M. Freiburger, Paramount Theater, Dewey, Oklahoma (May 1949)

"Good old Gene. We still love him. Enjoyed extra business." —Harland Rankin, Plaza Theater, Tilbury, Ontario, Canada (October 1949)

"Just the usual western stuff. Some fairly entertaining songs. My patrons don't go for Gene Autry nearly as well as they did. Did 85% normal business with fine weather and poor opposition." —Melvin M. Edel, State Theater, Centralia, Illinois (Feburary 1950)

"Played with a cartoon festival to above average Saturday business. Gene is popular here—on equal terms or better than Roy Rogers. I'm doubling Gene Autry soon to see what he will do in such a situation. 'Loaded Pistols' is okay but I think they should be in color."
—Fred G. Weppler, Colonial Theater, Colfax, Illinois (January 1950)

SOURCES:
1. Interview with the author. May 2005.

The Big Sombrero
Columbia, March 1949
A Gene Autry Production in Cinecolor

Teddy Powell)—sung by Gene Autry; "My Adobe Hacienda" (music and lyrics by Louise Massey, Lee Penny)—sung by Gene Autry and extras; "Goodbye to Old Mexico" (music and lyrics by Dwight Butcher)—sung by Gene Autry.

RUNNING TIME: 78 minutes

FILMING DATES: August 7 to September 9, 1947

LOCATIONS: Autry Ranch near Florence, Arizona; Saguaro National Forest; Tucson Mountain Park (including Starr Pass); Corriganville; Red Rock Canyon; Monogram Ranch; Rancho Maria; Columbia backlot

NEGATIVE COST: $278,043.49

Producer ....Armand Schaefer
Director ....Frank McDonald
Assistant Director........................Earl Bellamy
Screenplay....................................Olive Cooper
Photography ....William Bradford
Musical Supervisor ....Paul Mertz
Musical Director ....Mischa Bakaleinikoff
Film Editor..................................Henry Batista
Sound Dept...................................Howard Fogetti
Art Director.................................Harold MacArthur
Set Decorations ....George Montgomery
Cinecolor Supervisor ....Clifford Shank
Special Effects.............................Barney Wolff
Makeup ....Bob Keats, Paul
                                          Malcolm

SONGS: "You Belong to My Heart" (music and lyrics by Augustin Lara with English lyrics by Ray Gilbert)—sung by Gene Autry and studio singers; "I'm Thankful For Small Favors" (music and lyrics by Don Raye, Gene de Paul)—sung by Gene Autry; "Rancho Pillow" (music and lyrics by Allie Wrubel, Charles Newman)—sung by Gene Autry and extras; "Trail to Mexico" (Public Domain)—sung by Gene Autry; "O My Darling Clementine" (Public Domain)—sung by Gene Autry; "La Golondrina" (music and lyrics by Narciso Serradell with English lyrics by

CAST:

Actor	Character
Gene Autry ....Gene Autry
Elena Verdugo ....Estrellita Estrada
Stephen Dunne ....James Garland
George J. Lewis...........................Juan Vazcaro
Vera Marshe ....Angie Burke
William Edmunds ....Don Luis Alvarado
Martin Garralaga.........................Felipe Gonzales
Gene Stutenroth ....Ben McBride
Neyle Morrow ....Tico
John "Bob" Cason........................Stacy
Pierce Lyden...............................Farmer
Rian Valente ....Estaban
Antonio Filauri...........................Pablo
Jose Alvarado ....Border Patrolman Pedro
Jose Portugal ....Mexican Policeman
Cosmo Sardo, Alex Montoya.......Border Patrolmen
Artie Ortego ....Vaquero
Sam Bernard................................Pawn Shop Owner
Robert Espinoza ....Mexican Policeman Pepe
Joe Palma, Joe Kirk, Joe Dominguez........................Extras
Champion....................................Champion

STUNTS: Duke Taylor.

THE FILM: Filmed shortly after Gene Autry's only other Cinecolor Columbia release, "The Strawberry Roan", in August/September 1947, "The Big Sombrero" was held up for release for 18 months, for undetermined reasons, until March 1949.

Originally, producer Armand Schaefer and Gene planned to once again utilize Old Tucson for location shooting as they had on "The Last Round-Up", however they found the site unusable due to windstorm demolishment.

Other production problems, primarily weather, delayed filming as to where the company had only completed 12 hours work in three days. A sudden rainstorm in Tucson was one delay.

Eventually contending they had enough Arizona footage to get by, Schaefer and Autry moved the company back to California. Even then, extremely hot temperatures reaching 115 degrees in the San Fernando Valley stalled production. Hours were spent one day trying to get Champion to lay down behind a boulder. Either tired, temperamental or suffering from the heat, the usually agreeable equine refused to obey the cue given by Gene on this day. Eventually, the scene was shot with Champ hiding behind a much larger boulder.

Another incident occurred on September 3rd in Red Rock Canyon where 35 second unit crew members narrowly escaped serious injury when dynamite exploded 15 minutes ahead of schedule, collapsing a large section of the hillside. Boulders weighing two-hundred pounds narrowly missed producer Armand Schaefer by inches.

When "The Big Sombrero" wrapped, Gene came face to face with economic realities and wrote "finis" to any more productions in Cinecolor due to the horrendous cost factor…this one coming in at a whopping $278,043.49. Filming in Cinecolor also caused a great delay in printing and monetary losses in refilming needed sections.

The lavish music content of "The Big Sombrero" is as high as any of Gene's Columbia westerns and the color helps, but otherwise it's a rather lifeless affair, due in part possibly to the continual production problems.

The story concerns Gene's efforts to aid the Vaqueros of the vast Big Sombrero rancho in Mexico where confidence man, and old acquaintance of Gene's, James Garland (Stephen Dunne), through charm, has wormed himself into the good graces of Estrellita Estrada (Elena Verdugo), the lovely but flighty owner of the enormous rancho. Garland plans to gain control by marrying Estrellita, then sell the land for a tidy profit to businessman McBride (Gene Stutenroth).

Garland has simply, he believes, for show, appointed Gene as foreman, but fails to reckon with Gene's sense of fair play.

Overall, a rather tepid western involved with romantic misadventure more than standard action values. The screenplay is a bit episodic, failing to get down to business until halfway through, but the second half, with some nice action, manages to save the picture.

NOTES AND COMMENTS: Working titles for this film were "In a Little Spanish Town" and "Twin Sombreros".

The kiss that never made it onto the screen between Elena Verdugo and Gene Autry.

Gene's first screen kiss in many years was actually filmed according to leading lady Elena Verdugo. Apparently learning it was to be filmed, press representatives galore were on hand, which landed several stories in the newspapers. "That was the trouble," Elena explained. "Gene's fans definitely did not want Gene kissing and wrote to the studio. I saw the letters. So we shot the scene again, minus the kiss. But I have one satisfaction; Gene told me my kiss was undoubtedly the best kiss that ever landed on the cutting room floor." [1]

FILM COMMENTS: *Gene Autry:* "'The Big Sombrero' turned out to be my only other movie photographed in color. My dream had collided with an awful thing called economic reality. The process was simply beyond our budgets. But in a sense this picture did represent the bigger and better western I had envisioned. The plot was simple: I galloped off to Mexico and helped the small rancheros in their fight against the Big Enchilada. Twenty-five of (the film's) minutes were devoted to eight songs, including two of the year's biggest hits, 'You Belong to My Heart' and 'My Adobe Hacienda.'

Trivia fans might enjoy knowing that my leading lady was a then slender, sexy Latin named Elena Verdugo, who in the '70s was seen on television as Consuelo, answering the phone for Dr. Marcus Welby." [2]

Elena Verdugo: "I found Gene to be an interesting man. Working with him was a highlight. Right from the beginning, I noticed he was a great businessman. I remember the final scene, where I am on the veranda waving goodbye to Gene

Neyle Morrow, William Edmunds, Vera Marshe, Gene Autry, Stephen Dunne and John Cason at The Big Sombrero rancho.

and Champion. Gene and the horse turn around to ride off into the sunset, when Champion starts farting! All the way out. He kept on letting off wind, and we had all these important visitors on the set. Everybody was in hysterics. Gene was laughing as he was trotting off. That is typical when you work with horses. They are always relieving themselves during the love scenes! (Laughs)" [3]

Pierce Lyden: "Gene Autry was a fine rider, but the actor's beautiful horse Champion would have made any rider look good.

"Gene had made movies for Republic before he went off to war, but when he returned he found he'd been replaced by Roy Rogers. So he switched over to Columbia Pictures. It was there that I began appearing in the Autry flicks.

"Autry was a big name, but he wasn't big-headed. I was kind of in awe of him when we worked our first scene together, but he put me at ease then and many times after that. Gene was always nice, and very easy to work with. He wasn't doing his own stunts, fights or trick riding by that time.

"When Autry bought his own studio at Sunset and Highland and began making his own pictures for the movie theaters and TV, I continued playing the outlaw in Gene's films. Gene was a pilot and owned his own plane. He flew me and some of the other supporting cowpokes on locations with him to Arizona. We could get there in a few hours by plane. By bus or car it would take a day or longer.

"Autry had a tremendous following in the '30s, '40s and '50s. It was partly because of his personality, partly

his fine singing voice, partly the great songs he sang, and partly because of the western stories set against a modern background.

"He paid careful attention to business. He noted there was big money to be made in TV films and broadened out into the production of several series starring other actors. These included 'Range Rider' starring Jock Mahoney; 'Buffalo Bill Jr.' starring Dick Jones and 'Annie Oakley' starring Gail Davis.

"I had the impression Gene always knew what he was doing, and he wasn't about to let anybody or anything stand in his way. I guess he proved it." [4]

WHAT THE EXHIBITOR HAD TO SAY: "This one can't begin to measure up to 'The Strawberry Roan', and is just about average Autry western. We singled but should have doubled this one."
—Bob Halliday, Willamette Valley Theaters, Albany, Oregon (October 1949)

"Autry has been more popular here recently than Roy Rogers. This played to well above average gross and seemed to be well liked by those who came to see it."
—Fred G. Weppler, Colonial Theater, Colfax, Illinois (October 1949)

"This is in the class that our Saturday night patrons enjoy, so let's have more like it."
—Mrs. Denzil Hildebrand, Algerian Theater, Risco, Missouri (October 1949)

"Viva Autry! Need I say more? He is my box office hero."
—J. E. Willson, Majestic Theater, Cedar Lake, South Dakota (March 1950)

"This is what they like, and show it by turning out."
—Harland Rankin, Plaza Theater, Tilbury, Ontario, Canada (July 1950)

SOURCES:

1. Interview with author.
2. Autry with Herskowitz. p. 99.
3. *Westerns Women.* McFarland 1999. p. 252.
4. Letter to author, circa late '80s.

Riders of the Whistling Pines
Columbia, May 1949

A Gene Autry Production in Sepia Tone

Producer ....Armand Schaefer
Director ....John English
Assistant Director........................Carl Hiecke
Screenplay..................................Jack Townley
Photography ....William Bradford
Musical Supervisor ....Paul Mertz
Musical Director ....Mischa Bakaleinikoff
Film Editor ....Aaron Stell
Sound Dept.................................Lambert E. Day
Art Director................................Harold MacArthur
Set Decorations ....William Kiernan
Hair Stylist ....Flora Jaynes
Makeup ....Leonard Engelman

SONGS: "It's My Lazy Day" (music and lyrics by Smiley Burnette)—sung by Gene Autry; "Roamin' Around the Range" (music and lyrics by Smiley Burnette)—sung by Gene Autry and the Cass County Boys; "Hair of Gold, Eyes of Blue" (music and lyrics by Sunny Skylar)—sung by Gene Autry, Jimmy Lloyd; "Every Time I Feel the Spirit" (Public Domain)—sung by the Cass County Boys; "The Little Big Dry" (music and lyrics by Billie Weber)—sung by Gene Autry and the Cass County Boys; "Toolie Oolie Doolie" (music and lyrics by Vaughn Horton, Art Beul)—sung by The Pinafores; "Yellow Rose of Texas" (Public Domain)—sung by Gene Autry.

RUNNING TIME: 70 minutes
FILMING DATES: June 21 to July 8, 1948
LOCATIONS: Big Bear area; Janss Ranch landing strip; Columbia backlot
BUDGET: $41, 017

CAST:

Actor	*Character*
Gene Autry ....Gene Autry
Patricia White (aka Patricia Barry). Helen Carter
Jimmy Lloyd ....Joe Lucas
Douglass Dumbrille ....Henry Mitchell
Damian O'Flynn ....Bill Wright
Clayton Moore ....Pete
Harry Cheshire ....Dr. Daniel Chadwick
Leon Weaver ....Abner Weaver

The Cass County Boys: Jerry Scoggins, Fred Martin, Bert Dodson ....Foresters
The Pinafores: Beulah, Ione, Eunice......................................Foresters
Loie Bridge ....Loie Weaver
Virginia Carroll ....Townswoman at Hearing
Lane Chandler.............................Al, Forestry Officer
Roy Gordon.................................Superintendent John Hoaglund
Ted Mapes ....Logger
Merrill McCormick, Al Thompson .. Townsmen at Hearing
Frank O'Connor, George Bell......Men on Coroner's Jury
Jason Robards Sr. ....Charles Carter
Len Torrey...................................Marshal
Emmett Vogan ....Dr. Farley, Forestry Professor
Nolan Leary ....Rancher Brown
Britt Wood..................................Rancher Smith
Frankie Marvin............................Guitar Player
Steve Benton, Lynn Farr, Blackie Whiteford, Ray Jones, Bob Woodward, Sandy Sanders, Chuck Roberson ....Extras
Champion ....Champion

STUNTS: Sandy Sanders (Gene's double); Chuck Roberson; Bob Woodward.

THE FILM: Whereas Gene Autry's first few Columbia westerns retained much of the Republic Autry charisma, a certain post-WWII grimness, with a definite downplaying of humor and more concentration on harder-edged stories with a higher action content was beginning to settle in on Gene's films. It's notable in "Riders of the Whistling Pines" with its plot of the forestry service trying to stop exploitation of the forests by over-cutting, and the subplot of Gene attempting to aid his friend Joe Lucas (Jimmy Lloyd) to overcome his drinking problem after the death of his wife. Eventually, Joe purposefully flies his plane with he and one of the heavies aboard into the cabin of the crook who is about to shoot Gene. Far grimmer material than Autry fans were used to seeing. Although the song content in "Riders…" remains high, it would be the last time Gene's pictures would feature this much music. Gone too were the longer running times, Gene's films for the next couple of years would see a standardized 70 minute running time. Much of this cost cutting comes from the overruns of his two color features, but also the gradual reduction all theatrical B-westerns were beginning to see in revenue returns due to the encroachment of television. The B-western was struggling to survive.

Ex-forestry service man Autry, believing he has accidentally shot the father of Helen Carter (Patricia White), sells his Sportsman's Camp and prepares to leave the forestry country.

Learning someone murdered Carter's father and left him to take the blame, Gene returns and is assigned to supervise a program to spray the area with DDT to rid it of the dreaded Tussock Moth which he has discovered is laying blight to the trees.

Gene eventually learns lumberman Henry Mitchell (Douglass Dumbrille) and his associate Bill Wright (Damian O'Flynn) murdered Carter's forest ranger father to prevent him from spreading the word about the moth infestation which he also had discovered. If the infestation were not reported, the trees would die and would have to be cut, thereby profiting Mitchell and Wright.

After the first day's spraying, furious ranchers blame the DDT for the death of many animals found poisoned. A "phantom plane",

Badman Douglass Dumbrille (with gun) and henchman Clayton Moore have the drop on forestry men Bert Dodson and Gene Autry.

owned by Mitchell, full of true poison spray is actually responsible and is discovered by Gene's friend Joe Lucas who in the end sacrifices his life saving Gene.

NOTES AND COMMENTS: Working titles were "Wings Westward", "Ridin' Down the Old Pine Trail" and "Riders of the Whispering Pines".

The Pinafores, also known as the Kettle Sisters (Beulah, Ione and Eunice) were heard regularly on Gene's "Melody Ranch" radio program since 1945, but this was their only film appearance with the singing cowboy.

The idea for this film came from a rodeo appearance Gene made in Idaho in 1947. Hearing about the fight forest rangers were waging against the dreaded Tussock Moth with their light spraying planes over wooded areas,

upon his return to Hollywood, Gene told producer Armand Schaefer about it and had screenwriter Jack Townley develop a story.

The photo of Jimmy Lloyd's late wife, seen about 25 minutes into the film, is of young Columbia Pictures starlet Marilyn Monroe.

DDT, the spray that kills the destructive Tussock Moth in "Riders of the Whistling Pines", is stated in the film not to be harmful to wildlife. By 1972 this was proven not to be true and its use was banned.

Leading lady Patricia White came to Hollywood in 1946 via the Broadway stage. Born November 16, 1926, in Davenport, Iowa, she was the daughter of a doctor who owned clinics throughout the Midwest. Signed by Columbia, she appeared in some 15 features before "Riders of the Whistling Pines". In the early '50s she changed her name when she married and gained even more success in the '60s, '70s and '80s as Patricia Barry.

With the exorbitant cost overruns lensing "The Strawberry Roan" and "The Big Sombrero" in color, Gene made the economic decision not to film any other features in color. However, as a slight concession, "Riders of the Whistling Pines" and subsequent features were presented in Sepia Tone, a sort of antique brown, which is basically a lab bath of some kind rather than an actual filming process. However, even though other film companies such as Allied Artists advertised their Bill Elliott westerns as being in Sepia Tone, Gene's pictures were never referred to as such in print advertising. Unfortunately, Gene's personal screening prints were not treated with the process and it seems no surviving prints in Sepia Tone exist today.

FILM COMMENTS: *Gene Autry:* "The last few years I worked in pictures at Columbia I went back more or less to the regulation cowboy (clothes). I wore a dungaree shirt and dungaree pants. I stuck more or less to the traditional wear of the cowboy."[1]

WHAT THE EXHIBITOR HAD TO SAY: "Good business on this one and it is one of Autry's better pictures. Filmed in sepia-tone it was very pleasing to the eye, and his songs were pleasing to the ears, too. Autry's pictures do lack slapstick comedy that the fans like. Doubled with 'Henry the Rainmaker'."

—Bob Halliday, Willamette Valley Theaters, Albany, Oregon (August 1949)

"Very good little western. Autry pictures are much better than they used to be. Leon Weaver was in this. My folks really like him. Where is Elviry?"

—S. T. Jackson, Jackson Theater, F lomaton, Alabama (November 1949)

"Doubled this with 'The Mutineers' and did average Friday, Saturday business. Gene Autry of late does not draw them like he used to. We used to be able to bill him single feature and do business. His story material does not seem as good as it used to be. Does Gene need airplanes in his shows? We all know he can fly but so can a lot of people."

—Ernie Massman, Park Theater, Columbia Falls, Montana (November 1949)

"A very fine western drama. It did well for Friday and Saturday. Doubled with 'Daughter of the Jungle'. Made a fair profit. Autry brings them in. Well pleased."

—Harry A. Rolbiecki, Vogue Theater, Arcadia, Wisconsin (December 1949)

"Doubled with 'Ladies of the Chorus' to two-thirds of average gross. Can't account for the low gross because Gene Autry usually goes over very well here. It wasn't the weather, because it was perfect. The picture was the usual Autry with a slightly different plot. Was enjoyed by the Autry fans who came to see it."

—Fred G. Weppler, Colonial Theater, Colfax, Illinois (June 1950)

SOURCES:
1. "Melody Ranch Theater" showing of "Boots and Saddles" on Nashville Network, 1987.

Rim of the Canyon
Columbia, July 1949

A Gene Autry Production in Sepia Tone

Producer	Armand Schaefer		Photography	William Bradford
Director	John English		Musical Supervisor	Paul Mertz
Assistant Director	Carl Hiecke		Musical Director	Mischa Bakaleinikoff
Original Story	"Phantom .45's Talk Loud" by Joseph Chadwick in WESTERN ACES Magazine		Film Editor	Aaron Stell
			Sound Dept.	Russell Malmgren
			Art Director	Harold MacArthur
			Set Decorations	George Montgomery
			Hair Stylist	Beth Langston
Screenplay	John K. Butler		Makeup	Paul Langston

SONGS: "Rim of the Canyon" (music and lyrics by Hy Heath, Johnny Lange)—sung by Gene Autry and studio singers; "You're the Only Star in My Blue Heaven" (music and lyrics by Gene Autry)—sung by Gene Autry.

RUNNING TIME: 70 minutes

FILMING DATES: December 6-20, 1948

LOCATIONS: Vasquez Rocks; Corri-ganville; Columbia backlot

BUDGET: $46,784.

CAST:

Actor	*Character*
Gene Autry	Gene Autry/Marshal Steve Autry
Nan Leslie	Ruth Lambert
Thurston Hall	Big Tim Hanlon
Clem Bevans	Loco John
Walter Sande	Jake Fargo
Jock O'Mahoney	Pete Reagan
Francis McDonald	Charlie Lewis
Alan Hale Jr.	Matt Kimbrough
Denver Pyle	Cash Collins
Roy Bucko	Buck
Rory Mallinson	Sheriff Pat Nolan
Frankie Marvin	Cowhand
John McKee	Tex Rawlins
Sandy Sanders	Emerson Posse Rider
Bobby Clark	Posse Rider
Amelita Ward	Lily Shannon
Boyd Stockman	Stage Driver
Lynn Farr	Cowboy
Ralph Bucko	Extra
Champion	Champion

STUNTS: Boyd Stockman; Sandy Sanders (Gene's double).

THE FILM: "Rim of the Canyon" features a refreshing novel idea for a Gene Autry film, a ghost story with Gene playing a dual role, as himself and his father.

This is the first of Gene's films with a noticeable cut-back in the amount of songs, only two—with the title tune sung twice. As a cost-cutting measure, "Rim of the Canyon" incorporates more Columbia stock footage than previous Autry films.

When his stagecoach is disabled in a race, Gene is left stranded and limps to a nearby ghost town. There he finds lonely schoolmarm Ruth Lambert (Nan Leslie) who says she comes there to talk to the ghost of Big Tim Hanlon (Thurston Hall) who died 20 years ago.

Meanwhile, back in town, Gene's horse Champion is stolen by three escaped convicts, Jake Fargo (Walter Sande), Pete Reagan (Jock O'Mahoney) and Charlie Lewis (Francis McDonald). Fargo and Lewis had been captured by Gene's father, Marshal Steve Autry (Gene Autry with a mustache), 20 years earlier after the theft of $30,000 from Hanlon. Seems the crooks stashed the loot in the ghost

town before being imprisoned and are now back to find the money.

From there, it's a hunt for the loot through the spooky ghost town by everyone involved, with Gene getting an assist from the "ghost" of Big Tim.

NOTES AND COMMENTS: In playing the dual role of himself and his father, who sported a mustache, a dozen or so test photos of Gene with different mustaches were taken before a final decision of the one seen on film was made. These are only two of the test shots.

FILM COMMENTS: *Nan Leslie:* "Gene was in charge in a very different way on his series. He's a very affable man, easygoing. If he was a perfectionist, and I think he was, it was not so apparent. He was very much a friend to people on the set." [1]

Gene Autry: "My films at Columbia, after the first ones, had taken on a whole new look. Gone were the fancy shirts and pants and modern trappings and settings. What emerged for the most part was Gene Autry, frontiersman. The cycle had come nearly full circle. By then we were groping, guessing, trying to find a trend. The B-westerns were slipping. Once in a while we still found a good script with a modern viewpoint." [2]

Jock Mahoney: "Gene was a good man to work for. I had worked with him on some of his features, and he evidently liked my work as a heavy. When he decided to do 'Range Rider', he called me and Dickie Jones. He was always very helpful, and he was always a gentleman."[3]

CAST BIOS: "Jock Mahoney was one of the finest stuntmen and action men in movies," said Gene Autry. "He belongs up there with Yakima Canutt, David Sharpe, Cliff Lyons, Tom Steele, Chuck Roberson and a few others. He was a great 'Range Rider' too." [4]

Tall, rangy, 6'4" Jacques O'Mahoney made a name for himself doubling such stars as Charles Starrett (as the Durango Kid), George Macready, Errol Flynn, Gregory Peck and Randolph Scott.

Born February 7, 1919, in Chicago, Illinois, of French and Irish extraction, with some Cherokee Indian blood, Mahoney attended the University of Iowa where he excelled in swimming, basketball, boxing and gymnastics.

Jock O'Mahoney (later TV's "Range Rider" for Gene's Flying A TV Productions) battles with Gene in a ghost town hotel.

He endured two years of pre-med school before accepting a job as lifeguard and swimming coach at Long Beach Pacific Coast Club. Various other jobs followed until WWII broke out and he enlisted in 1941 as a Marine, eventually becoming a carrier fighter pilot earning the rank of Second Lieutenant.

He came to Hollywood as a stuntman at Columbia in 1946. Eventually, small speaking parts began to come his way in serials, Three Stooges shorts and Durango Kid westerns. Columbia then starred him in their "Cody of the Pony Express" and "Roar of the Iron Horse" serials in 1950 and '51 respectively.

Meanwhile, Gene spotted Jock (who varied his name from Jacques O'Mahoney to Jack O'Mahoney to Jock O'Mahoney to Jack Mahoney to Jock Mahoney over the years) while working as Tulsa Jack and doing stunts in Randolph Scott's "The Doolins of Oklahoma" ('49) and enlisted his talents for "Rim of the Canyon".

When Gene moved into television production, he expressly created "Range Rider" for Jocko (as his friends called him). The 78 episode half hour black and white series ran from December 1950 to June 1953 (plus syndication).

Jocko was later under contract to Universal-International where he starred in such films as "A Day of Fury" ('56), "Showdown at Abilene" ('56), "Joe Dakota" ('57) and "Slim Carter" ('57).

In 1958 Mahoney starred in another popular TV series, "Yancy Derringer" on CBS.

At age 43, he became the oldest man to play Tarzan in two features, "Tarzan Goes to India" ('62) and "Tarzan's Three Challenges" ('63). His role led to dysentery, dengue fever and pneumonia, canceling out any future roles as Edgar Rice Burroughs' famed apeman. Mahoney never fully recovered, and eased into character roles in films and on TV.

His second marriage was to actress Margaret Field, making him actress Sally Field's stepfather. Upon divorce from Margaret, he was wed in 1967 until his death to Autumn Russell.

Mahoney died in Bremerton, Washington, December 14, 1989, of an apparent stroke. He'd been hospitalized two days earlier following an auto accident resulting from a stroke.

WHAT THE EXHIBITOR HAD TO SAY: "These westerns are always popular with us. Autry still brings them in, but not as well as Rogers. However, we still enjoy checking the receipts after playing these pictures."

—Harland Rankin, Plaza Theater, Tilbury, Ontario, Canada (September 1950)

SOURCES:

1. *Westerns Women.* McFarland, 1999. p. 138-139.
2. Autry with Herskowitz. p. 101.
3. Knoxville, Tennessee, Film Festival audio tape, 1986.
4. *The Westerner #8.* 1986.

The Cowboy and the Indians
<u>Columbia, September 1949</u>

A Gene Autry Production in Sepia Tone

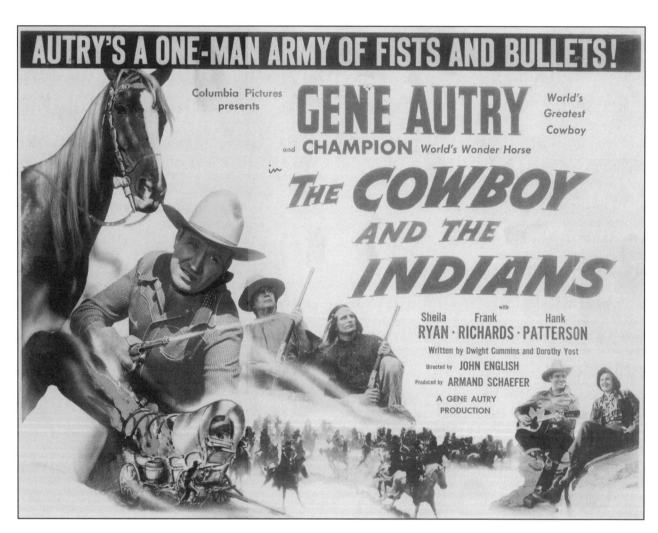

Producer ....Armand Schaefer
Director ....John English
Assistant Director........................Jack Corrick
Screenplay....................................Dwight Cummins,
　　　　　　　　　　　　　　　Dorothy Yost
Photography ....William Bradford
Musical Supervisor ....Paul Mertz
Musical Director ....Mischa Bakaleinikoff
Film Editor ....Henry Batista
Sound Dept...................................Frank Goodwin

Art Director.................................Harold MacArthur
Set Decorations ....Louis Diage

SONGS: "Indian Chant" (arranged by Paul Mertz)—sung by Chief Yowlachie; "One Little Indian Boy" (music and lyrics by Robert Bilder)—sung by Gene Autry; "America, The Beautiful" (Public Domain by Samuel A. Word, Katherine Lee Bates)—sung by Indian children; "Here Comes Santa Claus (Right Down Santa Claus Lane)" (music and lyrics by Oakley Haldeman)—sung by Gene

Autry and children; "Silent Night" (Public Domain by Franz Grüber, Joseph Mohr)—sung by Gene Autry and children.

RUNNING TIME: 70 minutes
FILMING DATES: March 14-28, 1949
LOCATIONS: Pioneertown; Columbia backlot
BUDGET: $44,375

CAST:

Actor	Character
Gene Autry	Gene Autry
Sheila Ryan	Dr. Nan Palmer
Frank Richards	"Smiley" Martin
Hank Patterson	Tom Garber
Jay Silverheels	Lakohna
Claudia Drake	Lucy Broken Arm
George Nokes	Rona
Charles Stevens	Broken Arm
Alex Frazer	Fred Bradley
Clayton Moore	Ed
Ray Beltram	Henchman
Iron Eyes Cody	Indian farmer
Romere Darling	Indian woman Two Mary
Felipa Gomez	Indian woman One Mary
Roy Gordon	Congressman Lawrence
Frank Lackteen	Joe Blue Eagle
Nolan Leary	Sheriff Don Payne
Harry Mackin	Bob Collins
Frankie Marvin	Frank
Maudie Prickett	Miss Summers
Charles Quigley	Henderson
Lee Roberts	Joe
Shooting Star	Indian
Chief Yowlachie	Chief Long Arrow
Sandy Sanders	Cowhand
Gilbert Alonzo	Lucy's Son
Jose Alvarado	Indian Boy
Champion	Champion

STUNTS: Sandy Sanders (Gene's double).

THE FILM: "The Cowboy and the Indians" portrays the Indian as something other than a blood curdling savage in this thought-provoking, intelligent western as Gene Autry fights to prevent the Indians' suffering from malnutrition and the theft of their valuable artifacts.

After Gene enlists the aid of Doctor Nan Palmer (Sheila Ryan) to help save an elderly starving Navajo lady, he runs afoul of burly trading post owner Smiley Martin (Frank Richards) who has been cheating the Indians for years. Martin and curio dealer Bradley (Alex Frazer) are scheming to obtain a priceless blanket from Lucy Broken Arm (Claudia Drake) and a symbolic turquoise necklace from Chief Long Arrow (Chief Yowlachie).

Gene finds he must defend the Indians against not only malnutrition but outright theft, with the crooks laying the blame on young brave Lakohna (Jay Silverheels).

NOTES AND COMMENTS: One Mary, the Navajo woman Gene saves from starvation was played by Felipa Gomez who was 103 years old at the time. She was born in Mexico in 1846.

Both The Lone Ranger—Clayton Moore—and Tonto—Jay Silverheels—are featured in the cast of this film. Coincidentally, "The Lone Ranger" was first seen on ABC-TV on September 15, 1949, and "The Cowboy and the Indians" was released to theaters in September 1949.

FILM COMMENTS: *Gene Autry:* "Although color was out, I tried to stick with my policy of including one or more popular songs in each picture. The plot of 'The Cowboy and the Indians' had me helping the Navajos defend their land against the palefaces. But we still managed to work into it that year's Christmas favorite, 'Here Comes Santa Claus'." [1]

CAST BIOS: Of Irish heritage, Sheila Ryan was born Katherine Elizabeth McLaughlin June 8, 1921, in Topeka, Kansas. Sheila's railroad official father transferred to Los Angeles when she was three months old.

While in high school, the 5' 5" Sheila began a career as a commercial model while she concentrated on an art career. Actress turned agent Sue Carol (Ladd) discovered Sheila at Hollywood High and had her cast in "What A Life" ('39) under the screen name Betty McLaughlin.

Placed under contract first to Paramount, she left over a salary disagreement and was picked up by 20th Century–Fox in 1940 where she remained until 1945, at which time she began to freelance.

She was first married to western star Allan Lane for a year in 1945-'46. She tried marriage again in 1947 to actor Edward Norris, but that also ended in divorce a year later. Her third marriage, however, was quite successful. She met Gene Autry's sidekick Pat Buttram when they worked together on "Mule Train" in 1949. They were married on December 26, 1952, with a daughter, Kathleen, born in '54.

Sheila co-starred in four features and nine TVers with Gene, as well as an episode of Flying A's "Annie Oakley".

Leaving the screen in the mid '50s, she was ill for several years and died of an unknown lung disease on November 5, 1975.

WHAT THE EXHIBITOR HAD TO SAY: "Kids loved it."
—Mrs. Denzil Hildebrand, Algerian Theater, Risco, Missouri (July 1950)

"A good Autry. Here is a different western story that pleased the action fans. Production values good. Doubled with 'Sons of Adventure' for a well balanced Saturday program."
—William Hayden, Vacaville Theater, Vacaville, California (March 1950)

SOURCES:
1. Autry with Herskowitz. p. 100.

Riders In the Sky
<u>Columbia, November 1949</u>

A Gene Autry Production in Sepia Tone

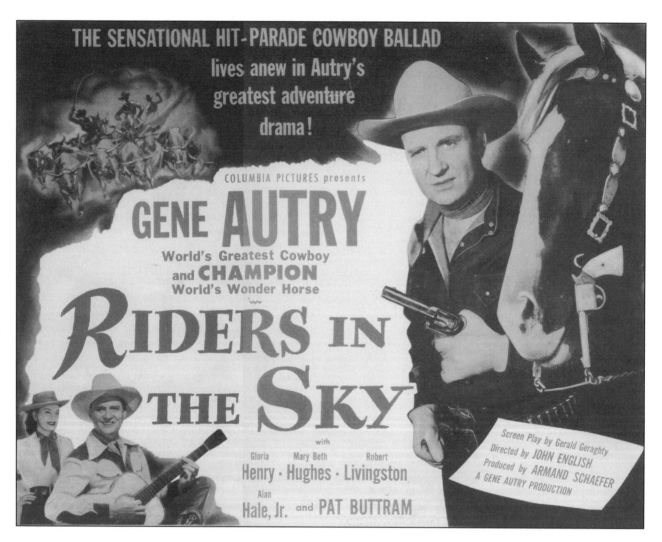

Producer ....Armand Schaefer
Director ....John English
Assistant Director........................Paul Donnelly
Original Story............................Herbert A. Woodbury
Screenplay..................................Gerald Geraghty
Photography ....William Bradford
Musical Supervisor ....Paul Mertz
Musical Director ....Mischa Bakaleinikoff
Film Editor ....Henry Batista

Sound Dept..................................George Cooper
Art Director................................Harold MacArthur
Set Decorations ....Frank Kramer
Makeup ....Newt Jones
Hair Stylist ....Irene Beshon

SONGS: "Ghost Riders In the Sky" (music and lyrics by Stan Jones)—sung by Gene Autry and studio singers; "The Cowboy's Lament" ("Streets of Laredo") (Public

Domain)—sung by Gene Autry; "It Makes No Difference Now" (music and lyrics by Jimmie Davis, Floyd Tillman)—sung by Gene Autry.

RUNNING TIME: 71 minutes
FILMING DATES: August 8-23, 1949
LOCATIONS: Pioneertown; Columbia backlot; Iverson's Ranch
BUDGET: $55,959

CAST:

Actor	Character
Gene Autry	Gene Autry
Gloria Henry	Anne Lawson
Mary Beth Hughes	Julie Steward
Robert Livingston	Rock McCleary
Steve Darrell	Ralph Lawson
Alan Hale Jr.	Marshal Riggs
Tom London	Old Pop Roberts
Pat Buttram	Chuckwalla Jones
Lynton Brent	Croupier
Loie Bridge	Widow Cathcart
Kenne Duncan	Travis
Joseph Forte	Willard Agnew
Roy Gordon	District Attorney J. B. Galloway
Herman Hack	Juror
Frank Jaquet	Coroner
Kermit Maynard	Henchman
Dennis Moore	Bud Dwyer
Bud Osborne	Juror Parkhurst
John Parrish	Sam Devlin
Hank Patterson	Luke (stagecoach driver)
Lee Phelps	Juror
Sandy Sanders	Sandy
Boyd Stockman	Well Guard
Robert Walker	Townsman
Ben Welden	Dave
Isabel Withers	Secretary
Bob Woodward, Art Dillard	Henchmen
Vernon Johns	Blaisdale
Pat O'Malley	Lowry
Cactus Mack, Victor Adamson, Jack Evans, Tom Smith, Stan Jones, Frank Ellis, Ed Peil Sr., George Bell, Guy Teague	Extras
Champion	Champion

STUNTS: Sandy Sanders (Gene's double); Boyd Stockman.

THE FILM: Gene Autry realized the advantage of the sensational hit song "Ghost Riders In the Sky" as a title and plot springboard for a movie.

Gene opens the picture with the song as he and his ranch hands herd cattle. When Gene's cowboys question the origin of the song, Gene relates the legend of how rancher Ralph Lawson (Steve Darrell) was accused of the shooting of a gambler in the border town of Desert Wells. Old Pop Roberts (Tom London) and other witnesses are threatened when they attempt to testify Lawson shot in self defense. When Lawson is convicted, Gene, as an investigator for the county attorney, and his pal Chuckwalla (Pat Buttram) try to help Lawson's daughter, Anne (Gloria Henry), clear her father's name.

Desert Wells is ruled with an iron hand by gambler Rock McCleary (Robert Livingston) whose henchmen fatally wound Pop, but not before Pop can give Gene all the evidence he needs to clear Lawson. He dies as he sees the eerie Ghost Riders in the Sky coming for him.

Gene reprises the title song to terrific effect three times in the film. The hit ballad literally comes alive at the end as the ghostly riders, led by Pop Roberts, echo across the song-filled sky. Merrill McCord in his book BROTHERS OF THE WEST saw the ending as "a fitting tribute to Tom London, the greatest of B-western character actors, and among the most memorable moments in B-western history."

On a 1987 "Melody Ranch Theater" TV program, Gene said, "I've been around these pictures so long I seldom ever get enthused about a picture, but I think the last scene in the picture with Tom London riding in the sky with those clouds was one of the most beautiful endings I ever worked on. It actually brought a few tears to my eyes."[1] Both Gene and partner Pat Buttram agreed London "stole the whole picture."

NOTES AND COMMENTS: Stan Jones was a

"Ghost Riders in the Sky" songwriter Stan Jones and Gene pause for a drink of water during the filming of "Riders In the Sky" in which Jones has a bit role.

National Park Service Ranger in Death Valley who passed the time by singing songs he had composed, when he was heard by a Hollywood press agent, Frank Daugherty of Columbia Pictures, and persuaded to come to Hollywood and try to sell his songs. The ranger was ready to give up and return to Death Valley when one day he ran into Eben Ahbez, the famous composer of "Nature Boy". Stan asked him desperately if he would listen to only four bars of a song he had written and give him an honest opinion. If Ahbez didn't think it had possibilities, Stan would return to Death Valley. When Ahbez heard the song, "Ghost Riders In the Sky", he rushed Jones to a music company headed by Burl Ives and Jones was offered a contract. The song was recorded by 13 different artists with a total sale of over four million records. Vaughn Monroe's version sold the most records but Gene Autry beat out several film companies to grab the movie rights when he and Jones met in a Sunset Boulevard radio station and Gene wrote out a check for a reported $10,000.

Leading lady Gloria Henry went on to star as Alice Mitchell, mother of "Dennis the Menace" on TV from '59-'63.

Alan Hale Jr. starred on TV as "Biff Baker, U.S.A." from '52-'53, as "Casey Jones" in '58 and finally, his greatest success as The Skipper on "Gilligan's Island" from '64-'67.

FILM COMMENTS: *Tom London:* "A star I owe a lot to was Gene Autry. I made around 18 pictures with him and he was one of the nicest guys to work with. He always saw that I got decent characters to play, and in 'Riders In the Sky', I got a great part playing a cowpoke in a big death scene. I've been told that this was the best acting of my whole career. Later on when I auditioned for some television work, I would bring along a 16mm print with that scene and show it on a casting agent's office wall and most of the time I got the part."[2]

Gene Autry: "Pat Buttram was just a natural comedian. Pat teamed with me on radio and through most of my movies at Columbia and the 'Gene Autry Show' on television."[3]

"Buttram always had that precious gift of being able to laugh at himself. He was the best of company but he honestly worried about the pace I kept and urged me to slow down and not push so hard. 'Someday,' he said, 'somebody will break your record for travel, for touring, for shows done and pictures made, rides and falls, rodeos and everything. But they are going to lose a helluva lot of sleep doing it.'"[4]

Pat Buttram: "I first met Gene when we were both appearing on the National Barn Dance over radio station WLS in Chicago. On the Barn Dance I used to play tricks on Gene. I would get one string of his guitar out of tune and I wouldn't tell him which one it was. I'd mix him up. (Chuckle) In the WLS days, I knew that Gene was destined for high achievements, yet he was a good friend to everyone who surrounded him. I thought he was a very talented man, a fine and generous person, and a tireless and industrious worker. When Gene came out of the service in 1946, he didn't have a sidekick in pictures, so he just put me in the pictures. Gene and I hit it off right away. He paid me money and I gave him a few jokes along the way. We both liked to drink and admire women. But he never loused up a show. He knew it would cost him money. Once we got him on a horse, we knew we were safe. Gene's word was impeccable. You could put it in the bank.

"When I first started (in films) with Autry, I knew Buster Keaton very well. I went out and talked with him, and he showed me how to do some falls. He said, 'If it's possible to do a stunt in a comedy yourself, do it—in a water trough, a cactus, or wherever you're to fall. It's not the fall that gets the laugh, it's your reaction as you hit the ground or whatever, then getting up. If they have to cut to a double and then cut back to you for your reaction, it's not as effective as if it's one big take.' Keaton also said, 'There's going to be kids watching your picture, so when you fall get up real quick because if kids think you're hurt, they won't laugh. When they see you're okay, then they'll laugh like Hell.' He helped me a lot.

"Autry is the life of the troupe on a P.A. tour. He enjoys each experience and enters all activities with great zest and energy. He loves to meet his public and takes great pleasure in being with them. The demands made on a star doing personal appearances are very heavy, but Gene seems to rise over fatigue and always has such a good time that his good humor pervades the whole cast.

"Gene is a wonderful boss. Kind, sympathetic, understanding and generous. He is never critical and often pretends the occasional errors that take place are his fault, in order to avoid embarrassing another performer or employee. He is easy to work with…never bad-tempered or touchy and he somehow manages to keep all his associates working together in friendship and harmony. Consequently, the group that surround Gene in his work seem to take on the feeling of a big, happy family. Gene is a wonderful, gifted, warm-hearted man—and a *real* man." [5]

Gloria Henry: "The limo took the actors to location. The assistant director said, 'Gloria you're in the next set-up.' So I had my wardrobe and makeup put on there. They had a scene with Gene and Pat Buttram and myself riding along talking, handing back and forth a canteen, drinking water. So—I'm fine. I got a good horse, I had a few lessons, I'm doing a bit better. Turns out the first horse they got me was a mare, and Champion was rather enamored with this mare…need I go further? (Chuckles) So they had to send the mare back and send up another horse for me. They sent this big old guy who was 16-17 hands tall—I don't know—but my legs would hardly go over him. I'm 5' 2". And they didn't bother to adjust my feet in the stirrups before the scene. Well, the horse had been in the corral all morning with his buddies and decided he didn't want to work, so he started taking off to the side—and I'm trying to rein in. Gene said, 'Rein in Gloria,' and I said, 'I am, I am.' But the horse keeps going away from the camera car in front of us. I remember thinking to myself, 'In the westerns I've seen, when the horse runs away with the young lady, Gene Autry comes running after her to save her. But I didn't hear any clip-clops behind me. I'm all by myself, taking off to Hollywood as far as I knew. (Laughs) The horse is now going lickety-split. I think, 'I don't intend to go all the way back on this horse,' so I do a slow roll of the back of the horse—only stunt I ever pulled and it worked. I fell down on the ground in the sagebrush and everybody came running over to me. And I said to Gene in a very hurt voice, 'Why didn't you come after me?' And he said, 'Well, if your horse had heard my horse he'd have gone even faster.' Well that convinced me, horses are dumb! (Laughs)"[6]

CAST BIOS: Pat Buttram had briefly appeared in "Strawberry Roan" but did not become Gene's regular sidekick until "Riders In the Sky". Pat had been on Gene's "Melody Ranch" radio program ("Mister Ar-tery…") since June 1948 and now became his movie sidekick as well as his TV sidekick on "The Gene Autry Show" beginning in July 1950.

The country-bumpkin comedian with a whining voice was born Maxwell E. Buttram, the son of a circuit-riding Methodist preacher June 19, 1915, in rural Winston County, Alabama.

The family endured a nomadic existence, living in several different places. A class play brought Pat to the

Gene's regular Columbia Pictures sidekick Pat Buttram.

attention of radio station WSGN in Birmingham, Alabama, where he obtained a job as a comedy announcer.

In 1934 Pat journeyed to Chicago to see the World's Fair. Pat was among the public interviewed by reporters for their reaction to the fair. His spontaneous answers were so hilarious that he was immediately hired by WLS, Chicago, for their popular radio show, "The National Barn Dance". It was here "The Sage of Winston County, Alabama", first encountered Gene.

As Smiley Burnette had moved on to the Durango Kid films while Gene was in the service, Gene remembered Pat's humor and brought him to Hollywood for a small role in "The Strawberry Roan" and elevated him to his comic sidekick with "Riders In the Sky". You'll notice in "Riders…" Pat is clean shaven, but by the time of his next film with Gene, "Mule Train", he had acquired the stubbly beard that worked well for the comic.

With his sharp wit, Buttram became a favorite of the Hollywood banquet circuit as a toastmaster—and roastmaster.

He and the co-star of "Mule Train", Sheila Ryan, were married from 1952 until her death in 1975.

When the westerns ended, Pat prospered in radio, films, TV and voice over commercials. His best known television work was as the crafty Mr. Haney on "Green Acres" which ran on CBS from '65 to '71. Pat did considerable work in animated films, supplying voices in "The Aristocats" ('70), "Robin Hood" ('73), "The Rescuers" ('77), "The Fox and the Hound" ('81), "Who Framed Roger Rabbit" ('88) and "A Goofy Movie" ('95).

In 1983 Pat instigated the Golden Boot Awards, the prestigious annual event that gives honor and recognition to western personalities of film and TV. He himself received the Award in 1984.

On January 8, 1994, 78 year old Pat Buttram died of kidney failure at the University of California Medical Center, leaving behind a rich legacy of comic performances.

WHAT THE EXHIBITOR HAD TO SAY: "Farmers were busy in the fields day and night. If they came in during this film, it was so late they did not want to see the show. Business terrible. I wonder each time if Autry is slipping."
—Fred G. Weppler, Colonial Theater, Colfax, Illinois (August 1950)

"Gene Autry stories and supporting casts are improving with each picture. However, between Rex Allen, Roy Rogers and Allan "Rocky" Lane, Gene Autry seems to have been lost in the parade for drawing power of western stars. Comment was good, particularly concerning Pat Buttram. Business was off, we feel, due to Autry's lack of draw."
—Tom S. Graff, Grand Theater, Pollock Pines, California (January 1951)

"Autry not the draw he used to be, but still did fair business."
—Harland Rankin, Erie Theater, Wheatley, Ontario, Canada (February 1952)

270

SOURCES:

1. "Melody Ranch Theater: showing of "Riders In the Sky" on Nashville Network, 1987.

2. Copeland, Bobby. *Trail Talk.* Empire, 1996. p. 94.

3. Rothel, David. *Those Great Cowboy Sidekicks.* Empire, 1984. p. 104.

4. Autry with Herskowitz. pg. 118.

5. Rothel, David. *Those Great Cowboy Sidekicks.* Empire, 1984. p. 105, 106. And *Autry's Aces.* January/February 1958. p. 16-17.

6. Author's audio tape of 1988 Charlotte, North Carolina, Film Festival panel discussion.

Sons of New Mexico
Columbia, January 1950
A Gene Autry Production in Sepia Tone

Producer ....Armand Schaefer
Director ....John English
Assistant Director......................Wilbur McGaugh
Screenplay.................................Paul Gangelin
Photography ....William Bradford
Musical Supervisor ....Paul Mertz
Musical Director ....Mischa Bakaleinikoff
Film Editor................................Henry Batista
Sound Dept...............................Lambert E. Day
Art Director...............................Harold MacArthur
Set Decorations ....Sidney Clifford
Hair Stylist ....Helen Hunt
Makeup ....Don Murphy

Marie Blake................................Hannah Dobbs
Clayton Moore ....Rufe Burns
Sandy Sanders...........................Walt
Kenne Duncan............................Ed
Roy Gordon................................Major Hynes
Pierce Lyden..............................Watson
Harry Mackin ....Cadet
Frankie Marvin...........................Joe
Steve Pendleton.........................Polo Umpire
Paul Raymond............................Brad
Bobby Clark ....Polo Player
Billy Lechner ....Corporal
Champion...................................Champion

SONGS: "New Mexico Military Institute March" (music by Capt. F. E. Hunt, Special lyrics by Paul Mertz)—performed by Military Band and studio singers; "Can't Shake the Sands of Texas From My Shoes" (music and lyrics by Gene Autry, Diane Johnston, Kenneth Pitts)—sung by Gene Autry; "There's a Rainbow On the Rio Colorado" (music and lyrics by Gene Autry, Fred Rose)—sung by Gene Autry; "The Honey Song" (Honey, I'm in Love With You") (music and lyrics by Curt Massey, Arbie Gibson)—sung by Gene Autry.

RUNNING TIME: 70 minutes

FILMING DATES: June 15-29, 1949

LOCATIONS: Agoura Ranch; New Mexico Military Institute in Roswell, New Mexico; Iverson Ranch; French Ranch; Lake Sherwood; Deerwood Stock Farm (now Ventura Farms aka Kentucky Park Farms) used for racetrack scene; Columbia backlot

BUDGET: $53,139.65.

CAST:

Actor	Character
Gene Autry ....Gene Autry
Gail Davis ....Eileen MacDonald
Robert Armstrong.......................Pat Feeney
Dick Jones.................................Randy Pryor
Frankie Darro ....Gig Jackson
Irving Bacon..............................Chris Dobbs
Russell Arms ....Chuck Brunton

STUNTS: Sandy Sanders (Gene's double); Bert LeBaron.

THE FILM: "Autry gunfire and cadet courage blast badmen off the map" read the advertising slugline for Gene Autry's latest Columbia picture which utilizes scenes filmed at the New Mexico Military Institute in Roswell, New Mexico.

Gene is appointed executor for a deceased friend and heads for New Mexico to care for the estate's ranch which comes complete with a rebellious teen son, Randy Pryor (Dick Jones), and his cute cousin Eileen (Gail Davis).

When he learns Randy is in deep with a gang of crooked gamblers headed by Pat Feeney (Robert Armstrong), Gene must get involved to save the boy.

To pay off his gambling debts to Feeney, Randy agrees to race his prize horse against one of Feeney's. The horse race (which, incidentally, is so excitingly filmed it gets your adrenaline pumping as if you were watching the Kentucky Derby) is fixed and Randy loses his prize horse to Feeney.

Attempting to straighten out the boy, Gene enrolls Randy in the New Mexico Military Institute but Randy disgraces himself in a polo match with a fellow student (Russell Arms) whom he's had trouble with before.

Returning to Feeney's gambling den-ranch, Randy is told by another youngster, Gig (Frankie Darro), that Feeney is preying on him because Feeney once loved Randy's mother, but lost her to the lad's father who also sent Feeney

272

Gene breaks up a fight between Dick Jones (left) and Russell Arms (right).

to prison for crooked gambling.

Enraged, Randy knocks Gig out. When Feeney discovers Gig has spilled the beans, he kills the unconscious boy and lays the blame on Randy. Feeney then convinces Randy he is guilty of Gig's death.

Randy flees with the gang in pursuit, but Gene, Eileen and cavalry cadets from NMMI come to the rescue.

Randy, cleared of the murder charge, realizes the wrong of his ways and re-enrolls in the Military Institute.

NOTES AND COMMENTS: New Mexico Military Institute in Roswell was formed in 1891, structured on the old cavalry regiments from the Civil War period. The NMMI polo team often rated in the top three in intercollegiate circles.

An example of early "product placement", Gene is clearly seen driving a Ford truck.

Again, as in "The Cowboy and the Indians", just before signing on to be TV's "The Lone Ranger", Clayton Moore is seen as one of Robert Armstrong's henchmen.

Frankie Darro's history with Gene stretches all the way back to Gene's serial, "The Phantom Empire", in 1935.

Roy Rogers was #1 and Gene Autry #2 in MOTION PICTURE HERALD's poll of "Money Making Western Stars of 1949". Gabby Hayes, Tim Holt and Bill Elliott followed at #3-5.

FILM COMMENTS: *Russell Arms:* "My second picture with Gene was 'Sons of New Mexico' and I didn't play cowboy in this one. I was the Cadet Captain of the school's polo team (I always thought of the part as Jack Armstrong, All-American Boy). Dick Jones was the troubled young kid whom Autry was rescuing this time and Dick and I wound up playing polo against each other. This was done on the studio backlot (Columbia backlot in Burbank) and the process screen. We did the close ups and they cut in long shots of an actual polo game in New Mexico. Riding a polo saddle with the double handful of reins, the polo mallet in the right hand, and no pommel to the little, flat saddle was a new experience for me but I only fell off once and that with a lot of rough riding, pushing and shoving between Dick and me. Fun!

"I didn't have many real scenes with Gene in this film, mostly some words on horseback on the polo field. But, again, I have to say it was a pleasure to work on an Autry film and, as I recall, with a good director, Jack English.

"Gene did have a bit of trouble with the 'sauce', so much so that they made it a point to shoot all his close-up scenes in the morning before 'lunch' which often was purely liquid. Later on in his life he got a handle on the 'sauce' and straightened out.

"Some time later I was emceeing a fashion show in Autry's hotel in Palm Springs and I made a point of seeking him out…where else but in the bar! (This was still in his drinking days.) I wasn't sure if he would remember me, but he did and we had a nice conversation over a beer." [1]

Gail Davis: "I went on several rodeos with Gene. I had to do all my own shooting and riding. We even went to England where I was billed as "Gail of the Golden West". Gene took Champion, his whole crew, and the entertainers. It was a wonderful experience. He was a fantastic man to work for. I did 14 films with Gene. He was a great boss and everyone loved working with him." [2]

Frankie Darro: "When this picture is released I'm going into hiding. At least I'm going to make sure I never set foot in Gene Autry, Oklahoma. You see, in this picture, besides just playfully bashing Gene over the skull with my gun, I shove him through a plate glass window and try my level-best to make life scarce for him. So after his friends see this picture, I'm a dead duck! (Laughs) Anyone who remembers me from ('The Phantom Empire' serial) is going to say, 'Now just look what happened to that nice young kid." [3]

CAST BIOS: "Sons of New Mexico" was the first of 14 pictures Gail Davis co-starred in with Gene Autry. Additionally she appeared in 15 of Gene's half-hour TV shows and co-starred three seasons for his Flying A Productions as "Annie Oakley" from January 1954 to February 1957, with reruns through 1960.

Born Betty Jean Grayson in Little Rock, Arkansas, on October 5, 1925, the daughter of a doctor, she was primarily raised in McGehee where her father built a hospital. She later attended Harkum Junior College for Girls in Bryn Mawr, Pennsylvania, and the University of Texas, majoring in drama at both schools.

Newly married to Army Captain Robert Davis, with acting aspirations, the 5' 2" Gail came to Hollywood at 20. Spotted by actor John Carroll, she was put under contract to MGM, making her screen debut in "The Romance of Rosy Ridge" ('47).

MGM sold her contract to RKO where Gail appeared in a few small roles, then she began to freelance with her first western being "The Far Frontier" ('48) with Roy Rogers.

Gail went on to co-star with Tim Holt, Jimmy Wakely, Monte Hale, "Rocky" Lane, Charles Starrett—and Gene Autry as of "Sons of New Mexico".

In 1953, Gene wrote, "Gail Davis is my idea of the perfect western actress. She not only rates tops in horsemanship and acting ability, but she has the knack of wearing western clothes well. Gail's good looks have always drawn attention." [4]

Even with that endorsement, when Autry's Flying A Productions acquired the rights to Annie Oakley, Gail had to convince producer Mandy Schaefer she was the right gal for the job.

For the next few years she spent six months a year filming "Annie Oakley" and the other six on the road touring the U.S. and Canada. Ceasing production after 81 episodes, Gail was hopelessly typecast as Annie Oakley, so much so that producers refused to cast her in anything.

For several years she was a partner in a personal management firm in Hollywood and later worked for a computer sales firm in Los Angeles. She also had her own public relations company, Gail Davis Enterprises.

She received the prestigious Golden Boot Award in 1994.

Married three times, she had a daughter, Terrie. Gail was widowed when she died of brain cancer March 15, 1997, at a Burbank hospital. Gene's most endearing leading lady left a large void in the western field.

WHAT THE EXHIBITOR HAD TO SAY: "Good old Gene—still love him. Always good for extra business. Not as popular as he used to be but still feel he has a big following."   —Harland Rankin, Rankin Enterprises, Chatham, Ontario, Canada (March 1951)

"This is a western with a little different twist to the plot. The sepia tone prints always draw lots of praise here, and the Autry fans are very loyal as ever. Freezing weather kept attendance very low."   —I. Roche, Vernon Theater, Vernon, Florida (January 1952)

Gene teaches a few rope tricks to Gail Davis who became "Annie Oakley" for Gene's Flying A TV Productions.

SOURCES:

1. Interview with author.

2. Knoxville, Tennessee Film Festival audio tape, 1989.

3. *Autry's Aces.* January 1949/February 1950. Interview with Virginia Siegers. p. 5.

4. *Who's Who In Western Stars.* Dell Pub. 1953. p. 31.

Mule Train
<u>Columbia, February 1950</u>

A Gene Autry Production in Sepia Tone

Producer ....Armand Schaefer
Director ....John English
Assistant Director........................Paul Donnelly
Original Story...............................Alan James
Screenplay....................................Gerald Geraghty
Photography ....William Bradford
Musical Supervisor ....Paul Mertz
Musical Director ....Mischa Bakaleinikoff
Film Editor..................................Richard Fantl

Sound Dept....................................Frank Goodwin
Art Director..................................Charles Clague
Set Decorations ....George Montgomery
Hair Stylist ....Helen Hunt
Makeup ....Dave Grayson

SONGS: "Mule Train" (music and lyrics by Johnny Lange, Hy Heath, Fred Glickman)—sung by Gene Autry (with an assist by Pat Buttram); Room Full of Roses" (music and lyrics by Tim Spencer)—sung by Gene Autry; "Old Chisholm Trail" (Public Domain)—sung by Gene Autry.

RUNNING TIME: 70 minutes
FILMING DATES: November 8-22, 1949
LOCATIONS: Lone Pine; Columbia backlot; Corriganville
BUDGET: $46,804

CAST:

Actor	*Character*
Gene Autry	Gene Autry
Pat Buttram	Smokey Argyle
Sheila Ryan	Sheriff Carol Bannister
Robert Livingston	Sam Brady
Frank Jaquet	Clayton Hodges
Vince Barnett	Barber Mulkey
Syd Saylor	Deputy Skeeter
Sandy Sanders	Deputy Bud
Stanley Andrews	Chalmers
Gregg Barton	"Keg" Rollins
Robert Carson	Bill Cummings
Kenne Duncan	Latigo
Roy Gordon	John MacKnight
Robert Hilton	Bancroft
Norman Leavitt	Homer
Frankie Marvin	Outrider
John Miljan	Judd Holbrook
George Morrell	Wagon driver for Gene
Pat O'Malley	Charley Stewart
Eddie Parker	Street Fighter Henchman
Robert J. Wilke	Henchman Bradshaw
Bob Woodward	Wagon Driver
Bobby Clark	Deputy
John McKee	Wilson
George Slocum	Brakeman
Mort Thompson	Posseman
Frank O'Connor	Bystander
Guy Teague	Extra
Champion	Champion

STUNTS: Sandy Sanders (Gene's double); Eddie Parker, Evelyn Finley (Sheila Ryan's double); Boyd Stockman.

THE FILM: U.S. Marshal Gene Autry rides into a situation where cement, something new in the west, is a motivating factor.

Gene comes to the aid of old pal Smokey (Pat Buttram) when Smokey's partner in the discovery of cement is killed. Sam Brady (Robert Livingston), a contractor, is the culprit secretly attempting to obtain the land.

Lady Sheriff Carol Bannister (Sheila Ryan) at first seems to be on Gene and Smokey's side, but is eventually revealed to be Brady's boss.

It's a simple B-western plot, but the angle of the lady heavy gives it some novelty. As usual with Autry, production quality is high all around.

NOTES AND COMMENTS: The genesis of such phenomenal song hits as "Riders in the Sky" and now, "Mule Train", is almost as fascinating as the songs themselves.

The crazy-quilt pattern of the song publishing business prevailed in the case of "Mule Train". Three Hollywood songwriters, Johnny Lange, Hy Heath and Fred Glickman, were returning to the film capital after a weekend in Las Vegas. As they drove through the borax country of Death Valley, they got to thinking about the fabulous mule teams that worked the desert mines. "We started working on a song as we drove," recalls Lange, "first we changed 'team' to 'train', which sounded better in a lyric. By the time we reached town we had the song pretty well worked out."[1]

Glickman then had the song recorded with a singer, but there the song languished. When the songsmiths got together again in Hollywood, Glickman dusted off the old record and played it for the other two. They became enthusiastic over their past effort, polished up the lyrics and put it on the market. This time it caught on like a house afire.

Frankie Laine and Vaughn Monroe recorded it, so did Burl Ives, Bing Crosby, and almost every recording artist of note, including Gene Autry. Over 30 different records were made. The most popular recording, besides Autry's, was Frankie Laine's whose sales have zoomed past the 1,000,000 mark.

Gene made a habit of using hit songs as the title of his films and springboard plot, and "Mule Train" was no exception. He reportedly paid $20,000 for the rights to use "Mule Train" as a film title and song within the film.

On November 27, 1949, Gene bought a $25,000 insurance policy on Champion. "I want to be sure if anything happened to me, Champ won't have to end his days pulling a milk wagon," Gene said. The money insured Champ be provided with $100 a month for feed and $100 a month for someone to look after Champ. [2]

FILM COMMENTS: *Gene Autry:* "The town sheriff (in "Mule Train") turned out to be a female, Sheila Ryan, and in cahoots with a scaggy band of claim jumpers. Pat (Buttram) and Sheila (Ryan) met on the set of that picture, eventually fell in love and were married. She was pretty and independent. He was country and fun-loving. No one thought it would last, but it did, until Sheila's death in late 1975. It seems to me that more than in most fields, people who stayed in the movie business any length of time formed relationships that were like vines of ivy, so that you could hardly tell where it had begun or ended or turned into the next vine. [3]

"When we went up to Lone Pine to make this picture it rained all night. I didn't expect to go out on location but I got up as usual around 5 or 5:30, went downstairs and ran into Armand Schaefer, my producer. It was still raining and looked like it was gonna stay that way all day. I said, 'Mandy, we're not going out in this weather are we?' He said, 'Yes, we're going out…we're going up to the location. I'm not happy and I don't want anybody else in this troupe

Deputy Syd Saylor, U.S. Marshal Gene Autry and lady sheriff Sheila Ryan in a tense moment from "Mule Train."

to be happy either.' So we all mounted up on a bus and went to the Alabama Hills. We sat out there in the buses for about an hour and a half and all at once the sun came out, it cleared up…but up at Mt. Whitney which is 14,900 ft. up, it was covered with snow. Then there was a layer of clouds below that, and below that was more snow on the Alabama rocks." [4]

Pat Buttram: "'Mule Train' shows you the character of Gene Autry, to let a guy come in and just take the whole part—it's *my* picture; it's the sidekick's picture for a change. Gene just encouraged it and helped out all he could to see that it held up as a picture rather than trying to hog it all for himself. A lot of guys in westerns, if the sidekick happened to get a little ahead of the star on his horse—now this is no joke—the star would stop the scene and say, 'You get back; I want to be six feet ahead.' This was often the rule a lot of them had, but Autry wasn't that way at all. We're very close; just like brothers today.

"Gene was one of the real great guys of the west, and he was the president of the Cowboy Hall of Fame in Oklahoma City. Gene's heart is still with the westerns, and we talk all of the time. Of course, what Autry liked most was the tours, the personal appearances. He says, 'Let's go on one more tour, just one more time.'

"'Mule Train' is in the library in New York City as the best B-western ever made. Columbia University has it as an example of the best B-western. I met Sheila Ryan on this picture, and we started going together during the picture, and, afterwards, we got married. She passed away in 1975.

She did a lot of pictures—westerns towards the end, and she was at 20th Century–Fox for years. We have a daughter who looks just like Sheila, but she's not in pictures. She went into banking. [5]

"But I never had such trouble in my life (as I did on 'Mule Train')! Did you ever try to lead six mules? (Chuckles) You can't do it! (Laughs) I tried and tried. I was trying to sing that song and lead the mules at the same time. You can't get mules to do anything you want 'em to do. They're stubborn. Finally, two of the prop men got behind the mules and they'd throw pebbles at 'em and hit 'em… that would make 'em run a little. Didn't hurt (the mules) but it'd goose 'em along. So I come along singing, they'd throw the pebbles and hit 'em, then they ran over me! (Laughs) Trying to get from getting stepped on by mules (laughs) we must have took a half day to get that song sung!" [6]

WHAT THE EXHIBITOR HAD TO SAY: "Can Gene Autry be slipping here? This one failed to do what I expected and was doubled with 'Kazan'. The song was worn out by the time I bought the picture and played it. This was one where I had a larger number of kids than usual. When Poppa and Momma bring junior to the show and then leave, something is wrong in 'Autryville'."
—Fred G. Weppler, Colonial Theater, Colfax, Illinois (July, 1950)

"This is the only bright spot in the week. If it weren't for a few of these boys, I don't know what we would do!"
—Harland Rankin, Plaza Theater, Tilbury, Ontario, Canada (August, 1950)

"Good Autry western which revived the song, 'Mule Train', here again. But it seems like something revived the boll weevils out here in the cotton patches again. Seems like everyone spent their extra money for poison again."
—Pat Fleming, Gail Theater, Round Park, Arkansas (September, 1950)

"Gene can always be counted on to make a bang-up western. For once we had a western with an honest to goodness pretty girl in it. Good story, good music, good production work and a pretty villain—what else could you ask for?"
—Curtis B. Willard, Victory Theater, Loxley, Alabama (November, 1951)

SOURCES:
1. "Mule Train" pressbook.
2. *San Bernardino Sun.* November 27, 2005.
3. Autry with Herskowitz. p. 100.
4. "Melody Ranch Theater". Nashville Network, 1987.
5. Rothel. p. 105-106, 109.
6. "Melody Ranch Theater". Nashville Network, 1987.

Cow Town
Columbia, May 1950
A Gene Autry Production in Sepia Tone

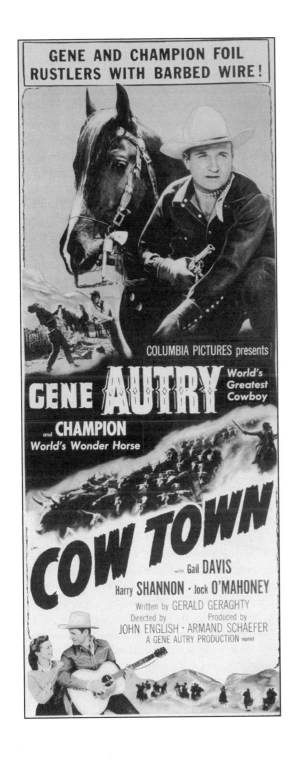

GENE AND CHAMPION FOIL RUSTLERS WITH BARBED WIRE!

COLUMBIA PICTURES presents

GENE **AUTRY** World's Greatest Cowboy

and CHAMPION World's Wonder Horse

COW TOWN

with Gail DAVIS

Harry SHANNON · Jock O'MAHONEY

Written by GERALD GERAGHTY
Directed by JOHN ENGLISH · Produced by ARMAND SCHAEFER
A GENE AUTRY PRODUCTION reprint

Producer	Armand Schaefer
Director	John English
Assistant Director	Paul Donnelly
Screenplay	Gerald Geraghty
Photography	William Bradford
Musical Supervisor	Paul Mertz
Musical Director	Mischa Bakaleinikoff
Film Editor	Henry Batista
Sound Dept.	Lambert Day
Art Director	Harold MacArthur
Set Decorations	Sidney Clifford
Hair Stylist	Helen Hunt
Makeup	Newt Jones

SONGS: "Down In the Valley" (Public Domain)—sung by Gene Autry; "Buffalo Gals" (Public Domain)—sung by Gene Autry; "Powder Your Face With Sunshine" (music and lyrics by Carmen Lombardo, Stanley Rochinski)—sung by Gene Autry; "Bury Me Not on the Lone Prairie (The Dying Cowboy)" (based on the poem "The Ocean Burial" by E. H. Chapin, music by George H. Allen)—sung by Gene Autry.

RUNNING TIME: 70 minutes

FILMING DATES: May 2-16, 1949

LOCATIONS: Lone Pine; Iverson Ranch; Columbia backlot

BUDGET: $127,332

CAST:

Actor	*Character*
Gene Autry	Gene Autry
Gail Davis	Ginger Kirby
Harry Shannon	Sandy Reeves
Jock O'Mahoney	Tod Jeffreys
Clark "Buddy" Burroughs	Duke Kirby
Harry Harvey	Sheriff
Steve Darrell	Chet Hilliard (aka Dave Hollister)
Sandy Sanders	Stormy Jones
Ralph Sanford	Martin Dalrymple
Holly Bane	Phillips
House Peters Jr.	Gill Saunders
Bud Osborne	Rancher George Copeland

Ted Mapes	Ed Loomis
Herman Hack	Rancher
Robert Hilton	Miller
Frankie Marvin	Ranchhand Frankie
Frank McCarroll	Rancher
Felice Raymond	Sheriff's Wife
Chuck Roberson	Mike Grady
Boyd Stockman	Boyd

Roy Bucko, Blackie Whiteford,
   Jack Tornek, Pat O'Malley,
   Frank O'Connor, Walt LaRue,
   Hank Mann, Buddy Roosevelt,
   Victor Cox, Kenny Cooper,
   Tom Smith, Bob Woodward,
   Ray Jones .... Extras
Champion .... Champion

STUNTS: Sandy Sanders (Gene's double); Jock O'Mahoney, Chuck Roberson, Walt LaRue, Ted Mapes.

THE FILM: By this point Gene Autry's westerns had settled into a routine-ish, comfortable niche—same director, producer, director of photography and crew on nearly every picture, a standard 70 minute running time, and fairly standardized B-western plots. Gone were the fancy clothes, big musical production numbers and fantasy world that gave the Republic features their originality. Gene had now settled in to rather serious, mostly straight B-westerns full of fisticuffs, gunplay and wild chases. No doubt the sobering effect of world events post WWII—and the ever increasing tension in Korea—was changing America and its films. The optimism of the Depression era that singing

Gail Davis and Gene have a good laugh over the final "mudpuddle scene" of "Cow Town."

cowboy heroes in white hats could ride in and save the day did not survive after the end of WWII. Times were changing. Gradually, Americans became more neurotic and realistic, and those changes were reflected in the movies being made. The "pure" cowboy hero was beginning to lose his foothold on the B-western range. Harder edged heroes like Lash LaRue were gaining in popularity. Soon the "adult" TV western would totally leave all the B-western heroes riding in the dust of a bygone era. Singing cowboy heroes like Gene and Roy Rogers adapted to the new mentality in their films as best they could—harder edged stories, rougher action, more conventional cowboy clothing and less music.

In his autobiography, Gene himself noted, "My films at Columbia, after the first ones, had taken on a whole new look. Gone were the fancy shirts and pants and modern trappings and settings. What emerged for the most part was Gene Autry, frontiersman. The cycle had come nearly full circle. By then we were groping, guessing, trying to find a trend. The B-westerns were slipping."[1]

Certainly serious issues are at work in "Cow Town" as Gene Autry introduces barbed wire to the range to end cattle rustling and straying cattle, thereby incurring the ire of pretty rancher Ginger Kirby (Gail Davis) and her kid brother Duke (Clark "Buddy" Burroughs). A murderous range war breaks out instigated by crafty livery stable owner Sandy Reeves (Harry Shannon) who wants the wide-open-unfenced-range for his sheep, planning to buy up rangeland for the taxes the cattlemen can't pay.

NOTES AND COMMENTS: Original title for this picture was to be "Barbed Wire", a title which was used later for another film.

During the filming of "Cow Town", Champion was borrowed for a special scene in Columbia's "The Good Humor Man" ('50) starring Jack Carson which called for a beautiful thoroughbred fitting Champ's description. Breaking precedent, Gene consented.

Clark "Buddy" Burroughs, the youngster of the picture, sang with the popular Hi-Los group.

More than three miles of barbed wire, 15,907 feet, were used in the filming of "Cow Town".

FILM COMMENTS: *House Peters Jr.:* "An amusing story came about on one of my days off from 'Cow Town'. I drove up a back road from the location to a lake and rented a boat. I rowed to just outside the point about 50 feet from shore and, lining up the spot with two trees and a small hideous cement restaurant, fished where my brother and Dad had done years before.

"On the set the following morning, I was approached by Frankie Marvin, one of Gene's permanent cowboy friends, who always worked when an Autry picture was made. He asked, 'I didn't see you around yesterday. Where do you go, House?' When I told him his eyes started to sparkle and he said, 'I've never fished. Would you take me the next time if I'm not scheduled to work?' I readily agreed to. The next time we worked together on that location on a day off for both of us, I took him up and showed him the ropes, which was accepted with extreme enthusiasm. We must have worked a number of times together after that day and perhaps a year or so later on a set I ran into Frankie and asked him how the fishing was. With his usual enthusiasm he described his many fishing trips with his boat, trailer and motor. What a great time he had had. But a sad expression came over his face as he told me, 'But my wife left me. I guess maybe I went fishing a little too often.'"[2]

CAST BIO: Veteran stuntman, actor and horse trainer Sandy Sanders doubled Gene Autry in many of his Columbia pictures as well as on some of Gene's half hour TV episodes.

Born in Deaf Smith County, Texas, May 23, 1919, Sandy grew up all over the country.

He served in the Army during WWII then put together a rodeo horse act out of Tulsa, Oklahoma. He rode a golden palomino named Sunlight. For a time in the '40s his act included a horse named Cherokee. In 1944 he participated in the Texas Rodeo at the Montreal, Canada, Forum.

While working in Kansas circa 1948 a film crew came through with one of the producers suggesting Sandy try his luck in Hollywood. Doing just that, it wasn't long before he was doubling for Gene and/or had roles in many of Gene's Columbia features and TV episodes as of 1947.

At the same time Sandy met Clayton Moore and a life-long friendship was born with Sandy doing many of Clayton's stunts on his "Lone Ranger" TV series.

Sandy was soon much in demand and worked on "Range Rider", "Roy Rogers Show", "Kit Carson", "Cisco Kid", "Wild Bill Hickok", and others.

Dick Jones ("Range Rider", "Buffalo Bill Jr.") told us, "Sandy was a talent that had not been exploited. He was an excellent horseman and a perfect photogenic double for Gene Autry. If Sandy dirtied his face up, grew a beard and kept his blond hair under a hat, he could pass as a pretty

Gene Autry, Harry Shannon, Gail Davis, Harry Harvey, Sandy Sanders and Frankie Marvin on the Columbia backlot for a "Cow Town" scene.

good villain. I enjoyed working with him; he was a heck of a good fight man. He became a member of Gene's stock company." [3]

Besides Sandy's stunt and acting work, he was a rope and horse trainer, riding stable owner and riding teacher.

Sanders died at 85, January 2, 2005, in California.

WHAT THE EXHIBITOR HAD TO SAY: "This is a very popular western, well produced by Columbia and well received for a very satisfactory weekend business."
—Harland Rankin, Plaza Theater,
Tilbury, Ontario, Canada (April, 1951)

SOURCES:
1. Autry with Herskowitz. p. 101.
2. Peters, Jr., House. *Another Side of Hollywood.* Empire, 2000. p. 127.
3. *Western Clippings #64.* March/April 2005. p. 14.

Beyond the Purple Hills
Columbia, July 1950
A Gene Autry Production in Sepia Tone

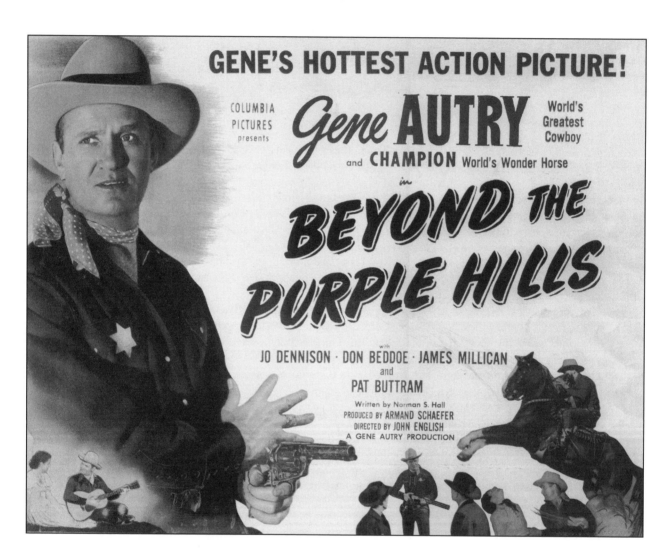

Producer ....Armand Schaefer
Director ....John English
Assistant Director........................Paul Donnelly
Screenplay....................................Norman S. Hall
Photography ....William Bradford
Musical Supervisor ....Paul Mertz
Musical Director ....Mischa Bakaleinikoff
Film Editor...................................Richard Fantl
Sound Dept....................................Frank Goodwin

Art Director..................................Harold MacArthur
Set Decorations ....George Montgomery
Hair Stylist ....Helen Hunt
Makeup ....Gordon Hubbard

SONGS: "Beyond the Purple Hills" (music and lyrics by Nick and Charles Kenny)—sung by Gene Autry and studio singers; "Dear Hearts and Gentle People" (music and lyrics by Bob Hilliard, Sammy Fain)—sung by Gene Autry,

The Cass County Boys, Sandy Sanders; "Square Dance Call" (Public Domain)—performed by Curt Barrett.

RUNNING TIME: 70 minutes

FILMING DATES: December 6-20, 1949

LOCATIONS: Lone Pine; Corriganville; Columbia backlot

BUDGET: $51,369

CAST:

Actor	*Character*
Gene Autry	Gene Autry
Pat Buttram	Mike Rawley
Jo Dennison	Mollie Rayburn
Don Beddoe	Amos Rayburn
James Millican	Rocky Morgan
Don Kay Reynolds	Chip Beaumont
Hugh O'Brian	Jack Beaumont
Roy Gordon	Judge John Beaumont
Harry Harvey	Sheriff Whiteside
Gregg Barton	Ross Pardee
Bob Wilke	Jim Conners
Ralph Peters	Bartender Tim
Frank Ellis	Corey
John Cliff	Dave Miller
Sandy Sanders	Doghouse
Curt Barrett	Square Dance Caller
Victor Cox, Jerry Ambler	Bank Robbers
Cass County Boys:	
Bert Dodson	Bass player
Jerry Scoggins	Guitar player
Fred S. Martin	Accordion player
Bobby Clack, Herman Hack	Cowhands on Fence
Frankie Marvin	Marty
Maudie Prickett	Agnes
Tex Terry, Merrill McCormick	Bar Patrons
Boyd Stockman	Ed
Robert Hilton	Voice in Crowd
Lynton Brent, Kermit Maynard, Joe Minitello, Frank O'Connor, Pat O'Malley, Fenton Jones, Ralph Bucko, George Bell	Extras
Champion	Champion
Little Champ	Little Champ

STUNTS: Sandy Sanders, Kermit Maynard, Boyd Stockman, Bob Woodward.

THE FILM: In this remake of screenwriter Norman S. Hall's "Sheriff of Las Vegas" ('44 Republic) starring Bill Elliott, Gene Autry becomes sheriff of the tough western town of Nortonville after the previous peacekeeper is gunned down in a bank robbery.

When Judge Beaumont (Roy Gordon) is murdered by saloon keeper Rocky Morgan (James Millican), suspicion falls on the judge's wild son Jack (Hugh O'Brian) due to an argument moments before the murder.

Believing Jack innocent, Gene and his new deputy Mike Rawley (Pat Buttram), foil a lynch mob with the aid of Jack's kid brother Chip (Don Kay Reynolds).

Hiding Jack and Chip, Gene tricks Morgan and his secret confederate, banker Amos Rayburn (Don Beddoe) into betraying themselves, completely exonerating Jack, leaving him free to romance his fiancée, Mollie (Jo Dennison).

Gene does break from the realistic formula for a moment or two by introducing Little Champ, having him, along with Champion, perform some tricks in the midst of the action-packed story. Both horses actually have important roles in the storyline, including some funny bits with Pat Buttram.

NOTES AND COMMENTS: Leading lady Jo Dennison was born in December 1923 in Florence, Arizona. Her folks were vaudeville performers. When her father died when she was 9, Jo's mother settled in Hale Center, Texas. After winning several local beauty pageants, Jo eventually became Miss America of 1942. Jo gives Gene an appreciative kiss on the cheek at a lakeside picnic. It's only a friendly gesture in thanks to Gene for saving her boyfriend's life so doesn't qualify as a true screen kiss for Gene. Dennison, whom Gene termed "a very cute girl,"[1] later married comedian Phil Silvers in 1945 and retired from the screen after 1951. Late in life she was involved for years with hospice care.

FILM COMMENTS: *Jo Dennison:* "My memories of working with Gene Autry are mainly what a considerate, kind, gentle man he was with me and those he worked with. One of my memories is of the pleasure while driving back in the dark on the bus after a long day's shooting to the parking lot of the studio. It was a beautiful location and, as I loved horses, the horse handler let me get a ride every now and then. My memories of the entire experience are happy and satisfying. Autry made his sets easy and smooth to work on. The drawbacks, as I remember them, were that I don't think I was very good in the movie, and Pat Buttram's raucous vulgarities shocked me at the time. But Gene Autry protected me where he could and was a lovely gentleman throughout. I think of him as a credit to show business and the movie industry."[2]

John Cliff: "I only worked this one show with Gene. He was pretty well liked. He wouldn't have make-up on the set. Somebody told me, 'You look awfully white…you better go get some makeup.' They told me it was down in the barbershop. I went down there and nobody was in there, just a bunch of make-up. They're hollering for me, so I came back. They said you still look white. I said I couldn't find the make-up man. They told me Gene won't allow it, and I said, then there's no make-up."[3]

Gene Autry: "We trained Champion to get up on a little platform…two of them…so Champion would get up on them, then Little Champion would go under his belly and do figure eights. Well, Champion was a stallion and he didn't like that very much so once in a while he would reach over and nip (Little Champion). But finally he got to where he was alright. We then taught Little Champion to walk across a board about 30-40 feet long. The first time he'd fall off. The next time he fell off I'd go right up to him and say, 'Listen, you better walk this plank this time.' … and one time he bit me on the finger! (Laughs)" [4]

Hugh O'Brian: "It was a great experience. Before we shot, I spent a week or two, little bit more than that, trying to stay in a western saddle without becoming a falsetto. I thought the world of Gene. Being the

Youngster Don Kay Reynolds brings urgent news to Gene Autry who is surrounded by (L-R) Jerry Scoggins, Bert Dodson, Frankie Marvin, Fred Martin and Sandy Sanders.

first film I ever did, I learned a great deal. Later on, when we did 'Wyatt Earp' we went out to the Autry Ranch (Melody Ranch) and did most of our exteriors out there. Gene was there almost every day for lunch, he remembered me, was very, very kind to me. I really trusted him totally. He was a good human being. On 'Beyond the Purple Hills' we filmed very quickly, I think it was 12 days, something like that. I do remember coming out of the house after Gene had come in saying 'Jack, Jack your Dad's just been murdered,' I run out and we jump on our horses. This is the first scene in which I am going to get on a horse. And I've got the professional, Mr. Autry, who's got on a few thousand horses in his time, and Champion who was such a great part of everybody's life. So, we come running out of the house in the very first take, he gets on his horse and I get on my horse and I went right over the other side and landed in the lawn. (Chuckles) I just leaped too far. Fell on my butt. After everybody stopped laughing, we did it again. Gene basically said something like 'Take your time. Just relax and don't try to do a fast mount.' Even Champion laughed! (Laughs) It was funny.

"Pat and Gene were very, very dear friends and had a lot of mutual respect for each other. Pat was very, very friendly. If he saw I was concerned about something, he was there. I thought it was a great partnership. I don't remember Gene ever doing more than one take, he was always right there. He was very much a professional. His whole being was embraced by the work ethic of the crew. I think the crew realized the professionalism of Mr. Autry and abided by that. There wasn't a lot of goofing around, I mean there were some laughs and so forth. Pat Buttram would alleviate the situation once in a while." [5]

WHAT THE EXHIBITOR HAD TO SAY: "This didn't go over. We had a very slow week as the spring season is so late and now that the weather is nice, the farmers are on the land with tractor lights glowing like firebugs everywhere."
—Harland Rankin, Plaza Theater, Tilbury, Ontario, Canada (May 1951)

SOURCES:
1. "Melody Ranch Theater" showing of "Beyond the Purple Hills" on Nashville Network, 1987.
2. Interview with Ray Nielsen. July 2006.
3. Interview with author.
4. "Melody Ranch Theater", Nashville Network, 1987.
5. Interview excerpts with Maxine Hansen on "Beyond the Purple Hills". Image DVD, 2006.

Indian Territory
Columbia, September 1950
A Gene Autry Production in Sepia Tone

Producer ....Armand Schaefer
Director ....John English
Assistant Directors ....Donald Verk, Wilbur
                    McGaugh
Screenplay...................................Norman S. Hall
Photography ....William Bradford
Musical Supervisor ....Paul Mertz
Musical Director ....Mischa Bakaleinikoff
Film Editor ....James Sweeney
Sound Dept................................Frank Goodwin
Art Director...............................Charles Clague
Set Decorations ....David Montrose
Hair Stylist ....Helen Hunt
Makeup ....Dave Grayson

SONGS: "Chattanoogie Shoeshine Boy" (music and lyrics by Harry Stone, Jack Stapp)—sung by Gene Autry; "When the Campfire is Low on the Prairie" (music and lyrics by Sam H. Stept)—sung by Gene Autry and cowboys; "Square Dance Calls" (Public Domain)—performed by Pat Buttram.
RUNNING TIME: 69 minutes
FILMING DATES: March 28 to April 8, 1950
LOCATIONS: Pioneertown; Corrigan-ville
BUDGET: $48,401.49

CAST:

Actor	*Character*
Gene Autry	Gene Autry
Pat Buttram	Shadrach Jones
Gail Davis	Melody Colton
Kirby Grant	Lt. Randy Mason
James Griffith	Apache Kid aka Johnny Corday
Philip Van Zandt	Curt Raidler
G. Pat Collins	Jim Colton
Roy Gordon	Major D. J. Farrell
Roy Butler	Townsman
Robert Carson	Capt. Wallace
Harry Cording	Cowhand
Kenne Duncan	Backshooter
Blackie Whiteford	1st man gunning for Apache Kid
Frank Ellis	2nd Man gunning for Apache Kid
Robert Hilton	Rider
Wes Hudman	Cook
Frank Lackteen	Indian
Frankie Marvin	Hank, short dancing cowhand with mustache
Bert Dodson	Curley
Sandy Sanders	Andy
Charles Stevens	Soma
Boyd Stockman	Apache Kid's rider
Chief Thunder Cloud	Indian
Chief Thundersky	Lookout
Chief Yowlachie	Indian Chief
Nick Rodman	Burns
Roy Butler	Rancher
John McKee	Cowboy
Roy Bucko, George Plues	Extras
Champion	Champion

STUNTS: Sandy Sanders (Gene's double); John Daheim, Boyd Stockman.

THE FILM: Cost cutting and lackadaisical production values are quite evident in "Indian Territory", a thus-far lowpoint in Gene Autry's Columbia output. Gene appears overweight and tired, perhaps due to the extra work and stress of gearing up for his half hour TV series which debuted in July 1950. Songs are minimal and don't truly seem logically inserted into the story. Stock footage is more noticeable than ever before, including oft seen opening shots of Indians crossing the Wind River near Landers, Wyoming, taken from Tim McCoy's "War Paint" in 1926 and plenty of footage from Gene's "The Last Round-Up" and Columbia's "Arizona" ('40).

There's much reliance on rear screen projection, poor character development, sloppy editing and a weak script that plays more like a series of incidents than a coherent story. All signs of cost-cutting and rushed production. Even the number of days in production was cut to 12, where all the previous Columbias had seen anywhere from at least

Champion, Gail Davis, Gene Autry.

15 days to as much as a month in lensing time. It took its toll and the evidence is on the screen in Gene's weakest Columbia outing to date.

Immediately following the Civil War, Cavalry Sergeant Gene Autry as a Special Assistant to the Chief of Indian Affairs, is assigned to break-up a series of Indian raids upon frontier settlers which are being perpetrated by the violent half-breed Apache Kid (James Griffith) and Curt Raidler (Phil Van Zandt), a renegade Austrian who is using the Indians to build himself an empire in America.

Subplot has Gene and Lt. Mason (Kirby Grant) in a running fistfight vying for the affections of Melody Colton (Gail Davis).

NOTES AND COMMENTS: Early in the film Gene mispronounces Chiricahua, the tribe of which he is a blood brother. A further sign of the rushed production, the script supervisor or director should have caught the glaring error and the scene should have been re-shot.

Kirby Grant had starred in a series of B-westerns at Universal in 1945-1946 and was currently starring with the German Shepherd Chinook in a series of Northwest Mountie films at Monogram when he made "Indian Territory". He reached his greatest fame on TV as flying cowboy "Sky King" from 1952-1959.

CAST BIOS: Wes (Wesley) Hudman became part of Gene Autry's TV and movie "stock company" of actors in 1950, just as Gene was developing his TV show through his Flying A Productions.

Hudman first appeared in Gene's "The Doodle Bug" TV episode in August 1950 and was subsequently in over a dozen of Gene's TVers. "Indian Territory" was Hudman's first movie of three with Gene, the other two being "Barbed Wire" and "Pack Train".

Hudman was a native of Texas but went to New York while still a youth. Interested in drama, he played in Broadway theatricals and came to Hollywood in 1949 where he played heavies and character roles in mostly westerns on radio, TV and movies.

Intensely interested in the lore of the west, he studied western history voraciously. While visiting an Aunt and Uncle in Yarnell, Arizona, he became acquainted with prospecting and mining. He became operator of a rock quarry in Drake, Arizona, a few miles from Williams and was also in partnership in another quarry.

Hudman continued to work sporadically in movies and TV, with his last being an unbilled role in Audie Murphy's "Posse From Hell" ('61).

Tired of the growing congestion in Los Angeles and happier in his prospecting and quarry work, he moved to the Drake area in early '62.

Hudman's life came to a tragic end on February 29, 1964. Hudman and a companion, James Dye, were working along the road about 25 miles south of Williams, picking up rocks and throwing them into a pickup truck. One man was working on each side of the road. Hudman heard a shot ring out. Dye called to Hudman who came to the front of the pickup where Vernon Oliver Martin, 50, jumped out from behind a tree brandishing a .30-.30 at Hudman, gritting his teeth. Hudman apparently pleaded, "Don't do that" as he backed around the truck. Martin followed and fired, hitting Hudman in the neck and killing him.

Dye witnessed the shooting then drove to Drake where he notified authorities. When deputies arrived back on the scene of the murder they found Martin in his cabin about a quarter of a mile away where they took him into custody.

Martin admitted the shooting and remarked Hudman was "trying to build a road into my copper mine." There are no copper mines in that area. Martin also accused Hudman of stealing goats from another Drake area resident.

Martin was charged with murder.

WHAT THE EXHIBITOR HAD TO SAY: "This did fair weekend business but do not feel it was strong enough to stand alone. If we had it to do over again, we would double bill it."
—Rankin Enterprises, Erie Theater, Wheatley, Ontario, Canada (April, 1950)

The Blazing Sun
<u>Columbia, November 1950</u>
A Gene Autry Production in Sepia Tone

Producer ....Armand Schaefer
Director ....John English
Assistant Director.......................Carter DeHaven Jr.
Screenplay...................................Jack Townley
Photography ....William Bradford
Musical Supervisor ....Paul Mertz
Musical Director ....Mischa Bakaleinikoff
Film Editor.................................James Sweeney
Sound Dept.................................Frank Goodwin
Art Directors ....Harold MacArthur,
                                       Charles Clague
Set Decorations ....George Montgomery
Hair Stylist ....Helen Hunt
Makeup ....Bob Meading

SONGS: "Along the Navajo Trail" (music and lyrics by Larry Markes, Dick Charles, Eddie DeLange)—sung by Gene Autry; "Brush Those Tears From Your Eyes" (music and lyrics by Oakley Haldeman, Al Trace, Jimmy Lee)—sung by Gene Autry.
RUNNING TIME: 70 minutes
FILMING DATES: April 24 to May 8, 1950
LOCATIONS: Lone Pine; Iverson Ranch; Columbia backlot
BUDGET: $48,604.31

CAST:

Actor	*Character*
Gene Autry	Gene Autry
Pat Buttram	Mike
Lynne Roberts	Helen Ellis
Anne Gwynne	Kitty Kelly
Edward Norris	Doc Larry Taylor
Kenne Duncan	Al Bartlett and Mark Bartlett
Alan Hale Jr.	Ben Luber
Gregg Barton	Trot Lucas
Steve Darrell	Sheriff Phillips
Tom London	Tom Ellis
Chris Allen	Old Man
Virginia Carroll	Townswoman
Sam Flint	Banker
Lewis Martin	Engineer
Frankie Marvin	Deputy Sheriff
Sandy Sanders	Carl Luber
Almira Sessions	Mrs. Purty
Boyd Stockman	Fireman
Bob Woodward	Telegrapher
Pat O'Malley	Smith
Nolan Leary	Small man
Jack Evans, Lew Morphy, Charles Coleman	Extras
Champion	Champion

Gene poses in an off-screen moment with his two leading ladies, Anne Gwynne (L) and Lynne Roberts (R).

STUNTS: Bob Woodward, Boyd Stockman, Sandy Sanders.

THE FILM: A locomotive on the loose, a vicious bank robber on the lam, a mysterious widow in danger, all serve to explode "The Blazing Sun", a scorching Gene Autry action western far superior in production values from his last film.

As an investigator for the banker's association, Gene and his pal Mike (Pat Buttram) hunt bank robbers Al Bartlett (Kenne Duncan) and Trot Lucas (Gregg Barton).

To throw off his pursuers, Bartlett kills his own twin brother (Kenne Duncan in a dual role) and Trot, hoping Gene and the Sheriff (Steve Darrell) will believe him dead. Bartlett then enlists the aid of crooked townsman Ben Luber (Alan Hale Jr.) to help him escape.

Also involved are Doctor Taylor (Edward Norris) and his assistant Helen (Lynne Roberts) whom Bartlett plans to have perform plastic surgery on his face to change his looks.

Into the mix comes a mysterious woman (Anne Gwynne) who claims to be Bartlett's "widow".

Gene, in a thrilling chase capped by a pulse-pounding fight atop a careening train, eventually brings Bartlett to justice.

NOTES AND COMMENTS: A short-line, narrow gauge freight train complete with crew were rented from the Southern Pacific Railroad for filming the initial scenes and the climatic fight of "The Blazing Sun". The railroad, at Lone Pine, California, is only 83 miles long. In order not to disrupt regular service of the line, the movie train was run onto a siding once a day so the regular train could pass.

Edward Norris (Doctor Taylor) was once married to another of Gene's leading ladies, Sheila Ryan, who was soon to be sidekick Pat Buttram's wife. Norris is also in "Back In the Saddle".

"The Blazing Sun" came during one of Autry's busiest years in the entertainment business. "The Blazing Sun" was his sixth movie in 1950, all directed by prolific western director John English, who had directed Gene in previous films and was to steer Gene through an additional five titles at Columbia in 1951.

In 1950 Gene also began his TV series, "The Gene Autry Show", produced by his Flying A Pictures, and he continued touring the U.S. and Canada with his Gene Autry Hit Show, live performances up to 85 cities seven days a week, two shows a day, with his troupe including Smiley Burnette, Pat Buttram, Rufe Davis, Gail Davis, The Cass County Boys and Carl Cotner, Johnny Bond, musical performers like banjo great Eddie Peabody, Frankie Marvin, Gene's pal from his earliest show business days, and guest artists like the Hoosier Hot Shots, among others.

FILM COMMENTS: *Anne Gwynne:* "'The Blazing Sun' with Gene Autry was a disappointment to me. It was far from his best, that's for sure. It was made near the end of my film career. I was married with two children and I don't recall much about Gene, except he seemed all business. There was no chitchat between us. A hit song 'Brush Those Tears From Your Eyes' came from that picture. Gene sang it to me, but I think the Weavers, not Gene, had the hit record of it." [1,2]

Kenne Duncan.

CAST BIOS: Gene Autry called Kenne Duncan "the meanest man in the movies" for Dell publication WHO'S WHO IN WESTERN STARS #3 in '53. "For my money," Gene continued, "he's the most convincing of all the badmen. Off screen, Kenne is a close personal friend of mine and nothing at all like the villain he's played in my pictures." [3]

Veteran heavy Pierce Lyden stated, "Kenne was white-haired and handsome; the pictures did not do his looks justice. He was an expert marksman and in demand making personal appearances throughout the south. They would show one of his pictures, and then a music group would perform. Next, would be Kenne and his shooting exhibition." [4]

Kenneth Duncan MacLachlan was born February 17, 1902, in Chatham, Ontario, Canada, of Scottish parents, both Canadian natives. Kenne later became a U. S. citizen.

Prior to entering films Duncan was a successful gentleman jockey who won races at Canada's Bluebonnet tracks and rode with the hounds in England. He later owned a brood farm "somewhere near where the Equestrian Center in Los Angeles is now," according to actor Dale Berry. "As I recall," Dale thought, "Kenne had around 11 thoroughbreds. He loved horses but hated to ride." [5] Between pictures, Kenne often trained horses at the Riviera Country Club.

Duncan was well educated, attending both St. Andrews College in Toronto and the Royal School of Infantry at Wolseley Barracks, London, Ontario.

Duncan reportedly made his stage debut shortly after he finished school. Acting was in Kenne's blood and, after a brief fling as an accountant, he found his way to Hollywood at the end of the silent era, managing to work in Universal two-reelers. Possessed of a solid, husky voice, Kenne moved easily into talkies with several uncredited bit parts. In 1934 he co-starred opposite Charles Starrett in the Canadian made "Undercover Man" for which he also contributed the original story.

From then until the late '50s Duncan worked continually, and often—some 225 westerns and serials— through 1959, primarily at Monogram, Republic and, later, with Gene Autry at Columbia and for Gene's various Flying A TV series. "The Blazing Sun" gives Duncan an excellent acting opportunity with a rare dual role.

Musician/actor Dale Berry first met Kenne Duncan in 1947 at the Ervay Theatre on Ervay St. in Dallas, Texas. "I toured with him on up into the '50s. And I stayed in touch with him practically every week after that. Personality wise, he was grumpy and grouchy. Not with me, but he was constantly being mistaken for Hopalong Cassidy, because of his white hair, and that irritated him! He wasn't grouchy with everybody…if it was a good lookin' girl he was the friendliest, nicest, sweetest person that ever was. If it was some guy he really didn't want to be bothered with…he was kind of a Pat Buttram type. He could be nice in one breath and testy the next. I'd often ask Kenne how he was doin', and he'd use the quotation, 'As the jockeys say at the track, I'm scufflin' for groceries.' When we were on the road on tour, he'd call his mother, who he called Duchess, he'd call her most every night. Also, you talk about a guy that was thrifty with a buck, he was tight. He wouldn't buy brand name beer. He'd buy off brand beer that tasted like… (Laughs) When he went to a restaurant, he'd grab up all those little bags of sugar. (Laughs) He *was* frugal! Kenne had an apartment in Hollywood where he'd lived forever." [6]

Duncan died at 69 February 7, 1972, at a Los Angeles hospital. He'd suffered a stroke a year earlier and many sources state, incorrectly, that was the cause of his death. Upon his demise, an investigation ensued with actual cause of death ruled a suicide from an overdose of barbiturates and alcohol. Friend Dale Berry disagrees, "I just do not believe that! He loved life. He loved living. Every day was a new adventure to him. Kenne did like to drink, and he'd had a light stroke and developed a little bit of a speech impediment. He was on whatever medication they gave you back then for strokes. So I think what happened, the booze mixed with the medication…I don't think he deliberately committed suicide. Statements in books that he was 'tired of living' are wrong…each day was a new conquest to him, especially if she was good looking. (Laughs)" [7]

WHAT THE EXHIBITOR HAD TO SAY: "Doubled with 'Blondie' (reissue) to above average grosses. Had about 150% kid attendance and 75% adult, which shows what the adults in my situation think of Autry and 'Blondie'. This Autry is one of the best I've had of him. However, he just doesn't draw the adults in, and one cannot make money on children's admissions."   —Fred G. Weppler, Colonial, Colfax, Illinois (May 1951)

"This is one of the best Gene Autry westerns we have had in a long while."   —J. W. Lawing, Palace Theater, Gastonia, NC (April 1952)

SOURCES:

1. *Westerns Women.* McFarland, 1999, p. 102.

2. *Western Clippings #27.* January/February, 1999. p. 7.

3. *Who's Who in Western Stars #3.* Dell Pub., 1953. p. 32.

4. Lyden, Pierce. *The Movie Badmen I Rode With.* Self published 1988. p. 2.

5. Interview with author.

6. Interview with author.

7. Interview with author.

Gene Autry and the Mounties
Columbia, January 1951
A Gene Autry Production in Sepia Tone

Producer ....Armand Schaefer
Director ....John English
Assistant Director......................James Nicholson
Screenplay..................................Norman S. Hall
Photography ....William Bradford
Musical Supervisor ....Paul Mertz
Musical Director ....Mischa Bakaleinikoff
Film Editor................................James Sweeney
Sound Dept...............................Howard Fogetti
Art Director...............................Charles Clague
Set Decorations ....Louis Diage

SONGS: "Love's Ritornella" (Public Domain)—sung by Elena Verdugo; "Blue Canadian Rockies" (music and lyrics by Cindy Walker)—sung by Gene Autry; "Onteora" (music and lyrics by Doris Anderson, Gene Andrea aka Theodore Snyder)—sung by Gene Autry.

RUNNING TIME: 70 minutes

FILMING DATES: June 12-24, 1950.

LOCATIONS: Big Bear Lake; Corriganville; Columbia backlot (interiors)

BUDGET: $50,495.39

CAST:

Actor	*Character*
Gene Autry	Gene Autry
Pat Buttram	Scat Russell
Elena Verdugo	Marie Duval
Carleton Young	Pierre LaBlond
Richard Emory	Terry Dillon
Herbert Rawlinson	Inspector Wingate
Trevor Bardette	Raoul Duval
Francis McDonald	Batiste
Jim Frasher	Jack Duval
Zoro (a Greenland Husky)	King
Chris Allen	Old Man Bettor
Gregg Barton	Sgt. Stuart
Roy Butler	Trapper Bettor
Bruce Carruthers	Sgt. McKenzie
Jody Gilbert	Squaw
Billy Gray	Boy
Teddy Infuhr	Boy

Nolan Leary ....Dr. Sawyer
House Peters Jr. ....Hogan
Boyd Stockman..........................Mountie McCloud
Bob Woodward ....Wagon driver Henchman
Tex Lambert, Carol Henry,
  Walt LaRue..............................Mounties
Blackie Whiteford, Robert Hilton,
  John McKee, Steven Elliott,
  George Bell, Frankie Marvin,
  Bob Burns, Bobby Clark ....Extras
Champion....................................Champion

STUNTS: Bob Woodward, Walt LaRue, Carol Henry, Boyd Stockman, Sandy Sanders.

THE FILM: U.S. Marshal Gene Autry and his deputy Scat (Pat Buttram) cross into Canada while pursuing bank robbers Pierre LaBlond (Carleton Young) and Raoul Duval (Trevor Bardette). In Canada they help young Mountie Terry Dillon (Richard Emory) fight off the bandits and take the wounded Mountie to a cabin where they meet Duval's niece, Marie (Elena Verdugo) and her brother Jack (Jim Frasher) who hates all peace officers and regards La Blond as a hero.

Gene finally convinces Jack that LaBlond, who is trying to establish an outlaw nation, is nothing but a crook when LaBlond forcibly carries away Jack's sister, intending to marry her against her will.

LaBlond's partner, Duval, also outraged by LaBlond's actions against his niece, has a change of heart and helps Gene and the Mounties defeat LaBlond in a blazing climax.

By this time, you may notice two trends in Gene's more action-oriented Columbias. Gene plays more "lawmen" rather than cattle ranchers or ranch foremen as he did at Republic and, not always, but there is a tendency for Gene to not actually be involved in the romantic subplots, but to assume the role of matchmaker as he does here with Elena Verdugo and Richard Emory. This was true in "Beyond the Purple Hills" as well and would be true in future Columbia titles.

Gene would be lost without John Brousseau, his general assistant who takes care of Gene's wardrobe, fan photos, musical instruments, cars and more.

NOTES AND COMMENTS: The town burning at the end of the film is stock footage from the finale of Columbia's "Man From Colorado" ('48).

Bruce Carruthers, portraying Northwest Mountie Sergeant McKenzie who is killed early in the film, was actually an ex-Mountie who was also hired as the picture's technical director.

FILM COMMENTS: *Gene Autry:* "Once in a while we still found a good script with a modern viewpoint. One was 'Gene Autry and the Mounties'. Buttram and I played a pair of U.S. marshals who crossed into Canada, chasing a gang of bank robbers. With right on our side, we didn't pay much attention in those days to international borders and other points of diplomatic nit-picking. This was the only other time, outside of a few Abbott and Costello films—as in 'Abbott and Costello Meet Frankenstein' ('48)—that the star's name had been used as part of the title." [1]

Gregg Barton: "I worked with Gene so many, many times and every time was a pleasure. He was a gentleman, a good friend and very, very generous to me. I think his contribution to the business was a great boon to the business at that time. I know he was well loved by his public. He and his agent, Mitch Hamilburg, started Flying A Productions. They worked out of Columbia. One day a group of us were sitting around and they were talking about how lucky Gene was. And Mandy Schaefer, in his dour, quiet way, said, 'Not lucky. Just country boy smart.' He knew when to duck and he knew when to move." [2]

Billy Gray: "The only thing I remember about Gene Autry is that he took us up to his Flying A Ranch to do the shows. More-so than Gene, I remember his line producer, 'Petty Cash' Parsons. If you needed some cash, he'd loan it to you!" [3]

House Peters Jr.: "I worked with Gene in six of his features. This gave me the opportunity to observe the off-camera Gene Autry. There was a lot more to him than being a successful singer, actor and businessman. He and his company treated actors fairly and honestly. He had a lot of bright people working behind the scenes, which helped immensely.

"The exteriors for 'Gene Autry and the Mounties' were filmed at Cedar Lake, located above the city of Big Bear. On the first morning the cast and crew boarded a bus at our motel and headed up a fogged-in, narrow, unpaved road to our location spot. Many of the early frozen north pictures were shot at this small well-known lake a mile above Big Bear. On this particular morning our driver, who apparently had never been there before, became completely disoriented as to where we were due to all the twists and turns; and frankly none of us were able to be of any help. There was dead silence from the passengers, which prompted me to say out loud over the bus driver changing gears, 'One of these days, folks, they'll find this bus out here loaded with nothing but scripts and skeletons.' Apparently, it was the correct thing to say because it broke the silence of our situation. It was shortly thereafter that the fog lifted and we pulled up to our destination for the first day's shooting at the lake.

"During the filming that day there was a tense moment when Emory Johnson (under his screen credit of Richard Emory), playing a Canadian Mountie, was kicked by Gene Autry's horse in a dialogue scene. The horse kicked out with his hind leg, striking my friend Emory above the ankle in an area covered by his boot, but it was obvious to everyone that he must have been in pain. He didn't let it interrupt the scene, however, and the camera kept rolling. After we got the take, Gene dismounted, and walking over to Emory asked, 'Are you okay?' He nodded that he was fine. Gene then called the wrangler over, saying, 'I've had it with this horse. This isn't the first time something like this had happened. Take him out behind the barn and geld him!'" [4]

CAST BIOS: "I've been knocked on my rear by every western star, including Annie Oakley. When the price is right, I'd let anyone knock me down."[5] One of the busiest heavies of the late '40s on through the '50s, particularly on the TV screen, was usually stubbly bearded Gregg Barton—especially in Gene Autry's Columbia westerns and TV series (11 features, 25 TV episodes).

Born Harold Wilsea Barker June 5, 1912, on Long Island City, New York of English/Scottish parentage, Hal's father died at 33 when Hal was only 3. As his father was a Mason, Hal and his older brother, age 4, were accepted into the Masonic Home and sent to their Home for Boys in Burlington, New Jersey, where Hal grew up.

Finishing high school, Hal attended the University of North Carolina at Chapel Hill on a football scholarship then went to work as a sales rep for a textile company but soon tired of this and headed west for greener pastures in California where he worked at odd jobs until he stumbled into the acting profession during a party at a friend's house circa 1939.

Hal studied at Bliss-Hayden Theatre, did little theatre work, and acquired an agent who switched his name to Gregg Barton to avoid confusion with Lex Barker or Jess Barker.

He was just getting started with a decent role in John Wayne's "Flying Tigers" ('42 Republic) when he enlisted in the Marine Corps the day after the attack on Pearl Harbor.

During WWII Gregg served as a tank commander with the 5th Tank Battalion, 5th Marine Division in the Pacific,

taking part in the invasion of Iwo Jima. For his heroism in that battle he received the Silver Star. Reminded of this in later years, Gregg remarked, "They're all heroes, all of them."

Back in Hollywood, ex-Major Barton was hired to play the lead heavy in Eddie Dean's "West to Glory" ('47) which started him on his villainous career.

Besides roles in A films, Gregg menaced B-cowboys Charles Starrett, Rex Allen, Whip Wilson, Johnny Mack Brown, Bill Elliott, Wayne Morris and, of course, Gene Autry in the waning days of the B-western. Dozens of other TV series used Gregg's talents as well.

Working on so many Autry productions, Gregg became close friends with Armand "Mandy" Schaefer of whom he said, "Mandy steered me very nicely, advised me what not to do and I'll be forever indebted to him for his clear-sightedness."[6]

For over ten years, in between his TV and movie work, Gregg managed a 1,600 acre cattle ranch at Bonsail, California. Retiring from films in '66, Gregg worked for Safeco Title Insurance for 22 years where he became top sales rep in Southern California.

Gregg was married in the late '40s, for about 14 years, then after a long stretch as a bachelor, Gregg and Bonita Cooper were wed in 1983 until the time of his death at 88 on November 28, 2000, in the Fallbrook, California, convalescent center. His health had been failing since he had knee surgery earlier in the month.

Another veteran heavy of Autry's films, Myron Healey, recalled, "We worked together a lot. I was doing the lead heavy and Gregg was doing the dog heavy. He was a very nice guy that I admired greatly. Back in the days of Flying A, Gregg mentioned he and his wife were moving onto a ranch down in Fallbrook. They were gonna raise strawberries. I said, 'That happens to be my favorite food. We're working together a lot, next time you're scheduled to work with old Dad, bring me a basket of berries.' For years after that, every few months we'd get a job together and I'd look at him and say, 'Well...?' and he'd say, 'Oh God, No strawberries.' This went on for years and years and

Leading lady Elena Verdugo, Gene, and Canadian mounties Gregg Barton (standing) and Herbert Rawlinson.

years. It got to a point where I'd really be disappointed if he ever brought me any strawberries. (Laughs) At the Golden Boot awards, I didn't have to ask him. When we went backstage, just before we came on, he looked at me and smiled, 'No berries.' (Laughs) [7]

WHAT THE EXHIBITOR HAD TO SAY: "A very entertaining outdoor action picture—plenty of action and comedy. Gene's singing is enjoyed here. With Roy Rogers' departure, now we'll have to build Autry back up, along with Rex Allen and a few others. This entry is very good."
—Carl F. Neitzel, Juno Theater, Juneau, Wisconsin (March 1952)

"Everyone is making westerns, which kind of kills business for Rogers and Autry. No draw."
—Harland Rankin, Plaza Theater, Tilbury, Ontario, Canada (September 1951)

SOURCES:
1. Autry with Herskowitz, p. 101.
2. Interview with author.
3. *Western Clippings #27.* January/February 1999. p. 6.
4. Peters Jr., House. *Another Side of Hollywood.* Empire, 2000. p. 138.
5. Interview with author.
6. Interview with author.
7. Interview with author.

Texans Never Cry
Columbia, March 1951
A Gene Autry Production in Sepia Tone

Producer ....Armand Schaefer
Director ....Frank McDonald
Assistant Director.......................Carter DeHaven Jr.
Screenplay...................................Norman S. Hall
Photography ....William Bradford
Musical Supervisor ....Paul Mertz
Musical Director ....Mischa Bakaleinikoff
Film Editor.................................James Sweeney
Sound Dept................................J. S. Westmoreland
Art Director...............................Charles Clague
Set Decorations ....George Montgomery

SONGS: "Texans Never Cry" (music and lyrics by Gene Autry, Oakley Haldeman, Hank Fort)—sung by studio singers over titles; reprised by Gene Autry; "Ride Ranger Ride" (music and lyrics by Tim Spencer)—sung by Gene Autry, Pat Buttram, extras.
    RUNNING TIME: 67 minutes
    FILMING DATES: July 17-27, 1950
    LOCATIONS: Lone Pine; Iverson Ranch; Columbia backlot
    BUDGET: $43,906.84

CAST:

Actor	Character
Gene Autry ....Gene Autry
Pat Buttram ....Pecos Bates
Mary Castle.................................Rita Bagley
Russell Hayden ....Steve Diamond
Gail Davis ....Nancy Carter
Richard Powers ....Tracy Wyatt
Don Harvey................................Blackie Knight
Roy Gordon...............................Frank Bagley
Holly Bane ....Henchman Rip Braydon
Roy Butler.................................Sheriff Weems
Frank Fenton ....Captain Weldon
Richard Flato.............................Carlos Corbal
Sandy Sanders..........................Ranger Bart Thomas
I. Stanford Jolley........................Red
Harry Mackin ....Ranger Bill Ross
Harry Tyler................................Dan Carter
Minerva Urecal ....Martha Carter
Duke York ....Baker
John McKee ....Ed Dunham
Frankie Marvin...........................Ranger Frankie
Bob Woodward ....Ranger #1
Dick Farnsworth.......................Ranger #2
Walt LaRue ....Ranger #3
Boyd Stockman.........................Ranger #4
Bobby Clark ....Ranger #5
Billy Williams ....Ranger #6
Guy Teague ....Ranger #7
Merrill McCormick, Victor Cox ..Extras
Champion...................................Champion

STUNTS: Sandy Sanders, Boyd Stock-man, Bob Woodward, Dick Farnsworth, Eddie Parker.

THE FILM: With a dynamite, unusual title, a strong cast and excellent story, "Texans Never Cry" continues Gene's Columbia adventures in the more action oriented mode.

Texas Ranger Gene Autry and his men save from eviction a family who has been swindled by Tracy Wyatt (Richard Powers) who heads up a counterfeit gang trying to pick up easy money by printing phony Mexican lottery tickets.

An initial spark of romance flares when Gene meets the family's pretty daughter Nancy (Gail Davis).

Paper for the phony tickets is being supplied by printer Frank Bagley (Roy Gordon) who uses his lovely daughter Rita (Mary Castle) as a spy, trying to woo Gene with her charms and secure information from him.

With Gene on his trail, Wyatt imports a hired killer, Steve Diamond (Russell Hayden) to get Gene out of their way.

Really interesting and offbeat plot twist has Gene saving Diamond's life from a rattlesnake, leaving the hired gun "in debt" to his savior.

Then meeting Nancy, Diamond also falls for the girl who now believes Gene is smitten by Rita, while actually Gene is only playing along with her spying ways to gain information from her. The romantic angle is emphasized pretty heavily for an Autry western at this point and gives the film much of its critical plot points and suspense.

The double-game eventually resolves itself in an unusual way during a blazing climax.

Hard action and plot manipulations are well handled by Frank McDonald (giving John English a break after directing 10 Autrys in a row). Without slowing the action, McDonald nicely employs a "romance montage" at one point to show the growing relationships between Hayden and Davis and Gene and Castle.

NOTES AND COMMENTS: After completion of "Texans Never Cry", Gene appeared for five weeks at the annual Madison Square Garden Rodeo September 27 through October 22.

"Texans Never Cry" cost Gene four pairs of the $150 boots he always wears in his Columbia pictures. Two days after production started, Gene injured the arch of his right foot. The arch swelled so that his beautiful, hand-tooled movie boots were too tight for comfort. He had to continue wearing them so they would match scenes already shot. Sorrowfully, Autry took out his jackknife and practically shredded the arches of the boots. Gene was able to walk comfortably, and a wax coating hid the slits from the camera. However, the boots were ruined.

Russell Hayden first came to film prominence as Lucky in the Hopalong Cassidy westerns of the late '30s and early '40s. After starring in his own series of westerns at Columbia, a couple at Universal and some Mountie films for Screen Guild, he teamed up with another former Hoppy saddlepal, Jimmy Ellison, for a series at Lippert. Hayden then entered television, starring in "Cowboy G-Men" and producing "Judge Roy Bean" on his newly built ranch sets at Pioneertown where so many of Gene's Columbias were filmed. Hayden also produced "26 Men" shot in Arizona.

Richard Powers first worked on Broadway and some early films as George Duryea. Switching to Tom Keene, he starred throughout the '30s and '40s in western series for RKO, Monogram, Paramount and Crescent. He used the Keene moniker for his westerns while reverting to Richard Powers when he played character roles in non-western films. However, by the '50s he employed the Powers name in western character roles such as "Texans Never Cry", several westerns with Tim Holt and many western TV episodes of "Judge Roy Bean", "Sergeant Preston", etc.

Russell Hayden and Gene Autry confront badmen Don Harvey and Richard Powers. Powers had been known as Tom Keene when he starred in B-Westerns in the '30s and '40s at RKO and Monogram.

The song "Texans Never Cry" was written by Gene in collaboration with Oakley Haldeman. The pair previously teamed to write Gene's perennial favorite "Here Comes Santa Claus" in 1947 as well as several other film tunes.

Early in the picture Gail Davis manages to kiss Gene on the cheek in appreciation for looking after her father, but one cannot consider this a "kissing scene" for the cowboy.

FILM COMMENTS: *Gene Autry:* "Shotgun Britton—the makeup artist—really talked Texas. He went to Hardin Simmons in Abilene, Texas. They used to have a great football player called Bulldog Turner. Ol' Shotgun was always talking about what a football player he was himself, but said Bulldog Turner kinda got more publicity than he did. So I was questioning a couple of people down there. They said yes ol' Shotgun really talked a good game. One time they were playing a tough team and ol' Shotgun came into the coach and said, 'Coach, you need me right now. There's a play coming up here. Just give me the ball and I'll carry it to the other end.' Coach said, 'Alright Shotgun, get in there.' They called the signals, gave the football to Shotgun and (the other team) hit him. The football went one way and he went the other. He jumped up and didn't even go back, just took off for the clubhouse. Says, 'So long Coach, I'll see ya later.' Anyway ol' Shotgun was always bragging about Texas. Said, 'Gene why don't you write a song about Texas, the title is 'Texans Never Cry'. Win, lose or draw, Texans never cry.' So, I wrote the song."[1]

WHAT THE EXHIBITOR HAD TO SAY: "A fairly good Gene Autry picture—plenty of action."

—O. Fomby, Paula Theater,
Humes, Louisiana (May 1951)

"How we wish Gene had the draw he used to have. There's not nearly the punch to his pictures."

—Harland Rankin, Rankin Ent.,
Chatham, Ontario, Canada (December 1951)

SOURCES:

1. "Melody Ranch Theater" showing of "Texans Never Cry" on Nashville Network, 1987.

Whirlwind

Columbia, April 1951

A Gene Autry Production in Sepia Tone

Producer	Armand Schaefer
Director	John English
Assistant Director	Paul Donnelly
Screenplay	Norman S. Hall
Photography	William Bradford
Musical Supervisor	Paul Mertz
Musical Director	Mischa Bakaleinikoff
Film Editor	Paul Borofsky
Sound Dept.	Lambert E. Day
Art Director	Charles Clague
Set Decorations	George Montgomery

SONGS: "Whirlwind" (music and lyrics by Stan Jones)—sung by studio singers over titles, reprised by Gene Autry and studio singers; "As Long as I Have My Horse" (music and lyrics by Gene Autry, Fred Rose, Johnny Marvin)—sung by Gene Autry; "Tweedle-O-Twill" (music and lyrics by Gene Autry, Fred Rose)—sung by Gene Autry, Smiley Burnette.

RUNNING TIME: 70 minutes

FILMING DATES: December 4 to December 15, 1950

LOCATIONS: Pioneertown; Columbia backlot

BUDGET: $46,702.15

CAST:

Actor	*Character*
Gene Autry	Gene Autry aka The Whirlwind
Smiley Burnette	Smiley Burnette
Gail Davis	Elaine Lassiter
Thurston Hall	Big Jim Lassiter
Harry Lauter	Wade Trimble
Dick Curtis	Lon Kramer
Harry Harvey	Sheriff Barlow
Gregg Barton	Bill Trask
Art Dillard	Henchman with bushy eyebrows
Kenne Duncan	Slim
Gary Goodwin	Carl
Tommy Ivo	Johnnie Evans
Stan Jones	Stan Jones
Frank Matts	Charlie
Frankie Marvin	Deputy Dave
Bud Osborne	Tom (stagecoach driver #2)
Boyd Stockman	Stage Driver
Al Wyatt	Bert
Jack O'Shea, John McKee, Pat O'Malley, Leon DeVoe, Frank O'Connor, Buddy Roosevelt, George Bell, Bob Reeves, Bobby Clark, Ken Cooper, Guy Teague, Herman Hack	Extras
Champion	Champion

STUNTS: Bob Woodward, Al Wyatt, Boyd Stockman, Dick Farnsworth; Duke Taylor.

THE FILM: While Gene Autry's normal sidekick Pat Buttram was recuperating from a terrible accident resulting in severe wounds inflicted when a small cannon exploded on the set at Pioneertown while Gene Autry and company were filming the television episode entitled "The Peacemaker", Gene's former partner in westerns, Smiley Burnette, came over from working on the Charles Starrett Durango Kid westerns to reunite with Gene for this feature. Buttram was back for the next feature, "Silver Canyon" and eight other features before Smiley eventually co-starred with Gene in his final six Columbias.

Advertising played up Smiley, giving him better billing than Buttram usually received, and stated "Smiley's back— funnier than ever!"

Stan Jones, who had written the hit "Ghost Riders In the Sky" used as the title tune for Gene's "Riders In the Sky", was also reunited with the singing cowboy for the title tune, "Whirlwind", although the tune never became the gigantic hit "Ghost Riders" was. Jones' name was also played up in the print ads, and Jones was afforded a cameo role in the film.

With Smiley aboard, there's a nostalgic charm to this feature missing in many other Columbias. Gene seems positively enlightened by the return of his old friend, displaying all of his smiling charisma. It's most noticeable when the pair, in a simple scene, are riding together on a

Gene's got the uper hand on outlaw leader Thurston Hall and Sheriff Harry Harvey.

wagon dueting on "Tweedle-O-Twill", a cheerful ditty first heard nine years earlier in "Home in Wyomin'" in 1942. Adding to the nostalgia, Gene sings "As Long as I Have My Horse", first performed in "In Old Santa Fe" and reprised in "Gold Mine In the Sky".

All that said, it is no bad reflection on Pat Buttram who was Gene's radio sidekick and, actually, preferred by many as Gene's film sidekick. But, as the final six Columbia entries show, when Smiley returned permanently, there was no doubt he and Gene had a special chemistry between them that worked. It's difficult to imagine Hardy without Laurel, Abbott without Costello—and it was the same when Gene was without Smiley.

A string of mail robberies bring undercover postal inspectors Gene Autry and Smiley Burnette to Red Valley where Big Jim Lassiter (Thurston Hall) is the head of the outlaw gang.

Preventing many of the robberies, Gene also masquerades as the masked Whirlwind.

Gene worms his way into Big Jim's confidence by romancing Big Jim's niece, Elaine (Gail Davis), and by pretending to be interested in land purchases. After Smiley finds partially burned fragments of stolen U. S. Postal bonds, Gene and Smiley force a confession from Big Jim's attorney henchman Wade Trimble (Harry Lauter) that Big Jim killed his own brother to rob Elaine of her estate and is also guilty of the mail robberies.

In a whirlwind of action, Gene rounds up the bandits. The reuniting of Gene and Smiley, along with Gene's "regular" leading lady, Gail Davis, fast action directed by John

English, top western support from Harry Lauter, Dick Curtis, Tommy Ivo, Thurston Hall, Gregg Barton and Kenne Duncan—plus the always intriguing element of a masked rider, all serve to make "Whirlwind" one of Gene's most enjoyable Columbias.

NOTES AND COMMENTS: Primarily a songwriter, Stan Jones went on to co-star on TV with John Bromfield in "Sheriff of Cochise" as Deputy Olson from '56-'58.

Tommy Ivo went from western movie child star to being TV Tommy Ivo, nationally known dragstrip star. He was the first inductee into the International Drag Racing Hall of Fame in Ocala, Florida.

Although Smiley Burnette's horse (with a ring around one eye) in the Republic films was known as Black Eyed Nellie, due to legal restrictions Smiley had to re-name the horse Ringeye in his Charles Starrett and Gene Autry Columbia titles.

Filming began December 10, 1951, on Flying A's newly built sound stage, the first designed specifically for television production. Flying A's "Range Rider" was the first to utilize the standing sets which included a barroom and saloon, barn, typical small town houses' living and bedroom, jail, cabin, office. The half million dollar building project began May 21, 1951, and was located at Sunset Blvd. and Orange Drive. Twenty-two offices, providing quarters for Gene's numerous enter-prises, were also housed there.

FILM COMMENTS: *Gene Autry:* "In early 1951, after a nine-year break, Smiley Burnette returned as my sidekick in 'Whirlwind'. There was no special emotion

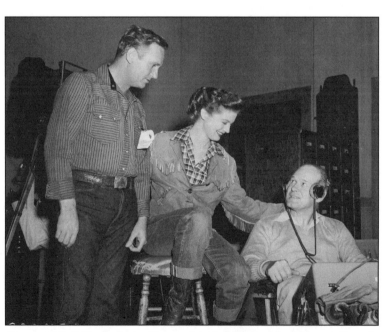

Gene and Gail Davis chat with sound technician Lambert Day on the set of "Whirlwind."

about it. Events and timing had caused us to split, and the same conditions brought us back. But Smiley and I had come to Hollywood together and there was always that bond between us.

"It ought to be explained that in all of his Columbia films, Smiley played a character called Smiley Burnette. The reason being that Frog Millhouse, the name he made famous in my films, and a few with Roy, was the property of Republic. Since Gene Autry happened to be my real name, there wasn't much Republic could do when I took it with me." [1]

Smiley Burnette: "My role as the veterinarian in 'Whirlwind' wasn't remarkable in itself. What made this part outstanding was getting together with Gene Autry after a nine year separation. Gene practically nursed me into pictures. He found me working for $12.50 a week at an Illinois radio station, hired me as an accordion player, then teamed up with me in pictures. We introduced singing westerns to the screen in 1934, and stayed together as friends, on and off the screen, for 20 years.

"When Gene went into the Air Force during the last war, I shifted to another series of westerns. I liked working with other actors, but I liked it even more when I got back with Gene again. It was like old home week. We sang a song, 'Tweedle-O-Twill', that we had first sung 15 years before. We made up our own dialogue as we went along, which we always do, and we had fun pulling old gags out of the past.

"The best gag in 'Whirlwind' was where I, as the veterinarian, had to vaccinate a 200-pound Brahma calf. I weigh 240, so I managed to put the calf on the ground. Then I 'accidentally' sat on the needle and vaccinated myself.

"I do my best work with Gene, and people say Gene works best with me." [2]

Tommy Ivo: "Gene was kind of mellow as I remember. I knew Smiley because I'd done so much stuff with him (on the Durangos). Actually, I'd heard Smiley wasn't an easy guy to get along with but I got the old rub on the head 'How ya doin' kid?' 'cause I always really liked him. Gene was a very humble person. He didn't have any airs about him despite what he'd done for himself."[3]

CAST BIOS: One of the most prolific heavies in Gene Autry's later Columbias and his TV series, Harry Lauter, appeared in six films and 15 TV episodes with Gene, as well as working on "Annie Oakley" and other Flying A TV series.

Coming close to stardom on several occasions in the mid '50s, he co-starred as Ranger Clay Morgan with Willard Parker (as Jace Pearson) on TV's "Tales of the Texas Rangers" for 52 episodes from '55-'58 and

Harry Lauter.

had running parts on two other TV series, "Rocky Jones, Space Ranger" ('54) and "Waterfront" ('53-'56). He had the lead in two of Republic's last serials, "Trader Tom of the China Seas" ('54) and "King of the Carnival" ('55).

There's no doubt, judging from his well over 300 TV episodes and some 150 movies plus commercials and other work, Harry was a popular and effective workaholic.

Herman Arthur Lauter was born June 19, 1914, in White Plains, New York. His grandparents were circus people, the world famous trapeze act, The Flying Lauters. Harry's father was also involved in the act as well as being a graphic artist.

His parents moved to Colorado when Harry was quite young which is where he learned to ride. Later moving to San Diego, when Harry was 13 he established California State Junior records in the 100 yard and 220 yard free style swimming sprints.

While still in high school in San Diego, he began working at radio station KGB as an announcer and general handyman. Whenever time would permit, he appeared in plays at the Globe Theatre in Balboa Park. This theatre experience convinced Harry he wanted an acting career and it led to his joining the Elitch Garden Theatre Group in Denver, Colorado, one of the oldest stock companies in the country.

Harry soon went to New York, where he worked in several radio dramas, and to New England for summer stock. He toured the country with Lillian Gish in "The Story of Mary Suratt" in 1947 and was doing "The Voice of the Turtle" at Martha's Vineyard in Massachusetts when Hollywood producer Frank Seltzer spotted him.

Drafted for the duration of WWII, upon his discharge 20th Century–Fox brought him out to California but never used him so he asked for a release.

After bit roles in a few films, Harry asked himself what movies would always be doing. Westerns. Being a good rider and with television coming on, westerns are what he concentrated on.

Harry said he liked playing heavies, "Because every part you do is a challenge. You got to watch yourself that you don't get into a set character. I used to like to work with makeup, not go overboard on it, but play with a scar, or the character itself. I like to play the heavy because they pretty well leave you alone, unless you go overboard. I love the heavies, and I love the reaction I get from people. 'Why are you so mean on screen? You're not a mean guy at all.' Most of the people I know that played really nasty heavies are the nicest guys in the world. I loved to play villains, especially in horse operas. That's what I'm best in and what I like most."[4]

When he worked on location, Harry became an accomplished artist, often spending time in between takes painting the Tetons, the Sierras, the Rockies, the Alabams at Lone Pine.

Myron Healey remembers, "Harry probably saved my life. We were up at Big Bear for a week's location shoot with Autry; Harry and I were doing heavies. I'm supposed to ride by a rock, Gene follows and bulldogs me into the lake for a fight in that cold water. Harry has to ride by with Pat Buttram pursuing him—Pat bulldogs him and he succumbs to Pat—on dry ground. Now, I had a bad cold all week—real sick, coughing, no medication. Unbeknownst to me, Harry talked to director George Archainbaud and said, 'What's the difference who goes in the water? Let us switch places.' So we did—If I'd gone in the water I would have come down with pneumonia and possibly died. To this day, I say Harry probably saved my life. He was always good for a laugh—take a bad situation and make it fun." [5]

One of the nicest western heavies—one of the best of the badmen—died October 30, 1990, of heart failure at his home in Ojai, California.

Often known as the meanest man in Hollywood, there was never any doubt when ox-like Dick Curtis came on screen he was a "heavy" in the truest sense of the word. He showed no mercy to the heroes on the Columbia lot.

Born Richard D. Dye May 11, 1902, in horse country, Newport, Kentucky, the 6' 3" Curtis started in films as an extra in 1919. He soon

Dick Curtis.

left, finding stage work more productive in the East where he had three years of New York stage experience and played stock in New Jersey and Massachusetts.

Curtis returned to Hollywood in 1930 and by 1932 was in four pictures that year.

Several months later, during the making of "King Kong" ('33), he was seriously injured and didn't work for over a year. Resuming work at a fever pitch by late 1934, westerns became his main niche.

Dick seemed to find a home at Columbia in '37 rustling, robbing and riding hell for leather against Charles Starrett and Bill Elliott.

Columbia kept Curtis busy not only in their B-westerns, but in virtually everything they made from horror films to Blondie movies, short subjects to serials, even bigger budgeted films.

His cohort in crime at Columbia, Kenneth MacDonald told an interviewer, "Socially, he was somewhat reclusive. This trait, in fact, was evident in production procedures. He was a thinker regarding his roles, and a strict professional. He found it uneasy to compromise. I felt, at one time, his thinking might lead him to an interest in direction. However,

this never occurred. He enjoyed cutting and assembling film clips for whatever purpose."[6]

There's a notable break in his film work from late '46 to mid '49. It was at this time Curtis discovered what he figured would be a terrific location site in the high desert above Twenty-Nine Palms, California, and, along with Russell Hayden, Roy Rogers, Bud Abbott and some members of the Sons of the Pioneers, 17 partners in all at $500 each, they developed the area for filming of westerns. Gene Autry's Flying-A Productions, ZIV TV's "Cisco Kid" and, eventually, Russell Hayden's production of "Judge Roy Bean" were the primary users of the locale they named Pioneertown.

Fellow badman Pierce Lyden once wrote, "Dick was so bad even the people who worked with him hated him. (Laughs) He was quite a talker, and was always going after the 'big one' (money). When the war was going on in Europe, Dick said, 'I remember the last one (WWI) and all the money people made. If we get into this one, I'm going to make mine.' Well, Dick got his chance—we got into war—and he started a project that was going to make him a millionaire: it was called Pioneertown. It was going to be a western picture location. Several people went in with him. He asked me to join them, but I didn't have the money. The project was a failure because there was not enough water (up on the high desert). Dick did not become the millionaire he had envisioned."[7]

In the early '50s Curtis found work on television, including "The Gene Autry Show", just prior to his untimely death January 13, 1952, at only 49. He'd been operated on for a brain tumor at Cedars of Lebanon Hospital in L.A. on Nov. 26, 1951. Cause of death was listed due to respiratory failure, lung cancer and a brain tumor.

WHAT THE EXHIBITOR HAD TO SAY: "Not like our old Gene, but his pictures are still enjoyable."

—Harland Rankin, Beau Theater,
Bell River, Ontario, Canada (October 1951)

SOURCES:

1. Autry with Herskowitz. p. 101.

2. *Saturday Evening Post, "The Role I Liked Best..."* by Smiley Burnette, 1953.

3. Interview with author.

4. Goldrup, Tom and Jim. *Feature Players Vol. 1.* 1986. (Self Published). p. 156-157.

5. Interview with author.

6. Magers, Boyd. *Best of the Badmen.* Empire 2005. p. 90.

7. Lyden, Pierce. *The Movie Badmen I Rode With.* 1988, Self Pub., p. 49.

Silver Canyon

Columbia, June 1951

A Gene Autry Production in Sepia Tone

Producer ....Armand Schaefer
Director ....John English
Assistant Director.......................Paul Donnelly
Original Story..............................Alan James
Screenplay...................................Gerald Geraghty
Photography ....William Bradford
Musical Supervisor ....Paul Mertz
Musical Director ....Mischa Bakaleinikoff
Film Editor...................................James Sweeney
Sound Dept...................................George Cooper
Art Director..................................Charles Clague
Set Decorations ....Frank Tuttle

SONGS: "Ridin' Down the Canyon" (music and lyrics by Gene Autry, Smiley Burnette)—sung by Gene Autry; "Fort Worth Jail" (music and lyrics by Dick Reinhart)—sung by Gene Autry.

RUNNING TIME: 70 minutes
FILMING DATES: March 12-22, 1951
LOCATIONS: Pioneertown; Iverson Ranch; Columbia backlot
BUDGET: $50,583.33

CAST:

Actor	*Character*
Gene Autry ....Gene Autry
Pat Buttram ....Pat
Gail Davis ....Dell Middler
Jim Davis ....Wade McQuarrie
Bob Steele ....Walt Middler
Edgar Dearing ....Colonel Middler
Richard Alexander ....Luke
Terry Frost...................................Irv Wyatt
Peter Mamakos...........................Laughing Jack
Stanley Andrews ....Major Weatherly
Stanley Blystone ....Soldier
Eugene Borden............................Gus Poppalardo
Steve Clark..................................Dr. Seddon
Kenne Duncan............................Corporal
Paul Frees...................................Narrator
Bill Hale ....Soldier driving wagon
Frankie Marvin...........................Telegrapher

John Merton ....Blacksmith
Eddie Parker...............................Mitchell
Jack Pepper ....Hotel Owner
Sandy Sanders............................2nd Pony Express Rider
Boyd Stockman...........................Stage Driver Sam
Duke York ....Sergeant Laughlin
Boyd "Red" Morgan, Art Dillard,
   Gary Goodwin, Jack O'Shea,
   Bob Woodward.......................Raiders
Bobby Clark, John McKee, Pat
   O'Malley, Martin Wilkins,
   Blackie Whiteford, Merrill
   McCormick, James Magrill......Extras
Champion.....................................Champion

STUNTS: Bob Woodward, Boyd Morgan, Eddie Parker, Sandy Sanders, Boyd Stockman.

THE FILM: It's 1861 and Gene Autry's an Army scout in "Silver Canyon", detailed to bring in Confederate guerrilla raider Wade McQuarrie (Jim Davis) who is interfering with Federal supply lines. With the assistance of Pat (Buttram), Gene tracks the raiders to an Union Army Post commanded (a bit naively) by Colonel Middler (Edgar Dearing) who has a daughter, Dell (Gail Davis), and a son, Walt (Bob Steele).

Walt secretly supports McQuarrie's actions but finally sees the right of things when his sister and Gene are captured by McQuarrie. Together they put an end to the guerrillas' plundering.

Many of the primary plot points are oddly reminiscent of "Gene Autry and the Mounties".

As with many of Gene's pictures at this time, "Silver Canyon" is pure western which caused many critics to hail Gene's Columbias of the '50s as one of the best B-western series ever made. Gene was now limiting himself to only a few songs per movie, stressing action instead. On the other hand, many older Autry fans longed for the cowboy to burst into song more often, but that would serve to nullify much of the authenticity of the pure western setting. It's a discussion that will never be settled.

As for the songs themselves, by this time Gene seemed

"Ridin' Down the Canyon" — Gene and his favorite leading lady Gail Davis.

NOTES AND COMMENTS: Working title for this film was "Silver Valley".

Jim Davis was in dozens of westerns from the '40s through the '60s, including his own series, "Stories of the Century" in 1955, but found his greatest fame late in life as Jock Ewing on the CBS nighttime soap opera "Dallas" in the late '70s.

Bob Steele had been one of the top B-western cowboy heroes since the late '20s, turning out series after series of pictures for FBO, Syndicate, Tiffany/World Wide, Monogram, Supreme, Republic, Metropolitan, PRC and Screen Guild while gradually turning to character roles in A films such as "The Big Sleep" ('46) and "Of Mice and Men" ('39) and many others.

Character player Stanley Andrews became best known as The Old Ranger, host of TV's "Death Valley Days" in its original conception, the first year of which was produced by Autry's Flying A Pictures.

FILM COMMENTS: *Peter Mamakos:* "One of the things I did when I first learned how to ride was 'Silver Canyon'. Gene told me what to do. He said, 'Don't grab the pommel, go with the rock.' I found him a very nice and easy man to talk to." [1]

to often rely on his choice of songs by reprising a hit from his Republic days that older fans were familiar with. In "Silver Canyon", "Ridin' Down the Canyon", first heard in "Tumbling Tumbleweeds", is one of those tried and true classics.

SOURCES:
1. *Western Clippings #27.* January/February 1999. p. 8.

Hills of Utah
Columbia, September 1951

A Gene Autry Production in Sepia Tone

Producer ....Armand Schaefer
Director ....John English
Assistant Director........................James Nicholson
Original Story.............................Les Savage Jr.
Screenplay...................................Gerald Geraghty
Photography ....William Bradford
Musical Supervisor ....Paul Mertz
Musical Director ....Mischa Bakaleinikoff
Film Editor..................................James Sweeney
Sound Dept..................................Lambert E. Day
Art Director................................Charles Clague
Set Decorations ....David Montrose

SONGS: "Peter Cottontail" (music and lyrics by Steve Nelson, Jack Rollins)—sung by Gene Autry; "Utah" (music and lyrics by Tex Atchinson, Billy Weber)—sung by Gene Autry.

RUNNING TIME: 70 minutes

FILMING DATES: April 16-26, 1951

LOCATIONS: Iverson Ranch; Agoura Ranch; Corriganville; Columbia cave set

BUDGET: $49,095.04

CAST:

Actor	Character
Gene Autry	Dr. Gene Autry
Pat Buttram	Dusty Cosgrove
Elaine Riley	Karen McQueen
Donna Martell	Nola French
Onslow Stevens	Jayda McQueen
Denver Pyle	Bowie French
William Fawcett	Washoe
Harry Lauter	Evan Fox
Kenne Duncan	Indigo Hubbard
Harry Harvey	Marshal Duffield
Tommy Ivo	Duncan McQueen
Tom London	Mayor Donovan
Teddy Infuhr	Boy
Lee Morgan	Man who brings boy
Stanley Price	Children's father
Peter Votrian	Jimmy
Sandy Sanders	Rio
Boyd Stockman	Stage Driver
Bob Woodward	Miner
Frankie Marvin, Roy Bucko, Victor Cox, Jack O'Shea, Cactus Mack, Billy Griffith, Ralph Bucko, Bob Reeves	Extras
Champion	Champion

STUNTS: Boyd Stockman, Bob Woodward, Sandy Sanders, Duke Taylor.

THE FILM: Without relinquishing his six-gun or neglecting the fisticuffs and hard riding action, for "Hills of Utah" Gene Autry's a doctor in Coffin Gap—"Where a killing a day keeps all other doctors away" read the print ads.

As explained in a film noirish opening, when he was young, Gene's father was shot by someone unknown and died because a physician was not available. Gene now returns as an M.D. to Coffin Gap where his father was killed to find an old feud still raging between mine owner Jayda McQueen (Onslow Stevens) and cattleman Bowie French (Denver Pyle) who claims the copper mines are polluting

Badman Harry Lauter is on the receiving end of Gene's punch.

the streams, thus causing the death of beef stock.

Autry attempts to steer clear of the feud, trying to confine himself to his doctoring, but that brings on complications when Gene responds to a request by Karen McQueen (Elaine Riley) to treat her younger brother, which he does, however the boy later mysteriously dies sending Jayda gunning for Gene.

When a miner shoots one of French's men, the feud escalates, eventually revealing who killed Gene's father years ago and why McQueen's son died.

One must applaud Autry for varying the themes in his westerns—from Army Scout, Post Office investigator, Texas Ranger, U. S. Marshal, Banker's Association investigator in previous films to medico in "Hills of Utah", but the Autry "healing touch" is still present.

NOTES AND COMMENTS: With two Christmas hits under his belt, "Here Comes Santa Claus" in 1947 and "Rudolph the Red-Nosed Reindeer" in 1949, America's favorite cowboy turned his attention to Easter and came up with the hit, "Peter Cottontail", in 1950. The inclusion of "Peter Cottontail" is offbeat and refreshing, even if "Hills of Utah" wasn't released at Easter-time.

FILM COMMENTS: *Gene Autry* explaining the difference between real boxing and movie fights, "The short snappy knockout punch that travels 12 inches or less may delight sports fans but for a staged movie fight it is strictly inadequate. The trouble is that the short straight blow isn't photogenic. I realize boxing fans sneer at screen fights that feature wild roundhouse swings, 'telegraphed punches' and gymnastics involving chairs, tables and whatever other furniture is handy. The fact is, much time and rehearsal is spent working out these battles. Experience has convinced us this type of fight is what western movie lovers want. The average person watching a prize fight fails to see 50 percent of the blows struck. There is so much weaving, ducking and clinching, and the punches are so short and fast, they are very difficult to spot. In our movie fights there is never such doubt. The audiences see the punch start, travel and land—or miss. The entire operation is visual. If two movie cowboys sparred, feinted and clinched the way boxers do, audiences would walk out. They demand and get continuously rough

action. Even a toe-to-toe slugging match would soon become monotonous to western fans. That's why we utilize chairs, tables, stairways and other props to vary the action and add to the excitement. And if you don't believe these screen fights are tough, you should have seen the shiner I got in a fight during filming of 'Hills of Utah'! They had to shoot around me for two days." [1]

Elaine Riley worked with Gene Autry in "Hills of Utah" and three TVers. "He was a sweetheart too. I have about two people in my mind, maybe three, that fell short of what I would say was, you know, nice. Not for any personal reason, anything they did to me, just statements they made. But aside from that, I got along with everybody; I think actors are a special group of people. Actors have a charisma about them, even the people in the craft part of the industry, as far as the sets and designers, they're all special. But Gene Autry is a doll. I spent a lot of time with Gene and (his sidekick) Pat Buttram on location in Pioneertown. We didn't have a personal phone, they had one probably in the studio, but at night anybody that wanted to use the phone, if Gene were going to town, Twenty-Nine Palms, he'd take you. So I'd always go down and call Dick (husband/actor Richard Martin). I'd drive down with Gene…he was just a nice man. Neat." A decision maker, according to Elaine was "…the little French person Gene Autry used to have around…George Archainbaud directed I don't know how many pictures. That's somebody who really did call me back to work. I think partly because I could get the horse on the mark and there weren't too many gals who could." [2]

Donna Martell: "Besides 'Hills of Utah' I also did six

Gene, Elaine Riley and Elaine's on-screen father Onslow Stevens.

or eight of the Gene Autry TV shows. They kept sending scripts and I'd do them! Gene used to do his own makeup and hair, so you had to do your own as well. They were very frugal at his Flying A Productions. You had to do *everything* for yourself. The script girl would be the only other female there, so she had to help me with some of the costumes. We'd do two TV shows at one time—so costume changes were frequent! Gene was very nice—and the shows were a great training ground. At Flying A I was up for the title role of 'Annie Oakley', but Gene Autry's agent wanted me under contract. I said 'No.' Stayed with *my* agent—and lost the show to Gail Davis. Gene was an icon of the business. He was a hero, a true American—he went to war, and everything he did, he did well. He was a giving, caring, good man. Those were my beginnings—working with and for Gene at both Columbia and Flying A Productions." [3]

CAST BIOS: It's hard to understand why Bob Woodward didn't get the recognition he deserved for his very prolific and enduring stunt career. He is as visible and active as any of the so-called well known stuntmen. Born March 5, 1909, in Oklahoma, Bob first appeared on the Hollywood scene in '31's Tom Tyler film, "Rider of the Plains". He spent the next 30 years as a stuntman, actor and double for such stalwarts as Gene Autry, Lash LaRue, Jimmy Wakely, Dick Foran and Buck Jones.

Forming an association with Gene Autry about the time Gene formed his Flying A TV productions in 1950, Bob can be spotted doubling Gene throughout his TV series as well as playing small roles (sometimes two parts in one episode) in nearly every episode. Woodward can easily be spotted as he always ducked his head close to his chest. Besides being a good fight man, Woodward was adept at horsemanship as well as team and buggy driving, even showing up as the stagecoach driver of a 4-up team on occasion.

Woodward worked A-westerns too—"Cattle Queen of Montana" ('54), "Wyoming Renegades" ('55), "Apache Territory" ('58), etc. By the time most of the westerns being done in Hollywood were for the television audience, Bob easily made the transition to the small screen, appearing in and performing stunts on over 100 episodic westerns including "Lone Ranger", "Annie Oakley", "Buffalo Bill Jr.", "Range Rider", "Tales of Wells Fargo" and others. When age and infirmity began to creep up on Bob, he kept his hand in doing bit parts and extra work on "Gunsmoke", "Wagon Train" and "Have Gun Will Travel".

After a four decade career in front of the camera, Bob Woodward succumbed to a massive heart attack February 7, 1972, in Hollywood, California. He produced a fabulous, productive career in stunt work that anyone could be proud of.

WHAT THE EXHIBITOR HAD TO SAY: "Poor old Gene, we feel, has pretty well shot his bolt. You can't play two horses, and now that he is on television, he seems to have lost his zip on the screen."

—Harland Rankin, Plaza Theater,
Tilbury, Ontario, Canada (May 1952)

"A good western with some good action. Did less than average business in this small town."

—Francis Gill, Panonia Theater,
Panonia, Colorado (March 1952)

"No special draw here but this one pleased them ok."

—Mrs. H. A. Fitch, Erin Theater,
Erin, Tennessee (February 1953)

SOURCES:
1. "Hills of Utah" pressbook.
2. Magers and Fitzgerald. *Ladies of the Western.* McFarland, 2002. p. 220, 222.
3. Magers and Fitzgerald. *Westerns Women.* McFarland, 1999. p. 158, 159 and *Western Clippings #27.* January/February 1999. p. 9.

Valley of Fire
<u>Columbia, November 1951</u>
A Gene Autry Production in Sepia Tone

Producer ....Armand Schaefer
Director ....John English
Assistant Director.......................Paul Donnelly
Original Story............................Earle Snell
Screenplay.................................Gerald Geraghty
Photography ....William Bradford
Musical Supervisor ....Paul Mertz
Musical Director ....Mischa Bakaleinikoff
Film Editor ....James Sweeney
Sound Dept................................George Cooper
Art Director...............................Charles Clague
Set Decorations ....David Montrose

SONGS: "Oh, Susanna" (Public Domain)—sung by Pat Buttram; "Here's to the Ladies" (music and lyrics by Gene Autry, Cindy Walker)—sung by Gene Autry and extras; "On Top of Old Smoky" (music and lyrics by P. D. Vernon)—sung by Gene Autry, Cass County Boys and extras.

RUNNING TIME: 63 minutes
FILMING DATES: June 5-15, 1951
LOCATIONS: Lone Pine; Columbia backlot
BUDGET: $48,358.01

CAST:

Actor	*Character*
Gene Autry	Gene Autry
Pat Buttram	Breezie Larrabee
Gail Davis	Laurie
Russell Hayden	Steve Guilford
Christine Larson	Bee Laverne
Harry Lauter	Tod Rawlings
Terry Frost	Grady McKean
Barbara Stanley	Laurie's friend, Gail
Teddy Infuhr	Virgil
Margie Liszt	Virgil's mother Blanche
Riley Hill	Colorado
Victor Sen Yung	Ching Moon
Gregg Barton	Blackie
Sandy Sanders	Banjo
Fred Sherman	Panhandle Jones
Wade Crosby	Window Washer

William Fawcett	Storekeeper Bundy
Al Haskell	Mexican
Ethan Laidlaw, Blackie Whiteford	Henchmen
James Magill	Bartender Tom
The Cass County Boys: Bert Dodson, Fred S. Martin, Jerry Scoggins	Musicians at Dance
Frankie Marvin	Cowhand
Bud Osborne	Beardsley
Syd Saylor	Drunk Miner
Duke York	Piano
John "Skins" Miller, Jack O'Shea, Pat O'Malley, George Magrill, Merrill McCormick, Boyd Stockman	Extras
Champion	Champion

STUNTS: Bob Woodward, Sandy Sanders, Boyd Stockman.

THE FILM: "Valley of Fire" is a lesser entry among Gene Autry's Columbia titles, with several roles miscast. Gail Davis, usually Miss Clean-cut All-American girl, is a spoiled gold-digger on the hunt for a rich westerner, making her a more unlikable character than the "bad girl", Christine Larson. There's also a bratty kid, Teddy Infuhr, who deserves a real good spanking but never gets one; some misplaced humor from wagon train driver Fred Sherman and one of the "brides to be" Margie Liszt; plus some slow spots that just don't hold together.

Even with a shorter running time than Gene's previous films, "Valley of Fire" seems longer. Fault lies with the script rather than the usual expert physical production from Armand Schaefer and director John English.

Yarn is a listless affair of gambler Tod Rawlings (Harry Lauter) trying to gain control of Quartz Creek and the efforts of newly elected Mayor Gene Autry to import a wagonload of women as prospective brides. The narrative lacks cohesion. A good encounter starts the proceedings and a humorous gun battle finale winds them up.

Gene's singing of "On Top of Old Smoky" is

Gene disarms badman Russell Hayden as storekeeper Willliam Fawcett and leading lady Gail Davis look on.

a standout, a hit song he would reprise as a title tune in 1953.

NOTES AND COMMENTS: According to veteran sound mixer George Cooper, the desert constantly produces more annoying noises than any other movie location site. The first day the troupe set up shop on "Valley of Fire" they were surrounded by rattlesnakes, judging from the frightening noises coming through the mike to Cooper's earphones. Each time the rattling was heard over the dialogue, Cooper halted the camera, and sound recorders walked around trying to catch the rattling on a "wild" sound track for use in a future picture when no snake was available. After hours of chasing the elusive rattlings over the desert, however, the recorders finally discovered they were pursuing swift desert locusts. Coughing horses, whose throats became irritated by the desert dust, ruined scenes, also, until Jay Berry, Gene's wrangler, dosed them with some good old-fashioned cough syrup. Several trees were brought along and transplanted for a certain scene, but the desert sun and wind dried the leaves so fast that their constant rustling came through the soundtrack like a machine-gun battle. To prevent this, the leaves were sprayed with a liquid-rubber solution. During a man-made rainstorm, the peculiarities of desert acoustics changed the natural sound of splashing raindrops to a noise like fat frying in a pan. This problem was solved by placing crumbled window-screening in the puddles to break the bigger raindrops into smaller ones.[1]

Even at a time when other B-westerns were curtailing production due to rising costs and lessening profits, Gene Autry's films were still more than doubling their cost in income. "Valley of Fire" cost $48,358.01 to produce. From November 1951 when it was released through May 1955 the film's net receipts were $110,799. Actually, within the first three months of release, "Valley of Fire" had earned over $57,000.

Oriental actor Victor Sen Yung is best remembered as Charlie Chan's #2 son, Jimmy Chan, in several 20th Century–Fox features.

WHAT THE EXHIBITOR HAD TO SAY: "A good western for the kids with some comedy thrown in."

—Francis Gill, Panonia Theater,
Panonia, Colorado (June 1952)

SOURCES:

1. *Autry's Aces.* Fall, 1951. Interview/article by Virginia Siegers. p. 9.

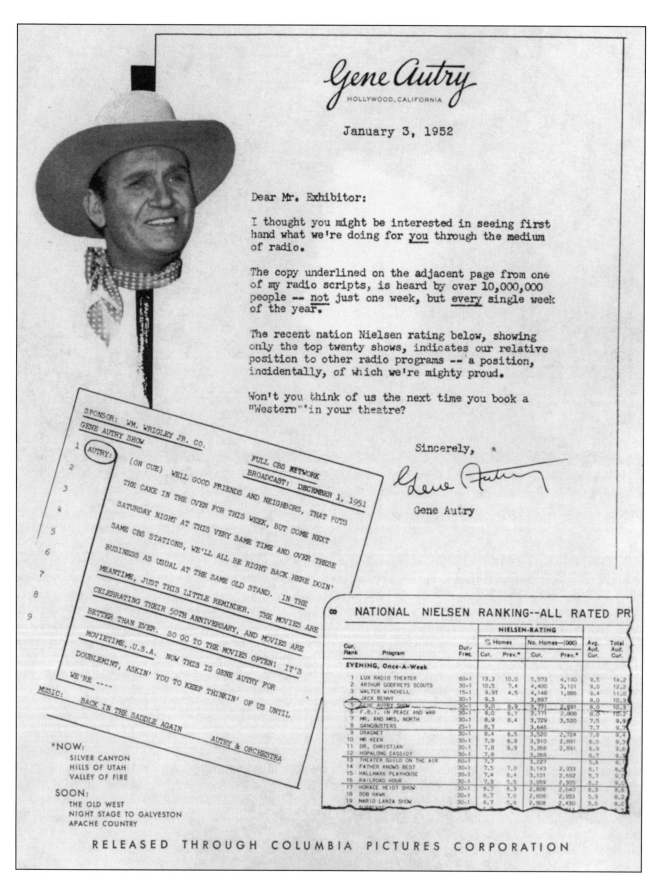

Gene Autry

HOLLYWOOD, CALIFORNIA

January 3, 1952

Dear Mr. Exhibitor:

I thought you might be interested in seeing first hand what we're doing for you through the medium of radio.

The copy underlined on the adjacent page from one of my radio scripts, is heard by over 10,000,000 people -- not just one week, but every single week of the year.

The recent nation Nielsen rating below, showing only the top twenty shows, indicates our relative position to other radio programs -- a position, incidentally, of which we're mighty proud.

Won't you think of us the next time you book a "Western" in your theatre?

Sincerely,

Gene Autry

Gene Autry

SPONSOR: WM. WRIGLEY JR. CO.

GENE AUTRY SHOW

FULL CBS NETWORK
BROADCAST: DECEMBER 1, 1951

1 AUTRY: (ON CUE) WELL GOOD FRIENDS AND NEIGHBORS, THAT PUTS
2 THE CAKE IN THE OVEN FOR THIS WEEK, BUT COME NEXT
3 SATURDAY NIGHT AT THIS VERY SAME TIME AND OVER THESE
4 SAME CBS STATIONS, WE'LL ALL BE RIGHT BACK HERE DOIN'
5 BUSINESS AS USUAL AT THE SAME OLD STAND. IN THE
6 MEANTIME, JUST THIS LITTLE REMINDER. THE MOVIES ARE
7 CELEBRATING THEIR 50TH ANNIVERSARY, AND MOVIES ARE
8 BETTER THAN EVER. SO GO TO THE MOVIES OFTEN! IT'S
9 MOVIETIME, U.S.A. NOW THIS IS GENE AUTRY FOR
  DOUBLEMINT, ASKIN' YOU TO KEEP THINKIN' OF US UNTIL
  WE'RE ----

MUSIC: BACK IN THE SADDLE AGAIN
                              AUTRY & ORCHESTRA

*NOW:
    SILVER CANYON
    HILLS OF UTAH
    VALLEY OF FIRE

SOON:
    THE OLD WEST
    NIGHT STAGE TO GALVESTON
    APACHE COUNTRY

NATIONAL NIELSEN RANKING--ALL RATED PR

Cur. Rank	Program	Dur./ Freq.	NIELSEN-RATING					
			% Homes		No. Homes--(000)		Avg. Aud. Cur.	Total Aud. Cur.
			Cur.	Prev.*	Cur.	Prev.*		
	EVENING, Once-A-Week							
1	LUX RADIO THEATER	60-1	13.3	10.0	5,573	4,190	9.5	14.2
2	ARTHUR GODFREYS SCOUTS	30-1	10.5	7.4	4,400	3,101	9.0	12.2
3	WALTER WINCHELL	15-1	9.9T	4.5	4,148	1,886	9.4	11.0
4	JACK BENNY	30-1	9.3		3,897		8.0	10.3
5	GENE AUTRY SHOW	30-1	9.0	5.9	3,771	2,891	8.0	10.3
6	F.B.I. IN PEACE AND WAR	30-1	9.0	6.7	3,771	2,806	8.0	10.2
7	MR. AND MRS. NORTH	30-1	8.9	8.4	3,729	3,520	7.5	9.9
8	GANGBUSTERS	25-1	8.7		3,646		7.7	9.7
9	DRAGNET	30-1	8.4	6.5	3,520	2,724	7.8	9.4
10	MR KEEN	30-1	7.9	6.9	3,310	2,891	6.0	9.3
11	DR. CHRISTIAN	30-1	7.8	6.9	3,268	2,891	6.9	9.6
12	HOPALONG CASSIDY	30-1	7.8		3,268		6.7	9.3
13	THEATER GUILD ON THE AIR	60-1	7.7		3,227		5.6	9.7
14	FATHER KNOWS BEST	30-1	7.5	7.0	3,143	2,933	6.1	8.6
15	HALLMARK PLAYHOUSE	30-1	7.4	6.4	3,101	2,682	5.7	9.0
16	RAILROAD HOUR	30-1	7.3	5.5	3,059	2,305	6.2	9.0
17	HORACE HEIDT SHOW	30-1	6.7	6.3	2,808	2,640	6.3	8.6
18	BOB HAWK	30-1	6.7	7.0	2,808	2,933	5.9	8.2
19	MARIO LANZA SHOW	30-1	6.7	5.8	2,808	2,430	5.6	9.0

RELEASED THROUGH COLUMBIA PICTURES CORPORATION

Motion Picture Herald, January 15, 1952.

The Old West
Columbia, January 1952
A Gene Autry Production in Sepia Tone

Producer ....Armand Schaefer
Director ....George Archainbaud
Assistant Director........................Paul Donnelly
Screenplay...................................Gerald Geraghty
Photography ....William Bradford
Musical Supervisor ....Paul Mertz
Musical Director ....Mischa Bakaleinikoff
Film Editor.................................James Sweeney
Sound Dept.................................John Westmoreland
Art Director................................Charles Clague
Set Decorations ....David Montrose

SONGS: Medley: "The Old West"/ "America the Beautiful" (music and lyrics by Paul Mertz/Public Domain)—sung by studio singers over titles; "Somebody Bigger Than You and I" (music and lyrics by Johnny Lange, Hy Heath, Sonny Burke)—sung by Gene Autry and extras; "Music by the Angels" (music and lyrics by Arthur Altman, Marty Symes)—sung by Gene Autry, Pat Buttram and extras.
RUNNING TIME: 61 minutes
FILMING DATES: August 18-28, 1951
LOCATIONS: Corriganville; Columbia backlot; Vasquez Rocks
BUDGET: $42,237.04

CAST:

Actor	*Character*
Gene Autry	Gene Autry
Pat Buttram	Panhandle Gibbs
Gail Davis	Arlie Williams
Lyle Talbot	Doc Lockwood
Louis Jean Heydt	Jeff Bleeker
House Peters Sr.	Parson Jonathan Brooks
House Peters Jr.	Mike Saunders
Dick Jones	Pinto
Kathy Johnson	Judie Bleeker
Don Harvey	Harve Evers
Dee Pollock	Eddie Jamison
Sandy Sanders	Rider with Chadwick/ Lockwood gunman
Bob Woodward	Lockwood gunman
Bobby Clack	Rider betting on race
James Craven	Daniels
Tom London	Chadwick
Frankie Marvin	Watkins
Lee Morgan	Duffield
Pat O'Malley, Herman Hack, Buddy Roosevelt	Townsmen
Syd Saylor	Whitey, takes bets
Rube Dalroy, Roy Bucko, Robert Hilton, Cactus Mack, Snub Pollard, Tex Terry, Blackie Whiteford	Extras
Champion	Champion
Little Champ	Little Champ

STUNTS: Sandy Sanders, Bob Woodward.

THE FILM: A religious element dressed up "The Old West" to make it slightly more than a routine Gene Autry Columbia, although the economy measures are firmly in place beginning with this outing. Running time is only 61

Gene with Little Champ and Champion.

minutes (later features dropped under an hour); plenty of stock footage from "Rim of the Canyon" is employed (a stagecoach race and a fight with Jock Mahoney being lifted from that film); there are editing or continuity lapses near the end; and—a new director is employed in the person of George Archainbaud who was also now helming many of Gene's TV episodes.

There's also an entertaining, but extended, sequence in which Gene puts Champion and Little Champ through a series of hoop tricks. It's welcomed by Autry devotees, but to be fair, it was film-padding and a definite economy measure.

The story, told in flashback, features Gene with a contract to tame wild mustangs to serve as horses for the stagecoach line in Saddle Rock managed by Arlie Williams (Gail Davis). The man who runs the town, Doc Lockwood (Lyle Talbot), has his eyes on that contract for himself. Control of the stageline comes down to a race between Gene and his horses and Lockwood's horses, dangerously driven by stagecoach driver Jeff Bleeker (Louis Jean Heydt) who is in denial about his failing eyesight.

The film features a sizable religious element as silent star House Peters Sr. makes a comeback as a traveling preacher who instills theology in Gene during his convalescence from a gunshot wound. Concordantly, both songs Gene sings in the picture are religious oriented.

It's a pretty thin story and Gerald Geraghty's screenplay gets a bit off track and involved with a number of characters outside the main theme, such as a pair of town toughs (Dick Jones and Don Harvey—blatantly mimicking Lon Chaney Jr.'s Lenny from "Of Mice and Men" ['39]), Bleeker's daughter Judie (Kathy Johnson) and her "boyfriend", stable boy Eddie (Dee Pollock) and Gail Davis who gets high billing but barely appears in a totally undeveloped role.

NOTES AND COMMENTS: This is the only film in which father and son, House Peters Sr. and Jr., worked together in a picture. Peters Sr. had been a matinee idol in the silent era, often working with legendary director Cecil B. De Mille.

Gail Davis took a break from filming after completion of "The Old West". She and husband Bob Davis were expecting "a visit from the stork" in January and they needed time to supervise the building of a nursery in their new home.

One of the stagecoaches seen in "The Old West" was purchased by Gene for $5,000 on a business trip back east. He had it shipped to California on a ton and a half truck. At the time, the stage was 221 years old and was said to have made the run from Boston to Worcester, Massachusetts. It was discovered in an old barn covered with years of accumulation of dust and cobwebs. However, it was still in such excellent condition that the oil lamps still shone. A luxury carriage in its day, it was outfitted with all-leather upholstery, springs, brass fixtures and gold trim. There is a five foot brake alongside the driver's seat which can be operated by hand or foot. Gene had the brakes tested in Boston and found the stagecoach could be stopped within a few feet.

FILM COMMENTS: *House Peters Jr.:* "One evening in 1951 I received a call from George Archainbaud asking me if Dad would be interested in a good role in an Autry western. The picture was pretty well cast, but he said that perhaps he could also work in a small part for me as a heavy. It was most unfortunate under these circumstances that Dad and I didn't have a substantial scene together. I worked for George many times over the years. George worked as an assistant director in many of Dad's films in the early silent days. When I told my father about the offer, he said he'd be delighted to do it. I think he also thought it might help me out if he did.

"'The Old West' had a good cast, including Gail Davis, Lyle Talbot, Dick Jones and Tom London. My father enjoyed meeting Lyle Talbot and talking over old times with Louis Jean Heydt, an actor who also had a background on the New York stage. Somebody who didn't get screen credit was Don Harvey in a significant role opposite Dick Jones, both of whom did a take-off of the characters in 'Of Mice and Men'.

"Despite not acting in over 23 years, my father

Gene and Lyle Talbot (center) disarm a couple of town toughs, House Peters Jr. and Lee Morgan, while James Craven (right) observes.

did very well in this picture—especially when you consider this was his first with sound. He had a very substantial role and had an excellent speaking voice, and had no problem with dialogue. Each morning as I drove him to the set he'd tell me about how he enjoyed working again." [1]

Dee Pollock: "I remember Champion more than anything. He was a beautiful horse. I was so impressed with Champion and the little pony jumping through the hoop. I thought, that's really something. I was only 14 or 15. My mother had a crush on Gene." [2]

CAST BIOS:

House Peters Jr.'s screen work began in 1936, but it was in the late '40s and early '50s that he hit his stride as a screen badman.

Robert House Peters Jr. was born in New Rochelle, New York, January 12, 1916. His father, silent screen matinee idol, Robert House Peters, was born March 12, 1880, in Bristol, England.

House Sr. left England and worked in a stock company in South Africa. Leaving there, he landed in Montreal and eventually New York about 1911. After working in New York theatre, he came to Hollywood in 1915 to do four films for Cecil B. De Mille.

House Sr. left the business after "Rose Marie" with Joan Crawford in 1928. He'd acquired enough wealth that he did not need to return to films.

However, in 1951, director George Archainbaud asked House Jr. if his father would play the preacher in the current Gene Autry western, "The Old West". Senior did the picture, the only one father and son made together.

As for House Jr., he began with small roles in films in 1936, including a role in Gene's "Public Cowboy No. 1" in '37.

He joined the Coast Guard Auxiliary when WWII broke out in 1941. Discharged in 1946, House returned to films and built a solid career over the next 18 years in films and TV.

At 50, in 1966, he retired from acting and went into real estate, eventually opening an office in Woodland Hills.

In 1976, he left real estate behind while he and his wife since 1946, Lucy, began a snowbird existence in their motor home.

In 2000, House was honored by the Motion Picture and TV Fund with a Golden Boot Award.

Today, he and Lucy live comfortably at the Motion Picture and TV Home in Woodland Hills, California.

George Archainbaud was already 60 when he became the workhorse of Gene Autry's Flying A Productions, directing both movies and TV episodes. His output during the six years he worked for Gene is staggering—Gene's last 12 Columbia movies (beginning with "The Old West") in '52-'53, 49 episodes of Gene's TV series, 28 "Range Rider" episodes, 32 of "Annie Oakley", 22 of "Buffalo Bill Jr." and at least 11 of "The Adventures of Champion".

Archainbaud was born in Paris, France, May 7, 1890.

Gail Davis as "Annie Oakley" with director George Archainbaud.

Early in life he was adopted by a French actor. The pair acted together on the Paris stage until 1910 when they both emigrated to the U.S., eventually moving to Hollywood when Archainbaud became an assistant director then, at 26, a director on his own, helming some 58 silent features between 1917 and 1929.

As sound came in, Archainbaud adapted easily, joining RKO in 1930. In '36 he moved to Paramount.

When Harry "Pop" Sherman was producing the Hopalong Cassidy features at United Artists, he hired Archainbaud who, up til then, had never directed a western. However, Archainbaud's Hoppys are quite good. Later, when William Boyd himself was producing the series, he hired Archainbaud to direct 12 features.

It was shortly after when Gene hired Archainbaud's considerable talents. "We used to call George Archainbaud 'The Old Frenchman'," Gene smiled. "He was from France. He worked at Paramount a number of years on some big features."[3]

R. G. Springsteen.

Stuntlady Alice Van, whose husband was western director R. G. Springsteen, often doubled for Gail Davis during the time "Annie Oakley" was in production. She told writer Mike Nevins that Archainbaud "...was very nice. They were kind of careful about different things with him because he'd had a heart attack. He had a French accent and was hard to understand, especially when he got nervous and started to holler." [4]

"He was a fast director," Jimmy Hawkins (Tagg Oakley on "Annie Oakley") stated. "Do this, do that, move here, move there. But every episode he directed, he had it all laid out in his mind before we started. I think his compositions, his setups, had more depth to them than most other directors on "Annie Oakley". He was a European. His attitude and approach were like Billy Wilder or Michael Curtiz: demanding but prepared. I can still see his hands forming squares in the air, framing shots." [5]

Dick Jones worked for Archainbaud on Gene's "Wagon Team" and "Last of the Pony Riders" and numerous times on "The Gene Autry Show", "Range Rider" and "Buffalo Bill Jr.". Dick exclaimed, "He was one of the best directors Gene Autry had! He cut the show before it ever got in the camera. Fantastic about putting it together. He was a real nice gentleman, a pleasure to be around, a nice conversationalist. But he didn't understand cowboys. I remember one time he came over and very quietly asked Jock (Mahoney) and me, 'Why do you guys get off the horse sometimes on this side, and sometimes on that side?' I said, 'It depends on where the camera is.' He thought about that for a minute and said, 'Oh. Okay.' (Laughs) He didn't like cowboy music. When they had the playback, he would sort of cringe. (Chuckles) (Interacting with Gene) it was strictly business. I kidded around and used to call him 'Archinbald.' But his name is actually pronounced Archain-bau. The 'd' is silent." [6]

When Gene folded production at Flying A, Archainbaud went on to direct various TV shows, signing on with Screen Gems, the TV subsidiary of Columbia.

On the evening of February 20, 1959, just short of his 69th birthday, Archainbaud suffered a fatal heart attack just after finishing the direction of a TV episode.

SOURCES:

1. Peters Jr., House. *Another Side of Hollywood.* Empire, 2000. p. 135.

2. *Western Clippings #27.* January/February 1999. p. 7.

3. "Melody Ranch Theater" showing of "Wagon Team" on Nashville Network, 1987.

4. *Western Clippings #55.* September/October 2003. p. 20.

5. *Western Clippings #55.* September/October 2003. p. 20.

6. *Western Clippings #55.* September/October 2003. p. 20.

Night Stage to Galveston
Columbia, March 1952
A Gene Autry Production in Sepia Tone

Producer ....Armand Schaefer
Director ....George Archainbaud
Assistant Director........................Paul Donnelly
Screenplay...................................Norman S. Hall
Photography ....William Bradford
Musical Supervisor ....Paul Mertz
Musical Director ....Mischa Bakaleinikoff
Film Editor ....James Sweeney
Sound Dept.................................Jack Goodrich
Art Director.................................Charles Clague
Set Decorations ....Al Rickerd

SONGS: "The Eyes of Texas" (music and lyrics by J. L. Sinclair)—sung by studio singers; "Down in Slumberland" (music and lyrics by Smiley Burnette)—sung by Gene Autry and studio singers; "Yellow Rose of Texas" (Public Domain)—sung by Pat Buttram; "A Heart as Big as Texas" (music and lyrics by Oakley Haldeman, Buddy Feyne)—sung by Gene Autry.

RUNNING TIME: 62 minutes
FILMING DATES: September 20-28, 1951
LOCATIONS: Iverson Ranch; Columbia backlot
BUDGET: $42,578.20

CAST:

Actor	*Character*
Gene Autry	Gene Autry
Pat Buttram	Pat Buttram
Virginia Huston	Ann Bellamy
Thurston Hall	Col. James Bellamy
Judy Nugent	Cathy Evans
Robert Livingston	Adj. General Slaydon
Harry Cording	Ted Driscoll
Robert Bice	Captain Yancey
Frank Sully	Kelly
Robert Peyton	T. J. "Bob" Wilson
Riley Hill	Policeman George Barnes
Harry Lauter	Evans
Clayton Moore	Clyde Chambers
Richard Alexander	Patrol Headquarters Leader
Frank Rawls	Capt. Kramer
Lois Austin	Martha Wilson
Steve Clark	Old Ranger
Sandy Sanders	State Police room Guard
Boyd Stockman	Stage Driver #1
Ben Welden	Arresting State Policeman
Bob Woodward	Slaydon Stage Driver
Frank Ellis	Gunman
Duke York	Arresting State Policeman
Carol Henry	State Policeman
Garry Goodwin, Kathleen O'Malley	Extras
Champion	Champion

THE FILM: Ex-Texas Rangers Gene Autry and Pat Buttram are asked by newspaper publisher Colonel Bellamy (Thurston Hall) and his daughter Ann (Virginia Huston) to obtain evidence of corruption in the Texas State Police run by Adjutant General Slaydon (Robert Livingston).

When attempts by Slaydon to have Gene and Pat killed fail, the crooked politician kidnaps Ann and little orphan Cathy Evans (Judy Nugent), now a ward of the crusading

Gene, Judy Nugent and Pat Buttram.

publisher. Cathy escapes and leads Gene to Ann and the outlaws.

NOTES AND COMMENTS: Upon completion of "Night Stage…", Gene appeared in October for the 20th annual World's Championship Rodeo at Boston Gardens. A total of 172,791 paid to see Gene over the eleven day run with one day's capacity turnout totaling 41,727 people.

Two ex-Lone Rangers are in "Night Stage to Galveston". Robert Livingston played the role in Republic's 1939 serial "The Lone Ranger Rides Again" and Clayton Moore was on a salary dispute hiatus from "The Lone Ranger" TV show when he worked in this film.

FILM COMMENTS: Judy Nugent: "I especially remember Gene's recitation of 'The Lord's Prayer' to me in the back of a wagon. It was cool! I later did an 'Annie Oakley' for Gene's company starring Gail Davis as Annie. Pat Buttram was in 'Night Stage'. He was a real character." [1]

SOURCES:
1. *Western Clippings #19.* September/October 1997. p. 25.

Apache Country
Columbia, May 1952
A Gene Autry Production in Sepia Tone

Producer ....Armand Schaefer
Director ....George Archainbaud
Assistant Director........................Paul Donnelly
Screenplay.................................Norman S. Hall
Photography ....William Bradford
Musical Supervisor ....Paul Mertz
Musical Director ....Mischa Bakaleinikoff
Film Editor ....James Sweeney
Sound Dept................................Russell Malmgren
Art Director...............................Charles Clague
Set Decorations ....Frank Tuttle

SONGS: "The Covered Wagon Rolled Right Along" (music and lyrics by Britt Wood, Hy Heath)—sung by Gene Autry, Carolina Cotton, Pat Buttram, Tom London; "Indian War Dance" (Public Domain)—performed by Tony Whitecloud's Jemez Indians; "I Love to Yodel" (music and lyrics by Carolina Cotton)—sung by Carolina Cotton; "Cold, Cold Heart" (music and lyrics by Hank Williams)—sung by Gene Autry; "Indian Eagle Dance" (Public Domain)—performed by Tony Whitecloud's Jemez Indians; "Crime Will Never Pay" (music and lyrics by Willard Robison, Jack Pepper)—sung by Gene Autry, Carolina Cotton, Cass County Boys; "Indian Buffalo Dance" (Public Domain)—performed by Tony Whitecloud's Jemez Indians.

RUNNING TIME: 62 minutes
FILMING DATES: November 12-20, 1951
LOCATIONS: Iverson Ranch; Columbia backlot
BUDGET: $39,786.08

CAST:

Actor	*Character*
Gene Autry	Gene Autry
Pat Buttram	Pat Buttram
Carolina Cotton	Carolina Cotton
Harry Lauter	Dave Kilrain
Mary Scott	Laura Rayburn
Sydney Mason	Walter Rayburn
Francis X. Bushman	Commissioner Latham
Tony Whitecloud's Jemez Indians	Tribal Dancers
The Cass County Boys: Bert Dodson, Jerry Scoggins, Fred Martin	Cass County Boys
Gregg Barton	Luke Thorn
Mickey Simpson	Tom Ringo
Harry Wilson	Henchman Steve Clayborn
Steve Raines	Duke Clayborn
Iron Eyes Cody	Indian with Pat
Byron Foulger	Bartlett
Tom London	Patches Witherspoon
Frank Ellis	Man at show
Frankie Marvin	Henchman
Eddie Parker	Brawler who catches ball
??	Lady selling lunches
Bob Woodward	Henchman
Carol Henry	Brawler
Bobby Clark, Guy Teague	Extras
Champion	Champion

STUNTS: Bob Woodward, Carol Henry, Eddie Parker.

Carolina Cotton and Gene Autry.

THE FILM: Chief of Scouts for the Southwest Cavalry Command Gene Autry and his pal Pat Buttram are commissioned by the Bureau of Indian Affairs (former silent matinee idol Francis X. Bushman) to break up a frontier ring headed up by Dave Kilrain (Harry Lauter) and Luke Thorn (Gregg Barton) who use phony Indian raids to cover up their bandit activities of hiding out wanted outlaws. Medicine show owner and entertainer Carolina Cotton assists Gene while searching for the killer of her father. The picture stops dead cold at 20 minutes, 34 minutes and 50 minutes while Tony Whitecloud's Jemez Indian dancers do the Eagle dance, the Buffalo dance, etc. while an off-screen Autry explains each dance. It simply doesn't work, giving the film a stitched together feeling. The slight story is padded by not only the Indian dances but several more songs than usual in recent Autry films, none of them memorable except Gene's rendition of Hank Williams' hit "Cold, Cold Heart".

Carolina Cotton, while a very likable personality performing her "I Love to Yodel" routine, just isn't up to the dramatic thespian qualities required of a leading lady.

There's also a free-for-all brawl that is played for comic effect. Again, like too many Indian dances, it seems out of place in an Autry film.

Overall, a low point in Gene's Columbia cañon.

NOTES AND COMMENTS: Tony Whitecloud's Jemez Indian dancers were four brothers who had never been off their New Mexico reservation until Gene took them to Madison Square Garden where they performed in the World Championship Rodeo. They toured Canada and New England with Gene, then went to Hollywood for roles in "Apache Country".

Mary Scott was married to noted British actor Sir Cedric Hardwicke.

Newspaper ad from Kansas City dated January 1951.

Barbed Wire

Columbia, July 1952

A Gene Autry Production in Sepia Tone

Producer ....Armand Schaefer
Director ....George Archainbaud
Assistant Director.......................Paul Donnelly
Screenplay...................................Gerald Geraghty
Photography ....William Bradford
Musical Supervisor ....Paul Mertz
Musical Director ....Mischa Bakaleinikoff
Film Editor ....James Sweeney
Sound Dept...................................Lambert Day
Art Director..................................Charles Clague
Set Decorations ....Frank Tuttle

SONGS: "Mexicali Rose" (music and lyrics by Helen Stone, Jack B. Tenney)—sung by Gene Autry and Cass County Boys; "Ezekiel Saw the Wheel" (Public Domain)—sung by Cass County Boys; "Old Buckaroo" (music and lyrics by Fleming Allen)—sung by Gene Autry.

RUNNING TIME: 61 minutes

FILMING DATES: December 10-20, 1951

LOCATIONS: Pioneertown; Columbia backlot; foothills of Mt. San Gorgonio, California

BUDGET: $58,874.36

CAST:

Actor	*Character*
Gene Autry	Gene Autry
Pat Buttram	Buckeye Buttram
Anne James	Gay Kendall
William Fawcett	Uncle John Copeland
Leonard Penn	Steve Ruttledge
Michael Vallon	August Gormley
Cass County Boys: Bert Dodson, Jerry Scoggins, Fred Martin	Cass County Boys
Terry Frost	Perry
Clayton Moore	Bailey
Eddie Parker	Ed Parker
Zon Murray, Stuart Whitman	Cattle Buyers
Wes Hudman	Ned Paulsen
Harry Harvey	Honest Bill Witson, Mayor
Sandy Sanders	Rancher Handley
Al Bridge	McGraw
Bobby Clark	Cowhand
Victor Cox	Cattle Buyer Goldie
Frankie Marvin	Spider
Frank O'Connor	Man at funeral
Pat O'Malley	Ed Gillifoil
Bud Osborne	Hendricks
Ralph Sanford	Cattle Buyer Buttons
Carol Henry, Cactus Mack, Roy Bucko, Bob Burns, Duke York, George Bell	Extras
Champion	Champion

STUNTS: Bob Woodward, Bobby Clark, Duke York.

THE FILM: "Barbed Wire" is a return to form for Gene Autry's Columbia westerns, making it one of his better efforts.

Gene is a cattle buyer who finds his source of supply for steers in Texas drying up due to a feud between homesteaders and cattlemen. The squatters have fenced off their range with barbed wire.

Newspaper publisher Anne James watches as Gene has a disagreement with unscrupulous Leonard Penn (center) and his henchman Carol Henry (right).

Investigation by Gene reveals it's more than a range war. Rich land owner Steve Ruttledge (Leonard Penn) has dreams of building a railroad over the land that he and his henchmen have claimed as homestead plots.

Gene foils the plot with the help of land agent Pat Buttram and newspaper reporter-publisher Gay Kendall (Anne James).

NOTES AND COMMENTS: Gene reprised his Gold Record "Mexicali Rose" which had been featured in "Rootin' Tootin' Rhythm" and "Mexicali Rose", as well as "Old Buck-A-Roo" that he'd sung in "Public Cowboy No. 1".

Since barbed wire was unknown in England, the film was oddly retitled "False News" for release in the U.K.

The excellent main title music written by Merlin Skiles was borrowed from the excellent 1948 Columbia western "Relentless".

After completing "Barbed Wire" Gene went on tour. In January and February of 1952 Gene made a series of 39 one-night stands ranging from Wichita, Kansas, to Miami, Florida. The tour grossed an all time high of $444,782, attracting an attendance of 243,844. The show was sold out in more than half the cities where it played. In Providence, Rhode Island, on February 8 Gene broke the attendance record at the auditorium when more than 15,000 turned out to see the two shows he gave. And that figure doesn't include the 4,000 that were turned away.

FILM COMMENTS: *Anne James* (who also worked with Charles Starrett under the name Delores Sidener in "Pecos River" ['51]) recalled, "I flew back from location with Pat Buttram and Gene on Gene's private plane back into Los Angeles. They were a lot of fun. They were very, very nice men. That was a nice experience. That was the first time I had been in a puddle jumper. In those days, because you're young enough, you don't know any fear and you're not in touch with your mortality. But I remember Gene put the plane on auto-pilot and came back and sat down. My heart started pounding because I didn't know anything about that. He and Pat Buttram got a big bang out of that. They thought it was so funny because I was starting to panic about who was flying the plane. I sat very still and was very nervous. Then they started laughing about it. Gene explained he had put it on auto-pilot, and it was flying all by itself."[1]

SOURCES:
1. Interview with Ray Nielsen. June, 2006.

Wagon Team
Columbia, September 1952
A Gene Autry Production in Sepia Tone

Producer ....Armand Schaefer
Director ....George Archainbaud
Assistant Director.......................Carter DeHaven Jr.
Screenplay...............................Gerald Geraghty
Photography ....William Bradford
Musical Supervisor ....Paul Mertz
Musical Director ....Mischa Bakaleinikoff
Film Editor...............................James Sweeney
Sound Dept...............................George Cooper
Art Director...............................Charles Clague
Set Decorations ....James Crowe

SONGS: "In and Out of the Jailhouse" (music and lyrics by Paul Mertz)—sung by Gene Autry; "I've Been Invited to a Jubilee" (music and lyrics by V.O. Stamps)—sung by The Cass County Boys; "Howdy Friends and Neighbors" (music and lyrics by Jack Pepper)—sung by Gene Autry and Cass County Boys; "Back In the Saddle Again" (music and lyrics by Gene Autry, Ray Whitley)—sung by Gene Autry and Cass County Boys.

RUNNING TIME: 61 minutes

FILMING DATES: April 7-15, 1952

LOCATIONS: Pioneertown; Iverson Ranch; Jack Ingram Ranch; Columbia backlot

BUDGET: $51,569.83

CAST:

Actor	*Character*
Gene Autry	Gene Autry
Pat Buttram	Deputy Pat Buttram
Gail Davis	Connie Weldon
Dick Jones	Dave Weldon, aka The Apache Kid
Gordon Jones	Marshal Sam Taplan
Harry Harvey	Daniel "Doc" Weldon
Henry Rowland	Mike McClure
George J. Lewis	Carlos de la Torre
The Cass County Boys: Bert Dodson, Jerry Scoggins, Fred S. Martin	Cass County Boys
John Cason	Slim
Bob Woodward	Henchman
Gregg Barton	Gandy
Pierce Lyden	Mangrum
Carlo Tricoli	Dr. Kunody
Syd Saylor	Jailbreak Deputy
Herman Hack, Frankie Marvin, Cactus Mack	Townsmen
Sandy Sanders	Deputy
Champion	Champion

STUNTS: Sandy Sanders, Bob Woodward.

THE FILM: Even a star with Gene Autry's draw can't continue forever without the benefit of strong story material, and "Wagon Team" is weak in this department. What it does provide is a return to the old ploy of Gene, as a stageline detective, joining a medicine show as he seeks the robbers of an Army payroll. As a singer with Doc Weldon (Harry Harvey) and daughter Connie's (Gail Davis) traveling show, Gene can introduce more songs into the movie than had been the case in recent times, including his theme-classic, "Back In the Saddle Again". It also gives a solid reason for the Cass County Boys to be there also.

Dick Jones as Connie's misguided teenaged brother provides most of the real plot interest as the only member in the gang of Mike McClure (Henry Rowland) who knows where a money box is hidden.

Gene sings and performs as well as ever, but the rambling plot fails to evoke much interest.

NOTES AND COMMENTS: Budgetary concerns (there were severe rain delays on this picture) continued to escalate for Gene's Columbia productions. Cost to make "Wagon Team" was $51,369.83 with the film only garnering $78,916 in revenue from its release in September 1952 through May 1955. Only a profit of $27,546.17 over a two and a half year period.

This was Gene's last picture to have a running time of over 60 minutes, with his final seven productions for Columbia all cut to between 56 and 58 minutes in order to trim a few dollars off the production costs.

In another budgetary move, an entire lengthy action segment from "The Big Sombrero" with Gene, John Cason

Gene Autry tries to help the misguided Dick Jones (center), on-screen brother of Gail Davis (left) and son of medicine showman Harry Harvey.

and George J. Lewis is intercut and reused in "Wagon Team".

During production Gene attempted a croupier mount (a leap over the back of the horse into the saddle, which he had done before) onto Champion, but that day the horse was restless and kept moving, so the crew tied the mount to a bush with invisible wires—but Champ still moved around, so, as you'll see, Gene finally did a moving horse vault by hanging on to the side of Champion as they took off.

Blue Canadian Rockies
Columbia, November 1952
A Gene Autry Production in Sepia Tone

Producer ....Armand Schaefer
Director ....George Archainbaud
Assistant Director.........................Frederick Briskin
Screenplay.................................Gerald Geraghty
Photography ....William Bradford
Musical Supervisor ....Paul Mertz
Musical Director ....Mischa Bakaleinikoff
Film Editor................................James Sweeney
Sound Dept................................Lodge Cunningham
Art Director...............................George Brooks
Set Decorations ....Louis Diage

John Merton ....Frenchy
David Garcia ....Met-Lik
The Cass County Boys: Jerry
  Scoggins, Fred S. Martin,
  Bert Dodson............................Cass County Boys
W. C. "Billy" Wilkerson ....Indian Joe
Maxine Gates ....Chubby Blonde
?? ....Sgt. Midler
Bob Woodward ....Dusty
Forbes Murray.............................Lodge Guest
Chick Hannon, Cactus Mack ....Extras
Champion ....Champion

STUNTS: Sandy Sanders, Bob Woodward.

SONGS: "Blue Canadian Rockies" (music and lyrics by Cindy Walker)—sung by Gene Autry, studio singers; "Yodel, Yodel, Yodel" (music and lyrics by Carolina Cotton)—sung by Carolina Cotton; "Mama Don't Like Music" (music and lyrics by Gene Autry, Smiley Burnette)—sung by Gene Autry, Cass County Boys; "Old Chisholm Trail" (Public Domain)—sung by The Cass County Boys; "Lovin' Ducky Daddy" (music and lyrics by Doc Hopkins)—sung by Carolina Cotton, Cass County Boys; "Big Rock Candy Mountain" (Public Domain)—instrumental by Cass County Boys; "Anytime" (music and lyrics by Herbert Lawson)—sung by Gene Autry, Cass County Boys.

RUNNING TIME: 58 minutes
FILMING DATES: May 19-27, 1952
LOCATIONS: Big Bear/Cedar Lake; Columbia backlot
BUDGET: $54,460.22

CAST:

Actor	*Character*
Gene Autry	Gene Autry
Pat Buttram	"Rawhide" Buttram
Gail Davis	Sandra Higbee
Carolina Cotton	Carolina Cotton
Ross Ford	Todd Markley
Tom London	Pop Phillips
Don Beddoe	Cyrus Higbee
Mauritz Hugo	Ed Mitchell
Gene Roth	Swede

THE FILM: Stylistically, "Blue Canadian Rockies" is a throwback to Gene Autry's Republic era with an easier pace, far more music, a modern day setting, a strong comedy element and two women for Gene to deal with. From the opening shots of the Rockies, followed by a cattle drive with Gene lazily riding Champ as he sings the title tune, there is a feeling of revival, of old fashioned Republic Autry westerns. All the elements are there, with the story of Gene as a ranch foreman sent to Canada by his employer Cyrus Higbee (Don Beddoe) to discourage the marriage of his daughter Sandra (Gail Davis) to Todd Markley (Ross Ford) whom Higbee suspects of being a fortune hunter, only interested in the girl's wealth. Arriving in Canada, Gene finds Sandra has turned the property into a dude ranch and wild-game preserve. Gene and pal Pat Buttram find themselves in the middle of trouble between the lodge and French-Canadian loggers bossed by Ed Mitchell (Mauritz Hugo), as well as some mysterious murder-attempts and the killing of a Mountie, with guilt seemingly pointing to Sandra's fiancé.

However, George Archainbaud's direction allows the picture to go overboard with parties, fancy dress and Carolina Cotton and The Cass County Boys singing, thereby slowing the pace to a crawl. Unfortunately, Archainbaud is not the helmsman Joe Kane, George Sherman and Frank McDonald were, and the whole thing doesn't blend as in Republic days.

The scenery is nice and Gene has one good brawl (played somewhat broadly for comic effect) but too much time is spent in the obvious studio-set lodge, no doubt as a budgetary move.

NOTES AND COMMENTS: The mirror gag by Pat Buttram can be traced back to Harpo Marx in "Duck Soup" ('33) according to movie authority Leonard Maltin, but Buttram manages to pull it off with panache.

Gene Autry said that luck was with him on his flight to Big Bear Lake in the San Bernardino Mountains, for location shooting on "Blue Canadian Rockies".

Autry took off from the Burbank airport in his twin-engined Beechcraft at seven in the morning with a heavy fog closing in so rapidly he barely became airborne before he was in the soup. The chartered transport plane, ready to take off right behind him with 40 members of the cast and crew, was forced to sit on the field for two hours before the fog lifted enough for them to take off.

Autry landed his ship smoothly and easily on the small mountain airport near Big Bear and with his six passengers drove to the location spot. However, when the big charter plane landed, two hours later, one wheel of the ship hit a soft spot and sank to the axle. Fortunately, the plane was taxiing slowly, did not nose over and all passengers were unhurt.

This was Gene's first Columbia film with a running time of under 60 minutes, an obvious concession to increasing budgetary expenditures.

Most people that knew Gene said he was not a "workaholic", but it would sure seem so. Gene obviously *loved* what he was doing. Few entertainers could keep up the sort of pace described in 1952 by Myrla McDougall

in the AUTRY'S ACES fan publication. "To borrow Mr. Autry's own words…'does anybody have an early morning paper route or milk delivery?'…and he might be open for suggestions as to how he can keep busy on Sundays! His Summer and Fall schedule makes me tired just *reading* it and I'd sure hate to have to *do* all that stuff! He finished 'Blue Canadian Rockies' at Columbia just before going into the Oriental Theatre in Chicago for a week (and we hope many of our members were able to see that show again). Returning home, he did four television pictures before starting another Columbia feature, 'Winning of the West' during the last week of June. From here on, it reads something like this: Starring in a rodeo in Nampa, Idaho, the middle of July; four more television pictures; then starring in another rodeo at Colorado Springs, Colorado, the first of August; a Columbia feature, 'On Top of Old Smoky' (and *you* figure out how he's going to be in Colorado and Hollywood both at the same time—as listed on the present schedule). His time from the middle of August to the end of October is almost equally divided between television and Columbia features and, at the last report, Herb Green was working on booking another tour beginning the first of November. Where Gene gets all his energy is a mystery to me—*and* to almost everybody who has ever been associated with him."[1]

FILM COMMENTS: By this time Gene had been in show business for over 20 years. For 15 years he was listed as one of the Top 10 western movie stars. He is one of the very few recording artists to have 10 songs sell over a million records. One of his recent personal appearance tours, in which he covered 37 cities in 37 days, grossed almost half a million dollars. Gene's radio show "Melody Ranch" is always listed among the top 15 shows on the air and his "Gene Autry Show" TV series is a ratings winner as well. Gene was convinced entertaining the public is a full time job. Expressing himself on that subject Gene stated, "There have been many stars who faded away after a few years because they just didn't work hard enough at their jobs. You don't find business executives away from their desks four, five and six months of the year. If they did, they'd soon find more ambitious men taking their places. The public has a fickle heart and a short memory. If you want them to remember you, stay in front of them.

"I have always tried to make the most of what I had, I never depend on luck, but I sure take advantage of it when it comes along. What success I've had has come mostly from hard work and concentration. And, most

Gene's in Canada's "Blue Canadian Rockies" with (L-R) Tom London, Gail Davis, Pat Buttram.

of all, the basis for a long life in show business is: don't let the public forget you." [2]

Gene Autry: "Hardest fight I ever had was up at Big Bear, California, in the (cold). I had to do a fight in that lake and it was about 6,000 feet high. I ran out of wind and I thought I was gonna drown. The director said, 'Cut. Now let's do a couple of good close-ups.' So I'd have to do that again. When I got out of there I never saw a fight end so happy on my part in my life. When I got out we had a first aid man there and he came running up to me and threw a couple of blankets around me; says, 'Here this'll help you get warmed up a little bit.' And he opened up a bottle of brandy, and he said, 'Here, take a drink of this, it'll warm you up.' Well, he turned the bottle up and drank about half of it before I got to it. Here I was shakin' and shiverin' and he was drinkin' all the brandy he brought to keep me warm."[3]

Gene and The Cass County Boys (Bert Dodson, Fred Martin, Jerry Scoggins).

CAST BIOS: Cindy Walker, who wrote the title tune, is considered by many as the outstanding female composer of country music. In 1970, Walker became a charter member of the Nashville Songwriters Hall of Fame and was elected to the Country Music Hall of Fame in 1997. She was known for her skills in writing songs for different stylists, and had top ten hits over five decades. She couldn't play a piano and used a guitar to help her compose.

Cindy's grandfather, F. P. Eiland, was a notable hymn writer and her mother, Cree, was an accomplished pianist. Walker, after appearing in Texas stage shows, came to Hollywood. Late 1940 found her singing with Mary Lee in Gene's "Ride, Tenderfoot, Ride". The gregarious lyricist/singer landed a 1941 contract with Decca and pitched several successful songs to their top recording star, Bing Crosby. In 1941, she filmed the first Soundie musical short, "Seven Beers with the Wrong Man", suggested by the hit "Seven Years with the Wrong Woman", featured by Gene Autry in "Colorado Sunset" ('39).

In 1944, Cindy scored a top ten hit, "When My Blue Moon Turns to Gold Again". Although she had movie star looks, Cindy preferred to compose rather than appear before the cameras. Gene Autry made "Blue Canadian Rockies" a big popular hit, and she wrote more than 50 numbers for Bob Wills and several for Ernest Tubb and Al Dexter. Among her other Autry hits were "Here's to the Ladies" featured in "Valley of Fire" ('51). Gene also used her "Cowboy Blues" song in both "Trail to San Antone" ('47) and "Winning of the West" ('53).

In 1954, Cindy returned to Texas and spent time in Mexia, as well as Nashville, Tennessee. In the '50s she wrote songs for Eddy Arnold, including his big hit "You Don't Know Me"; Hank Snow, Webb Pierce, Jerry Wallace and Jim Reeves. In the '60s, Roy Orbison, Stonewall Jackson and other well-known names recorded her songs. Glen Campbell, Ray Charles, Lacy J. Dalton, Riders in the Sky, Mickey Gilley, Merle Haggard and Willie Nelson kept her song-writing legacy alive in subsequent decades. In 1964, Monument Records issued the recording "Words and Music by Cindy Walker."

At 87, the prolific and highly respected Cindy Walker died at a Mexia hospital on March 23, 2006.

SOURCES:

1. *Autry's Aces.* June-August 1952. p. 11.

2. "Blue Canadian Rockies" pressbook.

3. "Melody Ranch Theater" showing of "Indian Territory" on Nashville Network, 1987.

Winning of the West
<u>Columbia, January 1953</u>
A Gene Autry Production in Sepia Tone

Producer ....Armand Schaefer
Director ....George Archainbaud
Assistant Director........................Paul Donnelly
Story and Screenplay ....Norman S. Hall
Photography ....William Bradford
Musical Supervisor ....Paul Mertz
Musical Director ....Ross DiMaggio
Film Editor ....James Sweeney
Sound Dept.................................George Cooper
Art Director................................George Brooks
Set Decorations ....Dave Montrose

Terry Frost...................................Brawler
Boyd "Red" Morgan ....Henchman Red
Eddie Parker................................Brawler
Bob Woodward ....Stagecoach Driver/
                      Henchman
Cactus Mack................................Henchman
James Kirkwood...........................Settler
Frankie Marvin............................Ranger
Charles Soldani ....Indian
Champion....................................Champion

STUNTS: Bob Woodward, Eddie Parker.

SONGS: "Five Minutes Late and a Dollar Short" (music and lyrics by Smiley Burnette)—sung by Smiley Burnette; "The Cowboy Blues" (music and lyrics by Cindy Walker)—sung by Gene Autry; "Fetch Me Down My Trusty Forty-Five" (music and lyrics by Smiley Burnette)—sung by Gene Autry and Smiley Burnette; "I'm a Cowpoke Pokin' Along" (music and lyrics by Gene Autry, Fred Rose)—sung by Gene Autry.

    RUNNING TIME: 57 minutes
    FILMING DATES: June 24 to July 2, 1952
    LOCATIONS: Pioneertown; Melody Ranch; Lone Pine; Columbia backlot
    BUDGET: $47,447.94

CAST:

Actor	*Character*
Gene Autry ....Gene Autry
Smiley Burnette ....Smiley Burnette
Gail Davis ....Ann Randolph
Richard Crane ....Jack Austin/Autry
Robert Livingston ....Art Selby
House Peters Jr............................Marshal Hackett
Gregg Barton...............................Clint Raybold
William Forrest ....Editor John Randolph
Ewing Mitchell............................Ranger Capt. Tom Hickson
George Chesebro.........................Boone
Charles Delaney ....Jules Brent
Frank Jaquet...............................Stage Line Manager
Rodd Redwing ....Pete Littlewolf

THE FILM: Smiley Burnette, Gene Autry's former longtime sidekick at Republic in all but one of Gene's pre-war westerns was reunited for the last six of Gene's Columbia pictures.

Under contract to Columbia, Smiley had finished his last of 56 westerns with Charles Starrett as the Durango Kid, "The Kid From Broken Gun", in mid 1952 and was now free to co-star once again with Gene in movies while Pat Buttram continued on as Gene's comic-foil in his TV adventures. "We had gone in together and we would go out together. Fair is fair," Gene said.[1]

Gene takes a different stance in "Winning of the West", risking his career as a territorial ranger to cover up a murder by his errant kid brother, Jack (Richard Crane), who is riding with bank robbers Art Selby (Robert Livingston) and Clint Raybold (Gregg Barton).

Relieved of his ranger duties because his boss (Ewing Mitchell) does not think Gene acted quickly enough in preventing the slaying of the town's newspaper publisher, Gene sets out on his own after both the outlaw gang and his own brother in an effort to set him straight.

Gradually, Gene wins back his brother to the side of the law, the confidence of the murdered newspaperman's daughter (Gail Davis) and regains his Ranger badge.

What mars the picture most is a cost-cutting measure in which the final wagon chase is nothing more than several minutes of stock footage lifted direct from Gene's "Mule Train" ('50) which also had Robert Livingston in the cast, therefore footage could advantageously be used here.

Footage from Columbia's big budget "Arizona" ('40) was also incorporated.

NOTES AND COMMENTS: Within a year, Richard Crane became the popular star of TV's "Rocky Jones, Space Ranger". The dimpled, handsome blond actor from Newcastle, Indiana, entered films in 1940 and became a "bobby sox dreamboat" in WWII after playing Don Ameche's ill-fated soldier son in 20th Century–Fox's "Happy Land" in 1943. However, his brief success did not translate into long lasting stardom and Crane quickly drifted into supporting roles in B-films and on TV. He got a bit of a career boost in 1953 as the star of Republic's "Commando Cody: Sky Marshal of the Universe" TV series and as the star of TV's low budget "Rocky Jones, Space Ranger" series. Roles after those series became fewer and fewer until he died at 50 of a heart attack in 1969.

"Winning of the West" received an extensive photo-feature treatment on its location filming and a scene-synopsis of the story in Dell Publishing's WHO'S WHO IN WESTERN STARS #2, their second annual edition in 1952. Under a Gene Autry byline (actually written by Gene's publicity department judging from certain phrases such as "oat burner", "leather pounder" and others) was a day-by-day log of interesting happenings while "Winning of the West" was in production. Whether Gene actually wrote it or not, we reprint that log here as an historical document of what it was like on location filming one of Gene's westerns.

"1st Day: Big day. One of the location trucks got stuck while fording a stream on the way to Pioneertown. We had to fetch 'er out by hitching on our horses. It appeared to me that the horses made less fuss than usual over this heavy job; sorta grinned as they settled into the traces. If Champion could have talked, I reckon he would have asked me, 'think these spavined, string-halt critters, these gas-eating mavericks, are here to stay?'

"Smiley Burnette is on the opposite side of the corral gate in this argument; he hopes the days of the oat-burner are numbered. Smiley came a cropper this afternoon. You see, these days he's a pretty good leather pounder (he's

made around 170 pictures), but he got his start as a musician. He can play about 100 musical instruments, some that you wouldn't be able to name to save your buttons. Practically none of these instruments help Smiley when the range gets thorny.

"Just to give Smiley his regular serving of the wide open spaces, the director usually says, 'Gene, you ride along this ledge of rocks, skirt this ravine, and gallop up this gully. Smiley, you ride beside Gene, on the outside.' Our route provides foothold for one horse, and Smiley would need a horse like Pegasus of the old myth to maintain his place beside me.

"Today we were rehearsing fast mounts for a break through the woods when Smiley's horse shied at a squirrel that jumped out of a clump of bushes. Smiley's buckskin pants were so tight he couldn't get his foot out of the stirrup, leastways not *fast* enough when you realize he was hanging onto the reins as well as a Winchester. He wound up on his back with the dust flying in every direction like a prairie twister.

"I dismounted and charged over, scared as white as a Brahma steer, to find out whether he was hurt or not. He insisted he wasn't and even grinned at my feeble joke of saying I thought he should be looked over by our vet. He went on with the day's shooting, but I noticed when he went to sit down he lowered himself kinda easy, like a puppy with a newly docked tail.

"2nd Day: The crew has been giving Smiley a bad time today. Whenever we're ready to shoot a scene they holler at him, 'Hang on, Smiley,' or 'Need any glue in your saddle?' or 'If you *please*, no trick riding, Mr. Cowhand.'

"Tonight, we had an indoor campfire meeting. Gathered around the fireplace of 'The Golden Lion' and sang the old songs. Paul Donnelly is our Irish tenor; Phil Coby plays real sweet piano and I fiddle with the guitar. It sure is a lot of fun. We made the hills ring with 'Down by the Old Mill Stream', 'Sweet Adeline', 'There's a Long, Long Trail A-Winding', 'When It's Springtime In the Rockies', 'When the Bloom is On the Sage', 'There's Silver On the Sage Tonight', and other pathetic little ditties.

324

Gene regains his Territorial Ranger badge from Ranger Captain Ewing Mitchell to the pleasure of Marshal House Peters Jr., Gail Davis and Smiley Burnette.

"3rd Day: Telephoned Ina as usual tonight to find out how things are going with her and Melody Ranch. She says Little Champ had been as jumpy as a tumbleweed in a Chinook wind for the past few days. Misses us, I reckon. Have to bring him along the next time, even if he decides to gnaw himself a chaps sandwich when Smiley Burnette isn't watching out for himself. Little Champ is partial to taking a regular nip out of Smiley.

"4th Day: I really get irked at Champion now and then. Today, in the midst of a shooting sequence, when I had dismounted and was firing from behind a boulder, Champ took off as if he'd been fired out of a cannon. I didn't think much of it at first, because usually he lounges into camp in 15 or 20 minutes, looking as sheepish as a cowhand bucked off in a chute. But this time Champ didn't come back. Finally we wound up in the Beechcraft, sky-searching for him, but he's a crafty coyote and hides at the sound of the plane motors. We couldn't locate him. I guess he'll ease back into camp now that it's dark; there's no sense hunting for him in this wild country at night. If I wasn't so hot under the collar, I guess I'd be worried.

"5th Day: Champ is back, but he didn't come home of his own accord. A pair of Mounted Scouts, one boy 13 and one 15, located the runaway last night, tethered him in their corral, and brought him back to home base this morning. Good wranglers, these Mounted Scouts; they had curried him and fed him, and Champ was in fine condition.

"6th Day: Champ and I are on speaking terms again. Today I was supposed to ride through the rock and brush to a fast stop, dismount and peer into the valley in search of an Indian war party. We tried the shot several times, but whenever Champ and I would reach the top of the rise, my chestnut pal would shy, swing wide, and start back down the

gully. That polka step is Champ's way of saying 'Snake!' Sure enough, when we checked, we found a big boy—14 rattles—sunning himself on the spot where I would have dismounted. Some of the boys killed the rattler, and we got through the scene without any more ruckus. Champ got a double order of oats tonight.

"7th Day: Had a little fun with Smiley this afternoon. For the past few days it's been hot enough on this spread to broil a steak in the sunshine. Smiley weighs around 240, so he feels the heat. He kept bawling like a herd of Herefords looking for a water hole, so somebody filled the horse trough and dropped him in. After that, every time we wanted to shoot a new scene, we'd have to send somebody to lasso the stray water buffalo.

"8th Day: We've moved to Lone Pine, a mountain location where the trees grow tall, the wind's sharp, and the fish in the streams are eager. We lose our light early up here, so we went fishing at dusk. Caught our limit and took the trout down to the Mt. Whitney Café where the chef broiled them for us. What chow! There's no music like the sound of the dinner triangle, especially when you've caught the meal yourself.

"9th Day: That Smiley Burnette is as crafty as a hungry coyote. Today he had a scene in which he was supposed to use the binoculars to sight a wagon train. His speech about the train was fairly long and complicated, so Smiley didn't try to memorize it. He just had the script girl hold up the pages—clear out of camera range across the street—and he read the script through the binoculars.

"10th Day: Picture is going fine, but there's trouble in the area. A stickup artist has been patrolling the highway (No. 395) between Mojave and Reno. He works by following a Cadillac for miles, them pulls alongside waving a flashlight over which he has drawn a piece of red cloth. The unlucky motorist, thinking he is being flagged down by a highway patrolman, stops. Then this road agent gets into the car, orders it to be driven to a side road, robs everyone in the car, orders then out into the desert, takes the car and drives back to the highway where he abandons it. Four of us spent several hours this evening, riding up and down the highway in a '52 Cadillac, hoping to lure the guy into jumping us. No luck.

"11th Day: Women do the dangdest things. Gail Davis, our leading lady, showed up today wearing toeless black suede slippers for a scene at a ranch house hoedown. Toeless slippers hadn't been invented at the time of our story, so I had the makeup man cover the toes with bicycle tape. By the time I got through, her shoes looked as neat as a $40 coffin and almost as square-cornered. Like as not, though, her feet won't even show in the shot—and after all that fixing, too.

"12th Day: Champ is giving me trouble again. He cut his right foreleg when we were unloading him from his trailer this morning. He just couldn't wait to get out, that short-eared jackass; got to lunging around and finally went over one of the tail gate chains like an Apache heading for a scalping party. The vet says it isn't serious, but I always do a little fretting whenever Champ is under the weather.

"13th Day: Champ is okay if disposition proves health. He's been lifting a lip at everybody who came within gunshot of him all day and he's kept his left hind foot flexed—just in case.

"Tonight I spent the evening fiddling with the guitar, which soothes the chestnut. I've got a genuine liking for a song named "Diesel Smoke", but for some reason it never made a hit. I play it often, have been toying with the idea that if the title could be changed to "Signal Smoke" it could be turned into an Indian festival number.

"14th Day: I finally got bitten by that old photography bug and bought myself a Rolleiflex camera. Today I drove the cameraman on the set crazy, asking for pointers. I've photographed Champ so many times that he strikes a pose whenever he sees my shadow. Poor Ina—now she'll have to keep up an album for me.

"15th Day: We wound up the exterior shots for 'Winning of the West' today, and we're moving to the Columbia ranch for interior shots tomorrow, which will represent the sunset finish.

"Champ always likes to get back to the Columbia ranch because he can count on a Coke machine being nearby. How that horse loves Coke; the picture crew buys him drinks just to watch him absorb them!

"Today was great for me, too. I had a chance to chin a little with Smiley about our next picture and to hear about his latest inventions—you wouldn't believe it if I told you about them, so you'll have to wait to see them in our pictures.

"I spent the late afternoon lassoing myself some new duds to wear when I go out on my next personal appearance tour. I always wear western harness; just feel more natural in boots and riding clothes. Also laid in a stock of 250 Stetsons. I plan to pass these out to the kids, hoping it will remind them, in some small measure, of our pioneer heritage. In these confused days, I figure it's mighty important for youngsters to bear in mind the frontier courtesy and hospitality, the good sense, the high courage and the untarnished honor that made up our western range law."[2]

FILM COMMENTS: *House Peters Jr.:* "Comparing Gene Autry and Roy Rogers is like comparing apples and oranges. They were that different. Gene was all business, but pleasant and in a position to always take care of his employees. I saw such concern many times, not only probably saving Pat Buttram's life (when he was injured during the filming of a TV episode) by using his private airplane and his concern when my friend Richard Emory was kicked by his stallion, but he would generally take members of his cast on location with his plane and full-time pilot. On occasion, if a member of his crew indulged a little too much the night before he never fired the person, but had a substitute do his job until he sobered up. There was generally always a room set aside on location for cast and crew with an open bar at the end of the day." [3]

Gail Davis, Champion, Gene Autry, House Peters Jr., Smiley Burnette — "Winning of the West."

SOURCES:
1. Autry with Herskowitz. p. 103.
2. *Who's Who In Western Stars #2.* Dell Publishing. 1952.
3. Peters Jr., House. *Another Side of Hollywood.* p. 134.

On Top of Old Smoky
Columbia, March 1953
A Gene Autry Production in Sepia Tone

Producer	Armand Schaefer
Director	George Archainbaud
Assistant Director	Paul Donnelly
Story and Screenplay	Gerald Geraghty
Photography	William Bradford
Musical Supervisor	Paul Mertz
Musical Director	Mischa Bakaleinikoff
Film Editor	James Sweeney
Sound Dept.	George Cooper
Art Director	George Brooks
Set Decorations	Frank Tuttle

SONGS: "On Top of Old Smoky" (Public Domain)—sung by Gene Autry; "I Hang My Head and Cry" (music and lyrics by Gene Autry, Fred Rose, Ray Whitley)—sung by Gene Autry and Smiley Burnette; "Trail to Mexico" (Public Domain)—sung by The Cass County Boys; "I Saw Her First" (music and lyrics by Smiley Burnette)—sung by Smiley Burnette; "If It Wasn't For the Rain" (music and lyrics by Gene Autry, Fred Rose, Edward Nelson)—sung by Gene Autry, Cass County Boys.

RUNNING TIME: 59 minutes

FILMING DATES: August 12-19, 1952

LOCATIONS: Pioneertown; Melody Ranch; Columbia backlot

BUDGET: $52,201.52

CAST:

Actor	*Character*
Gene Autry	Gene Autry
Smiley Burnette	Smiley Burnette
Gail Davis	Jen Larrabee
Grandon Rhodes	"Doc" Clint Judson
Sheila Ryan	Lila Maryland
Kenne Duncan	McQuaid
Robert Bice	Kirby
The Cass County Boys: Bert Dodson, Fred S. Martin, Jerry Scoggins	Cass County Boys
Zon Murray	Bud
Art Dillard, Jack Gargan, Frankie Marvin, Pat O'Malley	Extras
Champion	Champion

STUNTS: Bob Woodward.

THE FILM: A delight! One of Gene Autry's best of his latter-day Columbias. Incorporating a stronger-than-usual quota of music and humor, the film harkens back to Republic days, except Gene and Smiley Burnette are older.

Gene and The Cass County Boys are itinerant entertainers mistakenly taken for bonafide Texas Rangers. Seeing the bad elements in town, Gene decides to keep up the pretense and help pretty Jen Larrabee (Gail Davis) struggle to keep her toll road waystation from being taken over by crooked "Doc" Judson (Grandon Rhodes) who has designs on valuable mica deposits on Jen's property.

Gene's ruse is blown when bad girl Lila (Sheila Ryan) arrives in town amazed to find Gene and the Boys mistaken for lawmen because she knows better from a previous experience.

The Cass County Boys have some of their best roles, winding up in the jailhouse at one point and, in an almost surreal sequence, local postman Smiley digs a hole to free the boys in the midst of pouring rain while the Boys and Gene—in completely different locations!—both sing "If It Wasn't For the Rain". All concerned seem to be having great fun, and it's contagious, making this one of Gene's most enjoyable Columbia westerns.

NOTES AND COMMENTS: "On Top of Old Smoky", the title song of the film, was a tremendously successful recording hit, on a par with such ballads as "Mule Train" and "Riders In the Sky". Knowing the power of a great western ballad, Gene's movies frequently were labeled with the titles of hit songs. The tune was recorded by Burl Ives, Bob Atcher, George Cates, The Weavers, Libby Holmand, Josh White, George Siravo and Vaughn Monroe.

Diminishing returns continued to plague Gene's—and all B-westerns for that matter. Over a two year period "On Top of Old Smoky" generated only a $29,172.48 profit.

FILM COMMENTS: *Pat Buttram:* "Sheila (Ryan)

and I had been married about three years when this was made, and we were married for about 15 more years before she passed away, but she sure enjoyed making these westerns. She'd made a lot of pictures at Fox. The last big musical picture ever made, 'The Gang's All Here' ('43), directed by Busby Berkeley, starred Alice Faye and Sheila and Benny Goodman and his band. Then she started doing these pictures, we got married and had a real happy marriage."[1]

WHAT THE EXHIBITOR HAD TO SAY: "'On Top of Old Smoky'—doubled with 'Red Snow' and Stooges comedy. Did a nice Friday, Saturday business for a change. Sort of took the sting out of 'The Happy Time' which played the following two days.

—S. W. Booth, Booth Theater,
Rich Hill, Missouri (April 1953)

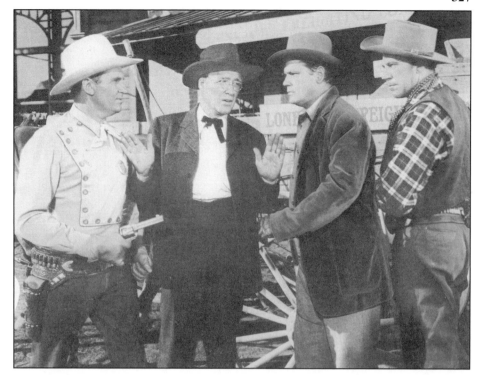

Crooked Grandon Rhodes (center) pretends he's helping Gene by preventing trouble between Gene and Rhodes' hendhmen, Robert Bice and Zon Murray.

SOURCES:

1. "Melody Ranch Theater" showing of "On Top of Old Smoky" on Nashville Network, 1987.

Goldtown Ghost Riders
<u>Columbia, May 1953</u>
A Gene Autry Production in Sepia Tone

Producer ....Armand Schaefer
Director ....George Archainbaud
Assistant Director........................Paul Donnelly
Story and Screenplay ....Gerald Geraghty
Photography ....William Bradford
Musical Supervisor ....Paul Mertz
Musical Director ....Mischa Bakaleinikoff
Film Editor.................................James Sweeney
Sound Dept.................................George Cooper
Art Director................................George Brooks
Set Decorations ....David Montrose

SONGS: "Pancho's Widow" (music and lyrics by Ned Washington, Sam Stept)—sung by Gene Autry, Smiley Burnette; "The Thievin' Burro" (music and lyrics by Smiley Burnette)—sung by Smiley Burnette; "Gold Mine In Your Heart" (music and lyrics by Gene Autry, Fred Rose, Johnny Marvin)—sung by Gene Autry.
    RUNNING TIME: 59 minutes
    FILMING DATES: September 9-16, 1952
    LOCATIONS: Columbia backlot; Lone Pine
    BUDGET: $48,668

CAST:

Actor	*Character*
Gene Autry	Gene Autry
Smiley Burnette	Smiley Burnette
Gail Davis	Cathy Wheeler
Kirk Riley	Ed Wheeler
Carleton Young	Jim Granby
Neyle Morrow	Teeno
Denver Pyle	Bernie Malloy
Steve Conte	Blackwell, Ghost Rider #1
??	Ghost Rider #2
??	Ghost Rider #3
John Doucette	Bailey
Blackie Whiteford, Cactus Mack, Herman Hack, Tex Terry, Frankie Marvin	Extras
Champion	Champion

STUNTS: Bob Woodward.

THE FILM: "Judge Gene Autry's dealing out swift six-gun justice…shooting it out with pistol-packing ghosts in a hate-haunted gold town!" Wow! Columbia was really going all-out to lure ticket-buyers into seeing Gene's latest western. Another ad read, "Gene's the judge…and Champ's the jury as flying fists and flying hooves carry the law into a ghost-ridden, fear crazed gold town." The copywriters were working overtime on this one.

The story gets underway fast when Ed Wheeler (Kirk Riley), after serving a 10 year prison sentence for the murder of a man named Mears, kills Jim Granby (Carleton Young), Goldtown's crooked boss.

Gene captures Wheeler who, in flashback, relates how Granby and Mears were the same person, Wheeler's partner years ago in a phony gold claim scheme. The pair sold the phony claims, then frightened prospectors away with a band of outlaws disguised as ghost riders.

When his daughter Cathy (Gail Davis) returned

Judge Gene Autry and Gail Davis mete out justice to conniving Carleton Young.

home from school back East, Wheeler attempted to reform, but Granby would not allow it.

Wheeler believed he had murdered Granby in a mine explosion, but during his 10 year jail sentence Wheeler learned Granby was not dead but had planted evidence pointing to the death of a man named Mears.

Knowing he cannot be tried for the same crime twice, Wheeler has now gunned down Granby.

Before Gene and Smiley can decide what to do, Granby's gang murders Wheeler, setting Gene on the trail of the killers whom he eventually finds mysteriously dead—justice apparently meted out by the legendary ghost riders.

Definitely back on the very serious side for Gene, with less music (no Cass County Boys) and a complicated plot. But it's to Gene's credit that he continually attempted to provide new twists and angles to his films that could otherwise become dull and repetitive.

NOTES AND COMMENTS: The script supervisor wasn't paying attention, as Gene's neckerchief changes from white to black and back to white in the first five minutes of the film.

There's a politically incorrect, by today's standards, bit of black-face humor when a keg of blasting powder blows up in Smiley Burnette's face.

Pack Train

Columbia, July 1953

A Gene Autry Production in Sepia Tone

Producer ....Armand Schaefer
Director ....George Archainbaud
Assistant Director.........................Paul Donnelly
Story and Screenplay ....Norman S. Hall
Photography ....William Bradford
Musical Supervisor ....Paul Mertz
Musical Director ....Mischa Bakaleinikoff
Film Editor ....James Sweeney
Sound Dept..................................Lambert Day
Art Director.................................George Brooks
Set Decorations ....Frank Tuttle

SONGS: "Hominy Grits" (music and lyrics by Smiley Burnette)—sung by Smiley Burnette; "God's Little Candles" (music and lyrics by Jimmy Kennedy)—sung by Gene Autry; "Wagon Train" (music and lyrics by Gene Autry, Smiley Burnette)—sung by Gene Autry, Smiley Burnette.

RUNNING TIME: 57 minutes
FILMING DATES: October 7-14, 1952
LOCATIONS: Iverson Ranch; Lone Pine; Columbia backlot
BUDGET: $47,595.60

CAST:

Actor	Character
Gene Autry	Gene Autry
Smiley Burnette	Smiley Burnette
Gail Davis	Jennifer Coleman
Kenne Duncan	Ross McLain
Sheila Ryan	Lola Riker
Tom London	Dan Coleman
Harry Lauter	Roy Wade
Jill Zeller	Blonde bargirl
Richard Alexander	Bartender Charlie
William Bailey	Old Timer
Wes Hudman	John, cleanshaven pack train traitor
Louise Lorimer	Martha Coleman
Frankie Marvin	Henchman
Rusty Wescoatt	Henchman
Kermit Maynard	Dave, Pack train member
B. G. Norman	Ted
Melinda Plowman	Judy
Blackie Whiteford, Bill Foster (aka Bill Coontz), Tex Terry, George Bell	Extras
Champion	Champion

STUNTS: Bob Woodward.

THE FILM: Another sound Gene Autry western, thoroughly competent on all levels but offering nothing new. However, there wasn't much new to offer in B-westerns by 1953 although Gene was in there trying in his third to last film.

The plot bears some resemblance to director Anthony Mann's A-western, "Bend of the River" ('52). When Sunshine Valley settlers face starvation and sickness because of a food and medicine shortage caused by the greed of storekeeper Lola Riker (Sheila Ryan) and her partner Ross McLain (Kenne Duncan), Gene Autry, Dan Coleman (Tom London), father of Gene's girlfriend Jennifer (Gail Davis), and Smiley Burnette eventually battle off all odds to get the supplies through to the settlers—just like James Stewart in "Bend of the River".

Gene and Champ in a "Pack Train" action moment.

Again, too much stock footage, the ending from Gene's "Blazing Sun" is reused, giving the viewer a bit of a gypped feeling. Obviously, the economic realities of making B-westerns in a dwindling market for them were taking its toll.

NOTES AND COMMENTS: Profits on Gene's Columbia releases continued to show decreasing returns. "Pack Train" cost $47,595.60 to make and reaped only $65,926 over a year's time, a profit of only $18,330.40.

Saginaw Trail
Columbia, September 1953
A Gene Autry Production in Sepia Tone

Producer ....Armand Schaefer
Director ....George Archainbaud
Assistant Director.........................Carter DeHaven Jr.
Story and Screenplay ....Dorothy Yost and
                                      Dwight Cummins
Photography ....William Bradford
Musical Supervisor ....Paul Mertz
Musical Director ....Mischa Bakaleinikoff
Film Editor ....James Sweeney
Sound Dept.................................George Cooper
Art Director................................Ross Bellah
Set Decorations ....Louis Diage

SONGS: "Mam'selle" (music and lyrics by Smiley Burnette)—sung by Smiley Burnette; "Beautiful Dreamer" (Public Domain by Stephen Foster)—sung by Gene Autry; "When It's Prayer Meetin' Time In the Hollow" (music and lyrics by Allan and Rice)—sung by Gene Autry.
RUNNING TIME: 56 minutes
FILMING DATES: January 5-13, 1953
LOCATIONS: Placerita Canyon; Columbia backlot; Melody Ranch
BUDGET: $49,106.95.

CAST:

Actor	Character
Gene Autry ....Gene Autry
Smiley Burnette ....Smiley Burnette
Connie Marshall...........................Flora Tourney
Eugene Borden.............................Jules Brissac
Ralph Reed...................................Randy Lane
Henry Blair..................................Phillip Brissac
Myron Healey ....Miller Webb
Mickey Simpson ....Jean "Frenchy" Leblanc
Gregg Barton...............................Lin Oakes
Charles Hayes ....Trapper
John Merton ....Trapper with Knife
John Parrish................................Trapper Walt
Rodd Redwing ....Huron Chief
John War Eagle ....Chief Red Bird
Billy Wilkerson ....Fox Chief
Frankie Marvin............................Settler on wagon

Evelyn Finley ....Settler's Wife w/baby
Ethan Laidlaw ....Trapper
Carol Henry.................................Renegade Indian
Champion....................................Champion
Little Champ ....Little Champ

STUNTS: Bob Woodward, Carol Henry.

THE FILM: Radically different in approach and setting for Gene Autry as he clears the Michigan Northwoods of renegades. He's not even wearing his usual gunbelt. The film is lacking in production values, much of it shot on one set. Too much time is spent with amateurish acting by juveniles Ralph Reed and Connie Marshall. More noticeable than ever before, at only 46 years of age, Gene's "heft" was

Gene relaxes between takes of his most unusual "western," "Saginaw Trail."

really beginning to show, and a more obvious than usual double for Gene was noticeable in the fight sequences.

Even though the setting is different, the yarn of white badmen murdering settlers and putting the blame on the Indians, hoping to stir up trouble, is a tired, hackneyed plot.

Jules Brissac (Eugene Borden) is the fur trader who, with Miller Webb (Myron Healey) is trying to run off homesteaders in order to keep his business going. Gene, as a captain in Hamilton's Rangers, is sent to investigate.

George Archainbaud's direction does little for the tired tale, the tempo dragging with minimal action interest. Gene plods through his role, calling for some silly disguises and clothing, and warbles Stephen Foster's "Beautiful Dreamer" in a toneless style, as if he knew the end was near. Smiley Burnette's brand of specialized humor collapses from exhaustion along the "Saginaw Trail".

It may have been a valiant try at something different, but the whole affair seems limited by budgetary influences.

Was it perhaps a glimpse into Gene's real thinking, when, at the end of the movie, Gene advises young Randy (Ralph Reed), "Don't try to stop progress, go with it, be a part of it."

NOTES AND COMMENTS: Connie Marshall was 14 when she made this picture. Born in New York City, she became a model at five and was in leading demand as a cover girl with New York artists and photographers. She made her screen debut at six in 1944. Marshall died in Santa Rosa, California, May 22, 2001.

With a profit on "Saginaw Trail" of only $4,597.05 over seven months' time, the handwriting was on the wall for Gene. Quitting time was nigh.

WHAT THE EXHIBITOR HAD TO SAY: "Typical Autry job, simple and straight forward, less than usual quota of action, with the rough stuff played in a minor key."

—Francis Gill, Panonia Theater, Panonia, Colorado (November 1953)

SOURCES:
1. *Western Clippings #27.* January/February 1999. p. 6.

Last of the Pony Riders
Columbia, November 1953
A Gene Autry Production in Sepia Tone

Producer ....Armand Schaefer
Director ....George Archainbaud
Assistant Director........................Carter DeHaven Jr.
Story and Screenplay ....Ruth Woodman
Photography ....William Bradford
Musical Supervisor ....Paul Mertz
Musical Director ....Ross DiMaggio
Film Editor ....James Sweeney
Sound Dept..................................Jack Lilly
Art Director................................Ross Bellah
Set Decorations ....David Montrose

SONGS: "Sing Me a Song of the Saddle" (music and lyrics by Gene Autry, Frank Harford)—sung by Gene Autry; "Sugar Babe" (Public Domain)—sung by Gene Autry, Smiley Burnette.

RUNNING TIME: 59 minutes
FILMING DATES: March 16-24, 1953
LOCATIONS: Pioneertown; Columbia backlot
BUDGET: Approximately $48,000

CAST:

Actor	*Character*
Gene Autry ....Gene Autry
Smiley Burnette ....Smiley Burnette
Kathleen Case ....Katie McEwen
Dick Jones...................................Johnny Blair
John Downey ....Tom McEwen
Howard Wright ....Clyde Vesey
Arthur Space ....Jess Hogan
Gregg Barton...............................Dutch Murdoch
Robert "Buzz" Henry...................Yank
Harry Hines.................................Bindlestiff
Harry Mackin ....Pony Rider Cliff
Kermit Maynard...........................Henchman
Bob Woodward ....Sam
Fred Krone ....Henchman
Frankie Marvin............................Office worker
Champion.....................................Champion

STUNTS: Bob Woodward, Fred Krone.

THE FILM: After 18 years and 89 starring feature pictures, the aptly titled "Last of the Pony Riders" ended an era for Gene Autry. It was a better than average Columbia entry for the Singing Cowboy.

"With pony riders under fire, the Pony Express route becomes a dead man's trail til Gene rides into the badlands and crushes the badmen out to cripple the Pony Express," stated the film's promotional material.

Gene is division superintendent for a section of the Pony Express run soon to be put out of business with the transcontinental telegraph nearing completion. When Gene's boss learns Gene intends to set up a stage line to carry the mail, he fires Gene for being disloyal, even though Gene fully intended to offer his boss a partnership.

With Gene no longer employed to protect the pony riders, the run is open prey for renegades.

Local schemers try to muscle in and get the government assignment for their own stageline, formulating a plan to discredit the Pony Express through a series of "accidents" and mail robberies.

Dick Jones (currently starring on TV in "Range Rider" and soon to star in "Buffalo Bill Jr." for Gene's Flying A Productions) has the technically prominent title role as

Watch out Gene, that's devious Howard Wright behind that door ready to ambush you.

Johnny Blair, a pony rider in love with attractive Katie McEwen (Kathleen Case). Blair comes close to physically breaking down after several raids and ambushes before he and Gene finally round up the heavies.

Dick recalled, "We knew beforehand this was Gene's last picture. They said, 'This is the last one he's gonna do.' I recall he said, 'It's been a good run, I'm gonna quit while I'm ahead.'"[1]

NOTES AND COMMENTS: "Last of the Pony Riders" features a slightly different opening, with a pony rider scene coming before the actual title comes on the screen.

Born Catherine Walker in Pittsburgh, Pennsylvania, in 1933, Gene's last leading lady, Kathleen Case, was once the prima ballerina of the renowned San Carlo Opera Company and the Ballet Theatre. She made her debut with the Metropolitan Opera Company in a production of "Aida" at age eleven. She dated Elvis Presley circa 1957-1960 and there was talk of marriage. Her brief 10 years before movie cameras also included work on TV episodes of Flying A produced "Range Rider" as well as "Kit Carson", "Hopalong Cassidy" and "Sugarfoot". She was only 45 when she died in Los Angeles in 1979.

Upon completion of "Last of the Pony Riders", Gene took his entire troupe (Pat Buttram, Carl Cotner, The Cass County Boys, Gail Davis, Rufe Davis, Tony Whitecloud and his Indians, Champion and Little Champ) in July and August, for a four week personal engagement at London's Empress Hall. The trip was Gene's first visit abroad (with the exception of his USO stint in the South Pacific) since 1939 when he made his successful tour of England, Scotland and Ireland. In London, 6,500 people lined up to see Gene ride Champion into the lobby of the Savoy Hotel and then into the ballroom of the luxurious hotel. 18,000 people lined Oxford Street, stopping all traffic, to see Gene ride Champion 20 blocks from historic Marble Arch to Selfridge's large department store. He rode Champion into the store and for three hours signed thousands of autographs. In his four weeks at Empress Hall, Gene played to over 600,000 people. Following the show, Gene and his wife Ina took off for a couple of weeks vacation covering practically the entire continent.

On September 20, 1953, "The Gene Autry Story" was featured on Ed Sullivan's "Toast of the Town" on CBS-TV.

Later in the year, after a two year absence, Gene returned to New York City to headline the Madison Square Garden Rodeo September 23 to October 18. Also on the show were Jock Mahoney and Dick Jones of Flying A's "The Range Rider".

"No one planned it that way, certainly not me," Gene wrote in his BACK IN THE SADDLE AGAIN 1978 biography, "but ("Last of the Pony Riders") pretty well closed the pages on the B-western chapter of Hollywood history. Allied Artists did make a few along into 1954, starring Wild Bill Elliott or Wayne Morris, but those were

Gene and Champion expect no more trouble out of Gregg Barton.

on a more adult scale and were sold as such. It is fair to say, I suppose, that the true Saturday afternoon matinee, the 'western pitcher', ended with 'Last of the Pony Riders'.

"There were no farewell toasts, no retirement dinner with someone handing out a pocket watch for 20 years of faithful service. Actually, 19 years between the release in November 1934 of 'In Old Santa Fe', when I made my first appearance with Ken Maynard for Mascot, until Columbia released my last in November of 1953. It just kind of slipped up on us. I don't recall ever saying that I had quit, or that I would never make another motion picture.

"Fact is, I never really left the business. The business left me. Hollywood started turning out a new type of western and half of the B-theaters that carried my films and others like them, closed down. Meanwhile, television swallowed up the rest, the old Autry and Rogers and Hopalong Cassidy movies, and swamped our homes with the made-for-TV series.

"It may not stretch a point to say we lost a little more of our innocence with the passing of the B-western." [2]

Gene's decision to cease making theatrical B-westerns and concentrate solely on television was the proper one both economically and physically. At 46, Gene was definitely starting to show his years, his face is rounder and that annoying double-chin and overall "heft" was catching up with him. Overall, Gene still looked and sounded fine, but he was definitely no longer cut out for the romantic lead, which is no doubt why he'd cut himself out of those type roles in his last few pictures.

Returns on Gene's films, which were lately in the near $50,000 range to produce, were less and less picture after picture, making it economically just not worth the effort to produce them any longer. "Last of the Pony Riders" returned $61,044 over about a year, only some $11,000 profit, of which Gene and Columbia split 50/50.

As Gene stated, the standard B-western had ended. Roy Rogers closed down his Republic series in 1951 and moved to TV later that year as had the Cisco Kid (in

September 1950) and Hopalong Cassidy (in 1952). Here again, Gene was the forerunner, having started his CBS TV series in July 1950. Johnny Mack Brown and Whip Wilson at Monogram, Charles Starrett at Columbia, Tim Holt at RKO, and Lash LaRue for Western Adventure all ended their B-series in 1952. Republic closed down Rex Allen's series in late 1953, although his final film wasn't released until February 1954.

To compete with older B-westerns being shown free daily on television, the B-western morphed into longer running, in color, minor A's, if you will, starring Audie Murphy, George Montgomery, Rod Cameron, Randolph Scott, Rory Calhoun, Jim Davis and others. Other big-budget westerns were capturing the marketplace also—"Winchester '73" ('50), "Broken Arrow" ('50), "High Noon" ('52), "Shane" ('53) and others.

The harder edge in B-westerns after World War II was certainly noticeable in the films of Gene, Roy and others. As the Korean War ended in 1953, the world changed again, becoming even more cynical and less innocent. Producers, and audiences, were turning to more adult themed pictures such as "A Streetcar Named Desire" ('51), "A Place in the Sun" ('51), "Quo Vadis" ('51), "Niagara" ('53), "The Wild One" ('53), "From Here to Eternity" ('53) and "The Caine Mutiny" ('54).

In 1952 profits were way down at theaters, bookings were off, exhibitors were no longer "reporting" on the few B-westerns they did play.

Television was certainly an influence, but the movie audiences' appetite was changing, as was the industry itself. As of 1953 to combat television the film industry was placing the emphasis on 3-D, bigger budgeted pictures, color, and Cinemascope. Science fiction pictures were also capturing the audiences' attention and drive-in theaters were proliferating. Box office champs in 1953 were "Shane", "Band Wagon", "Charge at Feather River" (in 3-D), "Second Chance" (in 3-D), "Gentlemen Prefer Blondes" and "Stalag 17".

The day of the B-western, and Gene Autry's film career, had come to a close. Gene, by continuing on into 1953 after most others had already left, was unique, and he'd made an unequaled contribution to western film history.

Gene's westerns, all recognizable from the over-riding presence of their star, provide a fascinating work. Seeing the Republic pictures today, one realizes just how fresh,

GENE HITS THE DANGER TRAIL!

COLUMBIA PICTURES presents

GENE AUTRY and CHAMPION

LAST OF THE PONY RIDERS

with
Kathleen Case · Dick Jones
and
SMILEY BURNETTE

Story and Screen Play by RUTH WOODMAN · Produced by ARMAND SCHAEFER
Directed by GEORGE ARCHAINBAUD · A GENE AUTRY PRODUCTION

exciting, amusing and satisfying they were. The Autry Republic westerns led the way; they set the pattern that Roy Rogers would follow in his second-period Republic films. Because Gene had done it first, the war-years ('42-'45) Rogers group never looked quite as fresh, since Republic used many of the same plot structures they had used for Gene's films in the later Rogers films.

And whatever the elements of Gene's appeal, or the arguments about his acting or riding abilities, there is no doubt it was Gene's singing voice that was the telling feature of his huge success. That and a natural country charm which he never lost through all the years of film and financial success. Gene was both simple and shrewd, likeable but tough, with a magical voice that endeared him to millions the world over. Critics never figured out Gene's boyish appeal, but the silent majority spoke, as they did at the box office, of their love for Gene Autry.

Gene's very best films are from '35 to '39. Western purists accustomed to the likes of Buck Jones, Ken Maynard and Bob Steele sneered. So be it, those Autry films are pure entertainment and we are the better for it. The period from '40-'42 lost a little freshness along the way, but there are still many fabulous moments. Gene's brief Republic work after the war is unremarkable and only served to mark time til his Columbia contract. His early Columbia films are the best of that period with good budgets and a fine balance between music and action. As the songs started to fade away with increasing budgets and declining returns, harder action became the hallmark of Gene's Columbia titles, and something of the essential Autry faded away too. Greeted in their time as superior B-westerns, which they are compared to much of the other product then available, they lacked the essential charm Republic gave to the Autry myth. It's notable when Smiley Burnette returned to Gene's series, there was a brightening up, both by Gene and the films. It was as if Costello had returned to Abbott, Laurel to Hardy, or Hepburn to Tracy. They were a team, and however one feels about Smiley, there is no doubt he and Gene formed a partnership that had genuine chemistry.

SOURCES:

1. Interview with author. February, 2006.

Other Gene Autry Film Shorts, Cameos, Guest Appearances and Oddities

We present here a list of Gene Autry's significant appearances in material other than his own full length movies or TV shows. Many of these were in Columbia's long-lived "Screen Snapshots" 10 minute short subjects which began in 1920 and ran through 1958. "Screen Snapshots" were an immediate success and turned a handsome profit because they could be made for peanuts. For the sake of publicity, stars graciously posed for pictures at various public events. At first they were hosted by Harriet Parsons, daughter of famed Hearst newspaper columnist Louella Parsons. She left Columbia in the late '30s and produced, directed and hosted a similar series for Republic in the early '40s, "Meet the Stars". Ralph Staub, who began as a director in 1936—and directed Gene in "Prairie Moon" and "Western Jamboree" in 1938—assumed control of the "Screen Snapshots" series in 1940, devoting himself to the 'Life in Hollywood' series from that time on. In later years many of the shorts used and reused footage from earlier shorts as well as public domain footage. His budget tightened by Columbia, after 1950 virtually every "Screen Snapshots" was comprised of footage from earlier entries framed by a new introduction featuring Staub himself talking with or reminiscing with a current star, often to promote a just-released picture.

"Hollywood Stadium Mystery"
(Republic, 1938)

In this B-murder mystery film, the key to the murder was indirectly provided by Republic's star Gene Autry, when the character played by Evelyn Venable sees a billboard advertising his 1936 film "Comin' 'Round the Mountain" and is thus able to identify the time the murderer whistled. Incidentally, Smiley Burnette plays himself in the movie.

"Screen Snapshots"
(Columbia, March 1938) Series #17, #7

Gene and Champion are shown amidst a mob of admiring kids. 10 minutes.

"Screen Snapshots: Seeing Hollywood"
(Columbia, 1940)

Gene Autry is shown at a rodeo and sings "There'll Never Be Another Pal Like You" to Champion. 10 minutes.

"Rodeo Dough"
(MGM, November 1940)
Sepiatone

Out of work actresses Sally Payne and Mary Treen attend a rodeo. A candid shot of Gene Autry signing autographs is included. 10 minutes.

"Meet the Stars"
10 minutes each

#4 (Republic, 1941) *"Between Scenes at Republic Studio"* includes a staged bit of tomfoolery with Gene Autry, Ann Miller, Jimmy Durante, George Hayes, Billy Benedict and director Joseph Santley while making "Melody Ranch".

#6 (Republic, 1941) *"An Intimate Tour of Several Stars' Homes"*. At the end of the short, various stars, including Gene Autry, are glimpsed at Santa Anita Park for the running of the $10,000 San Antonio Handicap.

#7 (Republic, June 1941) *"Meet Roy Rogers"*. Various stars, including Gene Autry, greet and congratulate Roy at his new Ranger Post store in the San Fernando Valley. Gene

Gene Autry congratulates Roy Rogers at the opening of Roy's Ranger Post store in Hollywood in this frame enlargement from "Meet Roy Rogers." (Photo courtesy Leonard Maltin.)

introduced as "The number one singin' western star", asks Roy about setting up a credit account at his store.

"Screen Snapshots"
(Columbia, March 1943) #43

The first half is a tour of a number of Army air centers in the Southwest with Gene Autry as the guide. The first stop is Luke Field where Gene joins the tour. 10 minutes.

"Screen Snapshots: Hollywood in Uniform"
(Columbia, September 1943)
Series #23 #1

Brief glimpse of Gene "home on furlough." Also seen—James Stewart, Alan Ladd, John Carroll, Clark Gable, George Montgomery. 10 minutes.

"Unusual Occupations"
(Paramount, late '40s)
In Cinecolor

At his home Gene sings "Back In the Saddle Again" and rides Champion. Gene also puts Champ through his tricks. 10 minutes.

"Screen Snapshots: Hollywood Cowboys"
(Columbia, September 1947)

Host Ralph Staub talks with Robert Young as he was currently making "Relentless" at Columbia. Footage of Gene, William Boyd, Johnny Mack Brown and others are glimpsed. 10 minutes.

"Screen Snapshots: Seeing Hollywood"
(Columbia, 1947 or 1948)

A visit to CBS Radio studios includes candid shots of Gene Autry. 10 minutes.

"Guns and Guitars"
(1947 or 1948)

Gene Autry's horse trainer John Agee sets up targets at Melody Ranch for Gene to shoot. Little Champ and Champion Jr. are shown with Champion Jr. doing all his tricks—prayers, hesitation waltz, bow, end of the trail, hula dance, backing up and x marks the spot with crossed front legs. Trainer John Agee taught Champion Jr. all these tricks but Gene, of course, had to learn to work with the horse as well. In an added segment, Gene sings "Private Buckaroo". This added segment was probably filmed circa 1941. 6 minutes.

"Screen Snapshots: Hollywood Rodeo"
(Columbia, 1949) Series #29

Gene Autry describes the annual rodeo held in the L.A. Memorial Coliseum. Attendees include John Wayne, Montie Montana, Jane Russell. 10 minutes.

"Erskine Johnson's Hollywood Reel"
(1949)

Gene and his fan club president with fan mail.

"Screen Snapshots: Hollywood's Famous Feet"
(Columbia, 1950) Series #29

Gene and Champion, John Wayne, Tom Mix and Tony are shown putting their prints in cement in front of Grauman's Chinese Theatre. 10 minutes.

"Hoedown"
(Columbia, June 1950)

A spoof of western filmmaking with Jock Mahoney as Stoney Rhodes (a play on Rocky Lane) as an out of work singing cowboy star. In a movie ("Bang 'Em Up Buckaroo") within the movie it's revealed Gene Autry dubbed Stoney's singing on "Can't Shake the Sands of Texas From My Shoes". There's also a cute scene when Stoney talks to a Gene Autry "Strawberry Roan" movie poster. 63 mintues.

"Screen Snapshots: Hollywood Goes Western"
(Columbia, 1951)

Interviewed are Gene Autry, Randolph Scott, Chill Wills at Sheriff Gene Biscaluiz's annual rodeo. 10 minutes.

"Columbia World of Sports: Rodeo Daredevils"
(Columbia, 1952)

Among other rodeo footage, Gene Autry puts Champion through a few of his tricks. 10 minutes.

"Screen Snapshots: Fun in the Sun"
(Columbia, 1952)

Actors seen relaxing include Gene Autry, Olsen and Johnson, and Johnny Weissmuller. 10 minutes.

"Screen Snapshots"
(Columbia, 1953) Series #32

Gene Autry and Smiley Burnette are shown in a chow line on location. 10 minutes.

"Screen Snapshots: Out West in Hollywood"
(Columbia, 1953) Series #32

Footage of Gene Autry, Tom Mix, William S. Hart, Charles Starrett, Buck Jones and others is used to promote Ken Murray and Hoot Gibson's "The Marshal's Daughter" film. 10 minutes.

"Screen Snapshots: Hollywood Cowboy Stars"
(Columbia, 1954) Series #34

Gene narrates rodeo footage from Sheriff Gene Biscaluiz' L.A. County Sheriff's Rodeo. John Wayne, Jane Russell, others. Gene is shown performing tricks on Champion. Footage recycled from "Screen Snapshots: Hollywood Rodeo" ('49). 10 minutes.

"Screen Snapshots:
Hollywood Stars on Parade"
(Columbia, 1954)
Recycled footage from "Seeing Hollywood". 10 minutes.

"Screen Snapshots:
Memories in Uniform"
(Columbia, 1954)
John Carroll is host Ralph Staub's guest as they reminisce and watch footage first seen in "Hollywood in Uniform" ('43). 10 minutes.

"Screen Snapshots:
Hollywood Bronc Busters"
(Columbia, 1955) Series #35
Host Ralph Staub talks with Jack Lemmon as they watch vintage footage of Gene Autry, William S. Hart, Charles Starrett, Hopalong Cassidy and others previously seen in "Screen Snapshots: Out West in Hollywood.". 10 minutes.

Gene and Pat Buttram ready for another session of "Melody Ranch Theater" on the Nashville Network.

"Screen Snapshots:
The Great Al Jolson"
(Columbia, 1955)
Many top composers, including Gene Autry, pay homage to Jolson. 10 minutes.

"Wide Wide World"
(June 8, 1958)
Gene hosted a wide array of western stars as he opened the door to his Melody Ranch film location for the biggest western spectacular in TV history. As Gene role Champion Jr. he sang a few refrains of "Back in the Saddle Again", then had Champ Jr. perform a few tricks. Little Champion was also shown. Hosted by Dave Garroway, the show also featured director John Ford, John Wayne, Gary Cooper, James Arness, Gabby Hayes, James Garner, Broncho Billy Anderson, Gail Davis, Clayton Moore and others. 90 minutes.

"Person to Person"
(CBS, June 10, 1960)
Gene and his wife Ina are interviewed by Charles Collingwood at their home in North Hollywood. Gene discusses his start in the entertainment business, his interest in baseball, contemporary western films and some of his western art collection.

Gene and his wife Ina pose in their home with "Person to Person" interviewer Chales Collingwood.

"The Melody Ranch Show"
(KTLA TV, 1964-early '70s)
"The Melody Ranch Show" began on KTLA-TV in Los Angeles in September 1964 and ran until the early '70s. Running one-hour on Saturday evenings, this color show presented top country talent with regulars Billy Mize, Johnny Bond and Carl Cotner and the Melody Ranchers. Guests included Rex Allen, Tex Williams, Hank Penny and Gene himself occasionally. It was later syndicated as "Gene Autry's Melody Ranch" in 52 edited half hour programs.

"Melody Ranch Theater"
(Nashville TV Network, 1987)

Gene Autry and Pat Buttram filmed "wraparounds" to all of Gene's Republic and Columbia pictures. In a western ranch house setting Gene and Pat would introduce and discuss each film. Often people such as director George Sherman, actress Ann Rutherford, musician Pee Wee King, historian Alex Gordon and others would appear as guests during the programs to reminisce about the films.

"Music of the West: A Tribute to Singing Cowboys"
(Warner Home Video, 1993)

Host Dennis Weaver and various musical acts pay tribute to Gene Autry (who accepts an award), Rex Allen, Roy Rogers and others. Filmed live at the Autry Museum. 70 minutes.

"Biography"
(Arts and Entertainment, October 30, 1993)

Bio of Gene Autry included interviews with Gene and many others—Alex Gordon of Flying A Productions, Monte Hale, George Gobel, Pat Buttram, Lupita Tovar, Ann Miller and Roy Rogers. 50 minutes.

"Melody of the West"
(Galen Films on American Movie Classics, October 1994)

Host Johnny Cash narrates the life and times of Gene Autry. Includes comments from Gene Autry, Gail Davis, Dick Jones, Richard Farnsworth, Peggy Stewart, Ann Rutherford,

Gene and Pat Buttram as they appeared with host Gary Collins on "Hour Magazine"'s "Gene Autry Show" reunion in November 1984.

Fay McKenzie, Dorrell McGowan, Jerry Scoggins, Freddie Martin, Monte Hale, Patsy Montana. 60 minutes.

Gene's guest star appearances on television from the '50s through the '90s are legion. He appeared on virtually everything, "Toast of the Town", "What's My Line", "Merv Griffin Show", "This Is Your Life", "Today", the KTLA Christmas Parade, "Hee Haw", "David Letterman", "Good Morning America", "Entertainment Tonight", "CNN", "Yesteryear in Nashville", "Hour Magazine", "Statler Brothers Christmas Show", "Prime Time Sunday", "Nightwatch", "Pat Sajak", the Grammy Awards, "Stuntmasters", "Showbiz Today", "Steve Allen", "Evening of Country Greats", "Perry Como", "Mike Douglas", and dozens more, including scores of news interviews regarding his California Angels baseball team.

Notes and Comments: Gene never appeared in either "The Silent Treatment" ('68) or "Alias Jesse James" with Bob Hope ('59). No footage of Gene for "The Silent Treatment" was ever filmed. Footage was shot for "Alias Jesse James" but was deemed not useable for the film which did guest star Roy Rogers, Ward Bond, Fess Parker, Gail Davis, James Arness, Jay Silverheels, Gary Cooper and Hugh O'Brian.

Songs written by Gene Autry often turned up in other (usually) B-western movies.

"Western Gold" (1937 20th Century–Fox)—Smith Ballew. Song "Echos of the Trail" was written by Fleming Allen and Gene Autry.

"Painted Stallion" (1937 Republic serial)—Ray "Crash" Corrigan. "Wagon Train" in Chapter 1 was written by Gene Autry and Smiley Burnette.

"Border G-Man" (1938 RKO)—George O'Brien. Ray Whitley composed "Back in the Saddle Again" for this B-western before Gene first used it and became a co-writer.

"Under Western Stars" (1938 Republic)—Roy Rogers. Originally intended as an Autry film, but given to Roy Rogers when Gene went on strike, the song "Dust" was composed by Gene Autry and Johnny Marvin, and "Rhythm of the Range" was written by Gene, Johnny Marvin and Fred Rose.

"Prairie Pals" (1942 PRC)—Lee Powell/ Art Davis/ Bill Boyd. "You'll Be Sorry" written by Gene Autry and Fred Rose.

"Shepherd of the Ozarks" (1942 Republic)—Weaver Brothers and Elviry. "Dreams That Won't Come True" written by Gene Autry and Fred Rose.

"Strictly In the Groove" (1942 Universal)—Leon Errol. "Be Honest With Me" composed by Gene Autry and Fred Rose.

"Cowboy In the Clouds" (1943 Columbia)—Charles Starrett. "There's a Rainbow On the Rio Colorado" music and lyrics by Gene Autry and Fred Rose.

"Man From Music Mountain" (1943 Republic)—Roy Rogers. "I'm Beginning to Care" music and lyrics by Gene

Autry and Fred Rose.

"Robin Hood of the Range" (1943 Columbia)—Charles Starrett. Reportedly contains a song written by Gene but the film is unavailable for viewing.

"Cowboy From Lonesome River" (1944 Columbia)—Charles Starrett. "(Let Me Ride Down In) Rocky Canyon" written by Gene Autry and Fred Rose.

"Cyclone Prairie Rangers" (1944 Columbia)—Charles Starrett. "Be Honest With Me" written by Gene Autry and Fred Rose.

"Saddle Leather Law" (1944 Columbia)—Charles Starrett. "Rhythm of the Hoofbeats" composed by Gene Autry and Johnny Marvin.

"Flaming Bullets" (1945 PRC)—Tex Ritter/Dave O'Brien. "Be Honest With Me" music and lyrics by Gene Autry and Fred Rose.

"Song of Idaho" (1948 Columbia)—Kirby Grant, Hoosier Hot Shots. "Nobody Else But You" music and lyrics by Gene Autry and Carola Wieland.

"Under California Stars" (1948 Republic)—Roy Rogers. "Dust" music and lyrics by Gene Autry and Johnny Marvin.

"Hoedown" (1950 Columbia)—Jock Mahoney. "Can't Shake the Sands of Texas From My Shoes" words and lyrics by Gene Autry, Diane Johnston and Kenneth Pitts.

In recent years, "Here Comes Santa Claus", "Back In the Saddle Again", "Be Honest With Me" and others have turned up in films such as "Semi-Tough" ('77), "Robocop 3" ('93), "Sleepless In Seattle" ('93), "The Polar Express" ('04) and others. For television Gene's songs have popped up on "M*A*S*H", "The Simpsons", "Chicago Hope" and others, including several commercials.

"The Gene Autry Show"

TV or not TV was the question facing Gene Autry as the new decade of the 1950s dawned. Time was running out on the B-western although, as we've seen, Gene struggled on into 1953. Television had begun to seduce the entire country, replacing our viewing with a small screen right in our living room.

William "Hopalong Cassidy" Boyd got the jump on everyone in the new medium. Major studios were at first hesitant to sell their films to television, but the Hoppy theatrical films were bought up by Boyd on a long-shot gamble that paid off handsomely. Overnight Hopalong Cassidy enjoyed a national revival as TV snapped up his pictures in the late '40s.

Like everyone else in the business, Gene saw the value and possibilities of television. On the other hand, Hollywood definitely considered TV a threat to their own business. This was particularly true of the theatre exhibitors who ran the local movie houses where films were shown; it was they who would suffer most from the encroachment of the new medium. Gene knew if he did go into small screen production, theatre owners might consider it a definite affront, an evidence of disloyalty.

After much consideration, and not wanting to make his TV debut in old movies he'd made 10 or 15 years ago, Gene formed Flying A Pictures to produce a series of half hour westerns for CBS TV, establishing another milestone by being the first movie cowboy to make a regular series for TV beginning on CBS on Sunday, July 23, 1950, sponsored by Wrigley's Doublemint Chewing Gum. Wrigley paid 30-50% of the production costs and obtained first transmission rights in return. Subsequent rights were retained by Gene's Flying A Pictures. In addition to Gene, producer Armand Schaefer and Gene's business agent, Mitchell Hamilburg, were in on the project. Columbia Pictures had nothing to do with Gene's Flying A TV episodes. Their deal with Gene was strictly for theatricals. Gene opened the door for others, the Cisco Kid followed Gene by only a few months, Roy

WTVM is in Columbus, Georgia.

Rogers came along a year later followed by made-expressly-for-TV Hopalong Cassidy episodes in 1952.

As Gene explained in a July 7, 1950, press release, "The reasons I decided to go ahead with this venture were (1) most of my movies play in small towns, whereas television sets are most numerous (per capita) in large cities, thus the areas of competition would not overlap to any considerable extent; (One must realize by mid 1951 there was still only 109 TV stations in the country, with Gene's TV films being shown on 90 of those stations.) and (2) and more important, television can and will serve as a boon to movie business. Children, and adults too, who see a certain star on television become interested in him and, as a result, will also go to see his movies…or his rodeos. It has worked that way in every other phase of the entertainment business. Stardom on radio, records, or movies immediately stirs up interest in that personality in other mediums—and it is going to be true in television. I firmly believe that."[1]

However, Gene's move into TV was not well accepted by the anxiety ridden theatre owners. An article in TIME magazine indicated theatre owners felt Gene was inflicting further financial suffering upon the several thousand theatres that had enabled him to reach his present enviable position in the industry. In protest, several exhibitors cancelled their contracts for Gene's Columbia features.

In response, Gene wrote the following, "I am not an enemy or traitor to the exhibitor. On the contrary, I have proved over a period of years that I am a friend of the industry, but let's look it square in the face—television is here, television is going to stay and the sooner we all start figuring out how to benefit from it rather than run away from it, the better off we all will be. In all the years I have made pictures the exhibitor has seldom given me a break as far as first runs in large metropolitan areas are concerned, and if they did run one in a downtown house, it was always at the bottom of a twin bill, giving the major companies a better break. My pictures have always played the smaller towns and communities. At the present time, television does not reach these areas, so how could television hurt my pictures at the boxoffice when they have not been given fair exhibition in the large cities in the first place? Also, the TV pictures are 27 minutes long, against an hour for my regular features. At the end of each TV feature this commercial is inserted: 'Be sure to see Gene Autry and Champion in their latest full-length feature at your local theatre.' This constitutes a trailer for each of my pictures run in your theatres. To buy this advertising would cost a great deal of money, so let's give it a try and see what the result will be."[2]

That Gene was right in making the move early to TV has been proven over the years. The end of the B-western era in theatres was in sight. Smaller budget films of any type simply could not compete with free entertainment in one's living room.

With a firm production staff headed up by Armand Schaefer and Louis Gray, before a single scene was ever filmed, Gene studied well how films made for TV would appear on a smaller screen. Long shots were mostly eliminated in deference to the fact home screens were smaller than theatre screens. In hard riding sequences the riders were photographed at closer range than usual and traveled across the screen rather than toward the camera, giving the TV viewers a constant close-up of the riders. Working with longtime director of photography, William Bradford, they made certain changes in the photographic technique, resulting in pictures where the contrast range was considerably lessened with more whites and lighter shades on the screen than usual. The darker portions of the picture were a blend of grays, easier on the eyes than blacks. In order to assure the utmost in film quality, all of Gene's TV shows were shot on 35mm film. Whereas other TV series used "canned" music, Gene's longtime friend and fiddle player from his "Melody Ranch" radio show, Carl Cotner, working with composer Walter Greene, composed all new musical cues for Gene's TV episodes, considerably enhancing the excitement of the episodes. Unlike the Roy Rogers and Rex Allen series that followed, obviously produced on a lower budget, Gene's shows prominently featured songs, making Gene the *only* singing cowboy on television. Also unlike the Rogers show and other early TV cowboys, which had a single locale week to week, Gene's shows featured him in a wide variety of places and jobs, just as his movies had done. Each episode found Gene and Pat Buttram as different characters in different locales, even though they retained the names of Gene Autry and Pat Buttram. In one episode they'd be Texas Rangers, in another Gene would be a rancher who did not know Pat at the start. Some episodes were set in the old west, some had a modern day setting.

Gene gathered long time associates around him to helm his series including producer Armand (Mandy) Schaefer (whom he'd first met at Mascot in 1934) and associate producer Louis Gray, formerly a producer at Republic. Their

Louis Gray.

lifelong relationships were based solely on handshakes. William Bradford, regular cinematographer on Gene's Columbia titles was added to the lineup. Stuntwork was primarily handled by Bob Woodward, Boyd Stockman, Sandy Sanders and Lou Morphy. Gene was loyal to his employees and tended to reuse hard working, faithful, competent actors such as Myron Healey, Sheila Ryan (married to Pat Buttram from 1952 til her death in 1975), Harry Lauter, Gail Davis, Dick Jones, Gregg Barton, the Cass County Boys, George J. Lewis, Don Harvey, Frankie Marvin, William Fawcett, Kenne Duncan and others. Of course, Pat Buttram continued over onto TV as Gene's regular sidekick, giving the shows even more recognizability. Veteran directors Frank McDonald (who'd guided many Republic and Columbia Autry features) and George Archainbaud (director of several Columbia titles) helmed the first 24 episodes. McDonald soon left but Archainbaud continued til the end of the series, abetted by Jack English, David Ross Lederman, Wallace Fox, George Blair, William Berke and Ray Nazarro—all men who knew their way around a horse and a sixgun. Scripts came from a wide variety of writers including many ladies such as Elizabeth Beecher (a writer of many Range Busters, Johnny Mack Brown and Charles Starrett scripts), prolific Betty Burbridge (responsible for plenty of Three Mesquiteers and Autry Republic titles among others), Polly James ("Redhead From Wyoming") and Virginia Cooke. Other regular contributors were Dwight Cummins ("Strawberry Roan", "Cowboy and the Indians"), Paul Gangelin ("Sons of New Mexico", "My Pal Trigger", "Daltons Ride Again"), John K. Butler (numerous Roy Rogers, Bob Livingston, Monte Hale, Gene Autry, Rex Allen movies), Oliver Drake (whose writing and directing date back to the late '20s), Maurice Geraghty (creator of Gene's "Phantom Empire" storyline and other Hopalong Cassidy, Charles Starrett, etc. westerns), Jack Townley ("The Last Round-Up", "Riders of the Whistling Pines", "The Blazing Sun"), Earle Snell (dozens of Buck Jones, Range Busters, Bill Elliott, Monte Hale, etc. westerns), Norman S. Hall (several of Gene's Columbia features as well as many Republic B's), J. Benton Cheney (many Hopalong Cassidy, Johnny Mack Brown and other westerns), as well as the prolific Robert Schaefer and Eric Friewald who wrote scores of TV westerns.

The first three seasons of "The Gene Autry Show" were filmed concurrently with Gene's Columbia features, something no other western star ever attempted. For instance, Roy Rogers' last Republic feature was released to theaters in December 1951 with his TV series beginning later that same month.

A permanent filming location was established at

Pioneertown (see locations section) where all the first season episodes were lensed. In later episodes, other locations were used as well.

With the familiar opening strains of Gene's theme music, "Back in the Saddle Again", two half hour episodes were filmed per week, usually utilizing the same basic casts. Although these episodes were seldom shown back to back, the viewer can match-up the companion episodes by checking the cast.

Thus Gene's TV shows became an extension of his theatricals, essentially becoming miniature B-westerns, efficiently and expertly produced. The entire series looked far better than all his TV competition and exhibited the friendly Autry personality the public had admired and loved since 1935.

Gene's TV series ran from July 23, 1950 until December 17, 1955, a total of 91 episodes, 15 of which were filmed in color. The series continued to air in syndication on through the '70s and has recently been revived in digitally remastered form on Encore's Westerns Channel.

It should be noted that Gene's TV shows were not aired on CBS in the exact order in which they were filmed. For our purposes here, we are listing the 91 episodes in the order in which they were shown.

SOURCES:

1. "Speaking of Television" CBS press release. July 7, 1950.

2. Letter to P. J. Wood, Ohio theatre exhibitor, and others. MOTION PICTURE HERALD, August 12, 1950.

The Gene Autry Show

1ˢᵗ season, 26 episodes (7/23/50-4/21/51). 30 minutes each.
Aired on CBS network on Sunday from 7-7:30pm EST

"Head For Texas"

ORIGINAL AIRDATE: July 23, 1950

Executive Producer ....Armand Schaefer
Associate Producer......................Louis Gray
Director ....Frank McDonald
Teleplay.......................................Dwight Cummins
Director of Photography ....William Bradford
Film Editor..................................Jodie Copelan
Musical Director ....Carl Cotner
Musical Score..............................Walter Greene
Assistant Director........................Rex Bailey

SONG: "Sing Me a Song of the Saddle" (music and lyrics by Frank Harford)—sung by Gene Autry.

CAST:

Actor	*Character*
Gene Autry	Gene Autry
Pat Buttram	Pat Jensen
Barbara Stanley............................	Sandy Dawson
Ben Weldon................................	Baldy Carter
George J. Lewis...........................	Rod Benton
House Peters Jr.	Lou Phelps
Ray Bennett................................	Sheriff Connors
Jim Frasher.................................	Billy Stone
Champion...................................	Champion

FILMING DATES: May 19-27, 1950 (Companion episodes "The Silver Arrow" and "The Star Toter.")
LOCATION: Pioneertown

THE FILM: Rustlers on the ranch of Sandy Dawson frame foreman Gene Autry for their acts but an ex-jockey Gene has befriended helps prove his innocence.

NOTES AND COMMENTS: Film editor Jodie Copelan started with Gene's Flying A Pictures, later editing dozens of features on through the '70s. He even turned director *once* for Clint Eastwood's "Ambush at Cimarron Pass" ('58). Dirk London, who had a role in that film called Jodie

"a real nice, helpful guy" who was "related to well-known character actor Ken Mayer."[1]

Jimmy Hawkins, Tagg Oakley on Flying A's "Annie Oakley" TV series worked many times with director Frank McDonald. "He was a great guy. Real good sense of humor. Always had a walking stick. Seemed to have a flair when he dressed. We were brother Scorpios. Our birthdays were both in November and we remembered each other for years by phone or through the mail. As a director he was good and fast. Didn't have the eye of a George Archainbaud, but made nice setups. Everyone on the 'Annie' set got along with him fine. There's a caricature of him at the bowling alley/post office in Pioneertown, where we shot many 'Annie' episodes."[2]

Dick Jones worked in several of Gene's TV episodes as well as starring in Flying A's "Range Rider" and "Buffalo Bill Jr." "The same crew did the TV shows as did the features only there was more of 'em 'cause they had a bigger budget (on the features). It was like family. As far as I was concerned, Bill Bradford (the director of photography) was just a figurehead. The camera operator and the camera assistant moved the camera and set the shots up. Bill had the title but the other two guys, Fleet Southcott and Joe August, really did all the work. As for directors, Frank McDonald and George Archainbaud, they could cut a show before it even got in the camera. No wasted motion, no wasted movement and they had an eye for selling the action.

"Producer Lou Gray, when he was on the set, when he was working, was very stern, all business. If there's a reason for things to slow down and stop he was very amiable and fun to be around. If you're not shooting, sittin' around talkin', nice guy. But when he was working, he was pacing the floor, looking at his watch, looking at the production board. I contribute Gene Autry's success to the people he hired, because he hired the best in the business. The best producer, the best cameraman, the best directors, the best agent…because he couldn't do it all himself. Gene surrounded himself with the best in their field 'cause that made him look good and that made him money.

"Gene's drive was he liked to be out in front of people. He liked to be on the stage. I remember at some point he was talking to me about going out on personal appearances.

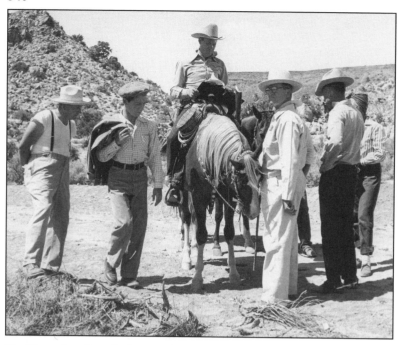

On Champion, Gene looks over the script for the initial scene from "Head for Texas," his first-shown TV episode, while members of the cast and crew prepare for the scene. Actor Jim Frasher has his jacket over his shoulder and Gene's usual director of photography, William Bradford, is seen next to Champ.

I said, number one, I will not do one-nighters. I will not go from town to town to town. I've traveled a lot when I worked and I don't like it and I wouldn't be worth a damn. He said all those people are gonna wanna see you and shake your hand. Then he went into the routine about going to see all the little kids in the hospitals and things like that. I said, well I can do it if I have to…and he said, 'Well you have to!' (Laughs) He said you're not gonna make any money doing this, you're gonna make your money out on the road.' The only time I traveled with his show was when I did the rodeos with him. Madison Square Garden, Houston Fat Stock Show, Boston Gardens." [3]

House Peters Jr.: "Gene was loyal to his employees… and that includes Lou Gray and Mandy Schaefer. Lou Gray was without a doubt one of the best fellows to work with. He was associate producer with Mandy Schaefer. Believe me, when I needed a job, I could always walk into Lou Gray's office and tell him my circumstances. He would do his darndest to help an actor out. I have yet to see prop men and so forth on the crew that didn't like Lou Gray.

"I remember the time we were to film the first Gene Autry TV shows. I remember Gene coming into the wardrobe room at Columbia and chit-chatting. He said, 'I got somethin' to show everybody.' He held up a check from CBS for $25,000…$12,500 for each episode. He was kinda proud of it. It shows what it cost in those days for two back to back. We did both shows at one time. When we did scenes, we'd change wardrobe and go back in the saloon or whatever for the second show, playing a different part." [4]

CAST BIO: Upon fiddler Carl Cotner rests the re-

sponsibility for the music and musical background of TV's "Gene Autry Show" as well as Gene's "Melody Ranch" radio program, Gene Autry Rodeos and other personal appearances.

The blue-eyed musician with the perpetual smile was born April 8, 1916, in Cocott, Indiana, the eldest of a family of three. They were raised in Kokomo, Indiana, where Carl's father played the violin and began teaching his son when he was four. At five, Carl was doing a single act on stage until child-labor laws caught up with the elder Cotner and he had to remove his son from the stage.

Carl studied with a private teacher in Indianapolis, then went to Cincinnati College of Music to study arranging, composing and harmony with every intention of becoming a "serious" concert violinist.

Carl was sidetracked by the Depression, finding his knowledge of country music and hoedowns served him well for making a dollar at dances and gatherings where a country fiddler was needed.

The story goes Carl was hitchhiking along a highway in 1933, violin case in hand, when Gene Autry, barnstorming in the area at the time, chanced to give Carl a ride. In need of a fiddle player, Gene hired Carl who stayed with him until Gene left for the movies. Carl then went to WLW radio in Cincinnati until he received a wire in 1937 from Gene who was preparing his first eastern tour of personal appearances. Carl rejoined Gene and this time came to Hollywood where he was Gene's musical arranger/director on "Melody Ranch".

With WWII, Carl enlisted in the infantry where he was placed in charge of an Army band in the South Pacific.

With the cessation of the war, Carl rejoined Gene where he remained for the rest of his professional career. Carl once referred to Gene as "One hell of a singer. Gene sounds good. He had a way with a song, he knew how to sing it, he knew how to sell it…to me he was a great artist." [5]

Carl Cotner.

The talented fiddler so integral to the music of Gene Autry died November 14, 1986, in Buena Park, California.

SOURCES:
1. Interview with author, November 2005.
2. Interview with author, August 2005.
3. Interview with author, February 2006.
4. Interview with author, December 2005.
5. Taped comment aired on A&E "Biography" (10/93).

"Gold Dust Charlie"

ORIGINAL AIRDATE: July 30, 1950

Executive Producer ....Armand Schaefer
Associate Producer......................Louis Gray
Director ....Frank McDonald
Teleplay.......................................Jack Townley
Director of Photography ....William Bradford
Film Editor..................................Jodie Copelan
Musical Director ....Carl Cotner
Musical Score..............................Walter Greene
Assistant Director........................Rex Bailey

SONGS: "The Cowboy Blues" (music and lyrics by Gene Autry, Frankie Marvin)—sung by Gene Autry and The Cass County Boys; "Home On the Range" (Public Domain)—sung by Gene Autry and The Cass County Boys; "Great Grand Dad" (Public Domain)—sung by The Cass County Boys; "Mexicali Rose" (music and lyrics by Helen Stone, Jack B. Tenney)—sung by Gene Autry.

CAST:

Actor	*Character*
Gene Autry	Gene Autry
Pat Buttram	Pat Buttram
Sheila Ryan	Betty Taylor
Alan Hale Jr.	Goss
Steve Darrell	Smith
Ralph Sanford	"Doc" Bailey
Tom London	The Sheriff
Sam Flint	Harry Taylor
The Cass County Boys	The Cass County Boys
Gregg Barton	Deputy
William Fawcett	Old Charlie
Frankie Marvin, Ray Jones, Frank Matts, Whitey Hughes	Townsmen
Champion	Champion

FILMING DATES: May 10-18, 1950 (Companion episodes "The Doodle Bug" and "The Double Switch".)
LOCATION: Pioneertown

THE FILM: Gene Autry and his friends come across a murdered prospector and his gold mine. While trying to see the mine goes to its rightful heirs, Gene is arrested for the old miner's murder.

"The Silver Arrow"

ORIGINAL AIRDATE: August 6, 1950

Executive Producer ....Armand Schaefer
Associate Producer......................Louis Gray
Director ....Frank McDonald
Teleplay.......................................Elizabeth Beecher
Director of Photography ....William Bradford
Film Editor..................................Jodie Copelan
Musical Director ....Carl Cotner
Musical Score..............................Walter Greene
Assistant Director........................Rex Bailey

SONG: "Can't Shake the Sands of Texas From My Shoes" (music and lyrics by Gene Autry, Diane Johnston, Kenneth Pitts)—sung by Gene Autry.

CAST:

Actor	*Character*
Gene Autry	Gene Autry
Pat Buttram	Pat Buttram
Robert Livingston	Frank Andrews
George J. Lewis	Sid Damon
Ben Weldon	Pete Clark
Jim Frasher	Randy Edwards
Ray Bennett	Sheriff Garner
House Peters Jr.	Myron Foster
Sandy Sanders	Jingo
Wes Hudman	Dave Edwards
Frankie Marvin, Bobby Clark	Extras
Champion	Champion

FILMING DATES: May 19-27, 1950 (Companion episodes "Head For Texas" and "The Star Toter".)
LOCATION: Pioneertown

THE FILM: Rodeo riders Gene Autry and Pat Buttram discover a dead man pierced with a silver arrow in his chest. This leads Gene to a man framed in order to get his silver mine.

"The Doodle Bug"

ORIGINAL AIRDATE: August 13, 1950

Executive Producer ....Armand Schaefer
Associate Producer......................Louis Gray
Director ....Frank McDonald
Teleplay.......................................Polly James
Director of Photography ....William Bradford
Film Editor..................................Jodie Copelan
Musical Director ....Carl Cotner
Musical Score..............................Walter Greene
Assistant Director........................Rex Bailey

SONG: "Ridin' Down the Canyon" (music and lyrics by Gene Autry, Smiley Burnette)—sung by Gene Autry.

CAST:

Actor	*Character*
Gene Autry	Gene Autry
Pat Buttram	Patrick Smith
Sheila Ryan	Lucy Lawrence

Alan Hale Jr.	"Kingpin" Tyler
Steve Darrell	Mason
Minerva Urecal	Mrs. Wilhelmina Wilkins
Tommy Ivo	Edgar Wilkins
Gregg Barton	Collins
Tom London	Sheriff Dawes
Wes Hudman	Walt
Frank Matts	Ben
Ray Jones	Extra
Champion	Champion

FILMING DATES: May 10-18, 1950 (Companion episodes "Gold Dust Charlie" and "The Double Switch".)
LOCATION: Pioneertown

THE FILM: While Gene and Pat are investigating numerous stagecoach holdups, they also help a lady schoolteacher.

"The Star Toter"

ORIGINAL AIRDATE: August 20, 1950

Executive Producer	Armand Schaefer
Associate Producer	Louis Gray
Director	Frank McDonald
Teleplay	Jack Townley
Director of Photography	William Bradford
Film Editor	Jodie Copelan
Musical Director	Carl Cotner
Musical Score	Walter Greene
Assistant Director	Rex Bailey

SONG: "Back In the Saddle Again" (music and lyrics by Gene Autry, Ray Whitley)—sung by Gene Autry.

CAST:

Actor	Character
Gene Autry	Gene Autry
Pat Buttram	Pat Buttram
Barbara Stanley	Martha Neill
George J. Lewis	Ben Foster
Billy Gray	Jimmy Foster
Robert Livingston	Curry
House Peters Jr.	Reynolds
Wes Hudman	Deputy Sheriff Joe
Frankie Marvin	Frankie
Frank Matts	Deputy
Beatrice Gray	Mrs. Taylor
Whitey Hughes, Ray Jones	Extras
Champion	Champion
Little Champ	Little Champ

FILMING DATES: May 19-27, 1950 (Companion episodes "Head For Texas" and "The Silver Arrow".)
LOCATION: Pioneertown

Gene on location at Pioneertown.

THE FILM: Sheriff Gene Autry pursues a vicious bank robber and reforms his ten year old wayward son.

NOTES AND COMMENTS: *Beatrice Gray:* "I remember, vaguely, taking (my son) Billy to Pioneertown for the Autry TV shows, but what I most remember about Gene happened when I was still back in Carthage, Illinois, and married to Bill's father. My in-laws owned a little gas station, and one day Gene Autry came in, on his way to Chicago. He needed $2 worth of gasoline to get him to Chicago, yet he had no money. Two dollars was a lot in those days! He was already known—we knew who he was, anyway. He went on to make so much money, but you know, he *never* did pay us back the two dollars! (Laughs)"

SOURCE:
1. *Western Clippings #27.* January/February 1999. p. 6.

"The Double Switch"

ORIGINAL AIRDATE: August 27, 1950

Executive Producer	Armand Schaefer
Associate Producer	Louis Gray
Director	Frank McDonald
Teleplay	Earle Snell
Director of Photography	William Bradford
Film Editor	Jodie Copelan

Musical Director ....Carl Cotner
Musical Score..............................Walter Greene
Assistant Director.........................Rex Bailey

SONG: "When the Bloom is On the Sage" (music and lyrics by Fred Howard, Nat Vincent)—sung by Gene Autry.

CAST:

Actor	Character
Gene Autry	Gene Autry
Pat Buttram	Pat Buttram
Alan Hale Jr.	The Bandit, Ben
Steve Darrell	Henry Harlow
Sam Flint	Chairman Clem Hughes
Tom London	The Sheriff
Gregg Barton	The Stranger
Bob Woodward	Stage Driver
Frankie Marvin	Doctor
Boyd Stockman	Wagon Driver
Champion	Champion

FILMING DATES: May 10-18, 1950 (Companion episodes "Gold Dust Charlie" and "The Doodle Bug".)
LOCATION: Pioneertown

THE FILM: Gene and Pat unmask an unexpected bandit leader when they investigate a series of stagecoach robberies.

"Blackwater Valley Feud"

ORIGINAL AIRDATE: September 3, 1950

Executive Producer ....Armand Schaefer
Producer ....Louis Gray
Director ....George Archainbaud
Teleplay.......................................Paul Gangelin
Director of Photography ....William Bradford
Film Editor..................................Sherman Rose
Musical Director ....Carl Cotner
Musical Supervisor ....Irving Friedman
Musical Score..............................Walter Greene
Assistant Director.........................Nate Barragar

SONG: "That's My Home" (music and lyrics by Sid Robin)—sung by Gene Autry.

CAST:

Actor	Character
Gene Autry	Gene Autry
Pat Buttram	Pat Buttram
Gail Davis	Lila Carson
Stanley Andrews	Carl Meecham
Francis McDonald	Tim Carson
Harry Lauter	Hank Bevins
William Haade	Jody Bowers

Jack Ingram	Sheriff
Art Dillard	Street Brawler with Pat
Bob Woodward	Street Brawler with Gene
Champion	Champion

FILMING DATES: July 31, 1950 to August 11, 1950 (Companion episodes "The Posse", "The Devil's Brand" and "Doublecross Valley".)
LOCATION: Pioneertown

THE FILM: Action packed episode in which a feud over a right of way escalates into murder, putting the blame on ranch foreman Gene Autry's boss.

"Doublecross Valley"

ORIGINAL AIRDATE: September 10, 1950

Executive Producer ....Armand Schaefer
Producer ....Louis Gray
Director ....George Archainbaud
Teleplay.......................................J. Benton Cheney
Director of Photography ....William Bradford
Film Editor..................................Jodie Copelan
Musical Director ....Carl Cotner
Musical Supervisor ....Irving Friedman
Musical Score..............................Walter Greene
Assistant Director.........................Nate Barragar

SONG: "Texans Never Cry" (music and lyrics by Gene Autry, Shotgun Britton, Hank Fort, Oakley Haldeman)—sung by Gene Autry.

CAST:

Actor	Character
Gene Autry	Gene Autry
Pat Buttram	Pat Buttram
Gail Davis	Susan Watson
Harry Lauter	Warren Kent
Stanley Andrews	Big Jim Watson
William Haade	Calico
Michael Ragan	Brent
Francis McDonald	Jason
Wade Crosby	Idaho
Jack Ingram	Jud Parker
Art Dillard	Raider
Bob Woodward	Shot Rancher
Boyd Stockman	Ranch Hand
Frankie Marvin	Henchman
Ray Jones, Herman Hack	Extras
Champion	Champion

FILMING DATES: July 31, 1950 to August 11, 1950 (Companion episodes "The Posse", "The Devil's Brand" and "Blackwater Valley Feud".)
LOCATION: Pioneertown

THE FILM: After the Civil War a renegade band of Quantrill's Raiders hide a cache of gold, only to be retrieved years later. Now the hidden gold is located on the ranch of a friend of Sheriff Gene Autry.

NOTES AND COMMENTS: In this episode, Gene spanks leading lady Gail Davis.

"The Posse"

ORIGINAL AIRDATE: September 17, 1950

Executive Producer ....Armand Schaefer
Producer ....Louis Gray
Director ....George Archainbaud
Teleplay......................................Betty Burbridge
Director of Photography ....William Bradford
Film Editor ....Jodie Copelan
Musical Director ....Carl Cotner
Musical Supervisor ....Irving Friedman
Musical Score..............................Walter Greene
Assistant Director........................Nate Barragar

SONG: "Pretty Mary" (music and lyrics by Gene Autry, Oakley Haldeman, Jim MacDonald, Bob Mitchell)—sung by Gene Autry.

CAST:

Actor	Character
Gene Autry	Gene Autry
Pat Buttram	Pat Buttram
Wendy Waldron	Mary Daro
Francis Ford	"Whopper" Daro
John Doucette	Ace Bolton
Bob Wilke	Charlie Bolton
Bud Osborne	The Sheriff
John Cason	Pete Bolton
Wes Hudman	Banker
Art Dillard	Posse Member
Bob Woodward	Ranch Hand
Frankie Marvin	Ranch Hand/Fiddler
Champion	Champion

FILMING DATES: July 31, 1950 to August 11, 1950 (Companion episodes "The Devil's Brand", "Blackwater Valley Feud" and "Doublecross Valley".)
LOCATION: Pioneertown

THE FILM: A rather tame episode in which rancher Gene helps a friend blamed for being an accessory to a bank robbery.

"The Devil's Brand"

ORIGINAL AIRDATE: September 24, 1950

Executive Producer ....Armand Schaefer
Producer ....Louis Gray
Director ....George Archainbaud
Teleplay......................................Elizabeth Beecher
Director of Photography ....William Bradford
Film Editor ....Sherman Rose
Musical Director ....Carl Cotner
Musical Supervisor ....Irving Friedman
Musical Score..............................Walter Greene
Assistant Director........................Nate Barragar

SONG: "Along the Navajo Trail" (music and lyrics by Dick Charles, Eddie DeLange, Larry Marks)—sung by Gene Autry.

CAST:

Actor	Character
Gene Autry	Gene Autry
Pat Buttram	Pat Buttram
Gail Davis	Nina Clagett
Wendy Waldron	Deborah Randall
John Doucette	Ward Clagett
Francis Ford	Jed Nolan
Bob Wilke	Monty Drake
Bob Cason	Spud Hicks
Wes Hudman	Henchman Hank
Bud Osborne	Sheriff
Bob Woodward	Tom Randall
George Lloyd	Clem Doyle
Champion	Champion

FILMING DATES: July 31, 1950 to August 11, 1950 (Companion episodes "The Posse", "Blackwater Valley Feud" and "Doublecross Valley".)
LOCATION: Pioneertown

THE FILM: Ranch foreman Gene Autry leads a manhunt for the killer of his employer. Gene sends for the owner's niece and heir, but outlaws have plans of their own to substitute the outlaw leader's sister for the niece.

NOTES AND COMMENTS: Pat refers to Gene as "Mr. Artery" as he often did on Gene's "Melody Ranch" radio show.

"Six Shooter Sweepstakes"

ORIGINAL AIRDATE: October 1, 1950

Executive Producer ....Armand Schaefer
Producer ....Louis Gray
Director ....Frank McDonald

Teleplay	Norman S. Hall
Director of Photography	William Bradford
Film Editor	Sherman Rose
Musical Director	Carl Cotner
Musical Supervisor	Irving Friedman
Musical Score	Walter Greene
Assistant Director	Rex Bailey

SONGS: "There's a Rainbow On the Rio Colorado" (music and lyrics by Gene Autry, Fred Rose)—sung by Gene Autry; "Back in the Saddle Again" (music and lyrics by Gene Autry, Ray Whitley)—two lines acapella sung by Jamel Frazier.

CAST:

Actor	Character
Gene Autry	Gene Autry
Pat Buttram	Hap Wallace
Virginia Herrick	Caroline Ewing
Harry Harvey	Sheriff Ewing
Kenne Duncan	Chuck Evans
Jamel Frazier	Corky
Tom Neal	Greasy
Zon Murray	Rocky Bowman
Wes Hudman	Doc Peters
Frankie Marvin	Slim
Art Dillard	Art
Buddy Roosevelt, Lou Morphy, Cliff Downing	Extras
Champion	Champion

FILMING DATES: August 14-19, 1950 (Companion episode "The Lost Chance".)
LOCATION: Pioneertown

THE FILM: When Pat loses Champion in a fixed horse race, Champ helps Gene track down the outlaws.

NOTES AND COMMENTS: This is a loose remake of the first film in which Gene appeared, "In Old Santa Fe" with Ken Maynard.
Virginia Herrick: "Gene's singing to me and I was thinking…I don't like his voice. 'Cause I was studying opera. To me he was kinda twangy…but it fit the role."[1]

SOURCE:
1. Magers–Fitzgerald. *Ladies of the Western.* McFarland, 2002. p. 86.

"The Poisoned Waterhole"

ORIGINAL AIRDATE: October 8, 1950

Executive Producer	Armand Schaefer
Producer	Louis Gray
Director	Frank McDonald

Teleplay	Polly James
Director of Photography	William Bradford
Film Editor	Jodie Copelan
Musical Director	Carl Cotner
Musical Supervisor	Irving Friedman
Musical Score	Walter Greene
Assistant Director	Rex Bailey

SONG: "Mellow Mountain Moon" (music and lyrics by Fred Howard, Nat Vincent)—sung by Gene Autry.

CAST:

Actor	Character
Gene Autry	Gene Autry
Pat Buttram	Pat Buttram
Sheila Ryan	Kate Judd
Bill Henry	Paul Judd
Chief Thunder Cloud	Chief Tejon
Leonard Penn	Ben Craig
Don C. Harvey	Reese
Tom London	Sheriff Baines
Frankie Marvin	Al
Wes Hudman	Deputy McDonald
Ray Jones, Frank Urten, Cliff Downing	Extras
Champion	Champion

FILMING DATES: August 20-25, 1950 (Companion episode "The Black Rider".)
LOCATION: Pioneertown

THE FILM: Gene discovers a poisoned waterhole belonging to an Indian friend. Attempting to find the culprit, Gene runs into badmen trying to seize a rich silver lode on Indian land.

"The Lost Chance"

ORIGINAL AIRDATE: October 15, 1950

Executive Producer	Armand Schaefer
Producer	Louis Gray
Director	Frank McDonald
Teleplay	Paul Gangelin
Director of Photography	William Bradford
Film Editor	Sherman Rose
Musical Director	Carl Cotner
Musical Supervisor	Irving Friedman
Musical Score	Walter Greene
Assistant Director	Rex Bailey

SONG: "Goodbye to Old Mexico" (music and lyrics by Dwight Butcher)—sung by Gene Autry.

CAST:

Actor	Character
Gene Autry	Gene Autry
Pat Buttram	Pat Buttram
Don Pietro	Pepito Garcia
Harry Harvey	Sheriff Mac Innis
Tom Neal	Buck
Kenne Duncan	Del Andrews
Zon Murray	Bo Hanlon
Wes Hudman	Art Daley
John Cason	Brawler
Frankie Marvin	Al
Art Dillard	Deputy
Buddy Roosevelt	Extra
Lou Morphy, George Steele	Henchmen
Champion	Champion

FILMING DATES: August 14-19, 1950 (Companion episode "Six Shooter Sweepstakes".)
LOCATION: Pioneertown

THE FILM: Gene helps a Mexican boy learn you can't get something for nothing when the boy is kidnapped by outlaws who believe he knows the location of a legendary gold mine.

"The Black Rider"

ORIGINAL AIRDATE: October 22, 1950

Executive Producer	Armand Schaefer
Producer	Louis Gray
Director	Frank McDonald
Teleplay	Elizabeth Beecher
Director of Photography	William Bradford
Film Editor	Jodie Copelan
Musical Director	Carl Cotner
Musical Supervisor	Irving Friedman
Musical Score	Walter Greene
Assistant Director	Rex Bailey

SONG: "When It's Night Time in Nevada" (music and lyrics by Will Dulmage, E. O'Reilly Clint, Richard Pascoe)—sung by Gene Autry.

CAST:

Actor	Character
Gene Autry	Gene Autry
Pat Buttram	Pat Buttram
Sheila Ryan	Sheila Dexter
Bill Henry	Doc Westover
Leonard Penn	Jeff Barker
Tom London	Sheriff Zeb Lorry
Don C. Harvey	Sim Conlon
Wes Hudman	Hardin
Ray Jones, Cliff Downing	Extras

Lou Morphy	Townsman
Frank Urten	Tom Harris
Champion	Champion

FILMING DATES: August 20-25, 1950. (Companion episode "The Poisoned Waterhole".)
LOCATION: Pioneertown.

THE FILM: Ex-Ranger Gene Autry tangles with the mysterious Black Rider who plans revenge on everyone connected with the execution of a captured killer.

NOTES AND COMMENTS: Pat calls Gene "Mr. Artery" as he frequently did on Gene's "Melody Ranch" radio show.

"Gunpowder Range"

ORIGINAL AIRDATE: October 29, 1950

Executive Producer	Armand Schaefer
Producer	Louis Gray
Director	George Archainbaud
Teleplay	Kenneth Perkins
Director of Photography	William Bradford
Film Editor	Sherman Rose
Musical Director	Carl Cotner
Musical Supervisor	Irving Friedman
Musical Score	Walter Greene
Assistant Director	Nate Barragar

SONG: "Cool Water" (music and lyrics by Bob Nolan)—sung by Gene Autry.

CAST:

Actor	Character
Gene Autry	Gene Autry
Pat Buttram	Pat Buttram
Gail Davis	Milly Parker
Dick Jones	Tim Parker
George J. Lewis	Bill Chapote
Lee Phelps	Deputy
Kenneth MacDonald	Sheriff Jack Jud
Dick Alexander	Dog-Iron Ned
Chuck Roberson	Wingo, Express Bandit
Wes Hudman	Two Spot, Express Bandit
Frank Matts	Breed, Express Bandit
Hal K. Dawson	Skeeter Martin
Frankie Marvin	Bill
??	Buck
Bob Woodward	Man in café with Button/also Indian
Art Dillard	Man in café
Victor Cox, Whitey Hughes	Extras
Champion	Champion

FILMING DATES: August 28 to September 8, 1950 (Companion episodes "Twisted Trails", "The Breakup" and "The Fight at Peaceful Mesa".)
LOCATION: Pioneertown

THE FILM: Gene and Pat risk disgrace and death in a desperate attempt to convince a boy there is nothing heroic about riding an outlaw's long trail.

"The Breakup"

ORIGINAL AIRDATE: November 5, 1950

Executive Producer ....Armand Schaefer
Producer ....Louis Gray
Director ....George Archainbaud
Teleplay.......................................Sherman Lowe
Director of Photography ....William Bradford
Film Editor ....Jodie Copelan
Musical Director ....Carl Cotner
Musical Supervisor ....Irving Friedman
Musical Score.............................Walter Greene
Assistant Director........................Nate Barragar

SONGS: "Painted Desert" (music and lyrics by Gene Autry, Ray Whitley)—sung by Gene Autry; "Broomstick Buckaroo" (music and lyrics by Gene Autry, Johnny Marvin, Frank Harford)—sung by Gene Autry.

CAST:

Actor	Character
Gene Autry	Gene Autry
Pat Buttram	Pat Buttram
Lynne Roberts	Susan Elwood
Alan Hale Jr.	Mort Craig
Jim Bannon	Slim
Rand Brooks	Jeff Elwood
Paul Campbell	Cactus
Ed Dearing	Sheriff
Stan Jolley	Ed Jackson
Wes Hudman	Charlie Tupper
??	Walt Darrington
Bob Woodward	Dr. J. M. Tripp
Art Dillard	Cowboy
Beatrice Gray	Neighbor Lady
Champion	Champion

FILMING DATES: August 28 to September 8, 1950 (Companion episodes "Gunpowder Range", "Twisted Trails" and "The Fight at Peaceful Mesa".)
LOCATION: Pioneertown

THE FILM: Helping a wounded rancher, Gene and Pat learn the man's son-in-law is suspected of the shooting. Investigating, they learn outlaws are trying to take possession of the wounded man's ranch.

"Twisted Trails"

ORIGINAL AIRDATE: November 12, 1950

Executive Producer ....Armand Schaefer
Producer ....Louis Gray
Director ....George Archainbaud
Teleplay.......................................Dwight Cummins
Director of Photography ....William Bradford
Film Editor ....Jodie Copelan
Musical Director ....Carl Cotner
Musical Supervisor ....Irving Friedman
Musical Score.............................Walter Greene
Assistant Director........................Nate Barragar

SONGS: "Room Full of Roses" (music and lyrics by Tim Spencer)—sung by Gene Autry; "Back In the Saddle Again" (music and lyrics by Gene Autry, Ray Whitley)—sung by Gene Autry.

CAST:

Actor	Character
Gene Autry	Gene Autry
Pat Buttram	Pat Buttram
Lynne Roberts	Felicia Summers
Alan Hale Jr.	Bill Watterson
Jim Bannon	Jim Baker
Rand Brooks	Deputy
Billy Gray	Eddie Baker
Ed Dearing	Sheriff Wade Clark
Paul Campbell	Andy McBride
Stan Jolley	Brad Owens
Carl Sepulveda	How Do
??	Mary
Wes Hudman	Louie
Art Dillard	Posse Member
Champion	Champion

FILMING DATES: August 28 to September 8, 1950 (Companion episodes "Gunpowder Range", "The Fight at Peaceful Mesa" and "The Breakup".)
LOCATION: Pioneertown

THE FILM: Rancher Gene Autry helps a 13 year old Eastern boy who has traveled west in search of his father, not knowing his father is an outlaw.

"The Fight at Peaceful Mesa"

ORIGINAL AIRDATE: November 19, 1950

Executive Producer ....Armand Schaefer
Producer ....Louis Gray
Director ....George Archainbaud
Teleplay.......................................Paul Gangelin
Director of Photography ....William Bradford

Film Editor ....Sherman Rose
Musical Director ....Carl Cotner
Musical Supervisor ....Irving Friedman
Musical Score..............................Walter Greene
Assistant Director........................Nate Barragar

SONGS: "Be Honest With Me" (music and lyrics by Gene Autry, Fred Rose)—sung by Gene Autry; "I'm Beginning to Care" (music and lyrics by Gene Autry, Johnny Marvin, Fred Rose)—sung by Gene Autry.

CAST:

Actor	Character
Gene Autry ....Gene Autry
Pat Buttram ....Pat Buttram
Gail Davis ....Anne Lawton
George J. Lewis...........................Jeff Forbes
Chuck Roberson..........................Tucson
Kenneth MacDonald ....Tom Lawton
Lee Phelps..................................City Marshal
Dick Alexander ....Dick
Wes Hudman...............................Pete
Frank Matts ....Barker
Champion....................................Champion

FILMING DATES: August 28 to September 8, 1950 (Companion episodes "Gunpowder Range", "Twisted Trails" and "The Breakup".)
LOCATION: Pioneertown

THE FILM: Texas Rangers Gene and Pat find an old friend killed by a masked gang. Attempting to carry out the man's oral will, the Rangers find themselves involved with a gang trying to take over the man's ranch.

"Hot Lead"

ORIGINAL AIRDATE: November 26, 1950

Executive Producer ....Armand Schaefer
Producer ....Louis Gray
Director ....George Archainbaud
Teleplay.......................................Dwight Cummins
Director of Photography ....William Bradford
Film Editor ....Jodie Copelan
Musical Director ....Carl Cotner
Musical Supervisor ....Irving Friedman
Musical Score..............................Walter Greene
Assistant Director........................Nate Barragar

SONGS: "Strawberry Roan" (music and lyrics by Curley Fletcher, Nat Vincent, Fred Howard)—sung by Gene Autry; "Good Old-Fashioned Hoedown" (music and lyrics by Gene Autry)—sung by Gene Autry.

CAST:

Actor	Character
Gene Autry ....Gene Autry
Alan Hale Jr................................Tiny Jensen
Harry Cheshire ....Bert Hodge
Harry Lauter...............................Sam Blake
Don C. Harvey ....Nat Ellis
Jim Frasher.................................Jeff Ellis
Marshall Reed ....Ed Dolan
Kenne Duncan............................Banker
Champion....................................Champion

FILMING DATES: September 18-23, 1950 (Companion episode "The Killer Horse".)
LOCATION: Pioneertown

THE FILM: When Gene befriends a young boy and a mistreated horse, his kindness is repaid in an unexpected way while on the trail of some bank robbers.

NOTES AND COMMENTS: Working title of this episode was "Fury".

"The Gray Dude"

ORIGINAL AIRDATE: December 3, 1950

Executive Producer ....Armand Schaefer
Producer ....Louis Gray
Director ....Frank McDonald
Teleplay.......................................Elizabeth Beecher
Director of Photography ....William Bradford
Film Editor ....Sherman Rose
Musical Director ....Carl Cotner
Musical Supervisor ....Irving Friedman
Musical Score..............................Walter Greene
Assistant Director........................Rex Bailey

SONG: "Red River Valley" (Traditional)—sung by Gene Autry.

CAST:

Actor	Character
Gene Autry ....Gene Autry
Chill Wills ....Chill Wills
James Griffith..............................Dude Devlin (Gray Dude)
Robert Filmer ....Sheriff Davis
Reed Howes ....Huck
Tom Monroe................................Slip
Kermit Maynard..........................Biff
Sam Flint....................................Townsman
Frank Urten ....Sheriff Tom Becker
Boyd Stockman...........................Deputy
Herman Hack, Cactus Mack, Lou Morphy, Cliff Downing ....Extras
Champion....................................Champion

FILMING DATES: September 11-16, 1950 (Companion episode "The Peacemaker".)
LOCATION: Pioneertown

THE FILM: U.S. Marshal Gene Autry and Sheriff's Deputy Chill Wills set out to capture The Gray Dude, the killer of Gene's friend, only to discover the Sheriff is in cahoots with the outlaw.

"The Killer Horse"

ORIGINAL AIRDATE: December 10, 1950

Executive Producer ....Armand Schaefer
Producer ....Louis Gray
Director ....George Archainbaud
Teleplay...Kenneth Perkins
Director of Photography ....William Bradford
Film Editor ....Sherman Rose
Musical Director ....Carl Cotner
Musical Supervisor ....Irving Friedman
Musical Score...............................Walter Greene
Assistant Director........................Nate Barragar

SONG: "Let Me Ride Down in Rocky Canyon" (music and lyrics by Gene Autry, Fred Rose, Ray Whitley)—sung by Gene Autry.

CAST:

Actor	*Character*
Gene Autry	Gene Autry
Alan Hale Jr.	Tiny
Harry Cheshire	Mike Hooper
William Kimbley	Chuck Jones
Harry Lauter	Uvade
Don C. Harvey	Scoop
Kenne Duncan	Sheriff Tub Mohan
Hal K. Dawson	Blowfly Jones
Marshall Reed	Stray Man
??	Young Girl
Jim Frasher	Fighting Boy
Boyd Stockman	Townsman in Checkered Shirt
Frankie Marvin	Deputy
Bob Woodward	Posse Member
Art Dillard, Cactus Mack, Tex Cooper	Extras
Champion	Champion

FILMING DATES: September 18-23, 1950 (Companion episode "Hot Lead".)
LOCATION: Pioneertown

THE FILM: Gene protects a young boy's wild horse accused of killing an old prospector. Evidence indicates the horse is at fault, but Gene sets out to find the real killer.

"The Peacemaker"

ORIGINAL AIRDATE: December 17, 1950

Executive Producer ....Armand Schaefer
Producer ....Louis Gray
Director ....Frank McDonald
Teleplay...Paul Gangelin
Director of Photography ....William Bradford
Film Editor ....Jodie Copelan
Musical Director ....Carl Cotner
Musical Supervisor ....Irving Friedman
Musical Score...............................Walter Greene
Assistant Director........................Rex Bailey

SONGS: "A Heart as Big as Texas" (music and lyrics by Oakley Haldeman, Buddy Feyne)—sung by Gene Autry; "Let Me Cry On Your Shoulder" (music and lyrics by June Hershey, Don Swander)—sung by Gene Autry.

CAST:

Actor	*Character*
Gene Autry	Gene Autry
Chill Wills	Chill Wills
Russ Hayden	Dave Anders
Peggy Stewart	Ellie March
James Griffith	Bill Hubbard
Robert Filmer	Bert Monaghan
Reed Howes	Orcutt
Sam Flint	George Hubbard
Tom Monroe	Tom
Kermit Maynard	Mike
Gary Goodwin	Ellie's Brother
Bob Woodward	Jim Hogan
Art Dillard	Henchman Johnny
Herman Hack, George Steele	Extras
John Kee	Well Driller Johnny
Champion	Champion

FILMING DATES: September 11-16, 1950 (Companion episode "The Gray Dude".)
LOCATION: Pioneertown

THE FILM: U. S. Deputy Marshal Gene Autry helps rainmaker Chill Wills and the honest ranchers to drive out land swindlers.

NOTES AND COMMENTS: Pat Buttram nearly died when a supposed rainmaker's cannon blew up, ripping open Pat's chest and stomach. It was about 6pm at Pioneertown during the filming of the TV episode "The Peacemaker" (originally titled "Scorched Earth"). The prop man, George McKinnon, had picked up a brass antique cannon—about 3 ft. long on wooden wheels. There was no licensed powder man, so McKinnon rigged it with a small pan of flash powder at the bottom (rather than taping it to the lip of the cannon), then covered the wire with dirt so it wouldn't show as it led

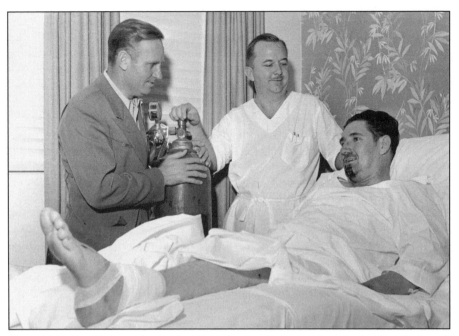

Gene visits Pat Buttram in the hospital following Pat's accident during the filming of "The Peacemaker" TV episode.

behind a rock where he was to set off the charge. When Pat pulled the string trigger, McKinnon tripped his wire and the powder inside the cannon literally exploded like a bomb, throwing shrapnel all over the area. Pat was less than three feet away. One large piece hit Pat in the chest, another in the jaw and a large chunk cut through his left boot, severing an artery. Shrapnel whizzed past Gene's head but Champion was nicked above one eye. One wrangler had his knee broken and a sound man was hit. Pat's entire chest was cut open and he was losing blood quickly in his boot. Loading Pat in a pickup truck, they rushed down the hill to Gene's airplane. Gene's pilot, Herb Green, flew to Twenty-Nine Palms for the doctor. Herb would be flying at night so Gene and the rest phoned ahead as there were no lights on the tiny airport's runway. The telephone operator called all over town and people jumped in their cars and drove to the airfield, turning on their lights, allowing Green to land the plane. As soon as Dr. Bill Ince (son of movie pioneer Thomas Ince, who'd produced William S. Hart westerns) was flown back from Twenty-Nine Palms, he began to work on Pat, immediately putting a clamp on the severed artery and picking shrapnel and dirt from Pat's open chest wound, all while Pat was conscious. Before an ambulance arrived, Green made two more hurried flights—one to bring plasma and another to fly in a second doctor from L.A. to assist Ince. Pat was laid up for nine months. Sheila Ryan, whom he'd been dating, moved to Twenty-Nine Palms to be near him. When he was on his feet again they were married.

Peggy Stewart recalls, "George McKinnon, the prop man, felt terrible. He had loaded the cannon. But when the cannon went off, it exploded. A little piece of lead flew past me and scraped my horse's shoulder, but a big piece hit Pat right in the chest. It also hit and hurt his horse. Man, Gene was right there. Herb Green, Gene's pilot…they had that plane and Pat on the plane down to the hospital in nothing flat. It was touch and go…a lot of people giving blood and happy to do it. Gene was so concerned. He'd call every two seconds to see how Pat was doing. His thoughts were there with Pat even though he was distracted…they picked up shooting the next day. Pat was in intensive care for several days. Gene loved Buttram. He liked Pat around, even in his personal life. Gene checked on Pat every single day. He was very loyal. The crew and wranglers loved him. That was kinda the criteria of everything, when that crew accepted you. Chill Wills called Gene and said I'll finish up for Buttram for free. Whether he really did it for free or not I don't know, but he came in to finish the show."[1]

Myron Healey said, "After Pat Buttram's accident at Pioneertown, when the cannon exploded and laid him open from his rib cage on down, Gene came into the hospital a few days later and said, 'Patrick, you whip this thing completely and you got a job for the rest of your life.' That was *beautiful* for a man to go in and say. And he meant it."[2]

House Peters Jr.: "No question about it, what Gene did for Pat Buttram when that cannon blew up in Pat's tummy saved his life. Gene sent his own plane and private pilot to Hollywood for blood. It was very late when he got back to Twenty-Nine Palms where Pat was hospitalized. They called ahead on the phone to put it on the radio to have people come down and keep their headlights on the runway so he could bring that plane in."[3]

Chill Wills replaced Buttram on two episodes, Alan Hale Jr. did two and Fuzzy Knight came in for four.

SOURCES:

1. Interview with author. January 2006.
2. Interview with author. 1998.
3. Interview with author. 1998.

"The Sheriff of Santa Rosa"

ORIGINAL AIRDATE: December 24, 1950

Executive Producer	Armand Schaefer
Producer	Louis Gray
Director	George Archainbaud
Teleplay	Polly James

Director of Photography ....William Bradford
Film Editor ....Jodie Copelan
Musical Director ....Carl Cotner
Musical Supervisor ....Irving Friedman
Musical Score..............................Walter Greene
Assistant Director........................Nate Barragar

SONGS: "Marcheta" (music and lyrics by Victor Schertzinger)—sung by Gene Autry; "Tweedle-O-Twill" (music and lyrics by Gene Autry, Fred Rose)—sung by Gene Autry.

CAST:

Actor	Character
Gene Autry	Gene Autry
Fuzzy Knight	Sagebrush
Dick Jones	Ted Doyle
Nan Leslie	Libby Blair
Stanley Andrews	Sam Blair
Mira McKinney	Mrs. Marquita Doyle
Dick Curtis	Hutch Logan
Chuck Roberson	Mr. Kenmore
James Harrison	Bill
Al Wyatt	Stan
Boyd Stockman	Mike
Art Dillard	Cowboy
Champion	Champion

FILMING DATES: November 7-12, 1950 (Companion episode "T.N.T.")
LOCATION: Pioneertown

THE FILM: Sheriff Gene Autry lets a young ranch owner, suspected of horse stealing, escape from jail in hopes he'll lead Gene to the rustler gang.

NOTES AND COMMENTS: *Nan Leslie:* "Gene was in charge in a very different way on his series. He's a very affable man, easygoing. If he was a perfectionist, and I think he was, it was not so apparent. He was very much a friend to people on the set. 'The Gene Autry Show' was fun to do. I remember I was in a jail cell in one of the episodes and he had to sing to me. That seems ordinary enough, but it suddenly struck me as funny—this cowboy serenading me through the bars of my jail cell with a pretty mournful tune. (Laughs) I suddenly found myself on the edge of breaking up completely. I tried to contain myself as I took in the surrounding atmosphere: Gene in his fancy cowboy outfit, I in my old-fashioned dress, the crew looking on earnestly as the camera rolled. I thought to myself, 'Gosh, is this for real?' Then another part of me said, 'No, of course it's not real, so keep your face straight.' (Laughs) It's very difficult to know what to do or what to look at while a singing cowboy is serenading you. I always felt superfluous when I found myself in that situation. But you're really not or you wouldn't be there. You want to react but you don't want to react too much. It *is* a dilemma. You cannot look enthralled or too romantic because it's a western, after all, and that's forbidden after a certain point. When a love song is being sung to you and you have close-ups, it's kind of difficult to maintain your composure and look as if you deserve all the nice things he's saying in song but not look too haughty about it. (Laughs) The bottom line is that it's just to be gotten through without breaking up! (Laughs)[1]

SOURCE:
1. *Westerns Women.* p. 138.

"T.N.T."

ORIGINAL AIRDATE: December 31, 1950

Executive Producer ....Armand Schaefer
Producer ....Louis Gray
Director ....George Archainbaud
Teleplay..Dwight Cummins
Director of Photography ....William Bradford
Film Editor ....Sherman Rose
Musical Director ....Carl Cotner
Musical Supervisor ....Irving Friedman
Musical Score..............................Walter Greene
Assistant Director........................Nate Barragar

SONGS: "She'll Be Comin' 'Round the Mountain" (partial) (Traditional)/"Tears On My Pillow" (music and lyrics by Gene Autry, Fred Rose)—sung by Gene Autry.

CAST:

Actor	Character
Gene Autry	Gene Autry
Fuzzy Knight	Sagebrush
Eilene Janssen	Theodora Natalie Towne (T.N.T.)
Stanley Andrews	Colonel Thaddeus Towne
Dick Curtis	Ed Simms
Chuck Roberson	Seth Weaver
James Harrison	Sheriff Downey
??	Jockey
Champion	Champion

FILMING DATES: November 7-12, 1950 (Companion episode "The Sheriff of Santa Rosa".)
LOCATION: Pioneertown

THE FILM: Rancher Gene Autry lands in explosive trouble when he befriends an apparently homeless little girl and is then accused of kidnapping by his neighboring rancher who wants Gene's property.

358

Gene and young Eilene Janssen in-between filming of scenes for "T.N.T." episode.

"The Raiders"
(In Kodachrome Color)

ORIGINAL AIRDATE: April 14, 1951

Executive Producer ....Armand Schaefer
Producer ....Louis Gray
Director ....John English
Teleplay......................................Betty Burbridge
Director of Photography ....William Bradford
Film Editor.................................Richard G. Wray
Musical Director ....Carl Cotner
Musical Supervisor ....Irving Friedman
Musical Score.............................Walter Greene
Assistant Director........................Stanley Neufeld

SONG: "The Angel Song" (music and lyrics by Gene Autry, Curt Massey, Mary Millard)—sung by Gene Autry.

CAST:

Actor	*Character*
Gene Autry ....Gene Autry
Fuzzy Knight...............................Sagebrush
Nan Leslie ....Faith Harding
Raymond Hatton ....Zeke Hawkins
George Cooper ...."Buckeye" Jack Hawes
Bill Kennedy ....Sheriff Dan Burke
Gregg Barton..............................Tom Watson
Reed Howes ....Spade
Michael Ragan ....Monte

Wes Hudman ....Jim
Jack Ingram.................................Deputy Sam
Boyd Stockman ....Stage Driver
Bob Woodward ....Wagon Driver
Art Dillard..................................Henchman
Champion....................................Champion

FILMING DATES: November 13-18, 1950 (Companion episode "Double Barreled Vengeance".)
LOCATION: Pioneertown

THE FILM: Rancher Gene Autry traps a notorious outlaw who has stolen the payroll from a construction company, fooling his own fiancé into helping him.

NOTES AND COMMENTS: "The Raiders" and "Double Barreled Vengeance" were two episodes loosely connected to Gene's first season episodes, but not shown until four months later (on two Saturday nights in April '51), technically as color "tests". The color episodes were seen during the special color broadcasting periods which CBS established in conformity with the Federal Communications Commission decision authorizing color television service beginning Nov. 20, 1950. Both of the color episodes offered a slightly different opening from the standard black and white shows.

"Double Barreled Vengeance"
(In Kodachrome Color)

ORIGINAL AIRDATE: April 21, 1951

Executive Producer ....Armand Schaefer
Producer ....Louis Gray
Director ....John English
Teleplay......................................Sue Dwiggens, Vy
                                                        Russell
Director of Photography ....William Bradford
Film Editor.................................Jodie Copelan
Musical Director ....Carl Cotner
Musical Supervisor ....Irving Friedman
Musical Score.............................Walter Greene
Assistant Director........................Stanley Neufeld

SONG: "I Wish I Had Never Met Sunshine" (music and lyrics by Gene Autry, Oakley Haldeman, Dale Evans)—sung by Gene Autry.

CAST:

Actor	*Character*
Gene Autry ....Gene Autry
Fuzzy Knight...............................Sagebrush
Nan Leslie ....Yvette Wilson
Raymond Hatton ....Slinger
Bill Kennedy ....Sheriff Tom Lash
Gregg Barton..............................Gus

Jack Ingram.................................Joe
Mike Ragan................................Dusty
Boyd Stockman...........................Stage Driver
Champion...................................Champion

FILMING DATES: November 13-18, 1950 (Companion episode "The Raiders".)

LOCATION: Pioneertown

THE FILM: As a special investigator for the express company, Gene has to turn outlaw to find money stolen 10 years ago.

The Gene Autry Show
2nd season, 26 episodes (10/7/51-3/30/52). 30 minutes each.
Aired on CBS network on Sunday from 7-7:30pm EST
(West Coast broadcasts were a day earlier on Saturday from October through December 1951 and on Fridays from January through February 1952.) All dates given are Sunday CBS airdates.

"Ghost Town Raiders"

ORIGINAL AIRDATE: October 7, 1951

Executive Producer ....Armand Schaefer
Producer ....Louis Gray
Director ....Frank McDonald
Teleplay..John K. Butler
Director of Photography ....William Bradford
Film Editor...................................Jodie Copelan
Musical Director ....Carl Cotner
Musical Supervisor ....Irving Friedman
Musical Score...............................Walter Greene
Assistant Director.........................Stanley Neufeld

SONG: "As Long as I Have My Horse" (music and lyrics by Gene Autry, Fred Rose, Johnny Marvin)—sung by Gene Autry.

CAST:

Actor	*Character*
Gene Autry	Gene Autry
Pat Buttram	Pat Buttram
Wendy Waldron	Lita Ormsby
William Fawcett	Crazy Charlie
George J. Lewis	Capitan Morales
Ray Bennett	Duke Travis
Reed Howes	Gunther
Kermit Maynard	Lance Preston
Sam Flint	J. L. Ormsby
Art Dillard	Thorpe
Bob Woodward	Telegraph Operator
Champion	Champion

FILMING DATES: February 26 to March 3, 1951 (Companion episode "Silver Dollars".)
LOCATION: Pioneertown

THE FILM: In an especially exciting episode, special mining agent Gene Autry risks his life to track down bandits who operate from a ghost town. The jigsaw puzzle is how they smuggle the gold across the border.

"Frontier Guard"

ORIGINAL AIRDATE: October 14, 1951

Executive Producer ....Armand Schaefer
Producer ....Louis Gray
Director ....George Archainbaud
Teleplay..Fred Myton
Director of Photography ....William Bradford
Film Editor...................................Richard G. Wray
Musical Director ....Carl Cotner
Musical Supervisor ....Irving Friedman
Musical Score...............................Walter Greene
Assistant Director.........................Nate Barragar

SONG: "Roamin' Around the Range" (music and lyrics by Smiley Burnette)—sung by Gene Autry.

CAST:

Actor	*Character*
Gene Autry	Gene Autry
Pat Buttram	Pat Buttram
Donna Martell	Diana Jamison
James Craven	Steve Kinney
Denver Pyle	Ed Slade
Francis McDonald	Dave Jamison
Gregg Barton	Joe
Riley Hill	Vic Cassidy
Ewing Mitchell	Sheriff
Tom Monroe	Pete
Art Dillard	Art
Boyd Stockman	Stage Driver
Champion	Champion

FILMING DATES: March 5-10, 1951 (Companion episode "Killer's Trail".)
LOCATION: Pioneertown

THE FILM: Border Patrol agent Gene Autry and pal Pat Buttram come to the aid of a rancher and his daughter who are being terrorized. Preventing the kidnapping of the rancher's daughter, Gene finds a land dealer attempting to link two ranches across the border for smuggling purposes.

"Silver Dollars"

ORIGINAL AIRDATE: October 21, 1951

Executive Producer	Armand Schaefer
Producer	Louis Gray
Director	Frank McDonald
Teleplay	Elizabeth Beecher
Director of Photography	William Bradford
Film Editor	Richard G. Wray
Musical Director	Carl Cotner
Musical Supervisor	Irving Friedman
Musical Score	Walter Greene
Assistant Director	Stanley Neufeld

SONG: "I Want to Be Sure" (music and lyrics by Gene Autry, Merle Travis)—sung by Gene Autry.

CAST:

Actor	*Character*
Gene Autry	Gene Autry
Pat Buttram	Pat Buttram
Wendy Waldron	Dorrie Tyler
Louise Lorimer	Mrs. Ada Mitchell
William Fawcett	Sheriff Eben Bailey
Ray Bennett	Nick Hatfield
Kermit Maynard	Chuck
Art Dillard	Mike
Boyd Stockman	Lou Goudy
Reed Howes	Henchman
George J. Lewis	Steve Tyler
Champion	Champion

FILMING DATES: February 26 to March 3, 1951 (Companion episode "Ghost Town Raiders".)
LOCATIONS: Pioneertown; one shot at Melody Ranch

THE FILM: Texas Rangers Gene Autry and Pat Buttram join forces with a sheriff to uncover the murdering outlaws behind a silver dollar counterfeiting ring.

"Killer's Trail"

ORIGINAL AIRDATE: October 28, 1951

Executive Producer	Armand Schaefer
Producer	Louis Gray
Director	George Archainbaud
Teleplay	Oliver Drake
Director of Photography	William Bradford
Film Editor	Jodie Copelan
Musical Director	Carl Cotner
Musical Supervisor	Irving Friedman
Musical Score	Walter Greene
Assistant Director	Nate Barragar

SONG: "Under Fiesta Stars" (music and lyrics by Gene Autry, Fred Rose)—sung by Gene Autry.

CAST:

Actor	*Character*
Gene Autry	Gene Autry
Pat Buttram	Pat Buttram
Donna Martell	Tonia Castelar
James Craven	Wade Morgan
Ewing Mitchell	Sheriff Jim Kent
Riley Hill	Mike
Gregg Barton	Hank
Francis McDonald	Felipe Mendoza
Denver Pyle	Frank Blake
Tom Monroe	Jed
Bob Woodward	Stage Driver/also Pedro
Art Dillard	Sam
Champion	Champion

FILMING DATES: March 5-10, 1951 (Companion episode "Frontier Guard".)
LOCATION: Pioneertown

Bob Woodward (left) not only played small parts on Gene's TV series, but doubled him in stunts as he's about to do here. Note the identical clothing to Gene.

THE FILM: As the Governor's special representatives, Gene and Pat discover the true identity of the outlaw known as El Avengador when they rescue a girl being pursued by three men. A banker and tax assessor are in cahoots to buy up all the area ranches for back taxes laying the blame on El Avengador.

NOTES AND COMMENTS: Oliver Drake's story is a loose remake of Bennett Cohen's original story made first in 1932 at RKO as "Come On, Danger" with Tom Keene. It was remade as "Renegade Ranger" at RKO in '38 with George O'Brien, "Come On, Danger" at RKO in '42 with Tim Holt and "Alias Billy the Kid" with Sunset Carson at Republic in '46.

"Frame For Trouble"

ORIGINAL AIRDATE: November 4, 1951

Executive Producer	Armand Schaefer
Producer	Louis Gray
Director	D. Ross Lederman
Teleplay	Joe Richardson
Director of Photography	William Bradford
Film Editor	Jodie Copelan
Musical Director	Carl Cotner
Musical Supervisor	Irving Friedman
Musical Score	Walter Greene
Assistant Director	Stanley Neufeld

SONG: "Ridin' Down the Canyon" (music and lyrics by Gene Autry, Smiley Burnette)—sung by Gene Autry (duets with phonograph).

CAST:
Actor	Character
Gene Autry	Gene Autry
Pat Buttram	Pat Buttram
Gail Davis	Virginia
Dick Curtis	Sam Taggert
Dennis Moore	Hank
John Halloran	Sheriff Maloney
Don Harvey	Clem
Marshall Reed	Skin
Bob Woodward	Black Jackson
??	Rutledge
Champion	Champion

FILMING DATES: March 26-31, 1951 (Companion episode "Revenge Trail".)
LOCATION: Corriganville

THE FILM: Investigating who and why someone hired a professional killer he's captured, Gene finds himself falsely accused of murder at the gunslinger's secret rendezvous.

"Warning! Danger!"

ORIGINAL AIRDATE: November 11, 1951

Executive Producer	Armand Schaefer
Producer	Louis Gray
Director	George Archainbaud
Teleplay	Dwight Cummins
Director of Photography	William Bradford
Film Editor	Richard G. Wray
Musical Director	Carl Cotner
Musical Supervisor	Irving Friedman
Musical Score	Walter Greene
Assistant Director	Nate Barragar

SONGS: "Down In the Valley" (music and lyrics arranged by Carl Cotner)—sung by Gene Autry; "She'll Be Comin' 'Round the Mountain" (Traditional)—sung by Pat Buttram; "Swing Low, Sweet Chariot" (Traditional)—sung by Gloria Winters and Gene Autry; "Nobody Knows the Trouble I've Seen" (Traditional)—sung by Gene Autry.

CAST:
Actor	Character
Gene Autry	Gene Autry
Pat Buttram	Pat Buttram
Dick Jones	Jerry Miller
Gloria Winters	Sue Miller
Gordon Jones	Mike Halen
Harry Lauter	Rick Carson
Teddy Infuhr	Bobby Miller
Leonard Penn	Hedge Nolan
Bill Kennedy	Vance Evans
Champion	Champion

FILMING DATES: April 2-7, 1951 (Companion episode "Bandits of Boulder Bluff".)
LOCATION: Iverson Ranch

THE FILM: Gene befriends two orphans, the older brother of whom has become involved with a notorious train robber.

NOTES AND COMMENTS: *Teddy Infuhr:* "I remember how nice Gene was to this little 12-year-old kid when I made a *big* mistake during the shooting of one of his TV shows. I'm in a small house and he's coming in the back window. I thought (in the film) he was an outlaw. What I was supposed to do was hit him on the head with a frying pan. What they gave me was a cast iron skillet with about four inches of sponge rubber painted black on the bottom of it, so it wouldn't hurt his head. When he came in I came down as hard as I could but the skillet turned sideways and I hit him right on the head with the side of that iron skillet and knocked him cold. I mean, he was out for about a minute. Everybody went crazy, but as it turned out, he came to, and about a half hour later we did the shot over again and I held it straight. But I know, for sure, he had a bump on the top of his head the rest of his life. I thought I'd never work in that town again! (Laughs) But he didn't get mad, blow up or anything"[1, 2]

Gloria Winters: "Everybody loved him! I am among his many thousands of fans; working with Gene made you even more of a fan. He was creative and an opportunist. What endeared him to me was that one day we were running lines and stopped to chat. I mentioned I had always wanted to be a singer, but never had the opportunity. He said, 'We'll take care of that,' and he rewrote the script of 'Warning! Danger!' I sang a warning to him to the tune of 'Swing Low, Sweet Chariot'. I was singing 'Bad Man Coming after You', something like that. I told him later, 'I owe you that big credit in my life. It made a dream come true.' Gene was a special man, ready to go with new ideas. He listened, mulled things over and was very successful as a result! He was a gentleman from the old school. I also want to pay tribute to his wife, Jackie. She gave him the happiest years of his life. She helped him achieve a lot of his goals. She did a lot for Gene—like helping get the museum going. Monte and Joanne Hale have also been a tremendous asset in both establishing and running the museum. It is first class."[3]

SOURCE:
1. *Western Clippings #27.* January/February 1999. p. 7.
2. Panel discussion at Memphis Film Festival, June 2006.
3. *Western Clippings #27.* January/February 1999. p. 7

"Revenge Trail"

ORIGINAL AIRDATE: November 18, 1951

Executive Producer ....Armand Schaefer
Producer ....Louis Gray
Director ....D. Ross Lederman
Teleplay.......................................Paul Gangelin
Director of Photography ....William Bradford
Film Editor ....Richard G. Wray
Musical Director ....Carl Cotner
Musical Supervisor ....Irving Friedman
Musical Score..............................Walter Greene
Assistant Director........................Stanley Neufeld

SONG: "Silver Spurs On the Golden Stairs" (music and lyrics by Gene Autry, Cindy Walker)—sung by Gene Autry.

CAST:
Actor	Character
Gene Autry	Gene Autry
Pat Buttram	Pat Buttram
Gail Davis	Hester Vance

Dick Curtis	Doc Leary (Johnny MacClain)
Dennis Moore	Ennis
John Halloran	Douglas Vance
Don Harvey	Milo Miller
Marshall Reed	Hod Baker
Boyd Stockman	Stage Driver
Bob Woodward	Henchman
Ray Jones, Art Dillard	Townsmen
??	Lady
Robert O'Byrne	Man in Café
Champion	Champion

FILMING DATES: March 26-31, 1951 (Companion episode "Frame For Trouble".)
LOCATIONS: Corriganville; Pioneertown stock footage

THE FILM: A trail of murders, each marked by a small hangman's noose, leads U.S. Marshal Gene Autry to a rancher, a Marshal and his daughter. Using hypnotism, Pat helps Gene solve the murders.

"The Bandits of Boulder Bluff"

ORIGINAL AIRDATE: November 25, 1951

Executive Producer ....Armand Schaefer
Producer ....Louis Gray
Director ....George Archainbaud
Teleplay.......................................Howard J. Green
Director of Photography ....William Bradford
Film Editor ....Jodie Copelan
Musical Director ....Carl Cotner
Musical Supervisor ....Irving Friedman
Musical Score..............................Walter Greene
Assistant Director........................Nate Barragar

SONG: "'Neath the Blue Montana Skies" (music and lyrics by Gene Autry, Johnny Marvin, Fred Rose)—sung by Gene Autry.

CAST:
Actor	Character
Gene Autry	Gene Autry
Pat Buttram	Pat Buttram
Dick Jones	Tom Colby
Anne O'Neal	Miss Lucy
Gordon Jones	Deputy
Harry Lauter	Ace Judkins
Leonard Penn	Mitch Lawson
Bill Kennedy	Bill
??	George Colby
??	Bearded Henchman
Boyd Stockman	2nd Deputy
Champion	Champion

364

FILMING DATES: April 2-7, 1951 (Companion episode "Warning! Danger!")
LOCATIONS: Iverson Ranch; Pioneertown

THE FILM: Marshal Gene Autry and Sheriff Pat Buttram expose the true murderer in a gold dust robbery after an innocent man is falsely accused.

"Outlaw Escape"

ORIGINAL AIRDATE: December 2, 1951

Executive Producer ....Armand Schaefer
Producer ....Louis Gray
Director ....George Archainbaud
Teleplay ....Earle Snell
Director of Photography ....William Bradford
Film Editor ....Richard G. Wray
Musical Director ....Carl Cotner
Musical Supervisor ....Irving Friedman
Musical Score..............................Walter Greene
Assistant Director........................Nate Barragar

SONG: "Crime Will Never Pay" (music and lyrics by Willard Robison, Jack Pepper)—sung by Gene Autry.

CAST:

Actor	Character
Gene Autry	Gene Autry
Pat Buttram	Pat Buttram
Gail Davis	Polly Glover
James Craven	Brad Bidwell
Ewing Mitchell	Hiram Glover
Ben Weldon	Pete
Robert Peyton	Red Lambert
Myron Healey	Blake
Lee Morgan	Sam Grover
??	Bartender Jim
Sandy Sanders	Brawler #1
??	Brawler #2
Bob Woodward	Henchman
Champion	Champion

FILMING DATES: April 30 to May 5, 1951 (Companion episode "Return of Maverick Dan".)
LOCATION: Pioneertown

THE FILM: As deputy sheriff, Gene Autry helps newly elected Sheriff of Goose Creek Pat Buttram bring a town boss and his highbinders to justice.

NOTES AND COMMENTS: *Myron Healey:* "Ol' Lou Gray, who was producing for Gene, sorta liked me, Harry Lauter…there were 8 or 10 people he really liked that he used quite a bit. It was great because my agent could call Flying A and say 'Myron's available' and they'd say, 'Send him over.' It was just that simple. Gene took care of a lot of guys…just by kindness, by being Gene Autry and having Flying A Productions goin'. Mandy Schaefer and Lou Gray were administrators of the whole thing and kept it going for him. Got to a point where he was able to sit back and let Mandy and Lou do it. When Gene got into baseball, it was more or less the same thing.

"His dedication and loyalty to people about him was fantastic. That's why his company was so solid, reliable and dependable—because the company could depend on Gene." [1]

SOURCE:
1. Interview with author.

"The Kid Comes West"

ORIGINAL AIRDATE: December 9, 1951

Executive Producer ....Armand Schaefer
Producer ....Louis Gray
Director ....George Archainbaud
Teleplay ....Joe Richardson
Director of Photography ....William Bradford
Film Editor ....Jodie Copelan
Musical Director ....Carl Cotner
Musical Supervisor ....Irving Friedman
Musical Score..............................Walter Greene
Assistant Director........................Stanley Neufeld

SONG: "On Top of Old Smoky" (Public Domain)—sung by Gene Autry.

CAST:

Actor	Character
Gene Autry	Gene Autry
Pat Buttram	Pat Buttram
Sherry Jackson	Frankie Scott
William Fawcett	Frank Graham
Steve Pendleton	Paul Greeley
Keith Richards	Duke Ferris
Craig Woods	Hench
Sandy Sanders	Monk
Boyd Stockman	Sam (Stage Driver)
??	Three Ladies
??	Male Party Guest
Champion	Champion

FILMING DATES: May 18-23, 1951 (Companion episode "Rock River Feud".)
LOCATION: Pioneertown

THE FILM: When his daughter dies, an elderly, wealthy, woman-hating rancher sends for his grandson, whom he plans to make his heir. Gene and Pat go to meet the boy's stage, only to discover he is a she. Gene then encounters

trouble from the rancher's nephew who hoped to inherit this ranch.

NOTES AND COMMENTS: Shooting began December 10, 1951, in Hollywood's first sound stage built specifically and solely for television production (above). Flying A's "Range Rider" was the first to utilize the interior sets at Sunset Blvd. and Orange Drive. The half million dollar facility contained numerous standing sets—a barroom, barn, living room, bedroom, jail, cabin and office. The building also housed 22 offices, quarters for Gene's numerous enterprises. Gene's personal office was upstairs. All of Gene's Flying A productions were soon making use of these interior sets. The building, still in existence, is now a shoe warehouse store. (Photo courtesy of Jimmy Hawkins.)

"Return of Maverick Dan"

ORIGINAL AIRDATE: December 16, 1951

Executive Producer	Armand Schaefer
Producer	Louis Gray
Director	George Archainbaud
Teleplay	Polly James
Director of Photography	William Bradford
Film Editor	Jodie Copelan
Musical Director	Carl Cotner
Musical Supervisor	Irving Friedman
Musical Score	Walter Greene
Assistant Director	Nate Barragar

SONG: "Roll On Little Dogies" (Traditional)—sung by Gene Autry and Pat Buttram.

CAST:

Actor	Character
Gene Autry	Gene Autry
Pat Buttram	Pat Buttram
Carol Nugent	Barbara "Bobbie" Blake
James Craven	Mayor Elliott Johnson
Ben Weldon	Rusty
Myron Healey	Clay
Ewing Mitchell	Sheriff
Robert Peyton	Maverick Dan Blake
Lee Morgan	Sam Grover
Bob Woodward	Townsman
Champion	Champion

FILMING DATES: April 30 to May 5, 1951 (Companion episode "Outlaw Escape".)
LOCATION: Pioneertown

THE FILM: On the trail of Maverick Dan, Deputy Marshal Gene Autry meets Dan's kid sister. Believing her brother innocent, she asks Gene to investigate, revealing a second Maverick Dan seeking rich ore land.

"Galloping Hoofs"

ORIGINAL AIRDATE: December 23, 1951

Executive Producer	Armand Schaefer
Producer	Louis Gray
Director	George Archainbaud
Teleplay	Dwight Cummins
Director of Photography	William Bradford
Film Editor	Richard G. Wray
Musical Director	Carl Cotner
Musical Supervisor	Irving Friedman
Musical Score	Walter Greene
Assistant Director	Stanley Neufeld

SONGS: "Pretty Mary" (music and lyrics by Gene Autry, Oakley Haldeman, Jim MacDonald, Bob Mitchell)—sung by Gene Autry; "Mexicali Rose" (music and lyrics by Helen Stone, Jack B. Tenney)—sung by Gene Autry.

CAST:

Actor	Character
Gene Autry	Gene Autry
Pat Buttram	Pat Buttram
Gail Davis	Mary Reed
George J. Lewis	Neil Pierson
Belle Mitchell	Emily Blake
Harry Harvey	Sheriff Henry Blake
Denver Pyle	Curt Wayne
Jim Brittain	Truant Officer
Champion	Champion

FILMING DATES: May 6-11, 1951 (Companion episode "Melody Mesa".)
LOCATION: Pioneertown

THE FILM: A convicted embezzler has escaped from jail and is accusing his partner of double crossing him. Gene intervenes to see that justice is done.

"Heir to the Lazy L"

ORIGINAL AIRDATE: December 30, 1951

Executive Producer	Armand Schaefer
Producer	Louis Gray
Director	Wallace Fox
Teleplay	Oliver Drake
Director of Photography	William Bradford
Film Editor	Jodie Copelan
Musical Director	Carl Cotner
Musical Supervisor	Irving Friedman
Musical Score	Walter Greene
Assistant Director	Nate Barragar

SONG: "Ridin' Double" (music and lyrics by John Rox)—sung by Gene Autry.

CAST:

Actor	Character
Gene Autry	Gene Autry
Pat Buttram	J. Patrick Buttram
Gail Davis	Pauline Logan
Alan Hale Jr.	Bart
Helen Servis	Hortense Appleby
Terry Frost	Cady
Hugh Prosser	Latimer
Sandy Sanders	Lem
Champion	Champion

FILMING DATES: May 12-17, 1951 (Companion episode "Horse Sense".)
LOCATION: Pioneertown

THE FILM: Gene inherits half of the Lazy L Ranch from his uncle. When he learns the owner of the other half, a headstrong female, plans to sell the other half, Gene suspects a plot.

NOTES AND COMMENTS: Oliver Drake's screenplay is a direct swipe from Gene's 1941 film "Under Fiesta Stars", written for the screen by Karl Brown and Eliot Gibbons.

"Melody Mesa"

ORIGINAL AIRDATE: January 6, 1952

Executive Producer	Armand Schaefer
Producer	Louis Gray
Director	George Archainbaud
Teleplay	Betty Burbridge
Director of Photography	William Bradford
Film Editor	Jodie Copelan
Musical Director	Carl Cotner
Musical Supervisor	Irving Friedman
Musical Score	Walter Greene
Assistant Director	Stanley Neufeld

SONGS: "Ages and Ages Ago" (music and lyrics by Gene Autry, Fred Rose, Ray Whitley)—sung by Gene Autry; "Back In the Saddle Again" (music and lyrics by Gene Autry, Ray Whitley)—sung by Gene Autry...and partial version by Pat Buttram.

CAST:

Actor	Character
Gene Autry	Gene Autry
Pat Buttram	Pat Buttram
Gail Davis	Joan Merritt
Belle Mitchell	Jessica James
George J. Lewis	Robinson
Denver Pyle	Professor Sharp
Harry Harvey	Sheriff Ed Jackson
Ewing Mitchell	Roger Merritt
Riley Hill	Cliff
Jim Brittain	Guard
Boyd Stockman	Stage Driver
Art Dillard	Art/and Street Extra
Champion	Champion

FILMING DATES: May 6 to 11, 1951 (Companion episode "Galloping Hoofs".)
LOCATION: Pioneertown

THE FILM: In a rather dull episode, Gene poses as a music teacher to trap a counterfeiting gang.

"Horse Sense"

ORIGINAL AIRDATE: January 13, 1952.

Executive Producer ....Armand Schaefer
Producer ....Louis Gray
Director ....Wallace Fox
Teleplay......................................Robert Schaefer, Eric Freiwald
Director of Photography ....William Bradford
Film Editor ....Tony Wollner
Musical Director ....Carl Cotner
Musical Supervisor ....Irving Friedman
Musical Score.............................Walter Greene
Assistant Director........................Nate Barragar

SONG: "Cowboy's Heaven" (music and lyrics by Gene Autry, Frankie Marvin)—sung by Gene Autry.

CAST:

Actor	Character
Gene Autry	Gene Autry
Pat Buttram	Pat Buttram
Gail Davis	Elaine Castle
Dick Jones	Jeff Castle
Alan Hale Jr.	"Trader" Adams
Terry Frost	Slade
Hugh Prosser	Matt Nixon
Sandy Sanders	Blackie
Boyd Stockman	Rider
Champion	Champion

FILMING DATES: May 12-17, 1951 (Companion episode "Heir to the Lazy L".)
LOCATION: Pioneertown

THE FILM: The uncanny intelligence of Gene Autry's horse Champion proves vital in bringing to justice a crook who killed the mare that foaled Champ years earlier.

"Rock River Feud"

ORIGINAL AIRDATE: January 20, 1952

Executive Producer ....Armand Schaefer
Producer ....Louis Gray
Director ....George Archainbaud
Teleplay......................................Earle Snell
Director of Photography ....William Bradford
Film Editor ....Jodie Copelan
Musical Director ....Carl Cotner
Musical Supervisor ....Irving Friedman
Musical Score.............................Walter Greene
Assistant Director........................Stanley Neufeld

SONG: "Yellow Rose of Texas" (Traditional)—sung by Gene Autry. (Exact same footage reused in "Cold Decked" on 9/15/53.)

CAST:

Actor	Character
Gene Autry	Gene Autry
Pat Buttram	Pat Buttram
Sherry Jackson	Bonnie Ford
William Fawcett	Jim Ford
Steve Pendleton	Lafe Ford
Keith Richards	Sam
Craig Woods	Big Mike
Sandy Sanders	Terry Buttram
??	Doctor
Champion	Champion

FILMING DATES: May 18-23, 1951 (Companion episode "Kid Comes West".)
LOCATION: Pioneertown

THE FILM: When Pat Buttram inherits a stageline from a distant relative, he and Gene become involved in a long-standing feud between the Buttrams and the Fords.

NOTES AND COMMENTS: The January 22, 1952, issue of tradepaper DAILY VARIETY reported "The Gene Autry Show" moved into 4th place during the week of December 9-15 (1951), topped only by "Lux Theatre", "Amos and Andy" and "Jack Benny".

"The Lawless Press"

ORIGINAL AIRDATE: January 27, 1952

Executive Producer ....Armand Schaefer
Producer ....Louis Gray
Director ....George Archainbaud
Teleplay......................................Robert Schaefer, Eric Freiwald
Director of Photography ....William Bradford
Film Editor ....Tony Wollner
Musical Director ....Carl Cotner
Musical Supervisor ....Irving Friedman
Musical Score.............................Walter Greene
Assistant Director........................Nate Barragar

SONG: "When You and I Were Young, Maggie" (music and lyrics by James Butterfield, George Johnson)—sung by Gene Autry.

CAST:

Actor	Character
Gene Autry	Gene Autry
Pat Buttram	Pat Buttram
Roy Gordon	Jud Halsey
George Pembroke	Lucifer Lane

Bruce Norman	Tommy
Dennis Moore	Abner Barnes
James Anderson	Burke Halsey
Gregg Barton	Pete
Ed Hinkle	Joe Bonner
Art Dillard	Henchman
Bob Woodward	Sheriff
Boyd Stockman	Stage Driver
Frankie Marvin	Henchman
Champion	Champion

FILMING DATES: July 10-15, 1951 (Companion episode "The Ruthless Renegade".)
LOCATION: Pioneertown

THE FILM: Sheriff Gene Autry faces a crooked newspaper publisher who prints headlines about robberies before they are committed—because he and his son, a crooked deputy sheriff, are behind the holdups.

"The Western Way"

ORIGINAL AIRDATE: February 3, 1952

Executive Producer	Armand Schaefer
Producer	Louis Gray
Director	George Archainbaud
Teleplay	Norman S. Hall
Director of Photography	William Bradford
Film Editor	Jodie Copelan
Musical Director	Carl Cotner
Musical Supervisor	Irving Friedman
Musical Score	Walter Greene
Assistant Director	Stanley Neufeld

SONG: "Billy Boy" (Traditional)—sung by Gene Autry.

CAST:

Actor	Character
Gene Autry	Gene Autry
Pat Buttram	Pat Buttram
Dick Jones	Billy Walker
Mira McKinney	Emily "Ma" Walker
Harry Lauter	Walt Brady
Steve Clark	Sheriff Dan Kincaid
Don Harvey	Deputy Paul Dixon
Bob Wilke	Russ
Bob Woodward	Bank Robber
Art Dillard	Henchman #1
??	Henchman #2
Champion	Champion

FILMING DATES: July 16-21, 1951 (Companion episode "Hot Lead and Old Lace".)
LOCATION: Pioneertown

Gene in another terrific fight scene with Harry Lauter.

THE FILM: Gene and Pat capture a bank robber who turns out to be the wayward son of their friend, Ma Walker. Helping the young man and his Ma, Gene captures an outlaw gang.

"The Ruthless Renegade"

ORIGINAL AIRDATE: February 10, 1952

Executive Producer	Armand Schaefer
Producer	Louis Gray
Director	George Archainbaud
Teleplay	Elizabeth Beecher
Director of Photography	William Bradford
Film Editor	Tony Wollner
Musical Director	Carl Cotner
Musical Supervisor	Irving Friedman
Musical Score	Walter Greene
Assistant Director	Nate Barragar

SONG: "Texas Plains" (music and lyrics by Stuart Hamblen)—sung by Gene Autry and Pat Buttram; partially sung by Bruce Norman and James Anderson.

CAST:

Actor	Character
Gene Autry	Gene Autry
Pat Buttram	Pat Buttram
Jane Frazee	Jane Winslow
Roy Gordon	Doc Armstrong
Bruce Norman	Timmy Winslow
Dennis Moore	Fred Mason
Gregg Barton	Gaffer
James Anderson	Paul Winslow
Ed Hinkle	Spike
Lee Morgan	Bartender
Champion	Champion

FILMING DATES: July 10-15, 1951 (Companion episode "Lawless Press".)
LOCATION: Pioneertown

THE FILM: Gene and Pat are drawn into the conflict between a crusading newspaperwoman and a ruthless town boss. Pat's composure of a song helps round-up the gang.

"Hot Lead and Old Lace"

ORIGINAL AIRDATE: February 17, 1952

Executive Producer ....Armand Schaefer
Producer ....Louis Gray
Director ....George Archainbaud
Teleplay ....Robert Schaefer, Eric Freiwald
Director of Photography ....William Bradford
Film Editor ....Jodie Copelan
Musical Director ....Carl Cotner
Musical Supervisor ....Irving Friedman
Musical Score..............................Walter Greene
Assistant Director........................Stanley Neufeld

SONG: "Home On the Range" (Traditional)—sung by Gene Autry.

CAST:

Actor	Character
Gene Autry	Gene Autry
Pat Buttram	Pat Buttram
Mira McKinney	Maud Munroe
Harry Lauter	Chad Matthews
Steve Clark	Pete Munroe
Don Harvey	Cody
Bob Wilke	Max
Bob Woodward	Pete Armstrong
Art Dillard	Stage Driver
Champion	Champion

FILMING DATES: July 16-21, 1951 (Companion episode "The Western Way".)
LOCATION: Pioneertown

THE FILM: Gene and Pat help a courageous old Bostonian lady defend her ranch from a takeover after the owner, her Uncle, is murdered.

"Blazeaway"

ORIGINAL AIRDATE: February 24, 1952.

Executive Producer ....Armand Schaefer
Producer ....Louis Gray
Director ....George Blair

Teleplay ....Paul Gangelin
Director of Photography ....William Bradford
Film Editor ....Tony Wollner
Musical Director ....Carl Cotner
Musical Supervisor ....Irving Friedman
Musical Score..............................Walter Greene
Assistant Director........................Nate Barragar

SONGS: None.

CAST:

Actor	Character
Gene Autry	Gene Autry
Pat Buttram	Pat Buttram
Mary Treen	Nettie Blinkensop
Richard Travis	Hack Watson
Pierre Watkin	Colonel
Bob Bice	Fighting Eagle
Kermit Maynard	Twig
Sandy Sanders	Stag
Bob Woodward	Gray Badger
Frankie Marvin	Man on Street
Champion	Champion

FILMING DATES: July 22-27, 1951 (Companion episode "Six Gun Romeo".)
LOCATION: Pioneertown

THE FILM: Following a series of tomahawk killings, Cavalry Sergeant Gene Autry helps prove the innocence of an Indian blood brother.

NOTES AND COMMENTS: There's a large continuity error in this episode. At one point both Hack (Richard Travis) and Twig (Kermit Maynard) give chase to Gray Badger (Bob Woodward) leaving *no one* by Pat Buttram's camera. In the very next shot, Twig is struggling with Nettie (Mary Treen) all over the camera.

"Bullets and Bows"

ORIGINAL AIRDATE: March 2, 1952

Executive Producer ....Armand Schaefer
Producer ....Louis Gray
Director ....George Blair
Teleplay ....Richard Schaefer, Eric Freiwald
Director of Photography ....William Bradford
Film Editor ....Anthony Wollner
Musical Director ....Carl Cotner
Musical Supervisor ....Irving Friedman
Musical Score..............................Walter Greene
Assistant Director........................Nate Barragar

SONG: "Rhythm of the Hoofbeats" (music and lyrics by Gene Autry, Johnny Marvin, Fred Rose)—sung by Gene Autry.

CAST:

Actor	Character
Gene Autry	Gene Autry
Pat Buttram	Pat Buttram
Elaine Riley	Joyce
Myron Healey	Sheriff
John Doucette	Frank
Denver Pyle	Burr Ramsey
Gregg Barton	Sloan
Bob Woodward	Stage Driver
Champion	Champion

FILMING DATES: August 5-10, 1951 (Companion episode "The Sheriff Is a Lady".)
LOCATION: Pioneertown

THE FILM: In an episode dominated by silliness, Gene's friend Pat, owner of the town's tailor shop, gets a shipment of ladies' clothing by mistake. The error provides a local big shot an opportunity to acquire Pat's prime-location property.

NOTES AND COMMENTS: This episode has Gene putting Champ through some of his tricks.

"Trouble at Silver Creek"

ORIGINAL AIRDATE: March 9, 1952

Executive Producer	Armand Schaefer
Producer	Louis Gray
Director	George Archainbaud
Teleplay	Howard Green
Director of Photography	William Bradford
Film Editor	Jodie Copelan
Musical Director	Carl Cotner
Musical Supervisor	Irving Friedman
Musical Score	Walter Greene
Assistant Director	Stanley Neufeld

SONGS: None.

CAST:

Actor	Character
Gene Autry	Gene Autry
Pat Buttram	Pat Buttram
Barbara Stanley	Alice Caldwell
George Pembroke	Kelly
Steve Conte	Buzz
Leonard Penn	Herb Higgins
Craig Woods	Chalky White
Francis McDonald	Sam Caldwell

Gene to the rescue in another action scene filmed on the desert near Pioneertown.

Tom Tyler	Hank
Champion	Champion

FILMING DATES: July 30 to August 4, 1951 (Companion episode "Trail of the Witch".)
LOCATION: Pioneertown

THE FILM: Sheriff Gene Autry and deputy Pat Buttram help a reformed outlaw turned rancher and his daughter when an unscrupulous businessman tries to blackmail them. When the blackmailer is murdered by his own henchmen, the rancher is blamed.

"Six Gun Romeo"

ORIGINAL AIRDATE: March 16, 1952

Executive Producer	Armand Schaefer
Producer	Louis Gray
Director	George Blair
Teleplay	Polly James
Director of Photography	William Bradford
Film Editor	Anthony Wollner
Musical Director	Carl Cotner
Musical Supervisor	Irving Friedman
Musical Score	Walter Greene
Assistant Director	Nate Barrager

SONG: "I'm Beginning to Care" (music and lyrics by Gene Autry, Johnny Marvin, Fred Rose)—sung by Gene Autry.

CAST:

Actor	Character
Gene Autry	Gene Autry
Pat Buttram	Pat Buttram
Elaine Riley	Jan Carter Gray

Mary Treen	Adele Tompkins
Richard Travis	Bryant Morgan
Pierre Watkin	Sheriff
Bob Bice	Chuck
Kermit Maynard	Biff
Boyd Stockman	Stage Driver
Bob Woodward	Shotgun Guard
Sandy Sanders	Joe, Outlaw
Art Dillard	Outlaw
Frankie Marvin	Outlaw/also Man who brings Jan her horse
??	Painter
??	Deputy in checkered shirt
??	2nd Deputy
Champion	Champion

FILMING DATES: July 22-27, 1951 (Companion episode "Blazeaway".)
LOCATION: Pioneertown

THE FILM: Unbeknownst to Gene, Pat has sent Gene's picture as his own to his mail-order-bride. Going to meet the bride-to-be, the pair encounter another stagecoach passenger who becomes involved with an outlaw leader in a bank holdup.

"The Sheriff Is a Lady"

ORIGINAL AIRDATE: March 23, 1952

Executive Producer	Armand Schaefer
Producer	Louis Gray
Director	George Blair
Teleplay	Dwight Cummins
Director of Photography	William Bradford
Film Editor	Jodie Copelan
Musical Director	Carl Cotner
Musical Supervisor	Irving Friedman
Musical Score	Walter Greene
Assistant Director	Nate Barragar

SONGS: "After Tomorrow" (music and lyrics by Gene Autry, Fred Rose)—sung by Gene Autry; "Sing Me a Song of the Saddle" (music and lyrics by Gene Autry, Frank Harford)—sung by Gene Autry.

CAST:

Actor	Character
Gene Autry	Gene Autry
Pat Buttram	Pat Buttram
Dick Jones	Horace
Elaine Riley	Kathy Vale
John Doucette	Gimme Porter
Denver Pyle	Dodge Hartman

Myron Healey	Jack Wells
Gregg Barton	Hurry Brown
Champion	Champion

FILMING DATES: August 5-10, 1951 (Companion episode "Bullets and Bows".)
LOCATION: Pioneertown

THE FILM: Border patrolmen Gene and Pat come up against a lady sheriff who mistakes them for gun smugglers.

"The Trail of the Witch"

ORIGINAL AIRDATE: March 30, 1952

Executive Producer	Armand Schaefer
Producer	Louis Gray
Director	George Archainbaud
Teleplay	Joe Richardson
Director of Photography	William Bradford
Film Editor	Anthony Wollner
Musical Director	Carl Cotner
Musical Supervisor	Irving Friedman
Musical Score	Walter Greene
Assistant Director	Stanley Neufeld

SONGS: None.

CAST:

Actor	Character
Gene Autry	Gene Autry
Pat Buttram	Pat Buttram
Almira Sessions	Mag
Steve Conte	Breed
George Pembroke	Judge
Leonard Penn	Marvin Green
Tom Tyler	Snake-Eye
Bill George	Sheriff Ned Rich
Francis McDonald	Jay Elston
Craig Woods	Jigger
Bob Woodward	Stage Driver
Sandy Sanders	Stage Guard
Art Dillard	Townsman
Champion	Champion

FILMING DATES: July 30 to August 4, 1951 (Companion episode "Trouble at Silver Creek".)
LOCATION: Pioneertown

THE FILM: Troubleshooters Gene and Pat are asked by a young, inexperienced sheriff to help stop a series of mine shipment robberies by an unknown gang. The trail leads Gene and superstitious Pat to a witch-like recluse's shanty-cabin.

The Gene Autry Show
3rd season, 13 episodes (7/14/53-10/6/53). 30 minutes each.
Aired on CBS network on Tuesday from 8-8:30pm EST

"Thunder Out West"

ORIGINAL AIRDATE: July 14, 1953

Executive Producer ....Armand Schaefer
Producer ....Louis Gray
Director ....George Archainbaud
Teleplay.......................................Dorrell and Stuart
                            McGowan
Director of Photography ....William Bradford
Film Editor ....Anthony Wollner
Musical Director ....Carl Cotner
Musical Supervisor ....Irving Friedman
Musical Score..............................Walter Greene
Assistant Director........................Harry Mancke

SONG: "Old Nevada Moon" (music and lyrics by Gene Autry, Johnny Marvin)—sung by Gene Autry.

CAST:

Actor	*Character*
Gene Autry	Gene Autry
Pat Buttram	Pat Buttram
Wendy Waldron	Lorna Evans
Lyle Talbot	George Evans
Harry Lauter	Jim Lear
William Fawcett	John Turner
Lane Chandler	Reverend Parker
Tom Tyler	Cobb
Larry Hudson	Bush
George Slocum	Oaks
Frank Ellis	Townsman
Bob Woodward	Safe Robber
Champion	Champion

FILMING DATES: April 25 to May 1, 1952 (Companion episode "The Bandidos".)
LOCATIONS: Corriganville; Pioneertown stock footage

THE FILM: A clever safe cracker uses Pat Buttram's mail order telescope to get the combination to a Cattleman's Co-op safe.

NOTES AND COMMENTS: Writers Dorrell and Stuart McGowan recycled their 1939 RKO Radio Pictures plot for "Trouble in Sundown" with George O'Brien for this episode. Coincidentally, co-scripter of "Trouble in Sundown", Oliver Drake, also re-used the idea in an episode of "The Cisco Kid", "Trouble in Tonapah" ('54).

"Outlaw Stage"

ORIGINAL AIRDATE: July 21, 1953

Executive Producer ....Armand Schaefer
Producer ....Louis Gray
Director ....Wallace Fox
Teleplay.......................................Robert Schaefer, Eric
                            Freiwald
Director of Photography ....William Bradford
Film Editor ....Jack Wheeler
Musical Director ....Carl Cotner
Musical Supervisor ....Irving Friedman
Musical Score..............................Walter Greene
Assistant Director........................Stanley Neufeld

SONG: "There's a Rainbow On the Rio Colorado" (music and lyrics by Gene Autry, Fred Rose)—sung by Gene Autry.

CAST:

Actor	*Character*
Gene Autry	Gene Autry
Pat Buttram	Pat Buttram
Don Harvey	Arnold Beeker
Steve Conte	Jim
Pierce Lyden	Red
Edmund Cobb	Hank
Frank Jaquet	Dr. Richard Moore
Kermit Maynard	Fred Manners
Julian Upton	Spence
Harry Mackin	Johnny Peters
Frank Ellis	Townsman
Bobby Clark	Young Townsman
Champion	Champion

FILMING DATES: May 2-8, 1952 (Companion episode "Border Justice".)
LOCATIONS: Burro Flats; Jack Ingram Ranch

THE FILM: Sheriff Gene Autry and hypochondriac deputy Pat Buttram clear a young stage driver in the fatal killing of a respected stage guard and the holdup of a jewelry salesman carrying a fortune in precious stones.

"Ghost Mountain"

ORIGINAL AIRDATE: July 28, 1953

Executive Producer ....Armand Schaefer
Producer ....Louis Gray
Director ....George Archianbaud
Teleplay..Dwight Cummins
Director of Photography ....William Bradford
Film Editor....................................Jack Wheeler
Musical Director ....Carl Cotner
Musical Supervisor ....Irving Friedman
Musical Score...............................Walter Greene
Assistant Director.........................Gilbert Kay

SONGS: "Ridin' Down That Old Texas Trail" (music and lyrics by Gene Autry, Smiley Burnette)—sung by Gene Autry; "If You'll Let Me Be Your Little Sweetheart" (music and lyrics by Gene Autry, Slim Bryant)—sung by Gene Autry.

CAST:

Actor	Character
Gene Autry	Gene Autry
Pat Buttram	Pat Buttram
Eilene Janssen	Wilma Markham
Clayton Moore	Slim Edwards
John Doucette	Brief Williams
Ross Ford	Professor Donald Markham
Sandy Sanders	Powder Kelly
Ewing "Lucky" Brown	Rush Norton
Champion	Champion

FILMING DATES: June 9-14, 1952 (Companion episode "Dry Gulch at Devil's Elbow".)
LOCATION: Pioneertown

THE FILM: Gene and superstitious Pat Buttram find themselves battling some very lifelike Conquistador ghosts when they become involved with an archaeologist, his kid sister and a clever outlaw gang.

NOTES AND COMMENTS: While making this episode Pat fell from his horse while wearing a full set of armor when his foot caught in the stirrup. Fortunately, Gene caught the horse and pulled him to a halt or Pat might have been dragged for a distance.

"The Old Prospector"

ORIGINAL AIRDATE: August 4, 1953

Executive Producer ....Armand Schaefer
Producer ....Louis Gray
Director ....George Archainbaud
Teleplay..Milton Raison
Director of Photography ....William Bradford
Film Editor....................................Jack Wheeler
Musical Director ....Carl Cotner
Musical Supervisor ....Irving Friedman
Musical Score...............................Walter Greene
Assistant Director.........................Stanley Neufeld

SONG: "I'm a Cowpoke Pokin' Along" (music and lyrics by Gene Autry, Fred Rose)—sung by Gene Autry.

CAST:

Actor	Character
Gene Autry	Gene Autry
Pat Buttram	Pat Buttram
Myron Healey	Les Wayland
Lyle Talbot	John Grimshaw
Terry Frost	Bill Daly
Ewing Mitchell	Sheriff
Bernard Szold	Hard Luck Finny
Sandy Sanders	Deputy
Herman Hack	Wagon Driver
Champion	Champion

FILMING DATES: July 21-26, 1952 (Companion episode "Gypsy Wagon".)
LOCATIONS: Jack Ingram Ranch; Lone Pine

THE FILM: Gene saves an old prospector from a pair of outlaws who believe the old fellow has found a gold mine.

NOTES AND COMMENTS: The episode smacks of a recycled radio script told partly by Gene in narration, but somehow it hampers the natural flow of the action.

"Narrow Escape"

ORIGINAL AIRDATE: August 11, 1953

Executive Producer ....Armand Schaefer
Producer ....Louis Gray
Director ....D. Ross Lederman
Teleplay..Virginia M. Cooke
Director of Photography ....Ernie Miller
Film Editor....................................Erma E. Levin
Musical Director ....Carl Cotner

Musical Supervisor ....Irving Friedman
Musical Score..............................Walter Greene
Assistant Director........................Stanley Neufeld

SONG: "Love, Burning Love" (music and lyrics by Gene Autry, Johnny Marvin, Fred Rose)—sung by Gene Autry.

CAST:

Actor	*Character*
Gene Autry	Gene Autry
Pat Buttram	Pat Buttram
Sheila Ryan	Marcie Nevers
Rick Vallin	Big Tim Brady
William Henry	Bill Barker
George Pembroke	Sheriff
Marshall Reed	Coley
David Coleman	Jimmy Nevers
Frankie Marvin	Man Struggling with Pat
Bob Woodward	Bob, Stagecoach Driver
??	Barber
??	Manicurist
??	Mr. Munroe
Ray Jones, Carl Mathews, Herman Hack	Townsmen
Art Dillard, Kermit Maynard, Reed Howes	Masked Outlaws (stock footage)
Champion	Champion

FILMING DATES: August 25-30, 1952 (Companion episode "Prize Winner".)
LOCATIONS: Corriganville; Pioneertown stock footage

THE FILM: While Pat awaits the arrival of his mail order sweetheart, Gene is busy solving the mysterious holdups of stagecoaches carrying silver bullion.

"Border Justice"

ORIGINAL AIRDATE: August 18, 1953

Executive Producer ....Armand Schaefer
Producer ....Louis Gray
Director ....Wallace Fox
Teleplay..Robert Schaefer, Eric Freiwald
Director of Photography ....William Bradford
Film Editor...................................Jack Wheeler
Musical Director ....Carl Cotner
Musical Supervisor ....Irving Friedman
Musical Score..............................Walter Greene
Assistant Director........................Stanley Neufeld

SONG: "Guns and Guitars" (music and lyrics by Gene Autry, Oliver Drake)—sung by Gene Autry.

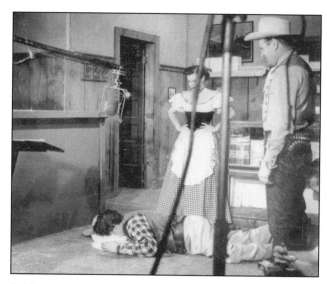

Behind the scenes shot . . . Sheila Ryan and Gene observe the aftermath of Pat Buttram's pie-in-the-face gag in "Border Justice."

CAST:

Actor	*Character*
Gene Autry	Gene Autry
Pat Buttram	Pat Buttram
Sheila Ryan	Mimi
Don Harvey	Ramon Ortega
Steve Conte	Ralph
Pierce Lyden	Ned
Julian Upton	Jose
Edmund Cobb	Sheriff
Bob Woodward	Mexican
Champion	Champion

FILMING DATES: May 2-8, 1952 (Companion episode "Outlaw Stage".)
LOCATIONS: Burro Flats; Jack Ingram Ranch

THE FILM: Gene and Pat help the Mexican government when they trail murderous men smuggling highly dangerous

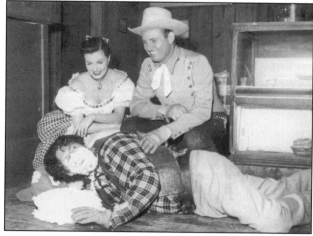

Gene and Sheila Ryan help Pat Buttram clean up after the pie-in-the-face scene in "Border Justice."

explosives across the border in bakery products.

NOTES AND COMMENTS: Gene "supposedly" celebrates a birthday in this episode, although his real birthday is September 29.

"Gypsy Wagon"

ORIGINAL AIRDATE: August 25, 1953

Executive Producer ....Armand Schaefer
Producer ....Louis Gray
Director ....George Archainbaud
Teleplay...Virginia M. Cooke
Director of Photography ....William Bradford
Film Editor....................................William Ziegler
Musical Director ....Carl Cotner
Musical Supervisor ....Irving Friedman
Musical Score...............................Walter Greene
Assistant Director.........................Stanley Neufeld

SONG: "Onteora" (music and lyrics by Doris Anderson, Gene Andrea aka Theodore Snyder)—sung by Gene Autry.

CAST:

Actor	Character
Gene Autry	Gene Autry
Pat Buttram	Pat Buttram
Gloria Talbot	Gerelda
Myron Healey	Clyde
Terry Frost	Spade Dunlap
Lyle Talbot	Judge Thaddeus Fawcett
Ewing Mitchell	Sheriff Clay Cody
Bernard Szold	Grandfather Alonzo
Sandy Sanders	Sandy
Bob Woodward	Payroll Rider/and/Dave Riley
Herman Hack	Deputy
Ray Jones, Frankie Marvin	Townsmen
Champion	Champion

FILMING DATES: July 21-26, 1952 (Companion episode "The Old Prospector".)
LOCATIONS: Lone Pine; Jack Ingram Ranch

THE FILM: A gypsy girl and her grandfather surprise a gang of stage bandits. Learning the gypsies can identify one of them, the outlaw leader tries to throw blame on the gypsies.

NOTES AND COMMENTS: Some blatantly mismatched stock footage mixed with new footage of Gene pursuing Terry Frost has Gene wearing two totally different shirts.

"The Bandidos"

ORIGINAL AIRDATE: September 1, 1953

Executive Producer ....Armand Schaefer
Producer ....Louis Gray
Director ....George Archainbaud
Teleplay...Dwight Cummins
Director of Photography ....William Bradford
Film Editor....................................Jack Wheeler
Musical Director ....Carl Cotner
Musical Supervisor ....Irving Friedman
Musical Score...............................Walter Greene
Assistant Director.........................Harry Mancke

SONGS: "Back in the Saddle Again" (music and lyrics by Gene Autry, Ray Whitley)—sung by Gene Autry; "Dixie Cannonball" (music and lyrics by Red Foley, Gene Autry, Vaughn Horton)—sung by Gene Autry.

CAST:

Actor	Character
Gene Autry	Gene Autry
Pat Buttram	Pat Buttram
Wendy Waldron	Verna Clayton
Harry Lauter	Frank Lassiter
Lyle Talbot	Senator Henry J. Murphy
William Fawcett	Mayor Green
Lane Chandler	Sheriff Asa Wendall
Larry Hudson	Bill
Tom Tyler	Outlaw
Bob Dominguez	Sombrero
George Slocum	Reid
Bob Woodward	Extra
Champion	Champion

FILMING DATES: April 25 to May 1, 1952 (Companion episode "Thunder Out West".)
LOCATION: Corriganville

THE FILM: A phony senator attempts to swindle townspeople into putting up money for a dam. Gene and the real senator join forces to thwart the crook's plans.

"Dry Gulch at Devil's Elbow"

ORIGINAL AIRDATE: September 8, 1953

Executive Producer ....Armand Schaefer
Producer ....Louis Gray
Director ....George Archainbaud
Teleplay...William Telaak
Director of Photography ....William Bradford
Film Editor....................................William Ziegler

Musical Director ....Carl Cotner
Musical Supervisor ....Irving Friedman
Musical Score............................Walter Greene
Assistant Director........................Gilbert Kay

SONGS: "Fetch Me Down My Trusty Forty-Five" (music and lyrics by Smiley Burnette)—sung by Gene Autry; "She'll be Comin' 'Round the Mountain" (Traditional)—sung by John Doucette.

CAST:

Actor	Character
Gene Autry	Gene Autry
Pat Buttram	Pat Buttram
Clayton Moore	Bud Drake
John Doucette	Snap Larkin
Ross Ford	Jack Hager
Joe McGuinn	Sheriff Higgins
Ewing "Lucky" Brown	Hank Jorday
Sandy Sanders	Chuck Dugan
??	Kid #1
??	Kid #2
??	Kid #3
??	Kid #4
Champion	Champion

FILMING DATES: June 9-14, 1952 (Companion episode "Ghost Mountain".)
LOCATION: Pioneertown

THE FILM: A sheriff buffaloed by stagecoach bandits sends for Gene and Pat to help but Pat's tall tales about outlaw Sly Fox and his buried loot get him in trouble with the bandits.

"Cold Decked"

ORIGINAL AIRDATE: September 15, 1953

Executive Producer ....Armand Schaefer
Producer ....Louis Gray
Director ....Wallace Fox
Teleplay......................................Elizabeth Beecher
Director of Photography ....William Bradford
Film Editor..................................Jack Wheeler
Musical Director ....Carl Cotner
Musical Supervisor ....Irving Friedman
Musical Score..............................Walter Greene
Assistant Director........................Harry Mancke

SONG: "Yellow Rose of Texas" (Traditional)—sung by Gene Autry. (Exact footage recycled from "Rock River Feud".)

CAST:

Actor	Character
Gene Autry	Gene Autry
Pat Buttram	Pat Buttram
Stanley Andrews	Ben Tansey
Alan Bridge	Sheriff Jeb Warner
Henry Rowland	Lee Strickland
Terry Frost	Snuffy
Myron Healey	Blake
Gregg Barton	Rich
Kenne Duncan	Ed Martin
Ted Mapes	Deputy Tom Elliott
Bob Woodward	Thompson
William Fawcett	Game Warden
Champion	Champion

FILMING DATES: May 9-15, 1952 (Companion episode "Santa Fe Raiders".)
LOCATION: Corriganville

THE FILM: Range detective Gene Autry searches for a banker who has mysteriously disappeared and is believed to have embezzled bank funds.

"The Steel Ribbon"

ORIGINAL AIRDATE: September 22, 1953

Executive Producer ....Armand Schaefer
Producer ....Louis Gray
Director ....William Berke
Teleplay......................................Robert Schaefer, Eric
                        Freiwald
Director of Photography ....William Bradford
Film Editor..................................Anthony Wollner
Musical Director ....Carl Cotner
Musical Supervisor ....Irving Friedman
Musical Score..............................Walter Greene
Assistant Director........................Stanley Neufeld

SONG: "Gallivantin' Galveston Gal" (music and lyrics by Milton Leeds, Steve Nelson, Fred Wise)—sung by Gene Autry.

CAST:

Actor	Character
Gene Autry	Gene Autry
Pat Buttram	Pat Buttram
Gail Davis	Billie Carter
Robert Lowery	Blake Jessop
Terry Frost	Lait
Dick Emory	Jeff Carter
John Hamilton	Dan Parker
Rusty Wescoatt	Cole
Tom London	Engineer
Bob Woodward	Mine Employee

Frankie Marvin..............................Extra
Champion....................................Champion

FILMING DATES: September 19-25, 1952 (Companion episode "Ransom Cross".)
LOCATION: Lone Pine

THE FILM: Assigned to stop a series of destructive railroad robberies, railroad investigators Gene and Pat are confronted by a thieving telegraph operator who is blaming a brother and sister who own a transport company.

"Rio Renegades"

ORIGINAL AIRDATE: September 29, 1953

Executive Producer......................Armand Schaefer
Producer.......................................Louis Gray
Director..George Archainbaud
Teleplay..Elizabeth Beecher
Director of Photography ....William Bradford
Film Editor..................................Paul Borofsky
Musical Director ....Carl Cotner
Musical Supervisor ....Irving Friedman
Musical Score..............................Walter Greene
Assistant Director........................Stanley Neufeld

SONG: "Let Me Ride Down in Rocky Canyon" (music and lyrics by Gene Autry, Fred Rose, Ray Whitley)—sung by Gene Autry.

CAST:

Actor	Character
Gene Autry	Gene Autry
Pat Buttram	Pat Buttram
Sheila Ryan	Corinne Sheldon
Stanley Andrews	Thaddeus Trigg
Myron Healey	Kansas
Effie Laird	Amelia Trigg
Lee Van Cleef	Hod
Harry Harvey	Sheriff
Ray Jones	Townsman
Champion	Champion

FILMING DATES: November 7-13, 1952 (Companion episode "Outlaw Warning".)
LOCATIONS: Monogram Ranch; Iverson Ranch; Lone Pine

THE FILM: Marshal Gene Autry and Pat Buttram aid an old prospector and his wife against a beautiful hairdresser and her cohorts who are trying to steal a map to the prospector's newly discovered gold mine.

"Ransom Cross"

ORIGINAL AIRDATE: October 6, 1953

Executive Producer......................Armand Schaefer
Producer.......................................Louis Gray
Director..William Berke
Teleplay..Robert Schaefer, Eric Freiwald
Director of Photography ....William Bradford
Film Editor..................................Jack Wheeler
Musical Director ....Carl Cotner
Musical Supervisor ....Irving Friedman
Musical Score..............................Walter Greene
Assistant Director........................Stanley Neufeld

SONGS: None.

CAST:

Actor	Character
Gene Autry	Gene Autry
Pat Buttram	Pat Buttram
Gail Davis	Bonnie West
Robert Lowery	Ron Corness
Terry Frost	Matt
Rusty Wescoatt	Ed
John Hamilton	Jonathan Diggers
Tom London	Engineer
Bob Woodward	Townsman
Frankie Marvin	Deputy
Champion	Champion

FILMING DATES: September 19-25, 1952 (Companion episode "The Steel Ribbon".)
LOCATION: Lone Pine

THE FILM: In this action packed, stunt filled episode, Sheriff Autry battles crooks who have stolen an archeological treasure known as The Cross of Wealth and are attempting to ransom it back to the archeologists who found it.

WMT is in Cedar Rapids, Iowa.

The Gene Autry Show

*4th season, 13 episodes (7/6/54-10/2/54). 30 minutes each.
Aired on CBS network on Tuesday from 8-8:30pm EST until
moving to Saturdays as of September 25, 1954*

"Santa Fe Raiders"

ORIGINAL AIRDATE: July 6, 1954

Executive Producer ....Armand Schaefer
Producer ....Louis Gray
Director ....D. Ross Lederman
Teleplay...Oliver Drake
Director of Photography ....William Bradford
Film Editor ....Anthony Wollner
Musical Director ....Carl Cotner
Musical Supervisor ....Irving Friedman
Musical Score...............................Walter Greene
Assistant Director.........................Harry Mancke

SONG: "Westward Ho!" (music and lyrics by Vern Spencer)—sung by Gene Autry.

CAST:

Actor	*Character*
Gene Autry	Gene Autry
Pat Buttram	Pat Buttram
Dick Jones	Tim Morgan
Gloria Saunders	Laura Bryan
Stanley Andrews	Judge Hiram Stone
Myron Healey	Miller
Terry Frost	Dugan
Alan Bridge	Sheriff
Gregg Barton	Hickey
Henry Rowland	Paul Nash
Kenne Duncan	Lane
Tom London	John Morgan
Bob Woodward	Rocky, Wagon Driver
Frankie Marvin	Shorty
Rocky Shahan	Extra
Champion	Champion

FILMING DATES: May 9-15, 1952 (Companion episode "Cold Decked".)
LOCATION: Corriganville

THE FILM: Gene helps an old friend's son take over the family freight business when the boy's father is killed by bandits who then frame Gene for a safe robbery.

"Johnny Jackaroo"

ORIGINAL AIRDATE: July 13, 1954

Executive Producer ....Armand Schaefer
Producer ....Louis Gray
Director ....D. Ross Lederman
Teleplay...Robert Schaefer, Eric Freiwald
Director of Photography ....William Bradford
Film Editor ....William Ziegler
Musical Director ....Carl Cotner
Musical Supervisor ....Irving Friedman
Musical Score...............................Walter Greene
Assistant Director.........................Gilbert Kay

SONG: "Gone With the West" (music and lyrics by Gene Autry, Frankie Marvin)—sung by Gene Autry.

CAST:

Actor	*Character*
Gene Autry	Gene Autry
Pat Buttram	Pat Buttram
Ann Doran	Lynne Moore
Harry Lauter	Ron Williams
William Fawcett	Steve Harper
Denver Pyle	Sheriff
B. G. Norman	Johnny Moore
Henry Rowland	Stan
Gregg Barton	Salesman
Champion	Champion

FILMING DATES: July 27 to August 1, 1952 (Companion episode "Carnival Comes West".)
LOCATIONS: Jack Ingram Ranch; Lone Pine

THE FILM: Pat Buttram, irritated by an eleven year old

incorrigible eastern boy, plans a mock stagecoach holdup to frighten some sense into the lad, but real bandits dress as Gene and Pat and really hold up the stage.

"Holdup"

ORIGINAL AIRDATE: July 20, 1954

Executive Producer ....Armand Schaefer
Producer ....Louis Gray
Director ....D. Ross Lederman
Teleplay..Norman S. Hall
Director of Photography ....William Bradford
Film Editor...................................Anthony Wollner
Musical Director ....Carl Cotner
Musical Supervisor ....Irving Friedman
Musical Score...............................Walter Greene
Assistant Director.........................Stanley Neufeld

SONG: "I Only Want a Buddy" (music and lyrics by Eddie Jones)—sung by Gene Autry.

CAST:

Actor	*Character*
Gene Autry ....Gene Autry
Pat Buttram ....Pat Buttram
Rochelle Stanton ....Gail Eastman
Arthur Space ....Jim Eastman
William Fawcett...........................Pop Wallace
Rory Mallinson ....Reb Stearns
Gregg Barton...............................Watson
Forrest Taylor..............................Eli Clark
James Best...................................Bank Teller
Red Morgan.................................Driver
Bob Woodward ....Man outside bank
Frankie Marvin............................Third man in fight
Champion....................................Champion

Gene waits while the crew adjusts the large reflectors for another scene on the desert near Pioneertown. Note the Flying A logo on the van.

FILMING DATES: June 15-20, 1952 (Companion episode "Hoodoo Canyon".)
LOCATION: Pioneertown

THE FILM: Gene and Pat, with the help of a brave telegraph operator, baffle an outlaw gang trying to defraud a rancher out of his valuable property.

"Prize Winner"

ORIGINAL AIRDATE: July 27, 1954

Executive Producer ....Armand Schaefer
Producer ....Louis Gray
Director ....D. Ross Lederman
Teleplay..Virginia M. Cooke
Director of Photography ....Ernie Miller
Film Editor...................................Paul Borofsky
Musical Director ....Carl Cotner
Musical Supervisor ....Irving Friedman
Musical Score...............................Walter Greene
Assistant Director.........................Stanley Neufeld

SONG: "God's Little Candles" (music and lyrics by Jimmy Kennedy)—sung by Gene Autry.

CAST:

Actor	*Character*
Gene Autry ....Gene Autry
Pat Buttram ....Pat Buttram
Sheila Ryan ....Doll
Rick Vallin...................................Doc McCoy
Louise Lorimer............................Agatha Baldwin
George Pembroke........................Spencer Baldwin
Ed Dearing ....Sheriff Cody
Ferris Taylor................................Mayor
Marshall Reed ....Tom Jenkins
Bob Woodward ....Bob, Stage Driver
Frank Ellis...................................Waiter
Frankie Marvin............................Henchman #1
?? ....Henchman #2
Herman Hack, Carl Mathews.......Extras
Champion....................................Champion

FILMING DATES: August 25-30, 1952 (Companion episode "Narrow Escape".)
LOCATION: Corriganville

THE FILM: In one of the most comedic episodes of the series, Gene exposes jewel thieves at the state fair who have stashed their stolen diamonds in the coop of Pat Buttram's prize rooster.

"The Sharpshooter"

ORIGINAL AIRDATE: August 3, 1954

Executive Producer	Armand Schaefer
Producer	Louis Gray
Director	Frank McDonald
Teleplay	Robert Schaefer, Eric Freiwald
Director of Photography	William Bradford
Film Editor	Harvey Manger
Musical Director	Carl Cotner
Musical Supervisor	Irving Friedman
Musical Score	Walter Greene
Assistant Director	Gilbert Kay

SONG: "Crime Will Never Pay" (music and lyrics by Willard Robison, Jack Pepper)—sung by Gene Autry.

CAST:

Actor	*Character*
Gene Autry	Gene Autry
Pat Buttram	Pat Buttram
Margaret Field	Peggy Barker
Dick Jones	Randy Barker
Stanley Andrews	Judge Alfred Stone
Denver Pyle	Will
Henry Rowland	Al Broderick
Tex Terry	Dike
Ray Jones, Herman Hack, Frankie Marvin	Townsmen
Champion	Champion

FILMING DATES: November 1-6, 1952 (Companion episode "Outlaw of Blue Mesa".)
LOCATIONS: Death Valley—Furnace Creek Camp #1; Corriganville

THE FILM: In one of the more movie-like episodes, Marshals Gene Autry and Pat Buttram track down a sharpshooting escaped criminal but, after hearing his side of things, help him clear himself of a trumped up charge by a brutal sheriff.

NOTES AND COMMENTS: Oops—watch for the boom mike shadow on the building wall when Pat is tangled up in the clothesline.

"Talking Guns"

ORIGINAL AIRDATE: August 10, 1954

Executive Producer	Armand Schaefer
Producer	Louis Gray
Director	D. Ross Lederman
Teleplay	Dwight Cummins
Director of Photography	William Bradford
Film Editor	Jack Wheeler
Musical Director	Carl Cotner
Musical Supervisor	Irving Friedman
Musical Score	Walter Greene
Assistant Director	Gilbert Kay

SONG: "The Cowboy's Trademarks" (music and lyrics by Gene Autry)—sung by Gene Autry.

CAST:

Actor	*Character*
Gene Autry	Gene Autry
Pat Buttram	Pat Buttram
Jim Bannon	Nate Tully
Emmett Lynn	Enoch Lesser
Harry Lauter	Mack Healy
William Fawcett	Grandpa Dekker
Stan Jolley	Jess Wheatley
Pierce Lyden	Vince Keys
Dee Pollock	Ronnie Dekker
Herman Hack	Extra
Champion	Champion

FILMING DATES: September 26 to October 2, 1952 (Companion episode "Civil War at Deadwood".)
LOCATIONS: Lone Pine; Corriganville

THE FILM: Special investigator Gene Autry helps a half crazy old mine owner and his grandson ward off a gang of claim jumpers.

"Hoodoo Canyon"

ORIGINAL AIRDATE: August 17, 1954

Executive Producer	Armand Schaefer
Producer	Louis Gray
Director	D. Ross Lederman
Teleplay	Fred Myton
Director of Photography	William Bradford
Film Editor	Jack Wheeler
Musical Director	Carl Cotner
Musical Supervisor	Irving Friedman
Musical Score	Walter Greene
Assistant Director	Stanley Neufeld

SONG: "Hillbilly Wedding In June" (music and lyrics by Buddy Moore, Freddie Owen)—sung by Gene Autry.

CAST:

Actor	*Character*
Gene Autry	Gene Autry
Pat Buttram	Pat Buttram
Rochelle Stanton	Linda McKee
Arthur Space	Jason McKee

Gene rides Champ in another exciting desert chase.

James Best	Ray Saunders
Forrest Taylor	Jim Saunders
Rory Mallinson	Slade
Gregg Barton	Burke
William Fawcett	Hank
Bob Woodward	2nd Stage Driver
Champion	Champion

FILMING DATES: June 15-20, 1952 (Companion episode "Holdup".)
LOCATION: Pioneertown

THE FILM: The owner of a seemingly jinxed stageline enlists Gene and Pat's assistance to find the real cause behind his troubles. Along the way Gene helps the owner's spoiled son to grow up.

"The Carnival Comes West"

ORIGINAL AIRDATE: August 24, 1954

Executive Producer	Armand Schaefer
Producer	Louis Gray
Director	D. Ross Lederman
Teleplay	Buckley Angell
Director of Photography	William Bradford
Film Editor	Paul Borofsky
Musical Director	Carl Cotner
Musical Supervisor	Irving Friedman
Musical Score	Walter Greene
Assistant Director	Gilbert Kay

SONGS: "Ridin' All Day" (music and lyrics by Gene Autry, Smiley Burnette)—sung by Gene Autry; "Silver Spurs On the Golden Stairs" (music and lyrics by Gene Autry, Cindy Walker)—sung by Gene Autry.

CAST:

Actor	Character
Gene Autry	Gene Autry
Pat Buttram	Pat Buttram

Ann Doran	Emma Conley
Denver Pyle	Sheriff Jim
Harry Lauter	Fresno
Henry Rowland	Santley
Clayton Moore	Tom Golden
Gregg Barton	Pete
William Fawcett	Slim
Pat Mitchell	Boy
??	Barker
Champion	Champion

FILMING DATES: July 27 to August 1, 1952 (Companion episode "Johnny Jackaroo".)
LOCATIONS: Lone Pine; Jack Ingram Ranch

THE FILM: The prideful social leader of a western town goes to surprising lengths to guard a secret from her past, leading Gene and Pat into the middle of a carnival in trouble.

"Battle Axe"

ORIGINAL AIRDATE: August 31, 1954

Executive Producer	Armand Schaefer
Producer	Louis Gray
Director	George Archainbaud
Teleplay	Virginia M. Cooke
Director of Photography	William Bradford
Film Editor	Harvey Manger
Musical Director	Carl Cotner
Musical Supervisor	Irving Friedman
Musical Score	Walter Greene
Assistant Director	Stanley Neufeld

SONG: "What's Gonna Happen to Me" (music and lyrics by Gene Autry)—sung by Gene Autry.

CAST:

Actor	Character
Gene Autry	Gene Autry
Pat Buttram	Pat Buttram
Mira McKinney	Belle Anderson (Battle Axe)
Rick Vallin	Vasco
Peter Votrian	Timmy
Terry Frost	Rolf
Francis McDonald	Sheriff Dan Carter
Gregg Barton	Barton
Kenne Duncan	Jed
Wes Hudman	Trask
Bob Woodward	Stage Driver
Fred Krone	Stage Guard
Jerry Scoggins, Fred Martin, Bert Dodson	Townsmen
Robert O'Byrne	Extra in street

Frankie Marvin............................Extra in bar
Herman Hack ....Extra loading stagecoach
Champion....................................Champion

FILMING DATES: December 15-20, 1952 (Companion episode "Boots and Ballots".)
LOCATIONS: Iverson Ranch; Monogram Ranch

THE FILM: When an elderly old maid known as "Battle Axe" pins on a sheriff's badge, she finds herself deceived by a smooth-talking confidence man, despite the warnings of the former sheriff and Gene Autry who have to round-up the outlaws themselves.

"Outlaw of Blue Mesa"

ORIGINAL AIRDATE: September 7, 1954

Executive Producer ....Armand Schaefer
Producer.....................................Louis Gray
Director......................................Frank McDonald
Teleplay.....................................Oliver Drake
Director of Photography ....William Bradford
Film Editor.................................Jack Wheeler
Musical Director ....Carl Cotner
Musical Supervisor ....Irving Friedman
Musical Score.............................Walter Greene
Assistant Director........................Gilbert Kay

SONG: "When the Bloom Is On the Sage" (music and lyrics by Fred Howard, Nat Vincent)—sung by Gene Autry.

CAST:

Actor	*Character*
Gene Autry	Gene Autry
Pat Buttram	Pat Buttram
Margaret Field	Sally Jackson
Dick Jones	Tom Jackson
Denver Pyle	Edwin Hadley
Claire Carleton	Marie Hadley
Henry Rowland	Neely
Hank Patterson	Idaho
Tex Terry	Sneed
Fred Krone	Pete
Ray Jones	Man in Restaurant
Herman Hack	Townsman
Champion	Champion

FILMING DATES: November 1-6, 1952 (Companion episode "Sharpshooter".)
LOCATIONS: Death Valley—Furnace Creek Camp #1; Corriganville

THE FILM: Insurance investigators save a young man from a "necktie party" and track down a banker and his wife involved in filing phony insurance claims.

"Civil War at Deadwood"

ORIGINAL AIRDATE: September 14, 1954

Executive Producer ....Armand Schaefer
Producer.....................................Louis Gray
Director......................................D. Ross Lederman
Teleplay.....................................Shelby Gordon
Director of Photography ....William Bradford
Film Editor.................................Paul Borofsky
Musical Director ....Carl Cotner
Musical Supervisor ....Irving Friedman
Musical Score.............................Walter Greene
Assistant Director........................Gilbert Kay

SONGS: None.

CAST:

Actor	*Character*
Gene Autry	Gene Autry
Pat Buttram	Pat Buttram
Gail Davis	Laurie Sampson
William Fawcett	Muskets Joe Corby
Emmett Lynn	Hannibal Sampson
Jim Bannon	Ed Talbot
Stanley Andrews	Sheriff
Harry Lauter	Curly
Stan Jolley	Joe
Pierce Lyden	Bank Teller
Champion	Champion

FILMING DATES: September 26 to October 2, 1952 (Companion episode "Talking Guns".)
LOCATIONS: Corriganville; Lone Pine

THE FILM: Rather weak episode with little action and no music as a feud between two Union and Confederate Army veterans gets out of hand when the two old men accuse each other of horse stealing and an ambushing.

"Boots and Ballots"

ORIGINAL AIRDATE: September 25, 1954

Executive Producer ....Armand Schaefer
Producer.....................................Louis Gray
Director......................................George Archainbaud
Teleplay.....................................Robert Schaefer, Eric Freiwald
Director of Photography ....William Bradford
Film Editor.................................Jack Wheeler
Musical Director ....Carl Cotner
Musical Supervisor ....Irving Friedman
Musical Score.............................Walter Greene
Assistant Director........................Stanley Neufeld

SONG: "Mama Don't Like Music" (music and lyrics by Gene Autry, Smiley Burnette)—sung by Gene Autry backed up by The Cass County Boys.

CAST:

Actor	Character
Gene Autry	Gene Autry
Pat Buttram	Pat Buttram
Mira McKinney	Mary Sanders
Rick Vallin	Yancy
Kenne Duncan	Thatcher Bowden
Gregg Barton	Austin
Terry Frost	Slater
Howard McNeely	Eddie
The Cass County Boys	Musical Group
Fred Krone	Fred
Bob Woodward	Al Walker
Frankie Marvin, Herman Hack, Robert O'Byrne	Townsmen
Champion	Champion

FILMING DATES: December 15-20, 1952 (Companion episode "Battle Axe".)
LOCATIONS: Monogram Ranch; Iverson's; Pioneertown stock footage

THE FILM: The fight for Mayor in a small town election gets out of hand when a murder and kidnapping of a small boy takes place, forcing Sheriff Gene Autry into action to fight for clean government.

NOTES AND COMMENTS: The sequence of Al Walker (played by Bob Woodward) being ambushed in a buckboard is stock footage from "Hot Lead and Old Lace".

"Outlaw Warning"

ORIGINAL AIRDATE: October 2, 1954

Executive Producer	Armand Schaefer
Producer	Louis Gray
Director	George Archainbaud
Teleplay	Robert Schaefer, Eric Freiwald
Director of Photography	William Bradford
Film Editor	Jack Wheeler
Musical Director	Carl Cotner
Musical Supervisor	Irving Friedman
Musical Score	Walter Greene
Assistant Director	Stanley Neufeld

SONG: "A Heart as Big as Texas" (music and lyrics by Oakley Haldeman, Buddy Feyne)—sung by Gene Autry.

CAST:

Actor	Character
Gene Autry	Gene Autry
Pat Buttram	Pat Buttram
Sheila Ryan	Louise Simmons
Myron Healey	Corey Fordham
Lee Van Cleef	Ray
Stanley Andrews	Judge Lockwood
Harry Harvey	Deputy Peters
Mickey Little	Billy Simmons
Melinda Plowman	Betsy Simmons
Gregg Barton	Bricker
Budd Buster	Telegrapher
??	Mr. Lewis
Francis McDonald	Old Timer
Bob Woodward	Clem
Fred Krone	Freddy
Frankie Marvin	Court Recorder
Ray Jones, Herman Hack	Townsmen
Champion	Champion

FILMING DATES: November 7-13, 1952 (Companion episode "Rio Renegades".)
LOCATIONS: Monogram Ranch; Iverson's

THE FILM: Gene Autry comes to help Pat Buttram when a killer, convicted on evidence supplied by Pat, swears revenge on both Pat and the presiding judge.

NOTES AND COMMENTS: The sequence in which Gene saves Mrs. Simmons' (played by Sheila Ryan) runaway buckboard is stock footage from an earlier episode.

Arden Farms Dairy was a sponsor in several markets.

The Gene Autry Show
5ᵗʰ season, 13 episodes IN COLOR 10/1/55-1/7/56). 30 minutes each.
Aired on CBS network on Saturday from 7-7:30pm EST

"The Million Dollar Fiddle"

ORIGINAL AIRDATE: October 1, 1955

Executive Producer	Armand Schaefer
Producer	Louis Gray
Director	Ray Nazarro
Teleplay	John K. Butler
Director of Photography	William Bradford
Supervising Film Editor	Anthony Wollner
Film Editor	Bruce B. Pierce
Musical Director	Carl Cotner
Musical Supervisor	Irving Friedman
Musical Score	Walter Greene
Music Editor	Erma E. Levin
Assistant Director	Stanley Neufeld

SONGS: "Yellow Rose of Texas" (Traditional)—sung by Gene Autry; "Back In the Saddle Again" (music and lyrics by Gene Autry, Ray Whitley)–sung by Gene Autry with Pat Buttram, Peter Votrian, Jean Howell, Nestor Paiva.

CAST:

Actor	Character
Gene Autry	Gene Autry
Pat Buttram	Pat Buttram
Nestor Paiva	Signor Luis Corelli
Harry Lauter	Buck Bowman
Peter Votrian	Reggie Regalado
Jean Howell	Miss Nona Nixon
Joe Besser	Railroad Conductor
Frank Jenks	Bradley
Mike Ragan	Cliff Maddern
Boyd Stockman	Keller
Bob Woodward	Handcar operator
Champion	Champion
Little Champ	Little Champ

FILMING DATES: August 9-14, 1954 (Companion episode "The Golden Chariot".)
LOCATIONS: Melody Ranch; Lone Pine

THE FILM: An eleven year old concert violinist with a valuable half million dollar Stradivarius falls into the hands of thieves when he runs away from home and the concert stage to visit Gene's Flying A Ranch.

NOTES AND COMMENTS: A special effects miniature train shot is quite noticeable and disconcerting in this episode. Also, the slapstick scenes with comedian Joe Besser really seem out of place in a Gene Autry episode.

With the beginning of the 5ᵗʰ produced group of 13 "Gene Autry" TV shows, all were filmed in color. This necessitated a new opening to the series be shot in color, which was filmed at Vasquez Rocks in California. Note that this entire new introduction of Gene riding out on Champ is a "flop shot", in other words, complete reverse photography which was never corrected. Quite obvious by noting Gene's gun is on his left side.

"The Stage to San Dimas"

ORIGINAL AIRDATE: October 8, 1955

Executive Producer	Armand Schaefer
Producer	Louis Gray
Director	George Archainbaud
Teleplay	John K. Butler
Director of Photography	William Bradford
Supervising Film Editor	Anthony Wollner
Film Editor	Bruce B. Pierce
Musical Director	Carl Cotner
Musical Supervisor	Irving Friedman
Musical Score	Walter Greene
Music Editor	Erma E. Levin
Assistant Director	Clark Paylow

SONGS: "Sing Me a Song of the Saddle" (music and lyrics by Gene Autry, Frank Harford)—sung by Gene Autry; "Mellow Mountain Moon" (music and lyrics by Fred Howard, Nat Vincent)—sung by Gene Autry and Barbara Knudson.

CAST:

Actor	*Character*
Gene Autry	Gene Autry
Pat Buttram	Pat Buttram
Barbara Knudson	"Diamond" Della Dix
Keith Richards	Cliff Barton
George J. Lewis	Captain Randy Jones
Myron Healey	Hal Keller
Steve Conte	Bert Nixon
Jack Daly	Pawn Broker Julius Smithers
Edward Clark	Station Agent
Jacquelyn Park	Emily
Bob Woodward	Stage Driver
Frankie Marvin	Stage Guard
Jimmy Noel	Army Sergeant
Champion	Champion

FILMING DATES: August 2-7, 1954 (Companion episode "Guns Below the Border".)

LOCATIONS: Iverson Ranch; Melody Ranch

THE FILM: U.S. Marshal Gene Autry escorts a diverse group of passengers aboard a stagecoach bound for San Dimas. All of the other runs have been cancelled due to an Apache uprising.

NOTES AND COMMENTS: *Barbara Knudson:* "I was a dance hall gal in this episode. Of course, everybody knew because of Gene's drinking that you better get the shots of Gene before noon. (Laughs) That was kind of cute. He was always so pleasant and cheerful, but the funny thing was he could absolutely not remember the names of cities when he was filming. He would do this whole big line and he'd get to a town name and he'd forget it. And they'd say cut. (Laughs) I was in this stagecoach with Pat Buttram. Pat and I are in this overturned thing, and the shot is for Gene to jump over and help me out of this stage. I have to jump down about four and half feet. Prior to that, we left really early, early in the morning. I had grabbed my things, met the limo and gone out on location. We get ready for the scene and I have this big long dress and I put my shoes on but I'd brought two left shoes. So I thought, there wasn't anything that was so major that I couldn't wear those. Now, I had to jump out of this stage. Pat gets me out and we jump down and I have this left shoe on my right foot and it's just killing me. Autry does his line but forgets the town he has to say. 'Cut!' then he'd do the next take. Gene would say, 'They're on the road to…uh…' 'Cut!' About this time, my foot is killing me, my whole leg is out of joint because I'm jumping down on this left shoe. Finally, they ended up, practically saying 'thataway'. It was San Dimas, but he *could not* remember it. (Laughs) That same day, I was sitting by the wardrobe trailer, touching up my makeup. I had this little pillbox hat, made out of cardboard. There was a big two by four, leaning against the trailer, and I guess people walking back and forth in the trailer rocked

Gene's ready for action on the Pioneertown desert.

this board. It fell and hit me smack on the head. If it hadn't been for that hat, I don't know if I'd be here today. (Laughs) Running around with a foot in the wrong shoe and getting hit on the head with a board and everything else in the same film. (Laughs) But I remember Gene, because we had a lot of fun on the set, and Pat was such a wonderful person."[1]

SOURCE:
1. Magers, Boyd and Fitzgerald, Michael. *Ladies of the Western.* McFarland, 2002. p. 128-129.

"The Portrait of White Cloud"

ORIGINAL AIRDATE: October 15, 1955

Executive Producer	Armand Schaefer
Producer	Louis Gray
Director	Robert G. Walker
Teleplay	John K. Butler
Director of Photography	William Bradford
Supervising Film Editor	Anthony Wollner
Film Editor	Bruce B. Pierce
Musical Director	Carl Cotner
Musical Supervisor	Irving Friedman
Musical Score	Walter Greene
Music Editor	Erma E. Levin
Assistant Director	Clark Paylow

SONGS: "Onteora" (music and lyrics by Doris Anderson, Gene Andrea aka Theodore Snyder)—sung by The Cass County Boys; "It's My Lazy Day" (music and lyrics by Smiley Burnette)—sung by Gene Autry, Pat Buttram and The Cass County Boys—reprised by Gene and Cass County Boys.

CAST:

Actor	Character
Gene Autry	Gene Autry
Pat Buttram	Pat Buttram
Jack Daly	Lennie Renault
Dick Rich	Jack Hastings
Glenn Strange	White Cloud
John Close	Sheriff Tim Davis
Steve Raines	Pete Crowder
Terry Frost	Carl McHenry
Joseph Michaels	Running Deer
The Cass County Boys	The Cass County Boys
Champion	Champion

FILMING DATES: November 4-10, 1954 (Companion episode "Go West Young Lady".)
LOCATION: Pioneertown

THE FILM: Gene crosses paths with an artist who has been "framing" his subjects in more ways than one.

"Law Comes to Scorpion"

ORIGINAL AIRDATE: October 22, 1955

Executive Producer	Armand Schaefer
Producer	Louis Gray
Director	George Archainbaud
Teleplay	Maurice Tombragel
Director of Photography	William Bradford
Supervising Film Editor	Anthony Wollner
Film Editor	Jack Wheeler
Musical Director	Carl Cotner
Musical Supervisor	Irving Friedman
Musical Score	Walter Greene
Music Editor	Erma E. Levin
Assistant Director	Stanley Neufeld

SONGS: "Somebody Bigger Than You and I" (music and lyrics by J. Francis Burke)—sung by Gene Autry and congregation (reprised later in the story); "The Angel Song" (music and lyrics by Gene Autry, Curt Massey, Mary Millard)—sung by Gene Autry; "I Wish I Had Never Met Sunshine" (music and lyrics by Gene Autry, Oakley Haldeman, Dale Evans)—sung by Gene Autry.

CAST:

Actor	Character
Gene Autry	Gene Autry
Pat Buttram	Pat Buttram
Arthur Space	Sheriff
Sydney Mason	Parson
Myron Healey	Jaycee Cady
Lisa Montell	Esther
Richard Avonde	Gantry
Earle Hodgins	Judge
John Cason	Henchman #1 (Bob)
Art Dillard	Henchman #2
??	Henchman #3
Tex Palmer	Pete Smith
Roy Bucko	Tom Brown
Bob Woodward, Herman Hack, Jack Perrin	Townsmen
Champion	Champion

FILMING DATES: November 11-17, 1954 (Companion episode "Feuding Friends".)
LOCATIONS: Iverson Ranch; Melody Ranch

THE FILM: When Gene and Pat try to help a crusading parson rid the town of Scorpion of a gambling ring and crooked politicians, Gene himself winds up faced with a homicide charge.

NOTES AND COMMENTS: *Lisa Montell:* "I had always loved riding horses and even won a jumping competition while living in Peru, where I made my first film. So riding horses was not a problem. I always looked forward to filming on location and getting to see parts of the country I had not seen before. I grew up in New York, attended my final year and graduated from high school in Florida, where I also attended the University of Miami, before moving to Peru.

"After Peru, I moved to Los Angeles to work in films. I fell in love with the American southwest which I consider to be quite unique on the planet, with its incredible landscapes, breath-taking beauty, and unusual foliage. It is a magical place full of wonder and spiritual power, as well as extraordinary history. I think that's one reason so many people are captivated by the films of the American West. I was introduced to the Mitchell J. Hamilburg Agency by a friend, after some unpleasant experiences with another major talent agency of the time that I had signed with. Hamilburg was Gene Autry's agent. I immediately liked the people working there and signed with them. They specialized in westerns, of course, so I ended up doing a lot of those.

"I had certainly heard of Gene Autry before working with him, who hadn't? But I had not met him personally. Working with him was a pleasure…he had the quality of many of those early western heroes: courtesy, gentleman-liness, dependability, courage and quiet strength. It felt good being around him—a thoroughly nice person.

"This was one of the first westerns I acted in. Another

early film was 'The Wild Dakotas'. Both these projects were unusual for me in the sense that both the characters I played were typical American western women and I used a 'western accent' playing them. Afterwards, I made numerous western films and TV shows, but was always cast in Native American, Mexican or Spanish (or Polynesian, Burmese, etc.) roles and spoke with those accents. I enjoyed this tremendously, though being plastered with body make-up (for the Indian roles) at 5 or 6am every morning at some desert location, in freezing weather with cold water being used on a sponge to apply the cake make-up, was pretty harrowing and required much more fortitude than anything the scripts called for.

"I did my own singing. I don't think the singing was the strongest suit for any of us in the show but I guess it was the thing to do for those early 'singing cowboy's. To sum it up, it was a most pleasant and enjoyable experience."[1]

SOURCE:
1. Email to Ray Nielsen. November, 2006.

"The Golden Chariot"

ORIGINAL AIRDATE: October 29, 1955

Executive Producer	Armand Schaefer
Producer	Louis Gray
Director	Ray Nazarro
Teleplay	Maurice Geraghty
Director of Photography	William Bradford
Supervising Film Editor	Anthony Wollner
Film Editor	Jack Wheeler
Musical Director	Carl Cotner
Musical Supervisor	Irving Friedman
Musical Score	Walter Greene
Music Editor	Erma E. Levin
Assistant Director	Stanley Neufeld

SONG: "Good Old-Fashioned Hoedown" (music and lyrics by Gene Autry)—sung by Gene Autry.

CAST:

Actor	*Character*
Gene Autry	Gene Autry
Pat Buttram	Pat Buttram
Junius Matthews	Michael Fitzpatrick
Jean Howell	Kathy
Harry Lauter	Charioteer
Ralph Sanford	Harper
Byron Foulger	Throckmorton
Elizabeth Harrower	Abigail Smith
Bob Woodward	Chuck
Tex Palmer	Stage Driver
Frankie Marvin	Sheriff
Ray Jones, Roy Bucko	Townsmen

Gene and Pat Buttram discover some evidence in a tense scene from "The Gene Autry Show."

??	Pete
??	Joe
Champion	Champion

FILMING DATES: August 9-14, 1954 (Companion episode "The Million Dollar Fiddle".)
LOCATIONS: Lone Pine; Melody Ranch

THE FILM: To raise money for a new schoolhouse, Gene enters his matched bay horses in a carnival chariot race and defeats some unscrupulous carnival operators.

"Guns Below the Border"

ORIGINAL AIRDATE: November 5, 1955

Executive Producer	Armand Schaefer
Producer	Louis Gray
Director	George Archainbaud
Teleplay	John K. Butler
Director of Photography	William Bradford
Supervising Film Editor	Anthony Wollner
Film Editor	Jack Wheeler
Musical Director	Carl Cotner
Musical Supervisor	Irving Friedman
Musical Score	Walter Greene
Music Editor	Erma E. Levin
Assistant Director	Clark Paylow

SONGS: "Marcheta" (music and lyrics by Victor Schertzinger)—sung by Gene Autry; "Under Fiesta Stars" (music and lyrics by Gene Autry, Fred Rose)—sung by Gene Autry.

CAST:

Actor	Character
Gene Autry	Gene Autry
Pat Buttram	Pat Buttram
Myron Healey	Jim Banning
Keith Richards	Steve Banning
Lane Bradford	Gregorio
George J. Lewis	Capitan Fernando
David Leonard	Padre Francisco Rio
Eugenia Paul	Marquita
Steve Conte	Cyclops
David Saber	Small Boy
Jimmy Noel	Cavalry Guard
??	Mexican Guard
Champion	Champion

FILMING DATES: August 2-7, 1954 (Companion episode "The Stage to San Dimas".)
LOCATIONS: Melody Ranch; Iverson Ranch

THE FILM: Border Patrol agent Gene Autry tracks down gun-smugglers, following them to the Mexican border where he joins forces with Mexican border guards to stop the crooked operation.

"Ghost Ranch"

ORIGINAL AIRDATE: November 12, 1955

Executive Producer	Armand Schaefer
Producer	Louis Gray
Director	George Archainbaud
Teleplay	Maurice Geraghty
Director of Photography	William Bradford
Supervising Film Editor	Anthony Wollner
Film Editor	Bruce B. Pierce
Musical Director	Carl Cotner
Musical Supervisor	Irving Friedman
Musical Score	Walter Greene
Music Editor	Erma E. Levin
Sound Editor	Arthur E. Klein
Assistant Director	Stanley Neufeld

SONG: "You're the Only Good Thing (That's Happened to Me)"—(music and lyrics by Jack Toombs)—sung by Gene Autry and the Cass County Boys.

CAST:

Actor	Character
Gene Autry	Gene Autry
Pat Buttram	Pat Buttram

Sally Fraser	Torrey Palmer
Harry Harvey Sr.	Gil Barnes
Maxine Gates	Marabelle Carroll
Bob Woodward	Ranch Hand
The Cass County Boys	Musical Group
Art Dillard	Buckboard Driver
??	Ranch Hand
Champion	Champion
Little Champ	Little Champ

FILMING DATES: October 28 to November 3, 1954 (Companion episode "Dynamite".)
LOCATIONS: Pioneertown; Melody Ranch

THE FILM: A hardheaded eastern businesswoman inherits a western ranch but finds efficiency is not the only consideration when running her ranch where Gene is foreman. A very tame episode, unique in that there are *no* outlaws to deal with.

"Go West, Young Lady"

ORIGINAL AIRDATE: November 19, 1955

Executive Producer	Armand Schaefer
Producer	Louis Gray
Director	Robert G. Walker
Teleplay	John K. Butler
Director of Photography	William Bradford
Supervising Film Editor	Anthony Wollner
Film Editor	Jack Wheeler
Musical Director	Carl Cotner
Musical Supervisor	Irving Friedman
Musical Score	Walter Greene
Music Editor	Erma E. Levin
Sound Editor	Harold E. Wooley
Assistant Director	Clark Paylow

SONGS: "Back In the Saddle Again" (music and lyrics by Gene Autry, Ray Whitley)—sung by Gene Autry; "When the Bloom is On the Sage" (music and lyrics by Fred Howard, Nat Vincent)—sung by Gene Autry and The Cass County Boys; "Back in the Doghouse Again" (music and lyrics by Gene Autry, Ray Whitley)—sung by Gene Autry and The Cass County Boys.

CAST:

Actor	Character
Gene Autry	Gene Autry
Pat Buttram	Pat Buttram
Nan Leslie	Mary Gridley
John Close	Big Jim Gridley
Dick Rich	Frank Layton
Jack Daly	Mr. Gillis
Muriel Landers	Little Mountain
Isabelle Dwan	Flora Layton

Gene, astride Champion, chats with his favorite photography director, William Bradford.

The Cass County Boys	Musical Group
Terry Frost	Sheriff Dixon
Bob Woodward	Stage Driver
Joe Michaels	Red Knife
Champion	Champion

FILMING DATES: November 4-10, 1954 (Companion episode "The Portrait of White Cloud".)
LOCATIONS: Pioneertown; Melody Ranch

THE FILM: Gene aids two women who have come west to marry him but are victims of a lonely hearts racket using Gene's name to defraud some 700 women.

"Feuding Friends"

ORIGINAL AIRDATE: November 26, 1955

Executive Producer	Armand Schaefer
Producer	Louis Gray
Director	George Archainbaud
Teleplay	Robert Blane
Director of Photography	William Bradford
Supervising Film Editor	Anthony Wollner
Film Editor	Bruce B. Pierce
Musical Director	Carl Cotner
Musical Supervisor	Irving Friedman
Musical Score	Walter Greene
Music Editor	Erma E. Levin
Sound Editor	Harold E. Wooley
Assistant Director	Stanley Neufeld

SONG: "Crime Will Never Pay" (music and lyrics by Willard Robison, Jack Pepper)—sung by Gene Autry.

CAST:

Actor	*Character*
Gene Autry	Gene Autry
Pat Buttram	Pat Buttram
Arthur Space	George Elkhart
Myron Healey	Gil Storey
Sydney Mason	Bill Grenner
Richard Avonde	Morrison
Dennis Moore	John Teal
Brad Morrow	Small Boy
Reed Howes	Passenger Agent Davis
John Cason	Charlie
Art Dillard	Outlaw
??	Outlaw
Bob Woodward	Stage Driver
??	Stage Guard
Frankie Marvin, Jack Perrin	Hotel Guests
Ray Jones	Hotel Guest in nightclothes
Champion	Champion

FILMING DATES: November 4-17, 1954 (Companion episode "Law Comes to Scorpion".)
LOCATIONS: Iverson Ranch; Melody Ranch

THE FILM: Gene and Pat pretend to be bitter enemies in order to foil a gang of counterfeiters.

"Saddle Up"
(Part 1 of a trilogy)

ORIGINAL AIRDATE: December 3, 1955

Executive Producer	Armand Schaefer
Producer	Louis Gray
Director	George Archainbaud
Teleplay	John K. Butler
Director of Photography	William Bradford
Supervising Film Editor	Anthony Wollner
Film Editor	Bruce B. Pierce
Musical Director	Carl Cotner
Musical Supervisor	Irving Friedman
Musical Score	Walter Greene
Music Editor	Erma E. Levin
Sound Editor	Arthur E. Klein
Assistant Director	Stanley Neufeld

SONGS: "Pretty Mary" (music and lyrics by Gene Autry, Oakley Haldeman, Jim MacDonald, Bob Mitchell)—sung by Gene Autry; "Gallivantin' Galveston Gal" (music and lyrics by Milton Leeds, Steve Nelson, Fred Wise)—sung by Gene Autry and The Cass County Boys.

CAST:

Actor	Character
Gene Autry	Gene Autry
Pat Buttram	Pat Buttram
Sally Mansfield	Abby
Sammy Ogg	"Lefty" Legan
Leonard Penn	Martin Pickett
Gregg Barton	Stan Richter
Will Crandall	Robson
Kenne Duncan	Sheriff Tim McBride
The Cass County Boys	The Cass County Boys
Boyd Stockman	Henchman Moody
??	Stagecoach Driver
Bob Woodward	Man at stage
Charlie Hayes	Stagecoach Guard
??	Dennis
??	George
??	Walter
??	Tony
Champion	Champion
Little Champ	Little Champ

FILMING DATES: December 6-15, 1954 (Companion episodes "Ride Ranchero", "The Rangerette".)
LOCATION: Melody Ranch

THE FILM: Gene takes over a ranch and turns it into a home for underprivileged boys. He faces a stiff challenge when an incorrigible lad arrives at the ranch and uncovers a rustling scheme involving two shady ranch hands.

"Ride Ranchero"

(Part 2 of a trilogy)

ORIGINAL AIRDATE: December 10, 1955

Executive Producer	Armand Schaefer
Producer	Louis Gray
Director	George Archainbaud
Teleplay	John K. Butler
Director of Photography	William Bradford
Supervising Film Editor	Anthony Wollner
Film Editor	Jack Wheeler
Musical Director	Carl Cotner
Musical Supervisor	Irving Friedman
Musical Score	Walter Greene
Music Editor	Erma E. Levin
Sound Editor	Harold E. Wooley
Assistant Director	Stanley Neufeld

SONG: "Ridin' Down the Canyon" (music and lyrics by Gene Autry, Smiley Burnette)—sung by Gene Autry and The Cass County Boys.

CAST:

Actor	Character
Gene Autry	Gene Autry
Pat Buttram	Pat Buttram
Emile Meyer	Big Jim Weston
Sally Mansfield	Abby
Leonard Penn	Martin Pickett
Peter Votrian	Pedro Gonzales
Sammy Ogg	"Lefty" Legan
Gregg Barton	Stan Richter
Kenne Duncan	Sheriff Tim McBride
The Cass County Boys	The Cass County Boys
??	Prison Warden
Will Crandall	Robson
??	Stage Driver
Charlie Hayes	Stage Guard
Bob Woodward	Cowboy
Champion	Champion
Little Champ	Little Champ

FILMING DATES: December 6-15, 1954 (Companion episodes "Saddle Up", "The Rangerette".)
LOCATIONS: Melody Ranch; Vasquez Rocks

THE FILM: Gene secures a parole for a confirmed criminal by giving him a second chance at the Flying A Ranch for underprivileged boys, but the man schemes to make Gene's work fail so he may obtain the ranch for himself.

"The Rangerette"

(Part 3 of a trilogy)

ORIGINAL AIRDATE: December 17, 1955

Executive Producer	Armand Schaefer
Producer	Louis Gray
Director	George Archainbaud
Teleplay	John K. Butler
Director of Photography	William Bradford
Supervising Film Editor	Anthony Wollner
Film Editor	Bruce B. Pierce
Musical Director	Carl Cotner
Musical Supervisor	Irving Friedman
Musical Score	Walter Greene
Music Editor	Erma E. Levin
Sound Editor	Arthur E. Klein
Assistant Director	Stanley Neufeld

SONGS: "'Neath the Blue Montana Skies" (music and lyrics by Gene Autry, Johnny Marvin, Fred Rose)—sung by Gene Autry; "Old MacDonald Had a Farm" (Traditional)—sung by Gene Autry and The Cass County Boys.

CAST:

Actor	Character
Gene Autry	Gene Autry
Pat Buttram	Pat Buttram
Emile Meyer	Big Jim Weston
Sally Mansfield	Abby
Leonard Penn	Martin Pickett
Nancy Gilbert	Geri Wentworth (Weston)
Peter Votrian	Pedro Gonzales
Sammy Ogg	"Lefty" Legan
Gregg Barton	Stan Richter
The Cass County Boys	The Cass County Boys
Kenne Duncan	Sheriff Tim McBride
Will Crandall	Robson
Boyd Stockman	Henchman Moody
Richard Farnsworth	Henchman
Champion	Champion
Little Champ	Little Champ

FILMING DATES: December 6-15, 1954 (Companion episodes "Saddle Up"; "Ride Ranchero".)
LOCATIONS: Melody Ranch; Vasquez Rocks

THE FILM: When Gene welcomes a young girl to his ranch for underprivileged boys, he discovers the girl is the daughter of a hardened criminal he'd tried to straighten out but who is now on his way back to prison. Gene must also deal with a crooked lawyer trying to obtain control of the Flying A Ranch.

"Dynamite"

ORIGINAL AIRDATE: January 7, 1956

Executive Producer	Armand Schaefer
Associate Producer	Louis Gray

Director	George Archainbaud
Teleplay	Maurice Geraghty
Director of Photography	William Bradford
Supervising Film Editor	Anthony Wollner
Film Editor	Bruce B. Pierce
Musical Director	Carl Cotner
Musical Supervisor	Irving Friedman
Musical Score	Walter Greene
Music Editor	Erma E. Levin
Assistant Director	Stanley Neufeld

SONGS: "Sierra Nevada" (music and lyrics by Joel Herron)—sung by Gene Autry and The Cass County Boys; "Trail to Mexico" (music and lyrics by Johnny Lange, Lew Porter)—sung by The Cass County Boys.

CAST:

Actor	Character
Gene Autry	Gene Autry
Pat Buttram	Pat Buttram
Francis McDonald	Ben (Harry Talbot)
Sally Fraser	Deborah
Glenn Strange	McCann
Harry Harvey, Sr.	Sheriff
Robert Bice	Charles Driscoll
John Boutwell	Garson
Bob Woodward	Tom Rankin
The Cass County Boys	Musical Group
Art Dillard	Henchman
Champion	Champion

FILMING DATES: October 28 to November 3, 1954 (Companion episode "Ghost Ranch".)
LOCATIONS: Pioneertown; Melody Ranch

THE FILM: A runaway empty stagecoach leads Gene into an adventure involving a mine disaster in which Pat is nearly killed.

Ridin' Down the Trail…

Gene Autry was far from ready to hang up his spurs even though his movie and TV series days were over. Gene's Flying A Productions of other series also wound down throughout the '50s. "Range Rider" with Jock Mahoney and Dick Jones ran from 1950-1953. Gail Davis' "Annie Oakley", with her kid brother Tagg (Jimmy Hawkins), aired from 1954-1957 and "Buffalo Bill Jr." starring Dick Jones and Nancy Gilbert was on from 1955-1956. There was also "The Adventures of Champion" in the '55-'56 season.

But times were changing, the advent of cultural changes in the country wrought by TV and rock and roll affected Gene's "Melody Ranch" radio show as well. In 1953 more pop songs were being utilized and the cast was reduced. The final broadcast came on May 13, 1956, after 17 years on the air for Wrigley Gum.

With Bill Haley, Little Richard, Fats Domino, Elvis Presley and other rock and rollers commanding more radio air time, Gene's recording career also slowly faded away with only a handful of releases through the mid-'50s, then consisted mainly of reissues and greatest hits albums.

Gene appeared on his last tour in 1961 with the Cass County Boys. Certainly there were the occasional talk-show guest shots but for all his love of entertaining there seemed to be no limit to Gene's energy and ambition, so his primary focus now became his growing business empire. He expanded, forming Golden West Broadcasters with radio and TV stations in Phoenix, San Francisco, Seattle, Detroit, Portland and Oklahoma City, also including KMPC radio and KTLA-TV in Los Angeles. "Melody Ranch" reappeared as a TV program in the Fall of 1963 and ran for seven years on KTLA. Although Gene didn't appear as a regular, he did make a handful of guest appearances. In the late '50s his Challenge Records label turned out hits by the Champs ("Tequila"), Jerry Wallace ("Primrose Lane", "Shutters and Boards") and others. Two years later he formed Republic Records. At one time or another the corporate cowboy owned a string of hotels (including the Mark Hopkins in San Francisco, the Gene Autry Hotel in Palm Springs) as well as a rodeo, the Flying A Ranch in Texas, a 20,000 acre cattle ranch in Arizona, ranches in Oklahoma and Colorado, three music publishing firms, interests in movie theaters around Dallas, Texas, and in the deep South, two newspapers in Arizona, a flying school and charter airplane service, even an oil well in partnership with good friend boxer Jack Dempsey. Pat Buttram once joked, "Gene Autry used to ride off into the sunset, now he owns it."

Gene became a major public figure in the business world when he bought and was approved to operate the California Angels baseball team in December 1960. Throughout the next four decades Gene turned more and more to his lifelong interest in baseball

Gene's Flying A Productions produced "Range Rider" with Dick Jones (left) and Jock Mahoney (center).

Gene and Jackie Autry.

while continuing to oversee his various business interests.

As we've seen, Gene's career was multi-faceted, eventually becoming the only individual to have five stars on the Hollywood Walk of Fame: Radio, Recording, Motion Pictures, Television and Live Theatre.

Throughout the '60s, '70s, '80s and '90s Gene truly became America's most honored star. The Autry home is filled with plaques, loving cups, scrolls, badges, keys to cities, and banners all proclaiming the many honors which have been bestowed upon him by civic and governmental dignitaries, charitable organizations, youth groups and others. Perhaps the most singular honor was having Berwyn, Oklahoma, change its name in 1940 to Gene Autry, Oklahoma, where a museum in his honor now stands. Gene has also been elected to the Country Music Hall of Fame, the Cowboy Hall of Fame, the Oklahoma Hall of Fame, received the Nashville Songwriters Hall of Fame Award, the Country Music Pioneer Award, the National Broadcasters Hall of Fame Award, the Golden Boot Award and hundreds more, including Grammy Hall of Fame Awards for "Rudolph the Red Nosed Reindeer" and "Back in the Saddle Again".

In 1987 The Nashville Network decided to screen Gene's B-westerns under the title of "Melody Ranch Theater" with Gene and co-host Pat Buttram providing lively banter and remembrances of making each film.

In November of 1988 The Gene Autry Western Heritage Museum (now the Autry National Center) in Los Angeles' Griffith Park opened to the public, a non-profit cultural and educational institution that acquires and preserves artifacts, art and archival material documenting the development and history of the American West. Built with a $54 million gift from the Autry Foundation, the museum is a world-class center and a monumental, lasting tribute to Gene.

Gene married Ina Mae Spivey in 1932. Their marriage endured 48 years until her death in 1980. In July 1981 Gene married Jacqueline Ellam who served as the 13th female vice president in the Security Pacific National Bank system. Jackie oversees Gene's estate and serves as president of his companies as well as the Autry Foundation and is chairwoman and a director of the Autry National Center. Long sharing Gene's love of baseball, and a savvy businesswoman in her own right, Jackie Autry is the honorary American League president of major league baseball.

Gene always believed his success was due to the fact he always played to "the real middle America." Every movie, TV show, radio program or personal appearance Gene made was designed to provide wholesome entertainment for eager audiences. The story of Gene Autry is an epic of America, equally inspiring as that of many time-honored figures of history who demonstrated the American promise that anyone, no matter how humble his beginnings, is endowed with the rich heritage of unlimited opportunity. Gene Autry proved that promise and fired the imagination of the world over seven decades.

When Gene died on October 2, 1998, President Bill Clinton wrote, "He lived the virtues he embodied on screen…fairness, integrity, kindness, courage and generosity. He was a hero to millions. Gene Autry's music and movies captured all that was good and inspiring about America's Old West." President Ronald Reagan said, "He put his heart and soul into every project he worked on and there will never be another like him."

394

Gene's Top Tens

To illustrate how various Gene Autry enthusiasts view his films as to their particular favorites, we solicited 'Top 10 Lists' from several noted authorities on Gene Autry, all of whom have viewed all of Gene's films many times over the years. It's interesting to note the differences in their selections. (Participants listed alphabetically.)

Les Adams
Author of SHOOT 'EM UPS

My choices are based on the ones where Autry was "in his element" persona-and-plot wise. Based on what I liked best and not what may have been best. I have no idea what constitutes a Best film. But I know what I like.

- ❖ "The Phantom Empire" ('35)—A table-setter…and Smiley had little to do. I really liked that part.
- ❖ "Tumbling Tumbleweeds" ('35)—For the title song, plus "That Silver Haired Daddy of Mine".
- ❖ "Springtime in the Rockies" ('37)—"You're the Only Star in My Blue Heaven" as one of the songs, and Gene devised a scare plan worthy of Smiley Burnette.
- ❖ "The Big Show" ('36)—It has a Texas Centennial background, the Sons of the Pioneers *and* The Light Crust Doughboys, a double doubling Autry doubling himself, "Nobody's Darling But Mine" and a real Texas Ranger in it.
- ❖ "Comin' 'Round the Mountain" ('36)—Autry in tailored buckskins as a Pony Express rider.
- ❖ "Guns and Guitars" ('36)—Autry and Earle Hodgins *both* in their elements.
- ❖ "Public Cowboy No. 1" ('37)—Because the first Big Little Book I ever owned was adapted from this film.
- ❖ "Boots and Saddles" ('37)—Bill Elliott, Judith Allen… and Ra Hould, a kid extremely easy to dislike.
- ❖ "Melody Trail" ('35)—Because it had a corral full of Sweet Young Thangs.
- ❖ "Melody Ranch" ('40)—Jimmy Durante, "Gabby" Hayes…and the most inept gangsters seen outside of a Columbia serial directed by James W. Horne. All hands seemed to be having a good time.

Doug Altizer

Trying to list 10 favorite Gene Autry movies is like comparing between my two children as to which one is my favorite. Both my children are my favorites and I make no comparison between either of them. So, I guess you know where I am going—all of Gene's movies are my favorites!

- ❖ "The Strawberry Roan" ('48)

- ❖ "The Big Sombrero" ('49)
- ❖ "Riders in the Sky" ('49)
- ❖ "Mule Train" ('50)
- ❖ "Shooting High" ('40)
- ❖ "South of the Border" ('39)
- ❖ "Sierra Sue" ('41)
- ❖ "Melody Ranch" ('40)
- ❖ "Whirlwind" ('51)
- ❖ "Cow Town" ('50)

Chuck Anderson
Old Corral Website

- ❖ "Down Mexico Way" ('41)—If I had to pick my favorite Autry, this is it. Nice performance by A and B film actor Sidney Blackmer as one of the con men trying to swindle the local populace into investing in a phony John Wayne movie. Great Autry tunes.
- ❖ "Sioux City Sue" ('46)—Nice blend of western and comedy with Gene hired by Lynne Roberts to do some singing in a film, unaware his voice will be used for a cartoon character. Wife and kids don't appreciate B-westerns? Show them this one.
- ❖ "The Phantom Empire" ('35)—Producer Nat Levine planned to star Ken Maynard in this cliffhanger. Instead, Gene got the hero role in this sci-fi western which has robots, death rays, "Thunder Riders", the underground city of Murania…and Autry always arriving in the nick of time to do his weekly "Radio Ranch" broadcast. I watched every episode over and over…and was mesmerized. Ask a fan to recall their favorite childhood memories of serials—good chance "The Phantom Empire" will be on their list.
- ❖ "Gaucho Serenade" ('40)—Great Autry adventure with Gene and Smiley as penniless rodeo performers who leave the hustle and bustle of New York and head west. Along the way, they meet June Storey, Mary Lee and Duncan Renaldo. But the storyline is about a stowaway English lad trying to connect with his father, unaware that his dad is in jail on an embezzlement charge.
- ❖ "Riders in the Sky" ('49)—I saw this at a little theater

in Georgia when I was about seven or eight. At the time, I was very impressed with the superimposed images of the "ghost riders" galloping on white horses in billowy cloud formations. Screen vet Tom London is a personal favorite, and in "Riders" he's showcased as the grizzled but nice "Old Man Roberts". He dies at the end, and becomes one of the mystic riders while Gene sings a great rendition of "Ghost Riders In the Sky".

❖ "Mexicali Rose" ('39)—Radio singer Gene Autry discovers his sponsor is involved in phony oil wells and a fraudulent stock scheme…and the local orphanage is affected. Playing a good guy for a change is ruff, gruff Noah Beery Sr. who really hams it up.

❖ "Colorado Sunset" ('39)—Gene, Smiley and milk cows versus a dairy protection racket. Buster Crabbe, sporting a moustache, is one of the gang. Rock solid Autry with lots of music and action.

❖ "Bells of Capistrano" ('42)—Gene's last film before he entered WWII is an exciting tale of two competing rodeo shows, one run by pretty Virginia Grey and the other by unscrupulous Morgan Conway. Grey's show becomes popular because Gene is her singing cowboy attraction.

❖ "Boots and Saddles" ('37)—Gene is the foreman of a ranch owned by an English youngster. The brains heavy is a moustached Gordon Elliott, a year or so prior to starring in westerns at Columbia and becoming "Wild Bill" Elliott. The ending includes a superbly filmed horse race with the winner getting the contract.

❖ "Blue Montana Skies" ('39)—As a kid, I wasn't a fan of the singing cowboy. Give me action and gunplay please—not songs. This one is a bit different than Gene's normal—there's less tunes and the theme is about fur smuggling blended against a snowy background. Memorable to me 'cause this was *the* Autry film in which I first realized that "Gene can ride".

Karla Buhlman
VP, Gene Autry Entertainment
(In chronological order)

❖ "Tumbling Tumbleweeds" ('35)—Has my favorite Gene Autry song "Ridin' Down the Canyon" and Gene sings it with a recording of himself. The film also uses one of my all time favorite plot points: tricking the bad guys with a recording of Gene singing. Also has Gene's "That Silver Haired Daddy of Mine" which was the first song to ever receive a Gold Record.

❖ "The Big Show" ('36)—With the Texas Centennial as the set of this movie, how can it not be great? Gene plays two roles, which is highly entertaining. Champion gets to do some acting as well. The music is excellent.

❖ "Home on the Prairie" ('39)—Smiley's song "There's Nothing Like Work", the plot with Hoof and Mouth disease, and a live elephant! I just love the bits with Smiley and the elephant.

❖ "In Old Monterey" ('39)—Smiley and The Hoosier Hot Shots are lots of fun in this movie with their comical numbers. Good story of Gene the rancher becoming Gene the soldier, pretending to still be a rancher to help persuade the farmers to sell their lands to the government for proving grounds. The movie also reflects America on the eve of WWII with serious and moving songs.

❖ "South of the Border" ('39)—Great songs, good plot and the introduction of Mary Lee. Things that I like: Gene and Smiley are government agents; Gene "kisses" the lady; Smiley and Gene ride their horses onto the ship headed south; Gene and Morse Code; Gene's escape from the bad guys; the end beach scene.

❖ "Gaucho Serenade" ('40)—It doesn't have a lot of action, but it does have one of my favorite Gene Autry plots: Gene pretends to be foreman of Rancho San Quentin so a young boy won't learn the truth about his father's imprisonment. This is a western road picture with great female roles of the runaway bride (June Storey) and little sister (Mary Lee). Gene and Smiley's friendship clearly comes through, especially in the "bat in the barn" sequence and you clearly see Gene laughing at the absurd situation.

❖ "Ridin' on a Rainbow" ('41)—Gene's performance of the song "Be Honest with Me" was nominated for the Best Song Academy Award. I like the showboat setting, and the musical numbers with Mary Lee are very good.

❖ "Sioux City Sue" ('46)—Opens with Gene riding Champion and singing "Oklahoma Hills". Gene has returned to movies after flying planes for Uncle Sam and he looks *great!* The whole self-reflexive movie theme is wonderful. Strong female roles and the movie notes the first time the Cass County Boys appear onscreen with Gene.

❖ "Whirlwind" ('51)—Smiley returns after a nine year absence. The film opens with a happy Gene riding Champion and he then proceeds to *rob a stagecoach!* Also, you may start to wonder if there is a "five minute fistfight rule" in this film—there are so many fights. I totally love Gail Davis' character transition via clothing: first she's mistaken for a man due to her cowboy outfit of jeans, fringe coat and hat. Then she goes riding with Gene, and she is wearing gauchos—a split skirt popularized by female rodeo riders in the 1900s. Then, at the end of the film, she's quite the "prairie princess" with her full length gingham dress and ribbon in her hair.

❖ "Blue Canadian Rockies" ('52)—This film has all the trademark Gene Autry Columbia things: Gail Davis, Pat Buttram, smart Champion, Gene in blue denim shirt, Gene shooting at the bad guy from a cluster of large rocks, and the Cass County Boys.

Brian Dalrymple
(In chronological order)

❖ "In Old Santa Fe" ('34)—When I first saw the film it

(and "The Phantom Empire") really cemented me as a life-long Gene Autry fan. A great cast, a great plot and a fine location. Some knew Gene from radio and records, but this was the first time people both saw and heard him. A quality film and historically the first real musical western.

❖ "The Phantom Empire" ('35)—The best musical western/science fiction film of all time. The television airing of this serial over 50 years ago firmed me in as a life-long Gene Autry fan. Autry, an inexperienced actor, does a fine job as he talks and sings his way through an encyclopedia sized script. This film is so good that every time I see it, I want to put a metal bucket on my head and join the junior Thunder Riders Club.

❖ "Melody Trail" ('35)—A great film with the earlier style cowboy music I love. Goes beyond the standard B-western formula with Gene and Smiley being robbed in their room, having a run-in with gypsies, a kidnapped baby, a band of cowgirl ranch hands, and a thieving dog. One of Gene and Smiley's best film comedy sequences of all time has them trying to come off as cooks as they prepare food for the band of cowgirl ranch hands.

❖ "Red River Valley" ('36)—The great outdoor Arizona settings lend a lot to the proceedings. During the action scenes, the overly dramatic orchestral accompaniment keeps us sitting on the edge of our seats as George Chesebro and Gene nearly drown in the rushing waters of the dam.

❖ "The Big Show" ('36)—There's nothing like this special Texas Centennial production. It's the inside story of a singing cowboy star and behind the scenes movie making. It's interesting to see a camera car as it is being filmed by another camera car and a visit to the front gate of Republic. The musical content of the film is excellent with both western and pop songs included.

❖ "Git Along Little Dogies" ('37)—Has the best beginning title credits of them all set to a fine rendition of the title song. There's something about hearing this traditional cowboy song done to its full visual and audio potential. Sing-a-long with the gang and follow the printed lyrics on the screen and soon arrive at the conclusion that "oils well that ends well."

❖ "Rootin' Tootin' Rhythm" ('37)—Who can resist the presence of one of the better western groups, Al Clauser and His Oklahoma Outlaws. Hal Taliaferro and Gene trying sneakily to out do each other is a priceless match of personalities. The adventure element mixed with fine early cowboy musical renditions makes this film a real gem.

❖ "Boots and Saddles" ('37)—Has all the necessary elements of quality western music, hilarious comedy and exciting action. I believe this film to be the most humorous of the Autry westerns. The shenanigans with the Colonel and his daughter and the action made this film a real winner.

❖ "Gaucho Serenade" ('40)—It's the best, if not the only, road picture Gene and Smiley made. Traveling the highways across the country by car opens opportunities for fine musical interludes and funny comedy sequences. The support of June Storey and Mary Lee is superb.

❖ "Heart of the Rio Grande" ('42)—A highlight of this film is the great accompaniment of the Jimmy Wakely Trio, one of the best western singing groups of all time. What a great message that exhorts a strictly business father to change his ways and spend more time with his kids.

Jimmy Glover

This is not an easy task but I'll settle on these:
❖ "The Strawberry Roan" ('48)
❖ "Whirlwind" ('51)
❖ "Ride, Tenderfoot, Ride" ('40)
❖ "Sioux City Sue" ('46)
❖ "Twilight on the Rio Grande" ('47)
❖ "The Last Round-Up" ('47)
❖ "Loaded Pistols" ('49)
❖ "Bells of Capistrano" ('42)
❖ "The Big Sombrero" ('49)
❖ "The Cowboy and the Indians" ('49)

Billy Holcomb

❖ "The Strawberry Roan" ('48)—An all around excellent motion picture, which ranks at the very pinnacle of any Hollywood film ever made. Photography, story, and location are fantastic, which proves the picture must be classed, in its rightful place, as a quality major production. It causes anyone to realize just how good Autry pictures really were.

❖ "Red River Valley" ('36)—Fast and furious, and never lets up from start to finish. Truly an exciting picture, which I feel really made Autry the most famous of all time cowboy greats. The song was older than Gene, but he introduced it to the world, and he is why it is as popular as ever.

❖ "Gene Autry and the Mounties" ('51)—A refreshing, believable, and much needed boost for the genre, made during a time when westerns were experiencing a decline in popularity. The Autry voice was unique, and never sounded better with a couple of super tunes.

❖ "The Big Sombrero" ('49)—This beautifully filmed romantic outdoor adventure is one of the biggest extravagant musicals. I wish the final kissing scene could be restored. It could prove Autry and Elena Verdugo were a true love team to be reckoned with.

❖ "Last of the Pony Riders" ('53)—A tremendous exit to musical westerns, and the man who brought them to the screen. Quality, and major production can be seen for the entire hour. The Autry stock company of actors paid the western farewell, in dignity and grace.

❖ "Mule Train" ('50)—Every Autry picture had excellent photography, and this one was especially handled with care. The scenery cannot be topped even by today's standard, and the cast was perfect. "Mule Train" raised Autry to higher acclaim, and the picture was chosen to represent westerns.

❖ "South of the Border" ('39)—Another Autry song which continues to live over half a century later. Possibly the most famous of all his pictures. Very well photographed, with something for everyone—action, songs, romance and comedy.

❖ "Riders in the Sky" ('49)—The easy going pace of the picture is enjoyed by casual western fans and newcomers to Autry alike. Others recorded the song, but when The Cowboy did his version, everyone else was forgotten.

❖ "The Big Show" ('36)—I only wish more westerns were like this, because I enjoy so much seeing old Dallas in '36, and would enjoy seeing other streets of old time downtowns, and musical groups.

❖ "The Phantom Empire" ('35)—This serial is a must for those who aren't familiar with the singing cowboy, which makes us want more, and that is probably what happened over half a century ago.

Mike Johnson

❖ "The Big Show" ('36)—Delightful movie within a movie. Big budget Republic entry.

❖ "Mexicali Rose" ('39)—One of the best examples of what made Gene a star. Music, action and a good story.

❖ "Gaucho Serenade" ('40)—Great production values, a good story with genuine humor.

❖ "Melody Ranch" ('40)—Almost an A-picture. Durante is priceless!

❖ "Sioux City Sue" ('46)—My favorite Autry. Again a movie within a movie. Great songs. Good use of Corriganville and the Republic backlot.

❖ "The Last Round-Up" ('47)—A great start for Gene's own production company. A different "look" than Republic but story and production values just as high.

❖ "Loaded Pistols" ('49)—Love the repeated used of a great song plus the Lone Pine setting. Offbeat story and no sidekick a bonus!

❖ "Mule Train" ('50)—Great action and shows Lone Pine at its best.

❖ "The Blazing Sun" ('50)—Sentimental favorite since I remember this one as a kid. Loved the railroad sequences.

❖ "Whirlwind" ('51)—Perhaps Gene's best Columbia that in some ways rivals anything he did at Republic.

Phil Loy
Author of BROTHERS OF THE WEST and WESTERNS AND AMERICAN CULTURE 1930-1955.

The first five films are ranked in order of preference. The next five are listed in no particular order. I am attracted to the first five because each of them is a bit unusual or has an interesting plot twist. I was somewhat surprised that most of my favorites were prior to 1940. The Gene Autry westerns I remember as a kid were all the late '40s and early '50s Columbia films.

❖ "Yodelin' Kid From Pine Ridge" ('37)
❖ "Hills of Utah" ('51)
❖ "In Old Monterey" ('39)
❖ "Rovin' Tumbleweeds" ('39)
❖ "The Cowboy and the Indians" ('49)
❖ "South of the Border" ('39)
❖ "Boots and Saddles" ('37)
❖ "The Big Show" ('36)
❖ "Prairie Moon" ('38)
❖ "Colorado Sunset" ('39)

Boyd Magers

In writing this book, I viewed every one of Gene's films in chronological order (some more than once). These, for various reasons, stood out in my eyes.

❖ "Rovin' Tumbleweeds" ('39)—I love the radical departure from previous Autry films. A perfect social commentary on real life problems of the time. Exactly the type material that set Gene apart from the rest of the B-westerns.

❖ "Gaucho Serenade" ('40)—This "road picture" is Gene at the top of his career giving the public exactly what it wanted. Some of the wittiest dialogue and the most contagious fun of any Autry western.

❖ "Texans Never Cry" ('51)—A dynamite, unusual title, one of his best Columbia casts in a strong story well developed. The romance angle is the best in all of his Columbias.

❖ "Sioux City Sue" ('46)—Gene's back, singing better than ever in a picture unlike any he made before or after the war. Pure fun!

❖ "On Top of Old Smoky" ('53)—One of Gene's best latter-day Columbias incorporating a strong story and more music than usual. This one harkens back to Gene and Smiley's Republic days, and the title song has always been one of my favorites.

❖ "South of the Border" ('39)—Gene's most romantic film. Director George Sherman mixes the love story with exciting drama to begin a new era for Gene.

❖ "Back In the Saddle" ('41)—Quintessential Autry, combining his themesong with slambang action.

❖ "Riders In the Sky" ('49)—A hit ballad folded into a great story. We agree with Gene, the ending is possibly the best in B-western history.

❖ "Red River Valley" ('36)—Perhaps the most fast moving, exciting, tightly-knit of Gene's early westerns.

❖ "The Phantom Empire" ('35)—Where it all began. Fun to see the raw undeveloped talent and to think how it evolved and grew. Besides, it's a great serial.

Gary Parmenter

❖ "Melody Ranch" ('40)—My all time favorite Autry film where Gene looked, sang and acted his very best. The only thing wrong, Smiley was not in it.

❖ "Whirlwind" ('51)—My all time favorite Columbia film. Smiley was hilarious and the songs were great.

❖ "Mexicali Rose" ('39)—Had some of the best songs Autry ever did and was a funny and entertaining movie.

❖ "Home in Wyomin'" ('42)—Some great songs. Smiley and Tadpole were great together.

❖ "The Strawberry Roan" ('48)—Gene's first color film and Champ was beautiful. Dick Jones, one of my favorite actors, was good in this one!

❖ "Riders of the Whistling Pines" ('49)—The scenery and songs were great. Wish it had been in color.

❖ "Back in the Saddle" ('41)—Has my all time favorite title song of Gene's.

❖ "Robin Hood of Texas" ('47)—Gene returns from the war and was just as good as ever. I loved this film!

❖ "Cowboy Serenade" ('42)—One of my favorite Republics with Gene. Slim Andrews and Smiley Burnette both were hilarious. Especially great after I got to see it uncut for the first time.

❖ "On Top of Old Smoky" ('53)—One of my very favorite Columbia films of Gene. Smiley and Gene were great together in this film.

David Rothel
Author of THE GENE AUTRY BOOK and others.

❖ "Mexicali Rose" ('39)—One of the best of the '30s films with a great title song, a sentimental but atmospheric plot, and a great supporting cast.

❖ "Ride, Tenderfoot, Ride" ('40)—This film has all the ingredients one would expect of a pre-war Autry film: Smiley's comedy, a snooty leading lady (June Storey) Gene has to win over, unscrupulous businessmen as the villains, Mary Lee providing the "kid sister" appeal, and a passel of fine western songs.

❖ "Bells of Capistrano" ('42)—Gene's last film before WWII is well written and appropriately patriotic for the times.

For some reason I am particularly drawn to the post-war films Gene made for Republic. Perhaps some of their appeal for me has to do with my age at the time they were released. I was 10 to 12 years of age and at the height of my hero worship for this cowboy. I must say, I still go back to these films today and appreciate them for the quality with which they were made. My favorites of these post-war Republic films are as follows:

❖ "Sioux City Sue" ('46)—Great song, my favorite western leading lady (Lynne Roberts), and a behind-the-scenes look at western filmmaking (sort of).

❖ "Trail to San Antone" ('47)—This one has another great leading lady (Peggy Stewart) and beautiful Lone Pine, California, as a background for the plot. The Cass County Boys assist Gene in the vocal department, and I think add a lot to these post-war Republics.

❖ "Twilight on the Rio Grande" ('47)—The most atmospheric of the Autry films with a well-handled murder mystery angle.

❖ "The Strawberry Roan" ('48)—Both "The Last Round-Up" and "The Strawberry Roan" (Gene's first two self-produced Columbia films) are very different in style and tone from his previous films. It's obvious he was attempting films with storylines that were a bit more sophisticated and mature in approach, and he was also upping the budgets considerably. I much prefer "The Strawberry Roan" of the two, and it has the advantage of Cinecolor.

❖ "Mule Train" ('50)—One of Gene's best title songs, a great plot (even a female heavy), and beautiful Lone Pine scenery.

❖ "Gene Autry and the Mounties" ('51)—This is a personal favorite because of the Big Bear, California, locations at Cedar Lake with the rock-strewn shoreline and tall pines; the two great songs Gene sings: "Blue Canadian Rockies" and "Onteora" and the interesting plot regarding Gene and the Mounties working together to catch some bank robbers.

❖ "Whirlwind" ('51)—One of the best of the later Columbia films, it reunites Gene with Smiley Burnette, has popular Gail Davis as his leading lady, and features a cameo by western songwriter Stan Jones—who just happened to write the title song.

Richard Smith III
Author of MORE COWBOY SHOOTING STARS.

❖ "The Big Sombrero" ('49)—Gene Autry at his B-western pinnacle. Sparkling Cinecolor use with the lavish fiesta scenes.

❖ "The Strawberry Roan" ('48)—Excellent Cinecolor screenplay. Gives humane treatment to Autry horse Champion.

❖ "Gold Mine In the Sky" ('38)—I love this rip-roaring Autry vehicle. Energy filled, having great songs and loads of hard riding.

❖ "Down Mexico Way" ('41)—Upped budgeting grants Gene the whole enchilada for colorful tunes, rough-and-tumble, laughs and romance.

❖ "Twilight On the Rio Grande" ('47)—Absolute best post-WWII Republic for Autry. That final cantina fight melee is a gem.

❖ "Git Along Little Dogies" ('37)—A real outdoor sagebrusher. Antics between Gene and his leading lady unparalleled for a B-western.

❖ "Guns and Guitars" ('36)—Texas cattle fever plus comedy. I never stray very far from this inviting Autry oatuner.

❖ "Rancho Grande" ('40)—Snappy comedy musical which contains robust singing. Gene has big-time fun which I like.

❖ "Loaded Pistols" ('49)—Engaging tunes and adventure combine expertly. Plenty of saddle time by Autry lifts the plot.

❖ "Mule Train" ('50)—Gene in an action-loaded "Hit Parade" song event. Personally satisfying.

Gene's Movie/TV Sidekicks and Comedy Relief at a Glance

Smiley Burnette
"In Old Santa Fe" ('34)
"The Phantom Empire" ('35)
"Tumbling Tumbleweeds" ('35)
"Melody Trail" ('35)
"Sagebrush Troubadour" ('35)
"The Singing Vagabond" ('35)
"Red River Valley" ('36)
"Comin' 'Round the Mountain" ('36)
"The Singing Cowboy" ('36)
"Guns and Guitars" ('36)
"Oh, Susanna!" ('36)
"Ride Ranger Ride" ('36)
"The Big Show" ('36)
"The Old Corral" ('36)
"Round-Up Time in Texas" ('37)
"Git Along Little Dogies" ('37)
"Rootin' Tootin' Rhythm" ('37)
"Yodelin' Kid From Pine Ridge" ('37)
"Public Cowboy No. 1" ('37)
"Boots and Saddles" ('37)
"Manhattan Merry-Go-Round" ('37)
"Springtime in the Rockies" ('37)
"The Old Barn Dance" ('38)
"Gold Mine In the Sky" ('38)
"Man From Music Mountain" ('38)
"Prairie Moon" ('38)
"Western Jamboree" ('38)
"Rhythm of the Saddle" ('38)
"Home on the Prairie" ('39)
"Mexicali Rose" ('39)
"Blue Montana Skies" ('39)
"Mountain Rhythm" ('39)
"Colorado Sunset" ('39)
"In Old Monterey" ('39)
"Rovin' Tumbleweeds" ('39)
"South of the Border" ('39)
"Rancho Grande" ('40)
"Gaucho Serenade" ('40)
"Carolina Moon" ('40)
"Ride, Tenderfoot, Ride" ('40)
"Ridin' on a Rainbow" ('41)

"Back In the Saddle" ('41)
"The Singing Hill" ('41)
"Sunset in Wyoming" ('41)
"Under Fiesta Stars" ('41)
"Down Mexico Way" ('41)
"Sierra Sue" ('41)
"Cowboy Serenade" ('42)
"Heart of the Rio Grande" ('42)
"Home in Wyomin'" ('42)
"Stardust on the Sage" ('42)
"Call of the Canyon" ('42)
"Bells of Capistrano" ('42)
"Whirlwind" ('51)
"Winning of the West" ('53)
"On Top of Old Smoky" ('53)
"Goldtown Ghost Riders" ('53)
"Pack Train" ('53)
"Saginaw Trail" ('53)
"Last of the Pony Riders" ('53)

Max Terhune
"Ride Ranger Ride" ('36)

George "Gabby" Hayes
"Tumbling Tumbleweeds" ('35)
"In Old Monterey" ('39)
"Melody Ranch" ('40)

Jimmy Durante
"Melody Ranch" ('40)

Sterling Holloway
"Sioux City Sue" ('46)
"Trail to San Antone" ('47)
"Twilight on the Rio Grande" ('47)
"Saddle Pals" ('47)
"Robin Hood of Texas" ('47)

Pat Buttram
"Riders In the Sky" ('49)
"Mule Train" ('50)
"Beyond the Purple Hills" ('50)

"Indian Territory" ('50)
"The Blazing Sun" ('50)
"Gene Autry and the Mounties" ('51)
"Texans Never Cry" ('51)
"Silver Canyon" ('51)
"Hills of Utah" ('51)
"Valley of Fire" ('51)
"The Old West" ('52)
"Night Stage to Galveston" ('52)
"Apache Country" ('52)
"Barbed Wire" ('52)
"Wagon Team" ('52)

"Blue Canadian Rockies" ('52)
Plus 83 TV episodes

Alan Hale Jr.
2 TV episodes

Fuzzy Knight
4 TV episodes

Chill Wills
2 TV episodes

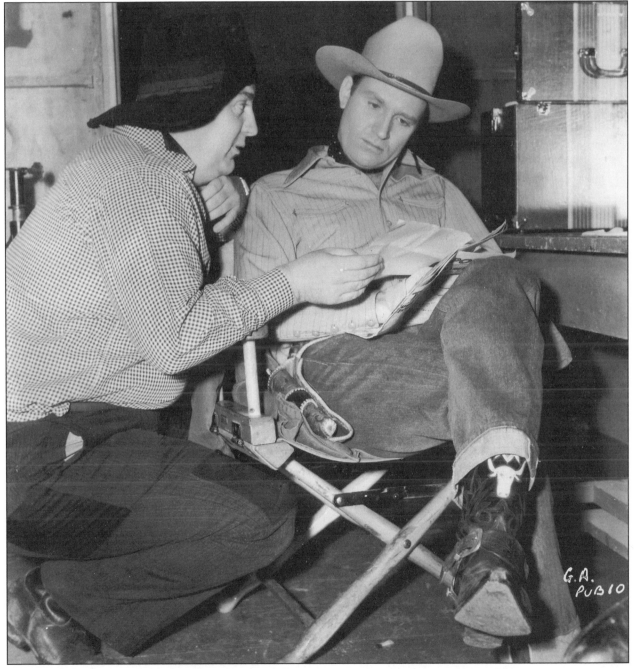

Gene and his most popular screen sidekick, Smiley Burnette, look over some last minute script changes. (Photo courtesy Neil Summers).

Gene's Movie/TV Leading Ladies at a Glance

Lucille Browne
"Tumbling Tumbleweeds" ('35)

Ann Rutherford
"Melody Trail" ('35)
"The Singing Vagabond" ('35)
"Comin' 'Round the Mountain" ('36)
"Public Cowboy No. 1" ('37)

Barbara Pepper
"Sagebrush Troubadour" ('35)

Frances Grant
"Red River Valley" ('36)
"Oh, Susanna!" ('36)

Lois Wilde
"The Singing Cowboy" ('36)

Dorothy Dix
"Guns and Guitars" ('36)

Kay Hughes
"Ride Ranger Ride" ('36)
"The Big Show" ('36)

Hope Manning
"The Old Corral" ('36)

Maxine Doyle
"Round-Up Time in Texas" ('37)

Judith Allen
"Git Along Little Dogies" ('37)
"Boots and Saddles" ('37)

Armida
"Rootin' Tootin' Rhythm" ('37)

Betty Bronson
"Yodelin' Kid From Pine Ridge" ('37)

Polly Rowles
"Springtime in the Rockies" ('37)

Helen Valkis
"The Old Barn Dance" ('38)

Carol Hughes
"Gold Mine In the Sky" ('38)
"Man From Music Mountain" ('38)
"Under Fiesta Stars" ('41)

Shirley Deane
"Prairie Moon" ('38)

Jean Rouverol
"Western Jamboree" ('38)

Peggy Moran
"Rhythm of the Saddle" ('38)

June Storey
"Home on the Prairie" ('39)
"Blue Montana Skies" ('39)
"Colorado Sunset" ('39)
"Mountain Rhythm" ('39)
"In Old Monterey" ('39)
"South of the Border" ('39)
"Rancho Grande" ('40)
"Gaucho Serenade" ('40)
"Carolina Moon" ('40)
"Ride, Tenderfoot, Ride" ('40)

Luana Walters
"Mexicali Rose" ('39)

Mary Carlisle
"Rovin' Tumbleweeds" ('39)

Lupita Tovar
"South of the Border" ('39)

Marjorie Weaver
"Shooting High" ('40)

Jane Withers
"Shooting High" ('40)

Mary Lee
"South of the Border" ('39)
"Rancho Grande" ('40)
"Gaucho Serenade" ('40)
"Carolina Moon" ('40)
"Ride, Tenderfoot, Ride" ('40)
"Melody Ranch" ('40)
"Ridin' on a Rainbow" ('41)
"Back In the Saddle" ('41)
"The Singing Hill" ('41)

Ann Miller
"Melody Ranch" ('40)

Carol Adams
"Ridin' on a Rainbow" ('41)

Jacqueline Wells
"Back In the Saddle" ('41)

Virginia Dale
"The Singing Hill" ('41)

Maris Wrixon
"Sunset in Wyoming" ('41)

Edith Fellows
"Heart of the Rio Grande" ('42)
"Stardust on the Sage" ('42)

Fay McKenzie
"Down Mexico Way" ('41)
"Sierra Sue" ('41)
"Cowboy Serenade" ('42)
"Heart of the Rio Grande" ('42)
"Home in Wyomin'" ('42)

Louise Currie
"Stardust on the Sage" ('42)

Ruth Terry
"Call of the Canyon" ('42)

Virginia Grey
"Bells of Capistrano" ('42)

Lynne Roberts
"Sioux City Sue" ('46)
"Saddle Pals" ('47)
"Robin Hood of Texas" ('47)

"The Blazing Sun" ('50)
    Plus 2 TV episodes

Peggy Stewart
"Trail to San Antone" ('47)
    Plus 1 TV episode

Adele Mara
"Twilight on the Rio Grande" ('47)

Jean Heather
"The Last Round-Up" ('47)

Gloria Henry
"The Strawberry Roan" ('48)
"Riders In the Sky" ('49)

Barbara Britton
"Loaded Pistols" ('49)

Elena Verdugo
"The Big Sombrero" ('49)
"Gene Autry and the Mounties" ('51)

Patricia White
"Riders of the Whistling Pines" ('49)

Nan Leslie
"Rim of the Canyon" ('49)
    Plus 4 TV episodes

Sheila Ryan
"The Cowboy and the Indians" ('49)
"Mule Train" ('50)
    Plus 9 TV episodes

Gail Davis
"Sons of New Mexico" ('50)
"Cow Town" ('50)
"Indian Territory" ('50)
"Texans Never Cry" ('51)
"Whirlwind" ('51)
"Silver Canyon" ('51)
"Valley of Fire" ('51)
"The Old West" ('52)
"Wagon Team" ('52)
"Blue Canadian Rockies" ('52)
"Winning of the West" ('53)
"On Top of Old Smoky" ('53)
"Goldtown Ghost Riders" ('53)
"Pack Train" ('53)
    Plus 15 TV episodes

Jo Dennison
"Beyond the Purple Hills" ('50)

Anne Gwynne
"The Blazing Sun" ('50)

Elaine Riley
"Hills of Utah" ('51)
    Plus 3 TV episodes

Virginia Huston
"Night Stage to Galveston" ('52)

Carolina Cotton
"Apache Country" ('52)

Anne James
"Barbed Wire" ('52)

Kathleen Case
"Last of the Pony Riders" ('53)

Margaret Field
    2 TV episodes

Wendy Waldron
    6 TV episodes

Virginia Herrick
    1 TV episode

Barbara Knudson
    1 TV episode

Barbara Stanley
    3 TV episodes

Lisa Montell
    1 TV episode

Jean Howell
    2 TV episodes

Sally Mansfield
    3 TV episodes

Sally Fraser
    2 TV episodes

Carol Nugent
    1 TV episode

Gloria Saunders
    1 TV episode

Mary Treen
    1 TV episode

Mira McKinney
    4 TV episodes

Almira Sessions
    1 TV episode

Gloria Talbot
    1 TV episode

Eilene Janssen
    2 TV episodes

Ann Doran
    2 TV episodes

Donna Martell
    2 TV episodes

Gloria Winters
    1 TV episode

Anne O'Neal
    1 TV episode

Sherry Jackson
    2 TV episodes

Jane Frazee
    1 TV episode

Rochelle Stanton
    2 TV episodes

Musical Groups and Singers in Gene's Westerns at a Glance

The Light Crust Doughboys
"Oh, Susanna!" ('36)
"The Big Show" ('36)

The Tennessee Ramblers
"Ride Ranger Ride" ('36)

Sons of the Pioneers
"The Big Show" ('36)
"The Old Corral" ('36)
"Call of the Canyon" ('42)

The Jones Boys
"The Big Show" ('36)

The Beverly Hill Billies
"The Big Show" ('36)

Cabin Kids
"Round-Up Time in Texas" ('37)
"Git Along Little Dogies" ('37)

Maple City Four
"Git Along Little Dogies" ('37)
"The Old Barn Dance" ('38)

Al Clauser and His Oklahoma Outlaws
"Rootin' Tootin' Rhythm" ('37)

Jimmy Lafevre's Saddle Pals
"Springtime In the Rockies" ('37)

Walt Shrum and His Colorado Hillbillies
"The Old Barn Dance" ('38)
"Blue Montana Skies" ('39)

Stafford Sisters
"The Old Barn Dance" ('38)
"Gold Mine in the Sky" ('38)

J. L. Frank's Golden West Cowboys
"Gold Mine In the Sky" ('38)

Polly Jenkins and Her Plowboys
"Man From Music Mountain" ('38)

Rodeoliers
"Home on the Prairie" ('39)

Hoosier Hot Shots
"In Old Monterey" ('39)

CBS-KMPC Texas Rangers
"Colorado Sunset" ('39)

The Ranch Boys
"In Old Monterey" ('39)

Pals of the Golden West
"Rovin' Tumbleweeds" ('39)
"Rancho Grande" ('40)

The Checkerboard Band
"South of the Border" ('39)

Jimmie Lewis and His Texas Cowboys
"Carolina Moon" ('40)

The Pacemakers
"Ride, Tenderfoot Ride" ('40)

Cindy Walker
"Ride, Tenderfoot Ride" ('40)

Kidoodlers
"Melody Ranch" ('40)

Herrera Sisters
"Down Mexico Way" ('41)

Texas Jim Lewis and His Lone Star Cowboys
"Down Mexico Way" ('41)

Jimmy Wakely Trio
"Heart of the Rio Grande" ('42)

KCBS Texas Rangers
"The Last Round-Up" ('47)

The Pinafores
"Riders of the Whistling Pines" ('49)

Cass County Boys
"Sioux City Sue" ('46)
"Trail to San Antone" ('47)
"Twilight on the Rio Grande" ('47)
"Saddle Pals" ('47)
"Robin Hood of Texas" ('47)
"Loaded Pistols" ('49)

"Riders of the Whistling Pines" ('49)
"Beyond the Purple Hills" ('50)
"Valley of Fire" ('51)
"Apache Country" ('52)
"Barbed Wire" ('52)
"Wagon Team" ('52)
"Blue Canadian Rockies" ('52)
"On Top of Old Smoky" ('53)
    Plus 9 TV episodes

Carolina Cotton
"Apache Country" ('52)
"Blue Canadian Rockies" ('52)

The Pinafores were regulars on Gene's "Melody Ranch" CBS radio program but were only featured in one film, "Riders of the Whistling Pines" in 1949. (Photo courtesy Neil Summers.)

Songs Heard in Gene's Westerns and Where to Find Them

A Boy from Texas, a Girl From Tennessee—Loaded Pistols ('49)

A Gay Ranchero (Las Altenitas)—Down Mexico Way ('41)

A Girl Like You—Rovin' Tumbleweeds ('39)

A Heart as Big as Texas—The Peacemaker (TV) ('50); Night Stage to Galveston ('52); Outlaw Warning (TV) ('54)

A Lone Cowboy on a Lone Prairie—Melody Trail ('35)

A Song at Sunset—Gaucho Serenade ('40)

African Chant—Round-Up Time in Texas ('37)

After Tomorrow—The Sheriff Is a Lady (TV) ('52)

After You've Gone—Git Along Little Dogies ('37)

Ages and Ages Ago—Melody Mesa (TV) ('52)

All Nice People—Man From Music Mountain ('38)

Along the Navajo Trail—The Blazing Sun ('50); The Devil's Brand (TV) ('50)

Amapola—Saddle Pals ('47)

America, the Beautiful—The Cowboy and the Indians ('49); The Old West ('52)

An Apple For the Teacher—The Last Round-Up ('47)

Angel Song, The—The Strawberry Roan ('48); The Raiders (TV) ('51); Law Comes to Scorpion (TV) ('55)

Any Bonds Today—Home in Wyomin' ('42)

Anytime—Blue Canadian Rockies ('52)

As Long as I Have My Horse—Gold Mine in the Sky ('38); Whirlwind ('51), Ghost Town Raiders (TV) ('51)

As Long As I've Got My Dog—In Old Santa Fe ('34)

As Our Pals Ride By—Oh, Susanna! ('36)

At Sundown—Bells of Capistrano ('42)

At the Old Barn Dance—The Old Barn Dance ('38)

At the Rodeo—Carolina Moon ('40)

Autry's Your Man (Campaign Song)—Colorado Sunset ('39)

Ava Maria—Rancho Grande ('40)

Away Out Yonder—Rovin' Tumbleweeds ('39)

Back in the Doghouse Again—Go West, Young Lady (TV) ('55)

Back in the Saddle Again—Rovin' Tumbleweeds ('39); Back In the Saddle ('41); Home in Wyomin' ('42); Unusual Occupations (late '40s); Twisted Trails (TV)

('50); Six Shooter Sweepstakes (TV) ('50); The Star Toter (TV) ('50); Melody Mesa (TV) ('52); Wagon Team ('52); The Bandidos (TV) ('53); Go West, Young Lady (TV) ('55); The Million Dollar Fiddle (TV) ('55); Wide Wide World (TV) ('58)

Back to the City Again—Melody Ranch ('40)

Balloon Song—Western Jamboree ('38)

Be Honest With Me—Ridin' on a Rainbow ('41); Sierra Sue ('41); Home in Wyomin' ('42); The Fight at Peaceful Mesa (TV) ('50)

Beautiful Dreamer—Saginaw Trail ('53)

Beautiful Isle of Somewhere—Colorado Sunset ('39)

Beer Barrel Polka—Down Mexico Way ('41)

Beyond the Purple Hills—Beyond the Purple Hills ('50)

Big Bull Frog—Home on the Prairie ('39)

Billy Boy—The Western Way (TV) ('52)

Blue Canadian Rockies—Gene Autry and the Mounties ('51); Blue Canadian Rockies ('52)

Blue Tail Fly—Loaded Pistols ('49)

Blueberry Hill—The Singing Hill ('41)

Born In the Saddle—In Old Monterey ('39)

Broomstick Buckaroo—The Breakup (TV) ('50)

Brush Those Tears From Your Eyes—The Blazing Sun ('50)

Buffalo Gals—Springtime in the Rockies ('37); Cow Town ('50)

Bugle Song, The—Ride Ranger Ride ('36)

Bury Me Not on the Lone Prairie (The Dying Cowboy)—Cow Town ('50)

By the River of the Roses—Trail to San Antone ('47)

Calamity Jane—Git Along Little Dogies ('37)

Call of the Canyon—Melody Ranch ('40); Call of the Canyon ('42)

Can't Shake the Sands of Texas From My Shoes—The Silver Arrow (TV) ('50); Sons of New Mexico ('50); Hoedown ('50)

Carolina Moon—Carolina Moon ('40)

Carry Me Back to the Lone Prairie—Ridin' on a Rainbow ('41)

Casey Jones—Sunset in Wyoming ('41)

Cave Man—Round-Up Time in Texas ('37)

Chattanoogie Shoeshine Boy—Indian Territory ('50)

Chinatown—Git Along Little Dogies ('37)

Chiquita—Comin' 'Round the Mountain ('36)

Cielito Lindo—Boots and Saddles ('37); Western Jamboree ('38)

Cimarron—Heart of the Rio Grande ('42)

Clementine—Home in Wyomin' ('42)

Climbin' Up D'Mountain—Carolina Moon ('40)

Cold, Cold Heart—Apache Country ('52)

Colorado Sunset—Colorado Sunset ('39)

Columbia, the Gem of the Ocean—In Old Monterey ('39)

Come to the Fiesta—South of the Border ('39)

Construction Song—Red River Valley ('36)

Cool Water—Gunpowder Range (TV) ('50)

Corn-Fed and Rusty—Tumbling Tumbleweeds ('35)

Coronation March—Call of the Canyon ('42)

Covered Wagon Rolled Right Along, The—Saddle Pals ('47); Apache Country ('52)

Cowboy and the Lady, The—Down Mexico Way ('41)

Cowboy Blues, The—Trail to San Antone ('47); Gold Dust Charlie (TV) ('50); Winning of the West ('53)

Cowboy Medicine Show—Tumbling Tumbleweeds ('35); Guns and Guitars ('36)

Cowboy Serenade—Cowboy Serenade ('42)

Cowboy, The—Trail to San Antone ('47)

Cowboy's Dream, The—Western Jamboree ('38)

Cowboy's Heaven—Horse Sense (TV) ('52)

Cowboy's Lament, The (Streets of Laredo)—Riders in the Sky ('49)

Cowboy's Trademarks, The—Talking Guns (TV) ('54)

Cowboys Don't Milk Cows—Colorado Sunset ('39)

Crime Will Never Pay—Outlaw Escape (TV) ('51); Apache Country ('52); The Sharpshooter (TV) ('54); Feuding Friends (TV) ('55)

De Camptown Races—The Singing Vagabond ('35)

Dear Hearts and Gentle People—Beyond the Purple Hills ('50)

Dear Old Western Skies—Oh, Susanna! ('36)

Deep In the Heart of Texas—Heart of the Rio Grande ('42); Stardust on the Sage ('42)

Defective Detective From Brooklyn—Public Cowboy No. 1 ('37)

Dinah—Round-Up Time in Texas ('37)

Dixie Cannonball—The Bandidos (TV) ('53)

Don Juan of Sevillio—Comin' 'Round the Mountain ('36)

Don't Bite the Hand That's Feeding You—Bells of Capistrano ('42)

Down Along the Sleepy Rio Grande—The Old Corral ('36)

Down In Old Santa Fe—In Old Santa Fe ('34)

Down In Santa Fe—Yodelin' Kid From Pine Ridge ('37)

Down In Slumberland—The Singing Cowboy ('36); Night Stage to Galveston ('52)

Down In the Land of Zulu—Springtime in the Rockies ('37)

Down In the Valley—Cow Town ('50); Warning! Danger! (TV) ('51)

Down Mexico Way—Down Mexico Way ('41)

(Down the) Trail to San Antone—Trail to San Antone ('47)

Dreaming Dreams that Won't Come True—Carolina Moon ('40)

Dreamy Valley—Guns and Guitars ('36)

Dude Ranch Cowhands—Gold Mine In the Sky ('38); Rancho Grande ('40)

Dusk on the Painted Desert—Heart of the Rio Grande ('42)

Dusty Roads—Boots and Saddles ('37)

Dying Cowgirl—Rootin' Tootin' Rhythm ('37)

Eating Wax—The Old Barn Dance ('38)

El Rancho Grande—Mexicali Rose ('39)

Eleven More Months and Ten More Days—Ride, Tenderfoot, Ride ('40)

End of the Trail—Sagebrush Troubadour ('35)

Every Time I Feel the Spirit—Riders of the Whistling Pines ('49)

Eyes of Texas, The—Night Stage to Galveston ('52)

Ezekiel Saw the Wheel—Barbed Wire ('52)

Famous Men of the West—Blue Montana Skies ('39)

Farewell Friends of the Prairie, Farewell—The Singing Vagabond ('35)

Fat Caballero—South of the Border ('39)

Fetch Me Down My Trusty Forty-Five—Red River Valley ('36); Winning of the West ('53); Dry Gulch at Devil's Elbow (TV) ('53)

Five Man Band—The Old Corral ('36)

Five Minutes Late and a Dollar Short—Winning of the West ('53)

Forgive Me—Bells of Capistrano ('42)

Fort Worth Jail—Bells of Capistrano ('42); Silver Canyon ('51)

Gallivantin' Galveston Gal—The Steel Ribbon (TV) ('53); Saddle Up (TV) ('55)

Gaucho Serenade—Gaucho Serenade ('40)

Georgia Rodeo—Yodelin' Kid From Pine Ridge ('37)

Ghost Riders In the Sky—Riders in the Sky ('49)

Girl In the Middle of My Heart, The—Prairie Moon ('38)

Girl of My Dreams—South of the Border ('39)

Git Along Little Dogies—Git Along Little Dogies ('37)

Give Me a Pony—Springtime in the Rockies ('37)

Give Out With a Song—Gaucho Serenade ('40)

God's Little Candles—Pack Train ('53); Prize Winner (TV) ('54)

Goin' Back to Texas—Robin Hood of Texas ('47)

Goin' Down the Road—Ride Ranger Ride ('36)

Gold Mine In Your Heart—Mountain Rhythm ('39); Goldtown Ghost Riders ('53)

Gone With the West—Johnny Jackaroo (TV) ('54)

Good Old-Fashioned Hoedown—The Singing Hill ('41); Robin Hood of Texas ('47); Hot Lead (TV) ('50); The Golden Chariot (TV) ('55)

Goodbye Little Darlin'—South of the Border ('39)

Goodbye Pinto—Man From Music Mountain ('38)

Goodbye to Old Mexico—The Big Sombrero ('49); The Lost Chance (TV) ('50)

Goodnight Ladies—Git Along Little Dogies ('37)

Goodnight Sweetheart—Stardust on the Sage ('42)

Great Grand Dad—Sioux City Sue ('46); Twilight on the Rio Grande ('47); Gold Dust Charlie (TV) ('50)

Green Grass Grew All Around, The (aka The Tree In the Wood)—The Old Barn Dance ('38)

Guadalajara—Down Mexico Way ('41)

Guns and Guitars—Guns and Guitars ('36); Border Justice (TV) ('53)

Hair of Gold, Eyes of Blue—Riders of the Whistling Pines ('49)

Happy Days Are Here Again—Git Along Little Dogies ('37)

Happy Go Lucky Vagabonds—The Big Show ('36)

He's a Jolly Good Fellow—Git Along Little Dogies ('37)

He's Gone, He's Gone Up the Trail—The Old Corral ('36)

Headin' For the Wide Open Spaces—Gaucho Serenade ('40)

Heebie Jeebie Blues—Public Cowboy No. 1 ('37); Sierra Sue ('41)

Here Comes Santa Claus (Right Down Santa Claus Lane)—The Cowboy and the Indians ('49)

Here's to the Ladies—Valley of Fire ('51)

Highways Are Happy Ways—Mountain Rhythm ('39)

Hike Yaa—Gold Mine In the Sky ('38)

Hillbilly Wedding In June—Hoodoo Canyon (TV) ('54)

Hittin' the Trail—Yodelin' Kid From Pine Ridge ('37)

Hold On Little Dogies, Hold On—Melody Trail ('35)

Home Corral—Call of the Canyon ('42)

Home on the Range—Stardust on the Sage ('42); Gold Dust Charlie (TV) ('50); Hot Lead and Old Lace (TV) ('52)

Hominy Grits—Pack Train ('53)

Honey Song, The (Honey, I'm in Love with You)—Sons of New Mexico ('50)

Honey, Bringing Honey to You—Git Along Little Dogies ('37)

Honeymoon Trail—The Singing Vagabond ('35); Oh, Susanna! ('36)

Horse Opry, The—South of the Border ('39)

Howdy Friends and Neighbors—Wagon Team ('52)

Hummin' When We're Comin' 'Round the Bend—Gold Mine In the Sky ('38)

Hunky Dunky Dory—Ridin' on a Rainbow ('41)

Hurdy Gurdy Man—Sagebrush Troubadour ('35)

Hurray—Rovin' Tumbleweeds ('39)

I Don't Belong In Your World—Rancho Grande ('40)

I Hang My Head and Cry—On Top of Old Smoky ('53)

I Hate to Say Goodbye to the Prairie—Rootin' Tootin' Rhythm ('37)

I Just Want You—Blue Montana Skies ('39)

I Love the Morning—Western Jamboree ('38)

I Love to Yodel—Apache Country ('52)

I Only Want a Buddy—Holdup (TV) ('54)

I Picked Up the Trail to Your Heart—Public Cowboy No. 1 ('37)

I Saw Her First—On Top of Old Smoky ('53)

I Tipped My Hat and Slowly Rode Away—Twilight on the Rio Grande ('47)

I Want to Be a Cowboy's Sweetheart—Colorado Sunset ('39)

I Want to Be Sure—Silver Dollars (TV) ('51)

I Was Born in Old Wyoming—Sunset in Wyoming ('41)

I Wish I Had Never Met Sunshine—Saddle Pals ('47); Double Barreled Vengeance (TV) ('51); Law Comes to Scorpion (TV) ('55)

I'd Love a Home in the Mountains—Sagebrush Troubadour ('35)

I'd Love to Call You My Sweetheart—Gold Mine In the Sky ('38)

I'll Be Thinking of You, Little Gal—The Singing Cowboy ('36)

I'll Be True While You're Gone—Sierra Sue ('41)

I'll Never Let You Go, Little Darlin'—Stardust on the Sage ('42)

I'll Wait for You—Heart of the Rio Grande ('42)

I'll Yodel My Troubles Away—Tumbling Tumbleweeds ('35)

I'm a Cowpoke Pokin' Along—Winning of the West ('53); The Old Prospector (TV) ('53)

I'm An Old Cowhand—Back In the Saddle ('41)

I'm Beginning to Care—Man From Music Mountain ('38); The Fight at Peaceful Mesa (TV) ('50); Six Gun Romeo (TV) ('52)

I'm Getting a Moon's Eye View of the World—The Phantom Empire ('35)

I'm Gonna Round Up My Blues—Home on the Prairie ('39)

I'm Mad About You—The Big Show ('36)

I'm Oscar, I'm Pete—The Phantom Empire ('35)

I'm Thankful For Small Favors—The Big Sombrero ('49)

I'm the Only Lonely One—Ridin' on a Rainbow ('41)

I'm Thinking Tonight of My Blue Eyes—Home in Wyomin' ('42)

I've Been Invited to a Jubilee—Wagon Team ('52)

I've Got Fine Relations—Guns and Guitars ('36)

I've Got No Use for Women—Under Fiesta Stars ('41)

If It Wasn't For the Rain—On Top of Old Smoky ('53)

If You Want to Be a Cowboy—Git Along Little Dogies ('37)

If You'll Let Me Be Your Little Sweetheart—Ghost Mountain (TV) ('53)

In and Out of the Jailhouse—Wagon Team ('52)

In Old Capistrano—Bells of Capistrano ('42)

In Our Little Shanty Town of Dreams—Shooting High ('40)

In the Heart of the West—The Old Corral ('36)

In the Jailhouse Now— Prairie Moon ('38); Back In the Saddle ('41)

In the Valley Where the Sun Goes Down—Git Along Little Dogies ('37)

Indian Buffalo Dance—Apache Country ('52)

Indian Chant—The Cowboy and the Indians ('49)

Indian Eagle Dance—Apache Country ('52)

Indian War Dance—Apache Country ('52)

Old Home Place, The—Rootin' Tootin' Rhythm ('37)

Old Lamplighter, The—Twilight on the Rio Grande ('47)

Old MacDonald Had a Farm—Mountain Rhythm ('39); The Rangerette (TV) ('55)

Old Nell—The Old Barn Dance ('38)

Old Nevada Moon—Thunder Out West (TV) ('53)

Old November Moon—Western Jamboree ('38)

Old Trail, The —Rhythm of the Saddle ('38)

Old West, The—The Old West ('52)

Ole Peaceful River—Rovin' Tumbleweeds ('39)

On My Merry Old Way Back Home—Colorado Sunset ('39)

On Revival Day—Round-Up Time in Texas ('37)

On the Melody Trail—Melody Trail ('35)

On the Prairie—Sagebrush Troubadour ('35)

On the Range—Ride, Tenderfoot, Ride ('40)

On the Sunny Side of the Cell—Rovin' Tumbleweeds ('39)

On the Sunset Trail—Ride Ranger Ride ('36)

On Top of Old Smoky—The Kid Comes West (TV) ('51); Valley of Fire ('51); On Top of Old Smoky ('53)

One Hundred and Sixty Acres—The Last Round-Up ('47)

One Little Indian Boy—The Cowboy and the Indians ('49)

One Rose That's Left in My Heart, The—Boots and Saddles ('37)

Onteora—Gene Autry and the Mounties ('51); Gypsy Wagon (TV) ('53); The Portrait of White Cloud (TV) ('55)

Painted Desert—The Breakup (TV) ('50)

Pancho's Widow—Goldtown Ghost Riders ('53)

Paradise In the Moonlight—Rovin' Tumbleweeds ('39)

Patsy's Birthday Routine—The Singing Hill ('41)

Perfidea—Stardust on the Sage ('42)

Peter Cottontail—Hills of Utah ('51)

Poor Little Dogie—Colorado Sunset ('39)

Powder Your Face with Sunshine—Cow Town ('50)

Prairie Rose—Round-Up Time in Texas ('37)

Pretty Knife Grinder, The —Twilight on the Rio Grande ('47)

Pretty Mary—Loaded Pistols ('49); The Posse (TV) ('50); Galloping Hoofs (TV) ('51); Saddle Up (TV) ('55)

Purple Sage in the Twilight—Under Fiesta Stars ('41)

Put On Your Old Gray Bonnet—Mountain Rhythm ('39)

Rainbow in the Night—Heart of the Rio Grande ('42)

Rainbow Trail—The Singing Cowboy ('36)

Rancho Grande—Rancho Grande ('40)

Rancho Pillow—Heart of the Rio Grande ('42); The Big Sombrero ('49)

Red River Valley—Red River Valley ('36); Git Along Little Dogies ('37); Yodelin' Kid From Pine Ridge ('37); Sioux City Sue ('46); The Grey Dude (TV) ('50)

Rhythm of the Hoofbeats—Prairie Moon ('38); Bullets and Bows (TV) ('52)

Ride On Vaquero—Oh, Susanna! ('36)

Ride Ranger Ride—The Big Show ('36); Ride Ranger Ride ('36); Texans Never Cry ('51)

Ride, Tenderfoot, Ride—Ride, Tenderfoot, Ride ('40)

Ridin' All Day—Guns and Guitars ('36); The Carnival Comes West (TV) ('54)

Ridin' Double—Sioux City Sue ('46); Heir to the Lazy L (TV) ('51)

Ridin' Down That Old Texas Trail—The Singing Hill ('41); Ghost Mountain (TV) ('53)

Ridin' Down the Canyon—Tumbling Tumbleweeds ('35); The Doodle Bug (TV) ('50); Frame For Trouble (TV) ('51); Silver Canyon ('51); Ride Ranchero (TV) ('55)

Ridin' on a Rainbow—Ridin' on a Rainbow ('41)

Ridin' the Range—Boots and Saddles ('37); Sierra Sue ('41)

Rim of the Canyon—Rim of the Canyon ('49)

Roamin' Around the Range—The Old Barn Dance ('38); Riders of the Whistling Pines ('49); Frontier Guard (TV) ('51)

Robin Hood—Mexicali Rose ('39)

Rockin' In the Saddle—Blue Montana Skies ('39)

Rocky Mountain Express—Rovin' Tumbleweeds ('39)

Rocky Mountain Rose—The Old Barn Dance ('38)

Rodeo Rose—Melody Ranch ('40)

Roll On Little Dogies—Return of Maverick Dan (TV) ('51)

Roll Wagons Roll—The Big Show ('36)

Room Full of Roses—Mule Train ('50); Twisted Trails (TV) ('50)

Rumble Seat for Two—Heart of the Rio Grande ('42)

Sail the Seven Seas—The Singing Hill ('41)

Salud Vaquero—Boots and Saddles ('37)

Say Si Si—Carolina Moon ('40)

Seven Years With the Wrong Woman—Colorado Sunset ('39)

Shame On You—Trail to San Antone ('47)

She Works Third Tub at the Laundry—Man From Music Mountain ('38)

She'll Be Comin' 'Round the Mountain—Comin' 'Round the Mountain ('36); Round-Up Time in Texas ('37); Git Along Little Dogies ('37); Yodelin' Kid From Pine Ridge ('37); The Old Barn Dance ('38); Home on the Prairie ('39); The Last Round-Up ('47); T.N.T. (TV) ('50); Warning! Danger! (TV) ('51); Dry Gulch at Devil's Elbow (TV) ('53)

Sierra Nevada—Dynamite (TV) ('56)

Sierra Sue—Sierra Sue ('41)

Silent Night—The Cowboy and the Indians ('49)

Silent Trails—The Old Corral ('36)

Silver Spurs On the Golden Stairs—Revenge Trail (TV) ('51); The Carnival Comes West (TV) ('54)

Sing a Song of Laughter—Ridin' on a Rainbow ('41)

Sing Me a Song of the Saddle—Yodelin' Kid From Pine Ridge ('37); Sunset in Wyoming ('41); Head for Texas (TV) ('50); The Sheriff Is a Lady (TV) ('52); Last of the Pony Riders ('53); The Stage to San Dimas (TV) ('55)

Sing Your Song Cowboy—Springtime in the Rockies ('37)

Singing Hills, The—Gaucho Serenade ('40)

What's Your Favorite Holiday—Ridin' on a Rainbow ('41)

When a Circus Comes to Town—Yodelin' Kid From Pine Ridge ('37)

When It's Chilly Down in Chili—Call of the Canyon ('42)

When It's Night Time in Nevada—The Black Rider (TV) ('50)

When It's Prayer Meetin' Time In the Hollow—Saginaw Trail ('53)

When It's Springtime in the Rockies—Springtime in the Rockies ('37)

When Mother Nature Sings Her Lullaby—Rhythm of the Saddle ('38)

When the Bloom Is on the Sage—Round-Up Time in Texas ('37); Western Jamboree ('38); Loaded Pistols ('49); The Double Switch (TV) ('50); Outlaw of Blue Mesa (TV) ('54); Go West, Young Lady (TV) ('55)

When the Cactus Blooms Again—South of the Border ('39)

When the Cactus is in Bloom—Back In the Saddle ('41)

When the Campfire is Low on the Prairie—Comin' 'Round the Mountain ('36); Indian Territory ('50)

When the River Meets the Range—Back In the Saddle ('41)

When the Roses Bloom Again—Stardust on the Sage ('42)

When the White Roses Bloom—The Strawberry Roan ('48)

When the Work's All Done This Fall—Ride, Tenderfoot, Ride ('40)

When You and I Were Young, Maggie—The Lawless Press (TV) ('52)

When You're Smiling—Under Fiesta Stars ('41)

Where a Water Wheel Keeps Turning On—Oh, Susanna! ('36)

Where Will the Wedding Supper Be—Melody Trail ('35

Which Way'd They Go—Saddle Pals ('47)

Whirlwind—Whirlwind ('51)

Whistle—Rancho Grande ('40)

Why Did I Get Married—Boots and Saddles ('37)

Wild and Wooley West—The Big Show ('36)

With All My Heart—The Old Corral ('36)

Woodpecker Song—Ride, Tenderfoot, Ride ('40)

Wooing of Kitty McFuty—Gaucho Serenade ('40)

Wouldn't You Like to Know—Stardust on the Sage ('42)

Ya-Hoo—The Singing Cowboy ('36)

Yellow Rose of Texas—Ride Ranger Ride ('36); Riders of the Whistling Pines ('49); Night Stage to Galveston ('52); Rock River Feud (TV) ('52); Cold

Decked (TV) ('53); The Million Dollar Fiddle (TV) ('55)

Yodel, Yodel, Yodel—Blue Canadian Rockies ('52)

Yodeling Cowboy—Red River Valley ('36)

You Are My Sunshine—Back In the Saddle ('41); Stardust on the Sage ('42)

You Belong to My Heart—The Big Sombrero ('49)

You Can Take the Boy Out of the Country—Rancho Grande ('40)

You Can't See the Sun When You're Crying—The Last Round-Up ('47)

You Stole My Heart—Saddle Pals ('47)

You'll Be Sorry—Stardust on the Sage ('42)

You're the Moment of a Lifetime—Robin Hood of Texas ('47)

You're the Only Good Thing (That's Happened to Me)—Ghost Ranch (TV) ('55)

You're the Only Star in My Blue Heaven—Springtime in the Rockies ('37); The Old Barn Dance ('38); Mexicali Rose ('39); Rim of the Canyon ('49)

Yours—Sioux City Sue ('46)

Gene Autry—on the air for CBS' "Melody Ranch" in December 1948. (Photo courtesy Neil Summers.)

Gene's Story and Screenwriters at a Glance
(S-Story SP-Screenplay)

Wallace MacDonald
"The Phantom Empire" ('35) *(S)*

Hy Friedman
"The Phantom Empire" ('35) *(S)*

John Rathmell
"The Phantom Empire" ('35) *(SP)*

Armand Schaefer
"The Phantom Empire" ('35) *(SP)*

Ford Beebe
"Tumbling Tumbleweeds" ('35) *(SP)*

Alan Ludwig
"Tumbling Tumbleweeds" ('35) *(S)*

Oliver Drake
"Sagebrush Troubadour" ('35) *(S+SP)*
"The Singing Vagabond" ('35) *(S+SP)*
"Comin' 'Round the Mountain" ('36) *(S+SP)*
"Oh, Susanna!" *('36) (S+SP)*
"Round-Up Time in Texas" ('37) *(SP)*
"Public Cowboy No. 1" ('37) *(SP)*
"Boots and Saddles" ('37) *(SP)*
 Plus 4 TV episodes *(SP)*

Joseph Poland
"Sagebrush Troubadour" ('35) *(SP)*
"The Old Corral" ('36) *(SP)*

Dorrell and Stuart McGowan
"Red River Valley" ('36) *(S+SP)*
"Comin' 'Round the Mountain" ('36) *(SP)*
"The Singing Cowboy" ('36) *(SP)*
"Guns and Guitars" ('36) *(S+SP)*
"Ride Ranger Ride" ('36) *(SP)*
"The Big Show" ('36) *(S+SP)*
"Git Along Little Dogies" ('37) *(SP)*
"Yodelin' Kid From Pine Ridge" ('37) *(SP)*
"In Old Monterey" ('39) *(SP)*

"Rovin' Tumbleweeds" ('39) *(SP)*
"South of the Border" ('39) *(S)*
"Down Mexico Way" ('41) *(S)*
"Stardust on the Sage" ('42) *(S)*
"Twilight on the Rio Grande" ('47) *(SP)*
"Saddle Pals" ('47) *(S)*
 Plus 1 TV episode *(SP)*

Sherman Lowe
"Melody Trail" ('35) *(S+SP)*
"The Old Corral" ('36) *(SP)*
 Plus 1 TV episode *(SP)*

Betty Burbridge
"Melody Trail" ('35) *(S)*
"The Singing Vagabond" ('35) *(SP)*
"Springtime in the Rockies" ('37) *(SP)*
"Gold Mine in the Sky" ('38) *(S+SP)*
"Man From Music Mountain" ('38) *(SP)*
"Prairie Moon" ('38) *(SP)*
"Colorado Sunset" ('39) *(SP)*
"Rovin' Tumbleweeds" ('39) *(SP)*
"South of the Border" ('39) *(SP)*
"Rancho Grande" ('40) *(SP)*
"Gaucho Serenade" ('40) *(SP)*
"Ride, Tenderfoot, Ride" ('40) *(S)*
"Melody Ranch" ('40) *(SP)*
"Stardust on the Sage" ('42) *(SP)*
 Plus 3 TV episodes *(SP)*

Harry Sauber
"Manhattan Merry-Go-Round" ('37) *(SP)*

Tom Gibbons
"The Singing Cowboy" ('36) *(S)*

Bernard McConville
"Ride Ranger Ride" ('36) *(S)*
"The Old Corral" ('36) *(S)*
"Public Cowboy No. 1" ('37) *(S)*
"The Old Barn Dance" ('38) *(SP)*
"Man From Music Mountain" ('38) *(S)*

Johnston McCulley
"Rootin' Tootin' Rhythm" ('37) *(S)*

Jack Natteford
"Rootin' Tootin' Rhythm" ('37) *(SP)*
"Yodelin' Kid From Pine Ridge" ('37) *(S+SP)*
"Boots and Saddles" ('37) *(S+SP)*
"Gold Mine in the Sky" ('38) *(SP)*
"Colorado Sunset" ('39) *(S)*
"Trail to San Antone" ('47) *(SP)*

Stanley Roberts
"Prairie Moon" ('38) *(SP)*
"Colorado Sunset" ('39) *(SP)*

Pat Harper
"Western Jamboree" ('38) *(S)*

Paul Franklin
"Rhythm of the Saddle" ('38) *(SP)*
"Home on the Prairie" ('39) *(S+SP)*
"Blue Montana Skies" ('39) *(S)*

Charles Arthur Powell
"Home on the Prairie" ('39) *(SP)*

Gilbert Wright
"Springtime in the Rockies" ('37) *(SP)*

Charles F. Royal
"The Old Barn Dance" ('38) *(SP)*

Luci Ward
"Man From Music Mountain" ('38) *(SP)*
"Colorado Sunset" ('39) *(S)*
"Mexicali Rose" ('39) *(S)*
"Trail to San Antone" ('47) *(SP)*

Gerald Geraghty
"The Phantom Empire" ('35) *(S)*
"Western Jamboree" ('38) *(SP)*
"Mexicali Rose" ('39) *(SP)*
"Blue Montana Skies" ('39) *(SP)*
"Mountain Rhythm" ('39) *(SP)*
"In Old Monterey" ('39) *(S+SP)*
"South of the Border" ('39) *(SP)*
"Riders in the Sky" ('49) *(SP)*
"Mule Train" ('50) *(SP)*
"Cow Town" ('50) *(SP)*
"Silver Canyon" ('51) *(SP)*
"Hills of Utah" ('51) *(SP)*
"Valley of Fire" ('51) *(SP)*
"The Old West" ('52) *(SP)*
"Barbed Wire" ('52) *(SP)*
"Wagon Team" ('52) *(SP)*
"Blue Canadian Rockies" ('52) *(SP)*
"On Top of Old Smoky" ('53) *(S+SP)*

"Goldtown Ghost Riders" ('53) *(S+SP)*

George Sherman
"In Old Monterey" ('39) *(S)*

Connie Lee
"Mexicali Rose" ('39) *(S)*
"Mountain Rhythm" ('39) *(S)*
"Rancho Grande" ('40) *(S)*
"Carolina Moon" ('40) *(S)*
"Ride, Tenderfoot, Ride" ('40) *(S)*

Norman S. Hall
"Blue Montana Skies" ('39) *(S)*
"Beyond the Purple Hills" ('50) *(SP)*
"Indian Territory" ('50) *(SP)*
"Texans Never Cry" ('51) *(SP)*
"Gene Autry and the Mounties" ('51) *(SP)*
"Whirlwind" ('51) *(SP)*
"Night Stage to Galveston" ('52) *(SP)*
"Apache Country" ('52) *(SP)*
"Winning of the West" ('53) *(S+SP)*
"Pack Train" ('53) *(S+SP)*
    Plus 3 TV episodes *(SP)*

Winston Miller
"Carolina Moon" ('40) *(SP)*
"Ride, Tenderfoot, Ride" ('40) *(SP)*
"Heart of the Rio Grande" ('42) *(SP)*

Jack Moffitt
"Melody Ranch" ('40) *(SP)*

F. Hugh Herbert
"Melody Ranch" ('40) *(SP)*

Peter Milne
"Rancho Grande" ('40) *(S+SP)*

Bradford Ropes
"Rancho Grande" ('40) *(SP)*
"Gaucho Serenade" ('40) *(SP)*
"Melody Ranch" ('40) *(SP)*
"Ridin' On a Rainbow" ('41) *(S+SP)*

Lou Breslow
"Shooting High" ('40) *(SP)*

Owen Francis
"Shooting High" ('40) *(SP)*

Doris Malloy
"Ridin' On a Rainbow" ('41) *(SP)*

Richard Murphy
"Back in the Saddle" ('41) *(SP)*
"The Singing Hill" ('41) *(S)*

Jesse Lasky Jr.
"Back in the Saddle" ('41) *(SP)*
"The Singing Hill" ('41) *(S)*

Olive Cooper
"The Singing Hill" ('41) *(SP)*
"Down Mexico Way" ('41) *(SP)*
"Cowboy Serenade" ('42) *(SP)*
"Call of the Canyon" ('42) *(S+SP)*
"Sioux City Sue" ('46) *(SP)*
"The Big Sombrero" ('49) *(SP)*

Joe Blair
"Sunset in Wyoming" ('41) *(S)*

Ivan Goff
"Sunset in Wyoming" ('41) *(SP)*

Ann Morrison Chapin
"Sunset in Wyoming" ('41) *(SP)*

Albert Duffy
"Down Mexico Way" ('41) *(SP)*

Maurice Rapf
"Call of the Canyon" ('42) *(S)*

Karl Brown
"Under Fiesta Stars" ('41) *(S+SP)*

Eliot Gibbons
"Under Fiesta Stars" ('41) *(SP)*

Earl Felton
"Sierra Sue" ('41) *(SP)*

Julian Zimet
"Sierra Sue" ('41) *(SP)*
"The Strawberry Roan" ('48) *(S)*

Newlin B. Wildes
"Heart of the Rio Grande" ('42) *(S)*

Lillie Hayward
"Heart of the Rio Grande" ('42) *(SP)*

Stuart Palmer
"Home In Wyomin'" ('42) *(S)*

Robert Tasker
"Home In Wyomin'" ('42) *(SP)*

M. Coates Webster
"Home In Wyomin'" ('42) *(SP)*

Lawrence Kimble
"Bells of Capistrano" ('42) *(SP)*

Bob Williams
"Saddle Pals" ('47) *(SP)*

Jerry Sackheim
"Saddle Pals" ('47) *(SP)*

John K. Butler
"Robin Hood of Texas" ('47) *(SP)*
"Rim of the Canyon" ('49) *(SP)*
    Plus 9 TV episodes *(SP)*

Jack Townley
"The Last Round-Up" ('47) *(S+SP)*
"Riders of the Whistling Pines" ('49) *(SP)*
"The Blazing Sun" ('50) *(SP)*
    Plus 2 TV episodes *(SP)*

Earle Snell
"Robin Hood of Texas" ('47) *(SP)*
"The Last Round-Up" ('47) *(SP)*
"Valley of Fire" ('51) *(S)*
    Plus 3 TV episodes *(SP)*

Dwight Cummins
"The Strawberry Roan" ('48) *(SP)*
"Loaded Pistols" ('49) *(SP)*
"The Cowboy and the Indians" ('49) *(SP)*
"Saginaw Trail" ('53) *(S+SP)*
    Plus 10 TV episodes *(SP)*

Dorothy Yost
"The Strawberry Roan" ('48) *(SP)*
"Loaded Pistols" ('49) *(SP)*
"The Cowboy and the Indians" ('49) *(SP)*
"Saginaw Trail" ('53) *(S+SP)*

Paul Gangelin
"Sons of New Mexico" ('50) *(SP)*
    Plus 6 TV episodes *(SP)*

Joseph Chadwick
"Rim of the Canyon" ('49) *(S)*

Herbert A. Woodbury
"Riders In the Sky" ('49) *(S)*

Alan James
"Mule Train" ('50) *(S)*
"Silver Canyon" ('51) *(S)*

Les Savage Jr.
"Hills of Utah" ('51) *(S)*

Ruth Woodman
"Last of the Pony Riders" ('53) *(S+SP)*

William Telaak
  1 TV episode *(SP)*

Sue Dwiggens/Vy Russell
  1 TV episode *(SP)*

Fred Myton
  2 TV episodes *(SP)*

Joe Richardson
  3 TV episodes *(SP)*

Howard J. Green
  2 TV episodes *(SP)*

Shelby Gordon
  1 TV episode *(SP)*

Robert Schaefer/Eric Freiwald
  12 TV episodes *(SP)*

Virginia M. Cooke
  4 TV episodes *(SP)*

Milton Raison
  1 TV episode *(SP)*

Elizabeth Beecher
  8 TV episodes *(SP)*

Polly James
  5 TV episodes *(SP)*

Maurice Tombragel
  1 TV episode *(SP)*

Maurice Geraghty
  3 TV episodes *(SP)*

Robert Blane
  1 TV episode *(SP)*
Kenneth Perkins
  2 TV episodes *(SP)*

Buckley Angell
  1 TV episode *(SP)*

J. Benton Cheney
  1 TV episode *(SP)*

Gene's Directors at a Glance

Otto Brower
"The Phantom Empire" ('35)

David Howard
"In Old Santa Fe" ('34)

Joe Kane
"Tumbling Tumbleweeds" ('35)
"Melody Trail" ('35)
"Sagebrush Troubadour" ('35)
"Guns and Guitars" ('36)
"Oh, Susanna!" ('36)
"Ride Ranger Ride" ('36)
"The Old Corral" ('36)
"Round-Up Time In Texas" ('37)
"Git Along Little Dogies" ('37)
"Yodelin' Kid From Pine Ridge" ('37)
"Public Cowboy No. 1" ('37)
"Boots and Saddles" ('37)
"Springtime In the Rockies" ('37)
"The Old Barn Dance" ('38)
"Gold Mine In the Sky" ('38)
"Man From Music Mountain" ('38)
"In Old Monterey" ('39)

Carl Pierson
"The Singing Vagabond" ('35)

B. Reeves Eason
"The Phantom Empire" ('35)
"Red River Valley" ('36)
"Blue Montana Skies" ('39)
"Mountain Rhythm" ('39)

Mack V. Wright
"Comin' 'Round the Mountain" ('36)
"The Singing Cowboy" ('36)
"The Big Show" ('36)
"Rootin' Tootin' Rhythm" ('37)

Charles F. Reisner
"Manhattan Merry-Go-Round" ('37)

Ralph Staub
"Prairie Moon" ('38)
"Western Jamboree" ('38)

George Sherman
"Rhythm of the Saddle" ('38)
"Mexicali Rose" ('39)
"Colorado Sunset" ('39)
"Rovin' Tumbleweeds" ('39)
"South of the Border" ('39)

Frank McDonald
"Rancho Grande" ('40)
"Gaucho Serenade" ('40)
"Carolina Moon" ('40)
"Ride, Tenderfoot, Ride" ('40)
"Under Fiesta Stars" ('41)
"Sioux City Sue" ('46)
"Twilight on the Rio Grande" ('47)
"The Big Sombrero" ('49)
"Texans Never Cry" ('51)
    Plus 16 TV episodes

Jack Townley
"Home on the Prairie" ('39)

Alfred E. Green
"Shooting High" ('40)

Joseph Santley
"Melody Ranch" ('40)
"Down Mexico Way" ('41)
"Call of the Canyon" ('42)

Lew Landers
"Ridin' on a Rainbow" ('41)
"Back In the Saddle" ('41)
"The Singing Hill" ('41)

William Morgan
"Sunset in Wyoming" ('41)
"Sierra Sue" ('41)

"Cowboy Serenade" ('42)
"Heart of the Rio Grande" ('42)
"Home in Wyomin'" ('42)
"Stardust on the Sage" ('42)
"Bells of Capistrano" ('42)

John English
"Trail to San Antone" ('47)
"The Last Round-Up" ('47)
"The Strawberry Roan" ('48)
"Loaded Pistols" ('49)
"Riders of the Whistling Pines" ('49)
"Rim of the Canyon" ('49)
"The Cowboy and the Indians" ('49)
"Riders In the Sky" ('49)
"Sons of New Mexico" ('50)
"Mule Train" ('50)
"Cow Town" ('50)
"Beyond the Purple Hills" ('50)
"Indian Territory" ('50)
"The Blazing Sun" ('50)
"Gene Autry and the Mounties" ('51)
"Whirlwind" ('51)
"Silver Canyon" ('51)
"Hills of Utah" ('51)
"Valley of Fire" ('51)
     Plus 2 TV episodes

Lesley Selander
"Saddle Pals" ('47)
"Robin Hood of Texas" ('47)

George Archainbaud
"The Old West" ('52)
"Night Stage to Galveston" ('52)
"Apache Country" ('52)
"Barbed Wire" ('52)
"Wagon Team" ('52)
"Blue Canadian Rockies" ('52)
"Winning of the West" ('53)
"On Top of Old Smoky" ('53)
"Goldtown Ghost Riders" ('53)
"Pack Train" ('53)
"Saginaw Trail" ('53)
"Last of the Pony Riders" ('53)
     Plus 47 TV episodes

Robert G. Walker
     2 TV episodes

Ray Nazarro
     2 TV episodes

D. Ross Lederman
     11 TV episodes

William Berke
     2 TV episodes

George Blair
     4 TV episodes

Wallace Fox
     5 TV episodes

Locations Where Gene Filmed

As with all B-western series, nearly every title was filmed in California. Budgets on B-westerns simply did not usually allow for travel to distant locations. However, when Gene filmed his own productions after WWII, he attempted to break the mold and traveled to Arizona to make his initial Columbia westerns. It ultimately proved too expensive and Gene returned to more familiar California locations.

In looking over the ranches, lakes and locations where Gene filmed his westerns, you'll find many popular spots were returned to frequently, other locations were only used once or twice. You'll also often note multiple locations utilized within one film. (Listed alphabetically.)

Acton Railroad Depot
"Gold Mine In the Sky" ('38)

The Acton depot, which was in Acton, California, on Highway 14 in Soledad Canyon northeast of Santa Clarita is no longer in existence.

Agoura/Albertson Ranch
"The Phantom Empire" ('35) serial
"Ride Ranger Ride" ('36)
"Blue Montana Skies" ('39)
"Ride, Tenderfoot, Ride" ('40)
"Ridin' on a Rainbow" ('41)
"Home In Wyomin'" ('42)
"Call of the Canyon" ('42) (*or* possibly Morrison Ranch. Unconfirmed.)
"Bells of Capistrano" ('42)
"Sons of New Mexico" ('50)
"Hills of Utah" ('51)

The Agoura Ranch was the site of Gene's Radio Ranch in "The Phantom Empire". Once a 14,000 acre working ranch, the large two-story main house framed by large oak trees played host to dozens of B-westerns. There was also a bunkhouse situated at an angle from the main house, a huge barn a bit farther away and rolling hills with excellent chase roads. The main house was constructed as a movie set, but the other buildings were authentic. The Agoura family originally owned the ranch as part of a Spanish land grant until publishing tycoon William Randolph Hearst acquired the property along with several other area spreads in the '20s. In 1943 Fred Albertson, a prominent area rancher and

car dealer, bought the 30,000 acre Hearst holdings. The now dilapidated spread can be found by taking Chesebro Road exit north off the Ventura Freeway. Proceed up Chesebro to Chesebro Park entrance on the right, walk east from a parking area up a hiking trail about half a mile to a locked and posted unmarked gate. Proceed, if you will, down the overgrown entrance road about half a mile to the ranch house area. The main house and barn are long gone, but the ramshackle bunkhouse is still standing. The main entrance road to the ranch, now closed to traffic, is about another quarter mile up Chesebro Road on the right. Gene rode up that road in "Sons of New Mexico" and serenaded Fay McKenzie on it at the end of "Home in Wyomin'".

Big Bear/Cedar Lake
"Blue Montana Skies" ('39)
"Sunset in Wyoming" ('41) (probable use)
"Riders of the Whistling Pines" ('49)
"Gene Autry and the Mounties" ('51)
"Blue Canadian Rockies" ('52) Cedar Lake

At more than 6,000 feet elevation, the gorgeous Big Bear Lake and Cedar Lake areas are about a three hour drive east of Los Angeles in the San Bernardino National Forest area. Big Bear City is on the eastern end of the lake. Big Bear Lake dam was built in 1911 to replace an original dam while a dam (with a millhouse, water wheel and waterside cabins) at Cedar Lake was built in 1914. Much of the Cedar Lake construction was done for "Trail of the Lonesome Pine" in 1936, although filming in the Big Bear/Cedar Lake area goes back to silent days. Cedar Lake is now a conference center/summer camp for the Congregational Church. Usually an advance call to them will allow you a visit. The church replaced the dilapidated millhouse and water wheel in the '80s with a reasonable facsimile. A cabin on the nearby Shay Ranch (on Hwy 38, now the Crausmeir House) hosted a few scenes of Gene's "Blue Montana Skies". The cabin was originally built for "Brigham Young—Frontiersman" in 1939.

Bishop and Mammoth Lakes Area
"Melody Ranch" ('40)
"Sierra Sue" ('41)
"Cowboy Serenade" ('42)

Gene and the Cass County Boys at Cedar Lake in the Big Bear, California, area.

Bishop, California, is way north of Los Angeles, about 50 miles north of Lone Pine, on Highway 395 in the Inyo National Forest. The Mammoth Lakes area is about 43 miles further northwest of Bishop on Hwy 395. Nearby June Lake and Lake Crowley were popular filming sites.

Brandeis Ranch
"The Singing Cowboy" ('36)
"Prairie Moon" ('38)

The Brandeis Ranch, often seen as a ghost town in B-westerns, was situated on the western edge of the upper Iverson Ranch. The property was once owned by members of the wealthy Brandeis family, whose patriarch owned large department stores. Besides the western street set, there existed nearby a small house with an unusual ramp-like entranceway with crude railing on the right side of the stoop to the house. Brandeis ended filming on the location in 1944. There are no standing structures on the now overgrown property.

Bronson Canyon
"Mystery Mountain" ('34) serial
"The Phantom Empire" ('35) serial
"Rancho Grande" ('40)
"Under Fiesta Stars" ('41)
"Heart of the Rio Grande" ('42)

"Call of the Canyon" ('42)

Looking much today like it did in 1935, the strangely shaped mid-sized tunnel at Bronson Canyon served as the entrance to the underground city of Murania for Gene's futuristic serial "Phantom Empire". Originally a rock quarry for construction of L.A.'s first street car system, Bronson Canyon has been a favorite filming site whenever a cave entrance was needed since 1919. Bronson is part of the 4,000 acre Griffith Park. There are four tunnel entrances—two large, one at each end of the main tunnel, as well as a medium sized tunnel entrance and a smaller cave opening which merge with the main tunnel. The walls of the canyon itself are quite steep, lined with rocky shale. Hundreds of westerns, sci-fi epics and TV episodes have lensed there. Take Hollywood Blvd. east to Bronson Ave. and go north until it becomes Canyon Blvd. which will lead you to a parking area.

Burro Flats
"Rovin' Tumbleweeds" ('39)
"Call of the Canyon" ('42)
"Outlaw Stage" (TV) ('53)
"Border Justice" (TV) ('53)

Burro Flats is a beautiful grassy plateau surrounded by huge boulders. The area, now owned by Rocketdyne Propulsion and Power of Canoga Park, California, formerly a division of North American Rockwell and currently a part of the Boeing Corporation, is off limits to visitors.

Calabasas area including Lasky Mesa

"The Singing Vagabond" ('35)
"In Old Monterey" ('39)

During the '30s, the Calabasas area (past Woodland Hills on the Ventura 101 freeway) was nothing but rolling hills, studded with oak trees. Lasky Mesa, so-named as the area to the west end of Victory Blvd., was acquired by the Lasky film company in late 1914. Scenes for many major motion pictures, including "Gone With the Wind" ('39), were lensed there. In 1963 Home Savings and Loan, the parent company of the Ahmanson Land Company, purchased the property. Washington Mutual Bank later took over the property which they sold in 2003. Lasky Mesa is now slated to become parkland.

Chatsworth Train Depot

"Rovin' Tumbleweeds" ('39)
"Rancho Grande" ('40)
"Ride, Tenderfoot, Ride" ('40)
"Back in the Saddle" ('41)
"Cowboy Serenade" ('42)
"Heart of the Rio Grande" ('42)

The Chatsworth, California, train station, at the end of Southern Pacific's Burbank-Chatsworth stretch, was popular for use in serials and westerns in the '40s. The depot succumbed to suburban sprawl in the '70s.

Columbia Backlot

"The Last Round-Up" ('47)
"The Strawberry Roan" ('48)
"Loaded Pistols" ('49)
"The Big Sombrero" ('49)
"Riders of the Whistling Pines" ('49)
"Rim of the Canyon" ('49)
"The Cowboy and the Indians" ('49)
"Riders In the Sky" ('49)
"Sons of New Mexico" ('50)
"Mule Train" ('50)
"Cow Town" ('50)
"Beyond the Purple Hills" ('50)
"The Blazing Sun" ('50)
"Gene Autry and the Mounties" ('51)
"Texans Never Cry" ('51)
"Whirlwind" ('51)
"Silver Canyon" ('51)
"Hills of Utah" ('51)
"Valley of Fire" ('51)
"The Old West" ('52)
"Night Stage to Galveston" ('52)
"Apache Country" ('52)
"Barbed Wire" ('52)
"Wagon Team" ('52)
"Blue Canadian Rockies" ('52)
"Winning of the West" ('53)

"On Top of Old Smoky" ('53)
"Goldtown Ghost Riders" ('53)
"Pack Train" ('53)
"Saginaw Trail" ('53)
"Last of the Pony Riders" ('53)

Columbia maintained studio facilities on Gower Street in Hollywood from 1924-1971. In 1935 Columbia established a backlot ranch (now owned by Warner Bros.) along Hollywood Way in Burbank. A western street set covered nearly the entire west end of the lot. Much of the western set was destroyed by a fire in the '50s and rebuilt but was torn down in June of '93.

Corriganville

"Mexicali Rose" ('39)
"Colorado Sunset" ('39)
"Rovin' Tumbleweeds" ('39)
"South of the Border" ('39)
"Shooting High" ('40)
"Carolina Moon" ('40)
"Ride, Tenderfoot, Ride" ('40)
"Sioux City Sue" ('46)
"The Last Round-Up" ('47)
"Loaded Pistols" ('49)
"The Big Sombrero" ('49)
"Rim of the Canyon" ('49)
"Mule Train" ('50)
"Beyond the Purple Hills" ('50)
"Indian Territory" ('50)
"Gene Autry and the Mounties" ('51)
"Hills of Utah" ('51)
"Frame for Trouble" (TV) ('51)
"Revenge Trail" (TV) ('51)
"The Old West" ('52)
"Thunder Out West" (TV) ('53)
"Narrow Escape" (TV) ('53)
"The Bandidos" (TV) ('53)
"Cold Decked" (TV) ('53)
"Civil War at Deadwood" (TV) ('54)
"Santa Fe Raiders" (TV) ('54)
"Prize Winner" (TV) ('54)
"Sharpshooter" (TV) ('54)
"Talking Guns" (TV) ('54)
"Outlaw of Blue Mesa" (TV) ('54)

Corriganville was one of the two most popular B-western filming sites, along with the Iverson Ranch. The 1,900 acre ranch was purchased in 1937 for around $11,000 by Ray "Crash" Corrigan of the Three Mesquiteers Republic film series. Filming began almost immediately with the rocky landscape being perfect for westerns. Corrigan originally built an artificial lake, a huge barn/stable and a ranch house on the location, adding a thriving townsite (called Silvertown) in 1943. He'd also increased the acreage to just over 2,000 acres. The famed "Fort Apache" Cavalry fort was built on the ranch in 1947. A special townset was constructed on the property in 1948 for Columbia's "The Man From Colorado" with Glenn Ford and burned to the ground in the closing scenes. Gene reused the burning town footage for "Gene Autry and the Mounties". Throughout the '30s, '40s and '50s some 2,000 movies and TV shows filmed at Corriganville. Even though filming on the ranch continued, in 1949 Corrigan turned the property into a western amusement park. Comedian Bob Hope purchased the ranch for development in 1965, paying Corrigan $2.8 million, renamed it Hopetown, then closed the ranch to the public in 1967. A fire swept through the ranch in September 1970, destroying a majority of the Silvertown sets. From 1967-1983, Hope sold off parcels of the ranch until only about 240 acres remained. In 1983 a developer took a $4.6 million option on some of the remaining property, however he filed for bankruptcy in 1994. Meanwhile, in 1987-1988, the Corriganville Park Master Plan was initiated, managed by the Rancho Simi Open Space Conservation Agency. Although much of the original ranch is now covered by condos, at least a portion of the once famous movie ranch reopened to the public as a park in May 1998.

French Ranch

"Sons of New Mexico" ('50)

Located in Hidden Valley near Thousand Oaks, California, the impressive French Ranch featured a distinctive white Spanish style main house, surrounding waist-high adobe wall, a fountain and a stable/bunkhouse. Although "Sons of New Mexico" is the only time Gene used the location, it is one of the striking uses of the ranch in B-westerns.

Griffith Observatory

"The Phantom Empire" ('35) serial

The underground world of Murania in "The Phantom Empire" was, in great part, played by the Griffith Observatory. A penniless Welsh immigrant who amassed a fortune in the golden state, Colonel Charles J. Griffith, donated the 3,015 acre parkland to L.A. in 1896. In 1912, he offered the city $100,000 to build an observatory on the property. Griffith envisioned an observatory and theater high atop Mt. Hollywood but an area on the slope of the mountain proved to be a more financially feasible site. Construction began in December 1933 and was completed 17 months later at a cost of over $655,000. The facility is a huge concrete structure topped by three copper-covered domes, the largest and most familiar a hundred feet across and the smaller two each 30 feet wide. The very first movie crew to utilize the site was Gene Autry's futuristic Mascot serial, "The Phantom Empire", filmed the year construction was completed in 1935. The observatory played the underground city of Murania, enhanced by many special effects and miniatures. Griffith Observatory, located at 2800 Observatory Road in Griffith Park, recently underwent a $90 million renovation.

Iverson Ranch

"Mystery Mountain" ('34) serial
"The Singing Cowboy" ('36)

"Oh, Susanna!" ('36)
"The Big Show" ('36)
"The Old Corral" ('36)
"Git Along Little Dogies" ('37)
"Man From Music Mountain" ('38)
"Prairie Moon" ('38)
"Rhythm of the Saddle" ('38)
"Western Jamboree" ('38)
"Mountain Rhythm" ('39)
"Back In the Saddle" ('41)
"Under Fiesta Stars" ('41)
"Heart of the Rio Grande" ('42)
"Call of the Canyon" ('42)
"Bells of Capistrano" ('42)
"Robin Hood of Texas" ('47)
"Loaded Pistols" ('49)
"Riders In the Sky" ('49)
"Sons of New Mexico" ('50)
"Cow Town" ('50)
"The Blazing Sun" ('50)
"Texans Never Cry" ('51)
"Silver Canyon" ('51)
"Hills of Utah" ('51)
"Warning! Danger!" (TV) ('51)
"Bandits of Boulder Bluff" (TV) ('51)
"Night Stage to Galveston" ('52)
"Apache Country" ('52)
"Wagon Team" ('52)
"Pack Train" ('53)
"Rio Renegades" (TV) ('53)
"Battle Axe" (TV) ('54)
"Boots and Ballots" (TV) ('54)
"Outlaw Warning" (TV) ('54)
"Stage to San Dimas" (TV) ('55)

Gene and Champion at a familiar Iverson Ranch pass in "The Big Show" ('36).

"Law Comes to Scorpion" (TV) ('55)
"Guns Below the Border" (TV) ('55)
"Feuding Friends" (TV) ('55)

Along with Corriganville, Iverson's was the most frequented B-western filming location. Located in Chatsworth, about a 40 minute drive from North Hollywood, Iverson's afforded fabulous rock formations, cliffs, chase roads and a western townsite. The ranch, which eventually encompassed some 500 acres, was first used for filming in 1912. The ranch reached its filming peak in the '30s, '40s and '50s, ultimately hosting some 2,000 features and TV shows. Construction of the Simi Valley Freeway (now Ronald Reagan Freeway) through the property in '65-'67 greatly diminished the site's value as a film location, then a 1970 fire destroyed most of the movie sets. Over the years, parcels of land were sold off so that by the early '90s a condo complex covered much of the lower Iverson and huge mansions covered the upper Iverson. An apartment complex covered the area where the middle Iverson ranch set had once stood. The most famous site on the ranch—the Garden of the Gods rock formations—were donated in the '80s to the Santa Susanna Conservancy for preservation as a nature area. There still remains about 140 undeveloped acres on the upper Iverson.

Jack Garner Ranch
"Melody Trail" ('35)
"Guns and Guitars" ('36)
"Springtime In the Rockies" ('37)
"Gold Mine In the Sky" ('38)
"Home on the Prairie" ('39)
"Colorado Sunset" ('39)

First developed in the 1860s, this working ranch was purchased by the Garner family in 1905. After WWII, then known as the Jack Garner Ranch, it encompassed nearly 10,000 acres. Located south of Banning, California, off Highway 74, near Lake Hemet, the Garner Ranch has a main house with a broad veranda, along with assorted barns and corrals and huge expanses of pasture land bordered by pine trees and rolling hills. The ranch remains today nearly as it did in the westerns of Gene Autry, Hopalong Cassidy and Tim Holt.

Jack Ingram Ranch
"Wagon Team" ('52)
"Outlaw Stage" (TV) ('53)
"Old Prospector" (TV) ('53)
"Border Justice" (TV) ('53)
"Gypsy Wagon" (TV) ('53)
"Johnny Jackaroo" (TV) ('54)
"Carnival Comes West" (TV) ('54)

In 1944 screen badman Jack Ingram bought property from PRC cowboy stars Dave O'Brien and James Newill off Topanga Canyon Road in Woodland Hills. (The area is now accessed by turning west on Mulholland for about half a mile. Mulholland did not extend that far at the time.) With the help of some friends, Ingram built sets on the ranch

which were used in many late '40s westerns and early '50s TV series. Ingram sold the ranch to Four Star Productions in 1956. All the sets except one western-style building have since been razed, although Ingram's old personal home still stands.

Janss Ranch
"Rancho Grande" ('40)
"Heart of the Rio Grande" ('42)
"Riders of the Whistling Pines" ('49) (landing airfield)

In 1910 Edwin and Harold Janss purchased about 10,000 acres of land in what is now central Thousand Oaks. The area was primarily used as a farm and to raise thoroughbred horses, although some filming was done on the wide open rolling hills and grasslands as well as the private airfield landing strip. In the '50s, the Janss brothers began buying more property and selling off parcels for development. What is now Wildwood Park was once on the Janss Ranch.

Jauregui Ranch
"Man From Music Mountain" ('38)
"Home on the Prairie" ('39)
"Mountain Rhythm" ('39)
"The Singing Hill" ('41)
"The Strawberry Roan" ('48)

The Andy Jauregui Ranch was used in dozens of B-westerns from the '30s to the '50s, with one of its most prominent uses in Gene's "The Strawberry Roan". Located near Newhall, California, about a 50 minute drive north from Los Angeles along Highway 14 in Placerita Canyon, the Jauregui, owned by noted rodeo performer Andy Jauregui, was an unpretentious working ranch. "The Strawberry Roan" crew added a large back porch to the main house giving it the advantage of having a front and back porch which could be utilized to suggest two different ranch houses. A large barnyard and outbuildings afforded cameras an excellent long shot of approaching riders. Advancing civilization brought change to the spread and in 1996 a long standing lease agreement allowed Chevron Oil Company to take over the property. They wasted no time in leveling the remaining barns, fencing and outbuildings, leaving, primarily, only the main ranch house standing.

Joe Yrigoyen Ranch
"Red River Valley" ('36)
"The Big Show" ('36)

Brothers Joe, Frank and Bill Yrigoyen operated property that included a horse barn on Main Street in Burbank, California, which they occasionally rented out to film companies. According to stuntman Jack Williams, Frank was the actual owner.

Keen Camp
"Yodelin' Kid From Pine Ridge" ('37)
"Springtime in the Rockies" ('37)
"Gold Mine in the Sky" ('38)

"Home on the Prairie" ('39)
"Colorado Sunset" ('39)
"Carolina Moon" ('40)
"Sunset in Wyoming" ('41) (possible use)

Keen Camp is located about a mile east of Mountain Center, California, on Highway 74, in the San Jacinto Mountain range. The oft-used Jack Garner Ranch is about 10 miles distant. The Tahquitz Lodge, the Keen Camp store, a school and a beautiful pine-bordered meadow made the area attractive for filming until the lodge was destroyed by fire in 1943.

Kentucky Park Farm
"Trail to San Antone" ('47)

Kentucky Park Farm was a thoroughbred ranch located in Hidden Valley, California (near Lake Sherwood), built by F. W. Matthiessen in 1923. Now called Ventura Farms, the track used in "Trail to San Antone" (and Roy Rogers' "My Pal Trigger") has long since been torn down.

Kernville
"Sagebrush Troubadour" ('35) including Pasco Ranch
"Oh, Susanna!" ('36)
"The Old Corral" ('36)
"Git Along Little Dogies" ('37)
"Public Cowboy No. 1" ('37)
"The Old Barn Dance" ('38)
"In Old Monterey" ('39)

Film crews began shooting in the Kern River Valley, three hours north of Los Angeles in the Sequoia National Forest, as early as 1916, but it became quite popular for westerns in the '30s and '40s. Most area filming was done in the original Kernville (now under Lake Isabella), along the raging Kern River, on various area ranches (including the Pasco Ranch), as well as in the surrounding hills of rocks and scattered pine trees. South of Kernville was a lagoon area used in many cliff fights. Just beyond the lagoon was a swinging bridge.

Lake Hemet
"Springtime in the Rockies" ('37)
"Gold Mine in the Sky" ('38)
"Ride, Tenderfoot, Ride" ('40)
"Ridin' On a Rainbow" ('41) (Unconfirmed)

Located near the picturesque Jack Garner Ranch, Lake Hemet is south of Banning near where Highways 243 and 74 intersect.

Lake Malibu
"Saddle Pals" ('47)

Located south of Highway 101 on Mulholland Highway near Malibu Creek State Park.

Lake Sherwood
"Yodelin' Kid From Pine Ridge" ('37)
"Blue Montana Skies" ('39)
"Sons of New Mexico" ('50)

First formed around 1905 with the completion of a dam, Lake Sherwood, near what is now Westlake Village (a 30 minute drive west on the Ventura Freeway from Los Angeles), was a popular filming locale for westerns and serials. Development now makes it mostly inaccessible to visitors.

Lone Pine
"Comin' 'Round the Mountain" ('36)
"Oh, Susanna!" ('36)
"Rootin' Tootin' Rhythm" ('37)
"Boots and Saddles" ('37)
"The Old Barn Dance" ('38)
"In Old Monterey" ('39)
"Melody Ranch" ('40)
"Down Mexico Way" ('41)
"Call of the Canyon" ('42)
"Trail to San Antone" ('47)
"Loaded Pistols" ('49)
"Mule Train" ('50)
"Cow Town" ('50)
" Beyond the Purple Hills" ('50)
"The Blazing Sun" ('50)
"Texans Never Cry" ('51)
"Valley of Fire" ('51)
"Winning of the West" ('53)
"Pack Train" ('53)
"Old Prospector" (TV) ('53)
"Gypsy Wagon" (TV) ('53)
"Steel Ribbon" (TV) ('53)
"Rio Renegades" (TV) ('53)
"Ransom Cross" (TV) ('53)
"Johnny Jackaroo" (TV) ('54)
"Talking Guns" (TV) ('54)
"Carnival Comes West" (TV) ('54)
"Civil War at Deadwood" (TV) ('54)
"Million Dollar Fiddle" (TV) ('55)
"Golden Chariot" (TV) ('55)

The Alabama Hills of Lone Pine, at the base of snow-capped Mt. Whitney, 200 miles north of Los Angeles on

The "Mule Train" rolls among the Alabama Hills of Lone Pine, California.

Highway 395, looks almost exactly today as it did when Gene filmed nearly 20 movies there from the '30s to the '50s. There's even a cucumber shaped rock in the Alabama Hills referred to as Gene Autry Rock, as Gene was seen sitting astride Champion by the unique formation in "Boots and Saddles". Lone Pine's actual train depot made a prominent appearance in "Boots and Saddles" also, with Republic not ever bothering to change the name of the station. Although now long gone, a depot and out buildings at nearby Keeler were seen in "The Blazing Sun".

Monogram Ranch (later Melody Ranch)

"Tumbling Tumbleweeds" ('35)
"Sagebrush Troubadour" ('35)
"Mexicali Rose" ('39)
"Bells of Capistrano" ('42)
"The Big Sombrero" ('49)
"Winning of the West" ('53)
"On Top of Old Smoky" ('53)
"Saginaw Trail" ('53)
"Rio Renegades" (TV) ('53)
"Battle Axe" (TV) ('54)
"Boots and Ballots" (TV) ('54)
"Outlaw Warning" (TV) ('54)
"Million Dollar Fiddle" (TV) ('55)
"Stage to San Dimas" (TV) ('55)
"Law Comes to Scorpion" (TV) ('55)
"Golden Chariot" (TV) ('55)
"Guns Below the Border" (TV) ('55)
"Ghost Ranch" (TV) ('55)
Go West Young Lady" (TV) ('55)
"Feuding Friends" (TV) ('55)
"Saddle Up" (TV) ('55)
"Ride, Ranchero" (TV) ('55)
"The Rangerette" (TV) ('55)
"Dynamite" (TV) ('56)

Gene Autry was closely associated with the Monogram Ranch, which became Melody Ranch in 1952. Locations expert Tinsley Yarbrough traced the history of the ranch in WESTERN CLIPPINGS #27 (Jan./Feb. 1999).

"Long owned by movie technical/art director Ernie Hickson and apparently used for filming as far back as William S. Hart's 'The Disciple' ('15), the spread, located at 24715 Oak Creek Ave., near the intersection of Oak Creek and Placerita Canyon Road, became the Monogram Ranch in 1937, when that little studio signed a long-term lease with Hickson which included the stipulation the ranch would bear the Monogram name. But it was to be even better known as Melody Ranch, the name Gene gave the spread when he purchased it shortly after Hickson's death on Jan. 22, 1952, and converted it into a thriving TV factory not only for such Autry Flying A series as 'Annie Oakley', 'Range Rider', 'Adventures of Champion', 'Buffalo Bill, Jr.' and his own series, but also for segments of Hoppy's video show, 'Wild Bill Hickok', 'Wyatt Earp', 'Cisco Kid', 'Sheriff of Cochise', 'Tombstone Territory'

and 'Gunsmoke', among other series, while continuing to lease it for B+ and A features as well. In 1958, the NBC series 'Wide, Wide World' hosted a western special there, directed by John Ford and featuring Autry and dozens of other western players. By the early sixties, Autry had plans to establish a museum and amusement park at the ranch, but then, tragedy struck. On August 28, 1962, a massive firestorm roared through the Santa Clarita Valley, destroying 54 structures on the 110-acre ranch, as well as Gene's extensive collection of western Americana and 17,000 recordings, with losses set at $1 million. Only the Melody Ranch entrance, a walled adobe ranch house and a few other buildings remained. Autry gave up plans for a museum, and over the next several decades gradually sold all but twelve acres of the property to developers. Scenes for 'Roots II' lensed at the ranch's train depot set. Otherwise, the spread's filming days seemed finished. But appearances can be deceiving. Not only did Gene's dream of a western museum become a wonderful reality, albeit in L.A.'s Griffith Park rather than Newhall, but in 1990, after

Gene rides Champion down a main street of his Melody Ranch.

the death of the last Champion stabled at the spread, Autry sold Melody Ranch, for a reported $975,000, to Renaud and Andre Veluzat, Santa Clarita Valley natives whose family had operated a film ranch in Saugus since the early '50s. Drawing painstakingly on photographs and videotapes, the Veluzat brothers restored much of Melody Ranch largely to its appearance during the early TV era, making it available once again for filming."

The rebuilt ranch is now open for tours and includes a newly established museum with items from Gene himself, "Bonanza", "Maverick", "Bronco Billy", and Autry's own guest house which was saved from the devastating fire of '62. Call to arrange a tour (661) 286-1188. Take Freeway 170 north from Los Angeles to I-5, I-5 north to Highway 14, Highway 14 north to the Fernando Rd. exit, Fernando Rd. west past Lyons Avenue to a street on the right that becomes Placerita Canyon Rd. and east on Placerita to the Melody

Ranch sign.

Morrison Ranch

"Blue Montana Skies" ('39)
"Colorado Sunset" ('39)
"Ridin' on a Rainbow" ('41)
"Cowboy Serenade" ('42) (unconfirmed)
"Heart of the Rio Grande" ('42)
"Stardust on the Sage" ('42) (unconfirmed)
"Call of the Canyon" ('42) (unconfirmed)
"Sioux City Sue" ('46)

In its filming days the Morrison Ranch in Agoura Hills (west on the Ventura 101 Freeway) offered open oak tree studded woodlands.

Old Tucson

"The Last Round-Up" ('47)

Old Tucson, Arizona, was originally built in 1939-'40 for Columbia's "Arizona" ('40). Columbia let its lease on the 320 acre site expire in 1944. In 1946 the Tucson Chamber of Commerce leased the Old Tucson site from the Pima County Board of Supervisors to whom Columbia had donated the acreage. In 1959, Robert Shelton formed Old Tucson Development Company and leased the site, opening it to the general public as a family fun park and movie location in January 1960. Shelton retired several years ago and the location is now operated by The Old Tucson Company.

Palmdale/Lancaster Area

"Rootin' Tootin' Rhythm" ('37)
"Mexicali Rose" ('39)
"South of the Border" ('39)
"Ride, Tenderfoot, Ride" ('40)
"Down Mexico Way" ('41)

The Palmdale/Lancaster area of California featured Joshua tree groves and scattered rock formations similar to those at Pioneertown, as well as a large dry lake. Now heavily developed, part of this area is now known as Lake Los Angeles; about an hour north of L.A. on Highway 14.

Pioneertown

"The Cowboy and the Indians" ('49)
"Riders In the Sky" ('49)
"Indian Territory" ('50)
"Whirlwind" ('51)
"Silver Canyon" ('51)
"Barbed Wire" ('52)
"Wagon Team" ('52)
"Winning of the West" ('53)
"On Top of Old Smoky" ('53)
"Last of the Pony Riders" ('53)

All 26 episodes of the first season of Gene's TV show ('50-'51) were filmed at Pioneertown as well as 24 of 26 in the second season ('51-'52), three in the third season ('53), two in the fourth ('54) and four in the fifth season (55). (See TV log for specific episodes.)

427

In the mid '40s screen badman Dick Curtis happened upon Yucca Valley in California's high desert, a 4,500 foot elevation about 30 miles north of Palm Springs. Convinced the area was ripe for development, Curtis persuaded some 17 investors to go into the project with him, including the Sons of the Pioneers, Roy Rogers, directors Tommy Carr and Frank McDonald, actor/producer Russell Hayden, comedian Bud Abbott and badman Terry Frost. In 1946, forming a corporation, each invested $500 in the project, acquiring 32,000 acres in the Valley. Pierce Lyden, a screen heavy who was invited to join Curtis and the others in the investment recalled, "He started a project that was going to make him a millionaire, it was called Pioneertown. It was going to be a western picture location. Several people went in with him. He asked me to join them but I didn't have the money. The project was a failure because there was not enough water (up on the high desert). Dick did not become the millionaire he had envisioned."[1] In fact, Curtis fell on ill health, being operated on for a brain tumor in November 1951. He died January 13, 1952. Russell Hayden replaced Curtis as corporation president. Several businesses, including the Red Dog Saloon, were built, arranged so they could double as a western street set. Dubbed Pioneertown after the singing group, by late 1948 on into 1949 four "Cisco Kid" movies and Gene Autry's "The Cowboy and the Indians" had been filmed in Pioneertown. A 1950 appraisal of the property valued it in excess of $1.5 million. The main problem, as Pierce Lyden said, was that the water supply was totally inadequate for further development of homes, resorts and dude ranches as the investors had envisioned, therefore Pioneertown never went any further than a modest small town and filming location. The surrounding landscape features very cinematic rock formations resembling huge mounds of giant pebbles, groves of Joshua trees and long stretches of chase roads perfect for B-western filming. The western street, dubbed "Mane Street" was far wider than a typical movie set, giving Pioneertown a unique authentic look. Gene's Flying A productions was the primary proponent of the arid area, filming ten of his Columbia movies and nearly all of his TV episodes there, as well as many episodes of Flying A produced "Range Rider",

The popular oft-used Red Dog Saloon at Pioneertown where so many of Gene's TV episodes were filmed.

428

"Buffalo Bill Jr." and "Annie Oakley". In fact, Gene spent so much time in Pioneertown his room at the local motel, Club 9, became the favorite after hours watering hole for actors and crews. The original corporation eventually lost the property to the finance company, but one hardy investor, Russell Hayden, was able to purchase acreage for a ranch house across the road from the town. He and his wife built their own ramshackle sets and filmed the Hayden-produced "Judge Roy Bean" TV series there ('55-'56). Hayden was living there at the time of his death at 70 in 1981. Hayden's wife, Lillian "Mousie" Porter, continued to live there until her death in 1997. Today, Pioneertown continues to trudge on, still hosting an occasional commercial or movie shoot. The Red Dog saloon has recently been refurbished and re-opened; the Pioneertown Palace and Pioneer Bowl continue to thrive among the less than 200 inhabitants. To reach Pioneertown, take I-10 east from Los Angeles to Highway 62. Go north on 62 to Yucca Valley and turn left on the road to Pioneertown, about 9 miles north.

SOURCE:

1. Magers, Nareau, Copeland. *Best of the Badmen.* Empire, 2005. p. 90.

Placerita Canyon and Walker Ranch
"Git Along Little Dogies" ('37)
"Home on the Prairie" ('39)
"Mountain Rhythm" ('39)
"The Singing Hill" ('41)
"Sunset in Wyoming" ('41)
"Sioux City Sue" ('46)
"Saginaw Trail" ('53)

One of the most oft used, scenic western film sites was the Walker Ranch east of Newhall along Placerita Canyon Road, near the Jauregui and Disney Golden Oak ranches. Placerita Canyon featured a clearing, in front of the small Walker Cabin, with scattered sycamore trees, a mine entrance to the left rear of the cabin, a running insert road in front of the cabin and a creek bed, usually found to be dry. Wooded hills surrounded the area, which was comprised of only about 300 acres. The small cabin with a rock chimney used as a hideout shack or relay station in so many westerns still stands today. The owner of the property during its filming days, Frank Evans Walker, sold the property to the state sometime in the early '50s. Placerita Canyon County and State Park is off of Highway 14 on Placerita Canyon Road.

Rancho Maria
"The Big Sombrero" ('49)
Elena Verdugo's comic swimming pool scene with Gene was filmed at Rancho Maria when inclement weather forced a cancellation of shooting plans at Tucson's Arizona Inn pool. Rancho Maria is along Sand Canyon Road near Newhall, California.

Red Rock Canyon
"The Singing Hill" ('41)
"The Big Sombrero" ('49)
Located on Highway 14, 100 miles north of Los Angeles, Red Rock Canyon, on the edge of the Mojave Desert, has been a very popular film site from the '20s on through today, furnishing filmmakers a spectacular backdrop of colorful cathedral-like cliffs. Rudolph Hagen settled there in 1896 and gained complete control of the canyon by 1913. He operated the Ricardo Land and Water Company and hosted movie companies by as early as 1925. After he died in 1937, his heirs continued filming arrangements. The area is now a state park, remaining untouched by civilization.

Republic Backlot
"Sagebrush Troubadour" ('35)
"The Singing Vagabond" ('35)
"Comin' 'Round the Mountain" ('36)
"Guns and Guitars" ('36)
"Oh, Susanna!" ('36)
"Ride Ranger Ride" ('36)
"The Big Show" ('36)
"The Old Corral" ('36)
"Yodelin' Kid From Pine Ridge" ('37)
"Public Cowboy No. 1" ('37)
"Boots and Saddles" ('37)
"Springtime in the Rockies" ('37)
"The Old Barn Dance" ('38)
"Gold Mine in the Sky" ('38)
"Man From Music Mountain" ('38)
"Prairie Moon" ('38)
"Rhythm of the Saddle" ('38)
"Western Jamboree" ('38)
"Home on the Prairie" ('39)
"Mountain Rhythm" ('39)
"Colorado Sunset" ('39)
"In Old Monterey" ('39)
"Rovin' Tumbleweeds" ('39)
"South of the Border" ('39)
"Rancho Grande" ('40)
"Melody Ranch" ('40)
"The Singing Hill" ('41)
"Sunset in Wyoming" ('41)
"Under Fiesta Stars" ('41)
"Down Mexico Way" ('41)
"Sierra Sue" ('41)
"Cowboy Serenade" ('41)
"Heart of the Rio Grande" ('42)
"Home In Wyomin'" ('42)
"Stardust on the Sage" ('42)
"Call of the Canyon" ('42)
"Bells of Capistrano" ('42)
"Sioux City Sue" ('46)
"Trail to San Antone" ('47)
"Twilight on the Rio Grande" ('47)
"Saddle Pals" ('47)
Republic arguably produced the best B-westerns of the

'30s and '40s, and Gene Autry was there from the beginning. The 43 acre studio was at 4024 Radford Avenue off Ventura Blvd. in Studio City. Bordered on the south by Ventura, on the west by Radford, east by Colfax Avenue and north by the Los Angeles River (now part of L.A.'s concrete aqueduct system), the studio was first constructed in 1928 as the home to comedy king Mack Sennett. When Sennett went bankrupt in 1933, Mascot became the tenant for two years before Herbert J. Yates formed Republic Pictures Corporation by joining together Mascot, Monogram and Liberty Pictures. Gene's "Tumbling Tumbleweeds" was one of the first two westerns made at Republic. (The other was "Westward Ho" with John Wayne.) Over the years, Yates gradually added new sound stages and buildings. The western street underwent changes with time, especially when a 1940 fire destroyed several sets. In 1959 Yates leased the studio to Lippert Pictures. CBS became the lessee in 1963, renaming it CBS Studio Center, eventually purchasing the property in 1967.

Reuss Ranch
"Under Fiesta Stars" ('41)

The Reuss Ranch was on Lake Malibu near where Cornell Road that runs by the current Paramount Ranch now intersects with Mulholland Drive. It's believed the Reuss Ranch was once owned by Ronald Reagan or one of his financial benefactors.

Russell Ranch
"Home in Wyomin'" ('42)
"Saddle Pals" ('47) (Possible use.)
"Robin Hood of Texas" ('47) (Possible use.)

The Russell Ranch was originally part of the huge El Rancho Conejo in the Agoura/Westlake Village area west of Los Angeles. Most of the property was sold to publisher William Randolph Hearst circa 1925. Hearst leased the property back to the Russell family who continued to rent the rolling woodlands, filled with creeks and small lakes to film companies.

Sedona
"The Strawberry Roan" ('48)

The spectacular and colorful rock formations of Sedona, Arizona, lured Gene to film his Cinecolor "The Strawberry Roan" there. Sedona, where some 76 movies were lensed, is about an hour south of Flagstaff on Highway 89A.

Saugus Train Station
"Oh, Susanna!" ('36)

The Saugus, California, train depot is now on display in Newhall, next to the William S. Hart Home and Museum.

Trem Carr Ranch
"Red River Valley" ('36)

Trem Carr was an early silent film producer. In 1931 he helped form Monogram. That same year, Carr took out a five-year lease on land in Placerita Canyon in the area which in now owned by the Disney Corporation. A western street was built on the property. Republic Pictures was formed in 1935 by combining several film companies, one of which was Monogram. Within a year, Carr walked away from Republic and reformed Monogram. Around the same time, Carr lost the lease on his property in Placerita Canyon.

Valsteve Ranch
"Saddle Pals" ('47)

It's unclear exactly where this ranch was in the San Fernando Valley, but it offered a jump arena for horses utilized in this film and one with Monte Hale.

Vasquez Rocks
"Rim of the Canyon" ('49)
"The Old West" ('52)
"Ride, Ranchero" (TV) ('55)
"The Rangerette" (TV) ('55)

Vasquez Rocks along Highway 14, about 50 minutes north of Los Angeles, is an impressive natural setting, little changed today from its filming heyday from the '30s to the '50s. Apparently the unusual rock formations rested on the floor of a prehistoric ocean. As the water receded and floods washed away the soil around the sandstone, violent earthquakes tilted the rocks upward at a 60 degree angle. The rocks derived their name from the Mexican bandit Tiburcio Vasquez who hid there until he was captured in 1875. Hundreds of movies, TV shows and commercials have been filmed in the 745 acre area which was acquired by L.A. County in the '60s and became a park in 1970.

Victorville Desert Area
"Tumbling Tumbleweeds" ('35)
"Back In the Saddle" ('41)
"Down Mexico Way" ('41)
"Twilight on the Rio Grande" ('47)

In the '30s and '40s the Mojave Desert around the ever-expanding Victorville, California, was perfect for desolate desert scenes in westerns. Located on I-15 south of Barstow.

Yuma
"Red River Valley" ('36)

The old territorial prison at Yuma, Arizona, was where scenes for "Red River Valley" were lensed. It's now a museum. Yuma's Laguna Dam spillway, on the Colorado River, is where Gene and George Chesebro staged a fight. The nearby Buttercup Valley in California's Imperial Sand Dunes, a few miles northwest of Yuma, were also utilized.

(This locations section would not be as complete or as informative without the specialized input of locations expert Tinsley Yarbrough. We are indebted to his knowledge.)

Gene's Movie Jobs

"The Phantom Empire" ....Radio Singer

"Tumbling Tumbleweeds" ....Medicine Show Singer

"Melody Trail" ....Rodeo Rider/Ranch Cook

"Sagebrush Troubadour" ....Undercover Ranger

"The Singing Vagabond" ....Ranger Captain

"Red River Valley" ....Ditch Rider

"Comin' 'Round the Mountain"...Pony Express Rider

"The Singing Cowboy" ....Rancher/Western Singer

"Guns and Guitars" ....Medicine Show Singer

"Oh, Susanna!" ....Radio Singer

"Ride Ranger Ride" ....Texas Ranger who joins
Cavalry

"The Big Show" ....Stuntman/Movie Star

"The Old Corral" ....Sheriff

"Round-Up Time in Texas" ....Horse Ranch Owner

"Git Along Little Dogies" ....Rancher

"Rootin' Tootin' Rhythm" ....Rancher

"Yodelin' Kid From Pine Ridge" .Wild West Show Star

"Boots and Saddles" ....Ranch Foreman

"Public Cowboy No. 1" ....Deputy Sheriff

"Springtime in the Rockies" ....Ranch Foreman

"The Old Barn Dance" ....Horse Trader

"Gold Mine In the Sky" ....Ranch Foreman

"Man From Music Mountain" .....Rancher

"Prairie Moon" ....Deputy Sheriff

"Rhythm of the Saddle" ....Ranch Foreman

"Western Jamboree" ....Ranch Foreman

"Home on the Prairie" ....Livestock Inspector

"Mexicali Rose" ....Radio Singer

"Blue Montana Skies" ....Cattle Rancher

"Mountain Rhythm" ....Rancher

"Colorado Sunset" ....Dairy Rancher

"In Old Monterey" ....Army Sergeant

"Rovin' Tumbleweeds" ....Rancher/Radio Singer/
Congressman

"South of the Border" ....Government Agent

"Rancho Grande" ....Ranch Foreman

"Shooting High" ....Movie Cowboy

"Gaucho Serenade" ....Rodeo Rider

"Carolina Moon" ....Rodeo Rider

"Ride, Tenderfoot, Ride" ....Cowboy

"Melody Ranch" ....Radio Star

"Ridin' On a Rainbow" ....Cattleman

"Back In the Saddle" ....Ranch Foreman

"The Singing Hill" ....Ranch Foreman

"Sunset in Wyoming" ....Rancher

"Under Fiesta Stars" ....Rodeo Star

"Down Mexico Way" ....Sage City Citizen

"Sierra Sue" ....State Board Inspector

"Cowboy Serenade" ....Cattle Rancher

"Heart of the Rio Grande" ....Dude Ranch Foreman

"Home in Wyomin'" ....Radio Star

"Stardust on the Sage" ....Cattle Rancher

"Call of the Canyon" ....Cattleman

"Bells of Capistrano" ....Rodeo Singer

"Sioux City Sue" ....Cattleman

"Trail to San Antone" ....Rancher

"Twilight on the Rio Grande" ......Rancher

"Saddle Pals" ....Rancher

"Robin Hood of Texas" ....Out of Work Cowboy

"The Last Round-Up" ....Cattle Rancher

"The Strawberry Roan" ....Ranch Foreman

"Loaded Pistols" ....Rancher

"The Big Sombrero" ....Ranch Foreman

"Riders of the Whistling Pines"...Ex-Forest Ranger/Owner
of Sportsman's Camp

"Rim of the Canyon" ....Owner of Flying A

"The Cowboy and the Indians"....Rancher

"Riders In the Sky" ....Rancher/Investigator for
County Attorney

"Sons of New Mexico" ....Cattleman

"Mule Train" ...............................U.S. Marshal

"Cow Town" ....Cattle Rancher

"Beyond the Purple Hills" ....Sheriff

"Indian Territory" ....Special Assistant to
Chief of Indian Affairs

"The Blazing Sun" ....Banker's Association
Investigator

"Gene Autry and the Mounties"...U.S. Marshal

"Texans Never Cry" ....Texas Ranger Sergeant

"Whirlwind" ....Post Office Special
Agent

"Silver Canyon" ....U. S. Cavalry Scout

"Hills of Utah" ....Medical Doctor

"Valley of Fire" ....Mayor
"The Old West" ....Wild Horse Wrangler
"Night Stage to Galveston"..........Texas Ranger
"Apache Country"........................Chief of Scouts for
                                        Southwestern Cavalry
"Barbed Wire"............................Cattleman
"Wagon Team" ....Stageline Detective
"Blue Canadian Rockies" ....Ranch Foreman

"Winning of the West" ....Territorial Ranger
"On Top of Old Smoky" ....Singer
"Goldtown Ghost Riders" ....Circuit Riding Judge
"Pack Train"...............................Trail Guide
"Saginaw Trail"...........................Captain in Hamilton's
                                        Rangers
"Last of the Pony Riders" ....Pony Express Division
                                        Agent

Gene leaves his home in Studio City for work at Republic Studios. Circa 1942. (Photo courtesy Neil Summers.)

Recurrent Themes in Gene's Westerns

Singing in Jail
"The Singing Vagabond"
"The Old Corral" (Sons of the Pioneers)
"Ride Ranger Ride" (Smiley Burnette and Max Terhune)
"Mountain Rhythm"
"Rovin' Tumbleweeds"
"Ride, Tenderfoot, Ride"
"Sunset in Wyoming"
"Sierra Sue"
"Bells of Capistrano"
"Saddle Pals"
"Mule Train"
"Silver Canyon"
"On Top of Old Smoky" (Cass County Boys)
"Double Barreled Vengeance" (TV)
"Frame For Trouble" (TV)
"The Sheriff is a Lady" (TV)
"Battle Axe" (TV)
"Law Comes to Scorpion" (TV)

Taming of the Shrew
"Sagebrush Troubadour"
"Git Along Little Dogies"
"Boots and Saddles"
"Springtime in the Rockies"
"Gold Mine in the Sky"
"Rancho Grande"
"Ride, Tenderfoot, Ride"
"Melody Ranch"
"The Singing Hill"
"Sunset in Wyoming"
"Under Fiesta Stars"
"Heart of the Rio Grande"
"Saddle Pals"
"The Big Sombrero"
"Loaded Pistols"
"Cow Town"
"Whirlwind"

Secret Recordings/Altered Trick Recordings
"Git Along Little Dogies"
"Rhythm of the Saddle"
"The Blazing Sun"
"Stardust on the Sage"
"The Old Barn Dance"
"Call of the Canyon"
"Saddle Pals"

Spanking Scene
"Sagebrush Troubadour"
"Twilight on the Rio Grande"
"Doublecross Valley" (TV)

Ride with Me or Walk
"The Singing Vagabond"
"Heart of the Rio Grande"
"Whirlwind"

Crowded off the Road
"Sagebrush Troubadour"
"The Old Corral"
"Boots and Saddles"

Gene whipping out his guitar to sing a song while confined in jail was a common occurence in his films. In this scene from "Bells of Capistrano" ('42) his audience is Smiley Burnette, Lucien Littlefield and Claire Du Brey.

"Man From Music Mountain"
"Prairie Moon"
"Mountain Rhythm"
"Bells of Capistrano"
"Saddle Pals"
"Blue Canadian Rockies"

Environmental Issues

"Red River Valley" (drought and irrigation)
"Git Along Little Dogies" (polluted water)
"Man From Music Mountain" (water problems)

"Rovin' Tumbleweeds" (flood control)
"Sierra Sue" (weed control and chemical spraying)
"Back In the Saddle" (polluted water)
"Sunset in Wyoming" (over logging and reforestation)
"Stardust on the Sage" (hydraulic mining)
"Riders of the Whistling Pines" (DDT and Tossock Moth)
"The Cowboy and the Indians" (plight of starving Indians)
"Hills of Utah" (pollution of streams by copper mines)

Champion

Gene and Champion.

untrained, but by 1939 he was worth a reported $25,000. It's thought he was given a dye job about 1940 to photograph sharper in black and white. The original Champion died at 17 at Melody Ranch on January 23, 1947, while Gene was filming "Twilight on the Rio Grande". He was buried at Melody Ranch by Gene's horse trainer, John Agee, who had previously worked 14 years for Tom Mix and who lived at the ranch with helpers who were caretakers while Gene was away.

Gene's most reliable horse to meet the public was best known as Touring Champ, a darker sorrel with four white stockings and a medium blaze. Gene reportedly paid $1,500 for what is believed was part Morgan and part Tennessee Walking Horse. Most people saw him in the late '40s and early '50s at rodeos and stage shows, including England in

Champion, the Wonder Horse, was as much a part of the Autry mystique as was the singing cowboy himself. But exactly which Champion was which? The original Champion was a dark sorrel with a blaze face and white stockings on three legs (all except the right front). He did travel on personal appearances during the '30s, but it's unsure when he stopped. However, he was not at the July 1942 rodeo in Chicago. The original Champ could untie knots, fall, roll over and play dead, come at Gene's whistle, rear up if someone else was riding him, bow, shake his head yes and no...even push Gene into the arms of June Storey. According to the HOLLYWOOD REPORTER tradepaper (10/8/40) Gene paid $75 for Champion whose sire was a Morgan trotting horse from Ardmore, Oklahoma. According to Gene, "The first horse I had was trained by Tracy Layne. He had trained a number of horses."[1] Making his film debut in "Melody Trail" ('35), this Champion was

Gene with Touring Champ.

Gene and Champ Jr.

unusually pretty because they bleached his mane and tail. This Champion was used in Gene's TV series, the feature films of the '50s and Flying A's "Adventures of Champion" TV series. This horse was evidently owned by Gene's wife Ina (as was "The Adventures of Champion" series), although she didn't ride.

A well-trained pony who knew many tricks, Little Champ joined Gene's stable and appeared in "Beyond the Purple Hills" ('50) and "The Old West" ('52) and made personal appearances beginning at Madison Square Garden in 1948. According to Gene, on a "Melody Ranch Theater" 1987 broadcast, Little Champ was a Hackney about 40 inches high. The word "Hackney" comes from the French "haquenee", a language commonly spoken in England in Medieval times, describing a riding horse with a particularly comfortable trot or amble. Over the years the term became synonymous with a general purpose ridden and driven animal whose stamina and soundness were greatly admired and whose favored pace was the trot. After WWII the emphasis on breeding shifted to producing a spectacular show harness animal with presence, athleticism, elegance, stamina and soundness. Little Champ had a crooked blaze and dark color over his left eye like the last Champion (referred to as Champion Three).

To hide these markings on Champion Three Gene tried to comb his mane into bangs. This horse, not in films, was used in personal appearances from roughly 1957-1960. Gene was seen riding this Champ on a Merv Griffin show. He was used in other '50s-'60s TV appearances. This horse was 41 when he died in 1990 at Melody Ranch where he's buried.

Yet another Champion was the Lindy Champ. A sorrel with four white stockings, an oval-topped blaze and a black dot on his nose (often powdered over or bleached), Lindy Champ was owned for the most part by John Agee. Lindy Champ was originally being trained to be a Tony Jr. for Tom Mix and is actually the "Champion" who took the well

1953. He appeared in bit parts in Gene's films, including the song at sunset number in "Gaucho Serenade" ('40). This horse, possibly the most photographed, was often referred to as Champion in magazine and comic book photos. Notice the back cover of GENE AUTRY COMICS #25 places Gene with leading lady Barbara Britton and this horse—even thought he *wasn't* in the movie. He was definitely on his way to replace the original horse, but was aging. This horse was at New York's Madison Square Garden in 1947 and subsequent appearances. His hoof prints are with Gene's handprints at Mann's Chinese Theatre. It's not known when he died.

After the war, Gene found the Champion he called Champ Jr., a lighter sorrel with four white stockings and a narrower white blaze on his face ending in an arrow tip. He's billed Champion Jr. (Wonder Horse of the West) in Gene's post war Republics and "World's Wonder Horse" in Gene's early Columbias beginning with "Loaded Pistols" but was retired around 1950 as being too high strung. He was replaced by the Touring Champ for personal appearances and in Columbia films by the TV Champ about the time of "Mule Train" ('50). Champion Jr. was in New York's Madison Square Garden in 1946. Champ Jr. was over 30 when he died in August 1977.

The TV Champ, also a light sorrel with four white stockings but with a wide white blaze face which comes down clear over his nose, was

Gene's between TV Champ and Little Champ.

Champion Three.

other mounts.

"Tennessee Walking Horses and Palominos are most applicable for high schooling. Gene Autry prefers the Tennessee Walkers because he wants an animal with an even gait and the Walkers have this. It is most important to start training a horse when he is between three and four years old.

"The first thing Gene teaches a horse is to walk in a circle approximately 20 feet in diameter. A halter with a 20-foot rope is put on the horse. Gene stands in the center of the ring with the loose end of the rope while an assistant, with a pail of oats as bait, urges the horse to follow him around the circle. At the same time, Gene flicks at the horse with a light whip.

"When the horse has learned to follow the boy with the oats, the rope and halter are removed and the animal is taught to follow unfettered. Once this is mastered, the horse is trained to move around the ring prompted only by Gene in the center flicking the whip.

"The second step of this same act is to train the horse to stop and start at a given signal during the circling. To do this, an assistant with a pail of oats who has been walking ahead of the horse stops. Naturally, the horse stops to get the food, and he is prompted by the flick of Gene's whip from the center of the ring. The pail is then withdrawn, Gene flicks

promoted 1940 TWA airplane flight from Hollywood to the Madison Square Garden World's Championship Rodeo. It's unclear how long he lived or what use he was put to after the war.

Collectively, the various Champions performed the world's largest repertory of horse tricks, including dancing the hula and the Charleston, jumping through a ring of fire, and playing dead. Along with Gene, these Champions greeted crowds from Texas to Ireland. Touring Champion even enjoyed a proper high tea at the Savoy in London. Champion received thousands of fan letters every month, proving that the World's Wonder Horse was an important element in Gene's success story.

An article on "How Gene Autry Trains His Horses" was supplied to AUTRY'S ACES fan club newsletter by George Lait, director of publicity at Columbia Pictures and was printed in AUTRY'S ACES in the July-August 1954 issue. Bear in mind, this was a publicity release and these many years later, we know John Agee and others trained horses for Gene. Nevertheless, Gene had to be involved in the training of Champion, Little Champ and his

Gene astride Lindy Champ beside trainer John Agee.

the whip twice and the horse is moving again. This routine is later repeated with no oats in the pail. But, instead, Gene brings the oats in his hand. In this way, the animal realizes he will always get oats for obeying the whip flicks.

"The third step is for the horse to leave his circle and put his head on Gene's shoulder. The same basic method is used to train the horse for this final phase as was in the first two.

"For what is known as the praying kneel, the horse's two front legs are flicked with the whip while Gene pulls down on the animal's neck. Oats are placed on the floor to induce the horse to put his head down and stretch out his neck.

"The easiest trick to teach a horse is dancing, although it might appear to be the hardest. Actually, the music follows the horse instead of the conventional procedure. During the training for the rhumba, Gene flicks the horse on the left hind flank, causing him to shy in the direction, then to the right. During an actual performance, Gene cues the horse with his spurs instead of the whip. For the Hesitation Waltz, the horse is trained by flicking the front legs up, one at a time. During the actual performance, Gene uses the reins to cue him.

"A horse is taught to rear by flicking him under the belly from between the front legs. He is taught to jump on a grand piano or platform in the same manner except oats are used to guide him until he understands what is expected.

"The most famous trick of a high schooled horse, known as 'The End of the Trail', was first done by Gene's Champion as a stunt. It emulates the well known picture of an Indian on his pony at the edge of a cliff, the horse's four legs close together and his head hanging low. Gene's horse steps up with four feet on a small box when doing this stunt, for which he was trained with oats and a flicking whip.

"To teach a horse to smile, Gene tickles his upper lip with a feather or fringe of the flicking whip, at the same time cueing him with a slight shake of the bridle. Then he is, as always, rewarded with oats or sugar. To make him nod or shake his head, Gene tickles his neck and cues him with the bridle.

"The flicking whip is not used for punishment, only for guidance and gentle urging. Gene uses a recording of applause in the final phase of training. This is to get the animal used to audience noises and to learn that applause at the end of the stunt means he did well. Gene says horses soon learn what applause means, and Champion actually gets stubborn if he fails to 'get a hand.'"[1]

It was trainer John Agee who did most of the training of Gene's horses at Melody Ranch, working with them two hours a day for a maximum of six months, maintaining that if a horse cannot master the training in that time, he never will. However, as Gene stated later, "Whoever trains a horse, the man that's going to ride him has to work with that horse himself. And that's a hard thing to do, because a horse that's trained to march, lie down, sit up, come to you and all that, you've got to know the cues to give him."[2]

SOURCES:
1. *Autry's Aces.* July/August, 1954.

Gene In Print

Gene as drawn by Jesse Marsh.

Autry was not only the forerunner of all the singing cowboys, he also was the first B-western cowboy to have a comicbook series. Fawcett's GENE AUTRY COMICS #1 went on sale for a dime in December 1941. It's now worth $775–$12,000, depending on condition…*if* you can locate a copy. Fawcett published ten issues from 1941-'43. Dell took over with #11-12 then put Gene into their Four Color Comics series in 1944 for six issues before resuming numbering with #1 in May 1946 and continuing for 121 issues til January/March 1959. By 1948 Dell was publishing more than one million GENE AUTRY COMICS every month. The title changed slightly with #102 to GENE AUTRY AND CHAMPION. With #112 the change was even more dramatic, with the established photo covers being abandoned in favor of painted covers of…Champion. Even Champ's name was now larger than Gene's! By #113 Gene's horse had even supplanted him as the lead story. (Dell also published GENE AUTRY'S CHAMPION for 19 issues from 1950-'55.) The first Autry photo cover was actually on Dell Four Color #100. Regular issue #1 was

again drawn, then photos were used continually from #2-111. Photo back covers ran from #4-65 (except for #19, #46, #47). All cover photos were specially posed by Gene except for the rare movie scene of he and Barbara Britton from "Loaded Pistols" on the back of #25 (3/49), released in conjunction with the film. Various Champions were shown on the front or back of 39 issues.

Many artists worked on GENE AUTRY COMICS including Till Goodan, Jim Chambers, Jesse Marsh, Nat Edson, Nicholas Firfires (second husband of Buck Jones' daughter Maxine), Ray Ramsey, John Ushler, Tom Massey, Mike Arens, Russ Manning and Dan Spiegle. Firfires, Marsh and Ramsey did the bulk of the work. The three rare photos below are among 18 I purchased from the Firfires collection. Gene posed for these to give the artist various angles from which to draw him. Comicbook stories came from writers Gaylord DuBois, Phil Evans, Dick Calkins (creator of Buck Rogers), Jean Klinordlinger, prolific Paul S. Newman, Eleanor Packer, screenwriter Eric Freiwald, Robert Ryder, John Wade Hampton and Kellogg Adams.

Predating all of these, POPULAR COMICS #28 (5/38) (published by Dell) featured a six page movie adaptation of Gene's "The Old Barn Dance". Gene also appeared in Dell's WESTERN ROUNDUP Giants #1-18, five small Quaker Puffed Wheat/Rice giveaway comics ('50), five 1953 3-D pocket-size giveaways and ten MARCH OF COMICS (an advertising venue for Weatherbird Shoes, Sears, etc.).

A June 9, 1940, panel from the Sunday comic strip "Gene Autry Rides" drawn by Till Goodan.

Beginning with a movie adaptation of "Public Cowboy No. 1" in 1938, Whitman issued eleven Gene Autry Big Little Books. The others were all original stories. In 1949-'50 Whitman produced two slightly taller Autry New Better Little Books. Then there were hardback novels, coloring books, paint books, paperdoll folios, Sandpiper and Little Golden Books and English publications all bearing Gene's likeness.

GENE AUTRY RIDES came out as a Sunday only newspaper comic strip in the Spring of 1940. Distributed by Gene's own organization, it was written by screenwriter Gerald Geraghty ("The Phantom Empire", "Mexicali Rose", "Riders In the Sky", "In Old Monterey" etc.) and drawn by cowboy cartoonist Till Goodan, who worked on the early Fawcett comics as well. The first story was a loose adaptation of "The Phantom Empire", with Gene's sidekick changed from Smiley/Frog to Frosty. The strip ended in '42 as Autry entered WWII service. Gene's renewed popularity on TV led to a second GENE AUTRY strip. General Features began a daily 9/8/52 with Sunday pages following 4/26/53. The strip, which often found Gene far from the western range—in Australia and Arabia for example, was written by Bob Stevens and competently illustrated by Bert Laws. The strip ended in 1955.

Panel from "Gene Autry" daily comic strip dated March 9, 1954. Illustrator was Bert Laws.

Afterword by Jimmy Hawkins

Did Gene Autry movies mold our lives?

It was a Saturday afternoon in August 1948 at my local theater, sitting there with 500 other kids. The summer vacation was almost over and school would begin in a couple of weeks. I was 6 years old with my cap pistol by my side holding a box of popcorn and ready for anything. As the movie began I heard a beautiful song and then this man came galloping on the screen, bigger than life, he was 40 ft. tall, riding this great looking horse. The movie "Strawberry Roan", the man, Gene Autry, the horse, Champion. Instantly, he was my hero. On the screen he was the model of fair play, someone who righted wrong and in 76 minutes

Jimmy Hawkins and Gene Autry.

was what you got.

Whenever we would go on personal appearance tours to fairs or rodeos he would always insist on stopping to visit local children's hospitals. He would bring his band with him and we'd put on a mini-show for the crippled and infirmed kids. I saw this happen time after time when he would sit at their bedside and listen to whatever the kids wanted to talk about. I would ask him questions about these visits and he shared with me that he did this because for that moment the kids forget all their pain, and if he could bring that gift to them then that's where he wanted to be. Gene Autry believed in giving back.

I saw his sense of humor and his

made the world a safer place. Little did I know but that day started a friendship that would last over 50 years. In 1953 I actually met Mr. Autry when he cast me to co-star as Tagg Oakley in the "Annie Oakley" series (1953-1958) produced by his Flying A Productions. Through time he proved to be the same man in person as he was on screen. What you saw

patience with his fans when a lady, oh she must have been 75 or 80 (Mr. Autry was in his late 40's at the time), came up to him and told him she had been a fan and saw all his movies when she was a little girl. She ended the conversation asking, "By the way, how's Trigger"? He just smiled, put his hand on her frail shoulder, thanked her and said, "Trigger's fine. When I see him, I'll tell him you asked." Gene Autry had a sense of who he was.

We were in a airport waiting for his plane to be serviced... I was walking by the counter where he was grabbing a bite. I asked him how long it would be before we took off; he said he would be getting word any minute. Knowing I liked mashed potatoes and gravy he handed me a spoon and told me to help myself to his plate. I was eating these potatoes when the man on a stool next to him made a sarcastic remark. I told Gene thanks for the potatoes but I guess I'm annoying the man. He told me to just keep eating that I wasn't bothering anyone. The man grunted something under his breath. Just then up came Mr. Autry's pilot/road manager (Herb Green) to tell us the plane would be leaving in about 10 minutes and he'd be back in a second. The man looked over and noticed Herb Green and said something derogatory about him being Jewish. Gene looked at the man and said he didn't like his remarks and how would he like to step outside. I started to put the spoon down and Gene said, "Keep eating." The guy started to have more of an attitude just as Herb came back and caught the essence of the conversation. Herb was diplomatic and just hustled us both out of the situation. But Mr. Autry in one fell swoop wanted to right the wrong he felt for two of his friends.

Gene Autry stood up to prejudice and bigotry.

During Christmas of 1958 I was invited to his home for a small holiday party. I watched him as I had many times with his wife Ina by his side being gracious to everyone they spoke with and making each guest feel as if they were the only person in the room. After dinner he announced that he was showing a TV pilot of a new series he was producing based on the title of one of his old movies. As the 16mm projector started the film flashed on the screen and I heard Gene Autry's familiar voice singing the title tune "Strawberry Roan". It instantly took me back to that August afternoon when I sat in my local theater and was transported into a fantasy world where good won over evil. It's not the world as it was, just as Mr. Autry thought it should be. As the film flickered... I looked over; there he was... still 40 ft. tall ... still my hero. A great man and a great American, Gene Autry is an inspiration to those who believe in the American dream. Plain and simple.

Did Gene Autry's movies help mold our lives? They did mine.

Jimmy Hawkins
TV's Tagg Oakley (The "Annie Oakley" Series)
Gene Autry's Flying A Productions (1953-1958) May, 2005

Bibliography

<u>Books</u>

American Film Institute Catalogs; 1931-1940; 1941-
1950. University of California Press, 1993.

Autry, Gene; Herskowitz, Mickey. *Back In the Saddle Again.* Doubleday, 1978.

Copeland, Bobby. *Trail Talk.* McFarland, 1996.

Dixon, Wheeler W. *The B Directors, A Biographical Directory.* Scarecrow, 1985.

Drake, Oliver. *Written, Produced and Directed by Oliver Drake.* Self published, 1990.

Dunning, John. *Encyclopedia of Old Time Radio.* Oxford University Press, 1998.

Fernett, Gene. *Next Time Drive Off the Cliff.* Cinememories Pub., 1968.

Goldrup, Tom and Jim. *Feature Players Vol. 1.* Self published, 1986.

Green, Douglas B. *Singing in the Saddle.* Country Music Foundation/Vanderbilt University Press, 2002.

Hall, Wade. *Hell Bent For Music.* University Press of Kentucky, 1996.

Lackmann, Ron. *Encyclopedia of American Radio.* Facts on File, 2000.

Lentz, Harris. *Western and Frontier Film and Television Credits.* McFarland, 1996.

Lyden, Pierce. *The Movie Badmen I Rode With.* Self published, 1988.

Magers, Boyd; Fitzgerald, Michael. *Ladies of the Western.* McFarland, 2002.

Magers, Boyd; Fitzgerald, Michael. *Westerns Women.* McFarland, 1999.

Magers, Boyd; Nareau, Robert; Copeland, Bobby. *Best of the Badmen.* Empire, 2006.

Mathis, Jack. *Republic Confidential: The Studio.* Mathis Advertising, 1999.

McCord, Merrill. *Brothers of the West.* Alhambra Pub., 2003.

Miller, Don; Smith, Packy; Hulse, Ed. *Hollywood Corral.* Riverwood Press, 1993.

Peters Jr., House. *Another Side of Hollywood.* Empire, 2000.

Rainey, Buck. *Sweethearts of the Sage.* McFarland, 1992.

Rothel, David. *The Gene Autry Book.* Empire, 1988.

Rothel, David. *The Singing Cowboys.* A. S. Barnes, 1978.

Rothel, David. *Those Great Cowboy Sidekicks.* WOY Pub., 1984.

Schneider, Jerry. *Corriganville.* Corriganville Press, 2004.

Shrum, Cal. *Presenting Cal Shrum.* Self published, 1986.

Tuska, Jon. *Vanishing Legion.* McFarland, 1982.

<u>Periodicals</u>

Autry's Aces, various issues (1949-1953).

Film Collectors Registry Vol. 2 #1 (January/February 1970).

Gene Autry's Friends, various issues (1996-2005).

Hamann, G. D. *Gene Autry in the '30s.* Filming Today Press, 2000.

Hamann, G. D. *Gene Autry in the '40s.* Filming Today Press, 1997.

Magers, Boyd. *Western Ladies #3.* (November 1997).

Magers, Boyd; Yarbrough, Tinsley. *Western Clippings*, various issues (1994-2005).

Malcolmson, Robert. *Those Enduring Matinee Idols V. 1 #7* (November 1970).

Motion Picture Herald, various issues (1935-1953).

Paige, Robert T. Article on "The Big Show" (2003).

Smith III, Richard. *B-Westerns in Perspective,* various issues (1983-1985).

Under Western Skies. (December 1983).

Who's Who in Western Stars #2. Dell, 1952.

Who's Who in Western Stars #3. Dell, 1953.

Los Angeles Examiner (June 10, 1937).

Los Angeles Evening Herald Express (August 4, 1937; January 1, 1946; May 24, 1947).

People (October 30, 1996).

Cliffhanger#10. WOY, 1989.

Hollywood Citizen News (October 3, 1940).

Lester, Jan. *Good Old Days* (May, 2005).

Westerner, The #8 (1986).

San Bernardino Sun (November 27, 2005).

Burnette, Smiley. *Saturday Evening Post* (1953)

Daily Variety (January 22, 1952).

Index

Text passages only are indexed. Gene Autry's name is not indexed as he's mentioned on virtually every page.

About the Author

Boyd Magers grew up at the right time and in the right place for a full appreciation of all westerns...the late '40s–early '60s. Born in Kansas City, Kansas, in 1940, he grew up with a western influence in Independence, Kansas (near where the Dalton and James Gangs rode) and Ponca City, Oklahoma (the site of the famed 101 Ranch). Beginning in late 1946 he attended the Beldorf in Independence and the Center in Ponca City, riding the range with the current crop of B-western heroes—Gene Autry, Monte Hale, Tim Holt, Eddie Dean, Jimmy Wakely, Roy Rogers, Charles Starrett, Johnny Mack Brown and others. By 1953 the new medium of television offered him a steady hour upon hour appreciation of the early screen cowboys—Buck Jones, Bob Steele, Hoot Gibson, Ken Maynard, George O'Brien, Rex Bell, Tim McCoy and the rest. The early '50s was also the time for the dawning of the TV western—"Gene Autry", "Range Rider", "Annie Oakley", "Hopalong Cassidy", "Kit Carson", "Cisco Kid" and the others which slowly matured into the so-called adult TV western of the late '50s early '60s, "Gunsmoke", "Cheyenne", "Sugarfoot", "Restless Gun" and dozens more. Therefore, he came to appreciate all eras of westerns.

Following Armed Forces Radio Network military service in Korea from '60-'61, and during a fifteen year career in radio on the air and as program director ('62-'77), Boyd began to contribute articles on westerns to publications such as COUNTRY STYLE and others.

In 1977 he established VideoWest which soon became the most respected source for western movies and TV episodes on video for over 25 years. From 1987 to 1994 he contributed a regular column on westerns to THE BIG REEL.

Boyd Magers

Over the ensuing years he wrote regular columns or contributed articles to COUNTRY AND WESTERN VARIETY, UNDER WESTERN SKIES, CLASSIC IMAGES, FILM COLLECTOR'S REGISTRY, among several others. Over the years he's also provided research data and material to over 40 books and several TV/video documentaries. He wrote hundreds of B-western film reviews still being used annually in VIDEO MOVIE GUIDE. In 2005 he wrote all the Roy Rogers and Gene Autry film reviews for Leonard Maltin's CLASSIC MOVIE GUIDE.

In 1994 he began self-publishing WESTERN CLIPPINGS which has become *the* primary source and authority for thousands of western readers. He also self-publishes SERIAL REPORT.

Knowledgeable about all phases of western films, over the last fifteen years Boyd has moderated nearly 200 western celebrity guest star discussion panels at western film festivals all over the country. In addition, Boyd currently has over 2,500 reviews and observations ("The Best and Worst of the West") of western films online at Chuck Anderson's Old Corral <www.b-westerns.com/magers.htm>

Boyd's first book, WESTERNS WOMEN, was published by McFarland in 1999 and was followed in 2002 by LADIES OF THE WESTERN. SO YOU WANT TO SEE COWBOY STUFF was his third book in 2003, followed by THE FILMS OF AUDIE MURPHY in 2004 and BEST OF THE BADMEN in 2005.

Boyd is dedicated to preserving the rich heritage and enduring memories of small and big screen westerns and the people who populated them.

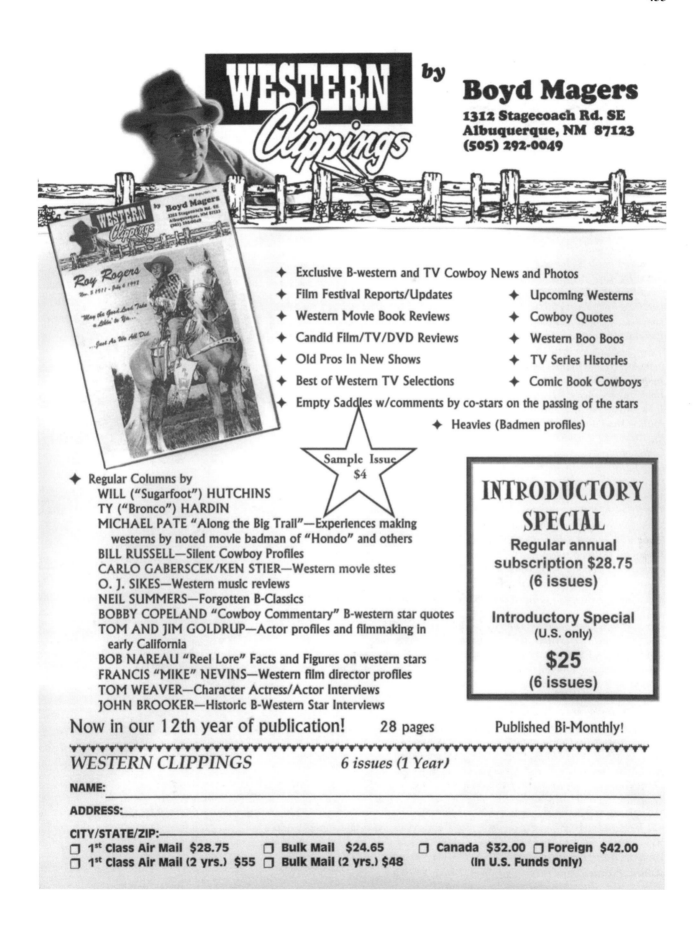

Other Fine Western Books Available from Empire Publishing, Inc:

ABC's of Movie Cowboys by Edgar M. Wyatt. $5.00.

Art Acord and the Movies by Grange B. McKinney. $15.00.

Audie Murphy: Now Showing by Sue Gossett. $30.00.

Back in the Saddle: Essays on Western Film and Television Actors edited by Garry Yoggy. $29.95.

Best of the Badmen by Boyd Magers, Bobby Copeland, and Bob Nareau. $39.00.

Bill Elliott, The Peaceable Man by Bobby Copeland. $15.00.

Brothers of the West: The Lives and Films of Robert Livingston and Jack Randall by Merrill McCord. $34.95.

B-Western Boot Hill: A Final Tribute to the Cowboys and Cowgirls Who Rode the Saturday Matinee Movie Range by Bobby Copeland

B-Western Actors Encyclopedia by Ted Holland. $30.00.

Buster Crabbe, A Self-Portrait as told to Karl Whitezel. $24.95.

B-Western Boot Hill: A Final Tribute to the Cowboys and Cowgirls Who Rode the Saturday Matinee Movie Range by Bobby Copeland. $15.00.

Charlie King: We Called Him Blackie by Bobby Copeland. $15.00.

The Cowboy and the Kid by Jefferson Brim Crow, III. $5.90.

Crusaders of the Sagebrush by Hank Williams. $29.95.

Duke, The Life and Image of John Wayne by Ronald L. Davis. $14.95.

The Films and Career of Audie Murphy by Sue Gossett. $18.00.

The First Fifty Years of Sound Western Movie Locations by Kenny Stier. $34.95.

The Golden Corral, A Roundup of Magnificent Western Films by Ed Andreychuk. $29.95.

The Hollywood Posse, The Story of a Gallant Band of Horsemen Who Made Movie History by Diana Serra Cary. $16.95.

Hoppy by Hank Williams. $29.95.

In a Door, Into a Fight, Out a Door, Into a Chase, Movie-Making Remembered by the Guy at the Door by William Witney. $24.95.

John Ford, Hollywood's Old Master by Ronald L. Davis. $14.95.

John Wayne—Actor, Artist, Hero by Richard D. McGhee. $27.50.

John Wayne, An American Legend by Roger M. Crowley. $29.95.

Johnny Mack Brown—Up Close and Personal by Bobby Copeland. $20.00.

Kid Kowboys: Juveniles in Western Films by Bob Nareau. $20.00.

Ladies of the Western by Boyd Magers and Michael G. Fitzgerald. $35.00.

Lash LaRue, King of the Bullwhip by Chuck Thornton and David Rothel. $25.00.

Last of the Cowboy Heroes by Budd Boetticher. $28.50.

More Cowboy Shooting Stars by John A. Rutherford and Richard B. Smith, III. $18.00.

The Official TV Western Roundup Book by Neil Summers and Roger M. Crowley. $34.95.

Randolph Scott, A Film Biography by Jefferson Brim Crow, III. $25.00.

Richard Boone: A Knight Without Armor in a Savage Land by David Rothel. $30.00.

Riding the (Silver Screen) Range, The Ultimate Western Movie Trivia Book by Ann Snuggs. $15.00.

Riding the Video Range, The Rise and Fall of the Western on Television by Garry A. Yoggy. $75.00.

The Round-Up, A Pictorial History of Western Movie and Television Stars Through the Years by Donald R. Key. $27.00.

Roy Rogers, A Biography, Radio History, Television Career Chronicle, Discography, Filmography, etc. by Robert W. Phillips. $75.00.

Roy Barcroft: King of the Badmen by Bobby Copeland. $15.00.

The Roy Rogers Reference-Trivia-Scrapbook by David Rothel. $25.00.

Saddle Gals, A Filmography of Female Players in B-Westerns of the Sound Era by Edgar M. Wyatt and Steve Turner. $10.00.

Silent Hoofbeats: A Salute to the Horses and Riders of the Bygone B-Western Era by Bobby Copeland. $20.00.

Singing in the Saddle by Douglas B. Green. $34.95.

Sixty Great Cowboy Movie Posters by Bruce Hershenson. $14.99.

Smiley Burnette: We Called Him Frog by Bobby Copeland

The Sons of the Pioneers by Bill O'Neal and Fred Goodwin. $26.95.

So You Wanna See Cowboy Stuff? by Boyd Magers. $25.00.

Sunset Carson - The Life and Times of Republic's Action Ace by Bobby Copeland

Tex Ritter: America's Most Beloved Cowboy by Bill O'Neal. $21.95.

Those Great Cowboy Sidekicks by David Rothel. $25.00.

Trail Talk, Candid Comments and Quotes by Performers and Participants of The Saturday Matinee Western Films by Bobby Copeland. $12.50.

The Western Films of Sunset Carson by Bob Carman and Dan Scapperotti. $20.00.

Western Movies: A TV and Video Guide to 4200 Genre Films compiled by Michael R. Pitts. $35.00.

Westerns Women by Boyd Magers and Michael G. Fitzgerald. $35.00.

Written, Produced, and Directed by Oliver Drake. $30.00.

Ask for our complete listing of WESTERN MOVIE BOOKS!

Add $3.00 shipping/handling for first book + $1.00 for each additional book ordered.

Empire Publishing, Inc. • 3130 US Highway 220 • Madison, NC 27025-8306 • Phone 336-427-5850